To Mark

MIXING POP AND POLITICS

If the kids are united
They'll never be defeated.

MIXING POP AND POLITICS

A Marxist History of Popular Music

Toby Manning

Published by Repeater Books

An imprint of Watkins Media Ltd

Unit 11 Shepperton House

89-93 Shepperton Road

London

N1 3DF

United Kingdom

www.repeaterbooks.com

A Repeater Books paperback original 2024

1

Distributed in the United States by Random House, Inc., New York.

ISBN: 9781913462673

Ebook ISBN: 9781913462680

Printed and bound in the United Kingdom by TJ Books Limited

CONTENTS

Mixing pop and politics, he asks me what the use is.
I offer him embarrassment and my usual excuses.

Billy Bragg, 'Waiting for the Great Leap Forwards',
Workers Playtime, 1988

Introduction: The Top 10

1. The Power of Popular Music

Erupting into suburban living rooms from valve radios and brand-new television sets in summer 1956, Elvis Presley's 'Hound Dog' announced a new reality, expressed through a new form: rock'n'roll. 'Hound Dog' and its performer were unalienated, uninhibited, free: a freedom of *being*, not *having*; an expression of pure feeling when feelings were suspect – disorderly, effeminate, probably dirty – delivered with a directness that disdained conformist convention. 'Hound Dog' demonstrated what popular music could *do*; what ordinary people could do. For rock'n'roll's origins lay in the music of the disenfranchised and disempowered – country and blues – in non-professional nobodies plugging into the electrical currents of modernity. Disreputable, ecstatic and defiant, rock'n'roll's expression of a liberated world was an offence to arbiters of taste, morality and control.

'Hound Dog' (UK 2; US 1) is a meta-song, a synecdoche both for rock'n'roll itself and for a popular music that's *of,* rather than *for*, the people. 'Hound Dog' wasn't the first rock'n'roll smash – that honour goes to Bill Haley's 'Rock Around the Clock' (UK 1; US 1) the previous year – it wasn't even Presley's first, but it was the first to sound adversarial. Rock'n'roll was the real starting point of post-war popular culture – youthful, multi-racial, unofficial – of music as a medium of rebellion, and thus the first looming of the counterculture, of a different kind of society. For all the intervening decades of co-option and self-incorporation, of buyout and sellout, 'Hound Dog' – played loud – still carries much of its original charge, its ability to excite, incite and inspire.

"You ain't nothin' but…" That opening *a capella* holler stops you in your tracks. What Elvis captured was not the timbre but the *abandon* of African American singers: most obviously Little Richard, but also bluesman Arthur Crudup and rhythm'n'blues shouter Big Mama Thornton, who cut the original version of 'Hound Dog'. Just as it's a vector of its precursors, 'Hound Dog' isn't just a vehicle for Elvis Presley but the sum of its social parts. In contrast to formally dressed balladeers, backed by a distant or invisible orchestra, scruffily attired *groups* were key to rock'n'roll's visceral visual and aural impact. After that opening shout, the sheer ferocity of D.J. Fontana's drumming slaps you in the face, gives you a few seconds to come to your senses... then does it again. Peppered with overexcited handclaps, the arrangement's stop-start approach is designed to mess with you – all disorientation, all excitement, all sex. Inspired by both Chuck Berry and jazz's improvisational freedom, Scotty Moore's first electric guitar solo (from 0:49–1:05) is channelled anarchy, his second – hitting discords and noteless reverb (1:20–1:37) – mere anarchy. The most conventional, ballad-like element of the track is the Jordanaires' unruffled backing vocals – the calm in the sonic storm, the orchestra playing on the *Titanic*, serving only to highlight the devastation that surrounds it.

The doggerel of 'Hound Dog' is defiantly beyond common sense, outside conventional thinking. It's also beyond authorised notions of authorship – an uncredited rewrite of a rewrite of a Leiber and Stoller Tin Pan Alley tune. Likewise, 'Hound Dog' pulls and pushes its mode of production, being louder, rawer and more aggressive than anything that preceded it in the pop charts. Yet the world that 'Hound Dog' announced would only have a year before the corporations would get the fix in, pull the orchestra out of the deeps and give it the kiss of life; before they'd pull a veil over Elvis's pelvis, push him into bland ballads and mawkish movies and reassert 'entertainment' as sedating rather than seducing.

The repressed would return (as the repressed does): each time music's adversarial energy has been contained or co-opted, something new emerges. Popular music's dialectic of repression and refusal charts and channels the political struggles of the last three-quarters of a century, and it's this relationship to which this book is dedicated.

2. Music Is Political

This book is a Marxist history of popular music, not a history of Marxist popular music – that would be a very short book, encompassing the Clash, the Jam, our titular hero, Billy Bragg, Public Enemy, Rage Against the Machine… and not much else. Or not much else that was *popular*, this book's focus being the chart music of Britain and America from 1953–2023, which has moved largely in lockstep. Beyond those putatively Marxist outfits, there is one act named after Karl Marx – 1993's one-hit wonder, Marxman ('All About Eve', UK 28) – 80s balladeer Richard Marx is no relation – and three hit songs that cite Marx, only one of which might be termed 'Marxist'. In the aftermath of the 60s, Don McLean's 1971 'American Pie' (UK 2; US 1) implicates Marxism in pop's politicised loss of 'innocence'. In the aftermath of punk's political refusal, the Clash's 1981 'The Magnificent Seven' (*Sandinista!* UK 19; US 24) captures Marx's concept of 'alienation', while giving the philosopher and his collaborator, Engels, surreal cameos at a 7/11. Amidst the depoliticised cynicism of the high 80s, Bros's 1987 'When Will I Be Famous' (UK 2) posits Marxism as a prop for the past-it and po-faced. Beyond that, there is one (loose) quotation from Marx in popular music, in ABBA's 1974 Eurovision winner, 'Waterloo' (UK 1; US 6), which theorises "The history book on the shelf/Is always repeating itself".

Pop and politics are part of the tragedy and farce – the fabric – of our lives and yet are rarely held to mix. Despite its Marxist terminology, Madonna's turn of the millennium claim that "music mix the bourgeoisie and the rebel", puts 'Music' *beyond* politics (UK 1; US 1). In our culture popular music is understood either aesthetically or affectively, critical approaches that, in Marxist terms, are 'idealist' (not rooted in the material). The aesthetic approach focuses on genre and 'influence' and thus mainly understands music in relation to other music. The affective approach reinserts the human factor, understanding music as the self-expression of the artist – thus the profusion of music biographies and autobiographies – while connecting 'universally' (and somewhat vaguely) to the emotions of its audience.

Of those who regard music more sociologically, Mark Fisher doesn't always mix his pop and his politics ('Acid Communism' being the major exception), Simon Reynolds is prone to exempting genres from the political (rave; grime), while Stuart Maconie dismisses Marx's "dialectical materialism" as antipathetic to music.[1] John Street asserts that political music is a minority report,[2] echoed by David Hesmondhalgh, who argues that such "protest music" isn't a politically effective medium,[3] while Tom Ewing extends this to protest itself.[4] These analyses rest upon a narrow concept of the 'political' in popular music – as progressive, as public-orientated, and as protest-based – and one which is essentially pessimistic, even passive.[5] For, if politics is a matter of governments and parties, it has little to do not only with music but with people's everyday lives, and can be left to politicians. However, just as politics encompasses the reactionary as well as the radical, so does pop, whose politics inform the private as much as the public sphere (the personal is political), while being expressed through more varied, subtle and unconscious means than protest (love songs, even instrumentals, can be political).

This book reads music in relation to the social and economic conditions of its production and reception, as an expression of the *mood* of its era, of what Raymond Williams called a "structure of feeling".[6] In comprehending the political as being *felt* as much as *thought*, this approach encompasses affect (that of music's creators *and* its listeners), while, in positing musicians' choice of a particular word or phrase, sound or style as expressive of a wider, social structure of feeling, it folds in the formal. By historicising music in this way, this book offers a materialist rather than an idealist analysis of cultural production, which, rather than closing music down didactically, as Maconie suggests, opens it up, providing new perspectives on old songs and radical reassessments of conventional assumptions. This approach doesn't merely illuminate music, but history itself, recounting the political events of the last three-quarters of a century through the living, democratic medium of popular music, rather than the dead medium of sequestered archives. The aim is not just to bring the past "back again, like a long-lost friend", as the Carpenters put it on 1973's 'Yesterday Once More' (UK 2; US

4

2) but also as an everyday adversary – and to capture the struggle between these impulses.

3. Music as a Charts-and-Minds Campaign

Amongst theorists and critics who *have* understood pop and politics as mixing, the process has usually been regarded as reactionary. For Theodor Adorno, popular music is pure commodity – "produced for the market, and… aimed at the market" – co-opting the masses into consenting, consuming subjects: "Before the theological caprices of commodities, the consumers become temple slaves."[7] Adorno's claim that popular culture is ideologically determined by capitalism derives from Marx's argument that, "The mode of production of material life conditions the general process of social, political and intellectual life".[8] So while Adorno is not *wrong*, and popular music is entirely imbricated in the production process and profit imperative of capital, Ellen Willis's counterpoint is critical. "Mass art is… never simply imposed from above, but reflects a complicated interplay of corporate interests, the conscious or intuitive intentions of the artists and technicians who create the product, and the demands of the audience".[9]

Music is, in Marxist terms, dialectical, a push and pull between product and affect, dominant ideology and popular imaginary, consent and refusal. As such, popular culture, Stuart Hall argues, is "the ground on which the transformations are worked" – a site of class struggle. Consequently, to regard listeners as "a purely passive, outline force" is, as Hall notes, "a deeply unsocialist perspective".[10] Marx argued that "every historically developed social form [is] in fluid movement… it lets nothing impose upon it and is in its essence critical and revolutionary".[11] Music-making, music-listening and music analysis are all part of that fluid movement.

Despite Hall's pioneering work in cultural studies, the left never really got a grip on pop – Dick Hebdige's *Subculture* (1979) being the major exception – with the topic either neglected or inadequately understood. For Alan Sinfield, for instance, popular music is "consumer capitalism writ too large".[12] Through ideological austerity or elitist snobbery, the left failed to comprehend popular music as *pleasurable* – indeed, for Adorno "pleasure always means not to think about anything... basically it is helplessness".[13] While pop's pleasures *can* be purely escapist – say, the Bangles' 1986 'Walk Like an Egyptian' (UK 3: US 1) – or appeal to the worst in us – Drake's entire catalogue – pop can also combine the pleasurable and the adversarial, as on M.I.A.'s 2008, Clash-sampling 'Paper Planes' (UK 19; US 4). In contradiction of both Adorno and contemporary conservatives, the fact that popular music is a product of capitalism – like iPhones, like nostalgia, like everything – doesn't preclude its potential to be adversarial to, ambivalent about, or revealing of the dominant ideology.

4. Ma-ma-say, ma-ma-sah, ma-Marcuse

Concurrent with rock'n'roll's rupture of the social fabric, Herbert Marcuse, a refugee from fascist Germany, published *Eros and Civilisation* (1955), which theorised the same new reality, encapsulated in the impulse which, following Freud, Marcuse called '*Eros*', the life drive. *Eros* is a sublimation of sexual release as a universal pleasure principle – unalienated, uninhibited, free – unmediated by the capitalist social relations of alienation, competition and subordination. A product of his patrician era, Freud called these same social relations the "reality principle" and regarded failure to adapt to them as mental illness.[14] Marcuse, however, renamed the reality principle the "performance principle", to emphasise that every aspect of capitalist society is predicated on productivity – not just the workplace but the nation and the individual too.[15]

Marcuse's argument rests upon Marx's theory of alienation, whereby "the external character of labour for the worker appears in the fact that it is not his own but someone else's, that it does not belong to him, that in it he belongs, not to himself, but to another".[16] Under capitalism, we are alienated from our human nature (which Marx called our "species-being")[17] and from nature itself, with capitalism transforming rural societies into urban populations, while treating nature as an exploitable resource. For all neoliberalism's rhetoric of 'freedom', this alienation has only increased since the 1980s, as the performance principle has encroached upon our leisure – the 'side hustle', the data-generating labour of social media – and our consciousnesses, meaning that, as Fredric Jameson famously remarked, "it is easier to imagine the end of the world than the end of capitalism".[18]

In contrast to the pessimism of Jameson and Adorno, Marcuse reaffirms the integral optimism of Marxism as a humanist philosophy – concerned with what's best for humans rather than for capitalism. This largely derives from Marcuse's comprehension of pleasure as political, and his insistence that, "in its refusal to accept as final the limitations imposed upon freedom and happiness by the reality principle, in its refusal to forget what can be, lies the critical function of fantasy".[19] For "fantasy" here, read 'music', while what Marcuse is articulating is utopianism.

5. A Word about Utopia

The *Oxford English Dictionary* defines 'utopia' as "a condition of ideal (esp. social) perfection". Amidst the 80s' growing gulf between rich and poor, Huey Lewis declared in 1988, "Ain't no livin' in a perfect world" (US 3): "a vision of the future is impossible to see". Capitalist realists form a curious coalition with Leninists in insisting that utopia has no postcode, and that utopianism is the indulgence of unrealisable fantasy – curious, because Soviet communism is a key centrist and conservative argument *against* utopianism. Yet prioritising the present – the struggle; the crisis; less excitingly, the institutions – over the future didn't work out so well in communist Eastern Europe and isn't looking so rosy in the capitalist West – whether we measure the results ecologically, economically or qualitatively.

Despite capitalism not being a subsistence economy – it's *all about* surplus – there's a constant slippage between 'realism' and 'austerity' in neoliberal politics and culture. This rhetorical and distributional scarcity serves to encourage us to work longer hours and accept lower standards of living, while perpetuating the competitive individualism that counteracts the collectivism which is capitalism's adversary. However, as Eric Olin Wright argues, a political utopianism – specifically, socialism – can counteract this conventionalisation of dystopia via the creation

7

of "real utopias",[20] exemplified by measures like universal basic income.

Popular music is not political strategy – and is all the better for it. Songs don't set out a "systematic utopia" in Williams' formulation – what Marx called "writing receipts... for the cook-shops of the future".[21] Rather, music expresses a "heuristic utopia", which Williams defines as "an imaginative encouragement to feel and relate differently".[22] Key to the power of popular music is that it can both *express* the desire for something more than is granted us and *induce* that desire in the listener. "Music is supposed to inspire", Lauryn Hill declares on 1998's 'Superstar' (*The Miseducation of Lauryn Hill*, UK 2; US 1). This inspiration doesn't just reside in music's lyrical content – Funkadelic's utopian 1978 'One Nation Under a Groove' (UK 9; US 28) asserting, "We're on the move/Nothin' can stop us now" – but in its sensory impact: the tonalities of a voice, the grain of guitars, the beat of the drum – the rhythm of music's refusal.

Utopianism isn't exclusive to the left. A running joke on TV comedy *Silicon Valley* (2014–19) is that tech-capitalists constantly claim they're trying to "make the world a better place". Key to capitalism's dynamism is its ability to co-opt its own critiques, and so neoliberalism incorporated countercultural utopianism in the 80s: consumerism would make us unalienated, uninhibited, free. Michael McDonald's 1986 'Sweet Freedom' (UK 12; US 7) uses the hippie language of liberation to celebrate the new dispensation: "Reaching out to meet the changes... there's no turnin' back". One boom-and-bust cycle later, neoliberal utopianism was phased out for what Fisher called 'capitalist realism', as the system went from "the best of all possible orders", to "the only possible order", as Luc Boltanski and Eve Chiapello put it.[23] There was no turnin' back from the usable parts of the counterculture either: but while our twenty-first-century freedoms are beyond 60s hippies' most tripped-out imaginings, so is the exponential encroachment of capitalism upon our time and our own imaginations.

No hegemony is ever complete, however. As Williams noted, "Beyond the snappy formulas of an instant and enclosed individualism... beyond the market schemes of obsolescent durables; beyond the widespread and reckless borrowing from the future to solve some current difficulty without discomfort... deeper impulses and reckonings persist".[24] So while this book will examine the realist reductions of snappy, individualist music and the dystopian world it reflects, it will keep returning to music's expression of those deeper, collective, impulses and reckonings, located in the past, but pointing always to the future – towards utopia.

6. A Short Thesis on History

Most accounts of the post-war period – from Dominic Sandbrook to Alwyn Turner, Andrew Marr to Ian MacDonald – are history as teleology, where all roads lead to neoliberalism. For as Marx remarked, "The ideas of the ruling class are in every epoch the ruling ideas, i.e. the class which is the ruling material force of society, is at the same time its ruling intellectual force".[25] History, therefore, is written by the winners, who, as Walter Benjamin argued, will always present their victory as providential, as "progress" through a linear "homogenous empty time".[26]

As a Marxist analysis, this book is written from the perspective of history's losers. Marx – chronicler of the defeats of the revolutions of 1848 and the Paris Commune of 1871, writing in exile – observed that "Men make their own history, but they do not make it just as they please, under circumstances chosen by themselves".[27] So, while defeat has been the lot of the left, Enzo Traverso argues that "the lost battles of the past [are] a burden and a debt, which are also a promise of redemption".[28] The winners' history denies agency to the defeated; a losers' history reinserts the struggle, "the courage, humour, cunning, and fortitude", as the exiled Benjamin put it in 1940, amid the Nazi occupation of Paris.

In order to "brush history against the grain" in Benjamin's terms,[29] this book homes in on the *hopes* of each historical moment, when struggle still seemed winnable and political change achievable. It thus regards popular music as an affective archive,[30] within a temporality that's neither linear, homogenous nor empty, but haunted. This book's periodisation is thus polemical, its divvying up of history an attempt to get beyond

9

the long sweeps of the 'post-war' or 'Pax Americana', to avoid assumptions of an inevitable endpoint, and to resuscitate the past's potentialities – its hopes – and thus the future's.

7. Fordism was Class Struggle

One of the potentialities of the past which this book locates is post-war social democracy, whose function, in the winners' history, can appear to have been the facilitation of neoliberalism. For Marx, society is formed of an economic base, or "foundation, on which arises a legal and political superstructure... to which correspond definite forms of social consciousness".[31] From the late nineteenth century, the dominant ideology of *laissez-faire* liberalism left capital and labour to fight it out in a long, bloody struggle. Marx claimed, "It would be possible to write quite a history of the inventions, made since 1830, for the sole purpose of providing capital with weapons against the revolts of the working class".[32] Accordingly, in the early 1900s, industrialist Henry Ford concluded that if he raised his auto-plant workers' wages, they'd be less likely to rebel, and this would have the additional benefit of turning workers into consumers of capitalist commodities. Indicative of a structure of feeling, British economist John Maynard Keynes hit upon a similar idea concurrently, prematurely declaring *The End of Laissez-Faire* in 1926.

Following the workers' revolution in Russian in 1917 and the collapse of the capitalist system in the Wall Street Crash of 1929, Ford's ideas gained traction, and by 1934, Italian Marxist Antonio Gramsci could identify a new 'Fordist' phase of capitalism. Fordism was a "technical rationalisation" not just of industry – with its assembly lines, mass production and mass consumption – but of humanity, creating a "new type of worker and of man" (and woman, in support), and Gramsci predicted that this "psycho-physical nexus" would transform society.[33] Fordism thus informed Franklin Roosevelt's interventionist New Deal (1933–39) and Clement Attlee's Keynesian post-war government (1945–51), wherein state guarantees of full employment and welfare provision ensured capitalism's survival. While this collectivist system is usually called 'social democracy', this book will deploy the term 'Fordism', as it acknowledges the 'regime of accumulation' of welfare capitalism and better fits the less social, less democratic, American system, as well as highlighting the automobile as a symbol of consumer-capitalist desire. What neither Gramsci, governments nor capital predicted was that Fordism would also empower the working class. Forged in struggle, Fordism would be *defined* by struggle – in the factory, on the street, at the ballot box – and where there is struggle, there is potential for change.

8. Fordist Music was Class Struggle – with a Beat

The post-war Fordist hegemony of mass-produced, mass-pacifying balladry was riven by rock'n'roll in the mid-50s. Like the Fordist system itself, Fordist music was defined by struggle: in the recording studio, as unschooled proletarian musicians battled patrician producers and patronising, white-coated engineers; in the record company office, as unschooled upstarts faced down smarmy suits and bovine bean counters; and in the music itself. From rock'n'roll to beat to psychedelia to glam to punk, Fordist period's most vital productions were protests *against* Fordism. Even pop *product* – from the Fordist factories of Motown, Stax, Mickie Most or Chinn and Chapman – was structured by this struggle. On the Crystals' Phil Spector-produced 1962 'He's a Rebel' (UK 19; US 1), its subject, expressing the Fordist era's class confidence, "holds his head up high". Such songs now sound like unfulfilled promises, the disposable acquiring depth through the hauntology of history.

The post-Fordist, neoliberal age, with its guitar-strumming, sax-playing heads of state and its mania for memorials and museums, has curated the Fordist musical past as a paradoxical "presentism", in Francois Hartog's term. Hartog claims that this "museified gaze [is] an invitation for collective amnesia".[34] As such, rock'n'roll becomes a dash of colour in the 50s consensus, the Beatles never stop being national treasures, glam becomes an escape from the "nightmare 70s", punk a tantrum against busted social democracy and hip-hop an expression of multiculturalism – a winner's history. Amidst the imperial phase neoliberalism that's the providential endpoint of such histories, middle-aged bankers

11

could sport Mohicans at 90s and noughties Sex Pistols reunions, while *School of Rock* (2003) could reframe rebellion as 'attitude', a simulacrum of Fordist struggle with the concept of *change* excised. No hegemony is ever complete, however, and the repressed will keep on returning.

9. Popular Music *is* Cultural Appropriation

Popular music is a particularly conducive environment for such returns of the repressed, repeatedly enabling subaltern groups to push into the mainstream, thereby altering the epistemology of culture and politics. Sometimes these groups have intervened on their own behalf – the working class with rock'n'roll and beat – at other times they've enabled *other* groups – queers with glam and disco. African Americans have done both: through blues, r'n'b, soul, funk and hip-hop's influence on rock'n'roll, 60s beat, heavy rock, glam, disco, punk and beyond. One name for this back-and-forth between social formations is 'cultural appropriation'; another is 'popular music'. The culture of sampling in 80s hip-hop and in concurrent black, queer Chicago house represented a belated reparation, a rejection of the property rights that underwrote liberalism but which historically excluded people of colour. While white artists exercised the historical legacy of bourgeois law to assert those property rights against hip-hop,[35] James Brown – probably the most sampled artist of all time – never sued anyone.

10. The Power of Popular Music (Remix)

Popular music's cycle of innovation, recuperation and regeneration hasn't ceased under neoliberalism, although it's returned to slower revolutions than the Fordist era's furious – and historically anomalous – rate of change. Created primarily from samples, post-Fordist music fits Jameson's definition of postmodern culture as "reproduction" – what Reynolds calls "post-production": "the scroll-and-click work of programming and processing, endless small decisions and obsessive-compulsive tweaking". In this both Jameson and Reynolds express a Fordist melancholic elevation of manual over service work, while

Reynolds imagines there was some past point of pure "Newness and Nowness",[36] whereas music has always looked backwards, as well as forwards and around. In defining innovation so narrowly and ahistorically, such futurism contradicts Fisher's (and Reynolds') own usage of 'hauntology'. The premise of this book is that *all* music is hauntological, given time, but sample-based music is hauntological at inception, the past always present in its mix, history processed – remixed – but perceptible.[37]

Just as what Jameson names "the nostalgia mode" doesn't neatly align with conservatism,[38] neither does futurism neatly align with utopianism: sci-fi has always had a dystopian stream. Jameson calls postmodernism – post-Fordism – "the cultural logic of late capitalism". If we regard pop and politics as *mixing* in this way, then to regard *remixing* – reproduction – as signalling an end to innovation – to change – isn't just inaccurate but also pessimistic, paralleling a belief that *political* change is at an end. The irony of fetishising futurism, therefore, is that it leads to that ultimate dystopian sci-fi trope that "Resistance is futile". From sci-fi's utopian stream, however, comes a more hopeful and usable concept: time-travel.

This book is a work of hauntology, a pursuit of the past which Fisher defines as "a refusal to give up on the desire for the future".[39] In our culture, the past is where the future is to be found, and music is a readily available – and electrically joyful – means of accessing it. Marcuse recognised this power of the past but warned that "remembrance is no real weapon unless it is translated into historical action".[40] This book views the past not as a place of mourning or escape, therefore, but as a resource of hope for the present, to inspire and incite us to push our way into the future – a future that is unalienated, uninhibited, free.

Chapter 1

"Raise a Fuss, Raise a Holler": Rock'n'Roll, Doo-Wop and the 50s (1953–58)

The 1950s are now 'classic' – from mid-century modern furniture to film noir, tail-finned cars to fashion staples like Converse, Levi's and Harringtons – and revisiting rock'n'roll has represented a hat tip to tradition for most subsequent popular music (not least classic rock). 'Classic' doesn't just suggest timelessness but tradition, conservatism: Dwight Eisenhower in the White House; women back in the house post-war; whiteness normative. The 1950s are fundamentally American in the popular imaginary, and fundamentally petit bourgeois in Marx's terms, fetishising "order", "religion" and "property".[1] Grey-flannel-suited 'organization man' drives his Chevy back to his two-garage tract home in sprinkler-suffused suburbia, where mom is baking a cherry pie in apron and curlers, while 2.5 kids play hopscotch on the tree-shaded sidewalk. As 80s sitcom *The Wonder Years* theorised, "Everybody was having babies and everybody liked Ike. Everybody knew that if they just worked hard and did all the right things, a sort of paradise of family life lay ahead".[2] Even in dowdier, war-battered Britain, prime minister Harold Macmillan could declare in 1957, "we've never had it so good", as the 'long boom' boomed, hemlines rose and television sets replaced radios as portals to the world.

During the volatile 1970s, the 50s became a utopia for the right, recalled as a time of national confidence after World War II's victory, of economic and social stability, its "lost innocence" becoming a cliché.[3] This 1950s hauntology was asserted politically by Eisenhower's VP, Richard Nixon being president, and culturally by a wave of nostalgia. The meta-50s of *American Graffiti* (1973) is suburban (thus white) and bar the occasional curled lip, conformist, a framing canonised by the cutely cool *Happy Days* (1974–84) and the goofball *Grease* (musical 1971; movie 1978). Disseminated by soundtracks and curated as 'golden oldies' on radio, rock'n'roll started to *sound* as quaintly classic as jukeboxes looked. Elvis's journey from rebellious pretty boy to all-American poster-boy became a pop cultural paradigm, the Presleys' previous poverty just backstory in the American Dream come true. While in this conservative 50s, the working class were mere colour on the road to Graceland, 'colored' people were nigh invisible. In *Back to the Future* (1985) not only does (white) time-travelling Marty McFly (Michael J. Fox) 'invent' rock'n'roll at a high-school prom, but he does so with a song by a black musician, Chuck Berry – even pinching Berry's patented duck-walk – while the *only* black characters in the film hail this "new sound" and alert cousin Chuck to it.

It's because of such cultural labour that the Diamonds' 1957 apple-pie doo-wop 'Little Darlin'' (UK 3; US 3) can be regarded as emblematic of the 50s (as per YouTube comments), while the Gladiolas' (better) original remains obscure. What underlies this labour is an attempt to resolve the contradiction in conservative claims to a stable, affluent society founded on an interventionist system they intrinsically opposed. It makes rather more sense that the 50s should be fetishised by the left: with Fordism creating an institutional framework of social security, this was, Jeremy Gilbert argues, "the first time in history since hunter-gatherer times… that most people weren't worried about how they were going to eat".[4] As such, Fordism produced a social interdependence, a collectivism that Williams calls "the habits of mutual concern and responsibility".[5]

Yet if everything was so peachy perfect, why *did* rock'n'roll happen? Why were the juveniles delinquent, the 'angry young men' angry, and the Beat Generation beaten? These faultlines have faded into 50s style and Fordist nostalgia, with African American experience parcelled off into a parallel universe of liberal 'progress'. The 50s New Left regarded Fordism as forging a "reified and abstract society, coordinated in ever greater bureaucratic complexes, everywhere negating human meaning and control", as Perry Anderson put it.[6] The period's authoritarianism was expressed politically by anti-communism, with the Rosenbergs executed in 1953, the Truman Doctrine of 'containment' creating the Korean War (1950–53) and the British Malayan Emergency consuming the entire decade (1948–60). Although the 50s are routinely referenced as "peaceful",[7] they were riven not just by war but the constant threat of nuclear Armageddon. Nothing says 'stability' like an atom bomb. The Cold War gets forgotten in Fordist nostalgia, but it was always a managed amnesia – there was nothing 'cold' about Korea – offset by consumer capitalism's shimmering showroom. So even the left is still looking the wrong way when it comes to the 50s.

The international containment of communism had a domestic corollary not just in McCarthyism and the repression of the civil rights movement but in the control of everyday behaviour, as Alan Nadel argues.[8] Just as post-war peace was underwritten by nuclear threat, so the nuclear family was underwritten by patriarchy, with the father the Fordist superego enforcing social conformity. Marcuse calls this patrolling of sexuality and work "surplus repression", its eye not just on the body but on the soul.[9] Similarly, the 'whiteness' of the 50s was underwritten by Southern segregation and Northern social apartheid. The flood of white working-class families into government-subsidised suburbs mirrored the black Great Migration from the South (1910–70), yet the suburbs were unofficially but strictly segregated. Indeed, it was white men who were Fordism's primary winners: after their liberating experience of war work, women were co-opted into "the cult of domesticity"[10] as producers of food, children, beauty and harmony. The pre-rock'n'roll pop charts' domination by close-harmonising suburban sisters was thus the *sound* of containment. Across 1955, on the McGuire Sisters' 'Sincerely' (UK 14; US 1), the Fontane Sisters' 'Hearts of Stone' (US 1) and the Chordettes' 'Mr. Sandman' (UK 11; US 1),[11] you can practically *hear* the hum of humongous fridges and *smell* the baking cookies – and see the neighbours' curtains twitching.

It was in youth that the faultlines in the 50s – and in Fordism – were revealed. Youth dissatisfaction was not, contra Gilbert, merely an expression of boredom,[12] but as Hall and Jefferson argue, of "social change", a harbinger of "the classless, post-protestant, consumer-society to come".[13] "I got some money in my jeans and I'm really gonna spend it right", Eddie Cochran crows on 1958's 'C'mon Everybody' (UK 6), voicing not just his individual freedom but youth's collective defiance against social repression. Cochran's cry of "Who cares?" is one of the most joyful in pop. While the development of youth culture was enabled by an income growth that outstripped even that of their newly affluent parents, Hall and Jefferson make too much of consumerism. Marxists can comprehend consumption without elitist dismissal of 'pseudo desires' or Hall's later mesmerisation by shopping: as Marx himself noted, commodities are a "social hieroglyph" which we need to decipher.[14]

Consumer objects can't 'contain' desire in the sense of summing up, restraining or closing down: desire precedes, exceeds and succeeds any commodity, a fact that built-in obsolescence both acknowledges and exploits. With Fordism giving the subaltern a stake in the system, 50s consumer desires *could* be conservative – to conform; to compete; even to condescend – and indeed consumerism was explicitly encouraged by Britain's Conservative government.[15] Not all previously unknown needs are nugatory, however: washing machines ameliorated women's domestic oppression somewhat, while television sets' new ubiquity meant rock'n'roll's revolt was transmitted directly into the conservative haven of the home.

Youth consumerism was expressive of wider, wilder desires than the Fordist settlement could satisfy – sexual liberty, racial intermingling, liberation from work – desires that rock'n'roll could capture but endless versions of orchestral bilge like 'Cherry Pink (and Apple Blossom White)' or schmaltz like 'A Blossom Fell' could not. Where music had hitherto been adult, sedate and moderate, it was now suddenly youthful, energetic and rebellious, resulting in a frantic *tripling* of record sales from 1955–59, with US sales in 1958 *five times* those of 1945.[16] Although vinyl records and transistor radios could be fetishised as *objects,* their material function was to access music, their affective function to access another world. Cars weren't just expensive consumer items, they offered freedom from adult oversight, a ride to that other world. Kids' customisation of cars as hot rods shows how commodities are souped-up by the consumer; repossessed. Bill Haley and his Comets' 'Rock Around the Clock' urges listeners to dance, not slash cinema seats, but audiences of 1955's *Blackboard Jungle* and 1956's *Rock Around the Clock* rendered the song a refusal of repression in both Marxist and Freudian senses. The association of youth with rebellion starts here.

Rock'n'roll represented a breach in the managed conformity of mass society – what Williams calls an "emergent culture" – and was one of the unexpected consequences of the working class entering history.[17] Rewriting the Fordist rules, publicly educated, non-professional musicians recorded songs in small studios and released singles on independent labels,[18] disdaining polite balladry and light jazz for a souped-up take on rural country and roustabout rhythm'n'blues. Sometimes they even sang their own rough-hewn songs, rather than those tailored by Tin Pan Alley. Where balladeers performed at a remove from their musicians, rock'n'rollers recorded and performed as a *group* – whatever the billing – expressing a collective sensibility, be that of youth, class or both. Although rock'n'roll appeared to be unsophisticated, un-Fordist, Fordism was integral to the form's sound – defined by Fender Stratocaster tremolo and analogue slapback echo – even as rock'n'roll's rural/urban, acoustic/electric, black/white dialectic pulled at Fordism's parameters. Sonically alone then, rock'n'roll was a form of protest: even Duane Eddy's 1958 instrumental 'Rebel-'Rouser' (UK 19; US 6) articulates a defiance that was like nothing heard previously in popular music.

Elvis has become the alpha and omega of rock'n'roll, although, arriving late and leaving the building early, he was just its lightning rod. Cuddly country-boy Bill Haley had the first rock'n'roll hit, with 'Crazy Man, Crazy' in 1953 (US 12), while his bowdlerised 1954 take on Big Joe Turner's 'Shake, Rattle and Roll' (UK 4; US 7) is still a facetious disruption of domestic placidity: "Get out in that kitchen and rattle those pots and pans". Yet Haley's 1955 game-changer 'Rock Around the

Clock' was quickly followed by three reminders of this music's origins – Fats Domino's 'Ain't That a Shame' (UK 23; US 10), Chuck Berry's 'Maybellene' (US 5) and Little Richard's 'Tutti Frutti' (UK 29; US 18) – with the latter's "A-wop-bop-a-loo-mop-a-lop-bam-boom!" amongst the most articulate expressions of liberation ever recorded.

Britain's response to rock'n'roll, 'skiffle' – an offshoot of Britain's New Orleans-jazz craze – was another music mined from the American cultural margins, a mix of blues and folk. Skiffle's broom-handle basses and cardboard guitars attested to continuing post-war austerity, contrary to Macmillan's claims of consumer plenty. In this make-do-and-mend culture, skiffle's repurposed washboards and preoccupation with the past were subtle protests against Fordist modernity. Articulated with a very un-British abandon, the whole scene was acutely discomfiting to sedately be-curlered and be-suited parents. That skiffle should become the soundtrack to the new Campaign for Nuclear Disarmament's (CND) opposition to militarised modernity was thus entirely in tune, prefiguring the austere radicalism of the folk boom.

Popular music's hitherto dominant balladeers were, by contrast, figures of order. During the Korean War, Frankie Laine's 1953 'I Believe' (UK 1; US 2) reassured anxious Americans that all was well with the world: "I believe that someone in the Great Somewhere hears every word". Conservatives were alarmed by this new youth music, therefore: by its black motifs, its overt sexuality and its class origins, and worst, by the potential for these elements to combine. After white workers' protests of the 20s and 30s, black soldiers' riots in the 40s and women's 1930s suffrage campaigns and 40s war work, conservatives sought to "keep... the working class divided against itself and labour weak in its relation to capital".[19] Rock'n'roll was the sound of class struggle, of cross-demographic sociality, so the press reviled it and politicians called it "raucous discord" made by "unwashed kids" – a not-so-subtle synonym for 'working class'.[20] Those kids' hero, DJ Allan Freed – self-proclaimed inventor of the term 'rock'n'roll' – was arrested for inciting a riot at a 1958 Jerry Lee Lewis concert in Boston and sacked from his radio show. With both rock and skiffle's public domain sources bypassing Tin

Pan Alley's stranglehold,[21] the new music attacked monopoly capitalism at its financial core, and so the publishing consortium ASCAP lobbied for federal legislation against broadcasting this literally unlicensed music.

Major labels initially attempted to ignore rock'n'roll, churning out ballads like Tony Bennett's schmaltzy 1953 'Stranger in Paradise' (UK 1; US 2), Patti Page's serene 1956 'Allegheny Moon' (US 2) and Dean Martin's smarmy 1956, 'Memories Are Made of This' (UK 1; US 1). The latter's "with His blessings from above... One man, one wife/One love, through life" makes domestic bliss seem like a life sentence. Doris Day's cute 1956 'Que Sera, Sera' (UK 1; US 2) expresses a pert complacency that events are beyond individual control, that the family is life's horizon. Similarly, the very charm of Page's 1957 'Old Cape Cod' (US 3) is coercive: the holiday as worker's playtime, a brief breathing-space inside the Fordist machine. When the pesky kids kept buying that dirty rock'n'roll, however, the Musicians' Union decried guitarists putting big bands and light orchestras out of work, while the major labels promoted more sedate forms of guitar-music. Slim Whitman's 1955 'Rose Marie' (UK 1), ostensibly country, is really an old Tin Pan Alley tune, owned, naturally, by ASCAP. Britain's answer to Elvis, Cliff Richard's propulsive 1958 'Move It' (UK 2) even commented on this containment – "They say [rock'n'roll]'s gonna die" but "ballads and calypsos have got nothin' on/Real country music that just drives along".

Finally, the majors conspired to co-opt rock'n'roll, to corner it in Tin Pan Alley. Crooning was the post-war's dominant vocal style, all soothing murmur and pacifying warmth, a close-microphoned technique that relegated rhythm to background. For Perry Como to cover rock'n'roll tune 'Ko Ko Mo (I Love You So)' (US 2) in 1955 was a neat idea, therefore: suaveness replacing savagery, a chirpy female choir channelling all those charmingly chorusing sisters. Conservative Catholic pinup Pat Boone was a more efficient vehicle of containment, however. Boone's thigh-slapping 1955 cover of 'Ain't That a Shame' made US 1 (UK 7) to Fats Domino's original's US 10 (UK 23), and this became a paradigm: radio stations played the white covers over the black originals. So while the Flamingos' 1956 r'n'b chart hit

'I'll be Home' didn't make the pop charts, Boone's cover was a transatlantic smash (UK 1; US 4). As early as 1956, though, Boone was ducking back to the safety of balladry with the straitlaced 'Friendly Persuasion' (UK 3; US 5) – "Put on your bonnet, your cape, and your glove" – and then 1957's controlling, patriarchal 'Remember You're Mine' (UK 5; US 6). Lest there be any doubt about the engine of containment, Boone was contracted to General Motors, and began presenting the *Chevy Showroom* the same year.

Yet, while Boone was second only to Presley in 50s record sales, the independents *still* outsold the majors, so the co-options kept coming. Kay Starr's 1956 'The Rock and Roll Waltz' (UK 1; US 1) is comically coercive in its subsumption of rock into swing (note the patrician punctuation), while balladeer Guy Mitchell's 1957 'Rock-A-Billy' (UK 1; US 10) is comically clueless, assuming repetitions of the word 'rock' will endow relevance. Yet the same year *American Bandstand* successfully incorporated rock'n'roll into family entertainment with its wholesome, tartan-skirted kids and Christian conservative presenter, Dick Clark. By 1958, the Kalin Twins' 'When' (UK 1; US 5) rendered rock'n'roll as bland as balladry, sexuality and racial otherness excised. Nik Cohn calls such contained, cutesy, bobby-sox-and-stripy-suits rock'n'roll, "highschool",[22] for, as Sinfield points out, rock'n'roll arose in opposition to *all* forms of institutionalised Fordist control – high school included.[23]

While Boone is thankfully lost to history, his work is done when rock'n'roll compilations, Spotify playlists and YouTube algorithms make no distinction between 50s ballads and rock'n'roll bangers and when Elvis's gloopy 'Can't Help Falling in Love' (UK 1; US 2) is, per Spotify, his *best-known song* – three times as familiar as 'Hound Dog'. Equally, prefab teen rock'n'roller Ricky Nelson is now, according to Spotify, more familiar than Fats Domino. This chapter will haul rock'n'roll out of the high school, recapture it from conservative nostalgia, restore its revolt against conformity and reveal it as the first strike in pop's countercultural revolution.

'Be My Guest': Race, Rock'n'Roll, Doo-Wop and Skiffle

The construct of 'race' was key to both the affront and appeal of rock'n'roll, which, along with the contemporaneous civil rights movement, contributed to the concept's gradual deconstruction. We've now moved beyond the poles of white denialism (Greil Marcus)[24] and black separatism (Amiri Baraka)[25] into a not-entirely-satisfactory equivalence. Karl Hagstrom Miller emphasises music as encounter, mutation and transformation, and rightly dismisses "a firm correlation between racialized music and racialized bodies" – the idea that "black people performed black music and white people performed white music".[26] Yet, you don't need to be an essentialist to recognise that rock'n'roll derived more from African American sources and idiom – phrasing, arrangement, presentation – than it did from country music's threadbare yearning. The point is not to establish ownership, but to understand why rock'n'roll was so repulsive to reactionaries and so attractive to the repressed.

Paul Gilroy quotes musicologist Alain Locke, who claimed white listeners experienced black music as a "revolt… against puritan restraint", which offered a "life-saving flight from boredom and oversophistication to the refuge of elemental emotion and primitive vigor".[27] If the 'noble savage' runs interference in such a mind/body duality, Locke's point is that by its very marginalisation, black culture expressed a liberation contrary to both its own political reality *and* to white culture's reality. The KKK's White Citizen's Council spokesman declared rock'n'roll "a designed reversion to savagery", without redeeming 'nobility': "The heavy beat music of the Negroes […] appeals to the base in man [and] brings out animalism and vulgarity". While it's striking that civilisation should be so fragile, the racist logic that black Americans were the *id* of white Americans expressed a social truth: that the cultural imbrication of races terrified the elites. Following the landmark integration case, Brown vs. Board of Education in 1954, segregationists held placards at Alabama rock'n'roll concerts declaring, "NAACP says integration, rock & roll".[28] The 'color line' at Little Richard's Southern shows was regularly breached without any involvement from Dr King's organisation, however.

Louisiana banned interracial dancing in summer 1956, while the torture and murder of teenage Emmett Till in nearby Mississippi testified to the stakes of crossing that cultural line.

Rock'n'roll pre-empted political desegregation, with African Americans no longer just appearing on film and television screens as janitors, maids and 'novelties' but as icons, role models and objects of desire. These musicians usually wrote their own music, appropriating no one's copyright or culture: indeed, Fats Domino's 'Be My Guest' (UK 11; US 8) can be read as a sly commentary on this cultural traffic – "I'm a king but you can wear my crown". In the film *Diner* (1982), a man berates his girlfriend for her failure to respect the genre-cataloguing of his record collection: he insists Domino isn't rock'n'roll but rhythm and blues. This is segregation sublimated as muso-pedantry, for while Domino's roll is less rocking than Presley's, his insistent backbeat is pretty much the *definition* of rock'n'roll – see 'I'm Walkin'' (UK 19; US 4) – as Elvis himself noted. With nine top-ten hits, and roles in *Shake, Rattle and Rock!* and *The Girl Can't Help It* (1956), Domino inspired a popular hysteria not far from Presley's, and established a style that survived rock's recuperation, probably *because* of its unthreatening mellowness. While most of Fats' lyrics are moon/June hokery, 'Blue Monday' stands out (UK 23; US 5), not just as one of the first songs to express Fordist alienation, but because its vocabulary links the specificity of African American experience – "Got to work like a slave all day" – to that of the entire working class.

Also from New Orleans, the criminally forgotten Lloyd Price's 1958 'Stagger Lee' still staggers (UK 7; US 1) – not just for its exuberance but for how the celebration of a black murderer got past the censors and segregationists. The details are grisly – the bullet "came through Billy and it broke the bartender's glass" – but the massed backing vocals gleefully egg the murderer on; "Go, Stagger Lee!" (tamed by Boone's cover to "Oh, Stagger Lee", while Google's transcription of Price's version primly follows suit). The song's power derives from its expression of the return of the repressed, revealing both the low value of life in black America *and* its population's latent potential for violent reprisal against the oppressors.

Little Richard's 1955 'Tutti Frutti' was a turbocharged

take on the New Orleans style, its sheer aggression becoming the template for subsequent rock'n'roll. Following the Boone-ification of 'Tutti' (UK 29; US 12), Richard's even faster and dirtier 1956 'Long Tall Sally' (UK 3; US 6) was intended to be uncontainable, but Boone was brave or dumb enough to try it (UK 18; US 8). Boone's falsetto "woo" is feeble compared to Richard's signature bullroar, while nobody could believe Pat was going to have any interesting "fun tonight". With rock'n'roll's emphasis on the visual as much as the musical a feature of its Fordist modernity, Richard's piano-bashing, cape-wearing, bouffant-barneted showmanship resulted in him being showered with female undergarments. This charisma enabled Richard to transcend the mockery of rock'n'roll in Jayne Mansfield vehicle *The Girl Can't Help It* (1956), his kinetic performance being gobbled up by teenagers, including the young Beatles. Richard's appeal is distilled in 1957's 'Lucille' (UK 10; US 21): words barely intelligible, it's pure feeling, the very *sound* of freedom, with a beat that seems to push into the future.

If Richard defined rock's aggressive dynamic, Chuck Berry created its guitar demotic, along with its visionary poetic. Berry's 1955 debut, 'Maybellene' (US 5) reversed and reclaimed Presley's musical amalgam by hot-rodding a rural country tune, 'Ida Red', with Chicago urban blues. As such, the song's car culture of Coup de Villes and V8 Fords was a fantasy for black Americans, as footage of the 1955 Montgomery bus boycott after Rosa Parks' arrest attests: *everybody* is walking. In subsequent hits, Berry seemed to consciously infiltrate white culture, changing the original "little coloured boy" on 1958's 'Johnny B. Goode' to a "little country boy", who lives the American dream through music (US 8). While it was a mark of conservatism for white commentators to act like America was a level playing field, for black musicians to do so was always either satirical or utopian.

Berry's 1957 'School Days' (UK 24; US 3) would be cutely 'highschool' were it not concurrent with the Little Rock school-segregation crisis. Its conclusion, "Hail, hail rock and roll/ Deliver me from the days of old", transforms the song from culturally humdrum to politically utopian, attesting to the power of music to effect social change. Equally, while the 'golly gee' language of 1958's 'Sweet Little Sixteen' (UK 16; US 2) suggests a white protagonist, the fact that she's dancing with "cats" in New Orleans is an insouciant vision of a desegregated world. Berry's stardom made this desegregation material, as a regular on TV and with roles in *Rock Rock Rock!* (1956) and *Go, Johnny, Go!* (1959). Moreover, Berry was under no illusion that American opportunities were equal: burned by the business's systematic exploitation of black musicians – he was coerced into giving Allan Freed a writing credit on 'Maybellene' – Berry demanded all payment in cash. So, Berry's last hit of the 50s, 'Back in the USA' (UK 6) does not, as Greil Marcus claims,[29] refuse irony by claiming, "I'm so glad I'm livin' in the USA", it *lives* irony: Berry's protagonist's search for a drive-in and "corner café" would be tricky enough in the North, let alone the segregated South.

Desegregation was the heart of rock'n'roll's appeal – and of its scandal. On Elvis's first hit, early 1956's 'Heartbreak Hotel' (UK 2; US 1), he sings the blues with connoisseur knowledge – all croak, rasp and shudder – which, combined with his trademark warmth, makes the track essentially *empathetic*. The narrator isn't just lonely, he's *alienated*, conveyed by the skeletal backing's ghostly hotel-band jazz and the eerie acres of echo that subsumes its empty spaces. The instrumental track sounds like it's coming from a distant past, while the vocal's close-mic'd intimacy is entirely modern, as is the sense that the hotel is erected *across* some southern town's railtracks, distinctions between white and black, self and other blurring.[30] Ricky Nelson's 1958 'Lonesome Town' (US 7) is an attempt to occupy the same location, even using Elvis's Jordanaires, but the effect, while pretty, is pure country, without the aura of racial encounter of 'Heartbreak'. Although country is a hybrid form, it signifies as 'white', and that Presley's follow-up, 'I Want You, I Need You, I Love You' (UK 14; US 1) was conventional country felt like a deliberate retreat. However, the track's B-side cover of bluesman Arthur Crudup's 'My Baby Left Me' was a more aggressive take on Presley's early Sun Studios sides, the stepping-stone to 'Hound Dog', itself initially merely the B-side to 'Don't Be Cruel' (US 1). The fix was in, however, because, while 'Don't Be Cruel' was *cute*, the threat was gone, so too the promise, except for Elvis's delighted "mmm!" at 0:47.

Jerry Lee Lewis was white from his voice to his suits to his hair, infusing rock'n'roll with a rebel yell and a raw, country crudeness. Yet Lewis's 1957 'Whole Lot of Shakin' Goin' On' (UK 8; US 3) isn't just an r'n'b cover, it evokes the young Jerry Lee's forays into black dives (solving the mystery of the line, "chicken in the barn" – it's barbecue). By contrast Ricky Nelson's version sounds like he's never been anywhere wilder than a high school hop (*Ricky*, US 1). Lewis doesn't so much cover Otis Blackwell's 'Great Balls of Fire' (UK 1; US 2) as *possess* it, espousing hellfire-preacher righteousness through Little Richard's gospel devilry, see-sawing in and out of a fierce 'Tutti Frutti' falsetto. On stage and in the films *Jamboree* (1957) and *High School Confidential* (1958), Lewis took Richard's piano-pulverising showmanship to perverse heights, standing on the instrument, even setting fire to it, his contempt for the liberal talisman of property paralleled by his abandonment of emotional restraint. The rules, Jerry Lee's scary stare tells you, simply don't apply.

Even a rock'n'roller as ramalama highschool as Buddy Holly – wholesome in his horn rims, candy sweet in his melodies – is *suffused* with African American influence. The stop-start syncopations of 1957's 'That'll Be the Day' (UK 1; US 1) – particularly the 1-2-3 drum stutter at 1:48 – are, compared to balladry, as leftfield as the lyric's morbid sentiment ("That'll be the day that I die"). Holly's electric guitar is equal parts Moore's mercurial sparking and Berry's bluesy chug – pure popular modernism. Holly's channelling of Bo Diddley's five-cornered African beat on 1957's 'Not Fade Away' (UK 3; US 10) is wildly syncopated, while its childlike lyric pitches for the eternal and utopian.

This emphasis on 'race' is not a matter of ownership or appropriation, therefore, but the utopianism of music's cultural encounter. Concurrently, Jack Kerouac in *On the Road* (1957), walking through Denver's "colored section" was "wishing I were a Negro, feeling that the best the white world had offered was not enough ecstasy for me, not enough life, joy, kicks, darkness, music". Despite not comprehending race as a *system*, Kerouac is attempting to upend hierarchies here, expressing the appeal of an oppressed group's culture to the dominant culture's doubters, trapped in what he laments as "white ambitions" – workplace alienation, domestic repression and racism itself. [31]

Direct from the ghettoes' street corners, doo-wop crossed the tracks concurrent with rock'n'roll and is one of the great art forms of the twentieth century. Vocal-based, because instruments were expensive – the baritone imitating a double bass – doo-wop's yearning derives from its descent from spirituals, hot-rodded by the rambunctiousness of r'n'b and is thus an encounter between the carnal and spiritual. The El Dorados' 1955 'At My Front Door' (US 17) is a joyfully unbridled explosion of handclaps, vocal blurts and ribald implication that breaks down its titular door. Boone's version (US 7) slams that door shut, swapping "Keep your little mama off my street" for "Teach your little mama right from wrong", failing to recognise that it was the licentiousness – the liberation – that *made* this music. The lothario of the Cadillacs' 1955 'Speedoo' (US 17) was uncontainable, however, and Martin Scorsese wasn't the only Italian American tuning in to doo-wop (see: *Goodfellas*). Frankie Laine gave Frankie Lymon and the Teenagers their first television exposure on his 1956 show, revealing no awareness of racial difference, and acknowledging their music as "rock'n'roll" before symbolically surrendering the stage. Yet, in 2023, the most popular YouTube video of the Teenagers' 'Why Do Fools Fall in Love' (UK 1; US 6) is a montage from *American Graffiti* featuring only white faces. Even in the segregated 50s, the Del Vikings broke through with a racially mixed lineup: 'Come and Go With Me' (US 5) is lively, but 1957's 'Whispering Bells' (US 9) is *giddy*, absolutely bursting with pop utopianism.

Doo-wop's pulse was slowed as the majors regained their grip. The Platters' 1958 'Smoke Gets in Your Eyes' (UK 1; US 1) and the Flamingos' 1959 'I Only Have Eyes for You' (US 11) turned the cultural clock back to post-war balladry, closer to the Ink Spots than the El Dorados, excised of excitement, oddity, carnality – making it easier for white acts to co-opt doo-wop's style. From their first hit, 1958's 'I Wonder Why' (US 22), Italian Americans Dion and the Belmonts were clearly intended as highschool – blazered, pocket-squared, finger-clickin' squares. Yet there was a depth to Dion that transcended his group's superficiality, an abandon in his body movements, a slyness in his facial expressions, an unbridled joy and pain in his voice that subtly articulated what Marcuse calls "the Great Refusal – the protest against what *is*".[32]

The bizarre British phenomenon of skiffle was another borrowing from black culture, with Lonnie Donegan's 1955 version of an old folk-tune, 'Rock Island Line' (UK 8; US 8), sparking a transatlantic craze. Get past the stilted spoken introduction – which crosses the line between amateurism and minstrelsy – and the track's raw, careening frenzy still carries a considerable charge. Donegan's 1957 'Cumberland Gap' (UK 1), with its electric guitar solo and gruffly abandoned vocal, is almost indistinguishable from rock'n'roll. Skiffle expressed both alienation from austerity Britain's stifled self *and* an empathy with its racial other, meaning that skifflers' instrumentality in new anti-racist organisation, the Stars' Campaign for Interracial Friendship, simply pursued their music's political logic.

This relationship of music to race wasn't always recognisable to the socially immobile. For rock'n'roll-loving Teddy Boys, immigration seemed "causal rather than coincidental" to their economic condition, Jefferson argues.[33] Unable to recognise the Windrush generation as class allies doing the same dead-end jobs, the Teds' misdirected resentment resulted in violent attacks on Caribbean communities in 1958. The music industry's concurrent championing of the calypso Caribbeans brought with them was less racially conciliatory than a misconceived attempt to stifle skiffle and rock'n'roll. For while 'The Banana Boat Song' superficially sounds 'exotic', it's a protest against dead-end work, while calypso was also an integrally anti-imperialist genre. The biographies of the hit versions' singers – civil rights activist Harry Belafonte (UK 2; US 5) and black Briton Shirley Bassey (UK 8) – were a statement in themselves, while Belafonte's 'Island in the Sun' (UK 3; US 30) professed a racial pride hitherto unheard in pop.[34]

This cultural encounter between races – on the radio, in coffee bars, across the colour line at concerts, within genres – was utopian, a vision of a world beyond the divisions of race, inevitably, provoked reactionary resistance. You could see that other world in the hot-rodded hybrid of Berry's America and in white women's libidinal reaction to Little Richard. In popular music, white demands for meaning in work and black demands for basic rights were part of the same desire for liberation, the same "revolt against the drabness of commonplace life". It was this capacity for class unity that meant rock'n'roll had to be contained, co-opted – or crushed.

"Tremors in the Thighbone": Sex and Gender in 50s Pop

When Nadel claims that 50s society "equated containment of communism with containment... of sexual license, of gender roles",[35] it's not meant as a metaphor. What Gramsci calls Fordism's "rationalisation" of sexuality repressed disorderly desire to focus the energies of the male worker, thus the emphasis on monogamous marriage, which also repressed female sexuality and post-suffragist revolt within the role of helpmeet.[36] Youth's sexuality was repressed through the systemic courtship culture of 'dating', going steady, the prom, good girls and bad girls – Sandra Dee vs. Rizzo – and the early age of the average marriage (20–22). Consequently, libertarian sexologist Albert Kinsey was lambasted by the media, harassed by the state, and had his research funding withdrawn. This was sexual containment.

With African American culture at an enforced remove from the 'mainstream' and possessed of its own record labels and radio stations, rhythm'n'blues enjoyed a sexual license denied to dominant balladry. With this stuff only a spin of the dial away, however, the pop charts began to be infiltrated by r'n'b raunch like Billy Ward and the Dominoes' 1951 'Sixty Minute Man' (US 17) – using the term "rock'n'roll" as synonym for sex – and Hank Ballard's 1954 'Work With Me Annie' (US 22). With rock'n'roll's sexual affront often relayed in racist terms – "animalistic", "jungle tom-toms" etc.[37] – the establishment put Elvis in palliative tails and banned movement from the waist down (*The Steve Allen Show*). When Presley had fun suggesting his pelvis had a mind of its own, they only filmed him from the waist up (*The Ed Sullivan Show*). Similarly, sex kept bursting 50s' society's bounds.

Sex as a seismic, uncontrollable force runs through Presley's spring 1957 'All Shook Up' (UK 1; US 1), Lewis's 1957 'Great

Balls of Fire' and 1958 'Breathless' (UK 8; US 7) – all by black songwriter Otis Blackwell – alongside a rare British gem, Johnny Kidd and the Pirates' 'Shakin' All Over' (UK 1). Where all this hyperventilation, shaking and shivering might traditionally have testified to masculine weakness, it instead evoked rupture – sexual, generational, racial – the rocking of foundations. Gene Vincent's leather-draped delinquent signalled a decadent sexuality, sleazily displayed on 1956's bluesily carnal 'Be-Bop-a-Lula' (UK 16). Vincent was smartened up on that year's *The Girl Can't Help It*, though his cheekbones still shouted 'danger', and nothing could clean up his coital whimper on the song's last verse. Little Richard's rendition of the film's title song (UK 9; US 7), meanwhile, uses kitchen metaphors to disrupt the temple of the domestic with unrepressed carnality – "If she winks an eye the bread slice turns to toast".

That the authorities viewed sex as just such a disruption of civilised order only fomented rock'n'roll's frisson. The Everly Brothers' 1957 'Wake Up Little Susie' knowingly plays out this moral panic – the teens who sleep through a movie will cause folks to declare, "Ooh la la!", so their "reputation is shot". Radio stations duly banned the song, giving it an unmerited risqué reputation that resulted in it shooting up the charts (UK 2; US 1). In Little Richard's 1958 'Good Golly, Miss Molly' (UK 8; US 10), that Molly "sure likes to ball" connects to the fact that, when she's "rockin' and rollin'", she "can't hear [her] mama call": rock'n'roll puts her sexuality beyond parental control. The narrator's father's warning – "Son, you better watch your step!" – is laughed off as envy. Parents are also up in arms in Johnny Otis's 1958 'Willie and the Hand Jive' (US 9), which, driven by another Bo Diddley beat, was taken to refer not to a demurely unbodily dance but to undemurely bodily masturbation. Parents and patrician radio stations somehow let Big Bopper's 1958 'Chantilly Lace' pass (UK 12; US 6), despite its lascivious yelp of "Do I what? Will I *what?*/Oh baby, you know what I like!"

The elites' response was to tempt teenagers with an alternative, asexual 'rock'n'roll' – Cohn's 'highschool' – given 'authenticity' by being, unusually, largely self-written. 16-year-old Paul Anka's 1957 'Diana' (UK 1; US 1) articulates youth as a yearning for adulthood – "I'm so young and you're so old/Oh my darling, I've been told" – its perky balladry having precious little to do with rock'n'roll, while, again, it's adulthood that's being fantasised in Jimmy Clanton's 1958 'Just a Dream' (US 4). Stood up on prom night, Marty Robbins' 1957 country ballad, 'A White Sport Coat' ("and a pink carnation") still reaffirms high school courtship rituals (US 2). Tommy Sands' 1957 mid-pacer 'Goin Steady' (US 16) lays out the process: "We ain't married/ But we're getting ready/To tie the knot" – pending her daddy's consent. Ricky Nelson's 1957 'Be-Bop Baby' (US 3) ups both tempo and temperature – "She got plenty of rhythm, got plenty of jive" – but just as this only prompts honourable thoughts – "My love for her is so tender and sweet" – the musicians' attempt at Bo Diddley barely has rhythm, let alone raunch. Nelson's 1958 'Believe What You Say' (US 4) allows some abandon into James Burton's guitar solo, but the warnings about taking sex lightly are dire on 'Poor Little Fool' (UK 4; US 1), as is the song.

Even Elvis wasn't Elvis anymore: the lilting Disney rock of 1957's '(Let Me Be Your) Teddy Bear' (UK 3; US 1) insists on his sexual tameness: "Don't want to be a tiger/'Cause tigers play too rough". The post-army, countryfied 1959 'A Fool Such as I' (UK 1; US 2) finds Presley *crooning* his uncarnal devotion. Despite the picture of Elvis in uniform on the cover, 'A Big Hunk o' Love' (UK 4; US 1) proclaims not sexual swagger but quantification of his commitment. In an indicator that sex itself could be co-opted, the Royal Teens' 1958 'Short Shorts' (US 3) offers *just* the right amount of sexiness to be both cute and commercial.

While theatre produced a Shelagh Delaney to counter the 'angry young men', 50s rock'n'roll is an unrewarding locale for feminism. Where in the early 50s one-third of American charting songs were by female performers, rock'n'roll led to a reassertion of masculine hegemony. In *The Girl Can't Help It*, elegant, unattainable women sing ballads – Julie London's haunting, jazzy 'Cry Me a River' (UK 22; US 9) – while raunchier female singers like Jayne Mansfield really just want to retire to be housewives. *Singing* sexily is left to the boys: Eddie Cochran's 'Twenty Flight Rock' is outrageous in its substitution of 'rock' for 'fuck' as he takes every flight.

Of the few female rock'n'roll hits, Georgia Gibbs' 1955 'Dance With Me Henry (Wallflower)' (US 1) was based on Etta

James' answer-song to Ballard's 'Annie', with neither raunch nor rock'n'roll surviving the transition. LaVern Baker's 'Tweedle Dee' (US 14) was eclipsed commercially by Gibbs' version (US 2), which copped the arrangement but chopped the only rock'n'roll element – Baker's seductive alto – leaving it merely twee. African American women contributed two great mid-pacers, however: Baker's 1955 'Jim Dandy' (US 17) and Shirley and Lee's life-affirming 1956 'Let the Good Times Roll' (US 20). While Connie Francis is commonly compiled as 'rock'n'roll', 1958's 'Who's Sorry Now' (UK 1; US 4) was a tatty old Tin Pan Alley ballad given a neat new r'n'b arrangement, although Francis's voice had a command that rose – indeed swooped – above the crooner quotidian. Better still, Francis's 'Stupid Cupid' (UK 1; US 14) offered a female take on the shivering, foundation-shaking song, enhanced by Francis's frantic hiccups and purrs. 'Fallin'' (UK 20; US 30) was an even bolder exercise in the same vein, with genuine grit to both lyric and performance, before Francis was pushed back into bland balladeering.

While this entire book is about re-reading music in retrospect, to regard rock'n'roll as queer seems entirely anachronistic – but only if you accept the quaint, cookies-and-curlers version of the era. Based on Little Richard alone, the 50s was queer to its roots: his original lyrics for 'Tutti Frutti' were "Good booty/If it don't fit, don't force it/You can grease it, make it easy". If overt queerness was suicide in 50s society, then Richard seemingly had a death wish: slavered in makeup and putting the 'pomp' in pompadour, he sang with an over-expressive abandon that mocked his own performativity while furiously asserting his sincerity. Little Richard was the *definition* of radical camp.

'Homoerotic' is referred on to 'homosexual' in the *Oxford English Dictionary*, while *Merriam-Webster* also emphasises homosexual "activity". Yet if the 'gaze' that frames visual culture is, as Laura Mulvey argues, male – objectifying women, subjectifying men[38] – then Elvis offering himself as an object of desire can only be termed 'homoerotic' (even as this linguistically excludes his gazing female fans), disrupting the ideological work asserting traditional masculinity in this era. Elvis even had one moment of literal queerness: 1957's 'Jailhouse Rock' (UK 1; US 1) was the bluesiest, raunchiest thing he'd done in months, and as the prisoners are partnering up for the titular dance, Number 47 tells Number 3, "You're the cutest jailbird that I ever did see". It's a clean joke only if you know nothing about what occurs in prisons – though the sequence in the accompanying film leaves little to the imagination. Presley's performance here is a last hurrah for his pelvis: soon he'd metaphorically be presenting *himself* from the waist up, containing his sexuality in his new role as wholesome family entertainer. Soon all music would sound as glazedly desexualised as Paul Anka's 1958 'You Are My Destiny' (UK 6; US 7), whose promise that "you share my reverie" makes heterosexual affirmation sound like hypnosis therapy.

"I'm Not a Juvenile Delinquent": Youth and 50s Pop

Youth violence is written out of the conservative narrative of the 50s for good reason, being indicative of what Hebdige calls "the breakdown of consensus in the post-war period".[39] As such, juvenile delinquency is an analogue of rock'n'roll's aggression and 50s fashion's informality, a rejection of patriarchal social control. Ballads like Eddie Fisher's 1954 'Oh! My Pa-Pa' (UK 9; US 1) – 'Oh Mein Papa' in Eddie Calvert's version (UK 1; US 6) – literally affirmed the name of the father. Skiffle's 'Don't You Rock Me Daddy-oh' took that name in vain, as a 1957 hit for both Lonnie Donegan (UK 4) and the Vipers (UK 10). Adorno calls the family "the fatal germ cell of society";[40] an "institutional state apparatus" in Louis Althusser's term, so the family was the arena in which 50s social conflict was played out.[41]

Youth rebellion is often patronised as a 'phase': with psychoanalysis the offspring of patriarchy, Freud's *id* is childish, unrealistic and needs to be corrected by the superego's – the patriarch's – reality principle. In Freud's family drama, the id (played here by bequiffed teens) *reaffirms* rather than rejects the superego (played by organization man), with "the liminality of adolescence giving way to inevitable reaggregation into the adult world", as Ross satirically notes.[42] For Phil Cohen, however, youth has agency within this drama, with its culture's role being to "express and resolve, albeit magically, the contradictions which remain hidden or unresolved in the parent culture".[43] Rather than repressing Fordism's faultlines, as their parents and their culture had, 50s youth *exposed* them, through the mediums of music and fashion – and the intermittent eruption of violence.

Chuck Berry's 1956 'Roll Over, Beethoven' (US 29) and 1957 'Rock and Roll Music' (US 8) are manifestos of this youth culture, rejecting patriarchal criteria – and in the case of 'Beethoven', the entire imperialist canon of high culture. Little Richard's 1956 'Rip It Up' (UK 30; US 17) refuses 50s frugality in favour of hedonism ("Fool about my money, don't try to save"), while its title and chorus urge the listener to rip up the societal rulebook. British rock'n'roller Tommy Steele's B-sides were far stroppier than his sedate, poorly-accented covers of American hits, with 1957's 'Teenage Party' (B-side, 'Knee Deep in the Blues', UK 15) asserting youth cultural difference – even the door is "teenage" – a difference rendered defiant by Steele's propulsive guitar solo. The same year's 'Rebel Rock' (B-side, 'Singin' the Blues', UK 1) declares, "If they say you gotta do it, don't... your life's your own". Directed at parents, the vessels of the societal superego, something rather more than domestic disputes is being dramatised in these songs.

Marx claims that capitalism creates its own gravediggers, unleashing forces it can't contain or control:[44] the proletariat of laissez-faire but also, less remarked, the youth culture of Fordism. Youth fashion was "style as a form of Refusal", in Hebdige's terms, "a symbolic violation of the social order".[45] Rolled up where parents were buttoned down, greased up where dad was smoothed down, youth favoured blue-collar and rustic fabrics like denim and plaid to organization man's modern nylon and seersucker. Yet capitalism also digs graves for its gravediggers: consumerism can contain as well as exploit rebellion and in Althusser's other key concept, consumerism "interpellates" youth into the system.[46] Yet because the capitalist imperative is fiscal rather than moral, the results are contradictory: the name Frankie Lymon and the Teenagers is both an interpellation of youth as a market demographic *and* an assertion of an oppositional identity. The Coasters' 'Charlie Brown' is Fordist factory hacks Leiber and Stoller's cynical satire of teen rebellion, but its titular rebel's complaint, "Why is everybody always pickin' on me?", adroitly captures youth

35

resentment at parental and societal pressure (UK 6; US 2). Conscious of these contradictions, Carl Perkins' 1956 'Blue Suede Shoes' (UK 10: US 2) both celebrates and satirises youth's fetishisation of fashion – the money and the show. Yet the song ultimately upends the priorities of the 50s property cult – "You can burn my house/Steal my car" – rhetoric that would have shocked the period's thrifty, materialist parents.

That 50s juvenile delinquency is now redolent of styling rather than violence is testament to the industriousness of capitalist containment. Brando's *The Wild One* (1953) and Dean's *Rebel Without a Cause* (1955) were fetishistically fashion-orientated, while *Jailhouse Rock* and *West Side Story* (both 1957) staged delinquency as dance routines, cultural threat contained by theatrical camp. This was followed by a series of products purpose-built to narrow the generation gap, written by professionals who'd literally never been teenagers (the term only becoming current in the mid-50s). Who better than the Teenagers to testify, 'I'm Not a Juvenile Delinquent' (UK 12) in 1957, therefore, and to advise, "Do the things that's right... Stay out of trouble and you'll be glad". Tommy Sands' 1957 theme from the cheese-promoting Kraft Television Theatre, 'Teen-Age Crush' (US 2), makes the cheesy claim that parents have "forgotten when they were young/ And the way tried to be free", again positing youth as a brief stop on the road to normative adulthood. Ricky Nelson's 1957 'A Teenager's Romance' (US 2) answers parental criticism – "They tell us... we haven't the right to decide for ourselves" – by pledging monogamy and marriage.

Literally 'highschool', Danny & the Juniors' 1957 'At the Hop' (UK 3; US 1) renders rock'n'roll not just innocuous but nerdy, with its passionless delivery of hipster demotic: "Where the jockey is the smoothest/And the music is the coolest" and "All the cats and the chicks can get their kicks at the hop". Compare this to Jerry Lee's 'High School Confidential' the following year (UK 12; US 21), where fun is expressed violently – "the juke box blows a fuse" – and hedonistic rapture becomes social rupture – "let's shake it up tonight". The likes of Lee were on their way out, however: Pat Boone's manual, *Twixt Twelve and Twenty* (1958), and Dick Clark's *Your Happiest Years* (1959) made the establishment's intent to contain youth culture explicit.

What was most threatening about rock'n'roll was its attitude to work. With the Depression a recent memory and full employment a relative novelty, the cult of work was central to 50s conservatism. Yet as Marx noted, "The worker feels himself only when he is not working; when he is working, he does not feel himself".[47] Thus for Marcuse, "the sphere outside labour" is freedom.[48] Bill Haley's 1955 'Rock Around the Clock' (UK 1; US 1) isn't just a celebration of hedonism but a rejection of capitalist temporality, life regulated by work, clocking on and clocking off. That Tennessee Ernie Ford's tough country tune 'Sixteen Tons' (UK 1; US 1) became a hit in 1956 was thus hardly coincidental. Presenting work as class oppression ("A poor man's made out of muscle and blood"), 'Sixteen Tons' depicts a life of drudgery and debt where aggression is the release-valve on this Fordist man-machine, with "one fist of iron, the other of steel", but also, crucially, its threat.

Black doo-woppers the Silhouettes' 1958 hit 'Get a Job' (US 1) is often taken literally – thus its use in an 80s ad for Brook Street Bureau recruiters – yet the tune's nonsense syllables are a raspberry blown at the performance principle, as the narrator's mother/girlfriend pushes want-ads at him. Once again, the hacks hacked into this affect: Leiber and Stoller's 1958 'Yakety Yak' for the Coasters' (UK 12; US 1) dramatises the parental performance principle that represses youth's rebellious id: "If you don't scrub that kitchen floor/You ain't gonna rock and roll no more". The bass voice's "don't talk back" tagline is ironic, for the *whole song* is talking back – to parents, to society, to the performance principle. In the Everlys' 'Problems' (UK 6; US 2), teachers in the institutional state apparatus enforce the Fordist compact which trades a modicum of leisure for a lifetime of containment: "Can't get the car, my marks ain't been so good".

Eddie Cochran's brief, brilliant career epitomised rock'n'roll as rebellion, channelling James Dean's style and Gene Vincent's attitude, despite industry attempts to Booneify him. 1958's 'Summertime Blues' (UK 18; US 8) is not just Cochran's major contribution to rock'n'roll but to any consideration of a counterculture. Its brusquely strummed chords and excited handclaps evoke a gang, an enclosed world with its own demotic, doing its own thing with utter seriousness. Yet its lyric looks outwards at the forces arraigned against it – bossy bosses ("No dice, son, you gotta work late"), pushy parents ("Son, you gotta make some money'") and the staid state (the congressman intoning, "I'd like to help you son but you're too young to vote"). As on 'Yakety Yak', the song's recurring bass drawl is the caricatured, hyper-masculine voice of patriarchal authority, insisting on the performance principle over the pleasure principle. The kid's vow to take his problem to the United Nations pre-empts parental mockery, but in its very flippancy makes clear quite how political the personal can be, for the summertime blues is the discovery that leisure is only guaranteed through labour, a contract the adult world both endorses and enforces. Marx's term for the summertime blues was 'alienation'. Consequently, the adult-youth conflict in the song – and in 50s culture – is a distraction: youth was only expressing the alienation experienced by adults too, a conflict otherwise known as 'class struggle'.

'High Class Baby': Class and 50s Pop Culture

There are, crucially, three components of class: economic, cultural – "accent, clothes, tastes, furnishing, food"[49] – and political – the power relations between rulers and ruled. If, under post-Fordism, the cultural has eclipsed the economic and political components, then under Fordism all three overlapped. Rock'n'roll's regional accents, 'unsophisticated' tastes and rough manners expressed culturally what trade unions expressed politically: the power of the working class as they marched across modernity's stage. Presley, Lewis and Holly were just the crest of a wave of proletarian culture that transformed conceptions of who and what could be admirable, heroic, influential. In Britain, former cabin boy Tommy Steele played on class dynamics with 1956's stereotype-satirising 'Rock with the Caveman' (UK 8) and by promoting the ditty at an aristocratic debutante ball. Cliff Richard's 1958 'High Class Baby' (UK 7) finds the plebs turning tables on the debs – "sable mink and a Cadillac... this pink champagne and caviar are all very grand", Cliff mocks – valorising the ordinary, voiced through music: "I prefer just rocking to a rock'n'roll band". The working class weren't just the mouthpieces of this new music but its performers and often its writers – the mass speaking in its own undubbed voice, its message diffused via mass media.

Williams noted at the time that "'mass' is a new word for mob",[50] and the music industry's disdain for rock'n'roll paralleled elite class condescension, cloaking fear of class power. In Britain, with 50s union unrest peaking at 2,832 strikes by 1960, this fear was relayed in the depiction of lazy workers and corrupt union bosses in the film *I'm Alright Jack* (1959), in the press's constant vilification of unions and in hysterical polemics like Woodrow Wyatt's *Peril in our Midst* (1956).[51] As Anderson notes, "The Cold War allowed capitalist regimes... to establish a powerful negative identification of socialism with... the Soviet Union under Stalin".[52] In America, the McCarthy anti-communist witch hunts, the strike-restricting 1947 Taft Hartley Act and the Marlon Brando-starring *On the Waterfront* (1954) – its unions both communist and corrupt – all deployed this association to keep the working class in check. Yet *Waterfront*, in a crucial distinction, while denigrating class revolt, valorises class *culture*, presenting the proletarian as pre-eminently *stylish*.

While this reification of working-class culture plainly had a pacifying purpose for the elites, it also opened up possibilities for plebeians. Mark Abrams reported in 1959 that "90 per cent of all teenage spending is conditioned by working-class taste and values".[53] Rock'n'roll fandom and fashion didn't just put the 'power' in 'spending power' therefore, but symbolically undermined dominant ideology. As Hebdige argues, style itself is a class issue: for the dispossessed to present themselves as objects of envy – and of desire – is a rejection of class hierarchy.[54] 1953's 'Teddy Boy murder' on Clapham Common was prompted by a Ted being called a "flash cunt", yet that unskilled working-class Teds were *getting above themselves* was the whole point. Teds' appropriation of the aristocratic style of Edwardian dandies – drape jackets, pleated trousers, brogues – was a symbolic rejection of the class hierarchy that had placed them on its lowest rung.[55]

The term 'establishment' was introduced via the *Spectator* in 1955 to describe society's upper echelons' domination of government, business and finance. Britain's 1956 imperial adventure in Suez offered a sterling example of establishment solipsism. This class stratification was protested by John

Osborne's 1957 *Look Back in Anger*, its incandescence as inchoate as the Teds' – and as misdirected: this time at gender rather than race. The term 'anti-establishment' was introduced by the leftist *New Statesman* in 1958: rock'n'rollers, Teds, spivs and greasers were all essentially anti-establishment, representatives of a class revolt – of the ruled against the rulers.

In all of this, the economic component of class can get lost, and nowhere is this more apparent than in accounts of how rock'n'roll's class revolt was quelled. With its major players all surrendering the stage, it can seem like rock'n'roll contained *itself*: Little Richard taking to the church, Elvis to the army, Jerry Lee to country's backwaters, Chuck Berry to prison and Buddy Holly and Eddie Cochran to the afterlife. But as that rock'n'roll-call of repressive state apparatuses – army, church, prison – suggests, the machinations of the rulers are implicated in all these biographical narratives. Marx and Melly both note that capitalists and conservatives alike seek order,[56] while rock'n'roll was clearly an expression of *dis*order.

By its very factual looseness and reduction to mythically representative personalities, Baz Luhrman's *Elvis* (2022) gives a better sense of this process than almost any historical account of rock'n'roll. The film dramatises how capitalism (played by Col. Tom Parker) first exploited and then contained rock'n'roll's anarchic energy (played by Presley): in the film it's Parker who gets Elvis drafted, pushes him into movies and recasts him as family entertainer. What *Elvis* leaves mysterious, however, is *why?* Why ditch the sex, the rebellion, the racial signifying – the *disorder* – that *pulled in* Parker and the punters? One answer is that, fuelled by fame, these visionaries of a liberated world sprang out of repression's traps with an anti-authoritarian abandon that pre-empted prudence, careening into moral traps that social conservatives had set. So, the revelation in 1959 of Lewis's marriage to his 13-year-old cousin and of Berry's affair with a 14-year-old girl were gifts to conservatives' equation of rock'n'roll with moral license. This is not to exonerate rock'n'roll excess: that Berry's first trial was suspended when he protested the judge's racism provides context rather than defence. With Little Richard also pursuing a lifestyle that wouldn't withstand moralists' scrutiny, it's hard not to regard his discovery of religion as a pre-emptive embrace of bourgeois order.

In fact, Richard's conversion was material rather than spiritual (sick of being exploited by Parker-types), and indeed it was money rather than morality that was the prime mover in rock's repression. Morality is always a flag of convenience for capitalism and its enablers. Rumbling throughout this era was the issue of 'payola' – indie labels' paying DJs 'sweeteners' to play records – and while ASCAP presented their anti-payola campaign as a moral crusade, Glenn Altschuler argues that it was "payback time, an opportunity to eviscerate rock'n'roll, its institutional infrastructure, and its principal proponents".[57] Yet this still leaves unclear why a publishing industry riddled with corrupt practices should take a stand on moral standards.[58]

The answer, as ever, is profit: rock'n'roll trespassed on established monopolies – those of the publishing companies and the major labels – and if even a *rigged* system couldn't compete in the charts, it could clean up in the courts. The legislature is the handmaiden of capital, and the congressional hearings on payola provide a parallel with the 1957 McClellan hearings into the Teamsters union, 'justice' deploying morality to contain class rebellion. Quite how payola differed from Boone's paid endorsement of Chevrolet is opaque, yet he and fellow establishment conservative Dick Clark escaped indictment, whereas the scandal shut down the indies, ended multiple DJ careers – the biggest scalp being Allan Freed's – and removed rock'n'roll from radio, charts and release schedules.

Holly and Cochran's careers both tanked post-payola. Ditching the Crickets, Holly barely charted across 1958 in America, while 'Rave On' (UK 5) – with Holly rasping and hiccupping his way through a celebration of disorder – didn't even make the US Top 30. The Parker paradigm thus beckoned: musicians as all-round entertainers, repressing their rebellion and singing from the Tin Pan Alley songbook. Holly recorded a session of string-laden ballads and signed up for a schedule of parochial concerts, the hasty decision to hire a private plane from Iowa to Minnesota proving fatal. With Cochran also barely charting across 1959 in America, and unable to get domestic bookings, he managed a minor British hit with a string-drenched ballad, 'Hallelujah I Love Her So' (UK 22) and so signed up for a provincial British tour. Once again, hasty travel between far-flung engagements had mortal consequences. An alliance of commercial and conservative pressure thus killed rock'n'roll.

As for Britain, lacking American rock's cultural roots, a music industry full of camel-coated, cigar-chomping hucksters only ever regarded rock'n'roll as a flash in showbiz's pan. The Parker paradigm was just the old-fashioned business of show – that was where the gold lay. Jack Good was Britain's Dick Clark, his TV show *Oh Boy!* (from 1958) adding rock'n'roll to the venerable variety formula. While Tin Pan Alley balladry was on the bill – for example, Billy Fury's 1959 'Maybe Tomorrow' (UK 18) – working-class music hall offered an even cosier containment of 50s rebellion, by speaking in the rebels' 'own' demotic. Cliff Richard's corny, Lionel Bart-written 1959 'Living Doll' (UK 1; US 30) splits the difference between balladry and music hall, paving the way for Cliff the family entertainer. The other British Elvis, Tommy Steele, ditched rock'n'roll for music hall with 1959's ghastly 'Little White Bull' (UK 6). Skiffle king Lonnie Donegan was right behind him, meanwhile, with 'My Old Man's a Dustman' (UK 1), whose subaltern stereotypes – dirty, lazy, lascivious – safely reasserted class as culture rather than politics. The establishment was thus re-established, the publishing companies were back in business, the majors had reasserted their commercial dominance and the subaltern was reassigned to its previous, unthreatening place. Order had been restored.

The different world that rock'n'roll had hailed now came to seem, in this golden age of sci-fi, less reachable than other planets – and rather less profitable. The success of arch-crooner Perry Como's 1958 'Magic Moments' (UK 1; US 4) didn't just triumphantly reassert balladry in the pop charts or restore the entertainer at the expense of the rebel-rouser in popular culture. 'Magic Moments' reasserted the square world of white picket fences and white middle-class families as *standard* – the horizon of desire and expectation. "The fun and the prizes", Como chortles, "the Halloween hop when everyone came/In funny disguises". Just when it seemed things couldn't get any duller or more sexless, fellow crooner Bing Crosby's seasonal perennial 'White Christmas' registered on the pop chart for the first time (US 12). The song reaffirms the same suburban, middle-class values of patrician orderliness within a naturalised traditionalism – "Just like the ones I used to know" – while excising anything unruly or *other*: "May all your Christmases be white". The old world, the establishment and capital had won. Yet, the new world of resentments and frustrations, of desires and hopes that rock'n'roll had revealed, couldn't be so easily repressed. The fuss and the holler had been raised.

Chapter 2

"In Beautiful Dreams": Morbid Symptoms, Dream-Work and Fordist Pop (1958–64)

If the 50s was all raw energy, the period that succeeded it was all sophisticated lethargy. The era between Elvis joining the army and the Beatles invading America is an interregnum, an interstice that produced what Ian MacDonald calls "an enervated pop scene",[1] and Nik Cohn dubs "Rue Morgue"– rock'n'roll's vault sealed by restoration balladry.[2] As the major labels reasserted the (moral) value of entertainment over excitement, it wasn't just record sales that were repressed in this period. The narrative of Bill Parsons' 1959 hit 'The All-American Boy' (UK 22; US 2) tracks the cultural trajectory, with rock'n'roll creating sexual licence and parental conflict, before the rebel's acceptance of the draft ultimately asserts his all-American conformity. Parsons' sleepy delivery imbues this assertion of conservative restoration with some ambiguity, however, and with the Elvis-figure standing in – if not standing up – for rock'n'roll's utopianism, hope still haunts the fatalism of both the song and this 50s' aftermath. This period's recurring songs of dreams and of death are the "morbid symptoms" Gramsci theorised as identifiers of an interregnum, and they lend an eerie luminosity to this ordered, ostensibly bright and breezy epoch.[3]

Like Bobby Vee's risible 1961 'Rubber Ball' (UK 4; US 6), this era keeps bouncing back, its cultural buoyancy deriving from its contradictions, which lend its Fordist pop productions a heightened intensity. For conservatives, this period is the height of the 'Long 50s', a period of stability and cultural self-confidence typified by the 1963 World's Fair: the apex of American hegemony. Consequently, much of what we think of as '50s' actually derives from this more sedate interstice,[4] with pop r'n'b tracks like Hank Ballard's joyous 1960 'Finger Poppin' Time' (US 7) or even Bobby Vee's pure pop featuring on 50s rock'n'roll compilations and Spotify playlists. Reynolds even calls Gene Chandler's doo-wop masterpiece 'Duke of Earl' (US 1) "50s", when it's from 1962.[5] Nostalgic film and television dramas, like *American Graffiti* (set in 1962), *Diner* (set in 1959–60), post-shark-jump *Happy Days* and Coppola's *Peggy Sue Got Married* (set in 1960), offer the 50s without delinquency, without utopianism – and largely without black people.

For conservatives, this era is sometimes framed as the "good sixties",[6] a preview of the conformist, technology-driven – and authoritarian – decade that might have been, more modern (and less quaint) than the 50s proper. This tendency was particularly evident in the 80s: in Morrissey's cover art and sartorial aesthetic; in the fashion for preppie retro and flattops; in David Lynch's small-town shtick; in Bratpack movies; and in Margaret Thatcher citing the Tornadoes' futuristic 1961 'Telstar' (UK 1; US 1) as her favourite tune. All these instances pause the tape at this moment of conservative technocracy, before the 'bad 60s' erupted. Yet Thatcher's choice highlights the era's contradictions: the Telstar satellite was an instrument of the Cold War – exemplifying modernity's technology-fuelled death drive, a futurism to end all futures – while its futuristic producer, Joe Meek, was a tortured homosexual who later shot himself and his landlady. Given these morbid symptoms roiling under modernism's efficiently sunny surface, Marcuse observes that "the powers-that-be have a deep affinity to death; death is a token of unfreedom".[7]

By contrast, it's this period's 50s/60s indeterminacy that provides its appeal for more progressive nostalgics: an Aladdin's cave of retro treasure, it's the platonic ideal of Fordist pop culture, while also possessing a covert counterculturality beneath its surface conventionality. Duckie's Long-50s threads in *Pretty in Pink* (1986) articulate his outsiderdom against the preppie elite's conformity, while *Dirty Dancing* (1987), set in

1963, captures the nodal point between restoration repression and countercultural liberation. Amy Winehouse's beehive and false eyelashes revived this period's working-class glamour in defiance of millennial 'classlessness'. Lana Del Rey's mining of the morbid sophistication of this interregnum, post-crash, is paradigmatic of what Paul Ewart calls "Fordist melancholia".[8] British teen drama *The End of the F***ing World* (2018–19) invokes Long-50s styles and sounds to express millennial disenfranchisement, more tamely echoed in *Sex Education* (2019–23). *Mad Men* (2007–15) is the meta-text of this mode – its guilty conscience – addressing its style-over-content tendency by historicising it. The series dramatises how advertising co-opted 50s discontent into consumerism and, as Thomas Frank argues, "made of alienation a motor for fashion".[9] While some of this era's hauntology derives from hipster irony towards an unimaginable historical innocence (a modality not itself without yearning), its magnetism derives from its alienation, the intensity that emerges from its repressed, deferred emotions.

For those who long for Long-50s cuteness, however, it's here in abundance, as a new "market segmentation" targeted an affluent youth demographic disenfranchised by rock'n'roll's repression. In what Frank calls "the construction of consumer subjectivities",[10] advertisements interpellated youth as middle-class, conformist and stylish – you didn't have to be a rebel to be cool anymore. This is visible in the new "Pepsi Generation" ads, in the period's proliferation of beehives, bangs and Alice bands, and in Lolita's stylised transistor radio in Kubrick's film (1962). It's audible in the songs those transistors played, broadcasting sensible teen sensibilities and wholesome youth desires. Ricky Nelson was paradigmatic: a politely stylish 50s' holdover, he performed professionally written, teen-branded hits like 1959's 'Young Emotions' (US 12), 1962's 'Young World' (UK 19; US 5) and 'Teen Age Idol' (US 5), without a glimmer of generational conflict.

Jerry Keller's 1959 'Here Comes Summer' (UK 1; US 14) captures this white-bread youth culture: swimming every day, "drive-in movies every night", going steady, meeting the gang at Joe's Café, with even its *freshness* adorably cute: "When we kiss, she makes my flattop curl". No longer a delinquent or malingerer, the teenager was now the all-American citizen of tomorrow. Consequently, Bobby Rydell's treacly 1960 'The Wild One' (UK 7; US 2) promises he's "gonna tame [the wild one] down", like teeth braces, while his almost lively 'We Got Love' (US 6) and Paul and Paula's pseudo-wop 1962 'Young Lovers' (UK 9; US 6) celebrate marriage as youth's aspirational apex. "We live and love by the golden rule", sings Rydell of the "cats" and "chicks" at his 1960 'Swingin' School' (US 5): "We'll have a house and car, a swimmin' pool". The 50s suburban dream was now being *voiced* rather than vetoed by teenagers, and as the kids themselves testified, it *swung*.

Arriving in 1961, the Beach Boys personified this Long-50s complacency, resolving 50s' contradictions by wedding ecstatic conventionality to unworryingly weedy 'rock'n'roll', and colonising doo-wop with Aryan barbershop cuteness, submerging the African American origins of both genres. From 1962, the Boys issued a sequence of surfing songs with Fordist efficiency: 'Surfin Safari' (US 14), 'Surfin USA' (US 3; Berry's 'Sweet Little Sixteen' rewritten) and the bouncy barbershop ballad 'Surfer Girl' (US 7). Jan and Dean were effectively a franchise, with Beach Boy Brian Wilson co-writing hits like 'Surf City' (US 1). Rakishly varying the formula, the Boys' own 'Be True to Your School' (US 6) hymns college football, complete with a cheerleader chant that now sounds like a cruel parody of this period but is delivered with serene sincerity. Wilson followed this with an even more Fordist automobile sequence from 1963–64: 'Little Deuce Coupe' (US 15), Jan and Dean's 'Drag City' (US 10) and the Beach Boys' 'Fun Fun Fun' (US 5) were all testaments to affluent, Long-50s modernity. The Beach Boys franchise was a fever dream of Fordist consumption – of clothes, of cars, of women – with "two girls for every guy".

Even amongst these teen-branded tunes there were intimations of restlessness, however, as on the untoward excitement of Sandy Nelson's percussive 1959 instrumental 'Teen Beat' (UK 9; US 4). Even the tame 'twist' craze – attested by Chubby Checker's joyous 1961 'Let's Twist Again' (UK 2; US 8) and Sam Cooke's 1962 'Twistin' the Night Away' (UK 6; US 9) – evidenced an enduring longing for liberation within the very repression of its movements. It was clearly a desexualised version of an African American dance. There's a hint of the sexually and racially risqué to the Crests' 1958 doo-wop hit '16 Candles' (US 2): even in an age of teenage marriage, its subject was racily young, its provocation accentuated by being performed by a racially mixed lineup. The (black) Shirelles' 1960 'Will You Love Me Tomorrow' (UK 4; US 1) – written by Goffin and King – was a risqué evocation of sexual restlessness: the heroine hopes her one night stand will still respect her in the morning, but anxiety is ramping up rather than damping down her anticipation. While, in an increasingly Italianised doo-wop, Dion and the Belmonts' tremendous, 1959 'A Teenager in Love' (UK 28; US 5) and Dion's solo, 1960 'Lonely Teenager' (US 12) removed the teenager's rebellion, his depiction as a mildly depressed mope was still hardly singing the company song.

Doo-wop's awed 'oohs' and 'aahs' were an effective way of communicating yearning for something beyond the conventional – sounding collective rather than corporate, these acts' vocal interconnection often seemed less corporeal than simply otherworldly. African American girl group the Chantels' extraordinary 1958 'Maybe' (UK 15) yearns so hard it sounds about to levitate. Black girl group the Cookies' 1962 hit with Goffin and King's 'Chains' (US 17) ostensibly expresses consent to conformity, to being "locked up in chains" by a benign authoritarianism: "chains of love". Yet in Earl-Jean's breakout verses, set against the wordless wonder of her fellow singers, it's the yearning for freedom that cuts through these social chains. With doo-wop tapped in all this period's pop, from Roy Orbison (1960's 'Only the Lonely', UK 1; US 2) to Neil Sedaka (1962's 'Breaking Up is Hard to Do', with the Cookies, UK 7; US 1), its vocalising could be used as a vessel for containment. Bobby Vee's breezy 1962 'The Night Has a Thousand Eyes' (UK 3; US 3) represents youth internalisation of patrician moral control, as he surveils his lover: "I'll know if someone is there."

For there was now no *yakety yak*, no talking back to parents, or to society. Paul Anka's 1960 ballad 'Puppy Love' (US 2) bleats blandly at familial interference in teen romance, but youth desire is instead repressed in the name of the father. Cliff Richard's *The Young Ones* film (1961) shadowplays generational conflict, only to 'resolve' it via family values: "someday, when the years have flown/Darling, then we'll teach the young ones/Of our own", Cliff coos on its theme tune (UK 1). On the Four Seasons' 1962 'Sherry' (UK 8; US 1), Frankie Valli respectfully pipes, "You – ooh – better ask your mama" if her daughter can join him tonight. Their 'Walk Like a Man' (UK 12; US 1) invokes the name of the father against the flightiness of youth: "My own father said, 'Give her up, don't bother'". Parental approval was largely granted to this period's pop, it being effectively a modernisation of post-war balladry. Indeed, the Fleetwoods merged balladry and doo-wop on 1959's lovely 'Come Softly' (UK 6; US 1) and 'Mr Blue' (US 1), while dressing in formal post-war evening wear.

All this era's music is adult, thus 'middle of the road' (MOR), with *Billboard*'s Easy Listening chart starting in 1961 and the soundtrack for the film of Leonard Bernstein and Stephen Sondheim's musical, *West Side Story* topping the album chart for over a year. As the latter's gangland setting indicates, *this* middle of the road was somewhat more 'street' than balladry's boulevardiers, indicative less of changing mores than of increasingly sophisticated containment strategies. This afforded some license around sexuality, and amid the increasing respectability of *Playboy* and John Updike's racy novel *Rabbit Run* (1960), Frankie Avalon's coyly sexy 1959 'Bobby Sox to Stockings' (US 8) and his tastefully flesh-filled *Beach Party* movies presented a demure, suburban sexuality – but sexuality nonetheless.

Pop was now largely tight-lipped on the struggle and stress of work, with even the hedonistic release of the weekend now repressed. Cliff and the Shadows' 1963 celebration of their 'Summer Holiday' (UK 1) is an affirmation rather than a rejection of Fordism: "Everybody has a summer holiday", Cliff assures us, but only "for a week or two" – leisure as containment. Two novelty songs about work, however, reveal that, while music hall was showbiz's chosen vessel of containment, it was a volatile one. Bernard Cribbins' George Martin-produced 1962 'Right Said Fred' (UK 10), coming in the wake of a wave of British strikes, *I'm Alright, Jack* and TV series *The Rag Trade* (1961–63), depicts workers as too busy gulping down tea to get the job done. Yet voiced by working-class Cribbins, well-known from the music-hall-continuity *Carry On* films, the effect was ambivalent. So while Cribbins' 'The Hole in the Ground' (UK 9) is easily seen as another class caricature – an angry workman murders a bowler-hatted busybody – it can also be read as a comic enactment of class *war*, the harassed worker becoming the bourgeois's literal gravedigger.

This puts Anthony Newley's bland-sounding hits in a different light. If the hints of cockney undercut the schmaltz of Newley's 1960 version of Avalon's 'Why' (UK 1), the music-hall rock of 'Do You Mind?' (UK 1) hints at presumption, while the 1960 music hall knees-up 'Strawberry Fair' (UK 3) is delivered in the empowered voice of the British worker, beholden to no-one. The cockney badinage of Mike Sarne's 1962 music-hall jive 'Come Outside' (UK 1), features Sarne recommending and Wendy Richard (*Are You Being Served?*, *EastEnders*) resisting the dangerously lascivious lure of what's outside the demure dance hall. However, the end-of-the-pier terminology ("slap and tickle") suggests this is not just about sexual but *class* freedom, not least when Richards concedes at the close. With Americans always keen to deny they have a class system, the redoubtable Dion's 1963 'Donna the Prima Donna' (US 6) offers a minority – if misogynistic – report, its would-be sophisticate a satire of Fordist social mobility. Played straight and sympathetic, the Four Seasons' 'Rag Doll' (UK 2; US 1) holds out a hand to Fordism's losers in a glorious piece of Spector-influenced pop (remarkably like the Beach Boys' concurrent 'Don't Worry Baby'): progressive in both sound and sentiment, it nags at the countercultural 60s.

For the most part, however, this period proffered a phoney modernism in both pop and politics. In Britain, with capitalism not just secured but seemingly valorised by an efficiently functioning Fordism, Harold Macmillan's restored Conservatives could assume Labour's mantle as technocratic modernisers.[11] "Life is better with the Conservatives", declared a typically complacent Conservative campaign slogan in 1959: "Don't let Labour ruin it". With Macmillan radiating an aristocratic somnolence, but still ruthlessly crushing union revolt, the era had an atavistically feudal air: everything – and everyone – in its place. The public's frustration at this neo-feudalism was indicated by the success of the new, iconoclastic satire, with *Beyond the Fringe* a huge success in 1960 and by that revue's Peter Cook opening a nightclub named the Establishment in 1961. While the social reality was a long way from this period's proclaimed 'classlessness', Labour was party to a consensus that society's economic problems had been solved, and, following three election defeats, tried to outflank the Tories from the right. Leader Hugh Gaitskell attempted to ditch the party's communist-sounding commitment to common ownership and succeeded in reversing Labour's CND-inspired pledge to nuclear disarmament.[12]

In America, for all the Kennedys' media-bruited modernity, beneath its surface stylishness their regime provided continuity with the staid Eisenhower era. The 0.2% margin between Eisenhower's VP, Nixon, and John F. Kennedy in the 1961 election was salient. Kennedy's inaugural address, "Ask not what your country can do for you. Ask what you can do for your country" was an affirmation that youth's – and the left's – demands would continue to be denied. Having run to Nixon's right on security, Kennedy was as inveterate a Cold-Warrior as that renowned red-baiter. Kennedy sent the first US troops to Vietnam (from 1961), while his role in the Bay of Pigs invasion of Cuba (April 1961), the Checkpoint Charlie tank standoff at the Berlin Wall (October 1961) and the Cuban Missile Crisis (October 1962) brought the world the closest it would ever come to nuclear war with the Soviet Union. If Kennedy's politics rested on the death cult of nuclear modernity, therefore, his political legacy was equally morbid. Kennedy's late 1963 assassination created a cult which caused the era's politics to keep ricocheting historically, like its popular music, Kennedy becoming a synecdoche of political statesmanship, even to those who'd previously opposed him, like Ronald Reagan.[13]

The period wasn't as politically placid as its reputation suggests, however. With the Cold War at its hottest thanks to Kennedy, Britain's CND hit its peak of popularity, with its annual Aldermaston marches becoming huge events. For youth, the mushroom-shaped shadow over their future was not just a single issue but, as Anderson notes, "the general truth of the present", the meaning of modernity itself.[14] CND was paradigmatic of the New Left, wherein frustration with the Fordist compact came from the ground up, outside formal political organisation, a return of the repressed signified not just through attitudes but through style – duffel coats and heavy-framed spectacles, a confluence of Beatnik cool and anti-modernist squareness. Here was a *mass* in opposition to 'mass society', collectivist liberation challenging liberal 'freedom'. These anti-Fordist frustrations were expressed in the American Students for a Democratic Society's (SDS) 1962 'Port Huron Statement', whose radicalism lay in the links it made between the disempowered and disenfranchised. Marx called such links 'class consciousness', while the SDS was another looming of the counterculture.

This solidarity was expressed on the ground via white youth involvement in the civil rights movement: sit-ins at segregated lunch counters; the Freedom Rides from 1961 testing Southern bus segregation laws; the Albany Movement in Georgia in 1961–62; and the 1963 Birmingham non-violent direct actions. With the socially conservative Kennedy unwilling to address the civil rights issue, the movement was met with literal repression, by police hoses and nightsticks, the state going to war with its own citizens. With patrolmen at Southern concerts similarly enforcing the colour line with dogs and batons, the repression of the emancipatory desires that rock'n'roll had unleashed was literal as well as psychological.

With Freud all the rage in the early 60s, the repressed returned in culture in tandem with politics, with Hitchcock probing 50s' patriarchy's controlling but ultimately impotent masculinity in *Vertigo* (1958) and *Psycho* (1960). Despite being channelled through middle-class performers, folk, the 'music of the people', was a literal version of this return of the repressed, with a lateral relationship to rock'n'roll's rural origins, its anti-Fordism strongly allied to the civil rights movement and CND's refusals of phoney, destructive modernity. When the most prominent of these new folkies, Joan Baez, made the cover of *Time* in November 1962, her protégée (and lover) Bob Dylan was only a cult figure, no more inventing the partnership of folk and protest than folk's anachronistic association with the acoustic guitar. It was the era-appropriate blandness of Peter, Paul and Mary that prompted folk's commercial breakthrough, which still meant a breakthrough of politics into pop via hit covers of Pete Seeger's 'If I Had a Hammer' in 1962 (US 10) and Dylan's 'Blowin' in the Wind' in 1963 (UK 13; US 2). The latter was an elliptical yet effective indictment of modernity's death drive, from racial oppression to nuclear threat, written in a Biblical mythical register given both moral authority and material heft by its borrowed spiritual melody.

Women were beginning to bridle at Fordism's sexual division of labour. If the sassiness of Doris Day and Mary Tyler Moore hinted at such frustration, they remained unthreatening. Yet pop was now producing more feisty female performers. Connie Francis' fantastic 1959 'Lipstick on Your Collar' (UK 3; US 5) tells a tale on the gendered hypocrisy of the dating game; British working-class schoolgirl Helen Shapiro's 1961 'Don't Treat Me Like a Child' (UK 3) asserts her right to "run wild" if she feels like it; while American teenager Lesley Gore's 1964 'You Don't Own Me' (US 2) warns, "Don't tell me what to do/Don't tell me what to say", and insists "I'm free/And I love to be free". This feminist space was quickly shut down: Francis's 1962, Spector-produced 'Second Hand Love' (US 7), Shapiro's 'You Don't Know' (UK 1) and Gore's 'That's the Way Boys Are' (US 12) are all doormat dirges, resigned to the gendered division of emotional labour. Gore makes being a doormat sound dreamily desirable on 1963's 'It's My Party' (UK 9; US 1), its feminine passivity a precise reversal of the refusal of Francis's 'Lipstick on Your Collar', despite a similar scenario. Traversing this trajectory, Betty Friedan's early 1963 *The Feminine Mystique* gave vent to suburban female frustration, while Valium arrived later that year to re-repress it. As we know, the repressed always returns, and it was provided with a path by the fissures these feminine refusals prised in the Fordist settlement.

While such frustrations as we've seen with that settlement have been localised, there were hints of a more totalising objection to Fordism, emerging in some unlikely locations. The question asked on Adam Faith's 1959 frivolous showbiz confection 'What Do You Want?' ("if you don't want money?") goes to the heart of the matter in a consumer society (UK 1). Paul Anka's Latinate ballad the same year, 'Lonely Boy' (UK 3; US 1), admits to alienation amidst the era's stifling plenty: although he's got "everything you could think of", he's got "nothin' to do" – as close as this enervated era came to confessing to existential crisis. The Marvelettes' marvellous

1961 'Please Mr. Postman' (US 1) is an intemperate outburst at Fordist bureaucracy – "Stop!" "Wait!" – and its stifling domesticity: *she's* stuck at home, *he's* exotically "so far away", probably burning Vietnamese peasants in Fordism and the father's name. Gene Pitney's 'Town Without Pity' (US 13), from the same year, proffers a protest at suffocating suburban conventionality: "We're like tigers in a cage… How can anything survive when these little minds tear you in two?" That the protagonist can't quite get beyond this 'reality', suggests how repression presses in upon everyday imagination. Yet the human desire for something more than what *is* will keep seeping out like nocturnal emissions; in dreams, as we'll see, and in hauntings.

'Dead Man's Curve': Morbid Symptoms

From prison, Gramsci famously declared, "The crisis consists precisely in the fact that the old is dying and the new cannot be born; in this interregnum a great variety of morbid symptoms appear".[15] The old dying fits this period's politics perfectly. Although Britain's Conservatives were rendered moribund by the Cold War scandals of the Profumo affair and Kim Philby's defection to the Soviet Union, their elite corpse continued to rule, with one decrepit aristocrat (Macmillan) replaced by another (Alec Douglas-Home). Concurrently, CND and the Labour left were unable to assert themselves against the literally dying Gaitskell and moribund former-left-winger Aneurin Bevan. If in America the white supremacy of the 'old' – Eisenhower – was no longer acceptable, the racial attitude of the 'new' – the popular-modern Kennedys – was equivocal. With attorney general Robert Kennedy endorsing and blocking civil rights simultaneously – attempting to divert the movement from direct action to voter registration – this was again the old refusing to die, while the grassroots of black activists and white students was the new multi-racial society, struggling to be born.

The old was dying in pop, too. It wasn't just that Presley's 1960 'Are You Lonesome Tonight?' (UK 1; US 1) and 'It's Now or Never' (UK 1; US 1) had nothing to do with rock'n'roll, but that they were stagy, 'performed' and square where this period's best ballads were dramatic, expressive and hip. While rarely as successful as Presley's efforts, the new balladry achieved its potency in a dialectic between the mechanisms of containment – orchestration, 'exotic' rhythms, girlie choirs (the old) – and a yearning, proto-countercultural utopianism, in concordance with Fordist technology (the new). You can hear this in gospel-sired Sam Cooke's sublimely sweet 1960 'Wonderful World' (UK 27; US 12) elevating the everyday to the epiphanic, in the way Brill Building alum Neil Sedaka's schmaltzy 1960 'Stairway to Heaven' (UK 8; US 9) merges doo-wop choruses with Hollywood heavenly choirs, and in the liminal affective space evoked by rocker-turned-balladeer Billy Fury's Latin, Goffin-King-written 1961 'Halfway to Paradise' (UK 3). You can *feel* it in the Shadows' Latin 1961 instrumental 'Wonderful Land' (UK 1), with its layers of reverb evoking space and freedom, in the giddiness of girl group the Chiffons' 1963 Goffin-King-penned 'One Fine Day' (UK 29; US 5), and in Ruby and the Romantics' futuristically Latinate 1963 'Our Day Will Come' (US 1), with its assertion that "we will have everything". This utopianism is underwritten by racial otherness – all those Latin rhythms and singers (Rosie of the Originals) at a time of postcolonial Latin revolution (Cuba's rebels were victorious by 1959).[16]

While such upbeat songs were overtly utopian, the period's many songs of loss were still subtly, if contradictorily, so. Freud theorised 'melancholia' as an obsessive mourning, a fetishisation of loss, resulting in an inability to function efficiently in the real world. Think of Del Shannon walking in the rain, haunted by his 'Runaway' (UK 1; US 1) and the sheer eeriness of the song's production, or the use of "hurt, hurt" as the hook on Dion's magnificent 1961 'Runaround Sue' (UK 11; US 1), managing to make morbid obsession sound immaculately 'pop'. As Traverso argues, what constitutes the 'real world' is always ideological, and so mourning represents an acceptance of loss in order to be productive in capitalist society, while melancholia is a failure to accommodate to social norms and be productive, and thus effectively a refusal of the performance principle.[17] Culturally, such morbidity was a contravention not only of Fordist pop conventions but of the period's *social* conventions, the obligation to be bright, breezy, upbeat. 'Morbidity' is thus another term for what would later be called 'hauntology', the spectres of other possibilities, other ways of being.

The protagonist of Johnny Leyton's 1961 'Johnny Remember Me' (UK 1) effectively *chooses* to be haunted by his dead lover, with Joe Meek's ghostly production echoing the past-haunted futurism of 'Runaway' in all senses. The lost lover in Bobby Vinton's 1963 remake of balladeer standard, 'Blue Velvet' (US 1) may or may *not* be dead, but the protagonist's fetishisation of her clothing is as morbid as it is creepy (even before the song got Lynched). The point is that something is absent, lacking, *lost*, but that the excessive yearning this inspires is, paradoxically, utopian. The point of hauntology is not purely the *past-ness* of the past – which is closed – but its futurity, which is open. We return to the past not to regain utopia, therefore, but to reaccess *utopianism*, from a time when other possibilities seemed possible.

Owen Bradley's 'Nashville sound' brought country to the city, the addition of pop sophistication and jazzy inflection giving a once raw, rustic genre a modernist sheen, while leavening its traditional morbidity with a spoonful of sugar. Former rock'n'roller Brenda Lee had an irrepressible voice that, pressed into Nashville balladry, produced a manic mournfulness on 1960's 'I'm Sorry' (UK 12; US 1) – as deployed in *End of the F*****g World* S01 – and 1961's 'Break It to Me Gently' (US 4) – featured in *Mad Men* S02 – whose excess threatened to burst the bounds of its format. The romantic morbidity of Skeeter Davis's 1962 'The End of the World' (UK 18; US 2), with its embrace of nuclear-gothic terminology, made it an apposite choice to soundtrack Kennedy's assassination in *Mad Men* S03. The marvellous Patsy Cline's 1961 hits 'Crazy' (US 9) and 'She's Got You' (US 14) obsessively fetishise loss, but delivered in her rich alto, they tap the serene, *adult* quality of 50s balladeers. Put in dialogue with a yearning morbidity derived from the church and the Southern gothic imaginary, her songs found resonance in this repressed conjuncture. Cline's death in a plane crash in 1963 only added to this eerie luminosity, this negative-image utopianism.

The era's recurring deaths of young singers in automotive accidents both embodied and fuelled this pop-cultural morbidity. Johnny Preston's 1959 teenage tragedy 'Running Bear' (UK 1;

US 1) was a hit after its composer Big Bopper's airplane death. Bopper's co-passenger Buddy Holly's own posthumous hit that year, a string-drenched cover of Anka's 'It Doesn't Matter Anymore' (UK 1; US 13), was hauntological from title on in, despite – or because of – its cutesy vocabulary ("golly gee", "oops-a-daisy"). Eddie Cochran's 1960 rock'n'roll tango from beyond the grave, 'Three Steps to Heaven' (UK 1), backed by Holly's surviving Crickets, is equally ghostly, but its next world sounds curiously proximate to this one, such is the hauntology of its utopian yearning.

Mark Dinning's 1959 automobile tragedy 'Teen Angel' (banned in the UK; US 1) and the Everly Brothers' 1961 airline tragedy 'Ebony Eyes' (UK 1; US 8) testify to modernity's deathly momentum with a fatalistic passivity, in line with Cold-War satires like Joseph Heller's *Catch 22* (1961) and Kubrick's *Dr Strangelove* (1964). The drivers on Ricky Valance/Ray Peterson's 1960 stock-car race song, 'Tell Laura I Love Her' (UK 1; US 7), and two drag-race dramas, Jan and Dean's 1963 'Dead Man's Curve' (US 8) and the Beach Boys' delightful 'Don't Worry Baby' (US 24), all articulate a fatalistic embrace of foreshadowed risk – "You won't come back from Dead Man's Curve" – that's quite the gear-change from this franchise's previously upbeat Fordist carols. Rather than simply being melodramatic, therefore, these songs, like the literary satires cited, offer a passive protest, an existential refusal of *what is*.

The Shangri-Las' stunning 1964 'Leader of the Pack' provides a female perspective on the same paradigm (UK 11, despite a ban; US 1).[18] Parental disapproval of the bad boy on the motorbike represents Fordist authoritarianism: that this results in another fatal automotive accident is more than just a personal tragedy, it's a societal rebuke. For Jimmy's countercultural allure outlives the girl's parents' pyrrhic victory; he even appears to be alive for the first half of the song, always being referred to in the present tense. She'll "never forget him" – and nor will we: for, as Traverso argues, even in defeat, rebellion haunts the cultural imagination.

With the leader of the pack coming from "the wrong side of town", crossing Fordism's colour and class lines was a deadly affair in this deadeningly ordered society – thus the demise of the cowboy in Marty Robbins' 1960 'El Paso' (UK 19; US 1) and the Native American lovers drowning in 'Running Bear'. That these songs were more than merely morbid self-indulgence was indicated not just by the recurring real-world deaths of pop singers but, more pointedly, by the regular killings of young civil rights protestors who challenged this society's order. Moreover, the patrician BBC's persistent banning of these death songs reveals what Gramsci calls a "crisis of authority".[19] Such overt repression was a revelation of weakness, of an inability to fully repress the period's morbid symptoms as ordinary people fumbled towards a critique of this patriarchal, authoritarian society.

Once Phil Spector would have seemed this age's spirit – youthful, Fordist, modernist, with his production factory's tagline "Tomorrow's Sound Today". Instead, he's now its grisly spectre, dying in prison a convicted murderer, a macabre realisation of modernity's death drive. Morbidity was written into Spector's teen dreams from his debut 1959 doo-wop hit 'To Know Him Is to Love Him' (US 2), however, with its title derived from his father's gravestone. Spector's Wall of Sound was a funeral vault of sound, an unstable multi-layered edifice encased in an ectoplasmic echo that put everything in the past – individual instruments a distant haze, voices coming from beyond the grave, tempos dirge-like and funereal.[20]

The lyrics, meanwhile, are fussily, fetishistically retrospective ("I met him on a Sunday", "The night we met", "Well he walked up to me/And he asked me if I wanted to dance"). Yet the result is utterly life-affirming, deriving once again from contradiction. For there are tangible utopian dreams here, given voice and credence by young working-class women of colour (the Ronettes, the Crystals, Darlene Love).[21] On the Ronettes' 1963 hits – 'Be My Baby' (UK 4; US 2), with its massed, echoing castanets, and 'Baby, I Love You' (UK 11; US 24), with its thunderous tympani eruptions – there's a radiance to Ronnie Spector's voice (and televisual presence) that pulls against the containment of the lyrics' aspirations (marriage and family) and of Phil Spector's patriarchal production. An expression of eternal *Eros* holding terminal *Thanatos* at bay, these songs capture the dialectic of the day, but the energy of futurity.

"Dreamin' till My Dreamin' Comes True": Pop Utopianism in the Interregnum

Dreams, in everyday usage, are just wish fulfilments – what Freud called "infantile" dreams – quite conscious articulations of daylight desire.[22] Freud established the idea that nocturnal dreams articulate *repressed* desire, while Marcuse expanded upon Freud's assertion in *Civilisation and its Discontents* (1930) that these desires are social rather than solely individual. This can produce capitalist dreams constituted in consumption, as well as utopian dreams constituted in social change – what Fisher calls "suggestive glimmers of worlds radically different from the actually existing social order".[23] If Fisher sounds like he's talking about music, that's because songs also articulate people's dreams – like Conway Twitty's 1958 wish-fulfilment ballad, 'It's Only Make Believe' (UK 1; US 1). Sometimes songs are aural dreamworks in themselves – the Crystals' 1963 'Then He Kissed Me', for instance (UK 2; US 6) – repression producing a luminous liminality suggestive of the state between sleep and waking, unconsciousness and consciousness.

Revenant in 1961's charts, the Everlys' 1958 'All I Have to Do Is Dream' (UK 1; US 1) established the template for both this period's recurring dream songs and the brothers' own post-rock'n'roll career: acoustic, balladic, wistful. The song concerns another conscious dream, but the *intensity* of the protagonist's desire to escape reality – "gee whiz/I'm dreaming my life away" – is utopian, a will to escape the very alienation such suburban language exemplifies (and which holds even if the song *is* about onanism). Like 'It's Only Make Believe', the chords for 'All I Have to Do Is Dream' follow the '50s progression', derived from doo-wop, a formal hauntology of that period's racial encounter, a dream of its rebellion. This somnambulant trend continued across 1959 with Johnny Mathis's jazzy 'Misty' (UK 12; US 12, and well chosen for the creepy 1971 *Play Misty For Me*), Santo and Johnny's spectral instrumental 'Sleepwalk' (UK 22; US 1) and Bobby Darin's yearningly breezy mid-pacer 'Dream Lover' (UK 1; US 2). Although Darin's is another waking, wish-fulfilment dream, his insistence that he won't quit dreaming *even when* his ideal lover is located ("I want a dream lover/So I don't have to dream alone") suggests the extent of the internalisation of this period's denial of desire, its repression producing an *excess* of yearning.

On Johnny Burnette's lovely, Orbison-esque 1960 'Dreamin'' (UK 5; US 11) and Roy Orbison's own 1962 'Dream Baby' (UK 2; US 4), what Freud calls the dream's "manifest" content is again the wish fulfilment of romance, but the songs' morbid obsessiveness and mantric repetitiveness suggest their "latent" content is a deeper lack than Fordist 'reality' – or Fordist plenty – can redeem.[24] Burnette's song would soon gain additional hauntological resonance via *his* death in another automotive accident. Johnny Mercer's theme for 1961's *Breakfast at Tiffany's*, 'Moon River', provided hits not just for Henry Mancini (US 11) but for two black singers – ex-Impression Jerry Butler (US 11) and South African Danny Williams (UK 1). Although the film's protagonists and the song's form signify as 'white' – there's no blues root, for instance – the lyric conjures the river voyage of Huckleberry and escaped slave Jim in Mark Twain's *Adventures of Huckleberry Finn* (1884), with its tentative exploration of a dream of a utopian other world beyond racial division. Hence, the song inhabits both the past and the future, in true hauntological style: "We're after the same rainbow's end".

Patsy Cline's 1963 'Sweet Dreams' (US 5) gave the pull of the past an eerier potency by emerging from beyond the grave, though hers was a modern, not a rustic, grave, all clean lines and technocratic emotional efficiency. Billy Fury's emulation of Elvis extended to his balladic turn and the film vehicle *Play it Cool* (1962), but in its somnambulant hit 'Once Upon a Dream' (UK 7), the dream possessed, then lost, provides an additional Elvis parallel – and works for the era's repression of desires too.

This evocation of a lost past full of possibilities is why Orbison's astonishing 'In Dreams' from early 1963 (UK 6; US 7) gives its name to this chapter. The song even *sounds* liminal – somewhere between sleeping and waking, haunted by a ghost of the past, but with a sonic sensibility that's a glimmer of the future.[25] 'In Dreams' depicts a classic wish-fulfilment dream: "*a thought expressed in the optative has been replaced by a representation in the present tense*":[26] i.e., the desire to have his lover back becomes her *being* back. As so often with the Long 50s, the 80s get in the way, and 'In Dreams' comes to us through the filter of Lynch's *Blue Velvet* (1987), which resurrected Orbison's career and provides what's now the song's official video (in an inferior, re-recording). Yet neither the film's toxic masculine creepiness nor its capitalist realism diminishes the song: indeed, they emphasise that, as Freud put it, "behind the obvious wish-fulfilment some other meaning may lie concealed" – a more existential or systemic loss.[27] In film and song alike, that loss is located in the 50s.

Orbison's opening verse uses the 50s progression, while the "candy-coloured clown they call the sandman" evokes the Chordettes' 'Mr. Sandman'. Yet this is an eerie, not a cosy nostalgia – Orbison's ghostly voice initially backed only by acoustic guitar, and channelling folk at its most spectral. This links to the sandman as folkloric spirit of sleep – key to Freud's 'uncanny' – and thus, contrary to the song's claim, everything is clearly not "all right". As the rhythm section enters (0:21), Orbison's voice remains foregrounded, before strings (0:41) gradually bury the drums (0:56), joined by first female (1: 15) then male choirs (1:18), balladic tricks deployed to convey conventional perception submerged by sleep. Then comes the reassertion of reality at 1:34: "I awake to find you gone" – the notes higher, the key now minor, melancholy – then the musical and emotional breakdown: "I can't help it if I cry" (1: 51). This taps the era's other motif of mourning, but its morbidity is again hauntological, because the finale (from 2:10) is a soaring major-key affirmation of the potency of dreams, Orbison's voice hitting its giddiest high note on "*on*-ly in dreams", modulating from the past into a utopian future. 'In Dreams' is smooth, stylish modernism for the ideal home, revealing that domicile to be far from ideal, loss and yearning built into its foundations, but the recognition of this loss leading to ultimate elevation.

British Beatlemania would begin concurrently, with 1963's 'Please Please Me' (UK 2), John Lennon's attempt to write in Orbison's style, though it's also indebted to the Everlys' interregnum approach. The Beatles' debut album, for all its raw energy, is still an artefact of the Long 1950s, a summary of the era's styles – doo-wop, girl group, Motown. Orbison's career – like all the acts in this chapter – would wane as the Beatles' waxed, but in the Orb's utopianism, and in writing and playing his own songs, Orbison was the latch that opened the door onto the counterculture.

'A Change is Gonna Come': Race and Utopia in Long-50s Pop

Despite the restoration of suburban cultural mores at the time and the 'whitewashing' of this period retrospectively, African American culture was integral to Long 50s popular modernity. Despite radio managers' best efforts, the cultural airwaves were full of the Fordist ecstasies of Motown, Stax and what Gillett dubs "uptown rhythm and blues".[28] Meanwhile, Colin MacInnes' Notting Hill-set novel *Absolute Beginners* (1959) bore white hipster witness to a new structure of feeling: a reverence for a distinctly black 'cool' – a proudly aloof mode far removed from Fats Domino or even Chuck Berry, and encapsulated by boxer Cassius Clay and jazz auteur Miles Davis. This, again, was another spectre of the counterculture to come.

So far in this chapter, the dreams have been modest, their radicalism in their mood or delivery rather than their ostensibly conventional desires. With repression literal for African Americans, their historical loss not just emotional but material, their utopian dreams – tracking the demands of the civil rights movement – were becoming more politically pointed – and more urgent. Black singers channelled the spirituals and gospel they were raised on – genres defined by an evocation of a better world – via their contemporary experience of the city, in contrast to the sub-urbanity of balladry. While, in uptown rhythm and blues, the songs were constructed in New York's Fordist Brill Building by white writers, and given arrangements poppy enough for suburban sensibilities, easy listening's containment techniques could produce *intense* listening when involving singers who could communicate something more than soporific smoothness.

Ben E. King had established this pull-and-push as his

provenance with the Drifters' haunting 1959 'There Goes My Baby' (US 2) and 1960's utopian 'This Magic Moment' (US 16). It's on his solo 1960 'Spanish Harlem' (US 10), however, that a *modern* black utopianism is articulated, beyond the exigencies of the spiritual or the love song. Despite being written by Spector and Leiber, it's King's gorgeous, haunted vocal that exemplifies the song's assertion that 'black is beautiful' and *inhabits* its evocation of African American communities' economic and social embattlement. The rose "growing in the street right up through the concrete" is a perfect popular-modern image, hope breaking through Fordism's functionalism and containment, growing towards the light, reaching for the future. The somewhat corny instrumentation, with its marimbas and sentimental strings, creates a *musical* concrete for King's vocal to break through. King's starker, acoustic, 1961 hit 'Stand by Me' (UK 27; US 1) is a literally spiritual lurch towards what was yet to be defined as 'soul music', using the 50s progression to assert social solidarity in the face of oppression. Couched as a love song, 'Stand by Me' comes across as a folk protest anthem.

King's former bandmates, the Drifters, also pursued this new social realism. 1962's 'Up on the Roof' (US 5) was another Goffin-King-written Brill Building project, another urban location ("Right smack dab in the middle of town"), with its rooftop's escape something black city-dwellers had more reason to seek than most. The repression here – the world getting you down – and the utopianism – the stars putting on a *free* show – are both vague, but the jollity of the arrangement is lifted far from the hustling crowd by the raw yearning of Rudy Lewis's vocal (and his *timing* – that lovely little pause in "You just have to wish to make it... so"). In the Drifters' 1963 follow-up 'On Broadway' (US 9), the desired utopia is modernity itself – exemplified by the neon signs of Broadway and the edgy mechanical whirrs and clicks of the track's electric guitar and percussion. In a trope that was then new, stardom functions as metaphor for aspiration. This dazzling utopia is presented in contrast to the narrator's reality – hungry, down to his last dime – so the song becomes a tussle between dreams and repression, brilliantly realised by the ascending key changes: equal parts utopian upwards motion and dizzying Escher staircase.

On Little Anthony and the Imperials' glorious 1964 'I'm On the Outside Looking In' (US 15), the svelte production signals the narrator's longed-for 'inside' – social acceptance, material comfort, modernity itself. Yet the song isn't content to window-shop with its nose against the glass: in the run-up to the Civil Rights Act, the narrator declares a determination to be on the other side of that barrier. Contrary to Gillett's dismissal, black musicians' desire to be on the inside didn't just chase white tastes, it *changed* them, helping to redefine mid-century modernity as multi-racial. Once again, the strength of this music is derived from the struggle to create freedom within the Fordist system, the internal tension between sweetness and rawness, uptown sophistication and down-home gospel grit.

The formula for soul was sketched as early as 1957 with Jackie Wilson's 'Reet Petite' (UK 6) and 'Lonely Teardrops' (US 7, written by future Motown boss Berry Gordy) and by Sam Cooke's sublime 'You Send Me' (UK 29; US 1). Both Wilson and Cooke were quickly constrained by the balladeer's evening jacket, however, as on Wilson's ghastly 1960 'Night' (US 4). Cooke's 1960 'Chain Gang' (UK 9; US 2) broke free, adding social commentary to this new music's technocratic tension. For all its joyfulness, the song's "Huh! Ah!" hook evokes the work songs of slavery; for all its modern, 'produced' quality, its percussion evokes the striking of prisoners' hammers against rock; for all its caution, the lyric doesn't passively place freedom in the past, it fixes it in the future. Increasingly politicised, Cooke refused to play segregated shows and asserted autonomy from the white-dominated industry by creating his own label, management company and publishing imprint. By contrast, Ray Charles followed the rare rawness of 1959's gospel-driven 'What'd I Say' (US 6) and 1961's poppy but gritty 'Hit the Road Jack' (UK 6; US 1) with 1962's softened *Modern Sounds in Country and Western* (UK 6; US 1). While the album was utopian in desegregating black and white styles – and declaring this to be modernity – country's formal rigidity and rhythmic restraint squeezed the heart (and the 'soul') out of Charles' music.

The very *fact* of Stax and Motown was utopian: black-run labels for black musicians. That Motown's tagline was "The Sound of Young America", not of *black* America, declared African Americans the acme of modernity – even as they fought for basic rights and recognition. Directly inspired by Henry Ford and Detroit's automobile plants, Berry Gordy was a bottom-line businessman: Motown's first hit was Barrett Strong's 'Money' in 1960 (US 23), followed by the market demotic of the Miracles' 'Shop Around' (US 2). Black capitalism doesn't solve systemic inequality, yet Cohn is entirely wrong to see Motown as "Uncle Tom",[29] for, as Greg Tate attests, "in the history of affirmative action Motown warrants more than a footnote beneath the riot accounts and NAACP legal maneuvers".[30] Moreover, the irony of Motown's assembly-line Fordism – its house bands, teams of writers, and unionised, on-the-clock sessions – was that it lent an urgency to horn-and-percussion-driven hits like the Miracles' 1963 'Mickey's Monkey' (US 8), freeing listeners from feeling like cogs in Fordism's machine. Once again, capitalism created its own gravediggers.

Rawer and more rural than its Northern rival, Memphis-based Stax always had a foot in the southern swamps, with the Mar-Keys' 1961 'Last Night' (US 3) recapturing much of rock'n'roll's excitement (and a sliver of its salaciousness). However, Stax was as much a Fordist factory as Motown, and as Carla Thomas's string-drenched 1961 'Gee Whiz' (US 10) reveals, no less inclined to sweeten the deal when scenting a hit. Carla's father Rufus's 1963 'Walking the Dog' (US 10) is punchier and rougher, and while its lyric is nursery-rhyme nonsense, the confidence in the assertion, "If you don't know how to do it/I'll show you how to...", is a manifestation of a broader racial confidence wherein African Americans lead and others follow.

Giving political substance to soul's yearning, Martin Luther King's "I have a dream" speech at the March on Washington in August 1963 was the political apex of this period. Suffused with biblical language, King's speech articulates the same utopianism that defines gospel and is implicit in soul. It was hauntological at the time – evoking the past while envisaging a utopian future – but after King's murder, the speech's dreaming combined with mourning: for King as a leader; for African

American freedom in the hinterland of the Civil Rights Act. The utopianism of King's speech, while vague, is still rooted in the material: the "appalling condition" of black communities; the "unspeakable horrors of police brutality". In the speech's subsequent containment within a liberal narrative of 'progress', with Bill Clinton co-opting King's dream as the American Dream,[31] King's socialism, the fact that Kennedy tried to get the march cancelled and that the FBI regarded King as a dangerous radical are written out of history. Equally obscured is the fact that the Ku Klux Klan's 16th Street Baptist Church bombing occurred the very next month in Birmingham, Alabama.

Inspired by King's speech, Sam Cooke's transcendent, early 1964 'A Change Is Gonna Come' (B-side, 'Shake', US 7), is the apex of this era's popular music, being located in a liminal space between mourning and dreaming. The song's chords are an adaptation of the 50s progression, with René Hall's sumptuous arrangement part supper club, part movie score, the pure gospel of Cooke's voice giving the song both street-level grit and emotional transcendence. Contrary to Gillett's claim,[32] 'Change' is no more an expression of Cooke's purely *personal* experience than 'I have a dream' was of King's: Cooke's lyric was triggered by a paradigmatic experience of racial prejudice. Unlike Spector's morbid origin stories, Cooke's opening, "I was born by a river", is collective: it's his *people* who've been "running ever since". Given this baleful history, there are morbid symptoms here aplenty: the times he thought he couldn't last too long; the fearful fatalism of "It's been too hard living, but I'm afraid to die". But the morbidity derives from the old refusing to die – the (white) men who tell the narrator, "Don't hang around" at a movie theatre symbolise enduring segregation; the (white) brother who'd *like* to help him (but...) represents the limits of liberalism. It's hard to see the road ahead for the barriers and blocks across it.

Yet the song's narrator is *determined* to see, as the new struggles to be born: "I *think* I'm able to carry on... I *know* a change gonna come" (emphases added). Mourning thus unites with dreaming here, the past with the future, a utopia that the song's narrator can't quite imagine but is haunted by – and so is the listener. This isn't *just* a vision of racial equality – any more than King's speech was – it's a vision of an equal *society*, the song's beatitude enhanced by the bitterness of the experiences it recounts, its hope exponential to the hate it has encountered. As such, 'A Change Is Gonna Come' both captures and closes this period of mourning, of dreaming and of repression, but it also opens onto the 60s proper. This era is thus revealed as an anticipation – a spectre – of the counterculture. Expressing the Long 50s' yearning directly, while amplifying its latent hopes for the future, ordinary people would now attempt to make this period's utopian "beautiful dreams" a material reality.

Chapter 3

"We Are All Together": High 60s' Beat, Soul, Folk-Rock and Psychedelia (1964–68)

The 60s began – or rather erupted – with the British Invasion of early 1964, which terminated post-war repression virtually on the spot. A new optimism swept away morbidity, sociality replaced conformity and colour eclipsed post-war greyness, as Fordism hit its functional peak with a deluge of social liberal legislation. With this political and cultural popular modernism rendering the progressive and experimental commonplace, the high 60s' pulse-racing rate of change represented a "widely shared feeling that... everything was possible", as Jameson put it: "a moment of a universal liberation, a global unbinding of energies".[1] With class deference and racial segregation officially dismissed, the subaltern now stormed the historical stage. The resultant, vibrant 60s popular culture, initially expressive of Fordism's accomplishments, gradually became a *counter*culture, expressive of Fordism's discontents. The counterculture was utopian where the dominant culture – even at its most progressive – was utilitarian, radical where the dominant was liberal, revolutionary where it was reformist. With each the condition for the other, however, the counterculture seemed for a time to be seeping into all aspects of society.

This is not how the 1960s are now viewed. For while the Swinging 60s get a free pass, the counterculture is increasingly regarded as counterfeit, 'hippie' synonymous with hypocrisy, as attested by Tarantino's *Once Upon a Time in Hollywood*'s "fuckin' hippies" (2019), the 'OK, boomer!' meme, and Generation Left's hippyphobia. The biggest hippyphobes have always been the right, however, whose 'bad 60s' makes no distinction between dominant culture and counterculture, Great Society and alternative society: the 60s was all one chaotic 'liberal' nightmare, its legacy a rocketing divorce rate, the 'welfare mother' and 'big government'. Indeed, Stuart Hall argues that neoliberalism "emerges in relation to the radical movements and political polarisations of the 1960s".[2] Lyndon Johnson's 1964 challenger, Barry Goldwater, opposed the Civil Rights Acts and Medicare, as did his protégé, Ronald Reagan, whose antipathy for both hippies and social liberalism took him from the California governorship (1967–75) to the American presidency (1981–89). When Reagan's ally Margaret Thatcher remarked, "We are reaping what was sown in the sixties. The fashionable theories and permissive claptrap set the scene for a society in which the old virtues of discipline and self-restraint were denigrated",[3] she didn't mean acid in the water supply, she meant claptrap like divorce and the criminalisation of racial discrimination.

With youth, as we've seen, the fulcrum of Fordist frustrations, Slavoj Žižek captures how "the 60s supplemented the traditional critique of socioeconomic exploitation with a new cultural critique: alienation of everyday life, commodification of consumption, inauthenticity of a mass society".[4] With its roots in the rock'n'roll culture and Beat Generation of the 50s, this critique was positive rather than negative, a vision of a better way of living, of thinking, of *being*. Capitalism's attempt to co-opt this cultural critique – 60s adverts advising, "Take a stand against conformity!" and "Tune in. Turn on. Step Out" – was an acknowledgement of its cogency.[5] Moreover, Boltanski and Chiapello's research demonstrates that to mitigate 60s workplace militancy, capitalism began to draw on this cultural critique to create a more 'flexible', post-Fordist regime of accumulation.[6]

For all the right's portrayal of 90s flexible politicians Tony Blair and Bill Clinton as the 60s redux, the pair's co-option of the cultural critique 'resolved' the contradictions of neoliberalism by making economic and individual freedom contiguous – and abandoning the socioeconomic critique. Yet the counterculture was *anti*-capitalist – "a disruption of late capitalist ideological and political hegemony"[7] – its cultural critique always collective. "No revolution without individual liberation, but also no individual liberation without the liberation of society", as Marcuse, the counterculture's favoured philosopher, remarked.[8] America's Civil Rights Acts, Education Acts, Social Security amendments and introduction of Medicare, alongside Britain's legalisation of homosexuality and abortion and introduction of the pill, enhanced individual freedom as a condition of collective responsibility. Arthur Marwick's replacement of Marcuse's concept of liberalism's "repressive tolerance" with "measured judgement"[9] elides the struggles in the streets that chivvied the elites towards change, activists always thinking bigger than the actuarial state. Moreover, Marwick and Sandbrook's characterisation of the counterculture as a middle-class enclave has to ignore 60s' industrial militancy.[10] Equally, Jeremi Suri's claim that "the counterculture was not about material needs" has to exclude the civil rights movement and Black Panthers,[11] despite black liberation providing "the nexus of social protest throughout the 60s".[12] Indeed, that all these groups would unite was the elite's greatest fear.

The counterculture's imbrication with black culture – from Freedom Rides to British Invasion to psychedelia – had an integral relationship to its anti-imperialism. With Vietnam revealing Fordism's authoritarian core and its paranoid anti-communism, opposition to the war was the ideological heart of the counterculture, which made Vietnam *the* dominant issue of the decade. Far beyond fear of the draft, ordinary young men and women faced being dragged by the hair, beaten with night sticks and shot dead on the street for standing with the postcolonial other as sisters and brothers. Universal love, in our cynical world, is the facet of the 60s most prone to mockery, the concept of 'kinship' having become biological rather than moral, with duty performed in the name of the father rather than the name of all. Yet the counterculture's veneration of love, its collectivity and solidarity are still tangible in the 60s' sounds and visions, in its forms and fabrics, which represent the enduring remnants of the era's attempt to attain utopia in the here and now.

1. Talking Back: Beat and Soul

The Working Class Talk Back: Beat

The years 1964–66 represent the peak of the Fordist settlement, politics and pop culture combining to create a social optimism unknown before or since. Coming to power concurrent with the British Invasion, and on the same wave of collectivist feeling, Lyndon Johnson and Harold Wilson were political popular modernists, their technocratic futurism balanced by a folksy populism which placed the previously subaltern at society's centre. Playing the proletarian rebel, Wilson shook up the state after the aristocratic enervation of Macmillan and Home, with a phalanx of socially liberal interventions, a modernist veneration of technology and a canny embrace of popular culture – awarding the Beatles MBEs. With similar energy, Johnson immediately broke the deadlock on the Civil Rights Act and launched a wholesale 'War on Poverty' that was the most ambitious programme of social engineering since the New Deal – a demonstration of what Fordist welfare capitalism could do.

From 1964 to 1966, Fordism's moving parts were in alignment, politics' leftward shift in creative dialectic with culture's discontents, sharing a concept of the greater good, differing only in how to define it. So, as Johnson took office and beat groups invaded the American charts, Bob Dylan's early 1964 declaration that 'The Times They Are a-Changin'' (UK 9) was as much promise as threat: "senators, congressmen", "mothers and fathers" all caught up in the indefatigable forward-motion of Fordism. Beat music was the sound of excitement, of possibility, and while 60s pop is often characterised as 'optimistic', the class character of that optimism is rarely acknowledged.[13] With an aristocrat prime minister until late 1964, bowler hats still staple dress for City gents, and patrician BBC presenters speaking like the Queen, class was key to the outrage beat produced in the British establishment. Noel Coward's derision and Paul Johnson's dismissal of beat fans as "a bottomless chasm of vacuity" were recognitions of the working class's refusal to accept their place.[14]

The security of full employment and the welfare safety net created a new class confidence, offering options beyond mere survival – not least the new art schools' democratisation of creativity. Enabled by Fordism's freedoms (and funding), beat music was also a response to its restrictions, deploying Fordist resources while disdaining its conventions – bought-in songs, professional accompaniment, the authority of patrician producers and white-coated engineers. Beat music is the sound of four self-taught musicians playing live and loud in a room, their affective directness and soaring harmonies voicing not just group solidarity but class consciousness. This music's very optimism was thus adversarial – talking back – and this push and pull between technocracy and feeling, repression and refusal, establishment and upstart was the motor of 60s pop.

A limitation of the term 'popular modernism' is that it elides the incorporation of the past. While beat was indisputably an emergent culture, it drew on a residual culture, rock'n'roll, and its ready-made vocabulary of refusal. This return of the repressed was audible in the Beatles' tentative 1962 'Love Me Do' (UK 17), but fully realised by the raucous Chuck Berry riffing of 'I Want to Hold Your Hand' (UK 1; US 1), which topped the American charts in early 1964. That EMI's American division initially refused to release the Beatles' records indicates how the musical establishment felt about this rebirth of rock'n'roll. Although the Beatles' sales on American indies and later, EMI's American wing, Capitol, couldn't be ignored, the company continued to treat this proletarian phenomenon with patrician condescension.

The Rolling Stones expressed this revivalism not just by hit covers of Berry's 'Come On' (UK 21) and Holly's 'Not Fade Away' (UK 3), but also by embodying rock'n'roll's *threat*. Beat fans embraced the original rock'n'rollers, with Holly having a wave of British hits,[15] Domino being given a hero's welcome and Berry's career reviving with 1964's 'No Particular Place to Go' (UK 3; US 10), which demonstrated to as-yet-contentless beat groups how to direct Fordism's frustrations. London's Kinks were quick to learn. With their live set and debut full of Berry covers, summer 1964's 'You Really Got Me' (UK 1; US 7) used Fordist technology against itself – Dave Davies slashing an amplifier to distort his guitar – rock'n'roll's atavistically adversarial energy rendered utterly modern. With brother Ray's self-made songwriting smarts talking back to Tin Pan Alley, 'You Really Got Me' was birthed in struggle – a standoff with the record company – and sounds it. The riff is an immediate affront, Ray's stroppy growl adding insult to sonic injury, his defiantly ascending chords creating a sense of unstoppable purpose. That this was a *class* purpose is communicated by the impatience with Fordist constraints upon desire expressed on 'Tired of Waiting for You' (UK 1; US 6) and with work-structured time on 'All Day and All of the Night' (UK 2; US 7).

In the interregnum there had been individual singers, *backed* by musicians, their vocals rarely harmonised, their space in the spotlight hymned by a subaltern chorus of 'oohs' and 'ahs'. Beat acts were collectives, *groups* who blurred individual identities with in-jokes and collective harmonies, the Beatles' hair-shaking a visualisation of this social symbiosis. On 'She Loves You' (UK 1; US 1), the lyric's unusual third-person narration gives a sense of the social beyond love songs' standard solipsism: the couple's love is commonly owned – we're *all* glad she still loves him. That Lennon and McCartney wrote every song on summer 1964's *A Hard Day's Night* (UK 1; US 1) was a statement of both class creativity and class confidence. "Up the workers and all that!" quips McCartney in the film's feature-length nose-thumb at the establishment. 'A Hard Day's Night' itself (UK 1; US 1) depicts alienated labour in uneasy alliance with affluence: "I work all day to get you money/To buy you things", Lennon laments, before cautiously affirming the Fordist compact ("why on earth should I moan?") because "When I'm home everything seems to be right". This pleasure in "things" is negated in the film's other hit, 'Can't Buy Me Love' (UK 1; US 1), its dismissal of aspirational accessories and its flip declaration "I don't care too much for money" de-libidinising Fordist consumerism with a very 60s positive-negativity, without an imperial ounce of cynicism or bitterness.

While the Beatles were cutely be-suited and polite, the Stones were unkempt and surly, with 1964's 'It's All Over Now' (UK 1; US 26) and 1965's 'The Last Time' (UK 1; US 9) articulations of pure scorn. Whatever Mick Jagger and Brian Jones' origins,

Cohn spoke for popular perception when he called the Stones "the voice of hooliganism"[16] – a *sexy* hooliganism, moreover, making the once-derided desirable – because they represented a threat to middle-class mores. The tabloid headline "Would You Let Your Daughter Marry a Rolling Stone?" said it all. A television clip for the Animals' summer 1964 'House of the Rising Sun' (UK 1; US 1) makes a mockery of their matching suits and corny choreography. Eric Burdon looks like he's been up for *weeks* doing unspeakable things, restoring all the carnality that's repressed in their bowdlerised version of a ribald folk song. Due to their bubblegum breeziness, it's forgotten that the Dave Clark Five were briefly the Beatles' main competitors – with 1964's 'Glad All Over' (UK 1; US 6) dislodging the fab four's chart dominance – and that singing drummer Clark exuded a saturnine working-class sexiness. Clark's hammering, four-square beat on both 'Glad All Over' and 'Bits and Pieces' (UK 2; US 4) is equal parts sex and threat.

The sound of the 60s, that four-square beat was derived from soul, and it's rarely acknowledged that the British Invasion was suffused with racial solidarity, from its music (the Beatles covering the Isleys' 'Twist and Shout', US 2), to its vocal stylings – Lulu's 1964 cover of the Isleys' 'Shout' (UK 7); Dusty Springfield; Stevie Winwood on Spencer Davis Group's supercharged 1966 'Gimme Some Lovin'' (UK 2; US 7) – to its content. With the urban increasingly associated with black America, two British Drifters pastiches offered different perspectives on city life: as salve for Fordist alienation in Petula Clark's delightful 1964 'Downtown' (UK 2; US 1); as alienation's *location* in the Animals' 1965 'We Gotta Get Out of This Place' (UK 2; US 13). The proles are "workin' and slavin' [their] life away"; thus Burdon's grinding repetition of the word "work", with class here clearly a *system* – the "dirty old part of the city where the sun refused to shine" – shortening lives and shutting off options. There's pride in this as well as refusal – in the roar of Burdon's voice; in the song's insistence that a better life is possible – alongside an implicit solidarity with the racial other. Wrong-footed by the Invasion, Americans began to breach their customary caution on class and race: hence the refusal of social divisions in the McCoys' 1965 'Hang on Sloopy' (UK 5; US 1) – Sloopy coming "from a very bad part of town" – heightened, like the Kingsmen's ornery 'Louie Louie' (UK 23; US 2), by the Latin otherness of its 'La Bamba' chord progression.

This racial solidarity was overt in the British subculture of 'mod', working-class kids with a love of soul and ska. As its name suggests, mod was popular modernism at its purest: proletarian, stylish, (suits, loafers, parkas), technological (scooters), and urgent (the songs, the speed). For Hebdige, mod's conspicuous consumption was "a parody of the consumer society",[17] taking a literally speedy, accelerationist approach to alienation – dive into it to destroy it. The Who's 1965 'Can't Explain' (UK 8) and glorious 1966 'My Generation' (UK 2) push Fordist technology beyond its limits, guitarist Pete Townshend's lyrics bridling at social restraint, less the voice of a generation than the voice of a class. Just as their lyrics *perform* working-class inarticulacy to explode the stereotype, so the Who's onstage destructiveness performed working-class violence – proper art-school boys, this was 'auto-destructive art' made material.[18] In mod itself, and in its skirmishes with rockers on the nation's beaches, the patrician media correctly perceived a class threat. "Nothin' gets in my way/ Not even locked doors", Roger Daltrey snarls on 1965's 'Anyway, Anyhow, Anywhere' (UK 10): "Don't follow the lines/That been laid before", as the track's buzzing, feeding-back guitars rip up the Fordist rulebook.

Fellow mods Small Faces squared up to all comers on 1965's soul-suffused 'Whatcha Gonna Do About It' (UK 14), while demanding unalienated gratification on 1966's explosive 'All or Nothing' (UK 1). With Steve Marriott increasingly flexing his cockney vowels, even the more innocuous British Invasion groups performed a pantomime proletarianism which thrilled America. Herman's Hermits scored a string of music-hall hits, with 1965's 'Mrs Brown You've Got a Lovely Daughter' (US 1) and 'I'm Henery the Eighth, I Am' (US 1) being assertive slices of working-class life, and with Peter Noone hamming up his Lancashire accent on 1966's cover of George Formby's 'Leaning on a Lamp Post' (US 9).[19] For all their quaintness, these tracks articulate working-class frustration with modernity, rather than a desire to return to the past, rendering them vitally popular modern rather than regressively retro.

If the Swinging 60s weren't as white as they're presented, neither were they as male. While, as Sheila Rowbotham points out, women usually appear in 60s retrospectives as legs under miniskirts,[20] working-class women were central to the 60s' soundtrack and style. Like Petula Clark, these women were interregnum balladeers reframed, and at this peak of Fordist functionality, such an embrace of MOR briefly belied the generation gap. Ignored by history because of her showbiz sheen, Cilla Black shared the Beatles' manager, producer and on 1964's 'It's for You' (UK 7), their songs, while bringing an unvarnished warmth to Bacharach-David's 'Anyone Who Had a Heart' (UK 1) and a hard-nosed aspiration to 1964's 'You're My World' (UK 1; US 26), which recalled Ronnie Spector. Working-class Londoner Sandie Shaw personified the informal stylishness of Swinging London, less with her Fordist, easy-listening songs – though her 1964 version of Bacharach-David's 'Always Something There to Remind Me' (UK 1) is definitive – than with her bare feet and Biba boutique clothes. Cathy McGowan's effervescence dissolved the division between fan and presenter on *Ready Steady Go!* (1963–66), a show whose energy captured the era's sense of *motion* – 'Keep on Running', as the Spencer Davis Group urged (UK 1).

As part of this forward motion, working-class models like Twiggy and mini-skirt queen Jean Shrimpton democratised fashion, making the ordinary glamorous. Shrimpton's boyfriend, Terence Stamp (*The Collector*, 1965), represented a new breed of working-class actors, alongside Michael Caine (*The Ipcress File*, 1965) and Sean Connery (the new James Bond series). Dramas like *The Likely Lads* (1964–66) and *Til Death Do Us Part* (1965–75) brought this social revolution onto television screens. 1965's John Boorman-directed *Catch Us If You Can* captures both this cultural convolution *and* the bid to contain it. As the Dave Clark Five and a model (Barbara Ferris), attempt to escape the system, they're literally pursued by capitalism, the troupe creating havoc in the petit-bourgeois suburbs, before running smack into modernity's military-industrial complex on Salisbury Plain. All this is vaguely tangible in the Five's title theme's insistence on freedom (UK 5; US 4). With Caine's *Alfie* (1966) suggesting the 60s swung more freely for men than women, its Bacharach-David theme by

Cilla Black (UK 9) and Dionne Warwick (US 15) meditates on instant gratification – "Is it just for the moment we live?" – and individualism – "Are we meant to take more than we give?" – not as a rejection of 60s values but as a reassertion of the era's ethos of collective responsibility.

It is, however, important to remember that, as Marcuse attests, "the majority of the people in the affluent society are on the side of that which is – not that which can and ought to be".[21] Marcuse calls this "the Happy Consciousness – the belief that the real is rational and that the system delivers the goods".[22] Such a consciousness was reflected in the soundtrack to *The Sound of Music* being the best-selling album of 1965, 1966 *and* 1968 (UK 1; US 1), in Dean Martin dislodging 'Hard Day's Night' from the top spot with 'Everybody Loves Somebody' in 1964 (UK 11; US 1) – alongside the popularity of his 50s-restoration variety show. Yet it was the Beach Boys who became America's primary defence against the British Invasion, ostensibly meeting it on its own terms. Yet where the Beach Boys mined Berry on spring 1964's 'Fun Fun Fun' (US 5), it was to invoke the reactionary, not the rebellious 50s, accepting the patriarch's authority to take the T-Bird away and call time on fun. The "real cool head" on 1964's oafishly infectious 'I Get Around' (UK 7; US 1) is a square who's "making real good bread", the song an attempt to harness 60s forward motion to an extant auto-franchise and getting nowhere.

The content of Paul Revere and the Raiders' 1965 'Just Like Me' (US 11) is innocuous for all its attractively Animal-istic aggression,[23] while their 1966 'Kicks' (US 4) is a paean to staying "straight". Even *within* the Invasion, Dusty Springfield's 1964, Bacharach-David-penned 'Wishin' and Hopin'' (US 6) reaffirms suburban gender norms ("Do the things he likes to do/Wear your hair just for him"), while 1966's 'You Don't Have to Say You Love Me' (UK 1; US 4) makes a (devastating) drama out of being a doormat. As early as 1965, Ray Davies was expressing reservations about the rate the times were a-changin'. 'Where Have All the Good Times Gone?' (B-side, 'Till the End of the Day', UK 8) yearns for high-Fordist security, even boredom: "Once we had an easy ride and always felt the same". Yet despite the dominant culture's defensiveness and the emergent culture's self-doubt about the direction of travel, the clash of Fordism's possibilities and limits had created an energy that was unstoppable.

The Stones' 1965 '(I Can't Get No) Satisfaction' (UK 1; US 1) is a beat-group meta-song, which adroitly – and coolly – captures Fordism's contradictions. With its four-square 60s beat both factory-regular and exuberantly *free*, 'Satisfaction' celebrates modernity (driving, TV, flying), while refusing what Marcuse calls Fordism's "renunciation and delay in satisfaction"[24] – communicated as much by the frustrated, circling, Stax-inspired guitar riff as by the lyric. 'Satisfaction' is a siren song for those who damn the 60s as self-indulgence, therefore.[25] Philip Norman, hearing only "the insufferable ennui of being handed everything",[26] misses that the song's collapse of consumer and sexual frustration is self-mocking (does Jagger even know what sexual frustration *is?*), while also exposing capitalism's false promise to fulfil every desire.

Although by 1965 even Pepsi ads were promising a Marcusian world beyond work, Sandbrook and Marwick both scare-quote 'alienation', because for conservatives there *is* no system by which to be alienated. 60s beat groups knew better. On Australians, the Easybeats' 1966 'Friday on My Mind' (UK 6; US 16), the clock-like riff invokes the "five-day grind", but the volatile vocal's escape from the riff's constraint adds threat to its complaint that "nothin' else bugs me more than workin' for the rich man". Expressing a riotous joy in the desire to let rip at the weekend, the track is pop modernism capturing Fordism's contradictions, the subaltern talking back to the power but still too exhausted to see beyond its own everyday experience. Like everything else in the 60s, this was about to change.

Black America Talks Back: Soul

That soul would provide America's most robust resistance to the British Invasion was ironic, given the South's contemporary campaign of 'massive resistance' to granting black Americans basic citizenship. While soul gets critically segregated from the 60s, it was as much the sound of modernity as (soul-suffused) beat, its crotchet bounce and four-square rhythm emphasising the 60s 'now!' so pressingly that it was pushing into the future. The Supremes broke through at peak Beatlemania to become the decade's second-most-successful group of any gender or race. The trio's mid-60s hits encapsulated 60s optimism, sounding victorious on 1965's forward-marching 'Back in My Arms Again' (US 1) and triumphalist on 'I Hear a Symphony' (US 1), its title declaring its ambition and sophistication, its musical twists and turns defining popular modernity's push forwards into a seemingly unstoppable future. The Southern white supremacists were stuck in the past, with Goldwater being decimated by a gold rush for Johnson in the fall 1964 election.

Despite this forward motion, the narrative of steady progress towards racial equality is a neoliberal one – heard in Reagan, Bush's and Clinton's speeches – with Martin Luther King's radicalism, Malcolm X's existence and economics all excised. Post-war affluence never became a 'right' for those on the wrong side of the colour line, so the fact that the northern ghettoes exploded the very summer of the Civil Rights Act – Harlem, New Jersey and Chicago all aflame – was hardly coincidental. If the Supremes' hits of that year – 'Where Did Our Love Go' (UK 3; US 1) and 'Baby Love' (UK 1; US 1) – suggested a sense of loss, it was too lightly delivered to resonate politically, while the Temptations' hits – 'The Way You Do the Things You Do' (US 11) and 'My Girl' (US 1) – remained a relay of positivity and progress, sunshine on a cloudy day.

One Motown group *did* capture this volatile moment, however, without relinquishing the company's command-Fordist positivity. Martha and the Vandellas' 'Dancing in the Street' (UK 4; US 2) is a party song, albeit a very 1960s party – "It's an invitation across the nation/A chance for folks to meet" – whose racial inclusivity encompasses racial pride, with its pointed roll-call of black-dominated conurbations, most of them aflame as the song burned up the charts. Heard in this way, 'Dancing in the Street' is the sound and celebration of riot, of refusal – 60s positive-negativity and popular modernity at its peak.

As much a bottom-line businessman as Berry Gordy, James Brown kept his distance from politics, yet his music was formally radical, its uncompromising rhythmic otherness both a form of racial refusal and an expression of racial pride –"a different rhythm of living and being", as Gilroy puts it.[27] On that same combustible summer's propulsive 'Out of Sight' (US 24) – and on 1965's 'Papa's Got a Brand New Bag' (UK 25; US 8) and 'I Got You' (UK 29; US 3) – Brown excised soul's sugar and fat, stripping it to raw energy: rhythm over melody, repetition over exposition, funk's syncopation over rock's steady roll. Curtis Mayfield's Impressions' 'Keep on Pushing' that summer (US 10) was an exhortation to the civil rights movement to maintain the pressure against the massive resistance campaign – "A great big stone wall stands there ahead of me". Following radical Malcolm X's murder in February 1965, the Impressions' gorgeous ballad 'People Get Ready' (US 14) offered a fitting elegy, making gospel's spiritual material and demanding its 'tomorrow' today. The song's "train coming" sounds both an intention and a warning to those who would stand in progress's tracks.

King and the NAACP were facing down Southern resistance with a new combativeness. Prompted by a state trooper killing a black protestor, the second of three marches from Selma to Montgomery in March 1965 resulted in the police riot of 'Bloody Sunday', which, in an era of Fordist mass communication, was broadcast to the entire nation, with the graphic reality of systemic racism offending liberal sensitivities. Johnson sent federal troops to secure the third march and brought the Voting Rights Act into law within weeks. That the Alabaman legislature called the activists "Left-Wing Pro-Communist Groups" told an inadvertent truth: King was becoming radicalised, increasingly focusing on economics rather than legal rights. As if to underline this distinction, riots erupted again in Watts, Los Angeles, within days of the Voting Rights Act in August 1965.

It was at this tense political moment that former child star Stevie Wonder rebelled against Motown's authoritarian, command-Fordist caution. Insisting on co-writing his own material, Wonder succeeded in addressing social issues without jettisoning Motown's positivity or pop sensibility. Winter 1965's 'Uptight (Everything's All Right)' (UK 14; US 3) taps racial tensions from title to content – "A poor man's son, from across the railroad tracks" – refusing to be restricted by class or race. With 'Uptight' repossessing the track-crossing 60s beat from 'Satisfaction',

Wonder's 1966 'A Place in the Sun' (UK 9; US 20) channels 'We Gotta Get Out' through King's language ("running towards a dream"), to evoke a world freed from repression: "There's a place in the sun/Where there's hope for everyone".

That "everyone" is crucial, for as Gilroy points out, the civil rights movement gave material heft to the potential not just of one race, but of the whole *human* race to live as three-dimensional women and men.[28] Similarly, rather than merely being 'race music' produced for a narrow demographic, soul stitched 60s popular culture together. From beat's pop-mod positivity to psychedelia's Technicolor utopianism, soul was a common factor in all 60s music – even folk-rock. The Supremes deployed 12-strings on their *A Bit of Liverpool* LP (US 21) and toured with the Lovin' Spoonful, while Wonder's 1966 cover of Dylan's 'Blowin' in the Wind' (US 9) gave folk protest the patented Motown pop bounce. Using the 60s' four-square snare-push, the Four Tops' revelatory 1966 'Reach Out I'll Be There' is Motown's literal shout-out to Dylan (UK 1; US 1), with Levi Stubbs' urgent, life-affirming vocal asserting the staple 60s affect of unconditional solidarity.[29] The collectivity and humanism for which 60s soul is a synecdoche surpasses demographics as the determinant of culture: Marx called such interconnection "class consciousness".

'War on Poverty' notwithstanding, Johnson's escalation of the war on Vietnam was removing the gloss from his presidency, giving his counterculture-friendly 1964 election campaign spiel – "We must love each other or we must die" – a bitter irony.[30] For the condition of Fordist modernity was to be both progressive *and* destructive, to be both liberal *and* authoritarian, and this dichotomy brought Johnson's ally Wilson, into conflict first with peace protestors, then with the working class he was presumed to represent. With the affluent West's technology deployed to napalm third-world peasantry, and technocracy deployed to defend capital rather than workers, the gloss was beginning to come off the concept of modernity itself. Spilling out of the New Left and the civil rights movement, ordinary people – and popular music – began to stand back from their immediate experience and to explore the workings of society as a *system*.

2. Standing Back – Folk-Rock

Folk-Rock as Social Observation

Folk-rock developed both from beat and from beat groups' frustration with the constraints of the Fordist industry, developing into frustration with the constraints of Fordist society itself. As the title of late 1964's *Beatles for Sale* (UK 1) suggests, the groups were feeling processed by the machine, and the album, recorded hurriedly between tour dates, sounded harried and atypically sour. This being the 60s, however, 'Eight Days a Week' (US 1) alchemised exhaustion into ecstasy, negativity into positivity, its electro-acoustic shimmer using the folk past to amplify the popular modern present, pulling at Fordist constraints to create new possibilities. With 'Eight Days' largely contentless, it was Lennon's dolorous, Dylan-esque 'I'm a Loser' that opened up new lyrical possibilities, standing back with a coolly observing eye. Coming up through the austerely politicised folk-protest movement, Dylan had developed a subject position that owed more to 1930s radical Woody Guthrie than to traditional balladry – the unalienated social observer, deploying a mythic register that conveyed a visionary authority. Dylan's spring 1965 'Subterranean Homesick Blues' (UK 9) married this folk observer to modern technology with a Berry-inspired rock'n'roll backing.

Yet it was Californian folkies the Byrds' version of another Dylan *Bringing it All Back Home* track, 'Mr. Tambourine Man' (UK 1; US 1), that established folk-rock's popular modern amalgam of past and present, art and commerce, form and content. The foregrounding of Roger McGuinn's Rickenbacker electric 12-string literally chimes with Dylan's folk-observer lyric, enlightenment rendered material by the instrument's luminosity, cutting through the sound, just as the mythic lyric cuts through modernity's 'reality'. Both in the moment ("ready to go anywhere") *and* distanced from it ("all my senses have been stripped"), the track isn't merely *druggy*, as critics like Savage aver;[31] its emphasis on social perception is entirely political.

Folk-rock became *the* sound and vision of the mid-60s, and the deployment of an electric 12-string would invoke the 60s ever after (the Smiths, R.E.M., the La's) – echoing folk-rock's *sound*, but with its vision – its social observation – removed. Beat's evolution into folk-rock revealed to the industry that this new music wasn't going anywhere, so an 'it smells but it sells' attitude set in. Following 'Tambourine Man', Simon and Garfunkel's folkie dirge 'The Sound of Silence' was literally electrified by Dylan-producer Tom Wilson for its 1965 single release (US 1) into an epiphany. The song's titular silence is not a rural hush but the spell urban capitalist modernity casts upon its subjects, who bow to it as a god, with its prophecy "written on the subway walls" in advertising hoardings and flashed across streets in "neon light". Wilson's gleaming, echo-drenched production evokes this mesmerising modernity but also, via the 12-string's bell-like clarity, the capacity to see through it: "the vision that was planted" in the narrator's brain is what remains.

While the Beatles' 1965 'Ticket to Ride' (UK 1; US 1) cut through modernity's noise with a sound both recreationally slurred and ringingly precise, it was only on 'Help!' (UK 1; US 1) that – catching up with their competitors – they matched sound with vision. While critics cite the lyric as expressing Lennon's personal alienation,[32] it's plainly a protest at Fordist pressure, Lennon's falsetto "please!" chiming with the arpeggiated guitars, while the song's solution to its existential crisis is the assistance of another – with this 60s sociality rendered material by the band's gloriously intertwining vocals. Equally personalised by critics, Lennon's 1966 'Nowhere Man' (US 3) adopts the mythic register to summon modernity's "nowhere land", the titular liminal figure unsure where the Fordist future is pushing him. Again, the solution – "Leave it all 'til somebody else lends you a hand" – is, *contra* MacDonald, social rather than sarcastic, underlined by the lushest harmonies on *Rubber Soul* (UK 1; US 1) and of the 60s so far.[33]

60s communality is constantly co-opted by centrist critics as individualism, as in Dorian Lynskey's line on Dylan's shift from acoustic folk protest to electric folk-rock, "the *I* protesting the *we*... a politics of the self".[34] Dylan's eschewal of activism and his 1965 broadside 'Positively Fourth Street' (UK 8; US 7) were rejections of the folk scene's *constraints*, not its politics. Contrary to critics and the "Judas!" man, Dylan betrayed nothing by plugging in at Newport in summer 1965: he simply amplified his social commentary. The song he plugged in with, 'Maggie's Farm' (UK 22), satirises both class hierarchy and the alienated labour it creates – Dylan, too, was being worked to death by the Fordist machine and was increasingly rejecting conventional verities. Far from being 'personal', summer 1965's 'Like a Rolling Stone' (UK 4; US 2) deploys the mythic register in what Mike Marqusee calls a "critique of all aristocracies – the rich, the famous, the hip"[35]: class, in other words. The social climber's loss of bourgeois privilege is mocked by the narrating social outsider, the dynamism of Wilson's production rendering Dylan's relentless critique almost ecstatic. Yet, just as the song's length pulls at Fordist strictures, so its cruelty stretches 60s positive-negativity to breaking point.

Simon and Garfunkel's summer 1966 'I Am a Rock' (UK 17; US 3) takes this outsider observer stance to its cold conclusion. Gazing from his window to the streets below, the social critic is cut off from social reality: "I have no need of friendship", Simon sings with clipped precision: "It's laughter and it's loving I disdain". The song thus satirises the very individualism centrist critics claim as the 60s' essence, while highlighting the danger in the outsider observer's moral certainty, the nomad as monad. By contrast, the social observation of the Kinks' spring 1966 Swinging London satire 'Dedicated Follower of Fashion' (UK 4) is systemic but not unsympathetic, for all its snickering flippancy. Combining the populist forms of music hall and folk, 'Follower' evokes individualism as a conformist subject position created by capitalism: "[His clothes] will make or break him so he's got to buy the best".[36] Individualism in all these cases is a loss, not a gain.

The scepticism about Fordism that folk-rock articulated was galvanised by the war in Vietnam, with Students for a Democratic Society organising America's biggest-ever peace protest in Washington in April 1965, and their campaign highlighting the contradiction in Fordism waging war on both poverty and peasantry. On the Byrds' fall 1965 take on Pete Seeger's 'Turn! Turn! Turn!' (UK 26; US 1), the Biblical mythic register and bell-like guitars evoke both a peaceful rural past and a warring technological present in a vision of the future. While Barry McGuire's summer 1965 'Eve of Destruction' (UK 3; US 1) was written to order by P.F. Sloan, it's as systemic as it is formulaic, linking Vietnam to the violence greeting the Selma-Montgomery marches. Its exhortation to "take a look around" allies the mythic observer to the observational potential of modern technology, with television exposing Selma and Saigon to public oversight. With the Cuban Missile Crisis a recent memory, 'Eve of Destruction' is alert to technology's death drive: "…the world in a grave… if the button is pushed".[37] Again there was a 'straight' counter-offensive to such countercultural critique: Sgt Barry Sadler's patriotic 1966 'Ballad of the Green Berets' (US 1) was at the American top spot for a month at the height of folk-rock.

With folk the music of the people, and workers central to modernity, class was an inevitable focus for folk-rock's social commentary. Another Byrds Seeger-setting, summer 1965's 'Bells of Rhymney', concerning a 1930s mining disaster, offers a systemic account of class: "Who made the mine owner… and who killed the miner?" (*Mr. Tambourine Man*, UK 7; US 6). Meanwhile, Lennon's caustic observation that "a man must break his back to earn his day of leisure" on the Beatles' late 1965 'Girl' (*Rubber Soul*) both cuts across *and* accentuates the Fordism of the song's electro-acoustic sophistication. The Animals developed an appropriately aggressive version of folk-rock's 12-string jangle, with spring 1966's 'Inside-Looking Out' (UK 12) deploying a traditional prison-song as a metaphor for class. Incarcerated in a system where the narrator has to "sell [his] time", his enforced labour creates "pains and blisters" not just on his hands but his *mind*, while his "thoughts of freedom" sound, in Burdon's roar, less a threnody than a threat.

The Who also funnelled their aggression through folk-rock, spring 1966's 12-string-charged 'Substitute' (UK 5) evoking not "teenage… confusion" as Cohn and Savage both claim,[38] but the falsity of proclaimed 60s 'classlessness'. Being "born with a plastic spoon in [your] mouth" is a perfect pop-mod image for poverty: the narrator can only ever be a substitute for one who can *afford* leather shoes and a "fine-looking suit" (the devil in the detail). The Kinks' autumn 1966 'Dead End Street' (UK 5) satirically spells out the social hierarchy – "We are strictly second-class" – while again anchoring the song in material detail – cracks in ceiling, kitchen sink leaking. Although the protagonists are "out of work and got no money", the track's folk/music-hall bounce sounds joyous, its shouted chorus defiant – that 60s positive-negativity again. At the other end of the social spectrum, the band's 1965 'Well-Respected Man' (US 13) observes the establishment archetype with indifference to deference, skewering a conservative morality that's undermined by hypocrisy, and a social standing born of inherited wealth. For Sandbrook, it's "the so-called Establishment", because, for conservatives, society is a level playing field:[39] there *is* no system. 60s folk-rockers saw through this with a visionary – and thanks to the 12-string, a *ringing* – clarity.

Folk-Rock as Feminisation

Folk-rock exemplified a "different kind of maleness" in sound and style.[40] The girly-boy in popular music travelled through Johnnie Ray's extravagant emotionality and Elvis's engagement with the gaze. Dormant in the interregnum, he was reawakened in McCartney's winsome, wide-eyed, curiously unsexual come-hither and Jagger's ability to sexually compromise the viewer. Folk-rock, however, was suffused with a fey masculine femininity for which 'Donovan' is a name. 'Feminine' and 'masculine' are used throughout this book in a Marcusian, relational sense, aggression and competitiveness being encoded as 'masculine', gentleness and nurture as 'feminine' in society's gendered division of labour. Marcuse's "female principle" doesn't thus essentialise 'feminine' characteristics but upholds such qualities as antinomies to a conditioned masculinity compelled towards mastery – of their own nature, of others and of external nature.[41] On Bob Lind's 1966 'Elusive Butterfly' (UK 5; US 5), the gossamer lightness of his lovely voice and the track's wafting instrumentation are a world away from beat aggression, yet they're just as adversarial in their defiant immersion in nature and distance from the world of work.

Folk-rock's aural feminisation and capacity to stand back from society was combined in its observation of Fordism's repression of sexuality and gender. Heard as an empathic address to homosexuals, the Beatles' 1965 'You've Got to Hide Your Love Away' (*Help!* UK 1; US 1) is preoccupied with social judgement – people staring; people laughing – with observation as regulation. The Kinks' concurrent 'See My Friends' (UK 10) flips the framing back to the folk-observer, gazing longingly at his friend, just as the song flips social conventions, the social otherness echoed by the track's sitar-like inflections (six months before the Beatles' used a genuine sitar on 'Norwegian Wood'). The performance principle can be applied to gender as well as work, via the double meaning of 'performance': both work and gender are productions; both are socially (and economically) productive. So just as the Who exemplified music's performativity, so they now amplified gender's: summer 1966's 'I'm a Boy' (UK 2) concerns a boy who's forced to 'be' a girl – or a girl who insists she's a boy – displaying a radical disinterest in biology, gender here is understood only as social performance. Even from within "monogamic reproduction"[42] – and Fordist production – husband-and-wife Spector-associates Sonny and Cher gesture at this gender performativity on 1965's folk-rock bubblegum 'I Got You Babe' (UK 1; US 1), citing (and Sonny exemplifying) the "different kind of maleness" whose blousons and flowing tresses blur conventional gender lines.

Folk-rock also allowed for a new male observation – as opposed to objectification – of the feminine in pop. The Stones' spring 1966 'Mother's Little Helper' (US 8) uses a softer 12-string-guitar sound to depict housewives' alienation within the Fordist division of labour – "Cooking fresh food for her husband's just a drag" – and consequent addiction to that most modern of domestic aids, Valium. While this tracks Betty Friedan's 1963 *The Feminine Mystique* precisely, the Stones were hardly feminists, tending to express their class resentment through gender. On 1965's 'Play with Fire' (B-side, 'The Last Time'), '19th Nervous Breakdown' (UK 2; US 2) and 'Stupid Girl' (*Aftermath*, UK 1; US 2), feminised music is deployed to express anti-feminist sentiments. In this respect, Dylan was also like the Rolling Stones, as were the Animals, whose 1965 'It's My Life' (UK 7; US 23) aims its class anger at women over a clarion-call 12-string riff.

Each of these male visions had their female counterparts, however, as women negotiated a path between enduring 50s' chauvinism and 60s' social shake-up. Following Jagger-Richard's fey 1964 'As Tears Go By' (UK 9; US 22), Marianne Faithfull went far deeper into folk-rock than the fellows on two UK and one US top 20 albums. Dylan was countered by mentor Joan Baez, with her hit albums *5* (UK 3; US 12) and *Farewell Angelina* (UK 5; US 10), though her singles were blacklisted by radio due to her leftist politics – ironically ensuring an enduringly high profile. As against Sonny, Cher had a self-possessed serenity that subverted feminine norms, while Nancy Sinatra's professional partnership with another Spector associate, Lee Hazlewood, created a gloriously kitsch collision of Long 50s and high 60s. Early 1966's caustically camp 'These Boots Are Made for Walking' (UK 1; US 1) combines sex and sass: while the promo clip fetishises Sinatra and her go-go dancers' 'kinky boots' (and legs), the male gaze is countered by the women's ironic expressions and topped by Sinatra's head-tossing "ha", which – on record and video – is one of the peak moments in the history of pop. Repeating the formula like good Fordists with 'How Does That Grab You Darlin'' (UK 19; US 7), Sinatra's growl/purr after "There's more than one way to skin a cat, you know" is both flirtatious and feisty. None of this is folk-rock feminism, quite, but it's pop audibly feeling its way towards the future.

Folk-Rock as Faulty Observation

Amidst the 60s' questing and questioning, folk-rock didn't always observe so clearly. The Hollies' 1965 'Look Through Any Window' (UK 4) and 1966 'Bus Stop' (UK 5; US 5), alongside Herman's Hermits' 1966 'No Milk Today' (UK 7), give a charming, chiming resonance to visions of ordinary lives, but their kitchen-sink narratives lack the bite of beat's class assertion, let alone folk-rock's social savvy.[43] Even the Beatles sound befuddled on 1966's 'Paperback Writer' (UK 1; US 1), a cutup of proletarian pride, class cliché and hipster square-baiting, making its brief ejection from the US top spot by Frank Sinatra's square-courting 'Strangers in the Night' (US 1) more than circumstantial. That same summer the Beatles' 'Eleanor Rigby' (UK 1; US 11) gave ordinary people's privation a baroque grandeur via a fancy string quartet. Yet while its observation is rich with material detail, privation's *cause* remains unilluminated, even existential – "Ah! Look at all the lonely people!" – again suggesting the social detachment of the 'objective' observer. By contrast, teenage Janis Ian's fall 1966 'Society's Child' (US 14) presents familial opposition to interracial romance as entirely societal – and does so with passion.

'Society' is a slippery term, because the social is integral to socialism and to 60s sociality, the counterculture being also known as 'the alternative society'. Yet Adorno influentially understood 'society' as the machine that subsumes individuals into the economic system.[44] While it's the societal *system* that smothers Janis's love affair, it's *insufficient* society that kills Eleanor. The concept of 'society' thus set a snare for 60s radicals, in which several got snagged. In its transcendence of societal strictures, the Beatles' revelatory, proto-psychedelic 'Rain' (B-side, 'Paperback Writer'; also US 23) overlooks the social, the enlightened chiding the conventionally benighted with a hipster condescension ("They might as well be dead") that Marcuse called "a pubertarian revolt against the wrong target".[45]

As the counterculture took off with *International Times'* Roundhouse launch in autumn 1966, Manfred Mann's 'Semi-Detached, Suburban Mr. James' (UK 2) aloofly condemns toast-buttering and dog-walking as sellouts to the system, running counter to nascent hippies' inclusive ethos. Even while hymning ordinariness, the Kinks could slide into hipster smugness, as on summer 1966's 'I'm Not Like Everybody Else' (B-side, 'Sunny Afternoon'). As pop's upstarts joined the economic elite, they risked losing touch both with their class origins and with social collectivity. From summer 1966, the Kinks' 'Sunny Afternoon' (UK 1; US 14) and the Beatles' 'Taxman' (*Revolver*, UK 1; US 1) are classily crafted tracks whose rejection of Labour's redistributive taxation is politically anti-social, making the counterculture seem like an exclusive club.

Folk-rock's Fordists were quick to follow such simplistic signposts to hipness. Sonny and Cher's 1965 'But You're Mine' (UK 17; US 15) squares up to the squares ("It ain't gonna be us who lose this fight") but their idea of the battle lines can't extend beyond hair-length, a preoccupation shared by Jody Miller's vaguely countercultural country hit, 1965's 'Home of the Brave' (US 25). The Turtles' Dylan-esque late 1965 'Let Me Be' (US 29) declares, "Society's goal is to be part of the whole" but opposes this only with individualism ("I'm just trying hard to be myself"). Marx insisted we avoid postulating 'society' as an abstraction confronting the individual, because the individual is still a *social* being.[46] So while the Lovin' Spoonful's jazzy spring 1966 'Daydream' (UK 2; US 2) is a delight, its unalienated hippie protagonist lolling on some square's suburban lawn is an individualist abnegation of sociality rather than a rejection of repressive society: "I couldn't care less about the dues you say I got", John Sebastian sneers. It was into this hip/square faultline that Nixon would drive a wedge in the late 60s, interpellating the 'silent majority' as the socially responsible upholders of a benign system, while casting the counterculture as anarchically irresponsible individualists.

Exemplifying the way the counterculture was founded on Fordism yet confounded it, the Mamas & the Papas were a manufactured derivative of the same folk-rock scene as the Spoonful, yet their more 'pop' sound and more populist sensibility rendered their counterculturality inclusive. Rather than *objectifying* the ordinary, spring 1966's 'Monday Monday' (UK 3; US 1) *occupies* it, its evocation of the weekly Fordist grind decrying alienation rather than the alienated, and its solidaristic communality given grain and substance by the group's glorious vocal unity. The best-selling song of 1966, 'California Dreamin'' (UK 23; US 4), doesn't just reject the greyness and flatness of the square Fordist world, it offers a vision of an alternative: a sun-drenched utopia that's exemplified visually and vocally by the group themselves – and to which *everyone* is invited. Created in and against Fordist musical and social strictures, the Mamas & the Papas were the sound and the sight of the counterculture emerging.

3. Standing Up – Psychedelia

Psychedelia and Reality

Psychedelia is the musical manifestation of what Marcuse heralded as "a world that could be free", the cultural logic of the counterculture.[47] Inspired rather than simply instigated by drugs, psychedelia intensified folk-rock's preoccupation with perception, Marcuse observing that "today's rebels want to see, hear, feel new things in a new way: they link liberation with the dissolution of ordinary and orderly perception".[48] This 'liberation' wasn't just a drug-induced delusion, an altered state, but an insight into how consensus reality naturalises ideology, and how repression resides in the grain as well as the grind of everyday life, in convention and in 'common sense'.

Despite being an outgrowth of both beat and folk-rock, psychedelia bears little relationship to what four people could play in a room, its transcendence of Fordist musical limits paralleling its lyrics' rejection of social limits. Psychedelia, therefore, isn't a genre for what Joe Kennedy calls "authentocrats" – or "reactionary traditionalists"[49] – critics like Cohn (for whom psychedelia is pop getting above itself) and Gillett (in whose pop history psychedelia simply doesn't occur), 70s rockists (from classic to punk) or 90s lad-rockers (Oasis panel-beating 'I Am the Walrus' into standard shape). Setting limits on what's imaginable, these anti-psychedelicists are capitalist realists, for whom alternative ways of living can only be fantasy and a counterculture thus a counterfeit.

The pace of change in this conjuncture has rarely been equalled, its energy, innovation and imagination rarely eclipsed. Month on month, the period 1966–68 was a constantly shifting kaleidoscope of the experimental yet accessible, the inward-looking but inclusive, the adversarial yet affirmative. As MacDonald admits, "a sunny optimism permeated everything and possibilities seemed limitless": a paisley-patterned positivity swirled across Western culture.[50] While the Beatles have become the paradigm of 60s possibility, they coalesced as much as catalysed the era's currents, and it was former blues revivalists the Yardbirds whose February 1966 'Shapes of Things' (UK 3; US 11) set psychedelia in motion. Pushing Fordist technology to its outer limits, the track's reverse-echo and ricocheting feedback's disordering of perception mirror not just the acid experience but the lyric's evocation of a disorientating ideology which conventionalises technology's destructive power.

Weeks later, the Byrds' 'Eight Miles High' (UK 14; US 24) again invoked and overtook technology, McGuinn's wild, almost atonal 12-string soloing producing a discombobulation which, again, to regard as merely 'druggy' is to avoid deeper questions.[51] For Marcuse, "the 'trip' involves the dissolution of the ego shaped by the established society": psychedelia was thus an attempt to see through an ideological reality.[52] That June, the Yardbirds turned that reality 'Over Under Sideways Down' (UK 10; US 13) – "All the things they said were wrong/Are what I want to be"– just as they turned Fordist music inside out, r'n'b dizzyingly circled by sitar-like riffs, everything gradually sucked into an echo vortex, and interspersed with excited shouts. Segregated by critics from psychedelia, Dylan's surreal visions on July's *Blonde on Blonde* (UK 3; US 9) are an entirely countercultural "deconstruction of the customary".[53] 'Rainy Day Women #12 & 35' (UK 7; US 2) plays upon reactionary responses to hippie refusal of norms through a relentless pun on being stoned – by drugs, by the establishment. Concurrently, the Lovin' Spoonful's giddy 'Summer in the City' (UK 8; US 1) sounds like a celebration of urban modernity, but its electronic evocation of pneumatic drills and car horns and the fact that riots broke out in Detroit that August make it a deconstruction of Fordism, technology deployed to question technological modernity.

Psychedelia's quest for unalienated quietude was pursued into the psyche itself on the Beatles' August 1967 'Tomorrow Never Knows' (*Revolver*, UK 1; US 1). Surrender to Timothy Leary's lysergic 'void' is exemplified by the track's single-chord, tambura-drone harmonic openness, its reordering of reality expressed by laughter electronically accelerated to become fluttering birdsong, and orchestral swells sucking in on themselves then disappearing. Disorientation becomes reorientation, individual ego death a communal epiphany – "Love is all and love is everyone". Drugs are just a means, even a *metaphor*, for transcending ideological perception in psychedelia, a way to "break on through to the other side", as the Doors put it in January 1967 (*The Doors*, US 2), who'd named themselves after Aldous Huxley's druggy *The Doors of Perception* (1954). "The membrane which separated the inner and outer worlds seemed to have become permeable",[54] Rowbotham recalls. Yet rather than being the musical equivalent of being told someone's dreams, psychedelia at its best is a radical merger of self and other, subject and object.

On the Beatles' extraordinary February 1967 'Strawberry Fields Forever' (UK 2; US 8), the narrator is synaesthetically spellbound by his lysergically enhanced perception. His ego decomposes as he returns to childhood, to the womb, to inanimate matter – thus the melancholically wheezing mellotron, the nostalgic northern brass emissions, the cymbals' backwards, womb-like sucks: a total disassembly of Fordist technology and identity. The song's yearning to escape from social engagement – "It doesn't matter much to me" – isn't solipsism but escape from social *repression*, gradually fumbling its way through the musical and conceptual undergrowth to the realisation "Ah yes, but it's all wrong/That is, I think I disagree". Such reimagining of reality is the refusal at the counterculture's core, and this motif of childhood recurs throughout psychedelia, a space of imagination beyond alienation, where every day is a trip.[55] On Jefferson Airplane's surging, surreal, *Alice in Wonderland*-inspired 'White Rabbit' that June (US 8), Grace Slick's command to "feed your head" is an imprecation not just to gorge on drugs and examine your navel but to open your mind and observe the world. For Marcuse, to "break with the familiar, the routine ways of seeing, hearing, feeling, understanding things" means that "the organism may become receptive to the potential forms of a non-aggressive, non-exploitative world".[56]

As the biographies of Brian Jones, Syd Barrett and Brian Wilson suggest, such a break with the conditioned familiar could be confounding. With its backwards guitar signalling a reversed reality, the Electric Prunes' November 1966 'I Had Too Much to Dream (Last Night)' (US 11) presciently soundtracks a bad trip. The Fordist First Edition's January 1968 'Just Dropped In (To See What Condition My Condition Was In)' (US 5) would be deployed in *The Big Lebowski* (1998) to deride Leary's acid utopianism: "I saw so much I broke my mind". Yet post-war minds were made to be broken when Fordist stability was underwritten by authoritarian force, from the 50s' patriarch, to the army, to the atom bomb. Love's late 1967 *Forever Changes* (UK 24) combines ecstatic psychedelia with images of blood, death and incarceration to evoke an authoritarian establishment which enforces societal norms with night sticks and rifles. Critical claims that *Forever Changes* conveys the immanent "darkness" of the counterculture thus implicitly endorse state authoritarianism as a societal norm.[57]

All societal norms were shifting from the mid-60s, however. The anti-drug James Brown was nobody's idea of a hippie, but his Summer of Love hit 'Cold Sweat' (US 7) represents as much an epistemological break in soul as 'Tomorrow Never Knows' in pop. Both prioritise rhythm over melody, both create an angularity that, through repetition, morphs into mesmerisation. Both tracks rethink *thought* itself, with Brown's repeated "I don't care about…" renouncing the past, social norms and conventional desires respectively. Motown's straight Fordist technicians were tuning into this structure of feeling too: amidst ricocheting electronics, the Supremes' July 1967 'Reflections' (UK 5; US 2) evokes being "Trapped in a world /That's a distorted reality", while the Fifth Dimension's MOR/soul take on Laura Nyro's 'Stoned Soul Picnic' (US 3), with its visionary neologism, "surry", is an ecstatic evocation of sensuous Marcusian play, with work hallucinatory worlds away.

If such a reimagination of reality had a particular relevance for black Americans, it spoke to the British working class too, whose flat caps, vowels and horizons were cast aside as the 60s took flight. Proletarian rock'n'rollers who embraced flower power didn't simply retreat into navel-gazing solipsism, as Cohn and MacDonald claim,[58] but homed in on the humdrum, with everyday reality "defamiliarised" or "'made strange'", in Viktor Shklovsky's terms.[59] The music-hall psychedelia of the Beatles' February 1967 'Penny Lane' pioneered such kitchen-sink surrealism (UK 2; US 1), its baroque trumpets and piping falsetto backing vocals transforming a suburban Liverpool street and its ordinary denizens into a transcendent utopia in which everyone is included. Sounding sunny even when depicting rain, eerie while hymning the dowdy, 'Penny Lane' locates a liminal space between the Fordist quotidian and the eldritch utopian.

Although the Kinks' wondrous May 1967 'Waterloo Sunset' (UK 2) is a folk-rock throwback, its shimmering melody and swooning backing vocal 'oohs' and 'ahs' transform rush-hour crowds and underground stations into a utopian vision of a psychedelically Swinging London, its friendless outside observer swept up by 60s sociality into melancholic ecstasy. Mere weeks later, the Beatles' *Sgt. Pepper's Lonely Hearts Club Band* (UK 1; US 1) became the pinnacle of this psychedelic realism, making strange such humdrum familiarities as home improvements, traffic wardens, taxis and stations. 'A Day in the Life' is both summary and summit of this psychedelic docu-dream, its refracted piano and iridescent orchestration lending the alarm clock, the daily newspaper and the commuter bus a lysergic luminosity, an everyday enlightenment, as the structures of capitalist time and the divisions between self and other, subject and object, collapse. This is the *real* news Lennon hears today: "Oh boy!".

For all their surreality, these songs were all immersed in Fordist 9-to-5 reality, in what *was*, but as the Summer of Love progressed, a sense of what *could be* emerged. Popular music displayed an increasing "awareness that [people] could both work less and determine their own needs and satisfactions", in Marcuse's terms.[60] So on Traffic's May 1967 'Paper Sun' (UK 5), sitars, flutes and tablas transfigure the dreary black-and-white world of empty electricity meters and scrabbling for phone-booth sixpences into a rainbow-hued wonderland without work or possessions. On the Small Faces' joyous 'Itchycoo Park' that August (UK 1; US 16), the shiftless narrator finds bucolic bliss in a shabby London park. A world away from the countercultural Eden of Golden Gate Park, his mind is "blown" by such Brit banalities as feeding the ducks with a bun, because, in this everyday transcendence, "it's all too beautiful".

Work has been rejected by the "raver" on Small Faces' April 1968 'Lazy Sunday' (UK 2), but lysergic mysticism is grounded here by larkish music hall, with "Here we all are sittin' in a rainbow" followed, gloriously, by "Cor blimey! Hello, Mrs Jones. How's your Bert's lumbago?" Mrs Jones' "Mustn't grumble" exemplifies the post-war stoicism that enraged the likes of Lennon, but the culture gap is negotiated here with the same inclusive warmth as the song's ebullient melody, showing no trace of hipster condescension. Everyone is embraced in the everyday utopianism of this endless, workless 'Lazy Sunday'.

Psychedelia and Femininity

The drafting of American male students from February 1966 was a literal weaponisation of masculinity, an authoritarian reassertion of the name of the father, and was refused actively by draft-dodging, passively by "dropping out" and symbolically by the adoption of feminine sounds and styles by contemporary psychedelia. 'Feminine' here is not, again, an essentialism but, as Marcuse claims, the obverse of aggressive 'masculine' conditioning, with the psychedelic sensibility "receptive... passive... tender... sensuous".[61] For authentocrats, as Kennedy never quite points out, the feminine is always either flippant (as in camp) or fake (only the masculine is real). In fact, fakeness is the *point* of feminisation: when gnarly rockers like the Stones, Pretty Things and the Seeds transformed into fey Aquarians in scarves and kaftans, while playing delicately filigreed music, they deconstructed the performance involved in both gender *and* genre, refusing the restrictions of either.

Dragging-up for the promo clip for September 1966's 'Have You Seen Your Mother, Baby' (UK 5; US 9), the Stones matched visual gender confusion to the track's decentred swirl. On January 1967's 'Ruby Tuesday' (UK 3; US 1), intricately rococo flourishes (recorders, bowed bass) enhance Jagger's uncharacteristically empathetic vocal. The song's unsexualised female subject personifies the counterculture: uncontained by class ("She would never say where she came from") or time ("Yesterday don't matter if it's gone"), Ruby is unalienated, uninhibited, free, insisting on a life beyond the bounded 'real' ("Catch your dreams before they slip away"). Intensely yearning at the time, 'Ruby Tuesday' is almost unbearably nostalgic now, and so removed from popular conception of the band it doesn't even register on Spotify's most-played Stones tracks. The Stones would go even further into feminised psychedelia with December 1967's *Their Satanic Majesties Request* (UK 3; US 2), swooning over the desexualised flower child of 'She's a Rainbow', while the mellotron-gauzed '2000 Light Years from Home' evokes space travel as a return to Eden and the womb. This is all too much for authentocrats – "boring... toothless" (Cohn); a "debacle"

(Reynolds); "a complete fiasco" (Sandbrook) – presumably preferring their Stones conventionally macho.[62]

If Syd Barrett was the ultimate fey, psychedelic dandy, Pink Floyd's June 1967 'See Emily Play' (UK 6) is the consummate female figuration of the counterculture, a psychedelic reverse-zoom utopianism that embraces both the future (its echo-drenched space-rock guitar) and the past (the sped-up baroque piano at 0:54) to "float on a river for ever and ever". Reynolds and Press call the images of childhood, the mythic and the cosmic on Floyd's August 1967 *Piper at the Gates of Dawn* (UK 6) "a yearning to go back to that fantastical no-place from which we've all been banished by the reality-principle": the womb.[63] Indeed, an increasingly dysfunctional Barrett disappeared into his own psychic womb before returning to live with his mother: "You'll lose your mind and play/Free games for May". That girly-boy Barrett could be violent to real-life women – his mother included – suggests the limits both to psychedelic feminisation *and* to a purely psychoanalytical approach to culture.

As against Fordist masculinity's mastery of human and organic nature, the "female principle" represents an antithesis, close to nature not through sexuality but sensuality – see Emily *play*.[64] Lennon had also been violent to women, but his psyche was audibly softening under the influence of LSD, and the Beatles' summer 1966 'I'm Only Sleeping' (*Revolver*) is less about a lazy lie-in than escaping a masculinity mired in the performance principle ("people rushing by at such a speed"). Inspired by the Fordist touring treadmill that still trapped the band, escape here is exemplified by the track's gauzy acoustic guitars, Harrison's back-to-the-womb guitar and Lennon's voice, sped up to remove its 'male' frequencies. The Beatles would soon literally refuse to perform, abandoning touring, and, as Fisher points out, proceed to produce their most imaginative, progressive – and least masculine – work.[65]

This blissful, feminised indolence recurs throughout the era's pop. In the Beach Boys' union of nature, the female principle and the cosmos on October 1966's 'Good Vibrations' (UK 1; US 1), Brian Wilson's vocal is an ecstasy of discorporated sensuality. You can *feel* this feminised bliss in the indolently sunny, blue-eyed soul of the Young Rascals' April 1967 'Groovin'' (UK 8; US

1) and the sleepy rapture of the Cowsills' Summer of Love hit 'The Rain, the Park and Other Things' (US 2) – "Flowers in her hair/Flowers everywhere". The Mamas & the Papas' concurrent 'Twelve Thirty (Young Girls Are Coming to the Canyon)' (US 20) proclaims a societal shift to the female principle,[66] while the Bee Gees' baroquely orchestrated, tremulously voiced September 1967 'Holiday' (US 16) offers a "soft pillow" against the performance principle's hardness ("throwing stones"). The decade's second-biggest film, *The Graduate* (1967), also explored work, masculinity and the female principle, centred on Simon and Garfunkel's ecstatic paean to 'Mrs Robinson' (UK 4; US 1).

It wasn't as if traditional masculinity disappeared from pop overnight, but that it now worked in dialectic with the female principle. The lysergically altered perception of social norms of the Move's March 1967 'I Can Hear the Grass Grow' (UK 5) is delivered with a holdover mod aggression (retrospectively dubbed 'freakbeat'). Yet by August's 'Flowers in the Rain' (UK 2), the orchestral overlay matches the way the narrator's masculinity, corporality and reality dissolve into nature's female principle. While Move-friend Jimi Hendrix's fanboys fainted over his cock-rock machismo, his music also possessed an evanescent feyness – May 1967's yearning 'The Wind Cries Mary' (UK 6); August's harpsichord-gauzed 'Burning of the Midnight Lamp' (UK 18; US 20) – fitting his fondness for frilly ruffs and feather boas. February 1967's 'Purple Haze' (UK 3) distils this dialectic: blues-rock bluster sucked into space; lyrics drifting from a corporeal woman to the cosmic feminine – "'Scuse me while I kiss the sky". That this was widely misheard as "kiss this guy" only augmented the gender confusion.

Hendrix's disciples were less dialled-into this dialectic, however. The Who's brilliant September 1967 'I Can See for Miles' (UK 10; US 9) combines confrontational 'heavy' music with a hectoring, controlling lyric. Cream's thrusting 'Sunshine of Your Love' in November (UK 25; US 5) is priapically preoccupied with the feminine as an external *object*, while even feminised language can't occlude the masculine mundanity of 1968's 'White Room' (UK 28; US 6). Equally unhip to the changing gender dialectic were the Doors, with Jim Morrison's misogyny ('You're Lost Little Girl', *Strange Days*, US 3) connecting to the deeper misanthropy of their late 1967 'People Are Strange' (US 12).

There's no filigreeing the fact that psychedelia's actually existing women were relatively few. America's best-selling single of 1967 was Lulu's 'To Sir with Love' (UK 11; US 1), indicating female singers' restriction to high-Fordist traditions: formally, easy listening and ideologically, affirmation of traditional hierarchies – here a tribute to a teacher, albeit with a 60s inclusivity (the teacher is black). As Rhian E. Jones notes, "While rock allowed women a measure of empowerment and escapism as fans and consumers, it had little space for women to tell their own stories or become their own creations".[67] While visually, Mama Cass and bandmate Michele Phillips *were* their own creations, they were still voicing 'Papa' John Phillips' vision, however inclusive, however feminised. While Nancy Sinatra voiced Lee Hazlewood's vision, December 1967's stunning 'Some Velvet Morning' (US 26) expands the feminine realm of Fordist easy listening *and* the psychedelic female principle. Hazlewood hymns nature goddess Phaedra, who Sinatra voices in the 60s plural – "Look at us, but do not touch" – as the music pivots between Western-theme grittiness and carnival giddiness. Rarely credited as psychedelia, the track is one of its pinnacles.

For all this psychedelic feminisation, the male hippie imagination was more attuned to the ethereal feminine *principle* than actual female *people*. From Sheila Rowbotham and Jenny Diski's memoirs, we know who got to vacuum and wash the dishes after such feminised, muse-worshipping men. Yet as Rowbotham argues, there's a tendency to blame the counterculture rather than patriarchy for such hippie chauvinism.[68] That feminism is leveraged by liberal Marwick and conservative Sandbrook to discredit the counterculture should make us wary of such framings,[69] which occlude the fact that, as Lynn Segal attests, feminism was an *outgrowth* of the counterculture rather than a *reaction* to it.[70] Feminism would produce its musical stars in due course, but in the high 60s the phenomenon of Grace Slick did a good job of filling this conceptual space. Beholden to no one, Slick wrote her own story *and* her own songs (including 'White Rabbit'), while opting to deploy her commanding presence collaboratively, her extraordinary voice melding with bandmates Paul Kantner and Marty Balin, audibly exemplifying a collective individuality that was the essence of 60s solidarity.

Psychedelia and Solidarity

In the era of the Love-in and the Be-in, the line between festival and demonstration dissolved, with hippie gatherings in peaceful communality exemplifying a different way of living, of being. This collectivity was misunderstood at the time – *Life*'s April 1967 issue explored "Modern Society's Growing Challenge: The Struggle to Be an Individual" – and is lost in contemporary culture's assumption of a scorched-earth self-interest. Yet it was the counterculture's collectivity that alarmed the establishment, its solidarity operating outside formal politics and crossing conventional demarcations of 'interest groups'. Civil rights, student rights and the Vietnam War were all linked in America, while in Britain, hippies marched with striking seamen in late 1966. With Wilson condemning all concerned and declaring a state of emergency in response, Muhammad Ali having his titles stripped for refusing the draft in April 1967 and police attacking the Century City Vietnam protest in June and Oakland anti-draft protestors that October, the Fordist state was revealing its authoritarian essence under pressure. "There's battle lines being drawn", sang Buffalo Springfield on January 1967's 'For What It's Worth' (US 7), evoking a peaceful hippie gathering harassed by police: "getting so much resistance from behind".

San Francisco had become the counterculture's fulcrum, with young people pouring in from across America, as captured by John Phillips' song for Scott McKenzie, 'San Francisco (Be Sure to Wear Some Flowers in Your Hair)', in May 1967 (UK 1; US 4): "There's a whole generation/With a new explanation". This sentiment was echoed gauchely by the Animals' 'San Franciscan Nights' (UK 7; US 9), Fordistly by the Flower Pot Men's 'Let's Go to San Francisco' (UK 5) – "Funny people, they have found their land" – and rapturously by the Byrds' early 1968 'Tribal Gathering' (*Notorious Byrd Brothers*, UK 12). Living communally in the city's Haight-Ashbury district, the Grateful Dead epitomised this countercultural collectivity, functioning onstage as a group mind, while their freak-filled entourage dissolved the demarcation between band and fan. The Dead's neighbours, Sly and the Family Stone, extended this solidarity, with their lineup transcending race, gender and traditional family relations, their live appearances a living expression of utopianism. The call-and-response vocals of November 1967's 'Dance to the Music' (UK 7; US 8) rendered gospel's collectivity psychedelic, and 60s pop transcendent. Concurrently, the Impressions' 'We're a Winner' (US 14) was one of the first musical expressions of Black Pride, its collectivity captured by a garrulous studio audience. 1967 was also the year Sidney Poitier became a star, with *In the Heat of the Night* and *Guess Who's Coming to Dinner* exploring racism in this newly receptive climate.

This most spectacular affirmation of this cross-cultural collectivity was the Beatles' worldwide satellite broadcast of 'All You Need is Love' in July 1967 (UK 1; US 1). 'Love' here is universal rather than individual, social rather than sexual, political rather than personal. The introductory brass fanfare from the French national anthem formally equates love with revolutionary solidarity, and the track embraces the older generation with quotes from 'In the Mood' and 'Chanson D'Amour'. Akin to a nursery rhyme in its surreal folk simplicity, 'All You Need is Love' has been much derided subsequently – by the Rutles' vulgar-Marxist 'All You Need is Cash'; by MacDonald's capitalist realism ("drug-sodden laziness… casual incoherence")[71] – and yet, reaching an audience of 400 million amidst the Vietnam War, this was music as mass consciousness-raising, a pinnacle of countercultural positivity.

What Fisher calls "love [as] collective, and orientated towards the outside" can be heard throughout the Love Generation's music.[72] It's in the invocation of the Youngbloods' July 1967 folk-rock 'Get Together' to "Smile on your brother/Everybody get together/Try to love one another right now". It's in Love's name and in their declaration on 'Alone Again Or' to be "in love with almost everyone". It's in Donovan's giddy November 1967 'Wear Your Love Like Heaven' (US 23), and in the Zombies' epiphanic March 1968 'Time of the Season' (US 3), which is a time "for loving". The otherworldly, opalescent sonics of these songs – glowing, shimmering, shifting across stereo and sensory spectrums – encapsulate their sentiments, shucking off the constraints of self and other, summoning another world that felt entirely attainable at the time and whose giddy ingenuousness now *itself* sounds like something from another world.

In the era of "make love not war", universal love now merged with interpersonal *Eros*, this structure of feeling infusing even assembly-line love songs. The prefab Fabs, the Monkees' 'I'm a Believer' (UK 1; US 1) has an ecstatic utopian tone; psychedelic harpsichords give the Supremes' 'Love is Here and Now You're Gone' a hippie resonance (UK 17; US 1); while the transcendent lift and language of Jackie Wilson's soul miracle 'Higher and Higher' commingles convivially with the Summer of Love (UK 11; US 6). The flower child on bubblegummers the Association's 'Windy' (US 1) diffuses this love, "Trippin' down the streets of the city/Smilin' at everybody she sees". Even Louis Armstrong's MOR ballad 'What a Wonderful World' that September (UK 1) explores this countercultural kinship infusing everyday life, with its friends shaking hands "really saying, 'I love you'".

The Fordist state was neither feeling this love nor expressing such solidarity, and was increasingly cracking down on the counterculture, with the police conducting symbolic, example-setting raids on *International Times* and international stars. The Rolling Stones' response to their drug bust was arrestingly counterintuitive: to the sound of clanging cell doors, August 1967's 'We Love You' (UK 8) declares love for their incarcerators. The tune's Dada-esque play with pronouns – "We love they… We want you to love they too" – represents a radical merger of self and other, while in tandem, its echoing, pummelling pianos and buzzing, ricocheting mellotrons attempt to break down Fordist pop's form.[73] 'We Love You' even draws its backing-singers – the lazy Lennon and cautious McCartney – into a countercultural call to arms: "Your uniforms don't fit we/We forget the place we're in" – but, being 1967, it's a *loving* call to arms. As such, Arthur Penn's bloody *Bonnie and Clyde* makes paradoxical sense as a Summer of Love hit, with its rebel outsiders hounded by the Man and ultimately dying for love. Yet the film's violence indicates how an authoritarian society will produce a corresponding hardness in its rebels, an affect increasingly audible in psychedelia from late 1967: the era of handing flowers to policemen was now over.

Evanescent, childlike and magical as the Beatles' 'I Am the Walrus' is (B-side, 'Hello, Goodbye', UK 1; US 1), there's a truculence to its anti-establishment wordplay, a teeth-clenched paranoia in its police-siren melody, a not-so-submerged aggression in its defamiliarisation of reality. Yet the song still begins with the most absolute statement of empathy in popular music: "I am he as you are me/And we are all together", the adversarial and the affirmative always united in the counterculture, which is why this line provides this chapter's title. Black hippies the Chambers Brothers' early 1968 'Time Has Come Today' (US 11) has a musical aggression that cuts through its echoey, druggy haze, insisting the forward motion of the 60s can't be arrested: "Can't put it off another day/I don't care what other people say". Hendrix's concurrent 'If Six Were 9' (*Axis: Bold as Love*, UK 5; US 3) evokes the "white-collar conservative" who hopes "my kind will drop and die", but in defiance insists he's going to wave his "freak flag high, high". Poised between psychedelia and heavy rock, far from being the "individualist anthem" that critics claim, 'If Six Were 9' is an affirmation of collectivist revolt against Fordist conformity.

That both these last-named performers were African American isn't coincidental: the ghetto riots that tore up Detroit, Newark and Buffalo during the Summer of Love weren't historical irony – the demands of both demographics coalesced. These links between counterculture and African American culture are rarely remarked – not least the influence of soul on psychedelia – except by the FBI, who worked hard to prevent them coalescing.[74] Still, the love-in between Otis Redding and the "love crowd" at the 1967 Monterey International Pop Festival was a sublime moment of cross-cultural solidarity, the more striking for Redding disdaining soul's sweetening for pop sensibilities.[75] Exuding even more gospel grit, Aretha Franklin's version of Redding's 'Respect' was also a huge Summer of Love hit (UK 10; US 1), demanding equal treatment for black Americans but – in flipping the song's gender – for women too, and again, 'Respect' is both adversarial *and* inclusive. This inclusivity is formalised by the gospel trick of having the backing-singers hold the hook ("just a little bit"), which frees Franklin to take flight: collectivity as the condition of individuality. Testifying again in solidaristic give-and-take with her backing-singers on 1968's 'Think' (UK 26; US 7), Franklin's fervent, urgent repetition of "freedom" compellingly captures its cultural moment, speaking across lines of colour and class.

This solidarity between self and other was the essence of the 60s, from the civil rights movement to the counterculture's opposition to the Vietnam War, which stepped up following the Viet Cong's early 1968 Tet Offensive. Demonstrators and police clashed in LA in January, in London's Grosvenor Square in March and at Columbia University in June, while LBJ's withdrawal from the forthcoming election was essentially a victory for the anti-Vietnam movement. It was solidarity that prompted Martin Luther King to speak out against Vietnam – incensing his liberal allies as much as his conservative enemies. It was solidarity for which white civil rights activists were murdered in Orangeburg, Carolina, that February, while King himself, visiting Memphis to stand with striking sanitary workers, was assassinated by a white supremacist in April. Waving away security, James Brown calmed a volatile audience in Boston the next day, standing shoulder-to-shoulder with his community at this moment of collective loss. Franklin sang at King's funeral, as she'd sung at his rallies, while riots erupted in the ghettoes of 125 American cities.

Solidarity was the essence of the worldwide rebellions that erupted across 1968. Dismissed by Sandbrook in a few pages,[76] and by Adam Curtis in a sentence,[77] the magnitude of this historical moment is captured by Žižek: "'68 was a rejection of the liberal-capitalist system, a 'NO' to the totality of it".[78] As police attacked protestors in Paris, workers across France came out on strike in solidarity, bringing the economy and government to a standstill and prompting President de Gaulle to flee the country. The protests in Paris, then Prague, Mexico and Madrid, were inspired by the American counterculture – the Fordist technology of television relaying this rejection of Fordist authoritarianism to the masses – in turn inspiring sit-ins in British universities and art colleges. Just as workers and students combined in Paris and Madrid, British students now joined striking female Ford machinists on the Dagenham picket line.

With a new sense of political power, the counterculture flocked to Chicago that August, to protest the war at the Democratic Convention, just as a year earlier it had flocked to San Francisco.

The mood was very different to that of the Summer of Love, however: 'peace and love' was no longer a relevant paradigm when law enforcement made no distinction between demonstration and riot. Yet if the counterculture's mood was militant, Chicago's Mayor Daley's tactics were militarist. The resulting clashes were effectively a civil war between the state and the counterculture: ragged, disorganised and bloody, and broadcast to a shocked nation as protestors chanted, "The whole world is watching", when, clearly, *observing* was no longer sufficient.

The high 60s ended there, in summer 1968, in Chicago. The left-wing candidate lost the nomination, the Democrats lost the election, and the Vietnam War was extended and escalated. Yet to dismiss the countercultural dream because it was defeated is to accept the logic – and the justice – of history's victors. The *radical* history of the high 60s is of the counterculture first talking back to power, then standing back from it in social critique and then finally standing *up* to it. We owe radical shifts in the status and perception of women, people of colour and homosexuals to countercultural conceptions of kinship and collectivity and to the political pressure the alternative society applied to the normative Fordist state.

With the counterculture always thinking far beyond reformism, the revolutionary utopianism of the 60s has been kept alive by its music, whose energy, despite co-option's best efforts, can't be quelled. The 60s' sunny optimism, empathic warmth and imaginative openness – the conviction that change isn't just possible but *inevitable* – still comes surging out of 'Reach Out, I'll be There', 'Penny Lane' and 'Dance to the Music'. The left should cherish the 60s and be inspired by it: not merely as nostalgia for what *was*, but for the counterculture's vision of what *could be*. This utopia is still tangible – almost graspable – in the grain and the giddiness, the timbre and transcendence, the energy and the ecstasy of high-60s popular music.

Chapter 4

"Forces of Chaos and Anarchy": Revolution and Restoration at the End of the 60s (1968–71)

While the counterculture had been countered by autumn 1968, it hadn't been crushed: while the Fordist order had reasserted control, it had been seen to flounder. Despite the conventional 'death of the 60s' narrative, the period from late 1968 to mid-1971 contains a striking number of countercultural highs: the 1968 Olympics' Black Power salutes, the Woodstock Festival, the trial of the Chicago Seven, the feminist disruption of 1970's Miss World and the glory of ghetto soul. Rowbotham recalls that, "caught in that maelstrom of international rebellion, it felt as if we were being carried to the edge of the known world".[1] Yet we hear rather more about this period's countercultural lows, what Reynolds and Press call "the tenor of desolation and fatalism [in] the aftermath of the 60s":[2] the Manson murders; the violence at the 1969 Altamont festival; a Black Panther declaring women's role in the revolution "prone"; the deaths of Hendrix, Morrison and Joplin; and the breakup of the Beatles. Once the standard-bearers of 60s optimism, the Beatles' valedictory statement was a defeatist dirge, a recommendation in such "times of trouble" to simply 'Let it Be' (UK 2; US 1). Todd Gitlin recalls that "the riptide of the Revolution went out with the same force it had surged in… activists cooled, beaten and disappointed in the measure they were once hopeful".[3]

These contradictory impulses reveal this period's polarities after the relative cohesion and stability of the high 60s. 1968 was the apex of Fordism, the peak of post-war income and the apotheosis of Western economic growth.[4] It was also when Fordism began to falter, real wages became a warzone and growth began to shrink. The Fordist consensus was increasingly contested not just in its actions – by the counterculture in the bloodiest period of the Vietnam War; by renewed working-class militancy – but in its *essence*: by capital cutting costs to compete globally; by a resurgent anti-Fordist conservatism. Hall recites the conservative refrains of this restoration as "law and order, the need for social discipline and authority in the face of a conspiracy by the enemies of the state, the onset of social anarchy, the 'enemy within', the dilution of stock by alien black elements".[5] Conservatives were alarmed by Black Panther militarism and countercultural militancy, and particularly by their potential to combine,[6] with Panther Huey Newton declaring, "only by eliminating capitalism and substituting it [with] socialism will... all black people achieve freedom".[7]

Yet the right positioning itself as representative of "property, family, religion, order" is, Marx argues, always a populist ruse to discredit anyone to their left as "the enemies of society".[8] As such, murderous hippie cultist Charles Manson was the right's best nightmare. The ruse worked: Richard Nixon and Edward Heath's election campaigns in 1969 and 1970 effected a conservative restoration by interpellating a 'silent majority' in opposition to what Nixon called the "coastal elites", conflating metropolitan liberal culture and counterculture. Soon Nixon would wage a 'war on drugs', whose symbolic priority-shift from his predecessor's 'war on poverty' pitted respectable straight society against an anarchic alternative society.

Jefferson Airplane's claim that "we are forces of chaos and anarchy" on winter 1968's 'We Can Be Together' (*Volunteers*, US 13) satirises such conservative attitudes: "We are obscene, lawless, hideous, dangerous, dirty, violent". The rump counterculture's increasingly revolutionary outlook was caught by Lindsey Anderson's *If* (1968) and Thunderclap Newman's stunning 1969 'Something in the Air' (UK 1). Lest anyone imagine "the revolution's here" is metaphorical, the song spells out how it'll be achieved: "Hand out the arms and ammo/We're going to blast our way through here". This paralleled the attitude of the Panthers, Yippies and Weather Underground – who, declaring war on the American government, bombed the Capitol Building in 1971 – and Britain's Angry Brigade. Yet given the crackdown exemplified by Chicago, the counterculture's calcification was clearly a response to the increasingly authoritarian countermeasures of the state.

As Marx remarked, "To defend oneself with a stick when attacked with a sword" is, to the establishment, chaos and anarchy.[9] Mainstream media presented popular protest as civil disorder, and the 'new journalism' did the same, with added pretension. Tom Wolfe conflated revolution with counter-revolution in his 'Me Decade' essay,[10] while Joan Didion claimed the counterculture to be "devoid of any logic save that of the dreamwork", and that hippie "disorder was its own point".[11] This has become a consensus on the late 60s: Reynolds invokes "the sixties sagging into decadence";[12] Bracewell laments "the significant role of violence in an epoch too frequently misrepresented by the truism 'Love and Peace'".[13] Yet there's no distinction in these accounts between what was done *by* or done *to* the counterculture. Indeed, Suri uses "violence" *only* to describe the actions of protestors, never those of the state, while also calling Marcuse an "international advertiser for romantic ideas of liberation through sex and violence".[14]

The state may be struck from the historical record, but it struck contemporary skulls and ribcages with tangible force. California Governor Ronald Reagan declared, "If it takes a blood bath, let's get it over with – no more appeasement", and crushed the hippie occupation of Berkeley's People's Park in May 1969 (one dead) and the Isla Vista 'riot' in January 1970 (one dead), while an FBI raid on the Black Panthers' HQ resulted in the "justifiable homicide" of Fred Hampton. Then the death toll stepped up. Nixon sent the National Guard against war protesters at Kent State University in May 1970 (four dead), at Jackson State days later (two dead), while police attacked the fall 1971 Attica prison protest (43 dead). Less bloodily, but equally bloody mindedly, the state also deployed black ops (the FBI's COINTELPRO exposed in 1971) and the judiciary (the British state vs. *Oz* magazine; the

US state vs. war protestors) to counter the counterculture, and used the legislature to tame trade unions, with Wilson's 1969 'In Place of Strife' only withdrawn under pressure. Capturing this authoritarian atmosphere, R. Dean Taylor's 1970 'Indiana Wants Me' (UK 2; US 5) fearfully observes: "Out there the law's a comin'... Red lights are flashin' around me", as bullets fly. Which were the forces of chaos and anarchy?

Tony Judt regards the counterculture as bringing this counter-revolution upon itself: "the narcissism of student movements, New Left ideologues and the popular culture of the 60s generation invited a conservative backlash".[15] Nina Simone's 1968 'Backlash Blues' (*'Nuff Said*, UK 11) captures this reaction as a specifically "white backlash". Segregationist Alabama governor George Wallace and maverick British Conservative Enoch Powell played on fears of the racial 'other' among sections of the working class that hadn't benefited from Fordist mobility, and on the paranoia of the petit bourgeoisie who *had*, shifting the direction of political discourse in the wake of 1968's Civil Rights (US) and Race Relations (UK) Acts. Carl Freedman argues that Nixon's 'law and order' campaign motif "was the dominant code phrase... for hatred and fear of blacks",[16] and with the issue also underlying Heath's 1970 campaign (and 1971 Immigration Act), race served as a repository for a broader *ressentiment* about the 60s' upending of hierarchies and habits of mind.

While popular culture reflected this resentment in reactionary, working-class Alf Garnett (*Till Death Do Us Part*) and his American analogue Archie Bunker (*All in the Family*), this tendency also testified to something progressive: the cultural power of the working class, underwritten by political power. West Virginian miners shut down the state in 1969,[17] a wildcat postal strike caused Nixon to call in the National Guard in 1970, while in 1971 dockworkers on Britain's Clyde staged a counterculture-inspired 'work-in' which forced the government to reverse planned closures. This class power was audible in music: Glen Campbell's jazzy country songs infiltrated AM radio with accounts of ordinary working men, like his 1968 'Wichita Lineman' (UK 7; US 3), who's proud of working for "the county", or the soldier in 1969's subtly anti-war 'Galveston' (UK 14; US 4). Nicky Thomas's 1970 reggae hit, 'Love of the Common People' (UK 7) posits pride against poverty when there's "a dream to cling to". Lennon donated to the dockworkers, while his late 1970 'Working Class Hero' raged, "You're still fucking peasants as far as I can see" (*Plastic Ono Band*, UK 8; US 6). McCartney's first post-Beatles single, 1971's 'Another Day' (UK 2; US 5), was derided by critics – and Lennon – for the one thing that made it notable: the depiction of a female office-worker's life.[18] Everything, for Jethro Tull's "common working man", is 'Up to Me' (*Aqualung*, UK 4: US 7). Even Benny Hill's 1971 novelty 'Ernie (The Fastest Milkman in the West)' (UK 1) depicts ordinary working people as mythic heroes embroiled in an eternal struggle.

For all this era's reactionary cultural currents and the restoration's authoritarian actions, radical right-wing ideas couldn't gain political or popular traction at this point. While Heath experimented with Powellite laissez-faire economics – with letting it be – he abandoned the approach amidst rising unemployment and public resistance and returned to interventionist Fordism. Even Nixon asserted "We're all Keynesians now", and for all his right-wing rhetoric, largely pursued socially liberal policies. Moreover, while we often hear about the level of public support for Powell's racist 'Rivers of Blood' speech, it's less remarked that mixed-race Britons the Equals scored a huge 1968 hit with 'Baby Come Back' (UK 1) the very same year, while their 1970 'Black Skin, Blue Eyed Boys' (UK 9) could confidently declare, "The world will be half-breed".

For all the corporate consolidation occurring in this period, countercultural concepts still held sufficient sway to be co-opted rather than coldcocked, from 1969's psychedelic bubblegum – Tommy Roe's 'Dizzy' (UK 1; US 1); the Archies' 'Sugar Sugar' (UK 1; US 1) – to *Men's Wear* magazine's "cool conservative" look,[19] to Coke's 1971 hilltop hippies' television advert. This was the period of the corporation 'house hippie', and if the cynicism could be transparent – "If you won't listen to your parents, the Man or the Establishment... why should you listen to us?"[20] – the creative space this created for countercultural production benefited both musicians and fans. Despite the Bunkers and Garnetts, television was a progressive redoubt: with American networks ditching game shows, laugh-track comedy and small-town dramas, the trippy, multicultural *Sesame Street* (1969–)

was emblematic of the era, while Britain's *Play for Today* (1970–84) represented popular modernism at its most progressive. The 'New Hollywood' combined countercultural attitudes – *Catch 22* (1970), *Zabriskie Point* (1970) – and psychedelic techniques – *2001: A Space Odyssey* (1968). The film whose huge commercial success sparked this cinematic golden age, *Easy Rider* (1969), captured the period's polarities: enduring hippie utopianism violently opposed by reactionary forces.

Just as the political settlement broke apart after 1968, so did popular music segment and fracture. Cohn calls this period's music "a return to sanity, to responsibility", [21] but this is simply a pop variant on Suri's claim that "citizens... longed to return to something they identified as 'normal' in a world undergoing dizzying change"[22] – an acceptance of conservative concerns as consensus. Such critical bubblegum occludes the contestation that now defined pop and politics. David Crosby's 'Almost Cut My Hair' places his desire to let his "freak flag fly" in direct relation to state surveillance, which "increases my paranoia" (*Déjà Vu*, UK 5; US 1). Mungo Jerry's skiffly 1970 'In the Summertime' (UK 1; US 3) confronts this conflict amicably, assuring conservatives, "We're no threat, people, we're not dirty, we're not mean", voicing the solidaristic countercultural credo, "We love everybody", while adding, defiantly, "but we do as we please".

"Count Me Out/In": The Counterculture, Radicalism and Revolution

The late 60s were the 'street fighting years',[23] the period of Mao Tse Tung and Che Guevara posters on bedsit walls, of the play-power of 'radical chic' and the firepower of Black Panthers. Revolution was in the air and on the airwaves, but its meaning – and merit – were contested throughout the period's popular music. The Beatles' aggressive autumn 1968 'Revolution' (B-side, 'Hey Jude', UK 1; US 1) responds to the new radicalism with liberal alarm – "when you talk about destruction/Don't you know that you can count me out". However, on the gentler version on late 1968's *White Album* (UK 1; US 1), Lennon sings, "count me out... in", with MacDonald making much of recording dates proving that "out" postdates "in".[24] Yet in 1971 Lennon would release 'Power to the People' (UK 7; US 11), dressed in full Maoist regalia, where he revised his previous caution: "Say you want a revolution?/We better get on right away".[25]

The Airplane confronted this political polarity on the grandiose title track to 1968's *Crown of Creation* (US 6): "In loyalty to their kind/They cannot tolerate our minds/In loyalty to our kind/We cannot tolerate their obstruction", their communal singing strident but stunningly harmonised – the adversarial as universal love. By 1969's *Volunteers* (US 13), they were declaring, "Gotta revolution/Got to revolution" on the title track, while 'We Can Be Together' deployed a Panther slogan – "Up against the wall motherfuckers" – as Panther Bobby Seale was concurrently gagged and chained to a chair in the Chicago Eight trial. The lyric is as close to Marxist analysis as popular music gets: "All your private property is/Target for your enemy/And your enemy is we". The Doors' summer 1968 'Five to One' (*Waiting for the Sun*, UK 16; US 1) also articulates this face-off between counterculture and establishment, Morrison drawling with lascivious threat, "They got the guns/Well, but we got the numbers/Gonna win, yeah/We're takin' over". Counting themselves out of this radical turn, Jethro Tull's 1969 prog-pop delight 'Living in the Past' (UK 3; US 11) tuts, "Now there's revolution/But they don't know what they're fighting".

The Rolling Stones managed to capture both this revolutionary conjuncture *and* the counter-revolution. With its Indianate instrumentation, 1968's 'Street Fighting Man' is a last gasp of psychedelic exotica amidst the authentocrat rootsiness of *Beggars Banquet* (UK 3; US 5). The song's assertion that "the time is right for palace revolution" is a counting-in that pulls against the Hobbesian pessimism of the album's 'Sympathy for the Devil', where the darkness of 'human nature' – "'Who killed the Kennedys?'… It was you and me" – is underlined by a frantic samba beat and banshee wails. Despite its lyrical conservatism, musically it's sheer radicalism, a swaggering demonstration of what the once-derided form of rock'n'roll could do. The apocalyptically haunting 'Gimme Shelter' on 1969's *Let It Bleed* (UK 1; US 3) draws energy from these contradictions: while again making no distinction between the violence of the state and its opponents, the focus on the female principle, with backing-vocalist Merry Clayton taking the spotlight from 2:43, lends the song a visionary radicalism. With Clayton's voice *disappearing* with the force of her screaming, "Rape, murder, it's just a shot away" (2:57–3:01), Jagger emits a startled 'Wooh!' (3:02), then his last chorus switches to "Love, sister, it's just a kiss away", the countercultural feminine catalysing an assertion of *Eros* against *Thanatos*.

The conventional account of the Stones' conservatism ignores the radicalism of their late-60s experimentalism, feminisation and queerness. While 1968's 'Jumpin' Jack Flash' (UK 1; US 3) announces the authentocrat trajectory of their subsequent career, its promo clip, with the band in lipstick and eyeliner, queers the musical conservatism. While 1970's *Performance* depicts Jagger's polymorphously perverse rock star breaking down James Fox's gangster's machismo, 1971's 'Brown Sugar' (UK 2; US 1), for all its brilliance, marries musical to masculine authentocracy to become the 'classic' or 'cock-rock' paradigm, with countercultural queerness parcelled off into glam's uncocked rock. That the queer Stones have no more place in gay history than in rock history is to the detriment of both. Amidst all this, New York's 1969 Stonewall Riot launched gay liberation, a countercultural, adversarial, indeed revolutionary movement concerned with deconstructing the social codes of sexuality, gender and the family – with *inauthenticity*.

As Adorno argued, "Authenticity is supposed to calm the consciousness of weakness, but it also resembles it. By it the living subject is robbed of full definition".[26] This offers a way of reading this era's 'classic rock' beyond its surface chauvinism. British heavy rockers Free are a case study in protesting too much: their stripped-down sound; the daft fighting talk of 1970's 'Mr Big' (*Fire and Water*, UK 2; US 17); their absurdly priapic – and absurdly great – 'All Right Now' (UK 2; US 4). Yet Andy Fraser, Free's bassist and co-writer of both tracks, later came out as queer. As the Kinks remodelled themselves as hard rockers for American arenas, they couldn't resist queering their pitch as they entered the big tent, gloriously hymning the trans 'Lola' in 1970 (UK 2; US 9). The song concludes with a gleeful deconstruction of gender – "Girls will be boys and boys will be girls/It's a mixed-up, muddled-up, shook-up world" – that's designed to mess with meat-head minds.

The Who's undersold queerness indexes their political ambivalence. With the blues-rock bluster of 1969's concept album *Tommy* (UK 2; US 4) aimed at American audiences, its depiction of child abuse still subverts the restoration family fetish, while the fact that Townshend voices all the female parts destabilises Daltrey's audibly bare-chested machismo. Townshend counted himself out by hitting speechifying yippie Abbie Hoffman with his guitar at Woodstock, prior to performing *Tommy*'s song of distrust in mass movements, 'We're Not Gonna Take It'. He counted himself in by producing Thunderclap Newman's insurrectionary 'Something in the Air', then out again on summer 1971's superb, cynical *Who's Next* (UK 1; US 4). Decrying "the new revolution", Daltrey howls, "Meet the new boss, same as the old boss", on the churning, chest-beating 'Won't Get Fooled Again' (UK 9; US 15), prior to purchasing a mansion and a trout farm.

With Townshend deep in Eastern mysticism, Wolfe could wishfully declare, "In the long run, historians will regard the entire New Left experience as not so much a political as a religious episode wrapped in semi-military gear and guerrilla talk".[27] This conflates the late-60s' revolutionary spirit with the spiritualism that co-opted its energies: what Gitlin calls the "transcendence industry".[28] With this materialist spiritualism sucking in several Fleetwood Mac members, their extraordinary 1970 'The Green Manalishi' (UK 10) acutely conflates 'Mahirishi' and 'greenback'. Its huge sound, howling guitars and Peter Green's ghostly vocal wails are poised in a liminal space between psychedelia and heavy rock: simultaneously vulnerable and aggressive, it represents a tantalising road not travelled for 70s rock, with Green quitting the Mac soon after.

Wolfe's 'Me Generation' polemic is as much of a mystification of the counterculture's revolutionary impulses as the mysticism he derides. He has no explanation for phenomena like the epic title track of Traffic's 1971 *The Low Spark of High-Heeled Boys* (US 7), which commends violence towards "the man in the suit [who] has just bought a new car/From the profit he's made on your dreams". With the imaginative potency of countercultural concepts meeting the material power of conservative reaction, it became imperative to take a side, "to speak out against the madness", as Crosby put it on spring 1969's 'Long Time Gone' (*Crosby, Stills & Nash*, UK 25; US 6). Doing just that, Crosby, Stills, Nash & Young's rapid-fire response to the Kent State killings, 'Ohio', in spring 1970 (US 14), was the countercultural elite being counted in, asserting the polarised political space between the reactionary state and a radical citizenry: "We're finally on our own".

"Everybody's Saying that Music Is Love": Countercultural Continuity

For all this countercultural calcification and the conservative rhetoric of chaos and anarchy, peace and love had far from disappeared from popular culture. Indeed, the Moody Blues' autumn 1968 *In Search of the Lost Chord* takes up where *Sgt. Pepper* left off, with the Timothy Leary-hymning 'Legend of a Mind' and sitar-saturated 'Om' (UK 5; US 23). Donovan's concurrent 'Atlantis' (US 7) is so hippie-dippie it's been a gift for parody ever since (see: 1990's *Goodfellas*), while Jefferson Airplane's beach-bum hero on 'Lather' that fall is at liberty while his classmates are claimed by the military-industrial complex (*Crown of Creation*).

In winter 1968, hippie musical *Hair* became a Broadway and West End sensation, its songs ruling the charts across 1969: Nina Simone's 'Ain't Got No, I Got Life' (UK 2); psychedelic family group the Cowsills' 'Hair' (US 2); MOR soulsters Fifth Dimension's 'Aquarius/Let the Sunshine In' (UK 11; US 1) – hymning "sympathy and trust abounding" – and Three Dog Night's 'Easy to Be Hard' (US 4), while the Supremes released the psychedelic-sleeved *Let the Sunshine In* (US 24). 'Get Together' was a hit in 1969 for the Youngbloods (US 5) and in 1970 for the Dave Clark Five (UK 8), with its invocation to "smile on your brother... Try to love one another right now" As late as spring 1971, Crosby, Nash and Young could declare not only that 'Music Is Love' – on Crosby's *If I Could Only Remember My Name* (US 12) – but that *everybody* was saying so.[29]

This enduring half-life of psychedelia transcended both the usual hippie suspects and mere co-option, indicating instead the extent to which countercultural concepts had suffused the dominant culture. Where Tommy James and the Shondells had once produced psychedelic bubblegum, their 'Sweet Cherry Wine' (US 7), not only opposed the Vietnam War, but woozily proclaimed, "The beauty of life can only survive/If we love one another". Square pop-combo Three Dog Night also rejected war in a spirit of universal love on 1971's 'Joy to the World' (UK 24; US 1). Even country was imbibing the love vibe. Soul sessioneer Joe South's 1969 'Games People Play' (UK 6; US 12) asserts, "to hell with hate", serenaded by psychedelic sitar; his 1970 'Walk a Mile in My Shoes' (US 12) attests to absolute empathy through ego dissolution, while his song for Lynn Anderson that year, 'Rose Garden' (UK 3; US 3), acknowledges that such countercultural affects will always be countered.

That we were now some distance from the Summer of Love was registered by a recurrent sense of loss in the period's pop. The Move's late-1968 'Blackberry Way' (UK 1) matches mournful sentiments to magical psychedelic sonics; the Bee Gees' 1969 'I Started a Joke' is 'A Day in the Life' as a day in the death (US 6); while Marmalade's early 1970 'Reflections of My Life' (UK 3; US 10) uses reversed guitar to mirror its backwards glance at the high 60s. Critics are rather too relieved to read the countercultural shopping-list on Lennon's 1970 anti-credo, 'God' – "I don't believe in…" – as political 'realism' (*Plastic Ono Band*). Yet, culminating in the proclamation that "the dream is over", it can equally be read as a litany of loss.

You can hear this loss even in easy listening: the nostalgia of Mary Hopkin's late-1968 McCartney-produced 'Those Were the Days' (UK 1; US 2) isn't conservative, for all its parent-pleasing folksiness, recalling that, "We'd live the life we choose/We'd fight and never lose". That loss is tangible even in Middle of the Road's 1971 bubblegum account of abandonment 'Chirpy Chirpy Cheep Cheep' (UK 1), with the child's hippie parents "far, far away". As Traverso argues, to articulate loss is a form of refusal, and the Raiders' early 1971 'Indian Reservation' (US 1) uses psyche-pop sweetness to link international imperialism against the Vietnamese to domestic imperialism against Native Americans. The Moody Blues' concurrent 'The Story in Your Eyes' (US 23) concedes the counterculture's defeats while – surging out of the speakers – expressing both hope and fear for the future.

The most inspiring expression of countercultural continuity is heard in the period's 'psychedelic soul'. Sly and the Family Stone's late-1968 claim to be 'Everyday People' (US 1) enunciates an empathy which lends "We got to live together" a nursery-rhyme communality. The Isley Brothers' Fordist love-song 'Behind a Painted Smile' (UK 5) emits a shimmering psychedelic rapture in the summer of Woodstock. Marvin Gaye and Tammi Terrell coo, "love is the answer", on fall 1969's 'The Onion Song' (UK 9), while even their square Motown colleagues Gladys Knight and the Pips urge everyone to "Learn to live with each other/ No matter what the race, creed or color" on 1969's 'Friendship Train' (US 17). With Motown staff producer Norman Whitfield letting his freak flag fly, the Temptations' 1970 'Psychedelic Shack' (US 7) is a mind-warping affirmation of cross-race togetherness, while the Ross-less Supremes hymn a 'Stoned Love' (UK 3; US 7), promising that "love for each other will bring fighting to an end".[30] The sitar even briefly became a soul instrument in 1970, with the Delfonics' 'Didn't I (Blow Your Mind This Time)' (UK 22; US 10) and Freda Payne's 'Band of Gold' (UK 1; US 3), carrying a waft of incense with it.

Blue-eyed soul became equally hippiefied in this era. The Rascals' fall 1968 'People Got to Be Free' (US 1) asks, "Why can't you and me learn to love one another?", while the underrated Jackie DeShannon's 1969 'Put a Little Love in Your Heart' (US 4) advocates lending "your fellow man... a helping hand". Chicago's horn-driven 1970 'Does Anybody Really Know What Time It Is?' (US 7) empathises with lives structured by the Fordist clock. With Eric Burdon uniting with soul act War – note their album title, *The Black Man's Burdon* (UK 21; US 28) – summer 1970's 'Spill the Wine' (US 3) is a giddy affirmation of togetherness. White South African John Kongos' 1971 tribal stomper 'He's Gonna Step on You Again' (UK 4) conflates sexism, capitalism and imperialism as the oppressive other. San Francisco jam band Santana fused Family Stone and Grateful Dead, their countercultural amalgam of white, black and Latin hitting big with 1970's 'Oye Come Va' (US 13) and *Abraxas* (UK 7; US 1). Even Elvis took a countercultural stance in his Christmas comeback special in 1968, with its finale, 'If I Can Dream', channelling Dr King's iconic speech to imagine "a better land/Where all my brothers walk hand in hand" (UK 11; US 12).[31] Presley's 1969 'In the Ghetto' (UK 2; US 3) goes further, situating race as an economic system that compartmentalises crime in black neighbourhoods, with the song rejecting the ghettoisation of responsibility: "Do we simply turn our heads/And look the other way?"

Presley would soon retreat to the restoration-50s balladry with which the industry was countering the counterculture. This was exemplified by Engelbert Humperdinck's conservatively nostalgic 1969 'The Way It Used to Be' (UK 3), Shirley Bassey's 1970 MOR co-option of the Beatles' 'Something' (UK 4) and Presley's bombastic 1970 ballad 'The Wonder of You' (UK 1; US 9), in whose privatised utopia the social no longer exists. The clock was turned back even further with the reanimation of pre-rock'n'roll crooners, via Dean Martin's variety show and Perry Como's 1970 comeback, 'It's Impossible' (UK 4; US 10), where asking for the world is reduced from the political to the personal. 1969's 'My Way' (UK 5; US 27) was tailor-made for Frank Sinatra by arch-container Paul Anka, the silent generation in collusion with the 'Me Generation', asserting a Hobbesian competitive individualism in order to sneer at 60s solidarity: "For what is a man, what has he got?/If not himself, then he has naught".

With Nixon invoking family as fundamental to 'order', and evangelical Christian groups proliferating as quickly as communes, 'family values' countered the counterculture at its collectivist core by privatising the concept of kinship. Motown's Berry Gordy responded to Gaye and Wonder's psychedelic rebellion with the family-affirming conservatism of the Jackson 5. 'Discovered' by wholesome Diana Ross, the Jacksons' songs were credited to 'the Corporation' in this period of capitalist consolidation, a crack team headed by Berry himself. Yet rather than reasserting Supremes-style sweetness, 1969's 'I Want You Back' (UK 2; US 1), 1970's 'ABC' (UK 8; US 1) and 'The Love You Save' (UK 7; US 1) are suffused with psychedelic sound-effects and Family Stone grooves. Sweetened and lightened, this psychedelicisation of soul-pop is a corporate co-option: love, in

'I'll Be There' (UK 4; US 1), isn't just privatised but sacralised – "We must bring salvation back".

This cult of the family caught on. Mormon siblings the Osmonds were 'Sweet and Innocent' (US 7), an Aryan Jacksons, their 1971 'One Bad Apple' (US 1) a facsimile of 'I Want You Back'. The Partridge Family was a containment of the psychedelic Cowsills, with their own sitcom (1970–74) and even a good song in the rapturous 'I Woke Up in Love this Morning' (US 13). As for sibling duo the Carpenters, for all Karen's vocal warmth, there was a Tupperware-party glazedness to her demeanour; for all Richard's music's charm, there was a controlling sterility to his Woolworths orchestrations (and in his removing Karen from the drumkit). The duo's joyous summer 1970 'We've Only Just Begun' (UK 28; US 2) originated as a bank advert, and its "horizons that are new to us" suggest closing down more than opening up. Still, that Tony Orlando and Dawn's 1970 MOR 'Knock Three Times' (UK 1; US 1) is the first truly dreadful song we've encountered in this restoration, and that Orlando was Latino and his female cohorts black, shows how capital was conducting its counter-revolution in rather subtler ways than was the state.

"Gonna go to the place that's the best": Gospel, Heavy and Progressive Rock

Vying with psychedelic soul as *the* sound of this period was another cross-race creation, gospel pop. Gospel provided the perfect portal to transcend (rather than ground) psychedelia, shedding its evanescence but retaining its utopianism and solidarity: the 'good news' of gospel, like that of the counterculture, is love. As gritty as it was giddy, gospel pop confronted the counter-revolutionary 'real' of this world as much as the spiritual ideal of the next, embodying the period's polarities.

The empathic, anthemic communality of the Beatles' autumn 1968 'Hey Jude' (UK 1; US 1) was echoed weeks later by soul-shouter Joe Cocker's take on their 'With a Little Help from My Friends' (UK 1), a song so redolent of 60s optimism it would be used as the theme for nostalgic 80s sitcom *The Wonder Years.*

Edwin Hawkins Singers' genuine gospel, the joyous 'Oh Happy Day' (UK 2; US 4), chimed with 1969's structure of feeling, as did the Supremes' atypically churchy but typically chirpy 'Someday We'll Be Together' (UK 13; US 1). Even MOR-gospel gloop like the Hollies' 1969 'He Ain't Heavy, He's My Brother' (UK 3; US 7) – with Elton John on piano – John-associates Blue Mink's 1969 'Melting Pot' (UK 3) and Brotherhood of Man's awful 1970 'United We Stand' (UK 10; US 13) expounded solidaristic, utopian sentiments – though the clunky racial language of 'Melting Pot' showed the distance yet to travel.

With evangelism a key component of the counter-revolution, the era's more-literal gospel pop was either ambivalent or plain conservative. Despite Norman Greenbaum's apparent hippiedom, the Christian imagery of his 1970 heavy-rock/gospel 'Spirit in the Sky' (UK 1; US 3) offers nothing evangelicals would oppose, with utopia safely postponed to the next life rather than the countercultural *now*. Judy Collins' luminous 1970 *a capella* rendering of spiritual 'Amazing Grace' (UK 5; US 15) could be read through its history in civil rights activism and CND's utopianism *or* through contemporary evangelism's conservative acceptance of life as it is.

On Simon and Garfunkel's 1970 'Bridge Over Troubled Water' (UK 1; US 1), the addition of Spector-esque orchestral bombast to gospel hymnal provides piety to the song's privatisation of empathy. In a decade suffused with sociality, only Paul Simon could find that "friends just can't be found". *Billboard*'s biggest-selling album of 1971, Andrew Lloyd Weber and Tim Rice's *Jesus Christ Superstar* soundtrack (UK 6; US 1), deployed pop gospel and a dilute acid rock to reject 60s utopianism. Like Judt, Judas believes the demands of the counterculture will prompt a backlash – "They'll crush us if we go too far" – so he sells out the revolution for silver before killing himself. If revolution doesn't work out so well for Jesus, his story is a salient reminder that revolutionaries play a long game.

The New Seekers' 1971 folk-hymn 'I'd Like to Teach the World to Sing' (UK 1; US 7) was derived from the hilltop Coke ad, and tracks capital's co-option of the counterculture, recasting the materialist as spiritual and the corporate as collective, while, in incorporating utopianism, announcing an ambition to possess people's souls, not just their savings. Jameson's claim that capitalism colonised the political unconscious at this point is premature, however.[32] That this counter-revolution was contested is revealed by the twilight trajectory of the Beatles. Just prior to McCartney's resigned 'Let it Be', Lennon – with Harrison in tow – rushed out 1970's 'Instant Karma!' (UK 5; US 3), reaffirming the hippie gospel, "Better recognise your brothers/Everyone you meet", its communal chorus given a soaring, ricocheting resonance by new producer Phil Spector. Where Spector's 60s Wall of Sound tended to *contain* its yearning content, its 70s iteration – given substance to literally bounce off – opened it up. Spector's campfire choirs and massed acoustic guitars bring an inclusive universality to Harrison's 1971 Hindu spiritual 'My Sweet Lord' (UK 1; US 1). Lennon's countercultural hymn 'Imagine' that autumn (US 3) is effectively a response to 'Let It Be' and needs recuperating from those who delight in discovering hippie hypocrisy. The invocation to "Imagine no possessions" only prompted mockery from the materialist 80s onward, and while we would get Lennon the venture capitalist soon enough, 'Imagine' was the last gasp of the countercultural vanguardist before the FBI hounded him out of politics. 'Imagine' is a vision of spiritual – utopian – solidarity realised materially in *this* world, whose citizens will then collectively "live as one".

The transcendent and the earthbound, the radical and the reactionary are contradictory but co-dependent in this period. In what this book names the 'boomer-pop paradigm', MacDonald, Cohn and Frith decry the shift from pop to rock after 1968.[33] Slower, simpler, more aggressive and – with LPs now matching singles sales – more album-orientated, rock also reified the musician as 'artist' rather than pop's 'entertainer'. While this could lead to aural and conceptual bluster to fill the sterile spaces of the new voluminous venues, FM stations and rock press, the boomer paradigm's antinomy between innovative, ingenuous pop and regressive, cynical rock lacks dialectical depth, short-changing pop's artistry in denigrating rock's pretensions. Nurtured by ambitious managers and music executives, with an eye to a longevity that pop had never pondered, rock was a dialectical form which combined the commercial and the creative, the corporate and the maverick, and while it reduced music's adversarial impulse, it didn't eradicate it.

Heavy rock, for example, is a countercultural outgrowth, as Led Zeppelin's feminised image, Tolkien imagery and folky tendencies testify, with the supposedly 'dark' Black Sabbath no less fond of fairies and filigreed acoustic textures. Yet in a dialectic that recurs in heavy rock from Hendrix to Humble Pie, a 60s-imbued countercultural ingenuousness is countered by a cock-rock cynicism that derives from conservative restoration and counter-revolution. In parallel, these acts' independent 'artistry' was countered by the bottom-line ruthlessness of a new breed of bruiser-manager typified by Sabbath's Don Arden and Zeppelin's Peter Grant. So while, on one hand, the priapic swagger of Zep's 1969 'Whole Lotta Love' (US 4) or 'Lemon Song' is contradicted by Robert Plant's feyly feminine falsetto, the tracks' assertion of authenticity via African American music is contradicted by their expropriation from African American *musicians* (Willie Dixon and Howlin' Wolf, respectively). Deep Purple were frequently *shallow* purple – hence the priapic chauvinism of 'Strange Kind of Woman' (UK 8) – but summer 1971's gleaming, mysterious 'Fools' (*Fireball*, UK 1) decries death-drive modernity for a vision of "a better kind", united "on some greener hill".

Progressive rock is anathema both to rock roots-authentocrats and boomer-pop-paradigmers, yet it's the true heir of 60s pop. Expanding on psychedelic experiment, prog tracked its contested time with its ambitious but disjointed song-suites. The stop-start structure of the Moody Blues' 1970 'Question' (UK 2; US 21) is paradigmatic, the acoustic-driven agitation of the verses abruptly switching to the mellotron-suffused yearning of the refrains. While the song could be read as a retreat from social engagement to solipsism, with Justin Hayward's voice as open-throated as his sentiments are open-hearted, the answer to every 'Question' here is "love". Atomic Rooster capture how the restoration proffered 'The Devil's Answer' (UK 4) on the morning after the 60s, co-opting "people [who] are looking but they don't know what to do". Reynolds and Press are too quick to assume the devil's answer was accepted, calling Pink Floyd's 1971 epic 'Echoes' (*Meddle*, UK 3) "an allegory of the counterculture's disintegration and disillusionment".[34] Yet the rapturous rippling of Floyd's music is pure "oceanic feeling", Freud's concept of universal consciousness, exemplified in Roger Waters' image of strangers passing on the street recognising "I am you and what I see is me". The reverse of Althusser's 'interpellation', this is the dissolution of the other into the self, of the defensive ego into collective consciousness. Rather than the 'rock' in 'progressive rock' entailing a conservative disengagement, therefore, its continued countercultural engagement simply comes to us through the filter of post-80s cynicism.

'You've Got a Friend': Singer-Songwriters, Sociality, Feminism

Where progressive rock dramatised the tensions of the times, singer-songwriters internalised them, an uneasy amalgam of the Love Generation and the Me Generation, the countercultural and the corporate. Singer-songwriters combined 60s folk with 70s MOR – often using the same sessioneers. Many of these acts were signed to Warner/Reprise and Asylum and/or managed by David Geffen, representative of a phenomenon Fred Goodman calls "the middle ground between bohemia and business",[35] the combination of artistry and commerciality, message and marketing produced by the shift from pop to rock, a pre-echo of 'non-interventionist' post-Fordism. Although feminised singer-songwriters get an easier critical ride than macho cock rockers, what they did with their share of artistic freedom was equally ambivalent.

With the title of Leonard Cohen's 1969 *Songs from a Room* (UK 2) saying it all, these artists' seemingly intimate bedsit confessions express both a democratised communality *and* an individualist solipsism that Ross names the "privatization of existences".[36] This tension is addressed directly in Cat Stevens' 1970 'Father and Son' (*Tea for the Tillerman*, UK 20; US 8) as an intra-generational argument: "From the moment I could talk/I was ordered to listen" is a lovely encapsulation of hierarchical social relations, yet that both sides are voiced by Stevens (low for the father; high for the son) affirms this conflict as integral to the genre. Wealthy scion James Taylor's counterculturality was as anaemic as his voice and bland backing. The title track of

1970's *Sweet Baby James* (UK 6; US 3) begins by romanticising the outlaw but ends by lullabying the domestic, while 'Fire and Rain' (US 3) turns the loss of a friend into loss of faith in sociality. Taylor's follow-up, 'You've Got a Friend' (UK 4; US 1), was written by Carole King in response to 'Fire and Rain', for 1971's defining singer-songwriter album, *Tapestry* (UK 4; US 1). While often viewed as a countercultural anthem, the song's solidarity is privatised, essentially *anti*-social. "People can be so cold/They'll hurt you and desert you/And take your soul if you let them" is a Hobbesian worldview that's antithetical to hippie humanism.

Co-option of the singer-songwriter genre was barely even necessary, therefore: indeed, aesthetically, the corporate version sometimes improved upon its slippery source. King's Brill Building colleague Neil Diamond's warm tones and melodic talent made his music manna for 60s squares, with 1969's 'Sweet Caroline' (UK 8; US 4) a joyful declaration of privatised existence: "We filled [the world] up with only two". 1970's 'Cracklin' Rosie' (UK 3; US 1) mocks countercultural utopianism, promising to "set the world right" via a tumble in the sheets, while embracing the world as it is: "find us a dream that don't ask no questions". Yet Diamond has to concede that the private realm has its pitfalls, with 1971's splendidly melodramatic 'I Am... I Said' (UK 4; US 4) answering its assertion of ego with a void, "leaving me lonely still".

Countercultural concepts weren't only co-opted from without, however. Coming from *inside* the archetypal hippie collective, CSNY, Steve Stills' 1971 'Love the One You're With' (US 14) is the kind of song that gets the Love Generation confused with the Me Generation, wolfishness in sheepskin clothing. "If you can't be with the one you love, honey/Love the one you're with", Stills and a gospel choir of hippie luminaries urge, presenting sexual opportunism as social idealism, furtive infidelity as universal love. By way of response, Curved Air's Sonja Kristina voices the feminist view that free love is paid for by women on 1971's art-pop 'Back Street Luv' (UK 4) and 'Young Mother' (*Second Album*, UK 11): "I'm not bound to bleed for you". Yet second-wave feminism – launched by 1970's Women's Strike for Equality – did not, as commonly claimed, merely counterbalance the counterculture but, as Rowbotham and Segal insist, expand upon its utopian concepts of solidarity and equality. 70s feminism's foundational text was Gloria Steinem's 'After Black Power, Women's Liberation' (1969), while Germaine Greer's *Female Eunuch* (1970) coincided with her starring role in countercultural fulcrum *Oz*. Both texts repeatedly use the term 'revolution', and any revolution worthy of the name will transform sexual as well as social relations. Marcuse didn't call his utopian ideal '*Eros*' idly.

Feminist activism coincided with far better female representation in music: that this was revolutionary can be seen in the way Yoko Ono became a lightning rod for negative conceptions of the counterculture – and remains one. MacDonald was still referring to Ono's "disturbing influence" in the 90s; Penman reproduced this trope in 2021.[37] It nevertheless quickly became clear that *representation* wasn't intrinsically radical: Tammy Wynette's late 1968 'Stand by Your Man' (US 19) might have modernised the country sound and tapped 60s self-expression, but its self-subjugation was as far from feminism as its sound was from psychedelia. Whether it was Janis Joplin's countercultural liberation or her conservative conditioning that killed her at 27, she functioned quite as effectively as an exemplar for moralists as for feminists. The chorus-line from Joplin's posthumous hit, Kris Kristofferson's 'Me and Bobby McGee' (US 1), "Freedom's just another word for nothing left to lose", captures this ambivalence, its narrative set in a liminal space between the high 60s and the "faded" 70s, and expressing equal parts utopianism and nihilism.

The prevalence of female singer-songwriters was no less ambivalent, partly *because* of their representation of typical female experience. Carly Simon's spring 1971 'That's the Way I've Always Heard It Should Be' (US 10) casts societal expectations as patriarchal control, making its climactic capitulation to marriage all the more of a let-down. While it was cynical of Wolfe to reduce feminism to individualism – "Let's talk about me" – both Carole King's material at this point and Joni Mitchell's best-known album, summer 1971's *Blue* (UK 3; US 15), represent retreats from the 60s' public sphere, with little indication that their personal is political. Carole weaves her tapestry and stays in bed mooning over her man ('It's Too Late', UK 6; US 1); Joni wants to knit her sweetheart a sweater ('All I Want') while clucking ruefully about the "rogue" who robbed her

('California'). The fact that two of the three men in these songs are James Taylor makes the genre as much a matter of celebrity solipsism as sisterly solidarity, turned away from the world in an elite Laurel Canyon enclave.

"We've Got to Get Back to the Garden": The Late 60s' Pastoral Turn

In the aftermath of the confrontation of '68, *everyone* seemed to be going back to the land, not just the cheesecloth denizens of LA's canyons. Musicians were always "getting it together in the country" – Dylan and the Band at Big Pink; McCartney at his Highland farm (note *Ram*'s cover, UK 1; US 2); Fairport Convention at Farley Chamberlayne; Led Zeppelin at Welsh farmhouse Bron Yr Aur. Young people flocked to the new outdoor festivals like Woodstock and Isle of Wight, while *Newsweek* declared 1969 "the Year of the Commune" and the UK's rural population increased for the first time in a century.[38] In tandem, musicians turned from psychedelia's astral flights to grounded, rustic forms like folk and country. Rather than this being merely escapism from political realities, as in Jameson's dismissal of a "fantasmic relationship with some organic precapitalist peasant landscape and village society",[39] this rural turn was more radical than it was reactionary, a progression into the future rather than a retreat into the past.

On 1968's bare-bones folk-rock *John Wesley Harding* (UK 1; US 2), Dylan warns of the lure of pastoral solipsism: "Don't go mistaking Paradise/For that home across the road" ('Ballad of Frankie Lee and Judas Priest'), before doing exactly that on 1969's *Nashville Skyline*'s smugly domesticated country (UK 1; US 3). The era's empty signifier, Eric Clapton, was constantly clutching at rural authenticity – with Cream, Delaney and Bonnie, and Derek and the Dominos, or solo – his lyrics forever returning 'home' (the etymological meaning of 'nostalgia'), his music blues without hurt, country that's earthbound rather than grounded. Sepia-tinted Californians Creedence Clearwater Revival proffered the pastoral as escape from political realities: 1969's 'Green River' (UK 19; US 2) opining, "You're gonna find the world is smolderin'/And if you get lost, come on home".

127

1970's 'Up Around the Bend' (UK 3; US 4) advises leaving the "sinking ship" to head to where "the neons turn to wood". This is what Svetlana Boym calls "restorative nostalgia" – a conservative longing for a perceived prior order (in both senses):[40] Elton John's 1970 'Country Comfort' hymns the rural as, effectively, "property, family, religion, order" (*Tumbleweed Connection*, UK 2; US 5). John Denver's summer 1971 MOR-country 'Take Me Home (Country Roads)' (US 2), meanwhile, merely adds hippie harmonies to conservative traditionalism: "Life is old there".

The Band's 1969 'The Night They Drove Old Dixie Down' (US 25) could be regarded as a reactionary "restorative nostalgia", mourning the Civil War defeat of the slaveholding South. Yet 'Dixie' also laments the loss of an agrarian society to a capitalist economy, whose imposition was the war's true purpose. This agrarian society had in turn wiped out that of Native Americans. So while the Western outlaw/hippie analogy of the Grateful Dead's 1970 *Workingman's Dead* (US 27) and *American Beauty* (UK 27; US 30) produced a great statement of solidarity with the working man in 'Cumberland Blues', their mystification of the frontier overlooked the imperialism folded into the pre-capitalist process of "primitive accumulation" – of land, of property, of capital.[41] Pulling against this, the Dead, like many hippies, adopted Native American clothing in solidarity with the dispossessed, as did Neil Young, who also stood with antebellum black Americans on 'Southern Man' (*After the Gold Rush*, UK 7; US 8), who'd never had possessions to dispossess.

For all its contradictions, the pastoral turn was essentially progressive. Communes were a material expression of counterculture, de-privatising social life while destabilising the liberal totems of property and family. Living together at rural Big Pink, the Band interweave the communality of their four vocalists with the collectivity of agricultural workers and the rhythm of the seasons on 'King Harvest' (*The Band*, UK 25; US 9). Moreover, returns to the pre-capitalist era didn't routinely fetishise feudalism in as per Jameson's formulation. In acid-folk murder ballads like Fairport Convention's 1969 'Matty Groves' (*Liege & Lief*, UK 17) and Pentangle's 1970 'Jack Orion' (*Cruel Sister*), the brutality of such a hierarchical system is starkly relayed. Yet because, as Marcuse argues, feudal social relations were "not yet organized as things and instrumentalities"[42] – neither commoditised nor yet competitive – they possessed relative agency. Traffic's use of an old folk tune as the title track of 1970's *John Barleycorn Must Die* (UK 11; US 5) beautifully captures this organic way of life, grain's death and resurrection as alcohol not just a metaphor for nature's decay and renewal but for the cycle of human despoliation and natural regeneration. This, then, is Boym's "reflective nostalgia" – the past invoked to inspire the present.[43]

Despite hippie cults like the Children of God offering a distorted reflection of restoration religiosity, there was also a radical spiritualism to the pastoral turn, an attempt to recapture the non-alienated state Marx called "the complete emancipation of all the senses", and which he materially located in "the supersession of private property".[44] Driven by Indian tamboura and acid guitar, Donovan's summer 1968 'Hurdy Gurdy Man' (UK 4; US 5) evokes the eternal musician as the conduit of nature's balm, "singing songs of love". Emanating from Donovan's influence and the same Indian trip, the woozy psyche-folk of McCartney's 1968 'Mother Nature's Son' brings another organic Orpheus to life, with Lennon's 'Dear Prudence' his female counterpart: "The wind will sing that you are part of everything" (*White Album*). This folky feminisation disassociates folk from authentocracy – male, earthbound, dirt-encrusted – being ethereal, transcendent, sensuous. Al Wilson's falsetto on Canned Heat's 1969 folk-blues 'Going up the Country' (UK 19; US 11) formalises its lyric's rejection of militarised masculinity – the rural as literal refuge from war via the draft – and was apposite for the credits of 1970's *Woodstock* film's documentation of this rural turn. "We've got to get back to the garden".

Songs of this era regularly hymn abandoning the city for an unalienated rural existence. Harry Nilsson's late-1969 *Midnight Cowboy* theme, 'Everybody's Talkin'' (UK 23; US 6), flees the "northeast wind" to go "where the weather suits my clothes". Across 1970, on Creedence's 'Proud Mary' (UK 8; US 2), the river is democratic where the city is class-stratified; on John's 'Border Song' (*Elton John*, UK 5; US 4) the pastoral is peaceful where the urban is "poison"; while the nomadic Romani life on Van Morrison's 'Caravan' is unalienated, uninhibited, free

(*Moondance*, US 29). At its most transcendent, this pastoralism evokes a shucking-off not just of alienation but of the corporeal itself. Fleetwood Mac's extraordinary late-1968 instrumental 'Albatross' (UK 1) evokes unity with the elements, the sky as freedom, the track's "oceanic feeling" articulated by its hauntologically harmonised guitars. Bodies dissolve into water on Morrison's folk-soul 1970 'And It Stoned Me' (*Moondance*) and Traffic's 1971 'Hidden Treasure' (*Low Spark*); into water, earth and air on the Beach Boys' ecstatic hymnal 'Til I Die' the same year (*Surf's Up*, UK 15; US 29). On the Groundhogs' 1970 psychedelic hard-rock 'Garden' (*Thank Christ for the Bomb*, UK 9), the narrator lets nature run wild in his city plot before himself living wild, getting "my clothes from heaps, my food from bins, my water from ponds".

This is the utopian, warm stream of late-60s pastoral, but there's also a dystopian, cold stream that reflects the period's growing awareness of ecological crisis. With the BBC's *Doomwatch* (1970–72) condemning Fordism's festishisation of growth – the economy's performance principle – even the conservative *Ecologist* magazine critiqued capitalism's effect on the planet, while Friends of the Earth was formed in 1971.[45] The elemental darkness of Dylan's 'All Along the Watchtower' – a hit in Hendrix's extraordinary late-1968 reading (UK 5; US 20) – and Creedence's 1969 'Bad Moon Rising' (UK 1; US 2), with its Biblical "hurricanes" and "rivers overflowin'", are rarely understood as ecological portents, but should be. Jefferson Airplane's 1969 'Eskimo Blue Day' (*Volunteers*) can't be read any other way than as premonition of global warming. On Led Zeppelin's folky 1970 'That's the Way' (*III*, UK 1; US 1), both the banishment of the narrator's flower-kissing friend and the "fish in dirty water dying" are decreed by parents/society "the way it's got to be". With *Lord of the Rings* all the rage, Zeppelin's 1971 'The Battle of Evermore' (*IV*, UK 1; US 2), with Fairport's Sandy Denny, taps Tolkien's equation of the destruction of nature with that of humanity, again all-too presciently.

As Marcuse argued, such symbiosis also links the *emancipation* of humanity with that of nature:[46] Fordism's technological future, once a promise, was increasingly viewed as a threat. Snapping out of her solipsism, Joni Mitchell's 1970 'Big Yellow Taxi' (UK 11;

Ladies of the Canyon, UK 8; US 27) condemns capitalist 'progress', which paves paradise and produces the insect repellent DDT ("Give me spots on my apples/But leave me the birds and the bees"). The key point about the same album's 'Woodstock' is not that Mitchell *wasn't there* but that she uses the festival to symbolise the urge to "get back to the garden", to reverse capitalism's repression of humanity – "a cog in something turning" – and of nature. With 'Woodstock' becoming a hit for both CSNY (US 11) and Fairport offshoot Matthews' Southern Comfort (UK 1), its climactic "bombers riding shotgun in the sky… turning into butterflies" is a vision of nature's life force defeating capitalism's death drive.

One of Marcuse's key political contributions was to synthesise the polarities of past/future and technology/ecology. Hence, agrarian society "haunt[s] the consciousness with the possibility of [its] rebirth in the consummation of technical progress":[47] a rural utopia that's futuristic not atavistic, technology creating leisure and equality rather than labour and disparity.[48] This ecological modernism is manifested in music through 'irrealism' – the iconography of fantasy, myth and sci-fi preferred to the conventions of an essentially capitalist 'realism'.[49] Hendrix's fall 1968 '1983… (A Merman I Should Turn to Be)' envisages a spaceship escaping from nuclear destruction to Atlantis (*Electric Ladyland*, UK 6; US 1). Both Crosby, Stills & Nash and the Airplane's 1969 versions of 'Wooden Ships' depict reversion to agrarian life as the literal fallout of nuclear modernity (*CS&N*, UK 25; US 6; *Volunteers*). Young's beautiful 1970 ballad 'After the Gold Rush' time-travels from a medieval past to a nature-curating future, with "silver spaceships… flying Mother Nature's silver seed to a new home in the sun". Similarly, Black Sabbath's summer 1971 'Into the Void' envisages "escape from brainwashed minds and pollution" to a distant planet "where love is there to stay" (*Master of Reality*, UK 5; US 8).

It was in progressive rock that this pastoral futurism was realised in form as effectively as content. On Pink Floyd's autumn 1968 *Saucerful of Secrets* (UK 9), Barrett's cosmic slide guitar renders the pastoral nostalgia of 'Remember a Day' spacey, while seagull cries make the sci-fi of 'Set the Controls for the Heart of the Sun' bucolic. On 1969's 'Cirrus Minor' (*More*, UK 9), rural idyll expands into cosmic vision, while despite the cow on the cover of 1970's *Atom Heart Mother* (UK 1), the epic title track is more futuristic than folky, reaching beyond conventional song-structure – at worst beyond melody, at best beyond conventional structures of feeling. Meanwhile, Yes's soaring, transcendent 1971 'Starship Trooper', simultaneously looks back to a fantasy rural Arcadia and forward to a sci-fi utopia (*The Yes Album*, UK 4).

The mellotron's ubiquity in this period is key to this retro-futurism: its sound simultaneously space age and steam age. Yes's Rick Wakeman uses the instrument to simulate a spaceship launching on David Bowie's 1969 'Space Oddity' (UK 5), while its tapes of choirs, flutes and strings evoke the classical European past on King Crimson's *In the Court of the Crimson King* (UK 5; US 28). Due to its wheezy volatility, the mellotron's past audibly decays, while is future is shakily prefab, hauntological at inception. Making the mellotron the axis of their sound, the Moody Blues' autumn 1968 'Ride My See-Saw' (*Lost Chord*) bids farewell to the world of exploitative work and "second-class" social relations to embark on a communal journey into space to "find another place that's free". Pastoral acoustics combine with spacey mellotron on the title track of Crimson's 1970 *In the Wake of Poseidon* (UK 4; US 30), in which "Mother Earth waits balanced on the scales": it lies with humans to adjust the balance. Poignancy permeates this pastoral turn from our twenty-first-century perspective, revealing a field of missed opportunities, a vista of unexplored possibilities, a countercultural reverence for nature that, far from fomenting chaos and anarchy, sought to nurture nature and to safeguard the future.

"Whoopee, We're All Gonna Die!": Vietnam, Imperialism and the Cold War

Fordist technological modernity was revealed at its most repressive and destructive of both nature and humanity in the relentless war in Vietnam. The war exposed liberalism's illiberal impulses, with America – and Britain in tacit support – preferring the deaths of thousands and the risk of nuclear Armageddon to the very existence of communism. Opposition to the Vietnam

War was neither a purely contextual nor a merely fashionable cause, as millennial hippyphobia suggests, but a systemic linking of imperialism and capitalism to domestic racism and ecological cataclysm.

The nuclear mushroom cloud on the cover of Jefferson Airplane's 1968 *Crown of Creation* makes precisely these connections, with the churning drama of 'House at Pooneil Corners' depicting the post-atomic dystopia this anti-communist crusade could create. With the Airplane climaxing their Woodstock set with the song, the festival was effectively the biggest anti-Vietnam demonstration yet – and boasting the best lineup. Forgotten black folkie Richie Havens captivated the crowd with 'Handsome Johnny', a personification of the proletarian universal soldier in wars against the Vietnamese, America's black citizens and, through nuclear weapons, the world itself. With Country Joe McDonald's 1969 'I Feel Like I'm Fixin' to Die Rag' also linking the Vietnam War to nuclear war, Jimi Hendrix closed the festival by both musically and literally setting the 'Star-Spangled Banner' aflame in protest. That same summer, Zager and Evans' 'In the Year 2525 (Exordium and Terminus)' topped American and British charts, its sci-fi depiction of humanity's 'progress' towards extinction not needing to mention Vietnam as a staging post. That November, Lennon and Ono's 'Give Peace a Chance' (UK 2; US 14) was sung by protestors at a "half a million strong" Washington demonstration that topped even Woodstock's massed protest.

Opposition to Vietnam wasn't just hippies hippying, with even the Beach Boys performing at protests and Motown producing anti-Vietnam songs. On 1970's 'War' (UK 3; US 1), as Edwin Starr demands, "War, what is it good for?", the backing-singers respond, "Absolutely nothing". On summer 1971's 'What's Going On?' (US 6), Marvin Gaye insists, "War is not the answer... only love can conquer hate", while Freda Payne demands, 'Bring the Boys Home' from "the senseless war" (US 12). Creedence are a metonym for (mis)perceptions of the late 60s. Taken for good 'ol boys, but really Californian, and for anti-hippies despite playing Woodstock, John Fogerty's macho bark suggests a chauvinist simplicity that his songs' egalitarian complexity don't support. 1969's 'Fortunate Son' (US 3) views Vietnam via class relations –

who gets to draft-dodge, who gets to die – the more effective for Fogerty having *been* drafted.[50] 1970's 'Run Through the Jungle' (UK 3; US 4) adroitly reverses partisan media presentation of Vietnam by depicting *America* as a jungle full of gun-toting savages.

Further disproving the boomer pop-paradigm equation of rock with reaction, Groundhogs' 1970 *Thank Christ for the Bomb* (UK 9) links Vietnam to nuclear war and class relations. Similarly, despite Black Sabbath's aggressive, doomy sound, their content was both peace-loving and utopian. 1970's 'War Pigs' (*Paranoid*, UK 1; US 12) depicts generals and politicians as "witches at black masses", using irrealism to confront the reality of class relations: "Why should they go out to fight?/They leave that role to the poor". Despite its gothic title, summer 1971's 'Children of the Grave' is a celebration of the counterculture, opposing both Vietnam and nuclear threat with the power of love (*Master of Reality*, UK 5; US 8). Even the more bozo Deep Purple produced, in their career-best 1970 'Child in Time', an anti-Vietnam epic that's countercultural from the Eastern otherness of its organ motif to the mythic register of its lyrics. Here, Ian Gillan's gruntingly macho vocals morph into something not only feminised but incorporeal, unearthly, uncanny (*In Rock*, UK 4).

Irrealism is the essence of progressive rock, pursued not for faerie flights of fancy as critical cliché has it, but to laterally address contemporary reality. The wild jazz-metal of King Crimson's '21st Century Schizoid Man' directly addresses Vietnam – "innocents raped with napalm fire" – while locating war's technological death drive in capitalism: "Death seed/ Blind man's greed".[51] Keith Emerson and the Nice's satirical assault on *West Side Story*'s 'America' (UK 21) was accompanied in live performance by the burning of another American flag. With Emerson joining Crimson's Greg Lake in Emerson, Lake & Palmer, 1970's 'Lucky Man' uses medieval imagery to mock militarism's ideological libidinisation (*ELP*, UK 4; US 18). On early 1971's *Tarkus* (UK 1; US 9), Lake's anti-war song (12:48–16:54) is given utopian uplift by his psychedelically reversed guitar, while Emerson's keyboards evoke war's ugliness and disharmony rather too literally. The ornate, irreal imagery of Yes's early 1971 'Yours Is No Disgrace' ("shining, flying purple wolfhounds") alternates with blunt evocations of the massacre of civilians by American soldiers at My Lai: "Mutilated armies scatter the earth/Crawling out of dirty holes... their morals disappear" (*The Yes Album*). Once again, the chaos and anarchy evoked here is that of the forces of order and democracy: the counterculture professes only peace and unity.

'Inner City Blues': Conscious Soul

Aside from the Vietnam War, the conditions in America's ghettoes were the biggest contradiction to the conservative restoration's claims to be the "party of order", undermining Cold-War proclamations of the liberal West as the location of 'freedom'. While the shift from civil rights' assimilationism to Black Power's autonomism was precipitated by King's assassination, the historical contiguity of high Fordism and the civil rights movement wasn't accidental. Following the state's crackdown on the counterculture and the Panthers, the 1968 Civil Rights Act's revelation of the limitations of legislative freedom, and the conservative restoration's curtailment of affirmative action, black radicals – paralleling rural radicals – effectively 'dropped out' of the Fordist system. Hence, the Panthers' free-breakfast programme, and the fact it so exercised J. Edgar Hoover. The growth of community-serving black capitalism – both legal and illegal – signalled this new autonomy, while the new 'Blaxploitation' films were as much an expression of cultural pride as of political protest.

James Brown's fall 1968 'Say It Loud, I'm Black and I'm Proud' (US 10) captures this structure of feeling, as he snaps, "We'd rather die on our feet/Than be livin' on our knees". Having stripped the sweetness from soul, Brown now stripped away its sentimentality, his lyrics acerbic but mantric, circling around the beat like Bootsy Collins' rubbery basslines. While Gilbert identifies funk's vitality as "immanent",[52] this doesn't, as he contends, lessen its transcendence: Brown's ability to both project *and* provoke ecstasy was his defining feature, his yelps and imprecations being as sampled subsequently as his drummers' breakbeats. While Brown's politics were essentially conservative – both 'Say it Loud' and 1969's 'I Don't Want Nobody to Give

Me Nothin' (Open Up the Door, I'll Get It Myself')' (US 20) posit black capitalism as the path to liberation – that he played 'Say it Loud' at Nixon's inauguration ball captures Brown's contradictions, while his restlessly innovative music assures his role in black radicalism.

In Brown's slipstream, the Isley Brothers also stripped back their sound on 1969's 'It's Your Thing' (UK 30; US 2), with its insistence that "I'm not trying to run your life/I know you wanna do what's right" capturing Black Power's self-determination ethos. While the 'self' here is clearly collective, self-determination always risks personalising the political, as two Brown-inspired songs prove. Sly Stone's 1969 'You Can Make It If You Try' (*Stand*, US 13) and the Staple Singers' 1971 'Respect Yourself' (US 12) both suggest it's individual failings that hold black communities back – a moralisation of poverty with which white conservatives readily concurred. However, in the Supremes' appearance on the *Ed Sullivan Show* to perform 'Love Child' in fall 1968 (UK 15; US 1), the song's ostensible moralism – the perils of premarital sex – is occluded by the iconography (the girls' modest Afros; the ghetto stage-set) and by the language of the lyric. 'Illegitimacy' here encompasses not just paternity but poverty, race and – 'love child' being interchangeable with 'flower child' – the counterculture, with the song's vaulting, swooning melody declaring every one of them legitimate.

Lynskey reduces soul's conscious turn to fashion and finance,[53] yet it's not as if *love songs* were ever above the commercial fray, and Lynskey's argument elides how such cynicism could produce such stunning music. Whitfield's injection of funk and social commentary into soul re-energised the genre both commercially *and* creatively. On the Temptations' 'Cloud Nine' (UK 15; US 6), Whitfield deploys communal Family Stone vocalising and funky wah-wah guitar to capture a Hobbesian "dog-eat-dog world" where "only the strongest survive", driving ghetto denizens into drug use. Quickly co-opted, the wah-wah sound would become TV- and film-soundtracks' shorthand first for 'black', and ultimately for 'crime'. With 1969's *Puzzle People* (UK 20; US 5) boasting a faded-brownstone cover, 'Message from a Black Man' replaces the atomised retreat of 'Cloud 9' with a collective advance: "No matter how hard you try", the Temps promise, "you can't stop me now". 1970's 'Ball of Confusion' (UK 7; US 3) depicts white flight to the suburbs, and bitterly summarises the civil rights movement as "segregation, determination, demonstration, integration/Aggravation, humiliation".

Curtis Mayfield's Impressions had pioneered conscious soul, but in largely cautious terms in line with civil rights' assimilationism. In the era of Black Power, Mayfield became blunter: fall 1968's grandiose 'This Is My Country' (US 25) asserts, "I've paid three hundred years or more/Of slave-driving, sweat and welts on my back". The new toughness was still countercultural, however, with both 1969's anthemic 'Choice of Colors' (US 21) and its B-side, 'Mighty Mighty Spade and Whitey', pushing for multi-racial unity. Mayfield's first solo album, 1970's magnificent *Curtis* (UK 30; US 19), further hardened his sound and sentiment, its lavish combination of orchestration, electronics and gospel so transcendent it felt like it could *itself* effect political change. The widely misheard line on the marvellous 'Move On Up' (UK 12), "Take nothing less than the second best", is actually the utopian "supreme best". 'The Other Side of Town' is a condemnation of the ghettoes' economic segregation, while '(Don't Worry) If There's Hell Below, We're All Going to Go' (US 29) conveys the polarities of the era's "political actors" – black, white, state, hippie – essayed with sincerity not cynicism, hope not hate, matched to the music's psychedelic darkness, with wah-wah funk its street-level base, the sweeping orchestration its utopian superstructure.

The trajectory of Sly and the Family Stone also tracks this toughening of psychedelic soul. Released just before they wowed Woodstock, 1969's 'Don't Call Me N****r, Whitey' (*Stand*) insists the multicultural love-in can't hold on to existing hierarchies. 1970's harder, funkier 'Thank You (Falettinme Be Mice Elf Agin)' (US 1) evokes police violence, alienated labour and racial stereotyping. Although its double A-side, 'Everybody is a Star' (US 1), is another of the Family's mic-passing communal celebrations, it's a skewering of the self-determination of 'You Can Make It': you can *think* you're a star all you like, but "the system" still "tries to bring you down". Consequently, 1971's murky, jerky *There's a Riot Goin' On* (US 1) expresses the period's political disintegration as much as the purely personal disintegration of Stone, to which critics give priority. While Lynskey does read *Riot* as political, it's as part of the 'death of the 60s' narrative – "grim songs for grim times",[54] and yet there's nothing "grim" about the emotional abandon of 'Family Affair' (UK 15; US 1), in which melancholy and ecstasy combine.

Off the back of 'The First Time Ever I Saw Your Face' (UK 14; US 1), Roberta Flack packed summer 1969's *First Take* (US 1) with political songs like 'Tryin' Times' ("riots in the ghetto… folks demonstrating about equality"). Even Aretha Franklin spoke out for imprisoned Panther activist Angela Davis and performed at an Attica benefit. Mayfield-protégées the Five Stairsteps' stunning summer 1970 'O-o-h Child' (US 8) expresses giddy optimism amidst ghetto realities, the song building and building until, by the end, its utopia seems entirely graspable, making it a fitting finale to Spike Lee's tribute to this era's transcendence and tragedy, *Crooklyn* (1994). Stevie Wonder's 'Heaven Help Us All' that fall (UK 29; US 9) turns downbeat observation – "Heaven help the black man if he struggles one more day/Heaven help the white man if he turns his back away" – into upbeat gospel. Bill Withers' 'Harlem' (B-side, 'Ain't No Sunshine', US 3) is a propulsive song of Black Pride, while concurrently, the Chi-Lites' '(For God's Sake) Give More Power to the People' excoriates the racialised gap between rich and poor (US 26).

Defying the Fordist authoritarianism of both Motown and the military, Marvin Gaye's summer 1971 *What's Going On* (US 6) coalesces this period's currents, linking its issues as seamlessly as its segued song-suite. A conscious-soul concept album, *What's Going On* is suffused with the utopian gospel that defines this era, while its orchestration offers continuity psychedelia, recalling the dreaminess of the Beach Boys' *Pet Sounds*, with the masculine frequencies of Gaye's voice feminised and the guitars' aggressive tones softened. This airiness is anchored by a taut, street-level funk, the album's conceptual flights grounded in the ghetto, in human community. *What's Going On* starts with a hubbub of convivial voices as the title track (US 6) laments the death toll in Vietnam, decries police "brutality" against civil rights activists and war protestors and positions itself as countercultural – "Who are they to judge us/Just because our hair is long?" – its politics centred on love (the backing vocals repeat "brother", "sister" like a gospel mantra). For Gilroy, the "political kinship between the African American nation and the world's colonised peoples" came from comprehending black America as an "internal colonisation" driven by the commodification of people. 'What's Happening Brother' thus tracks black veterans from America's war against Vietnamese peasants coming home to its war against the poor. Tapping into the period's pastoral turn, 'Mercy Mercy Me (The Ecology)' (US 4) conflates the capitalist pollution of water-systems with the military deforestation of Vietnam's jungles. Making a virtue of all those lists of post-60s ills, the album's closing track, 'Inner City Blues' (US 9), links ghetto immiseration to military imperialism. The album ends with a reprised reaffirmation of the title track's countercultural credo – "Who are they to judge us / Simply 'cause we wear our hair long?" – asserting a collectivity and empathy that completely transcend concepts of self and other.

Gilroy declares of this period's conscious soul that "the ideas of peace, love and harmony with nature that characterised their perilous time are still reminders of where important resources of hope might be located".[55] This claim can be extended to *all* the music of this era. For while there were retreats in the face of establishment reaction and defeats amidst conservative restoration, a heady cohort of the counterculture met that reaction and restoration head-on, whether through revolutionary rhetoric, anti-imperialist protest, ecological prog and folk, gospel utopianism or the politicised ecstasies of ghetto soul. If these responses represented "forces of chaos and anarchy", then force never felt so full of love, chaos was never so consummately crafted, and anarchy never so articulately utopian. As such, this period was simply the end of the 60s, not the *death* of the 60s.

Chapter 5

"The Children of the Revolution": The Glam and the Grim in 70s Pop and Politics (1971–74)

The early 70s were glam – not as a genre so much as a style, a cultural mode, a structure of feeling. Beam back to 1972 and every pop, rock, soul and even MOR star is in satin jacket, bell-bottoms and platform heels: so are shopping and football crowds. This period was a popular-modernist golden age of sartorial and musical ebullience, of flash, flare and flamboyance, captured by the urgent, *wicka-wicka* pulse of wah-wah guitar, the heat-haze shimmer of electric piano and the adversarial crunch of power chords. With 16- and 24-track technology producing both remarkable fullness and rich granularity, music never sounded so warm, or so full of well-being. Johnny Nash's joyous, lilting 1972 'I Can See Clearly Now' (UK 5; US 1) captures the conjuncture's character, acknowledging the obstacles since the high 60s, while still optimistically opining, "It's going to be a bright, bright, sunshiny day".

The standard depiction of the early 70s is as grim, not glam, however; a "grey landscape"; a period of decline – "shabby, backward-looking, falling to bits" – distinguished only by stasis: "directionless... going-in-circles".[1] This slough is variously – and vaguely – attributed to strikes, the collapse of the Bretton

Woods currency controls, the OPEC oil shock, the 1973–74 stock market crash and the unending Vietnam War. Paul Simon's 1972 'American Tune' (*Paul Simon*, UK 1; US 4) is paradigmatic of this perspective, perceiving an undifferentiated '70s malaise' which elicits a sighing, "We lived so well so long/I wonder what has gone wrong". For conservatives and centrists, the "'nightmare seventies" is a decade with which to frighten children, a conjuncture that cannot recur; the reason Thatcher and Reagan had to happen.[2] Alwyn Turner depicts the era in almost comically apocalyptic terms.[3] Dominic Sandbrook titles his early-70s history *State of Emergency*[4] – a crisis declared by Britain's Conservative government and South Africa's apartheid government alike – the assumption being that the natives rebelling must be revolting.

For the left, however, such resistance should be rousing, with the working class both lighting up this period culturally and turning its lights off politically, and even bringing the Conservative government down in 1974. This period's industrial unrest, feminist militancy and racial refusal is symbiotic with its musical efflorescence – an era bursting with ideas and initiatives, from alternative technology to collective squats, workers' occupations to concept albums. No longer the high 60s, this was still the *Long* 60s, as the blooded children of the revolution rejected the restoration's attempts to lower living standards and expectations, and did so with an uppity utopianism and ornery optimism that's audible throughout the era's music.

Inflation has become the index of 70s ills, indicative of social democracy's declared inability to deliver social stability. Wolfgang Streeck demystifies inflation as "a monetary reflection of a distributional conflict between a working class, demanding both employment security and a higher share in their country's income, and a capitalist class striving to maximise the return on its capital".[5] With international competition hitting capital's profits, workers were pressured to increase productivity, with growth-fetishising governments following the money – thus Britain's income policy and America's 'Nixon shock' wage freeze of 1972.[6] As workers took to the streets, students and hippie radicals joined them in solidarity, as Andy Beckett shows of Britain's 1972 miners' strike and Jefferson Cowie of America's

1973 miners' strike.[7] Despite winning re-election in 1972 against the pro-labour George McGovern, Nixon was forced to launch a commission into industrial disquiet, while the Senate held hearings on worker alienation.[8] Having inherited a healthy economy, Heath's ideologically driven attempt to discipline the working class with the Industrial Relations Act and increased council-house rents sparked a firestorm. That the 1972 miners' strike prompted power cuts across the country provided a material demonstration of class power, while that year's dockers' dispute provoked the very sympathy strikes the Act had banned, almost spiralling into a general strike. Consequently, Fisher claims that in this period, "we were as close as we were going to be to postcapitalism".[9]

Glam rock's proletarian flamboyance makes it the era's meta-form, the exemplification of what Hebdige calls "style as a form of Refusal". Working-class musicians and fans adopting aristocratic styles represented less a break with dress-down hippiedom than, for Hebdige, "a symbolic violation of the social order" – a performative redistribution via class drag.[10] "You look like a star, but you're really still on the dole", Mott the Hoople effuse on 1973's 'All the Way from Memphis' (UK 10). With this class confidence encompassing all genres, the refusal of authoritarian Fordism on Chicory Tip's 1972 'Son of My Father' (UK 1), of being "moulded and folded, preform packed", asserts a proletarian claim not just on the present but on the *future*, conveyed formally by producer Giorgio Moroder's use of the new fangled Moog synthesizer.

Urban folk-rock gave working-class culture glamour and drama, as on Rod Stewart's delightfully gritty 'Maggie May' in autumn 1971 (UK 1; US 1), or Lindisfarne's joyous Saturday night anthem 'Meet Me on the Corner' (UK 5) in 1972. On Stealers Wheel's Dylan-esque 1973 'Stuck in the Middle with You' (UK 8; US 6), Gerry Rafferty twice repeats, "You started off with nothing/And you're proud that you're a self-made man". Status Quo's *Piledriver* (UK 5) invokes heavy rock as heavy industry, the relentlessness of the band's riffing on the riproaring 'Paper Plane' (UK 8) leaving no doubt where the power lies. Black Sabbath reject a Fordist work-culture of 'Killing Yourself to Live' on early 1974's career-peak *Sabbath Bloody Sabbath* (UK 4;

US 11), while even the piano-ballad title track of Bad Company's debut (UK 3; US 1) finds these deserters from Free and Mott identifying as rule-defying renegades.

In soul, there was a blue-collar pride in the language of ex-Temptation Eddie Kendricks' "diesel-powered" 1973 funk hit 'Keep on Truckin'' (UK 18; US 1). Like Norman Whitfield's soul productions – the Undisputed Truth's fall 1971 'Smiling Faces Sometimes' (US 3) – progressive rock's instrumental extravagance and lyrical fancifulness was an affirmation of class ambition, as on the Moody Blues' 1972 re-release, 'Nights in White Satin' (US 2). You can hear class assertion in Argent's anthemic 1972 'Hold Your Head Up' (UK 5; US 5) and on Jethro Tull's album-long *Thick as a Brick* the same year (UK 5; US 1): in response to "tireless oppression", "the gutters run red" as the "losers" rise up in a "hellish chorus". Prog supergroup Emerson, Lake & Palmer's epic 1972 ballad 'The Endless Enigma' urges, "Won't you refuse to be used" by "hypocrite freaks" as "paupers" become "kings" (*Trilogy*, UK 2; US 5). This era's preponderance of concept albums wasn't so much a matter of pop getting above itself as of proles getting *ideas*. The size and scope of the Who's 1973 double-album, *Quadrophenia* (UK 2; US 2), is precisely the point: it takes working-class mod culture seriously, giving it glamour, and if that means taking *itself* too seriously, this still results in some seriously good music. Pushing Fordism to pop-modern limits, songs like '5.15' (UK 20) depict mod youth as "magically bored/On a quiet street corner", daring anyone to push them.

Even Fordist MOR lionised working-class culture in this era. Irish singer-songwriter Gilbert O'Sullivan's cloth cap bespoke a plebeian glamour that became a 70s style staple (the Osmonds; the Rubettes), while his spring 1972 'Alone Again (Naturally)' (UK 3; US 1) is all about the agony of the ordinary. American Jim Croce's 1973 hits 'You Don't Mess Around with Jim' (US 8) and 'Bad Bad Leroy Brown' (US 1) are depictions of wealthy hegemons struck down by the subaltern. The power of the working class was equally visible in television programming, in America's Archie Bunker-starring *All in the Family*; in its British equivalent *Til Death Us Do Part* (with even Alf Garnett losing faith in Heath); in *Steptoe and Son* (1970–74), *Whatever Happened to the Likely Lads* (1973–74) and the original reality TV contest, *Opportunity Knocks*.

Communist dockers' leader Jimmy Reid was almost as much a regular on chat show *Parkinson* as TGWU leader Jack Jones was at Downing Street. Because working-class power still strikes fear into the establishment, the Strawbs' jaunty 1973 folk singalong 'Part of the Union' (UK 2) has been put to work as an anti-union song,[11] whereas it's clearly a tools-down celebration: "Though I'm a working man/I can ruin the government's plan".

With the Attica riot a recent memory, the era's preponderance of prison songs is also expressive of this class conflict. As an exception – and for being execrable – Tony Orlando and Dawn's 1973 'Tie a Yellow Ribbon' (UK 1; US 1) can be forgotten, while Lennon and Ono's 1972 'Attica State' (*Some Time in New York City*, UK 11) deservedly already has. Art-poppers 10cc's 1973 'Rubber Bullets' (UK 1) is a flippant account of a jailhouse party and puts the state in the searchlight's beam: "I don't understand why they called in the National Guard/When Uncle Sam is the one who belongs in the exercise yard". Appearing as runaway convicts on the cover, McCartney and Wings' spring 1974 'Band on the Run' (UK 3; US 1) offers a blithe nose-thumb to the authoritarian state. Cloth-capped former Animal Alan Price's hokey hymn to 1930s hunger marchers, 'Jarrow Song' (UK 6) sounded – as Heath was driven from power by striking miners – like a victory march. If the government "won't give us a couple of bob", the marcher's wife advises, "with my blessings burn them down". The capitalist accumulation that underlies class conflict is highlighted on 10cc's 1974 'Wall Street Shuffle' (UK 10): "Let your money hustle/Bet you'd sell your mother/You can buy another".

Just as Fordism's political settlement was unsettled by industrial unrest, so was its cultural compact. With growing numbers of women joining the workforce, just as Britain's 1970 Equal Pay Act was achieved by struggle, so, in America feminist pressure provoked the Equal Rights Amendment of 1972, with the Coalition of Labor Union Women formed in 1974. As *Spare Rib* launched in 1972, this societal shift was visible in TV's *The Liver Birds* and *Man About the House*, in Billie Jean King's 1973 tennis victory over Bobby Riggs in tennis's 'Battle of the Sexes', and was audible in music. On Helen Reddy's 1972 MOR ballad 'I Am Woman' (US 1), the "I" is collective, as Reddy asserts, "No one's ever gonna keep me down again". As such, Carly Simon's 1972

'You're So Vain' (UK 3; US 1) can be seen to satirise masculine hegemony. Women are background colour in the male hero's narcissistic drama, beautifully realised by the attention-hogging 'background' vocal by one of the song's rumoured subjects, Mick Jagger (from 1:45), gradually fighting his way to the front of the mix to drown Simon out altogether (by 3:28).

Indicative of the decade's ongoing dialectic between the radical and the reactionary, the countercultural and the counter-revolutionary, feminism provoked a hunkering-down chauvinism that chimed with the music industry's corporate turn. As Neil Young moved towards MOR, his attitudes became more conservative: his musically lovely but lyrically loathsome 1972 orchestral ballad 'A Man Needs a Maid' seeks "someone to keep my house for me, cook my meals, then go away" (*Harvest*, UK 1; US 1). Fellow Canadian Gordon Lightfoot's 1974 MOR-folk 'Sundown' (US 1) expresses a patrician paranoia about female freedom as the fallout from feminism. Similarly, the possessive in Paul Anka and Odia Coates' MOR '(You're) Having My Baby' (UK 6; US 1) asserts patriarchal authority a year after the progressive *Roe vs. Wade* ruled that women had the right to choose.

As authoritarian promoters and managers pressed bands to pump up the performance principle on relentless American tours, their reward was lucrative live albums and a multi-date bacchanal. This culture is captured by Grand Funk Railroad's 'We're an American Band' (US 1), in which being "on the road for forty days" reduces men to loon-panted apes: "Booze and ladies, keep me right". Humble Pie's Steve Marriott's transformation from feminised hippie to be-denimed geezer was paradigmatic, from it all being too beautiful to the ugly cloddishness of 1973's 'Good Booze and Bad Women' (*Eat It*, US 13). By 1974, former psychedelicists Deep Purple were squealing "she was devil's sperm" on the brilliantly bovine 'Burn' (*Burn*, UK 3; US 9), while Bad Company's 'Can't Get Enough' (UK 15; US 5) proffered the ultimate cock-rock swagger: "I take whatever I want/And baby I want you". There was, however, a sunny, goodtime rootsiness to much of classic rock, its dialectic typified by the Faces' marvellous but misogynistic 'Stay with Me' (UK 6; US 17) and Steve Miller Band's lazily lecherous hippie on 1973's 'The Joker' (US 1) insisting he means no harm. Cock rock's absence from the pop canon is a casualty of feminism: in some cases deserved, but such was the form's dialectic that its proletarian grit would be missed once inoffensive soft rock succeeded it.

Race was another site of struggle in this era, with the National Front scapegoating immigrants and police harassing black youth and black businesses in Britain, while in America the bussing of kids to desegregated schools incensed social conservatives. Popular music rejected such populist attempts at racial restoration. Three Dog Night's reggaefied take on Pete Seeger's 'Black and White' celebrates educational desegregation (US 1); Hot Chocolate/Stories' 1973 account of an interracial relationship, 'Brother Louie' (UK 7; US 1), insists there "ain't no difference between black and white"; the Stones' funky 1974 'Doo Doo Doo (Heartbreaker)' (US 15) condemns racialised policing; while Frank Zappa's empathetically sarcastic 1974 'Uncle Remus' spits, "We look pretty sharp in these clothes/Unless we get sprayed with a hose" (*Apostrophe*, US 10). Even the just-so tidiness of MOR was ruffled by racial conflict, with fashion-plate Cher capturing the prejudice experienced by Romas on 1971's 'Gypsys, Tramps and Thieves' (UK 4; US 1) and by her own Native Americans on 1973's gauche 'Half Breed' (US 1).

For conservatives, the only desirable revolution is the clock turning back, the 70s right's platonic ideal of the past being the 50s – before, as Simon put it, everything had "gone wrong". Nixon was a figure of the 50s, deriding McGovern as a 60s libertarian,[12] while British housewife campaigner Mary Whitehouse waged moral war on the legacy of 60s "permissiveness" and the collapse of traditional hierarchies since the ordered 50s.[13] Whitehouse was commemorated on Deep Purple's 1973 'Mary Long' (*Who Do We Think We Are*, UK 4; US 15) and as one of the moralists "preaching sermons" on O'Sullivan's 'Permissive Twit' (*Himself*, UK 5; US 9).

In much of the era's 50s nostalgia, it's as if the 60s simply haven't happened, picket fences occluding picket lines in *That'll Be the Day* (1973), *American Graffiti* (1973) and *Happy Days* (1974-78). Middle of the road, middle class and middle-American, the Carpenters epitomised the glazed glamour of 50s restoration pop. On the yearningly lovely 1973 'Yesterday Once More' (UK 2; US 2), the comforting sound of 'golden oldies' "makes today seem rather sad", Karen Carpenter bemusedly observes: "So much has changed". Such wholesome family fare was a recurring feature of the period's charts, with British child star Neil Reid's cloying 1971 'Mother of Mine' (UK 2) – "You showed me the right way things had to be done" – Donny Osmond's teeth-grittingly cute 1972 take on Anka's 'Puppy Love' (UK 1; US 3) and his sister Marie's vile 1973 cover of anti-gay campaigner Anita Bryant's 'Paper Roses' (UK 2; US 5). Peters and Lee's 'Welcome Home' the same year made a dreary case for domesticity (UK 1), while Olivia Newton-John's 'Let Me Be There' (US 6), sounded like an emissary from an evangelical meeting.

Don McLean's 1972 'American Pie' (UK 2; US 1) deploys the death of Buddy Holly in 1960 as society's symbolic tipping point, "the day the music died". Set to a gently rollicking sock-hop beat, the song is a conservative co-option of 50s rebellion, its mythic tableau depicting the 60s not as rock'n'roll's legacy but its betrayal, a descent from calm and decency into chaos and anarchy, with the violence of Manson and Altamont the counterculture's logical conclusion. "When the world outside looks so unkind", as Dobie Gray observed on 1973's 'Drift Away' (US 5), the answer is to "get lost in your rock'n'roll", as 50s compilations glutted the British charts. In this conservative vein, Elton John's 1972 'Crocodile Rock' (UK 5; US 1) renders rock'n'roll's combustion cuddly, while Ringo Starr's 1974 cover of Johnny Burnette's 'You're Sixteen' (UK 4; US 1) is a cupcakes-and-circle-skirts 50s, complete with cutesy McCartney kazoo solo. Like contemporary cuisine's tinned fruit and frozen veg, the process of preservation always alters – contains – the past's essence. MOR monarch Barbra Streisand's question is apposite on 1973's 'The Way We Were' (US 1): "Can it be that it was all so simple then/Or has time rewritten every line?"

Time has certainly rewritten the 70s' relationship to the 60s, given that, David Edgar notes, "conventional wisdom sees the first half of the 1970s as either abandoning or exposing 1960s idealism".[14] Yet, conventional wisdom occludes the fact that a glammed-up countercultural continuity was as common in the early 70s as 50s nostalgia, and that the "nostalgia mode" isn't always conservative. Cat Stevens' 1971 'Peace Train' (US

7) depicts him "dreaming about the world as one"; soulful soft-rockers Chicago's 1972 'Saturday in the Park' (US 3) rapturously urges, "Will you help him change the world?"; Three Dog Night's 1973 'Shambala' is MOR hippie utopianism (US 3); while heavy rockers Free's 1973 'Wishing Well' (UK 7) longs for "love and a peaceful world". Even 50s holdover Sammy Davis Jr's 'Candy Man' has a distinctly countercultural quality (US 1): "He mixes it with love/And makes the world feel good". With Philadelphia International's Fordist house band named MFSB (mother, father, sister, brother), the O'Jays' 1972 'Love Train' (UK 9; US 1) is psychedelic soul at its most joyful. ELO were essentially a psychedelic Beatles tribute act on hits like 1972's '10538 Overture' (UK 9), as the public paid tribute via the Beatles' *1967-1970* compilation's success (UK 2; US 1). Concurrently, Harrison urged, 'Give Me Love (Give Me Peace on Earth)' (UK 8; US 1), while Lennon murmured, "Make love not war" on 'Mind Games' (UK 26; US 18).

McCartney's rejection of his former cohorts' hippie compassion for Hobbesian competition on Wings' brassily glam 1973 Bond theme 'Live and Let Die' (UK 9; US 2) better fits conventional wisdom of the 70s. "You've got to give the other fella hell", Macca screams. Lynskey treats the social paranoia of the O'Jays' 1972 'Back Stabbers' (UK 14; US 3) as paradigmatic of '70s malaise',[15] despite the song being a conscious-soul outlier. Ostensibly, Steely Dan's acerbic cynicism fits here too, but despite the pessimism of their brilliant 'Do It Again' (US 6), its spangling sitar runs hauntological hippie interference to its suburban bossa groove. This negative narrative finds fuel in films like *Dirty Harry* (1971) and *The Godfather* (1972), however, which dramatise the deficiency of ideals against what Maconie calls "the harsh realities of the 70s".[16] Yet Adam Curtis's claim that "everyone" concluded in 1973 that terrorism "is what all radical attempts to change the world inevitably lead to" reveals the ideological basis of this 70s narrative. "The fault is inside you, the individual, not in society",[17] Curtis asserts, endorsing an atomised individualism that reveals rather more about centrist ideology than it does about the early 70s.

There was nothing either cynical or escapist about the glories of glam or ghetto soul. Even fluff like Gallery's 'Nice to See You' (US 4) or King Harvest's 'Dancing in the Moonlight' (US 13) exude a sunniness that's entirely *1972*, while concurrently – and more credibly – Todd Rundgren's shimmering 'I Saw the Light' (US 16) attains near spiritual ecstasy through human connection. Among the era's few melancholy moments, Diana Ross's 1973 'Touch Me in the Morning' (UK 9; US 1) sports a supercharged melodic uplift, while Neil Diamond's 1972 'Song Sung Blue' (UK 14; US 1) is one of the happiest sad songs ever recorded (which isn't the same as it being good). Moreover, the enduringly countercultural Grateful Dead respond to the same constellation of crises as Simon's 'American Tune' on spring 1974's 'US Blues' (*From the Mars Hotel*, US 16) with an adversarial amiability that, paradigmatic of the period, is glam rather than glum.

Revision of the "nightmare 70s" narrative has begun, but is still burdened by shibboleths such as excessive union strength (Beckett; Turner), reversible decline (Medhurst) and inevitable neoliberalism (Cowie). Yet, from late 1971, when the 70s finally kicked in, until summer 1974, when Heath and Nixon were kicked out of office, the early 70s' ebullient, primary-coloured pop was entirely expressive of its explosive, play-at-maximum-volume politics. Defying declinism, embracing possibility and bullishly confident that the battles could be won, the early 70s, far from being grim, are fabulously, gloriously, *aggressively* glam.

Notes on Glam

Glam rock isn't just the meta-form for the 70s, it's a meta-text for the era's misrepresentation. All the critical verities on glam are misleading: that it rejected the 60s; that it was postmodern; that it was apolitical[18] – and that it made no impact on America. Taking this last point as paradigmatic, not only did Bowie, T. Rex, Gary Glitter and Sweet all have American hits, but the Osmonds' glammy, fizzy 1972 'Down by the Lazy River' (US 4) and Elton John's 1974, Bowie-biting 'Bennie and the Jets' (US 1), while dilutions of glam, are still more camply, flashily *outré* than anything their creators attempted thereafter. As befits a genre that delights in pastiche, the approach here is a tribute to Susan Sontag's 'Notes on Camp'.

1. Glam is political

Glam is the cultural logic of the era's industrial militancy. Glam's proletarian refusal was parlayed symbolically by Slade's gleefully misspelled titles – 1972's 'Look Wot You Dun' (UK 4) and 'Mama Weer All Crazee Now' (UK 1) – flippantly in the *Steptoe* grunts and groans of Lieutenant Pigeon's 1972 music hall-glam 'Mouldy Old Dough' (UK 1) and materially by the flashily-dressing council-estate kids on Mott the Hoople's 1972, Bowie-penned 'All the Young Dudes' (UK 3). "Is that concrete all around/Or is it in my head?" the narrator asks, capturing the brutalism of buildings and system alike, before the chargingly anthemic chorus renders class refusal utterly rapturous.

2. Glam is countercultural

Reynolds recites the standard refrain that glam was "a retreat from the political and collective hopes of the sixties into a fantasy trip of individualized escape".[19] Yet that T. Rex's 1971 chugging glam gauntlet 'Ride a White Swan' (UK 2) advises, "Wear a tall hat/Like a druid in the olden days/Wear your hair long", makes glam's continuity with psychedelic dress-up clear (Marc Bolan never really *stopped* being a hippie). T. Rex's delirious 1971 'Hot Love' (UK 1) lifts the hippie-gospel singalong of 'Hey Jude' to giddy heights, while 1972's glorious 'Metal Guru' (UK 1) gives 60s spiritualism a shiny 70s refurb. For all Bowie's disavowals of hippiedom, 1972's *Ziggy Stardust* (UK 5: US 21) is a homoerotic love letter to Hendrix and hippie-phase Bolan, while Roxy Music's avant-garde textures and surreal tape-effects are sheer souped-up psychedelia. "'68 was '68", Sweet insist on 'The Six Teens' (UK 9). Glam-rockers were thus 'Children of the Revolution', as T. Rex's 1972 hit had it (UK 2) – birthed by peace and love, blooded by chaos and anarchy, a fusion of hippie nonconformity and proletarian toughness, refusing to be fooled or ignored. The song's uncompromising guitar riff means business but means it with love: for all its "bump and grind" and Rolls Royces, this isn't Me-Decade self-indulgence or materialism but the We Decade's assertion of the power of ordinary people against the elites.

3. Glam is collective

As an expression of proletarian pride, glam's power lies in the group, the crowd, the class – 'collective' and 'co-op' being keywords of this era. At the Battle of Saltley Gate in February 1972, fellow unions flocked to striking miners' support, defeating management and defying government.[20] Inspired by union action, British schoolkids organised 'Pupil Power' strikes, and so Alice Cooper's raucous summer 1972 'Schools Out' (UK 1; US 7) perfectly matches this militant moment. The assertion that "We got no class/And we got no principles" isn't just a schoolyard pun, nor indeed, contra Reynolds (and Whitehouse), is it a statement of nihilism.[21] Class is a system, the principal its pinnacle, both of which Cooper rejects gleefully – "Can't salute ya/Can't find a flag" – as chorusing children cheer him on.

On Slade's celebration of the crowd, 1973's riotously exciting 'Cum on Feel the Noize' (UK 1), Noddy Holder's sinus-busting vocal, Dave Hill's gut-busting guitar and a combustible, football-terrace chorus taunt middle-class tribulations about the 'mass' as a mob. As warm as it is aggressive, as solidaristic as it is antagonistic, 'Cum on Feel the Noize' is a singularly proletarian piece of pop, strength in its sinew, wit in its wordplay, pride in its irrepressible power. Sweet's 1973 'Ballroom Blitz' (UK 2; US 5) is a bubbleglam companion piece, a delirious celebration of the crowd's destructive power, the band raised on collective shoulders to break through society's ceiling. Follow-up 'Teenage Rampage' (UK 2) spells out the threat: "So come join the revolution". *Of course*, 'revolution' is being used frivolously to titillate preteens by Sweet's Fordist Svengalis Chinn and Chapman here. Yet such a demotic was a combustible choice amid strikes and sit-ins, especially when egged on by such aggressive music.

Bowie's 1973 'Panic in Detroit' may be a liberal fret about the mob, but its frenzied Bo Diddley beat and Mick Ronson's guitar provocations make urban insurrection sound like a party you wouldn't want to miss (*Aladdin Sane*, UK 1; US 17).[22] As

Marcuse argues, "the regressive political content is absorbed…
in the artistic form".[23] So while the "juvenile product of the
working class" on Elton John's 1973 'Saturday Night's Alright
for Fighting' (UK 7; US 12) may be presented as a bourgeois-
tribulating thug, his assertion that "we've had it with your
discipline", and the sheer pulverising *power* of Davey Johnstone's
guitars, leaves no doubt whose side the listener should be on.
Aggression never sounded so amiable, because the adversarial in
glam isn't personal, it's political.

4. Glam is popular modern, not postmodern

Sontag's 'camp' superficially fits glam like a velveteen glove:
a "victory of 'style' over content" which "sees everything
in quotation marks",[24] making 'camp' and Jameson's
'postmodernism' virtually synonymous. Sontag bypasses Brecht's
materialist breakdown of 'performance', wherein the 'alienation
effect' – mannerism, overstatement, 'camp', in a word – makes a
point rather than merely striking a pose. Glam's radical camp is
thus a subversion of socially accepted meanings, not, as Sontag
claims, an embrace of *lack* of meaning.

    Bowie's 1972 'Starman' (UK 10) appears to tick all the
postmodern boxes – flippantly 'performed' rather than sincerely
expressed; cheekily repurposing the past as new while being
neither (per Jameson's definition) "ahistorical" nor "depthless".[25]
Indeed, it's the song's historical awareness that gives 'Starman'
its substance, mining 50s jive talk, folk-rock 12-string jangle,
Motown (the Morse-code guitar of 'You Keep Me Hanging On'),
showtunes (the melody of 'Somewhere over the Rainbow') and
hippie gospel (those "la-la-las"; the sci-fi deity Starman). These
reference points aren't idle *bricolage*, they invoke, respectively, a
countercultural, racial and sexual utopianism – aliens as escape
from alienation, the past as a teleport to the future.

5. Glam's nostalgia is retro-futurism

Rather than representing a retreat from the present, glam's
nostalgia takes what Benjamin called a "tiger's leap into the
past",[26] aggressively repossessing it. Glam's regular returns to

the 50s rip the throat out of its conformist complacency. Bowie's 1972 'Hang onto Yourself' drags Eddie Cochran to a gay club (*Ziggy Stardust*), while 'John, I'm Only Dancing' (UK 12) renders rockabilly's sweaty masculinity sexually ambivalent. Roxy Music are always depicted as 50s-fixated,[27] yet the swirling, oboe-driven art-pop of 'Virginia Plain' (UK 4) and the band's space-age couture landed in dowdy 70s living rooms like a visitation from the future. Still, with their cartoonish doo-wop, camp rock'n'roll and fondness for tacky tiger-print, Roxy both captured and subverted the 50s restoration. 1973's extraordinary 'In Every Dream Home a Heartache' (*For Your Pleasure*; UK 4) is a literal perversion of the Fordist domestic ideal. The playboy's blow-up doll isn't just a *solution* to the emptiness of his "penthouse perfection" but a *metaphor* for it: plastic, inert, soulless. The doll and Roxy's album-cover vamps *possess* retrograde 50s 'femininity' – woman as function, product, "disposable darling" – but distend its misogyny like latex, caricaturing it.

Even bubbleglam was initially onside in this regard – rock'n'roll revived not as pastiche but as riotous assembly: collective, joyful, adversarial. Gary Glitter's 1972 'Rock and Roll Part 2' (UK 2; US 7) literally mutes the nostalgia of 'Part 1', reduced to delinquent grunts and rumbling, threatening bass. Glitter revived this as bovine 50s biker-gang shtick on 1973's 'I'm the Leader of the Gang' (UK 1); reprised more quietly – and more creepily – by Alvin Stardust's Gene-Vincent leathers and eerie Elvis ventriloquism on 1974's 'Jealous Mind' (UK 1) and 'Red Dress' (UK 7). Even the most upbeat bubbleglam, like Wizzard's 1973 'Angel Fingers' (UK 1) – the 50s mauled by Phil Spector's clammy hands – and David Essex's 'Rock On' (UK 3; US 5) – as futuristic as it is 50s – possess a latent delinquent threat. By 1974 the delinquency had been diluted and Mud's irresistible 'Tiger Feet' (UK 1) is less a tiger's leap into the past than a teddy bear's picnic in a 50s theme park. Released amidst the three-day weeks Ted Heath called to combat the miners' strike, however, it still has a cheeky swagger in its sideways step.

6. Glam is utopian

There's no such thing as glum glam. Dented by the defeats of the 60s, glam's utopianism has scars from ripping off stars from its face, but gamely sticks them on again. Like most glam-rockers, Bowie was a working-class kid and a hippie youth, and 1972's radio hit 'Changes' speaks for both constituencies: "these children that you spit on/As they try to change their world", who are "quite aware what they're going through". Rather than the statement of 70s individualism it's usually credited as being,[28] 'Changes' is a collective refusal of patrician control: "Where's your shame? /You've left us up to our necks in it". Yet it's still looking *forward*, facing the strange, hailing the future. The camp melodrama of 1973 hit 'Life on Mars' (UK 3) uses Brecht's alienation effect to question mass entertainment's escape from the humdrum. The mousy-haired everygirl finds cinema's opiate glamour a "saddening bore" – contra Adorno, for whom the subaltern simply soak up mass entertainment's ideology.[29] With its swishy strings, thunderous tympani and Bowie's lungingly abandoned vocal, 'Life on Mars' is camp in Sontag's sense of "too much",[30] but rather than prompting humour, as Sontag claims, its excess expresses *yearning*, a longing for a utopia more substantial than cinema's gimcrack simulacras.

Elton John's 1973 career-best creation 'Goodbye Yellow Brick Road' (UK 6; US 2) is virtually a follow-up to 'Life on Mars' – another showtuney piano ballad with a spotlight on the glamorous life's aspirational lure: the glittery spell of Hollywood beckoning ordinary people to the utopia of Oz along the yellow brick road. Oz turns out to be another gimcrack utopia, but in the narrator's rejection of its pull and return to pushing his plough, this "mongrel who ain't got a penny" isn't accepting his place, as *The Wizard of Oz* recommends, but rejecting the class system altogether, looking "beyond the yellow brick road" with a visionary utopianism.

7. Glam is queerer than queer

Glam was the indirect product of Britain's 1967 Sexual Offences Act, but like all facets of the counterculture, gay liberation always thought bigger than the Fordist state, and represented a radical rethinking of the structures of sexuality, gender and the family. Liberation was less pioneered than *lived* by a New York *demimonde* centred on pop-artist Andy Warhol at his semi-ironic Fordist Factory, where "glamorous" was his favoured term of approval. Leaving the Warhol-patronised Velvet Underground, Lou Reed's 1972 'Walk on the Wild Side' (UK 10) was a montage of the Factory's maverick milieu which enacted a startling incursion of queerness into the 70s' mainstream. The song was produced by Bowie, whose own 'performance' of homosexuality – declaring he was gay to the music press; mock-fellating Ronson onstage – also presented a "form of resistance to the order which guarantees [queers'] continued subordination", in Hebdige's words (whatever Bowie's 'real' sexuality).[31]

While historically upstaged by Bowie, Bolan was initially the bigger star, camping up to the camera's gaze, nonchalantly avowing his bisexuality in interviews, while purring, in an androgynous warble somewhere between Syd Barrett and Donovan, "I'm gonna suck you" on 'Jeepster' (UK 2), "Take me!" on the glorious 'Get It On' (UK 1; US 10) and "I wanna be your toy" on '20th Century Boy' (UK 2). Bolan half-inched the same Berry riffs as cock-rock's be-denimed bozos, camping them up but conceding nothing in amped-up filth. Glam doesn't accept the binaries of machismo and femininity, toughness and tenderness – Mott's Lucy dresses like a queen but can "kick like a mule" – it mixes these polarities up, messes with them, *queers* them.

8. Glam's queerness is performative, not play-acting

If gender is work, with the performance principle 'producing' gender, then it is alienated labour, making glam's signalled gender performance akin to Brecht's alienation effect, parodying and thus questioning sexual conventions. Bracewell's affirmation of the tired 'builders in blusher' trope essentialises sexuality – along with class – and continues a tradition of trivialising glam.[32] Glam lit up the 70s with a sartorial radicalism that confounded conventions of both couture and gender, meaning that the 70s *is* Bolan in yellow satin trousers and glitter-spangled cheeks performing 'Hot Love' on *Top of the Pops*; Bowie draping his limp wrist around Ronson for 'Starman'; Slade guitarist Dave Hill's 1973 'metal nun' outfit; Rob Davis's femme customisation of Mud's matching 50s outfits on 1973's daft 'Dyna-Mite' (UK 4); and Sweet's Brian Connolly shamelessly showboating for the polymorphous gaze. Meanwhile, in the West End, 1973's *Rocky Horror Picture Show* made music theatre's integral campness overt with a radically anti-essentialist sexuality.

These moves don't simply perform *homo*sexuality but highlight the performativity of *hetero*sexuality – the masculine performance principle as a series of codes and tics that can be decoded and unticked. Sweet's effeminate guitarist Steve Priest queers the cock-rock bluster of 'Blockbuster' with the cock-blocked boyfriends' whinny of "We haven't got a clue *what* to do!" (UK 1). Dropping the Faces (and the misogyny), randy straight Rod Stewart, with his feather-cut, frilly shirts, exposed flesh and pancake slap, stripped the masculine codes from heterosexuality. Moreover, it wasn't just Freddie Mercury who queered heavy rock machismo in Queen: check out drummer Roger Taylor's pout in 1973–74 footage and listen to the sheer *swishiness* of Brian May's guitar. Americans Sparks made queering straightness their quotidian via the parodic polarity between Russell Mael's femme falsetto, flowing curls and rakishly belted cream trouser suits and brother Ron's masculine glare, moustache and bluff business suits. The epitome of popular modernism, Sparks represented Fordism straining at its strictures, refusing the regulation of clocking-on sexuality.

9. Glam is a lateral response to second-wave feminism

Bowie's 1972 'Suffragette City' (*Ziggy Stardust*) suggests glam's lateral relationship to feminism. While Bowie cheekily equates sexual emancipation with women's liberation, his "mellow-thighed chick" *still* puts his spine out of place: "Wham bam, thank you ma'am!" First-wave feminism crops up again on McCartney's joyously glammed-up 'Jet' (UK 7; US 7), where the patriarch's authority is undermined by being regarded as a "little lady suffragette". Sparks' stonking 1974 'This Town Ain't Big Enough for Both of Us' (UK 2) depicts heterosexuality as fear of women, with the macho bluster of its titular Hollywood cliché mauled by Russell Mael's archly hysterical delivery.

Glam's actually existing females were relatively few – the forgotten, delightful Lynsey de Paul (1972's 'Getting a Drag', UK 18); Sonja Kristina's call for revolution on Curved Air's 1972 'Marie Antoinette' (*Phantasmagoria*, UK 20); Lulu marvellously made-over in a man's suit and mobster fedora on Bowie's 'The Man Who Sold the World' in 1974 (UK 3). Then there was the wonder of Suzi Quatro, whose combination of raucous vocals, iconic bass guitar (no prop, she was a session player) and butch leather catsuit queered conventions of feminine appearance and attitude. Just as satin trousers could enhance masculinity, so the leathers emphasised Quatro's femininity, but this was all part of the confusion, of glam's polymorphous push and pull, and while Quatro's material was tailored by Mud and Sweet's Fordist pattern-makers Chinn and Chapman, it accentuated rather than contained her tomboy energy. On 1973's absurdly exciting 'Can the Can' (UK 1) Quatro reduces a disputed male sex object to tinned goods while flirting with her female rival; '48 Crash' (UK 3) uses capitalist collapse as a metaphor for male menopause. Quatro's music, like much of glam, *inhabits* crisis, draws energy from it: once the times quietened, so did her music; so did her muse.

10. Glam was futuristic but not the future

Glam was popular modernism personified: experimental and technological while capturing Fordism's futurist dialectic – and the decade's dialectic – between possibility and perturbation. Glam futurism thus presents both utopian desire – the Mars-dwelling astronaut on Elton John's yearning 1972 'Rocket Man' (UK 2; US 6) – and dystopian danger. On Bowie's 1973 masterpiece 'Drive-In Saturday' (UK 3), capital rules over an empire of ashes, the world a denatured desert ("the sea that raged no more"), sparsely populated by denatured humans (living a half-life in domes, unable to have sex; tethered to the machine). With the fearful future evoked by swooshing synths, the lost past located in 50s-progression chords and doo-wop backing vocals, 'Drive-In Saturday' incorporates everything that makes glam radical – queerness (Jung crashing out with Sylvian), feminism (women desexualised) and class-consciousness (the foreman keeping the drones in formation). 'Drive-In Saturday' is the closest glam will get to glum, and yet, as Jameson argues, dystopias are "premonitions", not predictions of the future, so the song is a warning of where untrammelled capitalism could take us, with the future still something to be fought for rather than something foreclosed.[33]

Strip-mined by the moneymen, glam itself had no future, expiring in a morass of bubbleglam nostalgia by mid-1974. Yet glam's obsession with the obsolescent had a considerable half-life, its aestheticisation of trash transforming commodity values. This is because glam was grounded in the historically material – a class and a culture once treated as trash – rather than the transient frivolity which it performed. That glam redux was always a dilution – in punk, in glam metal, in New Romanticism, in grunge, in Britpop – indicates glam's own depth, a synecdoche for the depth of this undeservedly denigrated decade.

"The World Is a Ghetto": Conscious Soul and Funk

70s soul is glam's sister under the skin: unrelentingly urban, musically ebullient and sartorially flamboyant, simultaneously confronting and transcending the harsh environment from which it emerges. Like glam, soul is a flank in the class struggle played out through popular music, the sound of the subaltern saying 'no' with defiant joy. With Nixon cynically declaring the "urban crisis" to be over and drastically slashing state housing subsidies in 1973, and the Panthers dissolved, music was effectively the political voice of the projects. This was articulated most clearly in conscious soul, but pride amid poverty produced such an embarrassment of riches that even love songs came across as statements of Black Pride. On Al Green's glorious 1971–72 hits – 'Let's Stay Together' (UK 7; US 1), 'Look What You've Done for Me' (US 4) and 'I'm Still in Love with You' (US 3) – his voice floats airily above the taut, street-level instrumentation, articulating a freedom that pulls against the regimentation of MGs' drummer Al Jackson's law-enforcing beat. 70s-iteration Isley Brothers added the acid-rock squall of Ernie Isley's Hendrix-inspired guitar to Ron's sublime falsetto, with the combination locating 'That Lady' (UK 14; US 6) and 'Summer Breeze' (UK 16) in an idealised otherworld that, sweltered in ghetto funk and slathered with gospel grit, is conceivable only in relation to concrete reality.

This grounded utopianism is captured by the image of the rose growing through the sidewalk concrete in Aretha Franklin's adaptation of ("black and") 'Spanish Harlem' (UK 14; US 2). On the Nina Simone-penned title track of Franklin's 1972 *Young, Gifted and Black* (US 11), these roses are the ghetto youth for whom, "There's a world waiting for you – you!" With Franklin at the peak of her powers, the album's self-penned hits – the "funky and lowdown feeling" of 'Rock Steady' (US 9); the everyday utopianism of 'Day Dreaming' (US 5) – are statements of Black Pride, pastel chalkmarks on the project paving. Franklin's only real female rival, Mavis Staples, lends a sensuous yearning to the Staples' utopian 1972 'I'll Take You There' (UK 30; US 1), transcending political obstacles – "Ain't no smilin' faces/Lyin' to the races" – as her extemporisations float free. Timmy Thomas's sublime 'Why Can't We Live Together' that same summer, (UK 12; US 3) is more universal: "No matter what color/ You are still my brother". Thomas's utopia pulls against the austerity of both his background and his backing, a parched gospel organ against the futuristic thrum of a newfangled drum machine.

More grounded, War's epic fall 1972 'The World Is a Ghetto' (US 7) hails the horizon of both black expectation and white comprehension, acknowledging the projects' privation while celebrating their culture – captured by its parent album's cartoon ghettoscape (US 1). On their 1973 'Me and Baby Brother' (UK 21; US 15), "the corner" is both where deals are done *and* community is created, the track's nervy funk overlaid with the group's joyfully communal singing. Few songs evoke the sun-baked brownstones of the 70s ghetto better than William de Vaughn's spring 1974 'Be Thankful for What You Got' (UK 30; US 3) – or better capture conscious soul's contradictions.[34] With car ownership a badge of American citizenship while ghetto dwellers, de Vaughn empathises, "may not have a car at all", the song sensually itemises the accessorised Cadillacs of local kingpins, "diggin' the scene with a gangster lean". Backed by Philadelphia sessioneers, the song's low-slung groove and drawling lyricism renders ghetto life glamorous. This expression of Black Pride is taken further in the Blaxploitation films launched by *Shaft*'s success (1971), where the pimp and the dealer, flamboyantly attired, refusing the Man's authority, become embodiments of style, rendering black culture enviably cool.

With even the James Bond franchise's *Live and Let Die* (1973) tapping this ghetto style, James Brown personified its inherent tensions, conveying both "the grind of the corner and the ecstasy of a Pentecostal prayer service", as Tate has it.[35] Brown's testament that "You got to use just what you got/To get just what you want" on 1971's 'Hot Pants' (US 15) isn't just a fetishisation of fashion or a downgrading of feminism, it's an assertion of *power* through style – "Make ya sure of yourself, good Lord!" – in clothing, in attitude, in music. So 'Make it Funky' (US 22) isn't just Brown self-advertising, it's a celebration of black culture – "Neckbones, candied yams, turnips/Smothered steak/Grits and gravy" and, yes, of funk itself – autonomous, street smart, uncompromising. 1972's 'Get on the Good Foot' (US 18) tautens that tension between "a whole lotta bills and my money's spent" and a ghetto glamour – "Where soulful people knows what it's about" – that (for now) is beyond co-option.

Less cool but more considered than Brown, Curtis Mayfield insists on the material factors behind this ghetto mystique on his superb 1972 soundtrack for Blaxploitation flick *Super Fly* (UK 26; US 1). Conventionally regarded as a counter-commentary, Mayfield's music is actually of a piece with the movie, acknowledging both the drug scene's glamour – "fly" being 'cool', the title track's aspirational refrain being "trying to get over" (US 8) – and its grimness: the stark statement that 'Freddie's Dead' (US 4) and the demystification of dealing as "pushing dope for the man". The magical, orchestral 'Little Child, Runnin' Wild' depicts both the economic system capitalism has created – "One room shack/On the alley-back/Control, I'm told/From across the track" – and the "jones" to escape it through narcosis, or the profits of narcosis. The 'Pusherman' is thus "a victim of ghetto demands"; with black male unemployment doubling in the mid-70s, he's "told I can't be nothin' else" and pushed into profiteering from his community's pain, as suspicions grew that the *state* was the real pusher, deploying drugs to pacify the projects.

Conscious soul's creativity suffused this period's Fordist productions: while Whitfield kept the commercial ballads coming for the Temptations – 'Just My Imagination' (UK 8; US 1) – 1972's 'Papa Was a Rolling Stone' (UK 14; US 1) was a peak of both ghetto funk and popular modernism. The lyric's evocation of the precariousness of project life, alongside the music's orchestral scope, gives the ghetto not just glamour but mythology. Yet while the mic-passing siblings capture a sense of a community under siege, the song offers no more answers than the mother does, with the *cause* of the errant father's shiftlessness left as open as the song's solitary, non-resolving chord. 1973's 'Masterpiece' (US 7) was Whitfield's Fordist replication, another trapped bass-riff circling the grimness of ghetto crime, narcotics and dilapidation. Yet while racism is suggested – "Nobody cares what happens to the folks that live in the ghetto" – the *system* shimmers above this as indeterminately as Whitfield's grandiose orchestration, its classicist bombast subtly invoking the imperial 'civilisation' that created slavery and its godless child, the ghetto.

Contrary to Philly soul's apolitical reputation, writer-producers Gamble and Huff, like Whitfield at Motown, used commercial confections to create space for more ambitious conceptions. Their follow-up to the O'Jays' *Back Stabbers* was 1973's *Ship Ahoy* (US 11), whose epic title track evokes the Middle Passage of slave ships from Africa to America – complete with crashing waves and cracking whips – while comparing *voluntary* immigration to slavery: "Coming to the land of Liberty/Where life's design is already made", and the American dream is a delusion. The implications of Whitfield's symphonic soul are taken to radical conclusions here, wherein 'civilisation' itself is a deception. The contrastingly stripped-back psychedelic funk of the album's early 1974 hit 'For the Love of Money' (US 9) is equally radical, depicting capital accumulation's infection of human relations – formally realised by the track's eerily surging, backwards-echoed backing vocals.

The towering commercial and creative force not just of 70s soul but of 70s *music* was Stevie Wonder, who abandoned Motown's Fordism and assimilationism to create music radical in both form and content, achieving crossover success entirely on his own terms. Wonder maximised the potential of minimalism – playing almost everything himself; substituting synthesizers for real instruments – the results as opulent as the Temptations (1973's 'You Are the Sunshine of My Life', UK 7; US 1) and as gritty as Brown. The raw, revelatory, 1973 'Superstition' (UK 11; US 1) offers a systemic depiction of how ideology works through irrational, unconscious means to pacify protest – "Keep me in a daydream" – as effectively as narcotics, because "you don't wanna save me".

Amidst a cinematically shimmering synthscape, fall 1973's 'Living for the City' (UK 15; US 8) condenses the twentieth-century history of African American experience: the segregated South; the Great Migration from country to city; the overpopulated powder keg of the ghetto; the lesser migration from project to prison, with a roiling anger clotting Wonder's usually serene voice by the song's last verse. Epic yet succinct, expansive yet compressed, 'Living for the City' expresses both the long journey and the political immobility of black America. As Wonder put it on summer 1974's 'You Haven't Done Nothin'' (UK 30; US 1), "the nightmare that's becomin' real life" wasn't a rhetorical 'malaise' for black Americans but a material reality. With the Jackson 5 joining the chorus of this funky but furious dismissal of Nixon's political record, black America effectively declares the Fordist state irrelevant. As the song hit the chart, Nixon was forced to resign by the Watergate scandal's revelation of Fordism's authoritarian underside – a fact already all too familiar to the ghettoes. What's notable though, is the *joy* of the song's vocals, united in righteous anger, the production's glamorous gleam butting-up against its ghetto realism, perfectly capturing the 70s' dialectic.

"Green and Quiet": Seven Landscapes of the 70s Pastoral

Although the early 70s' cultural landscape was largely urban, the pastoral didn't disappear, it was just given a popular-modern buff and polish. Mainstream 70s folk would no longer sound fustian, its country-rock no longer be rustic: instead, from singer-songwriters to progressive rock, the pastoral became *glamorous*, spinning out from the sticks into the cities and – in its quest for transcendence – off into outer space.

The counterculture's rural turn resulted in the earthiness of early-70s style, all cheesecloth, patched jeans and patchouli, while musicians, 'getting it together in the country' to write in a Welsh cottage or record in a decaying country house, gave the rural a reflected glamour. Pastoral locations offered a refuge from an increasingly corporate music industry – or from David Geffen, which came to the same thing. However, when Geffen-client Steve Stills hymns a place "Where I'm safe from the city blues/And it's green and it's quiet" on 1972's 'Johnny's Garden' (*Manassas*, US 4), his escape is protected by class privilege: "only trouble was – I had to buy it". On the same album, he declares the countercultural 'Song of Love' to be "empty now".

Political affiliations weren't always so neat, but among the new rock aristocracy it was notable who lived in communes (the Grateful Dead, the Incredible String Band) and who purchased a country pile (Zeppelin's Jimmy Page, the Who's Roger Daltrey); who reasserted this distance between fans and stars in the new, lucrative stadium tours (CSNY, Zeppelin, the Who) and who attempted to reduce that distance (the Dead again, their audience always part of the show). The 70s pastoral captures a political tension between an enduring countercultural radicalism and a contemporary retreat into conservatism. On Carole King's late 1972 'Peace in the Valley' (*Rhymes & Reasons*, US 2), she's caught between her own "selfish" individualism and the "brand-new light" of the collective, the pastoral transcendence that Yes term the 'Heart of the Sunrise' (*Fragile*, UK 7; US 4). This section explores this 70s' pastoral dialectic through seven representative landscapes.

1. The California desert

Having bought a ranch outside San Francisco, Neil Young's 1972 *Harvest* (UK 1; US 1) and its hit, 'Heart of Gold' (UK 10; US 1), were country music slicked by city sessioneers and mellowed by the harmonies of James Taylor, Linda Ronstadt and Crosby, Stills and Nash. Asserting class hierarchy, however, the unalienated 'Old Man' who Young hymns is his employee. Folk-rock trio America's concurrent 'A Horse with No Name' (UK 3; US 1) recalled Young in both sound and sentiment: the tremulous vocal, lush acoustic guitars and smooth harmonies, the horse carrying the alienated narrator into desert peace, where there "ain't no one for to give you no pain". The difference was in ownership: the desert is common land, ranches are private property, and America's CSN-esque 'Ventura Highway' (US 8) transports the listener to a countercultural California with "the free wind blowing through your hair". LA's Doobie Brothers' 1972 'Listen to the Music' (UK 29; US 11) equates the power of the pastoral with that of music – "Meet me in the country for a day/We'll be happy, and we'll dance... our blues away" – while vowing to "retreat and live off the land" in the California wilds of 'Ukiah' (*The Captain and Me*, US 7). With banjos and fiddles slicked by the new ARP synthesizer, the Doobies' fantastic 'Long Train Runnin'' (US 8) is roots music that glistens with glossy popular-modern futurism and analogue glam swagger.

2. The Western plains

Such was the polish of 70s pastoral that even Bob Dylan sounded mellow on 1973 Western *Pat Garrett and Billy the Kid*'s theme-song, 'Knocking on Heaven's Door' (UK 14; US 12), its choral gospel hymnal lending its atomised resignation transcendence. By contrast, the Grateful Dead mined the Old West as a metaphor for their continuing counterculturality – living communally, self-releasing records – while perennially alert to the agents of the law, from Warner Brothers to the police brotherhood. On official bootleg *Europe '72* (US 24) the outstanding outlaw ballad 'Jack Straw' passes the mic between singers like a canteen around a cowboy campfire, and glows accordingly.

Where the Dead's rural hippie outlaws struggled to uphold their freedom in a lawless landscape of primitive accumulation, the Eagles' hip urban cowboys wore their libertarian freedom complacently (hence, 'Peaceful Easy Feeling', US 22). Freed of countercultural idealism – "Lighten up while you still can", they urge on 'Take It Easy' (US 12) – the invocation to "find a place to make your stand" is unrelated to principle. With the

Eagles' lone riders corralled into a posse by homosexual bounty hunter Geffen, there's a link to glam not just in the band's homoeroticism but in the seductiveness of their suave country-rock and the weary vulnerability of their svelte voices. Yet, the Eagles' glamour was the opposite of glam's gender and class provocation, reaffirming heteronormativity, with their outlaw stance increasingly articulating elitist exceptionalism. In true frontier style, government is repression on the title track of the rockier, smoother 1973 *On the Border*, these libertarians "sick and tired of all your law and order" (UK 28; US 17). Concurrently, these lawyered-up outlaws deemed Geffen's accumulation *too* primitive and lighting out for corporate territory with an even *more* ruthless manager, became more urban, more commercial, less country. This, paradoxically, revealed the pioneering spirit of the Old West: greasing up the hicks for flexible accumulation.

3. The Deep South

With the redneck Deep South a no-go zone for hippies, 70s Southern rock isn't commonly regarded as countercultural. Yet the Allman Brothers' assimilation of soul, country and psychedelia (the Donovan-derived 'Mountain Jam' on 1972's *Eat a Peach*, US 4) and their near-mystical veneration of nature ('Blue Sky') suggests a Southern Grateful Dead. The multi-racial, multi-gender cover of summer 1973's *Brothers and Sisters* (US 1) encapsulates the sun-soaked, faded-jeans glamour of the early 70s. Hardly typical Marcusians, Southern rockers connected freedom to their region's wide-open spaces, human nature to organic nature, as on the Allmans' 'Ramblin' Man' (US 2).

Lynyrd Skynyrd's epic 'Free Bird' that same summer (UK 21; US 19), transforms swaggering country-rock chauvinism into a transcendent evocation of liberation. If the plains are presented as a masculine space in which to escape the domesticating feminine – every song on 1973's *Marshall Tucker Band* (US 29) – Skynyrd's tender, longing 'Tuesday's Gone' reverses the paradigm, with a woman who "had to be free" and has "gone with the wind" (*Pronounced 'Lĕh-'nérd 'Skin-'nérd*, US 27). This antebellum invocation proved prescient: on Skynyrd's spring 1974

Second Helping (US 12) the Southern landscape is more parochial: "Take that city hike", they cat-call in 'Swamp Music', fishing for bream as their hound dog catches "coons". In disparaging the metropolitan snobbery they perceive in Young's 'Southern Man', Skynyrd's irresistible 'Sweet Home Alabama' (US 8) appears to celebrate segregationist George Wallace – "the Governor" – as an authentically Southern man, and thus to reaffirm the racial resentments Wallace represented. Again, the 'real' effects a slide from countercultural to conservative across the early 70s.

4. Caledonia

Van Morrison gave his cross-racial, folk-soulful utopianism a local habitation and a name in 'Caledonia'. Music never sounded sunnier than on 1972's *Saint Dominic's Preview* (US 15), an ecstatic Morrison all but speaking in tongues as he growls and roars through his epic, acoustic voyage to utopia, 'Listen to the Lion'. The title track revives the outside folk-observer, gazing down on individualist stasis – "no one making no commitments to anybody but themselves" – before collectively "freedom marching" into liberation: heuristic utopianism at its most graspable and most glorious. By 1973's *Hard Nose the Highway* (UK 22; US 27) Morrison was in retreat, the music slicked by sessioneers, his songs constrained by conventional structures, his once-giddy lyrics grounded, ground down by the 'real'. 'The Great Deception' is Morrison's most regular-sounding and reactionary song, wherein "the plastic revolutionaries take the money and run", thereby blaming the wrong people for the loss of Caledonia, of utopia.

5. Arcadia

An idealised, irrealist pastoral Arcadia provided regular refuge for progressive and heavy rock in this period, sun-dappled folk fusing with fantasy fiction's mythic, medieval landscapes. With 'glamour' etymologically a spell, the magic here isn't prog's reputed faerie feyness, but in the era of *The Wicker Man* (1973), that of nature itself. In evoking a humanity in harmony with the pastoral, the past is used not as escape from the present but as inspiration for the future. That prog's musical and lyrical idealism was subsequently derided as inflationary 70s excess parallels a political cynicism in which 'reality' is always austerity. That ordinary people felt very differently is indicated by the commercial success of this complex, challenging music (e.g. the Moody Blues' 1972 *Seventh Sojourn*, UK 5: US 1).

The tension between rural and urban, past and present, is captured by the album cover of Led Zeppelin's late-1971 *IV* (UK 1; US 2), its brutalist tower blocks and bucolic woodsman coalescing in the album's transcendent centrepiece, 'Stairway to Heaven'. From its ancient Arcadia of forests, brooks and birds, evoked by plucked acoustics and woody recorders, a female-figured nature ("the May Queen") guides the listener into the present, the heavy riffing invoking heavy industry (from 6:44), but rather than overwhelming the pastoral, technology unites with it in a dazzling "white light", "where all is one and one is all". Yes's late 1972 *Close to the Edge* (UK 4; US 3) takes this futuristic pastoral to prog's outer limits – its edge – chiming 12-strings meeting spacey synths, popular music meeting the avant-garde, conventional song-structure shucked off like social convention. That 'edge' is the pastoral's proximity to both enlightenment *and* environmental catastrophe, a cosmic take on the 70s dialectic, a countercultural assertion of Arcadia against capitalist accumulation. Yes's 1973 *Tales from Topographic Oceans* (UK 1; US 6) has come to epitomise prog's – and the period's – excesses, but for all its flaws, it's a valiant attempt to capture a collective "oceanic feeling", to reconnect humans with each other and with nature in an increasingly alienated world.

The pastoral in prog is always pressed, however: even Mike Oldfield's dreamily Arcadian *Tubular Bells*, in summer 1973 (UK 1; US 3), is rudely interrupted by grunting aggression (Part 2, from 11:55–16:30), before transcendence is regained. The sleepy, sunny idyll of the narrator of Genesis's 1973 'I Know What I Like' (UK 21) is persistently disturbed by demands to produce: "There's a future for you in the fire escape trade – come up to town!" In the wake of the Club of Rome's *Limits to Growth*, productivity is presented as destructivity on Genesis's accompanying *Selling England by the Pound* (UK 3). The album's opening folk idyll 'Dancing with the Moonlit Knight' is reprised – repackaged – on the closing 'Aisle of Plenty', where nature's resources are now marked-down *product*, growth shrink-wrapped into a mean, shrunken thing, as the chiming acoustics, mellotron choir and strings yearn for the plenitude of a pastoral Arcadia. Britain joined the Common Market the same year.

Having exemplified prog's lazy English pastoralism, Pink Floyd aimed for American charts and minds with 1973's tense, metropolitan *Dark Side of the Moon* (UK 2; US 1). Ditching acoustic for electric guitars, pianos for synths and adding a panoply of contemporary sound effects (helicopters, trains, clocks, tills), their lyrics were now rooted in the real world – indeed, the crassly materialistic 'Money' (US 13) is deliberately anathema to the hippie ethos: "Grab that cash with both hands and make a stash". Not everyone clocked the satire, but that the album commences with the unalienated Arcadia of the pastoral, pedal-steel-swept 'Breathe (in the Air)', before being systematically assailed by real-world stresses – war, scarcity, overwork, mental illness – reveals the album's concept as being countercultural ideals confronting the 70s' 'real'. Rather than this confrontation being a rout, the album ends with the transcendence of 'Eclipse', an everyday Arcadia where "everything under the sun is in tune", yet where "the sun is eclipsed by the moon". The album thus captures the era's sense of possibilities as well as the forces threatening them.

6. Laurel Canyon

With the egalitarian musical elite lining the LA canyons, nature on their doorstep, the music industry a limo-ride away, the 70s West Coast sound was a liminal space between rural and metropolitan, folk-singer sincerity and city-slicker cynicism, the countercultural and the conservative. Having lived and breathed the 60s, singer-songwriters were children of the revolution, but mostly middle class, they were also the weathervanes of a changing climate. As the 70s corporate turn filled their patched pockets and cocaine became the Canyon's anti-social agent, so theirs became an increasingly scorched pastoral.

Crosby and Nash kept the countercultural faith, continuing as a democratic duo distinct from CSNY's bloated blowout, and on 1972's *Graham Nash, David Crosby* (UK 13; US 4) the sympathy of the pair's voices is an aural affirmation of 60s sociality. Carole

King and James Taylor played benefits for McGovern the same year, while even Paul Simon stumped for "the most left leaning candidate of any major party in the twentieth century".[36] Concurrent with McGovern's defeat in late 1972, Taylor's *One-Man Dog* (UK 27; US 4) turned inward, as its title suggests, into solipsistic whimsy and – pastoral sleeve notwithstanding – a more urban, slickly jazzy sound, as on 'Don't Let Me Be Lonely Tonight' (US 14). This would prove paradigmatic, a way out of folk's sonic enclosure *and* its social engagement. The Canyon scene's solipsism is typified by Carly Simon's 1973 'The Right Thing to Do' (UK 17; US 17), which posits her union with Taylor as a renunciation of 60s ideals – being "just a little too free" – married to an MOR arrangement. Carole King responded to McGovern's defeat with 1973's schmaltzily orchestrated *Fantasy* (US 6), and while 'Welfare Symphony' shows some awareness of a harsher world beyond the cushioned Canyons, King's affirmation of countercultural, universal love in 'Believe in Humanity' (US 28) is half-hearted, hedging that "if I really looked at what's going on/I would lose faith I never could recover".

West Coast rock's landscape became increasingly urban, both iconographically – reflecting the corporatisation of everyday life – and musically. Joni Mitchell's abandonment of folk for jazzy soft rock on early 1974's *Court and Spark* (UK 14; US 2) marked her return to social commentary, the solipsistic cynicism of which matched her new music's air-conditioned urbanity. The social here is *atomising* – listening for her lover's 'Car on a Hill' in her Canyon eyrie, lonely in a coked-up celebrity crowd at 'People's Parties'. On 'Free Man in Paris', Mitchell internalises Geffen's corporate rationalisation, coldly asserting, in her manager and label boss's voice, that "everybody's in it for their own gain". On the frostily lovely 'Down to You', Mitchell laments, "Things that you held high and told yourself were true/Lost or changing as the days come down to you", proclaiming the collapse of collectivist ideals amid the corporate individualism for which her music was now both soliloquy and soundtrack.[37]

"I hear that Laurel Canyon is full of famous stars", Neil Young whines on 1974's coruscating 'Revolution Blues' (*On the Beach*, US 16), "But I hate them worse than lepers, and I'll kill them in their cars". With revolution caricatured here as Young's acquaintance

Charlie Manson's murderousness, such cynicism doesn't betoken any more radicalism than the hippie comrades Young excoriates. Barney Hoskyns' account of cheesecloth revolutionaries becoming silk-draped celebrities leans heavily on a Hobbeisan human nature, with a hefty bump of narcotic determinism. The cultural logic of capitalism – containing, co-opting, monetising, disillusioning and demoralising – gets lost somewhere in the LA smog.[38]

7. Outer Space

Space was the 70s' metonym for the future, when the technological, multicultural utopia of TV staple *Star Trek*, and more mutedly *Dr Who*, still appeared achievable, their alternative worlds accessible. In Billy Preston's instrumentals 'Outa Space' in 1972 (US 2) and 'Space Race' in 1973 (US 4), Deep Purple's 1972 'Space Truckin'' (*Machine Head*, UK 1; US 7) – "rockin' the Milky Way" – and Hawkwind's 1973 space rock 'Silver Machine' (UK 3) and *Space Ritual Alive* (UK 9), technological progress creates a future of automated production and human leisure.

Yet, with Fordism's sci-fi future always a double feature, this period's popular culture was alive to technology's dystopian potential. Roger Dean's cover for Yes's late-1971 *Fragile* depicts a spaceship towing a broken planet, while its hit, 'Roundabout' (US 13), captures the contiguous fragility of nature and mankind: "hold the land, feel partly no more than grains of sand/We stand to lose all time". In *Silent Running* (1972) that catastrophe has occurred, and with earth unable to sustain plant-life, specimens are preserved in a spaceship, technology still possessing utopian potential in dystopia. However, *Soylent Green* (1973) dramatises the danger of endless growth, its dystopia an overcrowded, under-resourced urban landscape. Likewise, on Emerson, Lake & Palmer's early 1974 'Karn Evil 9', untrammelled capitalism has enslaved mankind to computers and rendered nature a museum exhibit (*Brain Salad Surgery*, UK 2; US 11). Bowie's early 1974 *Diamond Dogs* (UK 1; US 5) is the desolate culmination of this urbanisation, the pursuit of growth creating scarcity, survivors scavenging for food and yet, with capitalism's surplus now worthless, dressed literally to kill.[39]

Pastoralism and progressive rock would both soon disappear from popular music and culture. So these tracks represent a last stand in the face of an expanding, urbanising human society, which would ignore ecological warnings and whose ever-faster pace of life would leave no more space to luxuriate in music than in nature.

For all this, 1974 felt like a peak in pop and politics, not an ending. To break the deadlock of the miners' strike and end the three-day week, Heath called an election that spring to answer the question of who ran the country. Contrary to the apocalyptic scenarios of Sandbrook and Turner, the election's confirmation that the working class ran things was an indication of cross-class support of the unions. Despite the narrowness of the result, the victory was the more remarkable for Labour's manifesto being the most radical of any political party in British history. Harold Wilson's new government's promise of "a fundamental and irreversible shift in the balance of wealth and power in favour of working people and their families" represented a radical reformism hitherto unknown in British politics, and which sufficiently alarmed sections of the establishment that plans were made for a military coup.[40] That summer, American politics was in meltdown after the resignation of Nixon, as Watergate revealed the ruthlessly authoritarian nature of the conservative restoration, Vietnam dragged on, and American union militancy hit its highest point since the war, stacking up a staggering 6,074 strikes.

As T. Rex attested, "you won't fool the children of the revolution", as those who'd lived through the hopes of the 60s in relative ease now saw the Fordist guarantees of full employment and a reasonable standard of living beginning to be retracted. The political volatility and the musical creativity of this era are intrinsically connected, pop and politics mixing and matching. The week the Conservatives were defeated by the miners, Britain's chart-topper was Suzi Quatro's rambunctious 'Devil Gate Drive' (UK 1), with its cry of "Knock down the gates/Let me in! Let me in!" Bowie's chiming 'Rebel Rebel', meanwhile, was at UK 5, extolling another female rebel who refuses to abide by authoritarian social rules. Typical top-twenty fodder of the times – all killer, no filler! – these tracks capture the era's structure of feeling: the present is unstable, the future uncertain, but everything is to play for still. Edgerton entitles his 70s chapter 'Possibilities'; Rowbotham's 70s history is dubbed *Daring to Hope*. It was those possibilities, that potential – this hope – that had to be written out of the historical narrative by the austerity-reifying realists who rule us, but which can still be heard in almost every note of this era's music, in all its adversarial ebullience.

Chapter 6

'Take It to the Limit': Disco, Soft Rock and Soft Politics (1974–77)

The 70s got soft in the middle. The splayed collars, sagging flares and drooping moustaches of mid-70s fashion matched its overripe soft rock, saccharine MOR and decadent disco – as well as its ineffectual politics and inflated economy. An enervated excess infuses this interregnum – 'Take It to the Limit', as the era's archetypal act, the Eagles, wearily advised in 1975 (UK 12; US 4). Yet rather than *pushing* limits, both the song and the mid-70s were all about *hitting* limits: to innovation, as technocratic projects like Britain's Maplin airport were grounded and popular music entered a holding pattern; and to post-war growth, as Western economies stagnated. This era also hit the limits of social democracy, as Harold Wilson's Social Contract secured union pay restraint but not economic recovery, and Gerald Ford, the last Fordist president, failed to make an impression on anything or anyone.[1] Given the right's constant narrative of 'crisis', the social contract (without capitals) – between state, citizens and capital – became a central concern in this era's pop and popular culture, whether complained about, clung to, or, ultimately, canned. Consequently, while too flaccid to be a pivot, this period, like all interregna, has an historical importance and ideological intricacy that transcends its superficially bland surface.

Soft rock was the mid-70s' meta-form, enveloping every genre – even *heavy* rock – with its layered comforts: 'Rock Me Gently' as Andy Kim put it in fall 1974 (UK 2; US 1). For this was the soporifically seductive era of America's 1975 'Sister Golden Hair' (US 1) and Chicago's 1976 'If You Leave Me Now' (UK 1; US 1). While soft rock's plush sonics were inflationary, its sentiments were recessionary: "Some became disenchanted/ And some of us just got scared", Carly Simon confesses on 1975's *Playing Possum* (US 10). Soft rock charted the counterculture's commute to the conventional, as former hippies prioritised the mortgage and the office – what their younger selves had called 'the system'. "All those dayglo freaks who used to paint the face/ They've joined the human race", observed Steely Dan on 1976's 'Kid Charlemagne' (*The Royal Scam*, UK 11; US 15).

With Richard Dawkins' *The Selfish Gene* (1976) establishing the family as an extension of individualism,[2] the social now contracted into the domestic – 'You and Me Against the World', as Helen Reddy's sickly 1974 MOR hit had it (US 9) – the utopian into legal union. Bryan Ferry's 1976 cover of Wilbert Harrison's 'Let's Stick Together' (UK 4) avows, "The marriage vow is very sacred". Heart's 1976 'Crazy on You' (*Dreamboat Annie*, US 7) makes this social contraction explicit: in "a world cryin' in pain.../What you gonna do when everybody's insane?" You're gonna retreat to the private, with the abandon of Ann Wilson's vocal bounded by the elegant upholstery of the track's immaculate production.

The music of this era all *sounds* gorgeous, but the new 24-track technology produced technocratic proficiency rather than technical progress – *The Who by Numbers* (UK 7; US 8) was hardly a statement of creative innovation – just as placeholder Ford and former moderniser Wilson were ship-steadying preservationists. Ford held the Reaganite right at bay, Wilson the unions and the Bennite left, all notion of "a fundamental shift in the balance of wealth and power" abandoned. If such stagnation was some distance from a social-democratic utopia, it was an even greater distance from the 'nightmare 70s' of conservative myth. With the adversarial sidelined politically, this period's safe, sanded-down pop isn't simply the sound of resignation, but of *contentment*, of flock wallpaper, shag-pile carpets, bunk beds and Spanish holidays. This contentment is audible in Pussycat's 1975 Europop-country 'Mississippi' (UK 1), Paul Anka's 'Times of Your Life' (US 7) – "Collect the dreams you dream today" – and husband-and-wife Captain & Tennille's electric-piano-suffused affirmation of fidelity, 'Love Will Keep Us Together' (US 1).

Despite the right's restiveness, such conventional conservatism was a direct consequence of Fordism. Wholesome fare like the *Captain & Tennille TV Show* and Osmonds' spin-off *The Donny and Marie Show* gobbled up American TV schedules with bulimic blandness. With the Osmonds' beguiling 1974 'Love Me for a Reason' (UK 1; US 10) asserting primly, "I'm just a little old-fashioned/It takes more than a physical attraction", such adult sentiments in teen culture contradict any conception that pop was merely maturing with its audience. Rather, such moralism represented a bulwark against 'permissiveness', defined by Edgerton as the breaching of "the boundary between public and private".[3] Ray Stevens' irksome 1974 country novelty 'The Streak' (UK 1; US 1) captures this trespass of the private upon public space, the titular streaker personifying the counterculture as narcissistic, immature and individualistic. With Pink Floyd caricaturing the moral limit-setting of campaigner Mary Whitehouse on early 1977's 'Pigs' – "Gotta stem the evil tide/And keep it all on the inside" (*Animals*, UK 2; US 3) – repression was integral to the right's restoration of social standards.

The adult orientation of this era's music also tracked the times via a topic less amenable to conservatives: following 60s' liberalisations, marriage was declining and divorce increasing, becoming an unlikely source of some of the period's best music. In 1975 alone, Dylan's blistering, bitter 'Idiot Wind' (*Blood on the Tracks*, UK 4; US 1), Tammy Wynette's kitchen-sink country re-release 'D-I-V-O-R-C-E' (UK 12) and even its pathetic Billy Connolly parody (UK 1) all testified less to the joy of liberation than the fear of atomisation, the marriage contract here serving as a synecdoche for the fraying *social* contract. On ABBA's gnawing, early-1977 'Knowing Me, Knowing You' (UK 1; US 14), the bureaucratic chill of synths pulls against the human warmth of acoustic guitars, the unknown quantity of post-Fordism looming over the cosy familiarity of Fordism. "No more carefree laughter/ Silence ever after". As the longest recession since the war began to impose limits on people's daily lives, this was registered by the rising store prices on Wings' autumn 1974 'Junior's Farm' (UK

16; US 3) and the empty pockets of the "ordinary guy" in Philly soulsters the Stylistics' 1975 'Can't Give You Anything (But My Love)' (UK 1).

With the constant narrative of crisis an exhausting business, the charts were full of sleepy lethargy and idle dreams: as with the early 60s, this was the reflux of repression, the sound of limits being internalised. On Scottish soft-rockers Pilot's autumn 1974 'Magic' (UK 11; US 5), the disengaged narrator lazes alone in bed, to "dream of far away". Swaddled in a production soft as eiderdown, the lover in the Eagles' ballad 'Best of My Love' (US 1) "would be all right/If I could go on sleeping", whereas "every day I wake up and worry/What's gonna happen today". The subject of prog-poppers Supertramp's electric-piano-drenched 1975 'Dreamer' (UK 13) is stuck, immobilised; as is the recluse in Ozark Mountain Daredevils' 1975 'Jackie Blue' (US 3), who "lives a dream that can never come true".

Despite its futuristic synth-suffusion, Gary Wright's dreamy 1975 'Dream Weaver' (US 2) has abandoned the utopian for contemporary comfort: "Take away my worries of today/And leave tomorrow behind". The production on Boston's 1976 'More Than a Feeling' (UK 22; US 5), meanwhile, processes heavy-rock aggression into a soft-rock cocoon: "I close my eyes and I drift away". The "crystal visions" of Fleetwood Mac's gorgeous early 1977 'Dreams' (UK 24; US 1) are too fragile to share – "I keep my visions to myself", Stevie Nicks purrs, her hippie-chick image the haunt of a fading counterculture. 'This Ain't the Summer of Love', as once-heavy-rockers Blue Oyster Cult curtly put it, while their serenely morbid '(Don't Fear) The Reaper' cast its sleepy spell over 1976's charts (UK 16; US 11).

Rather than being a return of Gramsci's morbid symptoms, or an indicator of the end times summoned in Turner and Sandbrook's accounts, this interregnum's music occupies a liminal space between contentment and resignation, optimism and apprehension. "Faking my way through", as Peter Frampton put it on 'Wind of Change' from his stadium soft-rock smash *Frampton Comes Alive* (UK 6; US 1). Despite departing the cock-rock camaraderie of Humble Pie to go solo in an increasingly individualistic age, Frampton articulated a common structure of feeling here – that these were transitional times.

"More More More": Disco, Desire and Politics

As the recession kicked in, dancing at discotheques offered a cheap escape from toughening times, and the disco genre emerged from a resultant demand for upbeat, danceable music. In stripping away funk's syncopation, disco's relentless four-to-the-floor beat was expressive of economic contraction, while, strained of soul's grit, its extravagant instrumental accoutrement was a defiance of the downturn. There was defiance, too, in disco's flashy costumery, its slashed-open shirts and gold medallions, its spangly spandex pants and sequins. Despite Gilbert and Lawrence's claims,[4] chart disco purged conscious soul's political content, while, despite originating in black and gay communities, its removal of funk's rhythmic otherness made it a cinch for white and straight people to 'get down' to.

Disco-Tex and the Sex-O-Lettes' late 1974 'Get Dancin'' (UK 8; US 10) makes of disco's functionality a philosophy: "You can't think of all the wrong... of the world.../You just get out, get dancing". Former psychedelic soulsters Earth, Wind & Fire's 1976 'Saturday Nite' (UK 17; US 21) hymns the opportunity to "gather round in hope, to feel safe and sound", and forget "our stumbling nation". Also in 1976, the Jacksons warn, "You shouldn't worry about things you can't control" on 'Enjoy Yourself' (US 6). Once the conscience of conscious soul, Marvin Gaye, on early 1977's 'Got to Give it Up' (UK 7; US 1) proselytises, "Let's dance, and shout/That's what it's all about" – interspersed with whoops. For all its declarative energy, this period's disco was politically enervated, its beats per minute besting revolutions per minute.

Indeed, despite disco's intrinsic sociality, its sentiments tended to be individualistic, to opt out of the social contract. (Self-) defensively, Carl Douglas's huge-selling autumn 1974 'Kung Fu Fighting' (UK 1; US 1) posits individual success as a corrective to collective failure: "Be your own hero", because "the future is a little bit frightening". George McCrae's promo clip for 1974's delightful 'Rock Your Baby' (UK 1; US 1) frames the singer as an individual *star*, the musicians invisible, a presentation that would become paradigmatic in disco promos, as on Gloria Gaynor's glorious 1975 'Never Can Say Goodbye' (UK 2; US 9). Likewise, despite their countercultural image, Earth, Wind & Fire's 1975 'Shining Star' (US 1) – "Found I had to stand alone" – and 'Sing a Song' (US 5) – "Give yourself what you need" – are both carols to competitive individualism.

Even disco's recessionary attenuation of content had an individualist bent. After MFSB's 'TSOP' – whose entire lyric runs "Let's get it on/It's time to get down" (UK 22; US 1) – the content of Average White Band's 1974 'Pick Up the Pieces' (UK 6; US 1) is its title, followed by Van McCoy's 1975 'The Hustle' repeating "Do it!" (UK 3; US 1) and Silver Convention's 1976 Euro-disco chant 'Get Up and Boogie' (UK 7; US 2) (intermittently adding, "That's right"). Such contraction *is* content, however, this repetitive imperative being an assertion of pure id, spelled out on People's Choice's 1975 'Do It Any Way You Wanna' (US 11) and KC and the Sunshine Band's grating 'That's the Way I Like It' the same year (UK 4; US 1). On KC's 1975 'Get Down Tonight' (UK 21; US 1), the id's imperative is specifically sexual ("Do a little dance/Make a little love"), while Barry White's imprecations became increasingly carnal between 1974's 'Can't Get Enough of Your Love, Babe' (UK 8; US 1) and early 1975's stamina-attesting 'What Am I Gonna Do With You?' (UK 5; US 8). Donna Summer's fall 1975 'Love to Love You Baby' (UK 4; US 2) matches eight lines of lyrics to 16 stamina-testing minutes of groaning and grinding, announcing the arrival of the 12" single. With Diana Ross's 1976 disco conversion, 'Love Hangover' (UK 10; US 1), the sexiest she would ever get, libidinal disco became increasingly literal. Ohio Players deployed soft-porn sleeves on hits like 1976's 'Love Rollercoaster' (US 1), while Andrea True was an *actual* porn actress, whose 'More More More' (UK 5; US 4) makes a business of pleasure, with its knowing invocation to "get the cameras rolling".

Marcuse calls this capitalist co-option of desire "repressive desublimation",[5] whereby public acknowledgement of a repressed urge redirects and reduces it to the commodity form, rendering consumption erotic and sex a consumer item. Desublimation also reframes desire as consent rather than refusal, removing its unruliness. Disco was but one example, however, with sex now suffusing soul balladry like Roberta Flack's late-1974 'Feel Like Makin' Love' (US 1) and Major Harris' coercive 1975 'Love

Won't Let Me Wait' (US 5), complete with female shudders. Sex glommed onto the remnants of glam, with Roxy Music's 1975 'Love Is the Drug' (UK 2; US 30) tautly wound around a funk bassline and dogged disco beat, depicting sex less as narcotic than as performance principle: "The locked embrace/The stumble round". Priapic heavy rock was primed for repressive desublimation, thus Bad Company's creepy 'Feel Like Makin' Love' (UK 20; US 10) and Aerosmith's sleazy early-1977 'Walk This Way' (US 10). Even MOR revealed a new randiness, as on Starland Vocal Band's 1976 nudge-nudge 'Afternoon Delight' (UK 18; US 1) and Alan O'Day's disco ballad 'Undercover Angel' (US 1), with its sexy Moog squelches. For all the conservative complaints about permissiveness, the liberation of the id here is *anti*-countercultural, a prioritisation of individual over collective desire, *Eros* shrunk to the erotic, utopia confined to the bedroom.

That pop's libidinality should intersect with a fetishisation of automation at this historical moment is arresting: the Jackson 5's 1974 'Dancing Machine' (US 2) is "automatic, systematic"; the Smokey-free Miracles' 1975 'Love Machine' (UK 3; US 1) claims, "I'm not that hard to program... turn me on... set my dial"; and then there was the phenomenon of Bryan Ferry. Automation, libidinality and service-orientation were all facets of a new, post-Fordist capitalism reorganising in response to the 60s' cultural revolution, the 70s' industrial revolt and international competition – a 'flexible accumulation' that paradoxically represented a new rigidity, a setting of further limits.

"Go Your Own Way": The Individual and Society

Just as no one represented the collectivity of the 60s better than the Beatles, so did their mid-70s solo activities track the shift from countercultural sociality to conventional 'society'. Lennon's late-1974 'Whatever Gets You thru the Night' (US 1), with the era's spirit guide, Elton John, is a sax-slicked, soft-rock/disco frivolity that celebrates self-indulgence in semi-hippie terms, thereby trailing Lennon's abandonment of politics on *Walls and Bridges* (UK 6; US 1). McCartney's 1975 'Listen to What the Man Said' (UK 6; US 1) similarly uses sax-appeal and disco drive to encourage listeners to "leave behind a tragic world" and embrace the "wonder of it all – baby". With Wings always subsidiary to husband-and-wife-team Paul and Linda, 1976's even more discofied 'Silly Love Songs' (UK 2; US 1) affirms the personal with a new piety that would become McCartney's metier ("What's wrong with that?"). With the song being McCartney's response to Lennon's critique of his lack of content, that fact that it became McCartney's fifth US chart-topper prompted a piqued Lennon to abandon music altogether, contracting Ono to match Macca's fortune through venture capitalism instead. From countercultural rebels to capitalist competitors, this represents the most dispiriting political trajectory in pop history.[6]

Even silly love songs reveal social structures of feeling, however, with the form's mid-70s iteration increasingly contractual and anti-social. On 10cc's stunning 1975 ballad 'I'm Not in Love' (UK 1; US 2), the intricately detailed production's technocratic coldness is rubber-stamped by the narrator's fact-checking fussiness, as he bloodlessly belittles his lover to assert his independence – her picture covering a "nasty stain"; their affair a dirty secret she can't confide to her friends.[7] If the track's production is an inflationary Fordist blowout, its sentiments are recessionary, a retreat to a small, mean individualism, which, contrary to critical consensus, appears entirely sincere. The production on Paul Simon's 1976 '50 Ways to Leave Your Lover' (UK 23; US 1) similarly lends sonic warmth to affective coldness, as Simon ponders how best to divest his emotional investment. In Al Stewart's summer 1976 'Year of the Cat' (US 8), set in one of the era's many exotic locations, the currency of the mysterious "incense and patchouli" hippie chick is devalued by the transient traveller's emotional offshoring ("you know sometime you're bound to leave her"). Foreigner's heavy-rock heat, meanwhile, is cooled with layers of soft-rock synths, adding to the chill of early 1977's 'Cold as Ice' (UK 24; US 6), whose frozen-out lover gives as good as he gets, frostily promising, "Someday you'll pay the price".

In reifying individualism, these songs repudiate the social contract. Marcuse warned that "the entirely premature immediate identification of private [with] social freedom creates tranquilizing rather than radicalizing conditions and leads to withdrawal from the political universe in which, alone, freedom can be attained".[8]

Mid-70s music often positions such individualism as a rejection of 'society' in Adorno's – and the counterculture's – sense of the mechanism that subsumes individuals into the system.[9] Greg Lake's 1975 'I Believe in Father Christmas' (UK 2) conjures up the "fairy story" he's been "sold" – religion; state promises of "peace on earth" – with its inflationary choirs, sleigh bells and Prokofiev orchestration exemplifying the Fordist promise of plenty. Yet the piety of an all-seeing 'I' against a shadowy 'they' conflates citizenry and state in hipster condescension towards a public holiday. This is the problem with negative conceptions of 'society' – the concept gets collapsed into 'the social' (as in the 'social contract') and thus prioritises the individual over the collective.

The spurned fiancée in Elton John's expensively appointed 1975 ballad, 'Someone Saved My Life Tonight' (UK 22; US 4) represents a "haunted social scene", a suburban conventionality from which the narrator demands liberation to "run the field and play alone". In Queen's recession-busting blowout 'Bohemian Rhapsody' (UK 1; US 9), society is a literal prison, as the establishment condemns the protagonist: "Bismillah! We will not let you go!" Following this operatic orgy, Mercury's voice vaults free in the track's heavy-riffing finale, expressing a defiantly individualist liberation: "gotta get right out of here". That both these songs codedly concern their singers' homosexuality renders their anti-societal sentiments sympathetic, a rejection of heteronormativity. Yet Mercury's refusal to divulge the meaning of 'Bohemian' – making it thus the self-pitying plaint of a murderer – and John's insistence that 'Someone' concerns a suicide attempt – making it merely misogynist ("You almost had your hooks in me, didn't you dear?") – means these songs are scribbles on the closet wall, effectively assertions of privacy. Concurrently, the Jeremy Thorpe gay-sex scandal revealed the lengths some would go to protect such privacy. Credit therefore to the solidarity of John and Mercury's straight chum Rod Stewart, whose 1976 'Killing of Georgie' (UK 2; US 30) is a direct – even gauche – depiction of homophobia as a socially produced phenomenon, while still upholding the social contract: "Georgie was a friend of mine, oh yeah".

The concept of the social, then, is being tested and contested in this era, communicating itself in competing ways, not least the marked use of the mythic register in breakup songs. "Where are those happy days?/They seem so hard to find", ABBA sigh on 1975's 'SOS' (UK 6; US 15), its sonic sumptuousness enhancing its affective austerity. The downbeat blue-eyed soul of Hall & Oates' 1976 'She's Gone' (US 7) finds the abandoned lover socially atomised, haunted by the past, the production's eeriness offset by the solidaristic warmth of the duo's vocal interplay.

The sundering unions documented on Fleetwood Mac's *Rumours* (UK 1; US 1) are a synecdoche for a fracturing society in the aftermath of the 60s. Buckingham's stunning 'Go Your Own Way' (US 10) is a cynical appraisal of countercultural freedom – "Packin' up, shackin' up's all you wanna do" – gauzed in the final glimmer of 12-string folk-rock. Nicks' 'Gold Dust Woman' presages a more materialist, individualist world, while the forced cheer of Christine McVie's celebration of such a tomorrow on the dreadful 'Don't Stop' (US 3) isn't just a kiss-off to bassist husband, John, but to the counterculture: "Yesterday's gone... don't you look back". Throughout *Rumours*, the lavishness of the production expresses a utopianism that its lyrics simultaneously deny and mourn, but like almost all the music detailed here, the affect is less aggravated than enervated, a resigned embrace of limits.

"It's a Rich Man's World": Stars and the Social Contract

As capitalism globalised and the music industry corporatised, pop's superstars became increasingly distant from their fans, taking it to the limit in lifestyle, fashion and production costs. Cocaine audibly flows through mid-70s' music's sonic precision, yet the elite's fondness for an expensive, individualist drug amidst a recession is an *effect* rather than a cause of their social distance. As an analytic line, narcotic determinism floats free of the social sphere: the accumulation of capital and property can offload class consciousness and social conscience very efficiently – though sometimes it's useful to have a stiffener. Moreover, this cokey coldness is continually offset with a contemporary warmth, reflecting the period's cultural ambivalence.

Queen's autumn 1974 'Killer Queen' (UK 2; US 12) runs with Bowie's showtune rock, yet it celebrates the high life – "*naturally*" – without a hint of glam's parody of privilege. The song's pampered subject is a Marie Antoinette who "couldn't care less" for the recession, but still manages to charm. While supposedly self-satirising, Elton John's claim on the contemporaneous 'The Bitch is Back' (UK 15; US 4) that "times are changing now the poor get fat" is at best insensitive. In glam's end-times decadence, meanwhile, there's no performative distance from the aristocratic effervescence of Sailor's splendid 1975 'A Glass of Champagne' (UK 2): "I've got position, I've got the name", they chortle. Given Frampton's claim of consuming "champagne for breakfast", the public's answer to his 1976 hit's question 'Do You Feel like We Do' (US 10), was seemingly a 'yes'. ABBA's disco-driven delight, 1976's 'Money, Money, Money' (UK 3) offers superstar empathy to the economically pressed ("I work all night, I work all day/ To pay the bills I have to pay"), yet still seeks its solutions in the wealthy's citadels: winning in Monaco or in marriage, an exclusivity matched by the plushness of the track's roulette-wheel xylophones and neon-glimmering synths.

Elite disengagement from the social contract resulted in an unedifying resentment towards taxation, as on Loggins and Messina's fall 1974 'Changes' (*Mother Lode*, US 8), while the title of Rod Stewart's 1975 *Atlantic Crossing* (UK 1; US 9) celebrates his American exile to escape Labour's 83% high-earner tax rate. This repudiation of social responsibility was contiguous with a craven commerciality, Stewart jettisoning the Faces' proletarian heavy rock for jet-set soft rock, the smoothness of *Atlantic*'s hit, 'Sailing' (UK 1), seeming like a celebration of yacht ownership as much as a yearning for collective communion.[10] At live shows, Led Zeppelin dedicated 1975's 'In My Time of Dying' (*Physical Graffiti*, UK 1; US 1) to British Chancellor Denis Healey, decrying the progressive taxation of their earnings as expropriation, while fleecing the song's uncredited composer, Blind Willie Johnson.

Progressive rock was always an expression of Fordist plenty, but as the recession bit, its excess appeared in increasingly poor taste, morally and musically. Not content with a mere choir and orchestra, Rick Wakeman staged his unlistenable 1975 extravaganza, *The Myths and Legends of King Arthur and the Knights of the Round Table* (UK 2; US 21) *on ice* at Wembley Arena, sticking two fat fingers up at recessionary restraint. To tour their 1977 double album, *Works Vol. 1* (UK 9; US 12), tax-exiles Emerson, Lake & Palmer didn't just take along a choir and orchestra like any *normal* prog act, they also took a tour bus *per member*. On stage Emerson stuck knives into vintage Hammond organs, Lake performed on a priceless Persian carpet, and Palmer rotated the stage on a customised drum-riser.

The period's ultimate celebrity solipsism was a recurring griping about fame, from Carole King's 1975 'Nightingale' (US 9) – "Those spotlight shadows, how they lured him/And took him like all the rest" – to Bad Company's 'Shooting Star' the same year (*Straight Shooter*, UK 3; US 3). It wasn't merely ironic that Bowie's plaint about success, 1975's 'Fame' (UK 17; US 1), should become his American commercial breakthrough: the presence of Lennon in superstar solidarity and the grit-toothed grind of its guitar-riff suggest a determined pursuit of this poisoned prize. Barely had hearts stopped bleeding before Black Sabbath's 'The Writ' (*Sabotage*, UK 7; US 28) and Queen's 'Death on Two Legs' (*A Night at the Opera*, UK 1; US 4) were spitting bile at mercenary managers. While this is a *kind* of critique of capitalism, in being presented as individual venality versus individual virtue ("You suck my blood like a leech… you've taken all my money"), it's an assertion of the *literally* contractual, with little of the social left to account for.

As befitted a liberal democracy, there were regular attempts to cross the class divide and suggest that economic success was accessible to all. Yet Eddie Kendricks telling his 1975 'Shoeshine Boy' (US 18) that he'll "reach the top" and become a "star" sounds as hollow as the music, disco having taken the shine off soul as inflation took the shine off wages. Glen Campbell's radiant 1975 country/MOR 'Rhinestone Cowboy' (UK 4; US 1) frames success as a question of individual grit, its vaulting melody making aspiration material. Elton John's autobiographical, recession-busting 1975 *Captain Fantastic and the Brown Dirt Cowboy* (UK 2; US 1) similarly emphasises graft as the path to success, while Bill Conti's cheesy early 1977 *Rocky* theme, 'Gonna Fly Now' (US 1), keeps repeating, "Tryin' hard now", as if that were all it took to succeed. By contrast, this period's crime-caper pop actually seems more sympathetic. Steve Miller Band's 1976 'Take the Money and Run' (US 11) and Boz Scaggs' delightful early 1977 'Lido Shuffle' (UK 13; US 11) both depict ordinary people attempting antisocial shortcuts to a capitalist plenty no longer achievable by conventional means. The working-class couple on Alice Cooper's 1977 'You and Me' (US 9) have accepted this contraction of expectation, however: "You and me ain't no movie stars/What we are is what we are".

For all this, there were still examples aplenty of expansive sociality in this era. Depicting life on the road, Slade's blistering late-1974 ballad 'Far Far Away' (UK 2), is a riposte to celebrity solipsists: instead of having his "head up in the clouds", Holder has his "feet down in the crowds".[11] Billy Preston's fall 1974 'Nothing from Nothing' (US 1) asserts, "I'm a soldier in the war on poverty", its vocabulary pointed amid right-wing denigration of the Great Society.[12] Despite its Mantovani strings and heavenly choir, Ralph McTell's contemporaneous 'Streets of London' (UK 2) is a revival of folk's social observation, challenging middle-class exceptionalism ("How can you tell me you're lonely/And say for you that the sun don't shine?") to insist on an interconnection with society's marginalised.

Following CSNY's stadium blowout, Crosby & Nash's fall 1975 *Wind on the Water* (US 6) reaffirms countercultural ideals, expressing racial solidarity on 'Field Worker' – "Treat me like a human" – and collectivism on 'Love Work Out', with fellow faith-keeper Jackson Browne: "Before you get you got to give". The Commodores' 1975 soul ballad 'Sweet Love' (US 5) yearns for "a little peace and understanding", the condition of which is collectivity: "Together we can make a way". Even in the conservative medium of MOR, two 1976 songs assert music as the medium of sociality. On Barry Manilow's 'I Write the Songs' (US 1), his melodies "make the whole world sing", while on Neil Diamond's nostalgic 'Beautiful Noise' (UK 13), what inspires the Brill Building's writers is the sound "coming up from the street" – the "beautiful noise" is people. That there is still a sense of limits, however, is apparent in the sociality in these songs being passively serene where once it was joyfully adversarial.

"Getting Tougher Every Day": Fordism, Class and Counterculture

If this period's comedy, *Whatever Happened to the Likely Lads?* (1973–74) and police drama *The Sweeney* (1975–78) revealed the impact of the right's running anti-Fordist rhetoric, this still operated in dialectic with the working-class confidence curated by Fordism. Ken Loach's BBC series *Days of Hope* (1975) – set between 1916 and 1926 – and *When the Boat Comes In* (1976–81) – 1919–36 – historicised this Fordist confidence as forged through class struggle. Amid the politeness of this era's popular music, Status Quo's repetitive 1974 'Down Down' (UK 1) is a rousingly impertinent interruption, while the Who's smutty 1976 'Squeeze Box' (UK 10; US 16) is a welcome incursion of music-hall mores on middle-class sophistication. The mythic presentation of the gang's fucking and fighting on Thin Lizzy's barnstorming 1976 'The Boys Are Back in Town' (UK 8; US 12) is matched by the epic grandeur of its twin-guitar aggression. A similar plebeian pugilism is audible in Aerosmith, the hero of whose 1976 'Last Child' (US 21) has his "Hands on the plow/And my feets in the ghetto" (*Rocks*, US 3).

Nevertheless, with British and American governments applying limits to labour rather than capital – Wilson's wage freeze ensuring pay trailed inflation; Ford's approach being "help the rich, compel the poor to work harder"[13] – a sense of a class under pressure is also tangible. In the haunting country/soft rock of Michael Murphey's 1975 'Wildfire' (US 3), the titular horse is a means of escape: "We're gonna leave sodbustin' behind/Get these hard times right on out of our minds". The widescreen production of Bruce Springsteen's 1975 *Born to Run* (UK 17; US 3) professes proletarian aspiration, represented, in the era of *Badlands* (1973) and *Thieves Like Us* (1974), by the promise of the open road, with the couple vowing they'll leave their recessionary "town full of losers" on 'Thunder Road' and be "pulling out of here to win". On 'Born to Run' itself (US 23), the lower-class "tramps" long to escape their deindustrialised, "death-trap" town, full of resentful kids trying to look hard, while neurotically circling the city limits in their hot rods. Yet the song's nostalgia for the Long 50s, and the vagueness of its utopian vision – "someday", he doesn't know when, they'll "get to the place where we really wanna go", wherever that is – suggests its protagonists are as stuck as their peers "huddled on the beach in the mist". The *desire*, however – the expectation, the Fordist dream – is real. Economics pressing its limits on an ingrained utopianism is what gives *Born to Run* its burn, its inspirational spur. An aggressive frustration at these limits regularly bursts through the production's grandiosity: the garage-band filth of Springsteen's guitar on 'Thunder Road'; his yelled "1-2-3-4" before the final verse of 'Born to Run' (3:04) – one of the most wall-punching moments in popular music.

The reminiscing revolutionaries on ABBA's 1976 folkie fireside sing-along 'Fernando' (UK 1; US 13) "never thought that we could lose" but did. Yet as Traverso attests, the struggle inspires hope for the future, and the rebels promise, "If I had to do the same again/I would my friend". Although the addition of Michael McDonald's tremulous falsetto sanded down the Doobies' rawer, rustic edges, 1976's 'Takin' It to the Streets' (US 13) articulates a forthright urban toughness: demanding that the other "raised in poverty's despair" be recognised as a "brother", with its title line ambiguous – a riot, a demonstration? – but obviously adversarial. The everyman on Steve Miller's concurrent 'Rock'n Me' (UK 11; US 1) is "tryin' to find a job/But it just keeps getting tougher every day". While the times aren't so good for goodtime rock, the narrator is defiantly optimistic about his prospects, articulating this in social terms: "I got to do my part".

Queen's 1976 'Somebody to Love' (UK 2; US 13) is 'A Hard Day's Night' a decade on. With no social recompense now for working "til I ache in my bones", no amelioration for alienation in a failing economy, the narrator is as atomised as he is exhausted. Yet the vocal interplay between Mercury and his bandmates – echoing, sympathising, *intervening* – is an implicit reaffirmation of Fordist collectivism against the conservative revival of rugged individualism. The mythic register of blue-collar rocker Bob Seger's nostalgic 1976 'Night Moves' (US 4) suggests its tale of early-60s young love is a synecdoche. That the pair "weren't searchin' for some pie-in-the sky summit" parallels the Fordist compromise, posited as a social contract ("We were getting our share") but capturing the era's overwhelming optimism – "oh the wonder!" The acoustic bridge brilliantly effects a jump-cut to the recessionary present, when these modest desires seem ungraspably utopian and "you just don't have as much to lose", when limits have been set upon expectation. Yet that "oh the wonder!" does a lot of work here: a testament and affirmation of realisable desire, not just of individuals but of a class.

Responding to the industry's corporatisation, 70s pop showed an increasing awareness of its part in the capitalist system. David Essex's *Stardust* (1975) depicts an atomised "rock'n'roll clown", in the words of its brilliantly doomy theme-song (UK 7), who's ruthlessly manipulated by capitalist ringmasters. While, musically, Pink Floyd track the period's enervated mellowness on 1975's *Wish You Were Here* (UK 1; US 1), lyrically, it's distinctly acerbic. 'Have a Cigar' mocks the music industry's moneymen, while 'Welcome to the Machine' presents pop stardom as being processed by the system, Dave Gilmour's vulnerable vocal and delicate acoustic guitar gradually engulfed by the cold, whirring thrum of Rick Wright's corporate synth-bank.

With state corruption revealed both by Watergate and 1975's Church Commission into the CIA and FBI, the line "Forget it, Jake, it's Chinatown" has become paradigmatic of a 70s cynicism. Yet Jack Nicholson's detective in Polanski's *Chinatown* (1974) is defeated *because* he's a lone wolf, while, the same year, Pakula's *The Parallax View* and Coppola's *The Conversation* similarly depict atomised individuals defeated by corporate power. 70s cynicism thus itself becomes a reaffirmation of sociality. Moreover, despite the defeat of the musicians by the moneymen in Slade's *Flame* feature film (1975), the band's attitude still reads as refusal: "Every haunt has a hustler an' bustler with the tongue of a snake", Holder spits on 'Them Kinda Monkeys Can't Swing' (*Flame*, UK 6). For all the system's manipulations in *Network* (1976), its core is the collective cry, "I'm as mad as hell, and I'm not going to take this anymore!"

Behind all this lay not Fordism's failure but its *success*, as capital reorganised in reaction to proletarian power, deindustrialising, automating and offshoring in pursuit of the lower wages and production costs for which 'post-Fordism' is a name. Yet the desires had been triggered, the expectations raised – and wouldn't be so readily repressed. Even as it narrowed options for the working class, post-Fordism created opportunities for the *middle* class, flexible white-collar work expanding at the expense of regulated blue-collar work. This development was combined and uneven, but you can already hear it in the father who's too busy for his child in Harry Chapin's winter 1974 MOR saga 'Cat's in the Cradle' (US 1), in the lover hustling to keep up with his lover's consumerism and his colleagues' success in a "dog-eat-dog existence" on Scaggs' jazzy 1976 'Lowdown' (UK 28; US 3) and in the "people living in competition" and trying to "climb to the top of the company ladder" on Boston's 'Peace of Mind' (*Boston*, UK 11; US 3). This is some distance from the middle-class squeeze described by Turner, who accepts the conservative 'crisis' as a material rather than ideological issue, bruited amongst a nervy bourgeoisie.[14]

These unusual topics for pop songs indicate the cultural and political changes in progress, presciently captured by Jackson Browne on the title track of 1976's *The Pretender* (UK 26; US 5). Browne's businessman protagonist recalls the collective utopianism of the 60s – "the changes we waited for love to bring" – abandoned now for the individualist "paint-by-number dreams" of careers and consumerism: the setting of limits. Yet, like Scaggs' and Boston's protagonists, the pretender's heart isn't in this "struggle for the legal tender". So despite the track being accoutred with comforting soft-rock keyboards and a seductive disco undertow, Crosby and Nash's unmistakable harmonies hauntologically pull back to the hippie past, articulating a collective loss as "the ships bearing their dreams sail out of sight".

Always more acute than they're accredited, Browne's friends the Eagles offer a more jaded version of the same journey on early 1977's 'Hotel California' (UK 8; US 1). With the hotel representing the Californian dream, all that remains of the counterculture now is hedonism ("the pink champagne on ice") and libidinality (the "pretty, pretty boys" dancing in the courtyard; the production's sensory overload). Consumerism now stands in for utopianism (the "Tiffany twisted" heroine; her Mercedes-Benz), while competitive individualism has replaced the 60s' adversarial collectivism (the duelling guitar solos at the *denouement*). For all the hotel's glimmering promise, therefore, its plenty is no longer available to everyone; it's an exclusive, elite location.

"Winds of Change, Patriarchs": Women and Mid-70s Pop

History is a complex business, and a positive facet of the otherwise negative shift to post-Fordism was the increasing visibility and vocalness of women. As the workplace became increasingly feminised, "women were the real working-class heroes of civic and popular culture in the 1970s", Cowie argues.[15] Indicative of this new power, feminist pressure resulted in legislation on contraception, abortion, divorce and equal pay. Yet with formal politics having no commitment to transformative projects, the conservative backlash against 'permissiveness' ensured an inherent fragility to feminist achievements, with the US's 1976 Hyde Amendment, preventing federal funding of abortion, arriving a mere three years after *Roe vs. Wade*.

The charts were finally offering equal opportunity, with Rufus's Afro'd former Black Panther Chaka Khan emerging as a commercial force (*Rufusized*, US 7), while the very *fact* of Labelle was feminist: a black 'All-Girl Band', their material mostly written by member Nona Hendryx, their glam outfits evoking female superheroes. Labelle's joyous 1975 disco-funk 'Lady Marmalade' (UK 17; US 1) is Marcusian in its celebration not just of its titular sex-worker, but of an unalienated existence beyond her corporate client's "grey flannel life". Helen Reddy's surreal 1975 MOR ballad 'Angie Baby' (UK 5; US 1) depicts a teenage girl capturing her would-be abuser. Follow-up 'Ain't No Way to Treat a Lady' (US 8) updates 'You're So Vain' to evoke a man so self-involved he doesn't even notice Reddy leaving him. Janis Ian's summer 1975 'At Seventeen' (US 3) transcends both its cha-cha MOR arrangement and its 'teenage angst' tag,[16] its lessons far surpassing school. For even the dating game's 'winners', the "rich-relationed hometown queens" who are parcelled off in marriage, must eventually confront their commodity status in a patriarchal system. The lexical link of the economic to the emotional – "When payment due/Exceeds accounts received" – is rare in popular music (as, credit due, is the term "debentures"), though it leaves little prospect for escape. Re-engaging with the social realm, Joni Mitchell's expensively produced and expansively imagined 1975 *The Hissing of Summer Lawns* (UK 14; US 4) depicts women trapped as suburban or high-life trophies. Unlike Ian, Mitchell gives her heroines agency, with the domestic captive in 'Harry's House' escaping, while 'Don't Interrupt the Sorrow' invokes "Anima rising" against Mitchell's chauvinist lover, a "vengeful little goddess" who warns of "winds of change, patriarchs".

Female representation didn't always result in feminist rhetoric, however, with Carole King's *Wrap Around Joy* (US 1) having little to say about women's lives. While Fleetwood Mac had two female frontwomen, Christine McVie's 1975 'Sugar Daddy' (*Fleetwood Mac*, UK 23; US 1) celebrates a traditional patriarchal provider: "All that I want is someone to take care of me", while 1977's 'Oh Daddy' (*Rumours*) abjectly inquires, "Why are you right when I'm so wrong?/I'm so weak and you're so strong". Heart were a vital incursion into rock's locker room, but 1975's 'Magic Man' (US 9) expresses stock female helplessness before a male seducer. ABBA's frontwomen, meanwhile, sang songs composed by their husbands, with 1975's 'Mamma Mia' (UK 1) an immaculately appointed doormat song, demurely declaring, "You know that I'm not that strong". While Candi Staton's lovely 1976 'Young Hearts Run Free' (UK 2; US 20) endows disco with affective depth, its heroine's inability to break away from her domestic entrapment connects to her contained comprehension of freedom as individual: "Self-preservation is what's really going on today". As Marcuse warned, "The new individualism raises the problem of the relation between personal and political rebellion, private liberation and social revolution".[17]

The protagonist of ABBA's 1976 'Dancing Queen' (UK 1; US 1) is another individualist, but her levelling of the sexual scales is irresistible, for contemporary disco was full of male-gaze songs about dancing girls – Sylvers' 1975 'Boogie Fever' (US 1);

the newly discofied Bee Gees' 1975 'Nights on Broadway (US 7) and 'You Should Be Dancing' (UK 5; US 1), alongside Johnnie Taylor's dreadful 1976 'Disco Lady' (UK 25; US 1). By contrast, ABBA's dancing queen "leaves them burning" then she's gone, exercising a woman's right to choose from an identity parade of interchangeable males. Equally, while on Carly Simon's 1977 Bond theme 'Nobody Does It Better' (UK 7; US 2) the male remains the (not-so) secret *agent*, the song offers an all-too-rare avowal of female lust over an objectified male.

Given such feminist intervention in popular music, the quantity of songs parlaying women as pariahs wasn't coincidental. The Eagles' 1975 'Lyin' Eyes' (UK 23; US 2) is the more seditious for its vocal and instrumental seductiveness, Glenn Frey's wistful tones empathising with women who are economically ensnared in instrumental arrangements in the verse, before the chorus vocalises the misogynist trope of essential female mendacity. Featuring the ubiquitous Elton John, Neil Sedaka's fall 1975 MOR-disco 'Bad Blood' (US 1) is uncharacteristically unpleasant ("The bitch is in her smile"), as is ELO's concurrent 'Evil Woman' (UK 10; US 10), with its vengeful declaration, "It's so good that you're feelin' pain".

With attitudes as atavistic as their last-gasp glam, Sailor's 1975 'Girls Girls Girls' (UK 7) celebrates women who "know how to please a man". Neither glam makeup nor mawkish ballads like 'Beth' (US 7) could cover up Kiss's cock-rock chauvinism, with early 1977's 'Calling Dr Love' (US 16) demanding, "Please get on your knees". Yet that Kiss were still a *response* to feminism's winds of change is indicated by their glam-schlock peer Alice Cooper's attempt to grapple with domestic abuse and patriarchy on his 1975 ballad 'Only Women Bleed' (US 12). This suggests another way of reading the disengagement of this era – as a period of consideration, of a thinking-through, an approach that can also be apprehended in popular music's exploration of race.

"Who's that Kinky So-and-So?": Race and Mid-70s Pop

Where once the imperial West had been the cultural and political 'centre' and the rest of the world the 'periphery', this was changing in the mid-70s, given the postcolonial rebellions ricocheting across the 'Third World', and capital's reorganisation along global lines. With once-imperial Britain decimated by decimalised debt and superpower America disempowered by Vietnamese peasants, there were both negative and positive responses to this reduced state of the nation state. Negatively, the American Reaganite right and the fascist British National Front leveraged impotent imperialism as a populist *ressentiment* towards the racial other, cynically occluding America's historic institutionalised inequality and Britain's recruitment of Caribbeans and Asians as a reserve army of labour. More positively, if unevenly, Western musicians now looked beyond national and racial limits for lyrical and musical inspiration.

With former British colony Jamaica now led by socialist Michael Manley, the island's reggae was, as Hebdige attests, intrinsically anti-imperialist and anti-capitalist.[18] The genre was initially sweetened for colonial sensitivities: Ken Boothe's autumn 1974 Bread cover, 'Everything I Own', was soft-rock reggae (UK 1), Stevie Wonder's 'Boogie on Reggae Woman' (UK 12; US 3) confused the issue, while Bob Marley's albums were slavered with rock-sessioneer overdubs. Concomitantly, white musicians' attraction to reggae – Elton John's 1974 'Lucy in the Sky with Diamonds' (UK 10; US 1); the Stones' 1975 *Black and Blue* (UK 2; US 1); the Eagles' 'Hotel California' – expressed both a countercultural openness to the racial other *and* an enduring imperial entitlement.[19]

Eric Clapton's autumn 1974 cover of Marley's 'I Shot the Sheriff' (UK 9; US 1) flattened the song's syncopations and occluded its evocation of the political violence resulting from CIA destabilisation of Manley's regime. Clapton recorded 1975's reggae-saturated *There's One in Every Crowd* (UK 15; US 21) on the island, though the songs showed no awareness of events outside the studio. Nevertheless, it was Marley's raw, live version of 'No Woman, No Cry' (UK 22) that brought his

British breakthrough in 1975, its lyric steeped in poverty but also proclaiming a postcolonial optimism: "Everything's gonna be all right". Marley's American breakthrough was 1976's more political *Rastaman Vibration* (UK 15; US 8), with 'Crazy Baldhead' addressing colonial exploitation – "Didn't my people before me/ Slave for this country?" – and postcolonial war: "We gonna chase those crazy baldheads out of town". This broadens to class war on the Haile Selassie-quoting 'War': "Until there no longer/ First-class and second-class citizens of any nation... me say 'war'".

The Caribbean was a regular point of return for white musicians as they tentatively – sometimes tritely – explored the concept of race amidst postcolonial refusal. The orientalist stereotypes on 10cc's late 1974 'Hotel' (*Sheet Music*, UK 9) are undercut by its recurring refrain of "Yankee go home!" Typically Tropical's execrable 1975 'Barbados' (UK 1) affects Caribbean accents for reggaefied tourist-brochure exotica, while Elton John's ghastly 1975 account of a Jamaican prostitute, 'Island Girl' (UK 14; US 1), also deploys a caricature Caribbean accent in a gauche depiction of black exploiters and white saviours. However, Steely Dan's dazzling 1976 'Haitian Divorce' (UK 17) explores the relationship between centre and periphery with some acuity (*The Royal Scam*, UK 11; US 15). Set to a satirical appropriation of a reggae rhythm, the lyric unreels like a film, as an American woman seeking freedom from her failing marriage "takes a taxi to the good hotel" on an impoverished Caribbean island, where she beds a local "Charlie" with "kinky hair". Reuniting with her husband, she gives birth to a black baby, a return of the repressed which exposes both the imbrication of imperialism in American 'freedom' and its denial in domestic racism, as scandalised neighbours demand, "Who's that kinky so-and-so?"

Ranging beyond the Caribbean, Western attempts to connect with the racial other often stumbled into imperialist thinking. Maria Muldaur's yearning fall 1974 'Midnight at the Oasis' (UK 21; US 6) is stymied by stock orientalism – "I'll be your belly dancer, prancer/And you can be my sheik" – while colonising the Middle East with American cacti. Genesis's 1974 *The Lamb Lies Down on Broadway* (UK 10) tries to get inside the head of a Puerto Rican New Yorker, while the dialectic between the band's classicist Europeanism and Peter Gabriel's soul-suffused vocals attempts to transcend racial polarities. On Led Zeppelin's early 1975 'Kashmir' (*Physical Graffiti*), this utopian longing is expressed by the image of a vast road connecting East to West and by the track's epic spaciousness, driven by John Bonham's camber-rattling drums and the surging momentum of John Paul Jones's Eastern strings, while Robert Plant's keening, almost supra-physical vocal takes a trip out to transcendence.

On summer 1975's 'Mexico', James Taylor manages to proffer both unexamined exoticism and anti-imperialism, with Crosby and Nash in fainthearted support (*Gorilla*, US 6). Their old cohort Neil Young's 'Cortez the Killer' is a more trenchant consideration of the same territory, condemning Mexico's genocidal Spanish imperialists (*Zuma*, US 25). Joni Mitchell's late 1975 'The Jungle Line' is an extraordinary leap not just from singer-songwriter conventions but from Western pop's confines, splicing a not-yet-named 'sample' of tribal Burundi drums to a minimalist, buzzing Moog-riff, simultaneously folkie and futurist, with a lyric that samples and stretches language itself. Attempting to transcend the Western self, the lyric can't entirely overcome colonial conceptions, and like Conrad's searching, exploratory *Heart of Darkness* (1899), its equation of African heritage with an innate human primitivism challenges racialised conceptions of 'civilisation' at the expense of essentialising the racial other with whom it's trying to unite.

For all its missteps, popular culture remained the primary field through which race was explored, tending to push ahead of politics. The assertion of black Britishness via soul acts Sweet Sensation, Hot Chocolate and the Real Thing – 1976's 'You to Me are Everything' being the first all-black British UK 1 – and singer-songwriter Joan Armatrading – 1976's 'Love and Affection' (UK 10) – probably had as much impact on popular perceptions as 1976's Race Relations Act.[20] The fact that soul backing-singers became standard in mid-70s rock, from the Floyd to the Stones, Steely Dan to Carly Simon, and that Deep Purple, Roxy, ELO and the Bee Gees added funk, soul, then disco to their sound, represents something more utopian than cultural appropriation. With Funkadelic, Earth, Wind & Fire, the Isleys and Stevie Wonder's music incorporating rock dynamics and

Euro electronics, the idea that there should be a "firm correlation between racialized music and racialized bodies" isn't helpful, as Karl Hagstrom Miller argues.[21] However, racial power relations mean such cultural exchange doesn't occur on equal terms, as acknowledged by rockers Wild Cherry's 1976 'Play That Funky Music' ("white boy") (UK 7; US 1).

David Bowie showed sufficient awareness of these issues to call his work with Philadelphia International musicians on 1975's *Young Americans* (UK 2; US 9), "plastic soul". Yet in 1976, Bowie proclaimed fascism to be the political solution to social democracy's exhaustion, while – revealing this wasn't a slip of the tongue – his Thin White Duke tour persona was explicitly modelled on the Nazi Duke of York. Eric Clapton made a career of interpreting black music, yet in summer 1976 he invoked Enoch Powell's anti-immigration politics onstage, while deploying the National Front's "Keep Britain White" slogan. These incidents led directly to the formation of Rock Against Racism, and complicating Miller's argument, revealed a dangerous *disconnect* between racialised music and racialised bodies, a failure to comprehend the relationship between blues, soul and reggae, racial oppression and imperialism (of which fascism is but one articulation). In Bowie's partial defence, his occult fascism, however irresponsible, held no overt racial element. This was decidedly not the case for Clapton, who has defended his stance ever since and would have done far better to have *remained* an empty signifier.

If all this has been a question of the dominant culture's encounter with race, although conscious soul's golden age was over, the genre had neither become apolitical nor altogether devolved to disco. The magnificent Gil Scott-Heron finally broke through with 1975's *First Minute of a New Day* (US 30), its 'Winter in America' a doleful state-of-the-nation address that declared civil rights, the counterculture and trade unions to have been frozen out of politics. Nevertheless, one of 1975's biggest sellers, the Isleys' funk/disco 'Fight the Power' (US 4) is all about resistance, and if the repression it cites is vague, its refusal to "roll with the punches" is inspiring (not least for the future Public Enemy). The O'Jays 1975 *Survival* (US 11) was packed with songs about racialised poverty ('Rich Get Richer'), while 'Give the People What They Want' specifies those wants as "freedom, justice and equality". War's 1975 showtune-reggae 'Why Can't We Be Friends' (US 6) offers a rare affirmation of universal love – "The colour of your skin don't matter to me/As long as we can live in harmony" – and in one of the cuter moments of Cold-War *détente*, was used to soundtrack a NASA-Soviet linkup. Harold Melvin and the Blue Notes' 1975 'Wake Up Everybody' (UK 23; US 12) is alert to the risk of the retreat of utopianism: "The world won't get no better/If we just let it be".

Stevie Wonder's extravagant 1976 triple album, *Songs in the Key of Life* (UK 2; US 1), embraces the globe from Africa to Latin America, much of whose population seemingly appear in its vast supporting cast. Wonder expresses an inclusive communality in the life-affirming 'Love's in Need of Love Today' and hails the warmth of ghetto community in the joyful funk of 'I Wish' (UK 5; US 1), while condemning its systemic immiseration on synth ballad 'Village Ghetto Land'. 'Sir Duke' (UK 2; US 1) is both a jubilant articulation of African American music's centrality to Western culture and a glorious exemplification of that phenomenon. Wonder's music – optimistic, humanistic, hugely successful – is one of the most potent resources of hope in pop, encapsulating this era's excess while eliding its enervation, refusing to recognise the limits society places upon either his race or his music.

"Golden Years": The Past, the Future and the Mid-70s

The usual line on the mid-70s is that, as the present became increasingly precarious, the past became increasingly attractive, with its platonic ideal being that conservative favourite, the 1950s. With the charts full of Chubby Checker (UK 5) and Duane Eddy (UK 9), the risible Rubettes urged, "Do the juke-box jive" (UK 3), "just like they did in 1955". Or rather, like they did in *1975*, with heaped teaspoons of (white) sugar. This was rock'n'roll with its riotousness removed, nostalgia as a means of setting limits, rather than hauntology's revival of repressed possibilities. On Mud's late-1974 'Lonely This Christmas' (UK 1) and 'The Secrets That You Keep' (UK 3), '50s' means balladeer Elvis, and with Rob Davis toning down the queerness, the results are dully, wholesomely 'highschool'. On Showaddywaddy's cabaret 50s and the now-leatherless Alvin Stardust's hits, 'rock'n'roll' means Cochran ballads and Holly at his hiccupping cutest. Meanwhile, Mud Svengalis, Chinn and Chapman's soft-rockers Smokie piously rebuke 50s rebels on 1975's 'Don't Play Your Rock'n'Roll to Me' (UK 8). Art Garfunkel's 1975 Platters cover 'I Only Have Eyes for You' (UK 1; US 18) is doo-wop on Mogadon, while Linda Ronstadt's soft-rock resuscitations of Holly's 'That'll Be the Day' (US 11) and the Everlys' 'When Will I Be Loved' (US 2) manage to remove both their excitement *and* their innocence. Even Lennon's 1975 *Rock'n'Roll* covers album (UK 6; US 6) had all the inspiration of the contractual obligation it was, excised of the adversarial energy that drew the young greaser to the genre.

The mid-70s also regularly revisited the Long 50s, minus its morbidity or its utopianism. The Carpenters' late-1974 cover of 'Please Mr. Postman' (UK 2; US 1) excises the Marvelettes' intemperance and instead sounds accepting of both the lover's absence and the postman's parsimony. A reorientated Drifters were all soft-focus nostalgia ('There Goes My First Love', UK 3), while the discofied Four Seasons' 'December, 1963 (Oh, What a Night)' (UK 1; US 1) has nothing to say about 1963, though its family-values piety says plenty about 1975. Like Ronstadt, Shaun Cassidy's early-1977 glammed-up 'Da Doo Ron Ron' (US 1) sacrifices the innocence of the Crystals' original and thus the utopianism.

Even Long-50s refusal was now co-opted, with MOR swapping folk's protest for preservation. John Denver's autumn 1974 'Thank God I'm a Country Boy' (US 1) is a hokey hymn to parochial ignorance, while Briton Roger Whittaker's 1975 'Last Farewell' (UK 2; US 19) reconfigures the libidinal imperial gaze as racial equality. Teen-pop sensations the Bay City Rollers channelled the period's nostalgic elements into a postmodern potpourri – "ahistorical" and "depthless" in the Jamesonian mode – their charming 'Saturday Night' (US 1) managing to render both working-class hedonism *and* the British Invasion's four-square drum beat unthreatening. The only foundations Rollermania rocked were those of concert halls.

Given the critical presentation of this period as nostalgic, its pop charts reveal a surprisingly futuristic focus. Kraftwerk's sleeper summer 1975 hit 'Autobahn' (UK 11; US 25) celebrates the high-Fordist cult of the car, while its synthesizer-suffused production exemplifies the post-Fordist future, with the combination sounding intrinsically optimistic. On Bowie's stunning early-1976 *Station to Station* (UK 5; US 3), the synthetic, Kraftwerk-inspired coolness of the title track's opening gives way to an r'n'b-propelled optimism, as the emotionally numbed narrator realises "it's not the side-effects of the cocaine" but human connection he's experiencing: "I'm thinking that it must be love". The backing vocals' repeated admonition, "it's too late", is paradoxically positive: "It's too late to be late again", the motion is forwards, all limits removed. Even Bowie's reissued golden oldie that year, 'Space Oddity' (UK 1; US 15), has a stowaway utopianism in its spaceship – Major Tom's choice to float free into outer space is an escape from societal limits. Meanwhile, Bowie's contemporary 'Golden Years' (UK 8; US 10) rejects the attitude that "life's getting you nowhere" and promises "a thousand years" of fidelity while proclaiming the golden years to be occurring *now*.

Indeed, if we understand the 1970s as the golden age of sound – as we should – it reframes this period's pernickety production as an affirmation of futurism, an investment in technology – overdubbing, sound effects, synthesizers – that's utopian, refusing limits on either imagination or innovation. Parliament's 1976 *Mothership Connection* (US 13) name-checks "David Boohwie", while essaying a parallel funk heat/synthetic coolness to *Station to Station*, Euro and Afro-futurism uniting in a utopian "home of the extra-terrestrial brothers" in which such antinomies will be meaningless. The iconic use of the talk-box on Frampton's 1976 'Show Me the Way' (UK 10; US 6) renders regressive classic rock futurist, a man-machine music that, rather than being cold or robotic, is warm and romantic. Similarly, Steve Miller's repetition of "time keeps on slipping into the future" on 1976's jazzy 'Fly Like an Eagle' (US 2) is a promise of progress rather than a plaint of loss. The song's utopianism – "there's a solution" to hunger, poverty and homelessness – matches the futurism of the track's synths swooshing from speaker to speaker.

Stevie Wonder combines the electronic and organic throughout 1976's *Songs in the Key of Life*, with even the apocalyptic ecological landscape of 'As' – with electronic pioneer Herbie Hancock – ultimately affirming faith in the future. Even Captain & Tennille's 1976 MOR ballad 'Muskrat Love' (US 4) essays just such an eco-futurism in using synths to evoke the natural world. ELO's early 1977 'Telephone Line' (UK 8; US 7) is haunted by the past (the lover, the Beatles), yet its blips, bleeps and optimism are just as future-focused. Bowie's early 1977 *Low* (UK 2; US 11) buffs his music's synthetic sheen but retains its funk chassis. The fragmentary lyrics pull and push between affectless social withdrawal – 'Sound and Vision' (UK 3) invoking "Pale blinds drawn all day/Nothing to do, nothing to say" – and a craving for human connection ('Be My Wife'; 'What in the World'), an emotional future to match *Low*'s musical futurism.

All this rather complicates the conception of mid-70s popular music as past-fixated and safe-playing, a soundtrack to the plateaued, hopeless period that Sandbrook and Turner depict, the dog days of social democracy. As such, Gladys Knight's prediction on 1975's 'Try to Remember/The Way We Were' has proved prescient: "As bad as we think they are/These will become the good old days for our children" (UK 4; US 11). The gruesome 'Guilty Pleasures' club nights that began in 2004 and the related soft-rock revival, despite their defensive armouring in affectless irony, can now been seen as expressions of Fordist melancholia. Amid imperial-phase neoliberalism, soft rock's comforts ceased to sound stagnant or compromised and instead simply sounded content and secure. Neither Guilty Pleasures nor the mid-70s period would feature in the 'hauntology' that Fisher and Reynolds began to explore in 2005: their nostalgia for the "welfare-state era of benevolent state planning and social engineering" tended to focus on the early 70s – and on far cooler music.[22]

Yet contemporaneous with the millennial soft-rock revival, the New Economics Foundation's (NEF) 2004 'Measure of Domestic Progress' research revealed that 1976 represented the peak year of British national happiness.[23] If Britain's GDP didn't match that of other rich countries', human welfare and economic welfare do not, as Jim Tomlinson attests, necessarily tally: "Most welfare comes from non-market activities: from household production – or from not producing at all, that is, from leisure".[24] This then is history as hauntology, a reminder of a world that could be free, but not located where we would expect to find it. While Sandbrook turns rhetorical cartwheels attempting to dismiss the NEF's findings,[25] these aren't the era's only inconvenient statistics for conservatives. Research by Danny Dorling reveals that the rich's share of the UK's wealth was at its lowest point between 1974 and 1976.[26] With foreign holidays now common across social classes, and households packed with consumer objects, ordinary mid-70s lifestyles would have seemed like luxury as recently as the 60s,[27] meaning that even the economic pinch felt by those lower down the social strata now begins to look relative.

While this mid-70s period was some distance from a socialist utopia, it was an even greater distance from the "nightmare 70s", '70s malaise' or the failed Fordist social democracy of neoliberal history – and thus of popular cultural memory. This era is revealed as the location of a modest, everyday utopianism, enshrined in the conventional collectivity of the Social Contract and enmeshed in the assumption of steady progress towards an unspectacular but unthreatening future. Regarded as nostalgists rather than futurists, the Carpenters' sumptuously appointed 1975 ballad 'Only Yesterday' (UK 7; US 4) belies its title by not only venturing, "Feels like maybe/Things will be all right", but opining that "tomorrow may be even brighter than today". The song would begin to sound hauntological almost immediately.

For within a year, Jim Callaghan's cash-strapped Labour government would abandon social democratic solutions and subordinate the British economy to the dictates of the International Monetary Fund (IMF).[28] In America, Jimmy Carter's incoming 1977 administration would soon repeat this soft neoliberal coup upon social democracy via the anti-inflationary 'Volcker shock'. With these occurrences framed by the winners' histories as unavoidable responses to the exhaustion of social democracy, they can be better understood as the exhaustion of elite's will to make Fordism work, given the restiveness of reorganising capital and the right on one hand and the unions on the other.[29] Limits were now set not just on the economy, therefore, but on ordinary people's lives – and ultimately, on hope.

It's hard not to hear a warning in ELO's late 1976 'Livin' Thing' (UK 4; US 13), released as the British government hammered out the IMF deal that would impose the final, indeed terminal, limits on Fordism. "It's a giving thing/What a terrible thing to lose" Jeff Lynne keens, right at the limit of his range. Yet, rather than being merely melancholic – "taking a dive" – the song is upbeat, even exhilarating in its orchestral sweep, utopian in its recurring assertion that "it's magic". This testifies to the distinction between a passive Fordist melancholia and a politicised Fordist hauntology. For we can immerse ourselves in the past as a site of escape – as a comforter or pacifier – or we can return to the past as a resource of hope, grounded in its vision of the future. In choosing between an enervated or an energised hauntology, therefore, we can either embrace the imposition of politicised limits, or we can reject them.

Chapter 7

"Some Will Win, Some Will Lose": Punk, Disco and Authoritarian Pop (1977–81)

The period from 1977 to 1981 represents an epistemological break in pop and politics: between the post-war world and the world we inhabit now, between Fordism and post-Fordism, and between social democracy and 'monetarism', which we now call 'neoliberalism'. This break is defined by two songs from summer 1977, the Sex Pistols' 'God Save the Queen' (UK 2) and Donna Summer's 'I Feel Love' (UK 1; US 6). With British unemployment surging as the IMF-dictated spending cuts kicked in and America undergoing an energy crisis, both tracks are pared-down and cut back from inflationary mid-70s excess. Both pack a considerable punch after that era's enervation and both, in this time of transition, are focused on the future. That future is framed negatively in 'God Save the Queen', but rather than the nihilism usually attributed to punk, what's audible is a furious protest at the loss of prospects: "there's no future in England's dreaming". By contrast, the forward-motion of 'I Feel Love' affirms a future that's automated (Giorgio Moroder's synthesized production), female (Summer herself; the track's audible shrinkage of *man*power) and queer (the relentless disco beat). 'I Feel Love' is libidinal but detached, gospel grit excised from Summer's disembodied voice, the synths just *slightly* sinister – but the future is still to play for here.

For all its iconoclasm, 'God Save the Queen' looks to the past – not just the "mad parade" of imperialism that Britain's concurrent Jubilee celebrated, but to rock'n'roll's rebellion (being a direct descendant of Eddie Cochran's 'C'mon Everybody'). The track exhibits a Fordist, adversarial, masculine aesthetic (the aggression of its guitar attack; its football-terrace refrain), which, for all its despair, is still predicated on the collective (that recurring "we"). Yet in the statement "We're the poison in your human machine", and in Johnny Rotten's acidic whine, there's a cold front to the anger that's a new affect in popular music, and which connects to the detachment of 'I Feel Love'. Although derivatives of disco, electro or punk infuse all this period's music, it's this affective break that's crucial: a renegotiation of the interpersonal social contract, reconceiving the relationship between self and other as a polarity rather than a dialectic. Of her counter-revolutionary project to shift politics from "the collectivist [to the] personal society", Margaret Thatcher chillingly declared, "Economics are the method" but "the object is to change the heart and soul".[1]

This epistemological break preceded Thatcher and Reagan, however, and was messy and contested, being waged through class war (deindustrialisation, deflation, recession), renewed Cold War (world destruction risked for socialism's destruction),[2] race war (repression of the American projects; riots in British black communities) and finally, hot war (the Falklands; Grenada). Consequently, this period's music is a dialectic between affective disengagement and assertion of the human in the poison machine, between warmth and cold, between the enduringly utopian and the dystopian hopelessness of 'no future'.

Punk was class war

The standard line on punk is that it was a repudiation of social democracy, which Jon Savage calls an "inadequate... prison-like... consensus".[3] Yet this is to accept the right's narration of the 70s' crisis and, by implication, the right's solution: Thatcher's restoration of bourgeois power and her disciplining of the uppity proletariat. As Edgerton points out, there *was* no crisis of social democracy – 1976's happiness and income-gap statistics are proof that Fordism was far from a failure – but there *was* a crisis of capitalist accumulation, with profits pressed by competition and inflation. Yet, the supposed solution, the IMF-directed spending cuts, caused unemployment to rise and the number living in poverty to double.[4]

As an archetypal street-up emergent culture, punk was an inchoate reaction not to Fordism's failures but to its *abandonment* – an anti-social response to the Social Contract's voiding and the ensuing unemployment's contraction of social horizons. The Stranglers' summer 1977 'Straighten Out' (UK 9) snarls, "just tell me what we're living for/Frustrated intellect, the government capitulation". Whatever individual punks' political allegiances, Fordism presupposed a future that would be better than the present, whereas monetarism consigned a progressive future to the dustbin of history: the Stranglers' double A-side was titled 'Something Better Change'. Like most commentators, Hebdige is unwilling to pin punk down politically, but eventually admits that "beneath the clownish make-up there lurked the unaccepted and disfigured face of capitalism… beyond the horror circus antics, a divided and unequal society was being eloquently condemned".[5]

Punk was a cultural class war, an anarchic analogue to Britain's maverick political struggles from 1977 to 1979, as the Fordist consensus collapsed. Punk's championing of the disposable, the disavowed and the disapproved was a performance of the proletarian as other, as literal trash – "We're the flowers in your dustbin" sneered Rotten – enacted through exaggerated regional accents, names like Poly Styrene and Rat Scabies, and the use of toilet-roll holders and bin-liners as recessionary accessories. Even dressed-down, apolitical punks like the Buzzcocks and the Undertones performed this proletarianism through their market-stall clothes and blunt Lancashire and Derry accents. This class facet is confirmed by the media's patrician reaction, presenting punk as the personification of a contemporary crisis, as Matthew Worley notes, though he neglects to point out that this crisis was attributed to working-class power.[6]

Nothing better expresses punk's class war than the Clash's spring 1977 debut (UK 12), wherein 'Garageland' situates the band politically as proletarian (regardless of Joe Strummer's class origins), and asserts, "The truth is only known by guttersnipes".

'Remote Control' invokes a corrupt politics whose elites seek only self-advancement, cosying up to a "big business", whose "bank accounts [are] all that matters". 'Career Opportunities' confronts the threadbare Fordist compact – "They said I'd better take anything they got" – while marking a shift in the relationship between citizen and state, from social contract to social coercion, referencing the paid prescriptions and military conscription floated by (then) opposition leader Thatcher.

Class war is never pretty, as the Pistols confirmed that summer, playing up to class prejudice: "We're so pretty... pretty vacant" ('Pretty Vacant', UK 6). Nothing was uglier than punk's flirtations with fascism, however, but like the rise of the literally fascist National Front, this was a product of social democracy's abandonment, a venting of despair and despite, respectively. Fascism gains a footing in times of economic and political instability, and where its allure was metaphorical for demoralised, alienated punks, it was literal for the National Front. The Front's assertion of the imperialist self – "the fascist regime" – against the postimperial other was demonstrated on the streets and at the ballot box, and underwrote the Conservatives' rightward trajectory.[7] The punk-affiliated Rock Against Racism (RAR) and Anti-Nazi League (ANL) combated National Front attempts to recruit dispossessed punks, with the ANL facing down fascists in Lewisham and RAR staging concerts whose mixing of pop and politics had more influence on race relations than pop or politics did separately.[8] RAR participants, the Clash's 1977 'White Riot' pledges solidarity with the refusal of racialised policing erupting annually at Notting Hill Carnival. Tom Robinson Band's 1978 'Up Against the Wall' explicitly links the National Front to Fordism's collapse: "Rioting in Notting Hill Gate/Fascists marching on the high street/Carving up the welfare state" (*Power in the Darkness*, UK 4).

The long, bitter strike at London's Grunwick film-processing plant from 1976 to 1978 was paradigmatic of this period's class war: a revived union militancy in a multi-racial, multi-gender working class, weak support from a capital-conciliating Labour government and unrelenting attacks by right-wing press, pressure groups and militias. The defeat of the strike was an indicator of the changing power relations between working and ruling class, even before Thatcher came to complete this counter-revolution. As Gramsci had predicted, Fordism proved to be "a phase which [would] itself be superseded by the creation of a psycho-physical nexus of a new type… a part of the old working class will be pitilessly eliminated from the world of labour, and perhaps from the world *tout court*".[9] Punk was that class insisting on its continued existence.

Punk's radical/reactionary dialectic

The tendency to regard punk as the victor in a cultural turf war with prog makes music merely about other music, occluding the era's socio-political currents, while failing to explain Yes, Genesis or Rush's contemporary success. Punk as a response to soft rock has more political substance – soft rock representing the corporate containment of rock's aggression; punk representing the revival of music's adversarial impulse. It's likely there *was* a political conspiracy to keep Rod Stewart's slick Cat Stevens cover 'The First Cut is the Deepest' at UK 1 to block 'God Save the Queen'. Yet, with Stewart's career at its commercial zenith and the charts bilging with the likes of Wings' 'Mull of Kintyre' (UK 1) and Barbra Streisand's *A Star is Born* theme, 'Evergreen' (UK 3; US 1), the Pistols were caput and punk was co-opted by early 1978, whereas soft rock seemed to have won this cultural and political war.

The messiness of the era's epistemological break is furthered by the fact that while musically, soft rock and punk fit the roles of reactionary and radical, this wasn't affectively so neatly reflected. With weak links to the counterculture and a residual investment in Fordism, soft rock presented a cautiously critical perspective on the conjuncture. Paul Simon's fall 1977 'Slip Slidin' Away' (US 5) captures the epochal shift from Fordism: "We work our jobs/ Collect our pay/Believe we're gliding down the highway/When in fact we're slip slidin' away". Equal parts 'I'm Not in Love' and 'You Are the Sunshine of My Life', Billy Joel's concurrent 'Just the Way You Are' (UK 19; US 3) holds out for continuity against change – and puts his money where his mouth is in a sumptuous, inflationary production.

Soft rock was particularly attuned to the shifts in the

relationship of self to other in this polarising conjuncture. Misunderstood at such a moment, Randy Newman's late-1977 'Short People' (US 2) is a *satire* rather than an instance of an increased, divisive othering. The imagery of Kate Bush's 1978 gothic soft-rock 'Wuthering Heights' (UK 1) captures this cold front, embodied/disembodied by a spectre from the past's plea, "It's so co-o-o-old, pull me in-a-your window". Equally beautifully produced, Gerry Rafferty's 1978 'Baker Street' (UK 3; US 2) rues a society "so cold" that it's "got no soul", the protagonist doubting his friend's hippie dream of living off the land can ever now be realised in such a world. The Doobie Brothers' coolly lovely 1979 'What a Fool Believes' (US 1) dismisses the ties of the past to prioritise an unsentimental present, but a rueful haunt remains. On Supertramp's 1979 'Logical Song' (UK 7; US 6), the shimmer of electric piano has become chilly, processed, while the lyric notes the contemporary rightwards shift: "Watch what you say, or they'll be calling you a radical/A liberal". While none of this is reactionary, it expresses a resignation to the conjuncture's coldness, and soft rock would soon merge with punk's heir, new wave, in a conservative formation later dubbed 'yacht rock'.

Cut adrift from the social contract, punk was locked in a dialectic between the radical and the reactionary, only partly explained by its relationship to atavistic pub rock. Tom Robinson's 1977 '2-4-6-8 Motorway' (UK 5) is enjoyably oafish, the Stranglers' spring 1977 'Hanging Around' is even *about* a pub (*Rattus Norvegicus*, UK 4), while that summer's sexist double-whammy, 'Peaches'/'Go Buddy Go' (UK 8) reveals the band as punk's Bernard Manning. Eddie and the Hot Rods' riproaring pub-punk 'Do Anything You Wanna Do' (UK 9) pogoes between refusal of "doing day jobs", "politicians" who "tell me things I shouldn't be" and a heroically hedonistic individualism. That same combustible summer, Dr Feelgood-influenced Boomtown Rats' 'Lookin' After No. 1' (UK 11) responds to the era's dole queues and unequal distribution of resources with an icily calculated individualism: "I don't owe nobody nothing/'Cause it's me that must come through".

The Pistols' late 1977 *Never Mind the Bollocks* (UK 1) plays out this radical/reactionary dialectic – sometimes inside the same song. Lyrically 'Holidays in the Sun' (UK 8) could be anti-communist *or* anti-capitalist, but the martial riffing and jackbooted backing-vocals give it a fascistic undertow which Rotten's whinny peevishly pulls against. There's no simple polarity to the relationship between band and singer, however. The rockist riffing can be blokey ('Seventeen', 'Liar'), or libidinal ('Submission'); Rotten's refusal can be radical ('God Save', the scintillating 'Anarchy in the UK') or reactionary (the anti-abortion 'Bodies'); while the band's Fordist aggression renders Rotten's distant *froideur* ambivalent on 'No Feelings' ("for anybody else") and 'Problems' ("Don't come to me if you need pity").

Sham 69's terrace-chant proletarianism had none of the Pistols' ambiguity. They quickly shifted from the rousing rebellion of 1978's 'Angels with Dirty Faces' (UK 19) – "We're the people you don't wanna know/We come from places you don't wanna go" – and the stirring solidarity of 'If the Kids Are United' (UK 9) – with its countercultural "You are him and he is you" – to the lumpen atavism of 1978's 'Hurry Up Harry' (UK 10): "We're all goin' dahn the pub". Although their songs were articulations of beleaguered proletarian pride – "Council estates or tower blocks/ Wherever you live you get the knocks" on 1979's 'Hersham Boys' (UK 6) – Sham chimed with the NF's *völkisch* heroism and attracted an unwanted fascist skinhead following. This was hardly discouraged by a Sham/Pistols collaboration sporting swastika armbands.[10] In Sham and subsequent 'oi' bands, the warm front of regressive pub rock met the cold front of social disengagement to distinctly queasy effect, putting a chilly distance between the self and the other.

The Winter of Discontent was punk

The Winter of Discontent of wildcat strikes and the evolution of punk into post-punk were temporally contiguous, and while their political connection was tenuous, they were equally expressive of the conjunctural chill. Leaving the Pistols, John Lydon's new band Public Image Ltd's (PIL) composite corporate-branding mocked the market logic of capitalism as it co-opted punk: thus the near-identical titling of band, autumn 1978 single (UK 9) and album (UK 22). PIL turned punk inside out, removing rock's dynamics and machismo but also, by eschewing the blues root, its warmth and libidinality, transforming alienation into a virtue. "I wish I could die", Lydon whines indifferently on 'Theme'.

Occupying a hinterland between Fordism and post-Fordism, post-punk was a space women could occupy on their own terms, but this radically desexualised space was, dialectically, a wintry one. The Pistols' punk peers Siouxsie and the Banshees' remarkable late-1978 *The Scream* (UK 12) summons a totalitarian landscape ('Metal Postcard', 'Switch'), yet its music's taut, Teutonic coldness, with rock dynamics and emotions excised, causes critique and allure to combine. With two female members, X-Ray Spex's summer 1978 'The Day the World Turned Day-Glo' (UK 23) decries a world rendered plastic by consumerism, while late 1978's 'Germ Free Adolescents' (UK 19) depicts obsessive compulsion as a response to recessionary alienation: "Without fear she'd give up and die". With the music itself sounding plastic, processed – especially the sax – and the women provocatively sexless, it's again unclear whether dehumanisation is being celebrated or critiqued in lines like "You're deep-frozen like the ice". The partiality of post-punk fans for very long overcoats was thus a sensible precaution.

That winter, punk's prematurely old guard's releases came over as conservative compared to post-punk's radical rethink. Be-suited working-class mods, the Jam were overtly beholden to Fordist forms, while initially playing to proletarian stereotype on 1977's 'All Around the World' (UK 13). Compared to the concurrent *PIL* and *The Scream*, the corporate production of the Clash's major-label *Give 'Em Enough Rope* (UK 2) was staid and rockist. This was compounded by the racial chauvinism of 'Safe European Home', while the terrific 'Tommy Gun' (UK 19) was a liberal repudiation of leftist terrorists the Baader-Meinhof Gang. Yet on 'Guns on the Roof' it's clear who the *real* terrorists are: "This is a place where no judge can stand/Sue the lawyers and burn all the papers/Unlock the keys of the legal rapers". Indeed there's relatively little of post-punk's political ambiguity here: the folk-punk of 'English Civil War' (UK 25) protests and resists the fascism of the National Front – "The kids are shoutin' loud". There's the same sense of reactionary forces on the move on the Jam's concurrent *All Mod Cons* (UK 6), with the ground-down drone on 'Down in the Tube Station at Midnight' (UK 15) mugged by men brutalised by "too many right-wing meetings". The psychedelic guitars of their 'In the Crowd' expands punk's vocabulary to lend warmth to what would be hipster condescension did it not present conformism as something "the government sponsors underhand" and that cancels out collectivity and compassion: "They're just not thinking about each other". Indeed, early 1979's 'Strange Town' (UK 15) depicts such conformity as suspicion of the other, countering this with the refusal of "I'm so glad the revolution's here".

It wasn't quite a revolution, but the wave of unofficial strikes that became known as the Winter of Discontent had a puckishly punk spirit, and similarly struck a chill into the establishment. The media ensured the strikes scared the public too, disseminating images of unburied bodies and uncollected rubbish to demonstrate "the crisis of an overextended, overloaded and ungovernable state in which the trade unions were 'holding the country to ransom'".[11] The Winter of Discontent has been a gift for opponents of social democracy ever since, despite it being a *lack* of social democracy that unions were protesting. The unprecedented involvement of service-sector alongside manufacturing workers revealed the potential for a reconfigured proletariat, which explains the media's apocalyptic tone, enabling Thatcher to position herself as the upholder of bourgeois order against subaltern anarchy, in Marx's classic antinomy. Thatcher won the general election that followed in May 1979.

Thatcher's 'order' wasn't just a matter of defeating Labour, or even of dismantling social democracy, but of destroying the industrial working class, as Gramsci predicted. Thatcher's immediate introduction of anti-union legislation, creation of unemployment through deindustrialisation and reversal of Labour's progressive taxation indicated her intention, with her policies unleashing the most savage British recession since the 1920s.[12] If social democracy was dead, however, and socialist punk soon to follow, the class struggle wasn't over yet in politics or pop.

Disco, content, discontent

Largely eschewing the implications of 'I Feel Love',[13] disco represented a warm front in late-70s culture, from Donna Summer's own contentless, string-strewn hits to Heatwave's 1977 'Boogie Nights' (UK 2; US 2), the positivity of Kool and the Gang and the vague counterculturality of Earth, Wind & Fire. At its best, disco offered both content and discontent, however. Evelyn 'Champagne' King's superb fall 1977 'Shame' (US 9) refuses the conjuncture's authoritarianism: she's "tearing the rules apart".

Chic reintroduced funk into a stripped-down austerity disco, but by making the most of the least – the trim rhythm section; Nile Rodgers' economic guitar – appeared not just brand new but bedazzling. On late 1977's 'Dance, Dance, Dance' (UK 6; US 6), the "yowsah, yowsah, yowsah" refrain is a Depression phrase – heard in *They Shoot Horses, Don't They?* (1969) – a sly protest echoed by Chic's vocalists' 30s styling and the 'Stomping at the Savoy' reference on that winter's exuberant 'Le Freak' (UK 7; US 1). Offering empathy amidst a tautening economy – "All that pressure got you down/Has your head been spinning all around?" – Bernard Edwards' circling bass riff (from 1:38-2:40) expresses a refusal to be repressed, interlaced with the band's austerity strings, the track creating its own temporary utopia.

The Bee Gees weren't renowned for their content, but their domination of the charts across 1977–78 as artists and writers – e.g., Andy Gibb's 1978 'I Just Want to be Your Everything' (UK 26; US 1) and 'Shadow Dancing' (US 1) – gave their vaguely countercultural yearning a wide diffusion, countering the conjuncture's coldness. Moreover, the brothers made their sole venture into content count. The stunning 'Stayin' Alive' (UK 4; US 1), like the film it soundtracks, *Saturday Night Fever* (1977), isn't just about *escaping* hard times – "Life goin' nowhere"– but *refusing* them: "I'll live to see another day". Similarly, Gloria Gaynor's glorious late-1978 'I Will Survive' (UK 1; US 1) casts *all* who are cast aside as survivors – thus its adoption by gay men – her refusal to accept victimhood not individualist but countercultural: "As long as I know how to love, I know I'll stay alive". Philly soulsters McFadden and Whitehead's 1979 'Ain't No Stoppin' Us Now' (UK 5; US 13) urges the same resilience for African Americans amid right-wing backlash: "And if you've ever been held down before/I know you refuse to be held down anymore".

Sister Sledge's Chic-produced summer 1979 'Lost in Music' (UK 17) applies this refusal to work – "I quit my nine-to-five" – while "responsibility/To me is a tragedy" refuses monetarism's reassertion of the performance principle. Finding the electro-organic sweet spot between Fordist and post-Fordist disco, Michael Jackson's late-1979 'Off the Wall' (UK 7; US 10) advocates escaping the grind of work: "Gotta leave that nine-to-five upon the shelf/And just enjoy yourself". This is echoed in Donna Summer's 1980 new-wave disco 'The Wanderer' (US 3), again declaring "that nine-to-five life is a bore", and in Dolly Parton's camp country disco '9 to 5' (US 1). Despite newcomer Prince's 1981 'Let's Work' being a pared-back, post-Fordist electro-disco, rather than it being a Reaganite hymn to revitalising the economy, it's a reconfiguration of the performance principle as the pleasure principle (*Controversy*, US 21). These then are Marcusian disco songs.

However, as the Bee Gees lamented on 1978's 'Too Much Heaven' (UK 3; US 1). "Nobody gets too much heaven no more/It's much harder to come by/I'm waiting in line". The irony of all those rejections of work was that many would soon be "waiting in line" not for nightclubs but for welfare in the 1979 recession sparked by the anti-inflationary 'Volcker shock', the Carter administration's equivalent of Britain's IMF cuts. On the Bee Gees' 1979 'Tragedy' (UK 1; US 1), the incorporation of synthesizers makes the layered production sound corporate, cold, an affective shift signalled by its lyric depicting the loss of love as "you got no soul". Sonically and sentimentally, this cold front would continue to encroach as the recession bit.

Disco queered culture

Disco's infiltration of female and queer voices and visions into pop culture was one of this period's warm fronts. Contrary to Thatcher and Reagan's moral authoritarianism, post-Fordism's flexible accumulation undermined Fordism's patriarchal rigidity through deindustrialisation and increased female employment.[14] With the counterculture's embrace of *Eros* having attracted women and queers, capital was beginning to court these demographics, and disco – originating in gay clubs and popular with women – provided a perfect opportunity. You can hear a cautious, corporate feminism in Odyssey's female-starring fall 1977 'Native New Yorker' (UK 5; US 21), Chaka Khan's 1978 'I'm Every Woman' (UK 11; US 21) and, at a stretch, Kool and the Gang's 1979 'Ladies Night' (UK 9; US 8). If Sylvester's fantastic 1978 electro-disco 'You Make Me Feel (Mighty Real)' (UK 8) flaunted an uncontainable queer abandon, the corporate camp of Village People's 1978 'YMCA' (UK 1; US 2) and Odyssey's 1980 'Use it Up and Wear it Out' (UK 1) meant their queerness wasn't always recognised (and as Trump's fondness for the former shows, still isn't).

The queer signifiers of Sister Sledge's Chic-produced 1979 'He's the Greatest Dancer' (UK 6; US 9) are hard to miss, however – the gang "cruising" in San Francisco, renowned as a 70s gay capital; the amazing dancer with "the kind of body that would shame Adonis", and who "never leaves the disco alone". Terming such imagery 'homoerotic' privileges the male gaze, however, and it's the *female* gaze that gives 'Greatest Dancer' its libidinal thrill. The hanger-shuffling inventory of designer labels – "Halston, Gucci, Fiorucci" – evinces an equally libidinal consumerism that, in the age of glitzy venue Studio 54 and glamorous dramas *Dallas* and *Dynasty*, lionises wealth as style – the opposite of style as protest (Zandra Rhodes' designer-punk show notwithstanding). Yet Sister Sledge's reversal of the gaze is *still* liberating, just as the Bee Gees' boast of being "a woman's man" in feminine voices is subversive and Mick Jagger's sensual falsetto on 1980's discofied 'Emotional Rescue' (UK 9; US 3) undermines the Stones' machismo. Chic cleverly address this dialectic on Diana Ross's summer 1980 'I'm Coming Out' (UK 13; US 5), which works both as an assertion of the Ross brand *and* as a gay liberation anthem.

Rather than disco killing off cock rock, however, the genre enjoyed a renaissance, with Australians AC/DC's pared-back riffing chiming with punk, their machine-precision rhythm section analogous to synthpop (and indeed disco), even as their leeringly lascivious lyrics were (im)pure retro chauvinism. That 1980's terrific 'Touch Too Much' (UK 29) features cock rock's best couplet – "She wanted it hard, she wanted it fast/She liked it done medium-rare" – is no claim for its progressive sexual politics. After vocalist Bon Scott's death, his replacement, Brian Johnson, continued this theme of blaming women for male randiness, as on 1980's 'You Shook Me All Night Long' (*Back in Black*, UK 1; US 4) – "working double-time on the seduction line" – before reverting to the main (male) event from 1981's 'Let's Get It Up' on (UK 13):[15] cock rock at its most literal.

While the reactionary reassertion of sexual and racial norms in the 'disco sucks' movement and Chicago's summer 1979 Disco Demolition Derby derailed the genre's commercial dominance, it couldn't derail the cultural forces disco helped unleash. As ever with consumer culture, however, that these radical forces were unleashed by a reorganising capital – moving to the morally flexible accumulation of post-Fordism – meant they had the potential equally for liberation and co-optation.

Reggae was punk's conscience

Reggae was another warm front in this polarised conjuncture, exemplified by the unalloyed joy of Althea and Donna's 1978 'Uptown Top Ranking' (UK 1). While Bob Marley's hits were mostly love songs ('Is This Love', UK 9), his albums were as political as they were spiritual, with "Babylon" being both "the white colonial powers" and "contemporary capitalist society", in Hebdige's definition, while "Jah" functions as the revolutionary spirit.[16] The title track of 1977's *Exodus* (UK 8; US 20) prophecises, "Jah come to break downpression, rule equality", while urging the earthbound to remember, "where you stand in the struggle". On 1979's *Survival* (UK 20) the spiritual is increasingly material: "They don't want us to unite", but to "keep on killing one another" ('Top Rankin''). Yet these subaltern "sufferers" are adversaries of Babylon's "vampires", "destroying and melting their gold... We're more than sand on the seashore". On 1980's positively militant *Uprising* (UK 6), the folk-reggae 'Redemption Song' quotes black radical Marcus Garvey's "emancipate yourself from mental slavery", while 'Real Situation' advocates revolution, because "total destruction the only solution".

Reggae's formal and political radicalism provided punk

with a route out of its reactionary tendencies.[17] The Clash's 1977 cover of Junior Murvin's 'Police and Thieves' radically extended punk's range, while 1979's *London Calling* (UK 9; US 27) was suffused with reggae, affirming racial solidarity on 'Rudie Can't Fail', while 'Guns of Brixton' empathically ventriloquises the frustrations of downpressed black communities that would explode in riots in 18 months' time. Produced by Jamaican Mikey Dread, the Clash's 1980 triple album *Sandinista!* (UK 19; US 24), named after Nicaragua's Marxist revolutionaries, was riddled with radical politics and reggae stylings. The subaltern is presented as a threat throughout, from explosive ghettoes (Dread toasting over the *riddim* of 'One More Time') to imploding colonies (the reggae-calypso of 'Washington Bullets'; 'Kingston Advice'), while the dubby *Apocalypse Now*-quoting 'Charlie Don't Surf' vows, "So many armies can't free the earth / Soon the rock will roll over".

Britain's 'two-tone' explosion expanded on this racial solidarity, with its multicultural lineups and shotgun marriage between reggae's agitated antecedent, ska, and punk's attitude. After Coventry's Special AKA toured with the Clash and released 'Gangsters' (UK 6) on their own indie 2-Tone label, they released the Selecter's 'On My Radio' (UK 8), which rejected "the same old show", while 'Three Minute Hero' celebrated pop as an antidote to politics' "endless grey drone". The Specials' scrappy, Elvis Costello-produced late-1979 debut (UK 4) announced the dystopian 'Dawning of a New Era', with Thatcher's Britain defined by "master race masturbation" ('Do the Dog') and "getting chased by the National Front" ('Concrete Jungle'). By contrast to the Beat's forthright 1980, 'Stand Down Margaret' (UK 22), there was an ambivalence to the Specials – declaring both that "I won't fight for a cause" *and* insisting upon resistance ('It Doesn't Make It Alright'). The Specials' chauvinism – towards young mothers on 'Too Much Too Young' (UK 1); regarding university education on 1980's 'Rat Race' (UK 5) – made it easy to miss that the lumpen prole on 'Stereotype' (UK 6) "doesn't really exist".

Amplifying the ambivalence, the Specials' incorporation of working-class music-hall and lounge muzak on 1980's *More Specials* (UK 5) was both deadly satirical and dumbly serious. The dole dandy on 'Do Nothing' (UK 4), "trying to find a future" in a "life without meaning", occupies a liminal space between resignation and refusal. Perfectly timed for 1981's urban riots, summer 1981's 'Ghost Town' (UK 1) makes sense of both the Specials' ambivalence and their disparate musical ingredients, being simultaneously a passively resentful evocation of a violent, deindustrialised dystopia – "no job to be found in this country" – *and* a passionate lament for a modest Fordist utopia, evoked by the track's lurid lounge and music-hall stylings. "Do you remember the good old days before the ghost town?" they ask, "We danced and sang, and the music played in-a-de boomtown". 'Ghost Town' testifies to what popular music can *do* – capture *and* transcend its historical moment and genre; be entirely political *and* supremely *pop*; and evoke emotional complexity, in this case, both refusal and resignation – and thus what ordinary people can do.

By the time of Marley's death in 1981, reggae's radical associations were redundant. The Specials had split; the ska revival had expired; UB40 – their very name a protest at unemployment – had found lucrative employment as a bland mainstream pop act. Reggae became just one exotic flavour in pop's cultural melting pot. 10cc's dreadful 1978 'Dreadlock Holiday' manages to be both offensive and corny (UK 1), Blondie's 1980 cover of 'The Tide Is High' *in*offensive and corny (UK 1; US 1), but it was the Police who shut down reggae as a radical concern. It wasn't just the cringey cod-Jamaican of Sting's vocals, but his lofty imperiousness amidst the chilly inventiveness of Andy Summers' prog-dub guitar. 1980's grating 'De Do Do Do, De Da Da Da' (UK 5; US 10) manages to sound pertly pious about its political disengagement and its championing of "the meaningless and all that's true".

Neo wave: new wave and neoliberalism

Fusing punk's adversarial agitation and 60s pop songcraft, post-punk's warmer sibling, new wave, arrived concurrent with Thatcher, with 1979 being Britain's best-ever year for singles both commercially and creatively. Critics tend to conflate these occurrences, as if new wave were an accommodation with conservatism after punk's radicalism.[18] Such analyses occlude punk's ambivalence and the insecurity of Thatcher's position – as inflation rose and growth declined, she hit a 70% disapproval rating – while underselling new wave's near-unanimous opposition to the new politics. So it's not the Knack's frivolously fabulous 'My Sharona' (UK 6; US 1) that's the 1979 paradigm, but the Clash's 'London Calling' (UK 11), with its ebulliently adversarial fusion of punk and psychedelia, class politics and ecological alarm. Thatcher's advent revitalised the Clash musically and politically: "I'm not working for the clampdown", Strummer snaps on 'Clampdown', giving voice to the resistance occurring across the country, as local authorities refused to institute Thatcher's cuts and the left took over Labour's policymaking. "Kick over the wall, cause governments to fall… /Let fury have the hour, anger can be power" (*London Calling*, UK 9; US 27).

As a product of the conjuncture, new wave was a negotiation between 60s warmth and post-punk *froideur*, Fordist past and post-Fordist future. Despite Elvis Costello's 1978 *This Year's Model* (UK 4; US 30) featuring the anti-fascist 'Night Rally', his bristling sarcasm and brilliant wordplay were politically ambiguous. The misogyny targeted at a model on 'This Year's Girl' and a debutante on '(I Don't Want to Go to) Chelsea' (UK 16) could be either satirical or acidly sincere. Initially titled *Emotional Fascism*, 1979's *Armed Forces* (UK 2; US 10) adroitly captures the political in the personal, the shredded social contract underwriting exploitative sex on 'Busy Bodies', racism rendered respectable on 'Sunday's Best', the unemployed becoming imperialists on the stunning, ABBA-esque 'Oliver's Army' (UK 2). Yet following the song's use of the N-word as a metaphor for the marginalised, Costello used it as a provocation in a drunken tour run-in with Steve Stills. The new-wave soul of 1980's *Get Happy* (UK 2; US 11) provided a paradigm for the exorcism of this recurring fascist spectre, though Costello's enduringly withering lyrics hardly shook off the *emotional* fascism. 1981's *Trust* (UK 9; US 28) sharpened the political lines, with 'Clubland' capturing the era's free-market free-for-all as effectively as TV's *Minder* (1979–94), though the reggaefied 'Big Sister's Clothes" complaint that "compassion went out of fashion" could as easily have been directed at its author as its ostensible target, Thatcher.

The Jam's embrace of 60s pop – covering the Kinks' 'David Watts' in 1978 (UK 25) – gave them a warmth that gained them popular success without political compromise. On autumn 1979's 'The Eton Rifles' (UK 3) the scions of the establishment are pitted against the unemployed, while the middle classes desert the subaltern in the crucible of crisis. "What a catalyst you turned out to be/Loaded the guns then you ran off home for your tea" remains one of the greatest – and most politically acute – couplets in popular music, as the 70s bourgeoisie recoiled from class war. Even the cold greyness of the Jam's accompanying, post-punk-influenced *Setting Sons* (UK 4) was countered by its grounding in the sociality Thatcherism was sundering. On 'Burning Sky', Weller sarcastically spits, "There's no time for dreams when commerce calls… it's only us realists who are gonna come through" – pop's first recognition of looming capitalist realism. The lush strings on Bruce Foxton's 'Smithers-Jones' warm the album's instrumentation, while starkly exposing the cold instrumentalism of neoliberalism's deregulated corporate culture.

The Jam were commercially unstoppable, with spring 1980's gloriously insurrectionary 'Going Underground' going straight in at number 1. Weller's snarl of "kidney machines replaced by rockets and guns" tracks the epochal shift from welfare to warfare state, while decrying Thatcher's *völkisch* nationalism: "Brass bands play and feet start to pound". Another instant chart-topper that summer, 'Start!' (UK 1) captures the conjuncture's dialectic, a cold, post-punk spatiality pulling against its warmly psychedelic 'Taxman' riff, while its lyric longs for someone who "loves with a passion called hate" – distilling the hot/cold sonics and sentiments of the accompanying *Sound Affects* (UK 2). 'Set the House Ablaze' unites a four-square 60s drumbeat to a cyclical dub-guitar motif, as society's "cold, hard and mechanical" attitudes tilt towards fascism – thus the creepily jolly military whistling – while 'That's Entertainment' (UK 21) deploys *Revolver*-style acoustics and backwards guitar to depict the dystopian, post-industrial landscape of Thatcher's Britain.

More ambivalently, the Banshees' autumn 1979 *Join Hands* (UK 13) captures the conjuncture's coldness – its title mocking hippie collectivism – while its jagged gothic rock channels the Cold War death cult. Their cohorts, the Cure's 1980 *Seventeen*

Seconds (UK 20) absorbs the political into the personal on 'Play for Today': "It's not a case of share and share alike/I take what I require". By spring 1980's *Kaleidoscope* (UK 5) even the Banshees had embraced 60s pop, however, albeit with fingers crossed behind their backs. The psychedelic, Leslie-guitar-drenched 'Happy House' (UK 17) holds a mocking mirror to Sister Sledge's 1979 'We Are Family' (UK 8; US 2), countering its "Have faith in you and the things you do" with "There's room for you if you say, 'I do'/But don't say 'no' or you'll have to go". If this fusion of family values and authoritarianism satirises Thatcherism, it also satirises *sociality* – "It's safe and calm if you sing along" – while the production and performance render 60s warmth wintry. 1981's *Juju* (UK 7) digs deeper into gothic *grotesquerie*: the depiction of audiences dispassionately watching others' suffering on 'Monitor' is *itself* dispassionate. With no vision of utopia to counter dystopia, cruelty becomes gothic realism, and authoritarianism and affectlessness become quotidian.

Even the poppiest iterations of new wave enacted a dialectic of countercultural warmth and conjunctural cold. In XTC's jerkily agitated 1979 'Making Plans for Nigel' (UK 17), parents channel corporate aspiration for a teenager whose "future in British Steel... is as good as sealed". That British Steel's own future was being sealed by deindustrialisation reveals the shakiness of such Thatcherite 'aspiration'. The Boomtown Rats' 1979 'I Don't Like Mondays' (UK 1) reduces an American school shooting to nihilism (rather than, say, gun laws) – "because there are no reasons" – Bob Geldof's delivery pitched between performative passion and shrugging indifference. Dexy's Midnight Runners' fusion of acerbic punk attitude and melodic soul plenitude was again ambivalent. Summer 1980's stunning *Searching for the Young Soul Rebels* (UK 6) bitterly evokes the same class betrayal as punk ("Spat on and shat on... Losing and boozing") but directs its anger towards social democracy. Dexy's Kevin Rowland only rises from his resentful resignation on 'There, There, My Dear' (UK 7) to spit, "The only way to change things is to shoot men who arrange things".

New wave's absorption of soul and disco represented a warm front against this recurring, intermittently fascistic, *froideur*. Ian Dury's 1978 'Hit Me with Your Rhythm Stick' (UK 1) and 1979

'Reasons to Be Cheerful Part 3' (UK 3) combine disco with music hall, presenting dazzling displays of proletarian wit and warmth in the hinterland of Fordism. Squeeze's discofied 1979 'Cool for Cats' and 'Up the Junction' (both UK 2) are less kitchen-sink drama than sitcom, Fordist masculinity ironically celebrated and affectionately satirised, respectively. PIL's 1979 'Death Disco' (UK 20) unites 'God Save the Queen' and 'I Feel Love', but is so spacious – musically, imaginatively, affectively – that its mourning become electric, its personal political. Even the Clash absorbed disco on *London Calling*, which, along with a new emphasis on Mick Jones' feminised vocals, achieved a libidinality unreliant on Fordist archetypes, while critiquing post-Fordism. 'Lost in the Supermarket' brilliantly captures how, as classes become 'consumers', alienation expands into leisure.

This existential alienation is the focus of one of this period's pop's peaks, Talking Heads' early 1981, Brian Eno-produced 'Once in a Lifetime' (UK 14). David Byrne's arty ambiguity could drift into hipster condescension, as on 1978's 'The Big Country' (*More Songs About Buildings and Food*, UK 21; US 29). Yet there's a warmth to Byrne's ambivalence here, capturing the conjuncture's uncertainty in the track's one-chord harmonic openness. Byrne's yuppie evangelist espouses the era's socio-economic success as existentially elusive even for those who *achieve* it, while the track's bass-propelled Afrobeat funk and the band's collective chorus provide a balancing, humanist warmth.

As with punk and post-punk, race was a recurring concern in new wave, tracking the era's polarisation of self and other and the potential for fascism that accompanied it. As the only one-tone two-tone act, Madness attracted an unwanted fascist fanbase, and somewhat laterally (and jauntily), 1980's 'Embarrassment' (UK 4) is a repudiation of racial othering. Adam and the Ants' Burundi beat/post-punk combination was absurdly exciting and – like their Native American iconography – trod a provocative line between cultural appropriation and racial empathy: "Down below those dandy clothes/You're just a shade too white", Adam quips on 1981 hit 'Kings of the Wild Frontier' (UK 2). In tandem, the Ants also explored the self/other dialectic of class, with the video for 'Antmusic' (UK 2) depicting their proletarian rebels winning over an aristocratic audience, while the videos to

1981's 'Stand and Deliver' (UK 1) and 'Prince Charming' (UK 1) present ruffian Adam invading the aristocracy's citadels. All three promos reconfigure class – and class conflict – as *style* rather than substance, however, for in the age of Lady Di, aristocrats could be fashionistas, common highwaymen could be dandies and, possessed of sufficient style, *anyone* could be Prince Charming (or at least do the camp, arm-crossing dance).

New wave's women epitomised the genre's combination of 60s-pop warmth and post-punk *froideur*. Blondie were girl-group new-wave, its sole female member, vocalist Debbie Harry, alternating dead-eyed distance and bedazzling intimacy. Harry's lyrics for 1978's pitch-perfect 'Picture This' (UK 12) insouciantly appropriate the gaze as she watches her love object showering. The Pretenders combined folk-rock chime and punk-rock churn, with frontwoman Chrissie Hynde blending dandy swagger and de-objectified sexuality. 1979's gleaming 'Brass in Pocket' (UK 1; US 14) is coolly detached, without the distance of a Siouxsie, while on 1980's 'Talk of the Town' (UK 8), Hynde liberatedly refuses the rules, while repossessing the gaze on 'Tattooed Love Boys' (*The Pretenders*, UK 1; US 9), and reminding men to "Say 'Yes, ma'am', say, 'No, ma'am'" on 'Bad Boys Get Spanked' (*Pretenders II*, UK 7; US 10).

Rather than *Thatcher* being the inspiration for these female leaders, the counterculture produced something called 'feminism', to which Thatcher was fervently opposed. That countercultural influence was overt on the Pretenders' 1981 'Message of Love' (UK 11), insisting, over clangourous guitars and a pounding tribal beat, that "the reason we're here, every man every woman/Is to help each other/Stand by each other". This was an extraordinary sentiment in the hinterland of hippie-hating punk; released as hippie-hating politician Ronald Reagan became president, it was a defiant statement of collectivity in an increasingly individualist conjuncture.

Authenticity as hauntology

Masculine, be-denimed heartland rock appears the antithesis of effete, dandified new wave – grounded to its dreamy, authentic to its plastic, passionate to its ambivalent. Yet emerging from the same socio-economic conditions, heartland rock had a similar preoccupation with the 60s to new wave, with a Fordist hauntology in both its sonics and its sentiments. Heartland rock at its most performative, the title track of Meat Loaf's 1977 *Bat Out of Hell* (UK 9; US 14) filters Long-50s automotive morbidity through contemporary perceptions of a rusting, neglected Fordism. "Nothing ever grows in this rotting old hole/Everything is stunted and lost" manages to sound nihilistic, nostalgic and utopian simultaneously.

Blue-collar rock had few illusions about Fordism, as articulated on Bob Seger's 1978 'Feel Like a Number' (*Stranger in Town*, UK 30; US 4) and as Bruce Springsteen's 1979 'Factory' summarises the Fordist compact: "Factory takes his hearing, factory gives him life" (*Darkness on the Edge of Town*, UK 14; US 5). "Daddy worked his whole life for nothing but the pain", Springsteen howls on 'Adam Raised a Cain', but with the mid-70s recession hollowing out the heartlands, "now he walks these empty rooms looking for something to blame". Springsteen is channelling punk here – particularly Patti Smith, whose 'Because the Night' he co-wrote (UK 5; US 13) – and throughout *Darkness* there's an adversarial agitation and pared-back austerity that, like punk, matches the pinched late-70s economy. As Cowie observes, "It turned out that liberal economic success had been one of [workers'] key sources of power".[19] Recessionary realism infuses even a love ballad like Seger's yearning 'We've Got Tonite' (US 13), with its lovers "Longing for shelter from all that we see", and the future foreclosed: "All of my hopes... fading away".

Worse was to come for the American working class, however. Volcker's 1979 anti-inflation measures caused unemployment to soar and construction, manufacturing and agriculture to crumble, with furious farmers blockading the Federal Reserve building in protest. On Seger's autumn 1980 'Against the Wind' (US 5), the narrator, having "never worried about paying or even how much I owed", is now besieged by "deadlines and commitments". The line "Wish I didn't know now what I didn't know then" brilliantly suggests a reckoning with 'reality' – the Fordist settlement as a delusion – but also with experience, and with historical change.

Heartland rock's preoccupation with the past has nothing to do with postmodernity: it simply historicises working-class experience in human terms. The title track of Springsteen's late 1980 *The River* (UK 2; US 1) begins with 50s patrician conformity – "They bring you up to do just like your daddy done" – and progresses through high school and the hope symbolised by the river Mary and the narrator swim in and the car they drive to the reservoir. The narrator thrives through workplace unionisation and survives through domestic union ("for my nineteenth birthday I got a union card and a wedding coat"). Yet the marriage fails alongside the economy, and the narrator, unable either to find work or communicate with Mary, loses his sense of place in the world. Confronting the dried-up river, he conducts a reckoning in the song's extraordinary last verse: "Is a dream a lie if it don't come true/Or is it something worse?" The "dream" is Fordism's promise that better would come; the "something worse" is the political repudiation of that possibility. One of pop's earliest instances of Fordist melancholia, that 'The River' was recorded during the Carter administration and that Reagan would retain Volcker reveals that the abandonment of Fordism predated Republican victory.

Reagan accelerated the process with gusto, however, attacking the power of organised labour by breaking the 1981 PATCO air-controllers' strike, following which – as employers imitated his intransigence – strikes and union membership declined exponentially. Tom Petty and the Heartbreakers channelled these changes: the bratty, new-wave edginess of 1978's *You're Gonna Get It* (US 23) hunkering into a corporate heartland on 1979's *Damn the Torpedoes* (US 2). Petty's pained voice expresses a vulnerability that occludes his cold-hearted affect, as on the competitive individualism of 'Don't Do Me Like That' (US 10). When Petty chides his lover on 'Refugee' (US 15) not to "lay there, revel in your abandon", asserting, "Everybody's had to fight to be free", it's a rejection of Fordist melancholia for individualist Reaganite 'realism'. By 1981, Petty and his Heartbreakers were advising just holding on for dear life in 'The Waiting' (US 19): "Don't let 'em kill you, baby, don't let 'em get to you". The heartland's heart had been ripped out.

New wave in old bottles

The era's epistemological break was expressed by established acts retooling themselves via new-wave techniques. ABBA's terrific 1978 'Take a Chance on Me' (UK 1; US 3) balances the post-Fordism of its rigid rhythm and refrigerator synths with characteristically warm-hearted vocals, while its affective insecurity is evident from the title on in. Billy Joel's assertion of freedom on 1978's clipped, processed 'My Life' (UK 12; US 3) sounds coldly individualist rather than counterculturally idealist – "Go ahead with your own life, leave me alone". Joan Armatrading's drum-heavy 1980 'Me Myself I' (UK 21) moves into recognisably 80s sonics and sentiments: "I wanna be a big shot and have ninety cars". If the synthier, sinister 'I'm Lucky' is sarcastic – "Struck it rich… and the world/Loves a winner" – the satire is lost in its instrumental chill (*Walk Under Ladders*, UK 6).

Biking in on the 'new wave of British heavy metal', Motorhead's 1980 'Ace of Spades' (UK 15) possesses a more traditionally Fordist aggression, yet its agitated clip and affectless attitude – "You win some, lose some, it's all the same to me" – align it with post-punk detachment. On 'Motorhead' (UK 6) Lemmy longs for "mental anaesthesia" and chillingly promises, "I guess I'll see you all on the ice". Judas Priest's magnificently nervy 1980 'Breaking the Law' (UK 12) again incorporates new wave into metal, decrying class betrayal with punk rage rather than post-punk resignation: "So much for the golden future, I can't even start/I've had every promise broken, there's anger in my heart".

Christopher Cross's 1980 'Ride like the Wind' (US 2) is soft rock finding its way across the border into the 80s (sneaking Michael McDonald over with him): an edge of new-wave agitation, a hint of rebellion that chimes with both punk refusal *and* neoliberal assent. 'Sailing' (US 1) makes the dichotomy clear: 'freedom' here is a privatised affair, with the track providing the template for yacht rock. The wired, anxious backing of Rick Springfield's 1981 'Jessie's Girl' (US 1) tracks the narrator's paranoid desire to 'possess' his best-friend's girl. On Genesis drummer Phil Collins' 1981 'In the Air Tonight' (UK 2; US 19), what leaps out – apart from *that* drum-break – is the line, "If you told me you were drowning/I would not lend a hand": albeit addressed to his emotional rival, its denial of human empathy and its huge snare drum sound announce the arrival of the 80s.

By contrast, Collins' ex-colleague Peter Gabriel's new-wave conversion was paradigmatic of the genre's ability to reinvigorate and radicalise established artists. Gabriel's nervily glossy 1980 *III* (UK 1; US 22) shone a light on apartheid at home ('Not One of Us') and abroad ('Biko'), while its mockery of militarism on 'Games Without Frontiers' (UK 4) would prove prescient. Having been post-punk even *before* punk, Bowie's 1980 *Scary Monsters* (UK 1; US 12) is a masterpiece of popular modern experiment and political fury – "To be insulted by these fascists/Is so degrading", he shrieks on 'It's No Game' as Robert Fripp's guitars howl in solidarity. Yet this degradation isn't fought, perpetuating Major Tom's strung-out fatalism on 'Ashes to Ashes' (UK 1), one of the most stupendously *strange* songs ever to top the charts. The rebel on 'Scream Like a Baby', who "mixed with other colours", is sedated in a correction centre, "learning/To be a part of society", capturing neoliberalism's reverse-engineering of the state's role, from social liberalism to authoritarianism. With Bowie having some form regarding fascism, 'Fashion' (UK 5) finds him satirising contemporary 'style-fascism' as something more than mere metaphor: "We are the goon squad and we're coming to town/Beep-beep!".

Such artily cool distance is set aside on Bowie and Queen's late 1981 'Under Pressure' (UK 1; US 29). Where the track once sounded stadium-built for diva turns, it now sounds both empathetic and perceptive. Once dated and dashed-off-seeming lyrics about giving "love one more chance" now sound like a countercultural warm front protesting the conjunctural coldness. Mercury echoes "give love, give love, give love" into the epic distance, while Bowie dares us to "change our way of caring about ourselves", and the pair warn, "This is our last chance".

Futurism is now: thesis/antithesis/synthesis

Contrary to Fisher's claim,[20] Fordist futurism was never entirely utopian, always operating in dialectic with dystopianism,[21] reflecting modernity's potential to forge either a progressive or a destructive future.[22] In *post*-Fordist culture, however, with a progressive future off the agenda, the dystopian began to dominate. So, where disco *did* follow-through on the futuristic implications of 'I Feel Love', it tended to be pessimistic. On Cerrone's superb 1978 electronic Euro-disco 'Supernature' (UK 8), technological development has breached humanity's contract with the environment, which now reaps its revenge. In Dee D. Jackson's Moroder-produced 1978 'Automatic Lover' (UK 4), this dystopian futurism is *affective* – "There's no more feeling/ Automated love/Cold and unappealing" – chiming with the conjuncture's cold front. This is a facet even of Anita Ward's superficially upbeat 1979, syndrum-suffused 'Ring My Bell' (UK 1; US 1), as she offers comfort to a powered-down business-drone.

Rather than disco, it was rock that seized upon electro's innovations. On Blondie's 1979 'Heart of Glass' (UK 1; US 1), over bubbling Moroder-esque synths, Harry's coolly delivered "Riding high on love's true bluish light" and "We could have made it cruisin'" convey a cyborg affectlessness. In the promo, mannequin keyboardist Jimmy Destri sexily but creepily holds a patch cable in his mouth. 1980's 'Atomic' (UK 1) repeats the trick, with another machine-rhythm, a plastic-encased Harry dancing robotically in the video and the audience entwined in cables. Remodelled by Moroder as a slimmed-down electro enterprise, Sparks' 1979 'Number 1 Song in Heaven' (UK 14) presents heaven as a tech-capitalist dystopia – "In your homes [the song] becomes advertisements" – while 'Beat the Clock' (UK 10) mocks neoliberalism's recharged performance principle via an absurdist accelerationism. Moroder also created the soundtrack for 1980's *American Gigolo*, in which Richard Gere's preening prostitute is a synecdoche for the narcissistic individualism soon to be named 'yuppie'. "Take me out and show me off... /Dress me in the fashions of the 1980s", demands Harry, her human/cyborg persona a perfect fit for the film's sexily mechanical theme, 'Call Me' (UK 1; US 1). Here the 60s unconditional becomes the 80s transactional: "Call me any, any time" – at a price.

The standard assumption that synths are "sonic signifiers of the future", in Fisher's phrase,[23] simply doesn't hold: synths are clearly being deployed to depict the *present* in these songs, deploying a dystopian sci-fi demotic. Moroder's parallel pioneers, Kraftwerk began as tech-utopians,[24] but contrary to their reputation,[25] by 1978's magnificent *The Man-Machine* (UK 9) their electronics and emotions had become steely, the music's perfection clinical, its beauty cold. For androgynous, be-suited business mannequins to proclaim, "We are the robots", isn't to celebrate an automated future but to capture an affectless present, enslaved to the performance principle. Consequently, their 'Man-Machine' is a "pseudo-human being".[26]

Corporate-branded from music to affect to dress, Devo were Kraftwerk's American analogue. Summer 1978's Eno-produced *Are We Not Men?* (UK 12) renders organic instruments electronic, while the narrator's 'Uncontrollable Urge' is to repeat advertising slogans, and the subjects of 'Jocko Homo' are "monkey men all in business suits". Devo's proclaimed "de-evolution" wasn't just a degradation of intelligence but of that other defining facet of humanity – emotion, as on 1980's motivational satire 'Whip It' (US 14): "Go forward, move ahead... break your momma's back". Although parent album *Freedom of Choice* (US 22), depicts the "land of the free" as coldly totalitarian, Devo, like Kraftwerk, were accused of fascism – never far from technology fetishism, as Italian Futurism demonstrated. Both acts' deadpan delivery rendered their satire ambivalent, and alongside their excision of rock's blues root, lent their music a cold, Teutonic whiteness.

The British genre of synthpop was initially known as 'futurism', but generated by the new affordability of automating synthesizers, it was both materially and morally concerned with the post-Fordist present. The first of these acts to break through, Tubeway Army's stunning summer 1979 'Are "Friends" Electric?' (UK 1) is a chilling account of the erotic as automatic. Amid siren-like, paranoia-inducing synths, the narrator's humanity is trapped in a machine-world where "it hurts and I'm lonely". Going further than Kraftwerk or Devo, Gary Numan depicts his cyborgs' habitus as a literal dystopia on late 1979's *Replicas* (UK 1), a surveilled landscape of "rape machines", where "machmen... play kill by numbers". That Numan voted Conservative need not detain anyone: his dystopian, affectless vision captured the public imagination amidst Thatcher's ideologically driven recession. Going solo, Numan dropped his *Blake's 7* spacesuits for business suits, creating a Kraftwerkian satire of corporate culture on 1979's *The Pleasure Principle* (UK 1; US 16), as on 'Observer' and the blank, Ballardian 'Cars' (UK 1; US 9), which depicts that ultimate consumer object of desire as integrally alienating and atomising.[27]

As such, the corporate world that Buggles' 1979 'Video Killed the Radio Star' (UK 1) predicts was already in place and is as characterised as it is critiqued by the tune's ad-jingle jauntiness and cheesily chirpy chorus. Given that half of Buggles was future 80s production mogul Trevor Horn, the line "We can't rewind, we've gone too far" is as much promise as threat. Former Ultravox leader John Foxx's 1980 *Metamatic* (UK 18) offers a blank satire of a clinical business environment ('Plaza') populated by a 'New Kind of Man', with Foxx's grey flannel automat closely resembling Numan and Kraftwerk's businessman machines. The dystopian future on Human League's 1980 *Travelogue* (UK 16) thus seemed all too contemporary, 'Black Hit of Space', absurdistly evoking capitalist technological expansion, while 'WXJL Tonight' exudes a conjunctural Fordist melancholia that keeps returning to the phrase "as if it really mattered" – be that songs, emotions, employment or, indeed, meaning.

With electronics suffusing everything from Cars' new-wave pop to Michael Jackson's disco-soul, synthesizers gradually lost their dystopian associations, though their processed coldness meant they retained an ambivalent relationship to human affect. On synth-whizz Vangelis's collaboration with Yes's Jon Anderson, 1979's 'I Hear You Now' (UK 8), the yearning "Oh! Just to get the feeling!" sounds like it's reaching for human connection across its gorgeously frosty synth expanse. The duo's 1981 'I'll Find My Way Home' (UK 6) expresses a longing for collectivity – "One world we all come from/One world we melt into one" – emanating from someone cast out into the social cold. Jettisoning the affectless robotics, the human Numan was hardly less alien: self-pitying on spring 1980's 'We Are Glass' (UK 5), self-aggrandising on autumn's 'I Die You Die' (UK 6), anthemic choruses and guitars doing nothing to cancel the cold calculation of his electronics and his attitudes.

By deploying the more organic-sounding mellotron, alongside electric bass and emotive vocals, Orchestral Manoeuvres in the Dark's metier was humanity in dialogue with machines – literally, on summer 1980's 'Messages' (UK 13), where electronic comms presciently obstruct emotional communication. Invoking the plane that dropped the atomic bomb on Hiroshima, late 1980's excellent 'Enola Gay' (UK 8) expresses the subsumption of compassionate humanity by technological rationality. Rather than adopting a conventional 'protest' position, the track *inhabits* the contradiction, with Andy McCluskey virtually weeping the whimsically distanced lyric.

Even more ambivalent, Kraftwerk's superb spring 1981 *Computer World* (UK 15) is ostensibly a celebration of technological progress. Yet the logic of 'Computer Love' is circular – digital dating as solution to technological atomisation – while the title track's deadpan "Business, numbers, money, people" carols a creepily capitalist tech utopia. Over a relentless synthetic vocal pulse, the protagonist of New Yorker Laurie Anderson's 1981 'O Superman' (UK 2) discovers not just her answering machine but her emotional life to be colonised by the military-industrial complex. "Here come the planes/They're American planes," a sinister cyborg voice proclaims, informing her that individual agency is useless against technologically networked corporate power. "Hold me, Mom, in your long arms" the narrator sings, "Your petrochemical arms/Your military arms". The song is thus a chillingly dystopian vision of the Reaganite present.

In the second wave of British synthpop that invaded British and American charts across 1981, synths' familiarity caused their affective coldness less to fade than to become conventionalised. Kim Wilde's fantastic early 1981 new-wave-synthpop 'Kids in America' (UK 2; US 25) is as Numan as it is Blondie, a sliver of ice at its cyborg heart – "You know life is cruel/Life is never kind" – a coldness that the "new world coming" celebrates, because "kind hearts don't win any glory". That new world arrived that summer with Depeche Mode's 1981 'New Life' (UK 11), whose poppy insubstantiality waved through a paranoid, nihilistic lyric ("the road just leads to nowhere"), while the fizz-bomb superficiality of 'Just Can't Get Enough' (UK 8) renders amiable a greedy pursuit of gratification that would soon become familiar. Although Soft Cell's Marc Almond's warmly wobbly vocals couldn't be less cyborg, Dave Ball's synths lent a *froideur* to the duo's 1981

Northern Soul cover, 'Tainted Love' (UK 1; US 8), emphasising its complaints of emotional cruelty. 'Bedsitter' (UK 4) evokes both the heat of the night before and the chill of the morning after ("I've nothing in/I'm left without") via its queasy synths and queered vocals. The astonishing 'Sex Dwarf', meanwhile (*Non-Stop Erotic Cabaret*, UK 5; US 22), uses this hot/cold trick to communicate libidinal capitalism's contradictions: sexy but exploitative, social but transactional, exciting but cold.

The Human League abandoned futurist dystopianism for pop presentism with summer 1981's 'The Sound of the Crowd' (UK 12), while 'Love Action (I Believe in Love)' (UK 3) operated a push-and-pull between romanticism and transactionalism. The League's former colleagues Heaven 17 similarly adopted a soulful electro-pop, with the sleeve of autumn 1981's *Penthouse and Pavement* (UK 14) celebrating a networked, glossily corporate world. Sonically closer to Buggles than Kraftwerk, however, the inverted commas soon came off Heaven 17's corporate satire to become corporate soundtrack, contemporary with the irony-free yuppie. Consequently, rather than Kraftwerk's re-released 'The Model' being a ghost at the monetarist feast, its late-1981 success (UK 1) indicates quite how Thatcher had changed the heart and the soul. What was once satirical – a (wo)man-machine, exploited by shady patriarchs and shadowy corporations – was now a carol to an 80s exemplar. The synths that once articulated a cold transactionality now merely sounded contemporary, the track's emotional numbness normalised, its imbalanced power relations the way of the world.

The European turn

British pop's turn to Europe in the late 70s could be read as an instance of resistance to neoliberalism, a refusal of the Atlanticism reified by Thatcher and Reagan's special relationship and of the lockstep documented throughout this book. This trans-Europe express travels through the French lyrics of Blondie's 1978 'Denis' (UK 2) and 1979's 'Sunday Girl' (UK 1), ABBA's Balkanised summer 1979 'Voulez-Vous' (UK 3) and Adam and the Ants' 1980 pop-punk 'Young Parisians' (UK 9), in all of which 'European' signifies sophistication – possession of *style*. Yet, Old

Europe's Romanticism produced imperialism and fascism, while the new Europe was a centrifuge of diffused forces – markets, finance, cybernetics – which Michel Foucault's concept of an inescapable, decentred 'power' was both recognition of and resignation to. "Power is everywhere... because it comes from everywhere".[28] Equally, the European turn wasn't merely an expression of this disempowerment but a *glamourisation* of it in a non-interventionist age.

Recorded by the Berlin Wall with Eno, Bowie's late 1977 "'Heroes'" (UK 24) combines Old European Romantic grandeur with the contemporary continent's techno-*froideur*, into which Bowie's impassioned vocal interjects vital human warmth. When, as besieged lover, Bowie howls that "nothing will keep us together... nothing will drive them away", the shadowy 'they' that's denying human freedom is Foucault's faceless 'power'. While that power is refused – "We can beat them" – the title's quotation marks denote that such heroism is performative, given that, "We're nothing and nothing can help us" against the system. But their very failure is glamorous, stylish. The Stranglers' concurrent 'No More Heroes' (UK 8) taps the same Old European Romanticism – the line "They watched their Rome burn"; the swirling, neo-classical keyboards – to declare the demise of collectivist politics, citing both Trotsky and Lenin. On Magazine's coldly stunning early-1978 'Shot by Both Sides' (*Real Life*, UK 29), the politically unaligned protagonist takes the collectivist besieging of his individualism as valorising, proud to be "on the outside of everything", glamourising political disempowerment as performative disengagement.

While the Skids' 1979 singles were anti-imperialist – the punky 'Into the Valley' (UK 10); the synthy 'Masquerade' (UK 14) – their subaltern heroism was *völkisch*, especially given the Aryan sleeve of 1980's *The Absolute Game* (UK 9). Joy Division also exhibited this era's recurrent attraction to fascism, from their concentration-camp name to their photoshoots, working-class heroes presented in German Expressionist monochrome: "Here are the young men, the weight on their shoulders". Yet there's no potency to this *völkisch*ness, Martin Hannett's space-suffused production putting the band's aggression at a cold distance, foregrounding Ian Curtis's stentorian-voiced alienation. Curtis's lyrics on 1980's *Closer* (UK 6) look in on the world from outside, a disempowered detachment that, while personal, captures a political structure of feeling. Curtis's subsequent suicide meant the synthetically morbid, Moroder-influenced fatalism of 'Love Will Tear Us Apart' (UK 13) emerged from beyond the grave, a hauntology of impotence.

The apotheosis and terminus of this Europeanism, New Romanticism, arose from the London club scene Bowie identified on 'Fashion', arriving in charts and on televisions in autumn 1980 with Spandau Ballet's 'To Cut a Long Story Short' (UK 5). Named after a concentration camp, the cold hauteur of Spandau's look and sound (note: 'The Freeze', UK 17) was potently fascistic but, combined with a disco/funk libidinality, impotently narcissistic: "I am beautiful and clean/ And so very, very young/To be standing in the street/To be taken by someone". Unlike punk, there was no refusal in New Romanticism's style. Despite the evocation of the "bonds" of masculine work on Spandau's spring 1981 'Muscle Bound' (UK 10) – all leather and fire and steam – it doesn't celebrate the proletariat but deploys a heroic, homoerotic *völkisch*ness to valorise narcissism: the *self* as performance principle. On Duran Duran's 'Planet Earth' (UK 12) that spring, the heat of disco and funk pulls against cold Euro synths, while Simon Le Bon's melodramatic lyrics – proclaiming himself "New Romantic" – and his gesticulations in the video have no meaning beyond the assertion of self, an empty disengagement presented as heroic *style*.

New Romanticism frequently deployed Old European iconography to convey this glamourised disempowerment. Visage's gorgeous, dreamlike 1980 'Fade to Grey' (UK 8), with its snatches of French dialogue, exemplifies this European etiolation, expressing a morbid pleasure in fading, "Wishing life wouldn't be so long". Their forgotten 'Mind of a Toy' (UK 13) enacts a mesmerised ecstasy of disempowerment: "Controlled by a string/By a stranger/I've never met". Half of Visage were Ultravox, whose 1981 'Vienna' (UK 2), like '"Heroes"', combines Old and new Europe to convey this conjunctural powerlessness. The austere synths that track the video's empty, wintry streets segue into classically swirling viola and tinkling piano for the ball scenes, while the vaulting chorus – "This means nothing to me" – glorifies alienation as style, resignation as Romanticism. The Passions' concurrent 'I'm in Love with a German Film Star' (UK 25) swoons over its heroic subject – "Trying not to pose/ For the cameras and the girls" – while enervatedly sighing, "It's a glamorous world". Delighting that "these are the decadent days", Hazel O'Connor's 1981 'D-Days' (UK 10) depicts style-culture denizens "going out dancing, pose, pose", while its Weimar cabaret-new wave suggests they're partying into the arms of fascism.

In temporal and conceptual tandem with Kraftwerk, Duran Duran's summer 1981 'Girls on Film' (UK 5) celebrates the model as the platonic form of this glamorous disempowerment. Objectified, tracked, mauled ("the crowd all love pulling dolly by the hair"), "as she goes under again", the model's – and band's – powerlessness is surpassed by *style*: they're simultaneously victims *of* and victors *in* the spectacle. The music's processed funk doesn't so much offset as sublimate the Aryan implications of this impotent imbrication in spectacular power, the glamour of fascism 'resolved' by style fascism. The high 80s were about to begin.

Where there's authoritarian populism, there's authoritarian pop

As the paradox of Stuart Hall's definition of Thatcherism as 'authoritarian populism' suggests,[29] the radical right's *volk* amounted to little more than a clutch of paranoid petit bourgeois, repressed homosexual militiamen, National Front thugs and blackleg vigilantes. Colin Leys argues that few of the populace embraced neoliberalism, but rather resigned themselves to it,[30] sedated by its fantasy of populist empowerment, the gorgon glamour of its charismatic leader and the fascistic fetish of its 'strong state'. Indeed, those who refused that state's authority – strikers, rioters, squatters, metropolitan councils – were treated to an authoritarian 'law and order' entirely antithetical to neoliberal small-state orthodoxy. Given synthpop and New Romanticism's sublimated fascistic element, the Human League's 1981 'I Am the Law' (*Dare*, UK 1; US 3) is an instance of what can be regarded as 'authoritarian pop'. The track affectlessly declares the state a necessary control upon a Hobbesian war of all against all, a right-wing fantasy of rugged individualism which Thatcher and Reagan would endeavour to render a reality.

Heavy rock always had an authoritarian aspect, with Queen in particular revelling in their power over the crowd – Freddie Mercury playing the aristocratic potentate – and their music becoming less complex, more direct, and thus more populist in this period. With its jeer of "No time for losers", 1977's stadium power-ballad 'We Are the Champions' (UK 2; US 4) elides distinctions between the vanquished and the victim, as they're taunted by the rampant victor. On the track's football-terrace companion piece 'We Will Rock You' (*News of the World*, UK 4; US 3), charismatic leader Mercury incites the crowd not as a countercultural collective but as a populist mob. On Judas Priest's anthemic 1979 'Take on the World' (UK 14), leather-clad, whip-brandishing Rob Halford demands, "You got to follow your leaders", while the *volk* is flattered to deceive – "the spotlight's on you" – as long as they "put [themselves] in our hands". Retro-fitted knowledge of Mercury and Halford's homosexuality, or that the latter's Nazi-channelling leather and whips 'clone' regalia was a queer working-through of power relations, enhances rather than invalidates this analysis of these acts' affective authoritarianism.

In the narrative of Pink Floyd's 1980 concept album, *The Wall* (UK 3; US 1), the stadium rock star's walled-up feelings suddenly spill out into fascist incitement mid-show. The album's satire of conjunctural currents is conducted with such gusto – and such heavy riffing on 'In the Flesh' – that it comes across as an *exemplification* rather than condemnation of authoritarian pop, with its massing mobs marching on minorities, chanting "hammer-hammer". Entirely without satire, Journey's fall 1981 'Don't Stop Believin'' (US 9) fashions a *völkisch* air-punching anthem from authoritarian, 'survival of the fittest' ruthlessness: "Some will win, some will lose/Some are born to sing the blues". The song implicitly naturalises neoliberalism's politicised destruction of the industrial working class, alongside the immiseration of the projects' denizens whose forefathers first sang the blues. Journey communicate this cold sentiment through the performative pomp of the power ballad, which, during the 80s, would calcify into the consummate authoritarian pop form.

The epistemological break between the 70s and the 80s

The trajectory of the Human League charted the shift of post-punk from artiness to populism, and the mood of the populace from refusal of the new politics to acceptance. Phil Oakey's addition of two working-class teenagers from a Sheffield nightclub to the group's lineup was pure populism. Yet Joanne Catherall and Susanne Sulley didn't merely add a human factor to the League's cyborg setup: resplendent in their "fashions of the 1980s", and sporting variants on the Lady Di fringe, the duo's ordinary/elite style confirmed the ideological eclipse of class performed by proletarian New Romantics' hauteur and aristocratic Sloane Rangers' appearance in style-bible *The Face*.

Late 1981's 'Don't You Want Me' (UK 1; US 1) captures this cultural and political moment in both its sound and its sentiment. The bubbling Moroder-style synths no longer suggest a dystopian future *or* a disco past, just the push – and pushiness – of the contemporary, conventionalising a cold transactionality through the calculated seductions of authoritarian pop. The song both addresses and exemplifies the conjunctural concern of 'selling out' – be that your principles, your aesthetic, or your lover. Playing on the band's biography, Oakey complains of being transactionally treated by upwardly mobile Sulley, claiming he "turned you into someone new" and "put you where you are now", and with his usefulness over, she rejected him. Yet it's unclear exactly who used whom as 'raw material', in Williams' distillation of neoliberalism's affective mode.[31] Oakey's stentorian-toned insistence on his star-making potency and his threat that "I can put you back down too" are a coldly patrician power play. Sulley's assertion that she's a self-made woman articulates Thatcherite aspiration, in which individuals control their own destiny and others are competitors rather than collaborators. Even when singing, "I still love you", Sulley's vocals are affectless, musically and emotionally flat, while her kiss-off, "I guess it's time I tried to live my life on my own", captures the conjunctural shift from collectivism to individualism. Resignation has become participation: we're on the other side of the epistemological break.

The fact that 'Don't You Want Me' was widely taken as a love song demonstrates the extent to which cold sentiments and their sonic analogue – the track's layers of burbling, hissing synths – had become conventionalised by the early 80s. With harshness passing for humanity, affectlessness for 'ordinariness' and transaction for emotion, 'Don't You Want Me' says much about 1981, more about the distance travelled from the 60s and a great deal about what was to come in the high 80s.

Chapter 8

"It's a Competitive World": Post-Fordist Pop and the 80s (1982–87)

The 80s in popular memory is a primary-coloured montage from *Pretty in Pink*, *Dynasty* and *Miami Vice*, all hoop earrings and blonde highlights, shoulder pads and rolled-up sleeves, and possessed of an equally primary-coloured soundtrack. 80s pop now bests 60s soul as the music that can unite any social event across generation or class, while 80s sonics have become post-millennial pop's signifier of positivity. "Take your passion/And make it happen", urges Irene Cara on 1983's *Flashdance* theme, 'What a Feeling' (UK 2; US 1), extolling this age of opportunity: "You can dance right through your life".[1] With working and dancing the epoch's key motifs, 'What a Feeling' is the 80s distilled: an individualist optimism suffused with synths, energised by aggressive guitars and exemplified by soaring, soulful vocals. With every genre converging on a similar sonic palette, every second song a movie tie-in, heavy rockers Survivor's 1982 *Rocky III* theme, 'Eye of the Tiger' (UK 1; US 1), insists they're "Rising up, straight to the top". Driven by a disco beat and a competitive culture, they're "rising up to the challenge of our rival". A souled-out Spandau Ballet are equally incentivising on 1983's 'Gold' (UK 2; US 29). "You're indestructible", they smarm, invoking that very 80s alchemy, the ability to monetise *everything*: "Always believe that you are gold".

This high-80s positivity rode upon an economic boom which vindicated free-market economics and delivered Thatcher's landslide victory in 1983 and Reagan's in 1984. The neoliberal reversal of Fordist redistribution created a bonanza on deregulated financial markets for the period's winners – ambivalently parodied by Harry Enfield's Loadsamoney – while conventionalising unemployment for its losers. As Glenn Frey put it on 1984's *Beverly Hills Cop* theme, 'The Heat is On' (UK 12; US 2): "You can make a break, you can win or lose". With Michael Douglas's trader proclaiming, "Greed is good", both *Wall Street* (1987) and *The Wolf of Wall Street* (2013) recognise the cruelty of the conjuncture and the volatility of its venality. Yet it's these films' class-A rush of consumption, commercial display and social-contract-busting that stays with the viewer. As Kenny Loggins pants on 1986's Moroder-produced 'Danger Zone' (US 2, from *Top Gun*), "The further on the edge/The hotter the intensity". With Thatcher claiming to be anti-establishment, the reactionary was now rebranded as radical: the refusal of patriarchal authority in Madonna's 1986 'Papa Don't Preach' (UK 1; US 1) is also, amid fundamentalist Christian resurgence, an assertion of 'pro-choice' values – Madonna and child. Starship's 1985 claim to have "built this city on rock'n'roll" (UK 12; US 1) retains no remnant of their countercultural foundation as Jefferson Airplane: even the song's opposition to "corporate games" sounds corporate amid its synthetic bombast. Like everybody in the 80s, Starship "just want to dance", and so the fashionably attired zombies cavorting in formation in Michael Jackson's video for 1983's 'Thriller' (UK 10; US 4) provide a paradigmatic image for the age.

With *Newsweek* calling 1984 "the Year of the Yuppie" and Filofaxes and business cards becoming indispensable accessories, a central component of the 80s' conformist individuality was a new cult of work. After two decades in the cold, organization man was suddenly edgy, sexy, heroic. With Madonna's 1983 'Holiday' (UK 2; US 16) involving "just one day out of life", work was now "life", it seemed. This reaffirmation of the performance principle was achieved by the absorption of the pleasure principle, in Marcusian terms, making a pleasure of business: work was now *sexy*. In turn, Frankie Goes to Hollywood's stunning 1983 'Relax' (UK 1; US 10) makes a business of pleasure, not just by monetising libido, but by corporate auteur Trevor Horn's transformation of synthesizers' technocracy into a facsimile of libidinality which foregrounds the production – thus work. Grace Jones's Horn-produced 1985 'Slave to the Rhythm' (UK 12) is a corporate carol, employing erotica as its demotic: "Keep it up – never stop the action". The 'making of' conceit of Phil Collins and Philip Bailey's 1985 'Easy Lover' video (UK 1; US 2), makes a feature of pop's performance principle, paralleling the pair's exemplification of the phenomenon of "bands in business suits" noted by Huey Lewis and the News's 1986 'Hip to be Square' (US 3): "an idea whose time has come".

Market economics resulted in a decline in traditionally masculine, Fordist work. "The world is on a corner waiting for jobs", David Bowie laments on 1983's 'Ricochet', an off-note on his upbeat corporate makeover *Let's Dance* (UK 1; US 4). Hitting big with 1983's 'Down Under' (UK 1; US 1), Australians Men at Work's very name was a camp mockery of Fordism, as mass unemployment became mass culture. Billy Joel's discography tracks this trajectory: 1982's 'Allentown' (US 17) is Fordist melancholia – "Every child had a pretty good shot/To get at least as far as their old man got" – complete with a curiously homoerotic video, while on the promo clip for 1983's Four Seasons pastiche, 'Uptown Girl' (UK 1; US 3), the mechanics gesticulate and mince in a camp parody of blue-collar masculinity, towered over by an affluent female. By Joel's 1986 'Modern Woman' (US 10), the future is female: "She's got style and she's got her own money", because "times have changed". With its workaday evocation of a woman's working week, the Bangles' 1986 Prince-written 'Manic Monday' (UK 2; US 2) is the evidence of that cultural shift.

The success of such sassy, 'ordinary' all-female bands revealed how women were encroaching upon masculine strongholds. The Go-Go's fabulous 1982 'We Got the Beat' (US 2) is a pop-feminist manifesto, while the video for Donna Summer's 1983 'She Works Hard for the Money' (UK 25; US 3) features tired but triumphant female workers dancing in the street. This feminised new world is celebrated by Cyndi Lauper – "When the workin' day is done/Oh girls, they want to have fu-un" (UK 2; US 2) – while in the video, dancing women again take over the streets, symbolically pushing a hard-hat out of the way. The video for

Brits Bananarama's ebulliently melancholy 'Cruel Summer' of 1983 (UK 8; US 9) depicts the dungareed trio bettering male authority figures before, again, everyone dances together at the finale. After sex-workers turn on a macho harasser in Pat Benatar's 1983 'Love Is a Battlefield' promo clip (US 5), they all, again, dance in liberated formation, as Benatar belts out the air-punching chorus, "We are strong!"

Expressing this female strength alongside the new performance principle of gym fitness, Olivia Newton-John's lycra-fitted video for 1982's biggest seller, 'Physical' (UK 7; US 1), presents her as a personal trainer to weak, overweight men. Having been transformed into musclebound hunks, that the men pair off at the end is indicative of a concomitant queering of 80s culture – from Tom Cruise dancing in his pants in 1983's *Risky Business* to Nick Kamen stripping to his boxers in 1985's Levi's ad, or just the *fact* of INXS's Michael Hutchence. Yet homophobia was just as 80s as homoeroticism, and with Reagan claiming, "We're seeing rededication to bedrock values of faith, family, work",[2] while leaving AIDS to gut gay communities, 80s queers who weren't in a coffin were in the closet. If Bronski Beat were the exception, with 1985's 'Smalltown Boy' (UK 3) and 'Why' (UK 6) addressing anti-gay prejudice, the closeted Boy George, Limahl (Kajagoogoo's 'Too Shy', UK 1; US 5) and the Pet Shop Boys were the rule, whatever hints they offered (though PSB's 'It's a Sin' is more shame than liberation, UK 1; US 9). Bowie denied he'd dabbled; Elton John married a woman; George Michael duetted with him on 1985's male-gaze anthem, 'Wrap Her Up' (UK 12; US 20).

Homoeroticism, meanwhile, was absorbed into high-80s' iconography as a facet of libidinal capitalism. On Duran Duran's summer 1982 'Rio' video (UK 9; US 14), the band's tanned bodies are just one component in a capitalist showreel of women, yachts, champagne and designer suits. Made-up and effete, Dave Stewart as Louis XVIII in the Eurythmics' video for 1985's 'There Must Be an Angel' (UK 1; US 22) enacts an Epicurean sensuality – consuming alcohol, entertainment, bodies – that's entirely, homoerotically 80s. Yet the dandy is historically heteronormative, as the video for Falco's 1985 'Rock Me Amadeus' (UK 1; US 1) affirms. Queerness was co-opted into 80s culture as heterosexual camp: Godley & Creme's 1982 'Wedding Bells' video (UK 7); the dancing toughs in Toto's absurd 1982 'Rosanna' promo (UK 12; US 2); and John Oates. Both Bonnie Tyler's 'Holding out for a Hero' (UK 2) and its parent film, *Footloose* (1984), are queer, given producer Jim Steinman's synth-showtune production and the film's homoeroticised rebellion – handily compiled in Kenny Loggins' theme's video (UK 6; US 1). Queerness here simply lends contemporary gloss to traditional masculinity. Tyler's lustily sung "He's gotta to be strong and he's gotta to be fast/And he's gotta be fresh from the fight" *objectifies* machismo, while the song soundtracks the film's famed tractor-joust, playing "chickie run" with sublimated queer desire. Dancing tough guy Kevin Bacon was the poster boy for this queered machismo – with Tom Cruise running him close – a modality that merged with yuppie narcissism, but which, while softening masculinity's hard lines, neither jettisoned male aggression nor altered attitudes to homosexuality as an *activity* rather than an aesthetic.

The aestheticisation of female sexuality in this era was presented as feminist power, as on Madonna's peepshow video for 'Open Your Heart' (UK 4; US 1), defiantly – dismissively – courting the male gaze, its visuals neither erotic nor attaining *Eros*, Marcuse's transcendent state of liberation. The transformation of Sheena Easton from traditional housewife on 1980's '9 to 5 (Morning Train)' (UK 3: US 1) to glamorous sexpot on 1984's 'Strut' (US 7) is telling: "Strut, pout, put it out/That's what you want from women", she sighs, while doing much the same in the video. Easton's Prince-written 'Sugar Walls' (US 9) hymns her vagina while she coos, "Take advantage – it's all right". Marcuse calls such tropes "extend[ing] liberty while intensifying domination".[3] In an era of false eyelashes, glistening lipstick, huge hair and boob tubes, feminism, like gay liberation, could be co-opted into libidinal capitalism.

Indeed, capitalism recognised neither limits nor borders in the high 80s. Amid a Roman orgy of corporate mergers, record labels became just one division in multinational conglomerates, pushing music towards a more business-orientated model. Gone was the largesse and experimentalism of the 70s: A&R (artist and repertoire) departments now shaped the 'product' to a commodity logic, trimming costs, encouraging brand continuity and ensuring cross-genre sonic conformity. Like the state's strong hand on the free market, this corporate control was enforced by authoritarian auteurs like Horn, Moroder and Nile Rodgers, the strong hand on the studio controls. With singles strategically issued to re-ignite album sales, Epic's release of seven singles in a year from Michael Jackson's 1982 *Thriller* was refined by sister-label CBS into seven singles over two years, plus endless touring, for Springsteen's *Born in the U.S.A.* PR operations expanded to maximise media saturation via MTV, movie tie-ins, ad licensing and broadsheet and lifestyle magazine coverage. The development of the compact disc in the mid-80s was the cherry on the cake, dramatically boosting profits by CDs' inflated sales price, making 1987 the music industry's most profitable year ever – just as Thatcher scored her third electoral victory.

On Jackson and McCartney's video for 1983's 'Say Say Say' (UK 2; US 1), their nineteenth-century hucksters gleefully count the banknotes after gulling the public. Like the trajectory of Britain's Channel 4, municipal councils, post-punk or *Marxism Today*,[4] principles came to be regarded as square, uptight, snobbish. 80s pop, by contrast was hip, amiable, populist. "I'm a man without conviction", as Boy George put it on Culture Club's saccharine 1983 confection 'Karma Chameleon' (UK 1; US 1). Yet the great failure of 80s satire was *Spitting Image* presenting Reagan's folksiness as simplicity – as on Genesis's handwringing 'Land of Confusion' video (UK 14; US 4) – whereas Reagan's amiability overlaid a cold-steel conviction. Sometimes, there was a scampish innocence to 80s' pop's social disengagement, as on Madonna's glorious 1985 'Into the Groove' (UK 1), a cheerful cheapness retaining an aura of punky rebellion. Yet, as 80s pop's sonics and sentiments calcified as the dogma dug in, the genre came to sound increasingly coercive, every space filled with hooks, synth-washes and swimming-pool reverb, its positivity forced, autocratic. Former Go-Go Belinda Carlisle's 1987 declaration that 'Heaven Is a Place on Earth' (UK 1; US 1) pushes all the right, bright, 80s-pop buttons, but sounds attenuated, its booming drums hollow, while Carlisle's processed smile in the video makes authoritarian pop's populist coercion all too clear.

'Between the Wars': The Falklands, Cold, Race and Class Wars

There is another version of the 80s: the era of Iron Maiden's 1982 gothic-metal 'Number of the Beast' (UK 18) – "The evil face that twists my mind and brings me to despair" – and of Golden Earring's concurrent cyborg-synth makeover 'Twilight Zone' (US 10): "The place is a madhouse/Feels like being cloned". This 80s is the era of *Blade Runner* (1982) – a world run by corporations – of *1984* (1984) – a world turned totalitarian – and *Mad Max: Beyond Thunderdome* (1985) – a world destroyed by nuclear war. A recurring question in *Blade Runner* is what constitutes a human, and with the social contract shredded, the 80s' replicant winners were encouraged to renounce their humanity, while the era's losers had theirs discursively removed as scroungers, deadbeats, welfare queens and enemies within – or just 'losers'. Yet for the collective world, there's no such social separation, and as heartland rocker John Mellencamp insists on 1983's 'Pink Houses' (US 8), his ragged voice straining over raw acoustic guitar and solidaristic handclaps: "The simple man, baby/ Pays for the thrills with bills".

For the left there's a different 80s montage, therefore, one that's grainy and monochrome: dole queues, food banks and decaying inner cities; 1982 dole drama *Boys from the Blackstuff* ("gizza job"); the Greenham Women's Peace Camp by the cruise missile silos; 1983's huge CND demonstrations; ordinary people joining pickets during the miners' strike of 1984–85; the counterculture's remnant asserting their right to roam at 1985's bloody Battle of the Beanfield; the rebellions of Liverpool and London's councils in 1985–86; the Wapping British printers' strike of 1986–87; American ACT UP AIDS direct-action die-ins. This was the collective world doing battle with the competitive world, and though each one ended in defeat, such struggles are a forgotten facet of consensus-creation, as Gramsci argued.[5] "I fight authority", Mellencamp asserts on 1983's 'Authority Song' (US 15): "authority always wins". Yet, as the video dramatises, the defeated get up and fight again.

This 80s montage has a very different-sounding soundtrack:

"a public service announcement – with guitars", as the Clash put it on 1982's 'Know Your Rights' (*Combat Rock*, UK 2; US 7). Rawer, more aggressive and more melancholic than 80s pop, such music is a reminder of the sweat and grit eclipsed by the era's shine and gloss, a reassertion of Fordist graft and refusal against post-Fordist automation and assent. The austere Motown bounce of the Jam's 1982 'A Town Called Malice' (UK 1) matches its stark economic choices, "To either cut down on beer or the kid's new gear". In an era of synthesizers and Linn drums, Springsteen's acoustic 1982 *Nebraska* (UK 3; US 3), flecked by wheezy harmonica and the occasional mandolin, was a statement in *sound*, an analogue of its content and vocabulary – the "racket boys" safe in their 'Mansion on the Hill', the "losers" forced into crime or remaindered on "scrap-metal hill". Similarly, the Irish folk instrumentation of the Pogues' ramshackle 1985 *Rum, Sodomy & the Lash* (UK 13) – all rusty metal and dilapidated wood – gave a punky defiance to their songs of the dispossessed: "We'll sing a song of liberty for blacks and paks and jocks" ('The Sick Bed of Cúchulainn').

The danger of authentocracy is clear here, the boomer pop-paradigm redux, connecting to reactionary notions of 'real' or 'men's work'. When folk-rock revisionists the Smiths' answer to "panic on the streets" is to "hang the DJ" on 1986's 'Panic' (UK 11), they could as easily be damning multi-racial dance music as the bland banalities of radio's Smashies and Niceys. Yet the Smiths had their radical aspects – less their part in 'Red Wedge', backing Labour no-mark Neil Kinnock in feeble opposition to Thatcher, than in encapsulating 'indie', alongside the Cocteau Twins and R.E.M. A post-punk formation independent of label, production-sound and mind, indie's emergent culture created an austere space that, while hardly 'outside' capitalism, was at some distance from the cravenly corporate. As the 80s progressed, that space became harder to find – R.E.M. signed to a major, while a harder, spacier quality began to infuse the Smiths' production-sound.

80s protest music is full of the iconography of war, as pop musicians did the work politicians abnegated in protesting the Falklands adventure (Elvis Costello's scabrous 1983 'Pills and Soap', UK 16) and Britain's imperial war in Northern Ireland

(U2's elegiac 1983 'Sunday Bloody Sunday', *War*, UK 1; US 12). Music put a spotlight on Reagan's covert wars in Central and South America on Don Henley's 1984 'All She Wants to Do is Dance' (US 9) and in 1987, U2's 'Bullet the Blue Sky' *(The Joshua Tree*, UK 1; US 1) and R.E.M.'s 'Welcome to the Occupation' (*Document*, UK 28; US 10). Decrying the war on black South Africans were the Specials' 1984 Costello-produced 'Free Nelson Mandela' (UK 9) and Springsteen guitarist Little Steven's 1985 'Sun City' (UK 21), with Bono, Dylan, Springsteen and Run DMC.

If America's race war seemed repressed in this period, this was because 80s pop's corporate merger of soul and rock stifled soul's development into R&B, while MTV's resistance to black artists ensured emergent hip-hop's only hits were in Britain (casting doubt on *Billboard*'s assessment system). Hip-hop arose from a street culture of block parties and park jams, its music made from recycled old records and repurposed drum machines. Grandmaster Flash and Melle Mel's marvellous 1982 'The Message' (UK 8) systemically links poverty, racism and crime against a propulsive electronic backing: "You'll grow in the ghetto, living second rate/And your eyes will sing a song of deep hate". Suspiciously underpromoted in the US, Gary Byrd's 1983 'The Crown' (UK 6), with Stevie Wonder, is an effervescent return of the repressed, exemplifying an African American heritage and culture that's "never seen on your TV". While Reagan pursued economically racist policies, white acts co-opted hip-hop – overtly (and cleverly) on Tom-Tom Club's cute 1982 'Wordy Rappinghood' (UK7) – covertly (and stupidly) on Genesis's Grandmaster-referencing, drum-machine driven 1983 'Mama' (UK 4). Aerosmith's career was revived by Run DMC covering 'Walk This Way' in 1986 (UK 8; US 4), and while hardly exposing the realities of the projects, it still spirited a defiant, African American street-culture into the pop mainstream.

It was hardly coincidence that Thatcher and Reagan ramped up the Cold War as they rolled up social democracy: Stalinist communism had long functioned as a bogeyman for socialism.[6] Elton John's 1985 'Nikita' (UK 3; US 7) was thus a useful idiot, depicting the Soviet Union as the antithesis of Western freedom: "The human heart a captive in the snow". The West's renewed aggression sparked considerable domestic resistance, however, with CND membership peaking in 1985, Labour adopting unilateral nuclear disarmament and TV dramas (*The Day After*, 1983; *Edge of Darkness*, 1985), film (*War Games*, 1983) and even 80s pop protesting politics' apocalyptic brinksmanship. Initially pop's protest was performed with a light touch: Prince's 1982 '1999' (UK 2; US 12) flippantly but acutely conjoins 80s hedonism and nuclear nihilism: "Life is just a party/And parties weren't meant to last". The nuclear farce of Men at Work's 1983 'It's a Mistake' (US 6) doesn't disguise its tragedy, while for all its poppy chirpiness, Nik Kershaw's 1983 'I Won't Let the Sun Go Down on Me' (UK 2) is pretty cheerless: "Break your silence if you would/Before the sun goes down for good".

By 1984, the tone was grimmer but more fatalistic. On Nena's cute synthpop '99 Red Balloons' (UK 1; US 2), the end of the world is met with a melancholy sigh, while Ultravox's 'Dancing with Tears in My Eyes' (UK 3) proposes an utterly *80s* response: to *dance* through the apocalypse. The same year, Frankie Goes to Hollywood's 'Two Tribes' (UK 1) manages to be both flippant *and* frightening, with Holly Johnson's bombastic demand, "Are we living in a world where sex and horror are the new gods?", suggesting not just the normalisation of nuclear war but its incorporation into libidinal capitalism. Yet with Reagan and Chernenko depicted as wrestlers in the video, 'Two Tribes', like all these songs, enacts an equal opportunity blame game, eliding Thatcher and Reagan's provocations. At least Sting's gauche 1985 'Russians' (UK 12; US 16) questioned whether there *was* a Soviet threat. The political engineering of fear meant the era's sci-fi songs were taken for evocations of nuclear war, as on Genesis spinoff Mike and the Mechanics' dystopian 1985 'Silent Running' (UK 21; US 6) – under totalitarianism *all* songs will sound like Phil Collins – and glam-metallers Europe's escapist 1986 'The Final Countdown' (UK 1; US 8).

As for class war, metallers Judas Priest's *Screaming for Vengeance* (UK 11; US 17) protests an authoritarian 'Electric Eye' which "keep[s] the country clean" by crushing the masses. "Same old no tomorrow, kicked in the face", screams the title track. Despite its *völkisch* medium, 'Screaming for Vengance' evades being authoritarian pop both by its absence of synths and its aggressively adversarial lyric: "Send them screaming back through their hell's own gate". Several acts articulated this class war through the classless demotic of 80s pop. Pet Shop Boys' 1984 'West End Girls' (UK 1; US 1) plays out class conflict via club pickups, while "From Lake Geneva to the Finland Station" charts Lenin's route to the Russian Revolution. Sade's smooth, neo-soul 1984 'When Am I Going to Make a Living' speaks as a class, declaring, "We're hungry but we won't give in" (*Diamond Life*, UK 2; US 5), while Simply Red's 1985 'Money's Too Tight to Mention' (UK 13; US 28) references "Reaganomics" as the War on Poverty was replaced by a war on the poor.

The most concentrated expression of the 80s' class war was the British miners' strike. Thatcher's closure of the coal pits was a political strategy designed to provoke a confrontation which would, like Reagan's PATCO intervention, break the power of organised labour. Pitting both the army and the police against the strikers, the resultant massed battles in bleak landscapes resembled a civil war, the competitive world against the collective world. Despite the strike attracting public sympathy, neither the media, the Labour Party nor the TUC supported it, while the miners deserved better musical support than Sting's 1985 'We Work the Black Seam' (*Dream of the Blue Turtles*, UK 3; US 2), or Paul Weller's Council Collective's worthily dull 'Soul Deep' (a measly UK 24).

Released as the strike was facing defeat, Billy Bragg's stunning spring 1985 'Between the Wars' (UK 15) stands in exemplary solidarity, however. A raw song of sweat and toil, it's a modern folk-ballad hacked out on a solitary electric guitar, Bragg's universal worker bluntly but eloquently paying tribute to class power, offering a secular hymn to the social contract between citizen and state which was concurrently being crushed in the coalfields. While the song is unbearably moving, it doesn't surrender hope, for as Edgerton argues, "The miners were not doomed, they were *defeated*".[7] The universal worker's collectivist "faith in my fellow man" endures, while the fact that "we are *between* the wars" (emphasis added) means the class war isn't over.

The proof of that ongoing refusal was the links musicians made between the 80s' wars. The Clash's 1982 'Straight to Hell' (*Combat Rock*) connects Britain's industrial communities ("feel the steel mills rust") to Vietnam. Springsteen's 1984 'Born in the U.S.A.' (UK 5; US 9) evokes a demographic shot up in Vietnam, then shat on by Fordism's abandonment in a rustbelt "dead-man's town". Yet the song is so air-punchingly anthemic that Reagan wasn't alone in taking it as patriotic (the huge American flag on the cover didn't help).[8] Costello invokes the irony of the Clyde's maritime industry being reinvigorated by the Falklands on 1983's stunning 'Shipbuilding' (*Punch the Clock*, UK 3; US 24). Pink Floyd's pared-back 1983 *The Final Cut* (UK 1; US 6) is a morose masterpiece that links the destruction of the post-war dream to capitalism's pursuit of profit and, ultimately, the destruction of the world. "Oh Maggie, Maggie, what did we do?" demands Roger Waters.

These songs, like the left itself, were on the right side of history but the wrong side of politics – yet, as Traverso argues, "there [a]re no final defeats; defeats [a]re only lost battles".[9] The socialist Style Council's late 1984 'Shout to the Top!' (UK 7) acknowledges this recurrence of defeat – "when you're knocked on your back and your life's a flop" – but refuses to give up hope: "when you're down on the bottom, there's nothing else/But to shout to the top". With its surging Motown strings, rippling piano and soaring melody, the song is both a 60s hauntology *and* a typical 80s 'new pop' confection, deploying the era's cultural demotic against it, as the left dusted itself down for the next battle in the class war.

"Let's Make Lots of Money": New Pop, New Politics

'New pop' was the axis upon which popular music turned from countercultural to conservative. In throwing off the lyrical, sonic and literal overcoat of the punk era's "bleak midwinter", Bracewell argues, new pop embraced a "spring" which reasserted pleasure in popular music.[10] Former new-waver, Joe Jackson's delightful 1982 'Steppin' Out' (UK 6; US 6) is effectively a new-pop manifesto, declaring, "We are tired of all the darkness in our lives", while embracing soul cadence, disco beats and synthpop electronics. With Joy Division becoming New Order following Ian Curtis's suicide, their discofied, Moroder-inspired 1983 'Blue Monday' (UK 9) is paradigmatic of this shift from static post-punk chill to danceable new pop warmth. Yet Bracewell's language doesn't *coincidentally* invoke the Winter of Discontent, that conservative synecdoche for a 'socialism' which rhetorically (and inaccurately) covers the 70s in a chill mist. In affirming new pop, Bracewell, like Maconie, Beckett and its original proselytiser Paul Morley,[11] emphasise post-punk's *froideur* but excise new wave's fusion of warm affect and leftist politics. The clue to this sleight of hand is in the Thatcherite language of Morley's original new-pop manifesto: "overground brightness... modern excitement... choice and value... getting on with the job".[12] Morley's combination of work and play, grafting and dancing, reveals new pop as the cultural logic of Thatcherism – performance without principle. Bracewell's gloss is simply centrist defensiveness.

Complicating matters, however, with new pop declaring aggression passé and "rockism" phallocentric, post-Fordism's automated synths and drum machines *unmanned* music, much as it had unmanned manufacturing. Denim was ditched in tandem with hard hats, pushing women (Alison Moyet, Annie Lennox, Cyndi Lauper) and queers (Marc Almond, Bronski Beat, Pet Shop Boys) to the fore – alongside narcissistic straight men (Duran Duran; Paul King). With rockists deriding new pop 'haircut' bands in masculinist terms, Flock of Seagulls were as famous for Mike Score's bizarre *coiffure* as for their evocation of the incorporeal on spring 1982's nifty 'I Ran' (US 9). When, on the synth-suffused 'Wishing (If I had a Photograph of You)' (UK 10; US 26), Score taunts authentocrats by his preference for processed image over physical intimacy, it's not so much the affective coldness that's striking as the preoccupation with process and image. Such self-consciousness about co-option would characterise new pop, as it has characterised its critical champions.

The spark for Morley's new-pop manifesto, Sheffield post-punks turned soulboys, ABC, exemplified Thatcherite aspiration with their gold lamé jackets and glossy arrangements, while Martin Fry's performatively 'showbiz' stage persona was always at an ironic remove from its signalled 'soul' sincerity. Similarly, Horn's lavish production of summer 1982's *Lexicon of Love* (UK 1; US 24) is inorganic and incorporeal compared to soul's physicality, while the alienation effect of Horn's foregrounding of the apparatus is its own point, not a political one. This, combined with Fry's meaninglessly attention-seeking lyrics – "I know democracy/But I know what's fascist" ('Many Happy Returns') – makes the music's subject its own machinations in the marketplace.[13] Duran Duran had pioneered such an approach and, dropping Euro chill for rock libidinality, the 'meaning' of summer 1982's 'Hungry Like the Wolf' (UK 5; US 3) is thus the band's desire to break the States. Testament to an ongoing ambivalence about this process, however, Duran's lovely 'Save a Prayer' (UK 2) articulates an abiding Euro melancholy amid the mercenary advance (but note its absence from American charts).

Once-angular post-punks Simple Minds' autumn 1982 *New Gold Dream* (UK 3) matches instrumental giddiness to aspirational vocabulary – "gold", "silver", "shine", "dreams", "fame", "Glittering Prize" (UK 16) – again seeming like an annotation of its pop co-optation, with 'Promised You a Miracle' (UK 13) insisting, with Thatcherite assurance, "Everything is possible". Again, there's melancholia amid the miracles, however, a sense of loss that gives *New Gold Dream* a depth the band would soon disavow. Orange Juice's irresistible 1983 'Rip it Up' ("and start again") (UK 8) reads as a commentary on the commercial strategy of its synth-funk overproduction, undercut with an abiding anxiety about the implications: "I hope to God I'm not as numb as you make out". Aztec Camera's jaunty, kitchen-sink production on 1983's 'Oblivious' (UK 18) is the sound of trying too hard to be liked, again undercut by ambivalence about its incorporation: "Count me in and count me out".

In new pop's hinterland, however, something more adversarial was evident, centred upon this neoliberal cult of work. Madness's early 1982 disco-ska 'Cardiac Arrest' (UK 14) is a morbid tale of a conformist commuter not just failing to live up to the performance principle but dying of it. Tears for Fears' autumn 1982 'Mad World' (UK 3) distends synthpop sonics into proto-industrial territory, lamenting the commuting "daily race" of "worn-out faces… going nowhere". An unintended consequence of deindustrialisation was that its creation of unemployment produced a culture hostile to the performance principle. Wham!'s 1982 'Wham Rap!' (UK 8) rejects being "more dead than alive in a nine-to-five" while refusing to be unmanned by unemployment: "I *am* a man, job or no job" (accompanied by a ridiculously homoerotic video), insisting, "I'm a soul boy, I'm a dole boy/Take pleasure in leisure, I believe in joy!" In this engagingly gauche couplet on a ghastly song, Wham! double-handedly uncouple the pleasure principle from the performance principle.

From false eyelashes to drum machines to huge new workplace computers, the 80s was a denatured age, with several new-pop acts expressing ambivalence about such inorganic sterility. In the video for Eurythmics' 1983 'Sweet Dreams (Are Made of This)' (UK 2; US 1), Annie Lennox, with cropped orange hair and business suit, sternly brandishes a cane in a clinical office, as boffin Dave Stewart sits at a console, before the scene abruptly switches to the pair playing cellos in a field of cows. As this organic scene comically invades the office location, corporate culture is revealed as humourless, its hegemony consequently fragile. Similarly, Heaven 17 pit their corporate shtick against soul singer Carole Kenyon on 1983's 'Temptation' (UK 2). Glenn Gregory sternly demands, "You've got to make me an offer/That cannot be refused" – a business takeover of the love song's language: Kenyon's hyper-affective response is virtually in tongues. In the video the band are be-suited and monochrome; she's off-the-shoulder and in colour, but the satire is queasy, the inverted commas in danger of falling off. Heaven 17's former colleagues Human League's introduction of 'real' instruments on '(Keep Feeling) Fascination' (UK 2; US 8) and 'The Lebanon' (UK 11) evidenced an ambivalence about their commodity status as they struggled to follow up *Dare* (defensively playing a 'band' in the 'Fascination' video). With Horn giving proggers Yes a cyborg extravaganza production on 1983's 'Owner of a Lonely Heart' (UK 28; US 1), its video depicts a yuppie forced into Fordist labour, who thereafter yearns to rejoin the organic world.

Reversing synthpop's trajectory, Depeche Mode chose the peak of new pop to go Euro-dystopian on summer 1983's Berlin-recorded *Construction Time Again* (UK 6). Matching Martin Gore's gloomy lyrics, the Mode forged an 'industrial' sound, which is usually interpreted as Fordist melancholia amidst contemporary deindustrialisation.[14] Rather, their grinding, coldly automated electronics capture *post*-Fordist alienation, as do the lyrics of 'Everything Counts' (UK 6), where the corporate "contract" from which "there's no turning back" is the social contract's contrary: "The grabbing hands/Grab all they can/All for themselves, after all". This chorus is the more effective for being voiced in Gore's vulnerable tones, capturing the collective loss in individualism, before Dave Gahan returns to brusquely assert, "It's a competitive world!" The phrase performs two tasks for the performance principle, affirming the free-market demand to be 'competitive' in business, while conventionalising the war of all against all in both work and play.

The second wave of new pop, lacking any punk pedigree, took such competitive individualism not just as read but as radical. The video for Howard Jones' saccharine 1983 'New Song' (UK 3; US 27) features Jones and his creepy dancer inciting Fordist workers to quit their jobs and "throw off your mental chains", yet there's nothing Marcusian about this song of entrepreneurial incentive. Thomas Dolby's 1984 'Hyperactive!' (UK 17) also claims nonconformity, but the music's agitated synthetics parallel the lyric's post-human monad. Using a literally post-human figure in the video, Nik Kershaw's 1984 'Wouldn't It Be Good' (UK 4) deploys the Thatcherite trope of ridiculing envy of others' achievements. Scritti Politti went from indie Marxist post-punk to major-label postmodern pop (even naming a track 'Jacques Derrida'). Via pretty-boy Green's incorporeal falsetto, 1984's 'Wood Beez', voices aspiration (UK 10), 1985's 'Perfect Way' (US 11) antipathy to principle: "I don't have a purpose or mission".

There remained some ambivalence about this cult of work, however. The Thompson Twins were post-Fordist from their processed hair to their multi-racial, multi-gender lineup, to the ambiguity of who did what with what and to whom. 1984's 'You Take Me Up' (UK 2) decries work – "I know what it means to work hard on machines... going round in circles" – while in its chain-gang video, following the blowing up of the plant, there's another finale of dancing (former) workers. Tears for Fears' early 1985 'Shout' (UK 4; US 1) rejects both co-option – "In violent times/You shouldn't have to sell your soul" – and conformity: "You shouldn't have to jump for joy". Yet if spring 1985's ebullient 'Everybody Wants to Rule the World' (UK 2; US 1) was satirical, it was undercut by the video of the duo driving round California in vintage cars, demonstrating how "to make the most of freedom and of pleasure". Kershaw's concurrent 'Wide Boy' (UK 9) archly questions the Thatcherite dream he inhabits: "He no big deal, he's just an ordinary guy... but he got overnight success". Meanwhile, Pet Shop Boys' 1986 'Opportunities (Let's Make Lots of Money)' (UK 11; US 10) was easily taken straight, the crowded, corporate production putting Tennant's camply melancholic voice at a detached distance.

As Heaven 17 demonstrated, satire was an iffy business in this flippant but humourless era. Horn and Morley's ZTT label tracked capitalism rather too accurately, its merchandise tacky ("Frankie Says" T-shirts), Frankie's 1984 album *Welcome to the Pleasure Dome* (UK 1) lavishly packaged but musically lacklustre. The title track's satirical, "Using my power, I sell it by the hour/I have it, so I market it", fights it out with the corporate crush of Horn's production. Norwegians A-ha were seemingly beyond satire, being pure product from pretty-boy Nordic looks to processed hooks to corporate videos. For 1985's 'The Sun Always Shines on TV' (UK 1; US 20) viewers are invited to spot the difference between band and mannequins, as Morten Harket coos, "I reached inside myself/And found nothing there". Yet even in A-ha there's an ambivalence, an audible anxiety that illuminates the process of consensus-creation. The dialectical animation/live-action video for 1985's agitatedly effervescent 'Take on Me' (UK 2; US 1) pits the organic against the processed, offering an invitation to a Marcusian world beyond work – as the repressive state apparatus erupts into the frame.

"This Gun's for Hire": The Corporate Authentic

Dire Straits' summer 1985 'Money for Nothing' (UK 4; US 1) called time on new pop by ventriloquising Fordist workers' derision for MTV 'haircut bands'. "That ain't workin'", they mock, while resentfully noting, "that little faggot with the earring and the make-up... he's a millionaire". The problem isn't so much the homophobic language – queerness *was* new pop's demotic – as the weasel trick of attributing such views to workers when the intended contrast is clearly with the hands-on graft of 'real' musicians – such as Dire Straits. It's the more weaselly for its hypocrisy: 'satirising' MTV with a state-of-the-art video, co-opting superstar Sting to sing the channel's *actual* ad line ("I want my MTV"), then adding splashy synths and a processed ZZ Top guitar sound in a package as plastic as any new pop.

In fact, authentocrats had largely adopted new-pop conventions by this point – albeit with fingers crossed behind their backs. On 1983's 'Human Touch' (UK 23; US 18) Rick Springfield bemoans, "Everybody's talking to computers/ They're all dancing to a drum machine" – over computerised synths and drum machines, and with a homoerotic sci-fi video to match. Similarly, Springsteen queered his music with synthesizers, processed drums and the requisite homoerotic video on 1984's delightful 'Dancing in the Dark' (UK 4; US 2). Springsteen also had it both ways: the video's sweatily masculine 'live show', with the girl pulled out of the crowd, co-opts new pop into the Fordist traditionalism of 'real' rock and heteronormative sexuality. This, then, is that epitome of high-80s popular culture, the corporate authentic.

Rootsy r'n'b-veteran Tina Turner effected a comeback with her 1983 Heaven 17-helmed cover of Al Green's 'Let's Stay Together' (UK 6; US 26). With her leonine hair perfect for the 80s, Turner is queered in the video by ambivalently gendered dancers stroking her legs. Yet her 1984 *Private Dancer* (UK 2; US 3) was the ultimate expression of the corporate authentic, with its processed 'rock' dynamics and plastic-soul libidinality. Indeed, on the Knopfler-written title track (UK 26; US 7), Turner is a "dancer for money" for whom "any old music will do". On what Dylan Jones calls "a manifesto of independence",[15] formerly prolific composer Turner didn't write a single song: "You keep your mind on the money", she purrs. The video for 'Better Be Good to Me' (US 5) begins with the billing: "Tina Turner – sold out".

Queen took to the corporate authentic as to the manor born. In an era when ditching principles *was* principle, Queen abandoned their 'no synthesizers' authentocracy for authoritarian synthpop on 1984's 'Radio Ga Ga' (UK 2; US 16). Articulating a nostalgia for an authentic age, the track couldn't *sound* more artificial, while its anti-MTV *Metropolis* video couldn't *be* more MTV-friendly, accentuating the fascist camp inherent in such populist piety. However, Queen fell afoul of the corporate authentic's reactionary core when their fabulous drag video for follow-up 'I Want to Break Free' (UK 3) caused the track to bomb in America. So much for the post-Fordist unmanning of music. Queen's response was to authenticate with hard rock ('Hammer to Fall', UK 13) and pump up the fascist glamour (1985's 'One Vision', UK 7), a capitulation to reaction that revealed the moral redundancy of the age.

It was no coincidence that Queen's hair-metal heirs hit their commercial peak in tandem with new pop: 80s metal's palette-knife cosmetics, flouncy clothes and teased-up synthesizers made the genres kissing cousins, sharing a common progenitor in glam rock. Yet, typical of the corporate authentic, glam metal concurrently co-opted and denied its queerness. On 1983's poppy *Pyromania* (UK 18; US 2), Britons Def Leppard milked the macho trope of expressing gurning Fordist labour in every lubricious guitar lick, performance principle pulling against glam's performative queerness. With the videos for Quiet Riot's 1983 cover of Slade's 'Cum on Feel the Noize' (US 5) and Ratt's 1984 'Round and Round' (US 12) featuring disruption of suburban and aristocratic homes respectively, glam metal perpetuated convention-breaking radicalism, while its style and sound relayed corporate-branded reaction. Although Van Halen are queered by post-Fordist synths on 1984's 'Jump' (UK 7; US 1), the video presents an anachronistic doofus machismo, a push-and-pull reflected in the song, which may reference jumping ship or jumping off a building, rugged individualism or defeated atomisation.

With Van Halen's fall 1984 'Panama' (US 13) reviving the car/sex metaphor, Springsteen offers a similar single *entendre* on 1984's 'Pink Cadillac' (B-side, 'Dancing in the Dark'): "We can park it out in the back/And have a party in your pink Cadillac". These songs trade in the automobile as vehicle of liberation for that of libidinal consumer object, and, claiming blue-collar 'authenticity', do much the same to women. Prince's 1983 'Little Red Corvette' (UK 2; US 6) appears to turn the same corporate-authentic trick: after all, his sound is *constitutive* of 80s pop, its combination of synths and guitars, rock dynamics and soul sexuality having been 'new pop' long before Morley coined the term. Yet Prince was an 80s outlier, managing to make the automated human and the consumerist carnal, his lyrics and image simultaneously retro and futuristic, human and post-human, macho and queer. 'Corvette' spirits Fordist hauntology under the hood of post-Fordist pop:[16] amid the sense of regret – "I guess I should've known... it wouldn't last" – and the melancholia amid the carnality – "You're gonna run your little red corvette/Right in the ground" – the car metaphor becomes an invocation of an impotent Fordism rather than a tumescent post-Fordism.

The corporate authentic consumed 80s pop, with even acts whose ontology had been inauthenticity – Eurythmics, Tears for Fears, Thompson Twins – strapping on guitars, hiring a drummer, a brace of black backing-singers and a saxophonist (OMD's 1986 'If You Leave' from *Pretty in Pink*, US 4). Yet this Fordist superstructure rests on a synthetic post-Fordist base, and the combination sounds crushingly over-produced, with real and processed instruments fighting for space in the mix. There's a cry for help somewhere in Duran Duran's summer 1984 'The Reflex' (UK 1; US 1) – "I'm on a ride and I want to get off" – but the booming drum samples and migrainous melody bury it. Deploying Duran's guitarist, Andy Taylor, designer-suited Robert Palmer had fun with all this on 1986's 'Addicted to Love' (UK 5; US 1). The video's glazed, expressionless models overtly miming being a 'rock band' to an audibly automated backing offers a subtle satire of corporate authenticity in both music *and* gender. And yes, of course, Palmer is having it both ways, and – all but winking in the video – clearly knows it.

U2 had dabbled with automation on 1984's *The Unforgettable Fire* (UK 1; US 12), but their switch to authentocrat Americana on 1987's *Joshua Tree* cranked their commercial success up several notches. However, U2's was a peculiarly processed concept of the 'real' – the Edge's delay-saturated guitar, the omnipresent synths, the absence of 'feel' – while Bono's yearningly voiced *aspiration*, a will to be *more*, was 80s marketisation rendered messianic. On 'I Still Haven't Found What I'm Looking For' (UK 6; US 1) and 'Where the Streets Have No Name' (UK 4; US 13), U2's trick is to imbue the corporate authentic with a facsimile of transcendence. In similar vein, Australia's INXS seemed custom-made to a corporate conception of consumer desire – stadium guitars and hip-hop beats, synths and sax – "This is what you need/I'll give you what you need", Michael Hutchence promises sleazily on 1986's 'What You Need' (US 5), his solicitation of the gaze craven, his self-selling coercive. "Slide over here and give me a moment", he purrs creepily on 1987's 'Need You Tonight' (UK 2; US 1); "Can't think at all", he grunts, but it sounds *all too* thought out, a corporate goosing that insists its hands are on the table.

The corporate authentic had reached its apogee when atavistic glam metallers Mötley Crüe could be considered subversive. Their 1987 'Girls, Girls, Girls' (UK 26; US 12) affirms gender stereotypes both of men – "Friday night and I need a fight/My motorcycle and a switchblade knife" – and women – "Best when they're off their feet" – who are characterised in the video as half-naked dancers for the leering male gaze. Yet, just as it seemed that the corporate authentic was pop's Pacman, consuming everything in sight, this no-hope arena of hair metal produced something unexpectedly different. With a car accident leaving Def Leppard's drummer with one arm, the electronic kit his bandmates commissioned for him added a cyborg element to their sound that producer Mutt Lange maximised on summer 1987's *Hysteria* (UK 1; US 1). Lange deployed the cold distancing of digital sound to put metal machismo in acres of ectoplasmic space, the processing creating mystery even on a standard metal lust-song like 'Animal' (UK 6; US 19). Leppard's sample-saturated 'Pour Some Sugar on Me' (UK 18; US 2) sounds *off*, even queer, losing the *volk* from its inspiration, Queen's 'We Will Rock You'. Joe Elliott's lubricious gaze gets mirrored back at himself – "I'm hot, sticky sweet/From my head to my feet" – subverting the era's corporate authenticity from within.

'We are the World': The Individual and Society in 80s Pop

Thatcher's statement that "there's no such thing as society" was a rejection not just of socialism, or even of social democracy, but of *the social* itself. [17] As David Harvey observes, Thatcher and

Reagan's project targeted "all forms of social solidarity... in favour of individualism, private property, personal responsibility".[18] Unions were the most immediate target, with membership declining after the defeats of the PATCO and miners' strikes in what remained of Fordist industry. Meanwhile "flexible, mobile, and precarious" post-Fordist service work, Traverso argues, "eroded traditional forms of sociability and solidarity".[19] With class consciousness in retreat, the private realm was now the priority: an individual's income, their property – thus Thatcher's council-house fire sale – and their family. On Madness's joyous 1982 'Our House' (UK 5; US 7), there's only *their* family in the middle of their street, no neighbours, no community. The family is essentially an extension of the individual, and Thatcher's statement continues: "There are individual men and women and there are families... and people look to themselves first". Or as William Hurt put it in 1983's *The Big Chill*, "Wise-up folks, we're all alone out there!"

This individualism encroached upon music's reception (the Sony Walkman personal cassette player privatising listening), its sound (synths' sublimation of distance) and its sentiment (an audibly atomised affect). Donna Summer deployed a cast of 80s luminaries to proclaim her 'State of Independence' in 1982 (UK 14) across a majestic, frozen mountain-range of synths. Billy Joel's nervy, synthetic 1982 'Pressure' advises, "Don't ask for help, you're all alone" (US 20), its video depicting individuals in an endemically hostile environment. Men at Work's 1982 'Who Can It Be Now?' (US 1) simultaneously expresses and satirises such atomisation: "I keep to myself/There's nothing wrong with my state of mental health". Rick Springfield's 1982 'Don't Talk to Strangers' (US 2) posits both his lover and her imagined dalliances as untrustworthy – "You know he'll only use you up".

On Michael Jackson's brilliantly paranoid 1983 'Billie Jean' (UK 1; US 1), people are simply sources of pressure – ex-lover Billie; her disputed child; the video's stalking gumshoe – with Jackson defensively denying all social claims. The song is so familiar that its otherness is easily missed: mirroring the lyric, each sound sits in its own private space – a synth-waft here (1;13), a guitar fragment there (2:56), a discrete burst of strings in the distance (3:01) – and at a total remove from four people playing together in a room. Jackson guested on the funky synthpop of Rockwell's even more paranoid 1984 'Somebody's Watching Me' (UK 6; US 2). Going beyond the liberal equation of surveillance with totalitarianism, Rockwell's insistence on privacy – "All I want is to be left alone"– and his fear of the Inland Revenue Service are the tropes of conventional conservatism. The crashing drums and juddering synths of Pat Benatar's calculating 1985 'Invincible' (US 10) undergird an affective *realpolitik* – "We can't afford to be innocent/Stand up and face the enemy" – its Hobbesian assumption of the other's innate hostility absolving the absolutism of its self-interest.

The very thing that appeared to counteract this individualism, the collective Band Aid/Live Aid charity phenomenon of 1984–85, retrenched it. Prompted by an Ethiopian famine, Boomtown Rats' Bob Geldof and Ultravox's Midge Ure's all-star charity single, 1984's 'Do They Know It's Christmas?' (UK 1; US 13) was followed by Michael Jackson and Lionel Richie's even starrier spring 1985 'We Are the World' (UK 1; US 1) and that summer's transatlantic telecast, Live Aid. That Geldof never actually *did* say "Give us yer fuckin' money" on air is by-the-by: the project demanded individual citizens take up the work governments had once performed, an attitude entirely compatible with Thatcher, who knighted Geldof. With Live Aid making stars of U2 and reviving Queen's career, the ensuing charity trend's emphasis on celebrity rendered performative selflessness a form of self-promotion. "We're saving our own lives", 'We Are the World' declared, while sounding like a claim less of collectivity than of the global elite's *ownership* of that world.

As such, Live Aid merely insulated elite privilege with a pseudo-collective piety: note the title of Simple Minds' 1986 'Sanctify Yourself' (UK 10; US 14). The song's video contrasts monochrome communist iconography with the Minds' Technicolor live show – Western 'freedom' defined as narcissism (strutting frontman Jim Kerr) and passive consumption (the seemingly sedated audience) – authoritarian pop posing as humanitarian art. Whitney Houston's gruesome 1986 'The Greatest Love of All' (UK 8; US 1) reveals the paucity of this pop piety: the greatest love of all, it transpires,

263

is for *yourself*. Rather than being humanitarian, therefore, the song's repeated "I believe the children are our future" evokes *Cabaret*'s creepily authoritarian 'Tomorrow Belongs to Me'. With Houston singing into a mirror for much of the video, the song attributes success to individual effort, despite Houston's celebrity mother appearing throughout. Confirming quite how upended political logic had become, Paul Simon's *Graceland* that summer (UK 1; US 3) presented its breaking of the cultural boycott against apartheid South Africa as progressive. 'You Can Call Me Al' (UK 23; US 4) is a doozy of a pop tune, but its depiction of a Western man's mid-life crisis being solved by cultural imperialism is absent any sense of the political implications.

There was, however, a strand of 80s pop that rejected such pious individualism. On 1983's 'Get the Balance Right' (UK 13), Depeche Mode sarcastically recommend, "Be responsible, respectable... concerned and caring/Help the helpless/But always remain/Ultimately selfish". Hard as it is to credit, Paul Weller's socialist new pop collective, the Style Council played their 1985 revolutionary call-to-arms 'Walls Come Tumbling Down' (UK 6) at Live Aid: "The class war's real and not mythologized", Weller barks: "Governments crack and systems fall /'Cause unity is powerful". Prince's 'Paisley Park' (UK 18) in summer 1985 is radically utopian, hymning a communal space "of profound inner peace", where "love is the color this place imparts".

Godley & Creme's video for 1985's 'Cry' (UK 19; US 16) features humans of all genders, ages and races video-morphing into one another. Despite its piano-tinkling blandness, Bruce Hornsby's 1986 'The Way It Is' (UK 15; US 1) is a caustic critique of the era's moral atomisation, as the yuppie in his silk suit taunts the homeless man to "get a job". Erasure reassert the social contract on early 1987's 'It Doesn't Have to Be' (UK 12), against the dominant, Hobbesian ideology: "Always one against the other". This is put in class terms by John Mellencamp's 'We Are the People' on 1987's *Lonesome Jubilee* (US 6), the individualist self-congratulation of 'We Are the World' recast as collectivist revolution: "If you try to divide and conquer/ We'll rise up against you".

"No Romance without Finance": Love, Sex and the 80s

Politics infuse every aspect of society, and in this cold, un-empathetic era, "the language of love" that the Eurythmics hymn on 1983's 'Who's That Girl?' (UK 3; US 21) became markedly unromantic. On 'Love Is a Stranger' (UK 6; US 23), Annie Lennox calls love "glamorous and sleek by design/It's hard and restrained and it's totally cool". Love here is libidinal only as a consumer object is libidinal – all glossy surface, hard edges and straight lines – and in her affectless delivery, Lennox articulates a disdain for emotional clutter that's both Thatcherite and by this time unremarkable.

In this climate, a loveless transactionality became endemic to the love song. "You hold the percentage/But I'm the fool payin' the dues", sings Christine McVie on Fleetwood Mac's faxed-in synthpop hit 'Hold Me' (US 4), from 1982's corporate -makeover *Mirage* (UK 5; US 1), calculator in hand. Bonnie Tyler's 1983 gothic power ballad 'Total Eclipse of the Heart' (UK 1; US 1) evokes *emotion* being eclipsed – rather than doing the eclipsing, as is usually assumed. The clue is in the performative excess: Tyler's hair, her hoarse singing, and the extravagant but attenuated sonics of Steinman's authoritarian pop production. Love increasingly looked like a poor emotional investment: former punks Altered Images' new pop 1983 'Don't Talk to Me About Love' (UK 7) is emotionally frigid beneath Blondie-producer Mike Chapman's glossily pretty surface. Howard Jones's concurrent demand, 'What is Love?' (UK 2), is followed by "Does anybody love anybody anyway?", while on 1984's 'What's Love Got to Do With It?' (UK 3; US 1), Tina Turner yawns, "Who needs a heart when a heart can be broken?" T'Pau insist on 1987's 'Heart and Soul' that an inability to compromise is "the politics of life", while concurrently Whitesnake are committed to emotional disinvestment on their power ballad, 'Here I Go Again' (UK 9; US 1): "I ain't wasting no more time."

In such transactional times, the lover became mere product in the marketplace. "Every girl's crazy about a sharp-dressed man", ZZ Top asserted in 1983 (UK 22), accessorised with "gold watch, diamond ring/Cufflinks, stick pin": a yuppie. By

265

mangling grammar, Madonna's 1984 'Material Girl' (UK 3; US 2) manages to merge reality (the material) with acquisitiveness (materialism). Love here is an investment in futures which lives or dies by the profit imperative: "If they can't raise my interest then I/Have to let them be". Although Tina Turner's 1986 'What You Get Is What You See' (UK 30; US 13) satisfyingly objectifies *men*, as she haughtily huffs, "Before I buy/I always read the writing on the label", it's an assessment according to regressively Fordist criteria – the male as provider. Similarly, Gwen Guthrie's 1986 synthpop-soul 'Ain't Nothin' Goin' on but the Rent' (UK 5) complains, "Bill collector's at my door", while demanding of her suitor, "What can you do for me?" Guthrie's refrain, "No romance without finance", harks back to the good old days when sisters *weren't* doin' it for themselves, as Eurythmics and Aretha Franklin celebrated (UK 19; US 18). Newcomer Janet Jackson's 1986 'What Have You Done for Me Lately' (UK 3; US 4) likewise concerns what *he* can *do* for her, with Jackson's voice physically distanced in Jam and Lewis's tight, Princey production. Jackson's wonderful 'Nasty' (UK 19; US 3) captures this post-Fordist post-feminism, its deserved disempowering of lecherous Lotharios boasting one of pop's greatest asides: "No, my first name ain't 'baby', it's Janet – Miss Jackson if you're nasty".

It's not as if post-Fordism put an end to patriarchy, as Mötley Crüe's success made plain. Hall and Oates' digital Motown simulacra 'Maneater' in 1982 (UK 6; US 1) functions as a reply to post-feminist transactionality – "Money's the matter/ If you're in it for love/You ain't gonna get too far" – although reversion to trad misogyny is hardly a progressive solution. The Alan Parsons Project's creepy 1982 'Eye in the Sky' (US 3) is patriarchal authoritarian pop: "I can read your mind/I am the maker of rules": Big Brother as lover. Similarly, Sting insists, "I'll be watching you", on the Police's 1983 'Every Breath You Take' (UK 1; US 1) – a stalker soliloquy that's become a wedding song, such has been the subsequent sublimation of neoliberal affect. The video for Cars' 1984 'You Might Think' (US 7) features Ric Ocasek harassing a model, who, after being abducted and abused, is, naturally, won over to his charms. "I know when you're weak", he hisses. Wham!'s melancholic 1984 'Everything She Wants'

(UK 2; US 1) is another plaint about a material girl in which, like 'Maneater', the misogyny eclipses the anti-materialism.

With progressive forces perpetually on the back foot in this era, resistance to this cold, transactional trend was often itself problematic. When J. Geils Band's narrator sees his teenage crush in a porn 'Centerfold' in 1982 (UK 3; US 1), his "blood runs cold" because, "my memory has just been sold" – he's alienated by the marketisation of love. Yet, having it both ways, the song's promo is a soft-porn fever dream of half-dressed schoolgirls. The addressee of Hall & Oates' fantastic 1982 'I Can't Go for That (No Can Do)' (UK 8; US 1) is a business manager, but in this corporate takeover of the affective realm, it sounded like a love song. The track serves as a refusal both of the corporate turn *and* of transactional affect – "You got the body, now you want my soul" – even as its twinkling synths, body-popping rhythm and Hall's ecstatic vocal suggest this pair wouldn't "say no-go" to much (let's not even get into Hall's doe eyes in the video). Extending this blurring of the corporate and the libidinal, Billy Idol's 1983 'Eyes without a Face' (UK 18; US 4) neatly equates material and sexual greed as "a dip into someone else's pocket".

Sade's 1984 'Smooth Operator' (UK 19; US 5) matches a sleek, lounge-lizard Latin vibe to an evocation of a playboy who's as ruthless in love as in business: "Melts all your memories and change into gold/His eyes are like angels but his heart is cold". Travelling "coast to coast, LA to Chicago", the smooth operator is a personification of both global capital and the affective mode its logic deregulated, but he's also what Guthrie, Jackson and Madonna all seemingly desire. Tempting as it is to suggest they deserve each other, Carly Simon's 1986 'Coming Around Again' (UK 10; US 18) depicts the reality of women whose yuppie provider keeps them in contemporary style within a traditional servitude. "Pay the grocer/Fix the toaster" she enumerates, "Scream the lullaby". Imprisoned in her domestic paradise, Simon's narrator's insistence that she still believes in love connects both to the lovelessness of her situation and the universal love of her 60s past, a hippie hauntology that recurs throughout this profoundly anti-hippie era.[20]

"A Deadhead Sticker on a Cadillac": Hauntology in 80s Pop

Rather than the past becoming a postmodern pick'n'mix of depthless references during the 80s, it became a politicised space. Conservatives had long laid claim to the 1950s, and in the 80s-filtered 50s, rock'n'roll's rebellion was either absent (Shakin' Stevens; 1985's *Back to the Future*; George Michael's 1987 rockabilly 'Faith', UK 2; US 1), reconcilable with conservative mores (*Footloose*) or aestheticized as individualist style (*Rumble Fish*, 1983; Duckie in *Pretty in Pink*, 1986), or as homoeroticism (all the above, bar Shaky). Moreover, that the Kamen Levi's ad occupies the 50s visually but the 60s aurally – via Marvin Gaye's 1968 'I Heard It Through the Grapevine'[21] – is not merely 'ahistorical' in the postmodernist mode: it extends the long arm of the Long 50s into the 'bad 60s' to co-opt its rebellion as consumerism. While this is an example of how a palimpsest of competing periods can process dominant ideology, Jameson's take on postmodernism leaves both the past and the listening/looking subject – the 'consumer' – powerless in this process.

History is not hegemony, it's always a contested space. As such, hauntology restores both the power of the past *and* the power of the listening/looking subject. Fordist melancholia is the platonic form of Fisher and Reynolds' hauntology, providing a counter-narrative to the Thatcher/Reagan depiction of social democracy as strife, decline and failure, which is waved through by centrists. This melancholia is audible even in Mellencamp's joyful summer 1982 teen romance, 'Jack and Diane' (UK 25; US 1). With the heartland-rock rite-of-passage saga established as synecdoche for the historical transition from Fordism to post-Fordism, Mellencamp's rueful "life goes on/Long after the thrill of living has gone" is epochal as well as generational. With Dire Straits a pallid British take on heartland rock, that historical transition is relayed in mythic terms on their late-1982 epic 'Telegraph Road' (*Love Over Gold*, UK 1; US 19). With the workers told, "We're gonna have to pay what's owed/We're gonna have to reap from some seed that's been sowed", the implication is that deindustrialisation is payback for industrial unrest: a fair summary of the neoliberal project. Yet there's passivity as much as protest in the narrator's response – withdrawal to the private realm – which is Fordist melancholia's recurring pitfall.

There's no lack of energy in Big Country's stadium-filling sound, their skirling guitars, huge 80s drums and heroic vocals creating a Celtic heartland rock that, like Stuart Adamson's former band, the Skids, could be both rousing – 1983's 'In a Big Country' (UK 17; US 17) – and verge on the *völkisch*. However, Big Country also now took a melancholic turn: the "working man" narrator of 1984's 'Wonderland' (UK 8) historicises class struggle – "Fifty years of sweat and tears" – and hymns the class pride forged in that struggle, "when every head was high". Once again, with "that pride... torn apart", there's no resistance, just passive retreat to a privatised wonderland. On the title track of *Steeltown* (UK 1), later that year, Adamson sings, "We built all this with our own hands/But who could know we built on sand?" – again as if deindustrialisation were a matter of fate rather than political choice.

Despite its market-competitive confidence, Springsteen's 1984 *Born in the U.S.A.* (UK 1; US 1) is suffused with loss: "I had a job, I had a girl/I had something going, mister, in this world" ('Downbound Train'). In contrast to the anger of *Nebraska*, the melancholic mode here is, like Big Country and Dire Straits, fatalistic, the album's vacant stores and closed textile mills being presented as economic determination rather than political decision: "These jobs are going and they ain't comin' back" ('My Hometown', UK 9; US 6). Again, there's that redemptive escape into the private realm in 'Dancing in the Dark' and 'Cover Me' (US 7), and while there's still a kind of protest in this, its passivity is a precursor to Springsteen's retreat into the personal realm on 1987's *Tunnel of Love* (UK 1; US 1).

Springsteen's Amnesty cohort Peter Gabriel asserted his own commercial competitiveness and contemporary relevance with 1986's catchily contentless 'Sledgehammer' (UK 4; US 1). However, his electro-ballad 'Don't Give Up' (UK 9) concerns those experiencing contemporary *irrelevance* through competition. Gabriel's worker hymns the Fordist past – "we grew up strong/ We were wanted all along" – but as he fails to find work, the privatised personal realm exemplified by Kate Bush's chorus becomes the buffer against defeat – "You still have us" – replacing the political realm of class. There *is* a sense of class struggle in Bon Jovi's concurrent, Springsteen-like 'Livin' on a Prayer' (UK 4; US 1) – "Union's been on strike" – but again shutting out the social, Gina tells Tommy, "We've got to hold on to what we've got", as she works double shifts to support them. Note the amount of paid and unpaid female labour behind all these unemployed men. Erasure's 1987 'The Circus' (UK 6) is another memorial to Fordism, framed as an obituary: "There was once a future/ For a working man". While this Fordist melancholia functions to counter historical amnesia, by Traverso's criteria, its fatalism is the attitude of the victim, not the vanquished: the struggle has been subdued, defiance defeated.

The hauntology of Fordist melancholia is limited by its horizon being social democracy – locating utopia in a mythic past rather than a material future. However, there is an 80s nostalgia mode that's more utopian: countercultural hauntology. To be haunted is, it's rarely remarked, to be *frightened* – thus Marx's spectre of socialism haunting Europe. The fear the 60s inspired in the elites is indicated by the ideological labour devoted to countering the countercultural legacy – in Thatcher and Reagan's speeches and trickling down into popular culture. It's visible in the cruel caricature of hippie Neil in British TV comedy *The Young Ones* (1982–84), the assertion of the hippie as proto-yuppie in *The Big Chill* (1983) – as Lewis's 'Hip to be Square' notes, "Those that were the farthest out/Have gone the other way"– and the Beastie Boys' MCA symbolically smashing up a nerd's acoustic guitar in 1987's 'Fight for Your Right to Party' video (UK 11; US 7).

There is, however, a vein of 80s songs that venerate the counterculture, and that, rather than evincing the enervated stasis we've been seeing, convey a recurring sense of *motion* in their melancholia, and thus hope. For as Williams put it, "to be truly radical is to make hope possible, rather than despair convincing."[22] With punk spitting on the 60s ("Never trust a hippie"), it was quite the statement for Siouxsie and the Banshees to cover the Beatles' psychedelic 'Dear Prudence' (UK 3) in 1983, with the Cure guitarist Robert Smith. Sioux delivers its invocation of collective transcendence – "The birds will sing that you are part of everything" – without contemporary flippancy, while the arrangement even features a harpsichord (like fellow punks the Stranglers' 'Golden Brown', UK 2). Countercultural veteran Robert Plant's luminous 'Big Log' later that year (UK 11; US 20) evokes a journey from which "there is no turning back". Plant's adoption of electronic sounds isn't just an accommodation with the commercial present: he utilises their processed, disembodied quality to summon up the past. The thinned-out electric guitar and echoing drum machine, alongside Plant's keening wail, suggest an ectoplasmic, dead Zeppelin, "on the run" from a past that Plant's narrator can't stop regarding in his rear-view mirror.[23] There's no protest in the present, and no utopia ahead, but there's potency rather than passivity to the song's yearning, its sense of motion ultimately hopeful.

Like the Banshees, Prince's 1985 'Raspberry Beret' (UK 25; US 2) is a rare combination of 80s pop and psychedelia, violins and tinkling finger cymbals alongside churning synths and booming, processed drums. The tale of a shopworker's liaison with a flower child, the song's mythic register suggests a loss greater than that of a girl (or even of boyhood). Again, the past is full of motion alongside the melancholy – the girl and the narrator biking out to an ecstatic union with nature. Similarly, Bryan Adams' 1985 'Summer of '69' (US 5) is both salacious (the title's double entendre) and serene – "they were the best days of my life" – its mythic register again suggesting more than purely private loss. Tina Turner's 1985 theme for *Beyond Thunderdome*, 'We Don't Need Another Hero' (UK 3; US 2), surveys a dystopian "wreckage" and "ruin", "living under the fear", but it also promises "Love and compassion/Their day is coming". From a polar sonic universe, the Smiths' 1986 'Ask' (UK 14) focuses on the same choice between a positive or negative politics, albeit sarcastically: "If it's not love/Then it's the bomb... that will bring us together".

On its glossy surface, former Eagle Don Henley's autumn 1984 'Boys of Summer' (UK 12; US 5) is a cynical yuppie makeover of one of the original corporate hippies, its sound as slick as Henley's gelled hair in the video. Yet despite its acres of synth chords, its processed, skittish drums and spindly, spectral guitar, 'Boys of Summer' is so suffused with loss that it becomes otherworldly, luminous, eerie. As a spurned older lover drives around a mysteriously deserted Los Angeles, he spots "a

Deadhead sticker on a Cadillac". 'Deadheads' were fanatical followers of the Grateful Dead, the ultimate embodiment of the counterculture, and by the 80s, its ghost. Ostensibly, the bumper sticker – likely the Dead's skull insignia – is a metaphor for a morbid attachment: "Those days are gone forever/I should just let 'em go". But the counterculture is more than a metaphor for lost love here, as the neoliberal superego – "the little voice inside my head" – reasserts its reduced reality: "Don't look back, you can never look back". The empty streets, the deserted beach, the ex-lover's uninhabited house all operate as a hauntology of lost *sociality*, the narrator obsessively trying to chase its ghost down – the yuppie possessed by the hippie he once was, the skull beneath the 80s' perfect skin. Hardly a protest song, 'Boys of Summer' nevertheless possesses an affective potency in its hippie hauntology that, while achingly melancholic, is a resource of hope in a hopeless age.

With cultural memory throwing all these songs into a pot called '80s pop' – a set of sonic tropes conveying a positivity beyond politics – the neoliberal hegemony that's being engineered in the era's pop as much as in its politics gets occluded. Released at the high-80s' apotheosis, there's a *völkisch* triumphalism to Starship's 1987 power ballad 'Nothing's Gonna Stop Us Now' (UK 1; US 1). The theme for *Mannequin*, its aspiration is expressed in authoritarian terms – "We can build this dream together/Standing strong forever" – as the relentless push of the track's processed, crashing drums, chugging synths and strident vocals drive home its scorched-earth individualism: "Let the world around us just fall apart". It is, in such songs, a conventionally competitive world. The 80s pop that wasn't hegemonised has been homogenised by history, and songs that refused the competitive world or yearned for the collective past – like 'Boys of Summer' – are lost in the boom of Linn drums, the shimmer of synths and the huge reverb of a non-hauntological, 'I heart the 80s' nostalgia. Yet the anxious rhythms and affective ambivalence of tracks like A-ha's 'Take on Me' or Jackson's 'Billie Jean' provide an implicit commentary on the period's co-option, its consensus-creation, its affective processing.

"They come, they come to build a wall between us", Crowded House lament on 1987's 'Don't Dream It's Over' (UK 27; US 2), its language evoking deeper divisions than those between lovers: "Don't let them win". Yet it did feel like they'd won by that winter's failure of the British printworkers' strike, followed by Thatcher's third electoral victory in the summer. "The woman is invincible... the trend is irreversible", Robert Palmer purrs on 'Simply Irresistible' (US 2), again suggesting something larger than – indeed antithetical to – love: "She's a powerful force/ You're obliged to conform when there's no other course". There is no alternative.

Yet only months after Thatcher's victory, in October 1987, the stock market unexpectedly crashed. What became known as 'Black Monday' brought the high 80s to an end, removed the mystique from the 'economic miracle' and terminated the era's heady hedonism. Yuppies were no longer the heroes of the age. "Don't push too far, your dreams are china in your hand", T'Pau ruefully concluded that winter on what seemed a conventionally hateful 80s power ballad, 'China in Your Hand' (UK 1). Yet, the sonic harshness of the instrumentation, alongside Carol Decker's strident, slightly off-key vocals, revealed the indefatigable sonics of bombastic 80s pop to be as fragile, attenuated – and as the lyric told it, transparent – as a once indefatigable political system.

Chapter 9

'Everybody's Free': Rave, Rap and Grunge at the End of History (1988–92)

In November 1989, the Berlin Wall which symbolically divided Europe into communist and capitalist zones was breached by East German crowds, who flooded across no-man's land into the welcoming West. The Wall's official dismantling began the following year, with all Eastern Bloc states having disavowed communism by 1991. Conservative historian Francis Fukuyama announced that this represented not just the end of the Cold War but the end of history itself: "the universalization of Western liberal democracy as the final form of human government".[1] Folded into Fukuyama's thesis – and Western media's triumphalism – was the presumption that liberal democracy and neoliberalism were one and the same. The freedom that the crowds demanded at the Wall and in China's Tiananmen Square and celebrated at Nelson Mandela's release was thus, in Fukuyama's framing, the freedom of the market. Yet if neoliberal democracy was such a universally accepted solution, it left unclear quite what the free-world's restive ravers, rioters, rappers and grungers' *problem* was.

The fall of the Wall was greeted In Western pop with a three-gun salute. The video for Billy Joel's fall 1989 'We Didn't Start the Fire' (UK 7; US 1) presents suburban conformity as the height of human civilisation, as its rapid-fire lyric denies American responsibility for a shopping list of historical events. Shortly afterwards, President Bush (Sr) declared a "new world order" of American hegemony and invaded Panama, and by summer 1990, Operation Desert Storm had set oil fires burning across the Persian Gulf. Jesus Jones' 1990 indie-dance 'Right Here, Right Now' (US 2) approvingly cites Fukuyama – "Watching the world wake up from history" – while affirming, "There is no other place I want to be", with Western freedom demonstrated by a guitar solo. West-German metallers Scorpions' 1991 power ballad, 'Wind of Change' (UK 2; US 4) celebrates "a storm-wind that will ring the freedom bell" – rung in with another democratic guitar solo and a video of the crowds at the Wall, in Tiananmen, at Mandela's release and at a Scorpions' show, exemplifying freedom.

This rediscovered collectivity was really consensus, communal entropy rather than collective ecstasy, embracing neoliberal democracy as the only available option rather than as an optimal ideal. "It's not the way I hoped or how I planned/ But somehow it's enough" as Vanessa Williams put it on 1992's 'Save the Best for Last' (UK 3; US 1). With Panama and the Gulf followed by the Bosnian conflict, this consensus entailed a "resignation to endless crises and wars", as Raymond Williams had predicted.[2] "Exit light; enter night", Metallica intone on 1991's doomy 'Enter Sandman' (UK 5; US 16), summoning "dreams of war, dreams of liars".

With the future effectively cancelled, 'presentism' was the affective mode at the end of history – thus, on plastic Europoppers Roxette's joyless 1991 'Joyride' (UK 4; US 1), the journey "begins where it ends". The totalitarian domination of power ballads, pledging eternal changelessness helped make what Guy Debord called "the eternal present" feel particularly oppressive.[3] Bryan Adams' 1991 '(Everything I Do) I Do It for You' topped the British charts for 16 weeks (UK 1; US 1); Whitney Houston's 1992 'I Will Always Love You' (UK 1; US 1) ruled the American charts for 14 weeks, while radio was seemingly only ever a song away from another Mariah Carey mega-ballad.[4] Was this the best that neoliberal freedom could offer?

Following hard upon the dismantling of social democracy, the collapse of communism "paralyzed and prohibited the utopian imagination",[5] Traverso argues, making even the possibility of political alternatives – and thus *change* – essentially illiberal.[6] "I dreamt the impossible", Johnny Hates Jazz lament on 1988's saccharine 'Shattered Dreams' (UK 5; US 2), but then "woke up to reality/And found the future not so bright". Dreams led only to the gulag, it was declared, and with the left conceding the argument, the concept of 'utopia' disappeared from political and cultural discourse for a decade.[7] Even amid the countercultural hauntology of 'baggy' indie-dance, the Stone Roses' 1989 'What the World Is Waiting For' (UK 8) avows, "He needs a slave for his vision of the promised land", while Jesus Jones dismiss Tracy Chapman's 1988 'Talking 'bout a Revolution' (*Tracy Chapman*, UK 1; US 1), because the *real* revolution is the one that *rejects* utopia. In such a politics, "the crucial question… becomes not what kind of world we would like to collectively create, but what kind of world the 'economy' or 'market' necessitates".[8]

It was hard to see what there was to celebrate in all this when 1987's Black Monday had demystified the 'economic miracle' and reasserted capitalism as a cycle of boom and bust – 1992's Black Wednesday followed. In this post-80s comedown, the conservative utopianism of a "property-owning democracy" was replaced by uninspiring conceits like 'responsibility' and 'realism'. 'Back to Life' (UK 1; US 4), as Britain's Soul II Soul put it, "back to reality", more in weariness than in celebration, despite its house piano-line and diva vocalising. For Edgerton, the era was marked by "a culture of passive conformity, managerialism and imitation", in which "order and control were more obvious than freedom and imagination".[9]

In retrospect, this era seems as sepia-toned and monochrome as its pop videos. George Bush and John Major were dull understudies for neoliberalism's dazzling headliners – Reagan having retired after the Iran-Contra affair, Thatcher being ejected by her own party after the Poll Tax protests, although the pair's legacies long outlasted their regimes. 'There's No Other Way', Blur cooed on their baggy 1991 hit (UK 8), echoing Thatcher's "There is no alternative": "I don't wanna think at all… All that you can do is watch them play". Whether this was a serious or satirical affirmation of what Debord called "the spectacle", it captured a structure of feeling in which "all that was once directly lived has become mere representation",[10] and in which capitalism was the only real beneficiary of Western freedom.

Dull as they were, that Bush and Major could be regarded as 'non-ideological' revealed how far the political dial had turned to the right. Major's *Spitting Image* puppet, presenting him as head-to-toe grey, occluded his assaults on the remnants of Fordism: cutting benefits, deregulating railways, privatising docks and turning health and education into service industries. Indicative of the left's failure to capitalise on Black Monday or the Poll Tax, Labour's puppets presented no challenge to Major's complacent claim that class had been superseded – as the gap between rich and poor visibly widened. While leaving the mouth-frothing moralism to his VP, Dan Quayle, Bush's refusal of federal responsibility for America's citizenry and attribution of poverty to individual failings was a free-market fundamentalist take on 'freedom'.

As America's urban conurbations became sci-fi dystopias, this wasn't coincidentally the era of *Die Hard* (1988, 1990) and *Terminator II* (1991). 'Welcome to the Jungle', metal sensation Guns N' Roses declared in 1988 (UK 24; US 7), with the track's video capturing the era's information overload, its air of crisis, and sense of the world as a hostile environment amid neoliberal freedom's free-for-all. Radical hip-hoppers Public Enemy's 1990 'Welcome to the Terrordome' (UK 18) is the *sound* of overload, of crisis, of hostility, reattributing responsibility from society's subaltern to its elite. With Public Enemy and N.W.A. in the charts, Spike Lee's *Do the Right Thing* (1989) and John Singleton's *Boyz n the Hood* (1991) in cinemas and Rodney King's 1991 police-beating and the 1992 LA riots on TV, race made the faultlines in Western freedom glaringly, violently visible. "I was a time bomb... I'm mad, plus I'm the enemy", Chuck D booms on Public Enemy's 'Don't Believe the Hype' (UK 18).

'New jack swing' kingpin Bobby Brown's fall 1988 'My Prerogative' (UK 6; US 1) defensively asserts his freedom to "do what I wanna do", derived from the fact that "*I* made this money, you didn't!" With most people sharing no such prerogative in this period's harsh economy (as the riots demonstrated), the end of history wasn't the end of political resistance or thus of a genuine, radical collectivity. Resistance to the homophobic Section 28 resulted in a concerted wave of British protests, while American ACT UP actions exposed the intersection between laissez faire economics and leaving queers to die (even if queer music failed to step up to the plate). Public antipathy to the authoritarian Poll Tax destabilised Thatcher's last days and helped prompt the superficial political softening of the Major era. In reaction to 80s capitalist excess, this era expressed an anti-commercial structure of feeling that, paralleling politics' performative softening in mainstream pop, was more trenchantly articulated in alternative rock and acid house. The latter's free rave movement championed a freedom not covered by the free market, enshrined in a collective ecstasy which peaked at the week-long rave at Castlemorton common in 1992. As the climate crisis escalated, the 1991–92 anti-roads protests at Twyford Down and a new vein of ecological pop articulated an antipathy to a neoliberal democratic freedom that was increasingly understood as capital's prerogative to "do what I wanna do".

The woodland site of a projected road, like the no-man's land between communist East and capitalist West, was a liminal space – like the disused warehouses and factories of rave, the post-industrial wastelands of grunge, the urban devastation of the American projects, and the field of political opportunity between Black Monday and Black Wednesday. Despite its apparent sepia-toned stasis, the end of history was a period of possibilities – another interregnum. The fact that those possibilities ended in acquiescence, co-option or defeat – and that centrism was the ultimate beneficiary of this liminal political space – doesn't neutralise the radicalism of those possibilities, or diminish the potency of their hauntology. It's to that liminality that this chapter is dedicated.

"It's Time to Give a Damn": Politics in Post-80s Pop

Following Black Monday, popular music performed an affective stock-take. "What have we become?" glam metallers White Lion lament on 1988 power ballad 'When the Children Cry' (US 3): "All that we destroyed we must build again". American boyband New Kids on the Block's 1989 'This One's for the Children'

(UK 9; US 7) urges everyone to "remember we are all brothers", to "help others in need/And show them there's a better way". Reynolds argues that "positivity emerged as the pop ideology of the new decade", which "emphasised caring and sharing... a shift from materialism to idealism".[11] Or as Gloria Estefan put it on 1989's 'Get on Your Feet' (UK 23; US 11): "We've all been through/Some nasty weather", so we need to "understand that we're here/To handle things together". A new "touchy-feely' demotic developed in popular culture: note the titles of Kate Bush's 1989 'Deeper Understanding' (*The Sensual World*, UK 2) and Massive Attack's magnificent 1991 'Unfinished Sympathy' (UK 13).

80s pop acts who'd previously sung of love, work and dancing suddenly discovered a social conscience: "Join voices in protest/To social injustice", Janet Jackson purrs inspiringly on 1989's 'Rhythm Nation' (UK 23; US 2). Brother Michael's 1988 'Man in the Mirror' (UK 21; US 1) rejects the 80s' "selfish kind of love", insisting that we "see the kids in the street/With not enough to eat... see their needs". That recurring "see" is revealing, an emphasis on *awareness* – on spectacle – in which economics has no purchase, and where social change flows from the individual: "If you wanna make the world a better place/Take a look at yourself and then make a change". This emphasis on *image* spotlights the star – their humility, their sensitivity, their starring role in the spectacle – in what's effectively an enlightenment trickledown that changes nothing. Such pseudo-collectivity is revealed as 80s continuity, therefore, a revival of Live Aid's spectacular sanctimony, but like Major and Bush as against Thatcher and Reagan, more boring and more sententious.

Pop's handwringing about the increasingly visible homeless crisis was particularly hypocritical. Not because, in the old 'Imagine' saw, pop stars inhabited mansions, but because they framed homelessness as individual misfortune rather than political creation. Conservative-voting Phil Collins' atrocious 1989 ballad 'Another Day in Paradise' (UK 2; US 1) pins the problem on "the man on the street" who turns away from the spectacle, with Collins' pious repetition of "Think twice!" accusing the listener while urging them to *keep* looking. Again, the song is about nothing but Phil Collins, his hammy humanitarianism merely fuel for the spectacle. On Crystal Waters' 1991 house hit 'Gypsy Woman' (UK 2; US 8), her assertion that a begging busker is "just like you and me/But she's homeless", rests on both women "singing for money" rather than on any social responsibility beyond, again, *awareness*. Finally, the outsider romanticism of hippie-hoppers Arrested Development's 1992 'Mr Wendal' (UK 4; US 6) presents homelessness as a lifestyle choice – "Free to be without the worries of a quick-to-diss society" – rather than the waste material of Western freedom.

During the high 80s, the natural world was virtually absent from music's iconography, but in another rejection of 80s recklessness, ecology now spilled into mainstream pop. Enya's video for her twee, new-age 1988 'Orinoco Flow' (UK 1; US 24) is fecund with birds, plants and water. Indie dance videos' iconography gave rave's rural impulse an eco-spin on the Stone Roses' 1989 'I Wanna Be Adored' (UK 20), the Shamen's 1991, Tenerife-filmed 'Move Any Mountain' (UK 4) and James' 1992 Monument Valley-set 'Born of Frustration' (UK 13).[12] Yet it was rare to travel beyond *awareness*, again: nature as spectacle. The video for former choreographer Paula Abdul's 1991 'Promise of a New Day' (US 1) merges humans and nature in Marcusian *Eros*, with Abdul and her dancers writhing in jungle fronds and drenched by waterfalls in their underwear. Yet not only are the human images clearly projected *against* the nature footage, it's *all* image – Abdul's body, Abdul's *awareness*, the video's quote from the Rainforest Foundation – the socially concerned spectacle.

The upholders of post-punk's political legacy offered a more trenchant critique. Talking Heads' 1988 *Naked* (UK 3; US 19) connects ecological disaster to capitalism's reckless endangerment, while R.E.M.'s 'Orange Crush' (*Green*, UK 27; US 12) invokes the Vietnam-deployed defoliant Agent Orange. Michael Stipe's repeated assertion that "We are agents of the free" acerbicly defines Western freedom as America's right to destroy the planet. Williams noted that under neoliberalism, "there is nothing but raw material: in the earth; in other people".[13] As such, Erasure's autumn 1989 'Drama' (UK 4) connects "Do unto yourself as you see fit for your brother" to the planet, while, in the video, a deluge of plastic detritus rains down on the duo. On the Cure's lovely, gothic 'Lullaby' in 1989 (UK 5), the earth takes revenge on humanity, consuming the hapless Robert Smith alive, although there were plenty more deserving candidates.

This period also produced a gloomier strain of ecological pop with *no* promise of a new day: Pet Shop Boys' 1989 house cover 'It's Alright' (UK 5) bewails "Forests falling at a desperate pace/The earth is dying and desert taking its place", before returning to the reassuring (or just resigned) chorus. On George Michael's elegiac, psychedelically Beatlesy, 1990 'Praying for Time' (UK 6; US 1), his lament that "the wounded skies above/ Say it's much too late" is a hauntology that *closes* rather than opening options. On Tasmin Archer's similarly psychedelic 1992 'Sleeping Satellite' (UK 1), she suggests that by literally reaching for the moon, Fordism's technological drive destroyed the earth, the future cancelled by futurism. These songs are the end of history at its most literal, with their resigned acceptance of "the dream that died" making for an impotent kind of protest.

This fatalistic passivity passes for positivity throughout this period's popular music. Bobby McFerrin's excruciating *a capella* 1988 'Don't Worry, Be Happy' (UK 2; US 1) recommends insouciance as response to economic hardship. Former hippie Stevie Winwood urges everyone to 'Roll With It' (US 1): "People think you're down and out/You show them what it's all about." Sinead O'Connor recites the Alcoholics Anonymous credo on 1990's stunning, string-propelled 'Feel So Different' (*I Do Not Want What I Haven't Got*, UK 1; US 1) – "God grant me the serenity to accept the things I cannot change" – a particularly joyless declaration of freedom. With Queen always the darlings of the spectacle, their 1991, Middle Eastern-influenced 'Innuendo' (UK 1) bemoans a world where "We live according to race, colour or creed/While we rule by blind madness and pure greed" – before concluding, "Yeah, we'll keep on smiling... And whatever will be, will be". The song's social awareness is superficial, its empathy instrumental, a gateway to the reassertion of the status quo, while its invocation to "be free, be free" is exemplified by a Brian May guitar solo (4: 37–5:10).

As Adorno had predicted, "tragedy [is] made into a carefully calculated and accepted aspect of the world".[14] As such, mainstream pop's post-80s social conscience was a cover for its capitulation to capitalism, its apparent collectivism a lateral individualism, its performative 'caring' conducted with an acute consciousness of the flashing paparazzi bulbs and rolling, 24-hour broadcast of the spectacle.

"What Are You Playing, Who Are You Obeying?": Dominant, Residual and Emergent Culture in Post-80s Pop[15]

All popular music is a commodity, participating in consumer capitalism's spectacle. Possessed of no pretensions to social conscience, the new swathe of cheap and cheerful, sweatshop-produced, post-Fordist pop gleefully presented its commodity status as both its appearance *and* its essence. Of course, such presentation is entirely political, naturalising the commodity form while upholding the spectacle as the substance of democratic freedom. These acts were produced, managed and manipulated by pound-shop impresarios like Britain's Stock Aitken Waterman (Kylie Minogue, Jason Donovan, Rick Astley, Sonia) and Tom Watkins (Bros, East 17), following the lead of America's Maurice Starr (New Edition, New Kids on the Block) and are a defining example of dominant culture.

Stripped of the bombast of the corporate authentic, this factory-produced post-Fordist pop sounded so thin it was virtually transparent – a belated reveal of the 80s' essence – while offering a supermarket own-brand version of several high-80s tropes: unabashed commerciality, synthetic automation and populist ordinariness. American teen Tiffany's tinny, off-key take on Tommy James' 60s hit 'I Think We're Alone Now' in 1988 (UK 1; US 1) removes the original's generational conflict, while its shopping-mall video defines ordinariness as consumerism. Liverpudlian girl-next-door Sonia's video for 1989's 'You'll Never Stop Me from Loving You' (UK 1) presents her working her socks off to nail her dance moves (and her hunky dance teacher). The 'behind-the-scenes' conceit ostensibly deconstructs the spectacle but actually affirms it – as a meritocracy for those sufficiently dedicated to the performance principle. See also: New Edition in their rehearsal space, dressed down, limbering up, quaffing water, sweating, on 1988's 'If It Isn't Love' (US 7). Pretty-boys Bros' 1988 demand 'When Will I Be Famous?' (UK 2) and Roxette's 1989 boast of getting 'Dressed for Success' (UK 14; US 18) merge this awareness of the spectacle with an openness about 'aspiration' that, prior to the 80s, would have been regarded as tacky, but was now seen as bracingly democratic.

With Boyz II Men's 1991 'Motownphilly' (UK 23; US 3) featuring nine costume changes, and Kylie's 'What Do I Have to Do?' (UK 6) boasting nearer fifteen, videos became adverts not just for clothes and accessories, but for what Debord calls the "commodity as abstract form"[16]: consumerism as a *concept*, a way of life. The videos' constant cutting between scenes glories in the spectacle's information overload, consuming the past – 60s Motown, 70s Philadelphia, the disco age – while insisting upon the eternal, inescapable present.

An old hand at the pop spectacle, Cher's summer 1989 power ballad 'If I Could Turn Back Time' (UK 6; US 3) addresses this endless present – she *can't* turn back time and everything will remain broken. Yet Cher's vocal doesn't suggest philosophical acceptance of this static state so much as – stirring, uplifting, air-punching – a *celebration* of it: even *before* you get to the video where Cher is singing the song *on a fully primed warship*. Dressed in ripped fishnet basque and leather jacket, Cher winks and wiggles for the marines and intermittently strokes the ship's guns, before straddling the cannons as the by-now hysterical sailors whoop and cheer. This, then, is the Pax Americana, whereby Western freedom – exemplified by Cher's eternal sexuality – is underwritten by military might, the end of history from which no return to any chickenshit past is possible.

The past is never easily repressed, however: 'It's So Hard to Say Goodbye to Yesterday' (US 2), as new jack swingers Boyz II Men put it in 1991. Williams' concept of 'residual culture', whereby an outmoded ideology disrupts that of the dominant, is heard in the countercultural hauntologies of Michael and Archer and in George Harrison's 1988 'When We Was Fab' (UK 25; US 23), with Ringo Starr and Beatles tribute-act Jeff Lynne. Yet, 'Fab' is hauntology at its most conservative, patronising the past by keeping the counterculture's politics at a safe, cynical distance. On the Bangles' charming 1988 'In Your Room' (US

5), its tambourines, Eastern strings, sitar-like guitars and trippy video offer a glucose hit of nostalgia, but the past here is just dress-up, evacuated of social meaning. Where the last two songs are containment, Madonna's 1989 'Dear Jessie' (UK 5) is a co-option of the counterculture. In psychedelia, the child's-eye view is pre-ideological; on 'Dear Jessie' it's just *cute*, affirming family values where psychedelia questioned them.

Containment and co-option are recurring issues for residual culture, creating a hauntology of enervation rather than inspiration, "drift[ing] off into the sweet memories", as MC Hammer's Chi-Lites-derived 1990 'Have You Seen Her' (UK 8; US 4) puts it. Here the past is as generalised as the lyric's everywoman, the ghetto soul from which the track derives providing nostalgic colour rather than political context. This, then, is Jameson's ahistorical "nostalgia mode", 'Set Adrift on Memory Bliss', as PM Dawn's contentless 1991 hip-hop tune had it (UK 3; US 1).

Released after Mercury's death in 1991, Queen's 'These Are the Days of Our Lives' (UK 1; US 2) was hauntological at inception, and ostensibly indulges a 70s nostalgia: "When we were young/Things seemed so perfect". But this line is followed, in the monochrome video, by a painfully frail Mercury winking at the camera and declaring, "You can't turn back the clock/ You can't turn back the tide", before adding, candid camply: "Ain't that a shame!" The conclusion, "Better sit back and go with the flow", is a prioritisation of the present over the past, and as Hartog never quite makes plain, presentism's purpose is to naturalise neoliberalism. History, at the end of history, has no meaning, and in Queen's inheritors' Erasure's delightful drag video for 1992's 'Take a Chance on Me' (*Abba-esque*, UK 1), the past is only ever a costume-change away, a prop-box of ironic iconography rather than a socio-political location, detached from issue, reduced to comforting kitsch.

Popular music that comes from the street up rather than the marketing department down is an expression of emergent culture. Yet while hip-hop arose from block parties and park jams, it's also a *residual* culture, based on recognisable samples of older music, carrying the charge of the past and able to "make the present waver", in Jameson's resonant phrase.[17] De La Soul's combination of Steely Dan's 1978 'Peg', Otis Redding's 1968 'Dock of the Bay' and a *Sesame Street*-style video on 1989's delightful 'Eye Know' (UK 14) invokes a multicultural utopianism that pulls against the era's grey realism, expanding the concept of the counterculture from the 60s to the 70s and into the 80s. That former hippies the Turtles sued De La over a sample on *3 Feet High and Rising* (UK 13; US 24) wasn't just a betrayal of countercultural values but an assertion of cultural dominance. For Marx, all law is bourgeois law: sampling is a rejection of property rights by those long denied them, with African Americans' cultural property having been appropriated by everyone from Elvis to the Turtles. Likewise, Lou Reed's insistence on full remuneration for A Tribe Called Quest's letting his 'Walk on the Wild Side' meet on equal terms with jazz and soul on 1990's 'Can I Kick It?' (UK 15) ran counter to the track's utopian transcendence of property and race. Deee-Lite's glorious 1990 'Groove Is in the Heart' (UK 2; US 4) combines Swinging-60s iconography with 70s funk (Bootsy Collins), acid house with hip-hop (Q-Tip's rap), and again this amalgam evokes an elastic conception of counterculture, as a *commons* which transcends not just property, but time, genre and race.

Although acid house also contained elements of residual culture – the appellation 'acid', its sample base, 1988's 'Second Summer of Love' – it's better understood as an emergent culture. Like hip-hop, acid's free parties operated, initially, outside commerce. The tracks created for these parties, inspired by Chicago house, reconfigured not just how music could be made but also what it *constituted*, being largely instrumental, composed of sample snippets, and prioritising rhythm and mood over melody. Home-made, independently released tracks like A Guy Called Gerald's 1988 'Voodoo Ray' (UK 12) and Humanoid's 1988 'Stakker Humanoid' (UK 17) became hits through a countercultural network of fanzines, pirate radio and word of mouth. Orbital, named after illegal raves off London's Orbital motorway, wore anti-Poll Tax sweatshirts to perform 1989's 'Chime' (UK 17) on *Top of the Pops*, adding to acid house's air of revolt. Even a Europop cash-in like Black Box's cheesily exciting 1990 'Ride on Time' (UK 1) dismissed property rights via its unauthorised, explosive vocal sample,[18] while pop-ravers

Nomad's 1990 anthem '(I Wanna Give You) Devotion' (UK 2) excoriated the Poll Tax and Thatcher.

Despite this refusenik sensibility, Reynolds asserts that acid house was "never overtly political",[19] while Matthew Colin argues it "lacked any ideology bar the ceaseless pursuit of sheer pleasure".[20] This represents a narrow conception of both 'political' and 'ideology', and also underestimates the impact of the industry's co-option of this emergent culture. As early as 1989, London Boys' Euro excrescence 'London Nights' (UK 2) fused acid-house optimism with consumerism: "If there's hope and love across the nation/Everybody find a recreation". The addition of rap to house, as on Europoppers Snap!'s 1990 'The Power' (UK 1; US 2) was a corporate acid-house tactic, with Turbo D's aggressive individualism – "Stay off my back or I will attack" – anathema to acid's loved-up collectivity.

What Williams *didn't* allow for was emergent culture's willingness to co-opt *itself*. Smart E's' snickering 'Sesame's Treet' (UK 2) is an infantile performance of defiance, housing an adult understanding of the commercial power of 'controversy'. Contradicting its title, N-Joi's 1990 'Anthem' (UK 8) is entirely contentless. This diffusion of acid house's political potential meant its culture was easily absorbed into mainstream clubbing after the Entertainments (Increased Penalties) Act of 1990. If this didn't make dance a dominant culture, two acts of rave pranksterism did. The Shamen's shameless whoop of "E's are good, E's are good" on 1992's 'Ebenezer Goode' (UK 1) reduced acid house to *conventional* hedonism, while half of techno novelty-mongers Altern 8 stood as a candidate in the 1991 election as the Hardcore (Altern8-ive Party). The media's framing of such reactionary interventions as radical was part of the re-drawing of political lines after the Wall's fall. Yet this gap between presentation and reality also made visible the ideological labour engaged in containing and co-opting emergent and residual culture and in reasserting the rule of the dominant.

"Let Yourself Go Wild": Women and Queers in Post-80s Pop

The sheer number of female stars in this era's pop was a progressive development, the direct result of feminist struggle over the previous decades. Yet with utopianism no longer viable after the Wall's fall, the radicalism of these performers was relative and tended to be critically overstated – and not just by Camille Paglia.[21] Madonna unquestionably lit up a grey period in popular culture and restored a sense of *event* to pop, yet she and her fellow female stars' post-feminist understanding of 'freedom' was at some distance from 'liberation'. As Gilbert puts it, "While... some of the goals of women's liberation have been achieved... this has only been to the extent that they were compatible with the emergence of neoliberal post-Fordism".[22] Female performers were constrained to confront the world as it *was*, not as it *could* be, and with the power of sex central to libidinal capitalism, sex could thus be repossessed as female power, with Madonna, Janet Jackson, Paula Abdul and Kylie Minogue all radically sexualising their images in this era.[23] Yet sex also *sells*, driving the consumption not just of music but of makeup, clothes and accessories, and these stars' sexualisation coincided with a stylistic shift from youthful 'ordinariness' to mature glamour.

In Abdul's image-relaunching 1989 'Cold Hearted' video (US 1), her dance troupe's sexualised routine and the corporate executives' 'shock' are equally stagy, there being no conflict between sexual and market freedom in libidinal capitalism. That MTV banned Madonna's glamorously monochrome, implicitly bisexual, vaguely sado-masochistic videos for 1990's 'Justify My Love' (UK 2; US 1) and its 1992 reprise 'Erotica' (UK 3; US 3) justified the presumption that Madonna was promoting something repressed, rather than something unrepressed: herself.[24] Indeed, Madonna's exploitation of her own raw material was, by her 1992 *Sex* book, wearying the public rather more than it was worrying the moral majority. There is no utopia in *Sex*, no *Eros* in 'Erotica', instead this is what Marcuse calls "de-erotization",[25] whereby "sexual freedom... becomes a market value",[26] attesting merely to Madonna's commercial power within patriarchal capitalism. Similarly, Betty Boo's claim on 1990's pop-rap 'Doin' the Do'

(UK 7), "You called me rebellious… you think I'm a threat", declares a feminist radicalism that's really brand-building – "I'm fully in control… a go-getter" – which is confirmed by Boo referring to herself in the third person. 'Freedom' in these songs is a market value, but, crucially, not one that's available to all.

Alternative rock's feminism was far less corporate, new wave stripped of the winsome sugar-coating of the Bangles and Go-Go's, closer to the confrontation of a Siouxsie or Patti Smith. The Pixies were essentially as good as bassist Kim Deal's husky vocals were audible – which was very good indeed, up until 1990's *Bossanova* (UK 3). The updated psychedelia of 'shoegaze' indie brought female musicians to the fore – note the chart positions of My Bloody Valentine's 1991 *Loveless* (UK 24) and Lush's 1991 *Spooky* (UK 7) – their affectless disengagement simultaneously challenging female stereotypes and channelling dominant ideology. Likewise, the aggressive victimhood of PJ Harvey's dramatisation of the bleeding, suffering female body on 1992's *Dry* (UK 11) simultaneously reaffirmed and rejected female stereotypes, while her black-clad, lipstick-daubed look ambivalently combined the conventionally sexualised with the radically *de*sexualised. All-female grungers L7's songs equated masculinity with war ('Wargasm') and represented women fighting back physically on 1992's 'Everglade' (UK 27), but their exploitation of their own raw material – stripping off while playing 'Pretend We're Dead' (UK 21) on Britain's schlockfest *The Word* – was a refusal that the objectifying male gaze read as assent.

There was an attempt in this era to subvert the gaze by turning it back on men. On Belinda Carlisle's 1988 'I Get Weak' promo (UK 10; US 2), images of model Tony Ward appear on every surface Carlisle encounters. With Ward a polymorphous object of desire in Madonna's 'Justify' video, Kylie's housey 1991 'Shocked' (UK 6) repeats a tamer version of the same trick with another objectified hunk. On tomboy R&B trio TLC's 1992 'Ain't 2 Proud 2 Beg' video (UK 13; US 6), the male model is passive as the girls playfully mess with him, while Chilli's delighted double take at his packet is pure joy. The half-naked hunk that Siobhan Fahey and Marcella Detroit fight over in the video for Shakespears Sister's 1992 power ballad 'Stay' (UK

1; US 4) is *literally* an object – a corpse. There's an undeniable pleasure in this balancing of gender's scales, which undermines the male privilege of active subjecthood. Whether presenting men as passive objects made women any freer is debatable, however, and with the raw material of male bodies becoming a common commodity – Athena's half-dressed, baby-holding hunks; the Chippendales strip troupe – the main beneficiary of this spectacle was again the market.

As homoeroticism became mainstream, it lost its association with queerness and thus its transgressive potential. Where the homoerotic subtext of Pet Shop Boys' 1988 'Domino Dancing' video (UK 7; US 18) might once have subverted its heteronormative narrative – competition between two men for an attractive woman – with the Boys still not officially 'out', it came over as evasion. With the British government's concurrent Section 28 targeting the "promotion" of homosexuality, it was ironic that most gay stars didn't even promote the campaign *against* it, let alone their own sexuality.[27] Beyond the Communards' Jimmy Somerville and Erasure's Andy Bell, it was left to allies like Billy Bragg to take up the slack. "Your laws do not apply to me", Bragg ventriloquises sweetly on 'Sexuality' (UK 27), though we could have done without "And just because you're gay, I won't turn you away"

Months after Section 28 became law, the Pet Shop Boys' claim, on the Trevor Horn-produced 'Left to My Own Devices' (UK 4), to be "Che Guevara and Debussy to a disco beat" was revolutionary chic but political passivity, part of the reframing of radicalism this chapter has been recording. Consequently, Tennant's archly rapped "we'll do some shopping" is the song's key line, queer liberation in a transformed society replaced by gay *freedom* in the existing dispensation ("Left to my own devices I probably will"). This was a freedom guaranteed by the market and ultimately defined by it – as long as queers left the 'promoting' to corporate PR departments.

"This Wonderful World of Purchase Power": Anti-Materialism and Anti-Commercialism in Post-80s Pop

In another post-80s structure of feeling, this period's music was full of rejections of the materialism that defined the previous age. "No moneyman can win my love", insists Neneh Cherry on 1989's brilliant hip-pop/dance 'Buffalo Stance' (UK 3; US 3), rejecting the transactional machinations of gigolos and pimps. This anti-materialism was exemplified by street style becoming high style: ripped jeans for pop stars; plaid for slackers; baggy sportswear for ravers and hip-hoppers; Timberland work boots for almost everyone. De La Soul testified in 1989: "Style is surely our own thing/Not the false disguise of showbiz/De la Soul is from the soul" ('Me Myself and I', UK 22). With 'keeping it real' regularly blurring into building a brand – including Cherry's 'Buffalo' posse – this is a reminder of Marcuse's claim that "the music of the soul is also the music of salesmanship",[28] with the era's anti-materialism a constant pull-and-push between refusal and reification of the spectacle.

With Madonna often referred to as the 'Material Girl', her reversal of that song's sentiments on 1989's 'Express Yourself' (UK 5; US 2) exemplifies this era's anti-materialism. "You don't need diamond rings or eighteen-karat gold", Madge promises, invoking Marx's theory of built-in obsolescence: "Fancy cars that go very fast/You know they never last". However, the fact that the video, featuring Madonna as a Fordist factory owner, remains one of the most expensive ever made expresses the material security which affords the luxury of anti-materialism. Less ambiguously, the refutation of transactional affect in Paula Abdul's 1989 new jack swing hit '(It's Just) The Way That You Love Me' (US 3) is virtually an answer to 'Nothing Goin' on But the Rent': "It ain't your black limousine/It ain't your ninety-foot yacht... Honey I ain't impressed with your material things".

The starkness of Sinead O'Connor's stunning 1990 reading of Prince's 'Nothing Compares 2 U' (UK 1; US 1), alongside its literally tear-jerking graveyard video, are anti-materialist statements even before you get to the song's rejection of consumerism. The freedom to "eat my dinner in a fancy restaurant" is "nothing" compared to the human connection she's lost. Depeche Mode's 1990 'Enjoy the Silence' (UK 6; US 8) is a paean to peace to counter the commercial world's noise, its video depicting a king – someone who has everything – unable to locate a space in which he feels free. Or, as Bon Jovi put it on 1988's 'Bad Medicine' (UK 17; US 1): "I got lots of money, but it isn't what I need". The many who were growing poorer in this period might, of course, have a different perspective on both money and 'need'.

The anti-materialism is more pointedly political on the psychedelic hauntology of Tears for Fears' 1989 'Sowing the Seeds of Love' (UK 5; US 2), with its demand for "an end to need/And the politics of greed". On Prince's eerie 1992 'Money Don't Matter 2 Night' (UK 19; US 23), capitalist economics drive both personal and state overaccumulation: "So what if we controlling all the oil?/Is it worth a child dying for?" In Spike Lee's accompanying monochrome video, the political message is even starker, accusing Bush of perpetuating a hostile environment for African Americans. Concurrently, Manic Street Preachers' majestically chugging 'Motorcycle Emptiness' (UK 17) derides "this wonderful world of purchase power", and questions whether the shift "from feudal serf to spender", with its integral narcissism ("ego loaded") and unending alienation ("neon loneliness") is freedom in any meaningful sense. None of these songs are utopian: they can only lament how things *are*, not imagine how they might be, yet in a world of resigned consensus, they remain refusals of market logic.

Alongside this anti-materialism, popular music expressed a new anti-commercialism, asserting an awareness of – and distance from – the spectacle. Music videos were now typically set in rehearsal spaces, soundstages or empty venues, with visible scaffolding, ladders, lighting rigs and stagehands deconstructing the spectacle, and the non-diegetic (overlaid) music regularly interrupted by raw snatches of diegetic (live) sound. Pop stars were similarly authenticated – Whitney giggling and sticking out her tongue on 1988's 'So Emotional' video (UK 5; US 1); Kylie's 'home movie' footage for 1989's 'Wouldn't Change a Thing' (UK 2); Janet hanging with her homies at the pool hall on 1989's 'Miss You Much' (UK 22; US 1) – asserting a commonality with the ordinary consumer in contrast to the remote starriness of the 80s.

Ironically, this tendency kept snagging on celebrity solipsism. George Michael's refusal of the spectacle on 'Freedom! '90' (UK 28; US 8) is accompanied by a video where Michael is replaced by not one but *five* supermodels lip-syncing the lyrics. Not only does such emphasis on celebrity reveal an inability to think beyond the spectacle – or the celebrity address book – it patronises models as better symbols of commercialism than pop stars. Similarly, Right Said Fred's gruesome 1991 pop-house novelty 'I'm Too Sexy' (UK 2; US 1) mocks models' participation in the spectacle, as if the band's own branded 'ordinariness' wasn't invested in the same commercial system. Their piety is disavowed by a distancing, wipe-clean irony which would become very familiar as the decade progressed. Meanwhile, metallers Extreme's 1991 uncharacteristic ballad 'More Than Words' (UK 2; US 1) renders this anti-commerciality 'authentic' by its acoustic form and monochrome video, set in another rehearsal space, with the remaindered drummer and bassist 'ironically' holding up lighters.[29] Genesis's dreadful 1992 'I Can't Dance' (UK 7; US 7) deploys uncharacteristically rootsy rock to assert the trio's ordinariness in opposition to the spectacle's glamour. Again, the assumption that authenticity is a matter of style rather than substance makes nonsense of the band's performative anti-commercialism.

While all this renders Debord's totalisation of the spectacle persuasive – "the world of the commodity ruling over all lived experience" – it's also politically passive, disallowing the potential for change.[30] Acid house, grunge and hip-hop all demonstrated the possibility not of evading the spectacle, but of subverting it. Acid house's very ontology was anti-commercial: free parties, home studios, unlicensed samples, 'faceless' producers. For their 1992 'Blue Room' (UK 8) *Top of the Pops* performance, the Orb sat and played chess. KLF were acid house's anti-commercial apotheosis, a Situationist prank to gladden Debord's heart. With their content reduced to corporate branding – "KLF is gonna rock you"; "This is what KLF is about" – while their KKK robes and sparking chainsaws projected authoritarian pop at its most fascistic, KLF out-spectacled the spectacle. Hugely entertaining as this was, KLF's provocation lacked political purpose: 1991's '3 AM Eternal' (UK 1; US 5) simply celebrates an unchanging present. As with Frankie and Heaven 17, KLF's fake corporation soon lost its satire by its emphasis on commercialism rather than capitalism – a style, an image, an attitude, rather than an economic system. Consequently, KLF's prank of burning the million pounds they'd won from the music industry seemed less a kiss-off to capitalism than to the system's losers.

What KLF were to rave, a relaunched U2 were to alternative rock – or so they hoped. 1988's gauchely rootsy 'Desire' (UK 1; US 3), with its 'home movie' video and accompanying heartland rock album *Rattle and Hum* (UK 1; US 1), had been successful commercially but reviled critically. Consequently, the quartet, tapping the contemporary structure of feeling, abandoned authentic sincerity for satirical artificiality, playing up to the spectacle. On 1991's information-overloaded, breakbeat-driven 'The Fly' (UK 1) and Berlin-recorded *Achtung Baby* (UK 2; US 1), U2 deploy irony to *authenticate* themselves, though the emptily clever boast of 'Even Better than the Real Thing' (UK 12) articulates little more than their current promotional strategy. The Cure's insouciantly surreal video for 1992's 'Friday I'm in Love' (UK 6; US 18) says more about the spectacle in four minutes than U2's irony achieved over an entire album and a sequence of costly videos. On yet another soundstage, the constant, comic collapse of the Cure's backdrops mocks the pop video's capitalist showroom of scene-changes, while, without a trace of irony, the band plays on.

The fact that grunge is read backwards, through the filter of Kurt Cobain's suicide, taps into Debord's totalisation of the spectacle, meaning a successful emergent culture becomes a pre-incorporated failure, eliding both grunge's politics and ultimately the *point* of protest.[31] Fisher's claim that grunge morbidly channelled the "dead style" of punk contradicts his own use of hauntology. Cobain was haunted both by punk's defiance *and* the counterculture's utopianism (as his band's name suggests), however defensively he draped this in slacker irony. Joshua Clover's argument that grunge represented a "turn away from social engagement", directing punk's social rage inward, captures the grunge generation's psychic scarring but not its economic underpinning.[32] Grunge expressed the generational and class betrayal of those born amid Fordism's promise of a progressively improving future, then thwarted by the advent of deindustrialising neoliberalism and the steady withdrawal of the state's safety net. The resultant decaying, post-industrial landscapes of the Pacific Northwest didn't look much like the land of the free. Grunge's unkempt anti-fashion, its ripped and torn workwear, was thus a performative enactment of the remaindered Fordist worker reduced to post-Fordist poverty.

In signing to major label Geffen, Nirvana were publicly acknowledging the power of global capital, but their refusal to be bought and sold by it wasn't merely 'style' or its vapid 90s corollary, 'attitude', but something approaching a thought-through anti-capitalism. The cover of 1991's *Nevermind* (UK 7; US 1) is so recognisable it's no longer seen, its image of a baby chasing a dollar bill conveying humanity's immersion in capitalism from cradle to grave. 'Smells Like Teen Spirit' (UK 7; US 6) is so played it's no longer heard, yet its fractured lyric struggles to articulate a frustrated fury at generational and class betrayal. The song's sepia-filtered video has been so viewed it's no longer processed, but an audience passively entertained by pom-pom-wielding cheerleaders is the perfect image for the society of the spectacle. 'Teen Spirit' is a mockery of slacker apathy – "It's fun to lose"; "Oh well, whatever, nevermind" – rather than an articulation of it. Suitably incited, the crowd, by the video's end, is running riot while Cobain repeatedly howls, "a denial, a denial" – a refusal not of *reality* but of capitalist realism, of corporate common sense.

In the spirit of Adorno's "negative dialectic", alternative rock's refusal wasn't utopian, proposing no alternative, and of *course* its affect would be bottled like the deodorant invoked in 'Teen Spirit', the spectacle of rebellion used to pacify the masses. Nirvana pursue this theme on 'In Bloom' (UK 28), through the band's meta-fan who "likes all our pretty songs/And he likes to sing along... But he knows not what it means". Again, this isn't a pre-incorporated shrug, it's a *protest*, a provocation, designed to ignite the adversarial teen spirit which Cobain both mocks and mourns. This is crystal clear in the video, whose monochrome, 50s-television cuteness fails to contain the song's fury, as the band disdains the pop video's performance principle of lip syncing, then trashes the cardboard set and parades around in drag. This may not be utopian, but it *is* a howl of refusal – a denial – of the spectacle, of capitalism, roared from the belly of the beast. Let's not let them bottle that denial and sell it back to us as defeat.

"Brothers that Try to Work It Out/They Get Mad, Revolt, Revise, Realise": Radical, Gangster and Pop-Rap[33]

During the Cold War, America's proclaimed 'freedom' was realised in its housing projects not in human but in economic terms, via an unregulated free market based successively on smack, crack and guns. Such a eugenic solution to capitalism's waste material, out of political sight and mind in racially demarcated zones, was protested only by ghetto soul, which, eclipsed first by disco then by 80s pop, left the projects without a cultural – let alone political – voice. Now, however, at the end of history, when the answer to all social and economic ills was declared to be the system we already had, the problem of the projects erupted again – as rap, as riot, and as spectacle.

As with grunge, there's a tendency to read hip-hop *backwards*, assessing the genre through gangster rap's late-90s dominance, as if the demise of radical rap were preordained.[34] Not only do Clover and Lynskey reduce history to teleology, therefore, they overstate the division between radical and gangster rap, in another narrowing of what constitutes the 'political', and reduce the golden age of hip-hop to a turf war between Public Enemy and N.W.A. (N****z Wit Attitudes). Most egregiously, Eric B. & Rakim get written out of this history, although Eric B. was one of hip-hop's musical visionaries and Rakim deferred to no one in street realism – as on the brilliant 'Paid in Full' (UK 15) – or, in a broader understanding of the 'political', linguistic facility. Summer 1988's 'Follow the Leader' (UK 21) not only raised hip-hop's game musically – being both hauntological *and* futuristic – but conceptually, Rakim presenting the patented brag-rap as a cultural weapon – "I came to overcome before I'm gone/By showin' and provin' and lettin' knowledge be born". Rakim rhetorically invokes hip-hop as a replacement for the welfare state: "Since you was tricked, I have to raise ya/From the cradle to the grave", going beyond Fordist reformism to utopianism: "You're not a slave… I'm here to break away the chains/remake the brains".

Such sentiments don't only resonate beyond race, but also make common cause with Public Enemy's rarely cited utopianism. The aggression of summer 1988's *It Takes a Nation of Millions to Hold Us Back* (UK 8) doesn't just articulate the rage and evoke the violence of the projects, it relays a history of black refusal, the radical political projects of Malcolm X, Martin Luther King and the Panthers. Like Nirvana, Public Enemy's is a negative dialectic, its radicalism focusing on the betrayal not the promise of liberalism, but unlike Nirvana – and Adorno – Chuck D insists this presentist dystopia isn't the endpoint of history. Like Nirvana too, Public Enemy were preoccupied by the spectacle – 'She Watch Channel Zero?!'; "False media, we don't need 'ya" – and the potential of the subaltern to inhabit and disrupt it – 'Bring the Noise'; 'Don't Believe the Hype' – realised by their backing's restless, rolling-news bricolage of massed, sampled snippets. If Public Enemy's techniques were post-Fordist, their collectivity was Fordist (the Bomb Squad production trio; their camply paramilitary dancers), as were their sources, drawing from black America's heritage while reappropriating what had been appropriated from it. "They say that I stole this", Chuck D thunders on 'Caught: Can We Get a Witness': "I rebel with a raised fist". Public Enemy represent a radical hauntology.

Released a month after *Millions*, N.W.A.'s *Straight Outta Compton* emerged from the same political conditions, the same cultural memory bank and the same anger. Yet *Compton* did not, *contra* Clover and Lynksey, eclipse *Millions*, barely charting in the UK or US (although ultimately reaching US platinum). Unlike Public Enemy, N.W.A.'s music is presentist, neither hauntological – despite its ghetto-funk samples – nor future-orientated, thus dystopian rather than utopian. The title track's "with a crime record like Charles Manson" co-opts the counterculture as a war of all against all, while all that remains of revolution is refusal. A refusal not just of "the authority, laws, and norms of white culture", as Douglas Kellner has it,[35] but of almost *all* social codes: hence the casual murderousness towards black peers and contemptuous misogyny towards "dirty-ass hos". Nevertheless, 'Fuck Tha Police' crystallises what made this music so exciting to listeners and so frightening to the establishment. It's not merely a matter of the track's conscious-rap aspect – "So police think/ They have the authority to kill a minority" – but its raw threat to the repressive state apparatus. Althusser's illustration of citizens' interpellation into ideology is being hailed by a policeman. The N-word in N.W.A.'s name and lyrics didn't just *reclaim* the epithet with which police interpellated black men but *inhabited* it and played it back as meta-spectacle, transcending both irony *and* ideology.

Even the video for female duo, Salt-N-Pepa's pop-rap 'Shake Your Thang' (UK 22) expressed this structure of feeling in that febrile summer of 1988. Meanwhile the state's attempt to silence this racial rebellion managed to radicalise puerile party rappers 2 Live Crew by prosecuting 1989's misogynistic 'Me So Horny' (US 26) for obscenity. The Crew's 1990, Springsteen-mining follow-up, 'Banned in the USA' (US 20), could be seen as liberal, or as holding a mirror to liberalism's preoccupation with property rights – "What I do in my house is my business" – and 'freedom' of speech: "This is America, not the place where they brought down the Wall". As it is, the disconnect between the spectacle and the reality of liberal freedom is revealed by the video's images of burning KKK crosses and police attacking civil rights and hippie protestors, mirroring everyday life in the projects at the end of history.

Neither Public Enemy 'Minister of Information', Professor Griff's anti-Semitic misinformation nor the media furore that greeted it could crush radical rap's political potency. Nor could it crush its commercial potency, as the success of Public Enemy's uncompromisingly hook-free 1990 *Fear of a Black Planet* (UK 4; US 10) demonstrated. With Public Enemy's shows' combining gig, church service, rally and guerrilla insurrection – as the Spike Lee video for their incendiary masterpiece 'Fight the Power' reveals (UK 29) – the phenomenon truly was "a work of art/ To revolutionize". On 'Revolutionary Generation', Chuck D addresses rap's recurring problem of blaming peers rather than power via black-on-black violence and its sister issue, misogyny. "America took her, reshaped her, raped her" is the history lesson: "They teach us how to diss our sisters", the analysis of divide and rule. Meanwhile, the title track's declaration, "All I want is peace and love on this planet", places conscious rap within its countercultural lineage: the revolution always *was* love and peace.

The significance of Ice Cube guesting on *Black Planet*, then quitting N.W.A. to work with the Bomb Squad isn't simply Public Enemy's influence but their exemplification of a visceral structure of feeling. On the resultant 1990 *Amerikkka's Most Wanted* (US 19), Cube's gangster bragging gets politicised – "When I was robbin' my own kind/The police didn't pay it no mind" – the eugenic solution to the projects problem again. On 1991's *Death Certificate* (US 2), Cube gets tough on crime – "Do I have to sell me a whole lot of crack/For decent shelter and clothes on my back?" – the crime being the state's abandonment of its black citizens: "Or should I just wait for help from Bush?" The president did, in fact, weigh in the following year, but to condemn Ice-T's 'Cop Killer'. A hip-hop/metal hybrid released as Body Count (*Body Count*, US 26), the track is a revenge fantasy "for Rodney King", whose political message – "Fuck police brutality!" – still communicated through the contrived controversy.

This media-generated furore created a rep for gangster rap as integrally anti-social, meaning many kept the genre at a distance, unaware that beyond its hostile surface, it was both affectively complex and – relatively – political, though again in the spirit of Adorno's negative dialectic. Ice-T's 1991 'New Jack Hustler' (*O.G. Original Gangster*, US 15) initially appears to revel in consumerism, but then astutely asserts that "the system" "turned the needy into the greedy", giving ghetto kids a "capitalist migraine". "Is this a nightmare", Ice asks of the gangster life, "or the American dream?" Such analyses of the contradictions of capitalism are not, as we've seen, common in popular music – and almost never are they associated with gangster rap. The same year, Geto Boys' 'Mind Playing Tricks on Me' (US 23) viscerally conveyed the vicious cycle of gangster life, evoking both the prize ("I make big money, I drive big cars") and the price, the perennially primed violence preventing the enjoyment of peace ("Is it that n***a last week that I shot?").

For all this, gangster and radical rap were not, in this golden age of hip-hop, the only games in town. Amiable rather than adversarial, the hippie-hop Native Tongues collective of the Jungle Brothers, A Tribe Called Quest, Queen Latifah and De La Soul – heard ensemble on 1989's 'Buddy' (UK 7) – appears polar to Public Enemy and N.W.A., yet, emerging from the same structure of feeling, they possess more commonality than is conventionally allowed. Not only is Native Tongues' music as infused with ghetto soul as N.W.A.'s, but, like Public Enemy, they deploy this past hauntologically to evoke Black Pride, of which their lyrical dextrousness and sartorial stylishness are also demonstrations. When Native Tongues were more directly political, they tended to be vague: positively so on De La Soul's cute attestation of collectivity over individualism, 'The Magic Number' (UK 7); negatively on their confrontation with crack as a personal rather than systemic issue, on the Hall & Oates-sampling 'Say No Go' (UK 18).

In emerging from the same violence and poverty of the projects, even pop-rap operated within the terms that Public Enemy and N.W.A. established. Following MC Hammer's Rick James-sampling 1990 'U Can't Touch This' (UK 3; US 8), hubris prompted Hammer to symbolically 'solve' gang violence on the video for 'Pray' (UK 8; US 2), while fatuously flipping Public Enemy's aphorism to "*believe* the hype!" on 1991's absurd '2 Legit to Quit' (US 5), roping in James Brown to affirm Hammer's authenticity. With even party rapper LL Cool J channelling Public Enemy on 1990's 'Mama Said Knock You Out' (US 17), if DJ Jazzy Jeff & the Fresh Prince's "air of love and of happiness" on 1991's 'Summertime' (UK 8; US 4) was polar to Public Enemy/ N.W.A., Will Smith was soon doing his best Chuck D on 'Boom! Shake the Room' (UK 1; US 13). While all of this was some degree of co-option of radical rap, it was also a manifestation of a newly uncompromising attitude in African American music that provided an unremarked parallel to gangster rap.

A literal collective, Arrested Development's combination of hippie, party and political rap also rendered them figuratively collective. Returning to the South on 1992's 'Tennessee' (UK 18; US 6), rapper Speech learns to "see the importance of history" as he "climb[s] the trees my forefathers hung from". The inability to "get the ghosts from my skull" attests to hip-hop as a hauntological genre, with scratching and sampling sensual articulations of black history. Thus 'People Everyday' (UK 2; US 8) redeploys Sly Stone's psychedelic-soul classic to counterpose contemporary gangster glamour and assert black history's continuity beyond the end of history. If the revolution *is* peace and love, it's not so much an issue that hippie-hop should descend to violence – "I had to take the brother out for being rude" – but that it adds to the spectacle of black-on-black violence, to which the authorities had no objection. Similarly, the growing white market for hip-hop fed on precisely such spectacular aspects of rap culture.

Fear of a Black Planet: Race, Hip-Hop and Pop

'Race' as an issue – or as a spectacle – now swept through this period's pop. It's never remarked that Madonna's spring 1989 'Like a Prayer' (UK 1; US 1), with its video featuring her kissing a black Christ and dancing in front of burning KKK crosses, came mere months after *Nation of Millions*. For all its managed controversy, with Madonna self-cast as a white saviour, the video's racial politics are merely liberal pluralism; those of the song non-existent. Its key line, "Everyone must stand alone", positions individualism as the source of liberation. Far from standing alone, Madonna – and the song – are carried by a gospel choir, a reminder of both individualism's imbrication in social relations *and* popular music's enduringly unequal racial division of labour.

Janet Jackson's fall 1989 'Rhythm Nation' (UK 23; US 2) represented a dramatic reinvention in the wake of radical rap, its Sly Stone and James Brown samples and monochrome video's paramilitary dance routine pure Public Enemy. Or rather, *impure* Public Enemy, the track not just being more new jack swing than hip-hop but also invoking racial unity rather than political insurgency – "People of the world unite/Strength in numbers, we can get it right" – while its claim that dancing is the way "to break the colour line" is more rave utopianism than rap radicalism. Jackson's brother Michael's 1991 'Black or White' (UK 1; US 1) also mines new jack swing and hip-hop – thus his new propensity for grabbing his crotch – while asserting "equality" and claiming he isn't "scared of no sheets" (KKK). Again, the message of racial unity – "If you're thinking of being my brother/It don't matter if you're black or white"; the video's appropriation of Godley & Creme's morphing multi-racial faces – elides systemic divisions to brotherliness. Racism is simply a decision, racial unity a spectacle. Female R&B troupe En Vogue's 1992 explosive 'Free Your Mind' (UK 16; US 8) similarly urges, "Be colour-blind". Yet their bowdlerisation of Funkadelic ("and your ass will follow" becoming "and the rest will follow") indicates the track's containment, the period's recurring preoccupation with perception – "Before you can read me/You got to learn how to see me" – a fetishisation of the spectacle affirmed by the hyperactive, flashbulb-popping video.

If the spectacle was the measure, then racial equality had been achieved, with Public Enemy's black planet a cultural and commercial reality, not just white-supremacist paranoia. Hip-hop and new jack swing ruled charts and minds, 1992's second biggest-selling song in any genre being Sir Mix-a-Lot's 'Baby Got Back' (US 1). While boasting "I like big butts" is hardly "fucking up the government", like Chuck D, 'Baby Got Back' still addresses the racialisation of sexuality. Flowing from hip-hop, James Brown's 'Funky Drummer' sample now undergirded teenpop (Kylie's 1989 'Wouldn't Change a Thing', UK 2) and adult pop (George Michael's 'Freedom! 90'). The Brown-derived 'Whoo! Ha!' sample similarly underwrote both credible hip-house (Tyree Cooper's 1989 'Turn Up the Bass', UK 12) and incredible bilge (Timmy Mallet's 1990 'Itsy Bitsy Teeny Weeny Yellow Polka Dot Bikini', UK 1).

Former Page-3 girl Samantha Fox collaborated with hip-hoppers Full Force on 'Naughty Girls' (US 3), while Duran Duran, Fine Young Cannibals and Roxette all went new-jack swing. Boybands began biting B-boy style – New Kids on the Block's breakdancing on 1990's 'Tonight' (UK 3; US 7); their black vernacular on 'Hangin' Tough' (UK 1; US 1); East 17 offering a reedier, rougher British variant. Moreover, white musicians couldn't *stop* rapping, from Neil Tennant, to Madonna, to the Shamen's Mr C, to Vanilla Ice, who (defensively) conceded the cultural appropriation – "A white rapper with some street knowledge"[36] Irish American homeboys

House of Pain's joyfully ridiculous 1992 'Jump Around' (UK 8; US 3) was taken in good part, while the Beastie Boys went from being viewed as minstrels to the acme of hipster cool (1992's *Check Your Head*, US 10). While there were sideswipes at 'wiggers' and some mockery of appropriation in Run-DMC's 1988 'It's Tricky' video (UK 16),[37] such imitation was largely regarded as flattery. This was what liberal pluralism looked and sounded like: the spectacle would deliver racial equality where social democracy could not.

Yet although African Americans were now, if anything, *over-*represented in popular culture, the fact that they were also over-represented in prison populations, unemployment statistics and police executions evidenced the limitations of cultural rather than political change. For ordinary African Americans, the freedom of neoliberal democracy would continue to be situated elsewhere – beyond the projects, the other side of a cultural, political and ideological wall. For that majority of African Americans who didn't make the charts or inspire imitators, the 'end of history' was just another term for stasis, for the status inequalities of the status quo.

"Come Together as One": Collectivity and Dance

"We wanna be free… to do what we wanna do", a young man on Primal Scream's 1990 indie-dance hit 'Loaded' exclaims (UK 16), sampled from hippie-exploitation flick *The Wild Angels* (1966): "We wanna get loaded and have a good time". The same year, the Soup Dragons' Rolling Stones cover, 'I'm Free' (UK 5) was, similarly, as defiant as it was celebratory: "Don't be afraid of your freedom!" Such defensive articulations of 'freedom' would recur throughout acid house. Purely hedonistic as these desires appeared to be, the key question was *why* dance musicians and ravers were demanding freedom, when, only a year previously, the end of history had asserted neoliberal democracy as the embodiment of freedom.

The eruption of illegal raves in disused warehouses in British cities across 1987–88 surprised and unnerved the authorities, being "the first large-scale mobilisations of people since the miners' strike", as Jeremy Deller observes, and accordingly, the full force of the law was brought to bear upon these riotless assemblies.[38] Police crackdown pushed raves out to rural areas during 1989, but state harassment continued, with bills introduced in parliament and roadblocks erected across access points, while, in another echo of the miners' strike, violent clashes with police erupted as ravers fought back. While the impetus here was hedonic, ravers' refusal to abide within statutory provision of pleasure, and their desire to do so collectively, not only expressed dissatisfaction with the socio-political dispensation, but did so on neoliberalism's chosen ideological ground of 'freedom'. Hence 1990's Freedom to Party protest in London and that defiance in indie-dance assertions of liberty. So rather than rave's collectivity being, as Reynolds claims, a purely cultural reaction to 80s individualism,[39] its collective utopianism was possessed of considerable political potential. For Fisher, "Rave's ecstatic festivals revived the use of time and land which the bourgeoisie had forbidden and sought to bury", thereby summoning the seemingly vanquished "spectre of a world that could be free".[40]

Rave's callbacks to the counterculture weren't idle aestheticism therefore: ecstasy (MDMA) broke down social barriers just as cannabis and LSD had in the 60s, and to be "loved up" was to experience collective, platonic *Eros* rather than individual erotic gratification. Acid house commonly expressed this collective sensibility in utopian terms: Sydney Youngblood's 1989 'If Only I Could' (UK 3) attests, "United we're stronger"; Primal Scream's 1990 indie-dance hit advises people to 'Come Together' (UK 26), echoed by the Beloved's 1991 'Sweet Harmony' (UK 8) – "Let's come together right now… to be as one" – while, the same year, Sabrina Johnston's diva-house anthem 'Peace' (UK 8) extols, "Love… it's the part of us that keeps us all alive". Vague as this was, it was still a countercultural vision of collective liberation, a freedom that had nothing to do with the individualist freedom of the market.

Named after the Prodigy's 1992 hardcore carol to the collective (UK 2), Deller's 2018 documentary *Everybody in the Place* argues that, rather than escapism, what drew revellers to disused warehouses and factories was a "death-ritual to mark the transition of Britain from an industrial to a service economy".[41] This ritual marked the shift from Fordism to post-Fordism – and, as Deller does *not* say, from social democracy to neoliberalism. The factories in Madonna's concurrent 'Express Yourself' and Jackson's 'Rhythm Nation' videos suggest Deller's argument isn't entirely fanciful. Moreover, acid house ushered into the mainstream an identifiably post-industrial working class – disparaged by the elite press as 'the underclass' – for whom 'the Happy Mondays' is a name. Resentful, bohemian, hedonistic, this was Fordism's living, breathing, dancing, post-industrial waste, a living – if dead-eyed – hauntology. "You're twisting my melon man", Shaun Ryder sneers on 'Step On' (UK 5), "call the cops!"

Moreover, for an ostensibly ecstatic, immanent medium, there was a melancholic nostalgia in dance that was intrinsically, transcendently hauntological. With tracks composed of fragments of Fordist music, this melancholy is audible even in Lil Louis's orgasmic 1989 'French Kiss' (UK 2), while 808 State's 1989 'Pacific State' (UK 10) actually *sounds* sepia, and Future Sound of London's 1991 'Papua New Guinea' (UK 22) is rapturously dolorous, its layered, subliminal sound-fragments the essence of hauntology. Occasionally, this melancholy was verbalised, as on the Source's 1991 'You Got the Love' (UK 4), whose opening line, "Sometimes I feel like throwing my hands up in the air", combines a gesture of despair with that of a raver's joyful abandon, Candi Staton's heartbroken tones drawing melancholy from the machines, which twinkle like lasers.

Regardless of such subliminal resonances from the past, the present's material world left young people plenty to feel melancholic about, with little to look forward to beyond the next rave or club night. As against Deller's argument, rave's radical potential didn't reside in its melancholy but in its energy. On Wiz's video for Flowered Up's 1992 indie-dance epic 'Weekender' (UK 20), the opening voiceover proclaims raving "feels like we could do, like, fucking anything". Yet having captured this communal, utopian possibility in the club scenes, the film's final image shows the solitary weekender suspended in mid-air, transpiring, as the camera tracks back, to be sleeping in his window-cleaning boom, ready to start the cycle of work/escape/work again. Here, the utopian potential in acid house's collective freedom – "We could do, like, fucking anything" – wears off with the drugs, leaving

305

the individual isolated in their comedown, their quantum of 'freedom' getting recycled back into the system. However, Reynolds' observation that "Ecstasy culture [was] a useful way of dissipating the tensions generated by wage-slavery... channelling idealism and discontent out of the political arena" allows too little agency to ravers and too *much* agency to the state.[42]

In respect of rave's political potential, it's necessary to take a middle course between Reynolds' under-sell and Fisher's overstatement. Rave was pincered between repressive and ideological state apparatuses: the police and the Graham Bright 'acid house bill' on one hand; neoliberal individualism on the other. As such, a tension between individual and collective freedom is audible throughout acid house. Adamski and Seal's 1990 'Killer' (UK 1) asks, "Solitary brother/Is there still a part of you that wants to live?/Solitary sister/Is there still a part of you that wants to give?" – individualist ecstasy counterposed with collectivist solidarity. New Order's 'World in Motion' (UK 1) was claimed to combine the national collectivity of summer 1990's World Cup with the utopianism of acid house. Yet while "Love's got the world in motion" gives the chorus collective momentum, the verse's recurring "It's one-on-one" cheers on an individualism which highlights the star player, not the team: "Express yourself – it can't be wrong!" The Happy Mondays' masterpiece, 1990's 'Kinky Afro' (UK 5), meanwhile, is an acid-house inversion of Cat Stevens' 'Father and Son', the son castigating the feckless, freedom-chasing father, who, unforgivably, utters one of the greatest opening lines in pop: "Son, I'm thirty/I only went with your mother 'cause she's dirty".

This question of freedom is central to acid house's tension between the individual and the collective. On Soul II Soul's house-adjacent 1989 'Get a Life' (UK 3), the chorus, "Elevate your mind, free your soul", opens up a collective freedom that is then privatised in the verse: "Dreaming of your goals/Ambitions and feeling free". With rave renowned for its entrepreneurialism, this tension recurs in club promoters the Shamen's 1991 'Move Any Mountain' (UK 4): the communality of "one nation, one tribe" counterposed by the self-actualisation of "I will not fail nor falter, I shall succeed".[43] This renders ambivalent their statement, "You can be what you want to be/Let your soul and your body and your mind be free". On Rozalla's 1991 piano-house anthem 'Everybody's Free' (UK 6), the verses espouse a utopian, countercultural communality – "We are a family that should stand together as one/Helping each other" – yet the chorus's declaration that "Everybody's free to feel good" espouses an individualist freedom that contradicts such collectivity.[44]

Rozalla's song gives its name to this chapter because it captures how the collective freedom that constituted rave's radical, countercultural, impulse was in constant tension with the individualist (neo)liberal 'freedom' of the end of history. That this competitive freedom triumphed in acid house was as much due to internal as external pressures. Lacking a utopian project to house its collectivist impulses – a vision of the future rather than the endless extension of the eternal present – rave's political potential couldn't be realised, and its hedonic impulse could easily be absorbed into a market economy. As the history of both top-down and ground-up politics repeatedly reveals, to aim low in capitalist society can *only* result in containment and co-option, because the enemy never sleeps (while even the most dedicated ravers eventually do). So Castlemorton's week-long rave in summer 1992 is now revealed as a collective mourning as much as a celebration, a hauntology not of Fordism, as in Deller's reading, but of rave itself. Even as the revellers danced, rave's collectivity was being subsumed by capitalist clubbing's simulacra of sociality, with acid house's utopian aspiration excised.

"We Get to Carry Each Other": Alternative Rock at the End of History

From the Berlin Wall to Tiananmen Square, from riots to raves, and from Heysel to Hillsborough, the crowd was a recurring motif of this era, expressive of an enduring cultural collectivity in the face of a politicised individualism. That this collectivity was increasingly excoriated and pressurised in this interregnum between conservative and centrist neoliberalism is audible and visible in a vein of songs from this era. Occupying a cultural no-man's land between grunge and rave, these songs combine Fordism with post-Fordism, guitars with electronics, drums with breakbeats, while their collectivity is melancholic to rave's ecstatic, passive to its active, and dystopian to its utopian.

The Farm's 1990 indie-dance 'All Together Now' (UK 4) uses the iconic World War I football match in no-man's land as an emblem of utopian collectivity. Yet the song sounds unbearably sad even *before* you get to the video of elderly people in a working-men's club miming the words. It's clearly not about a world war won but a class war lost and thus relates to Deller's post-industrial death ritual. The chorus's yearning "All together now in no-man's land" harks back to the end of history as a loss rather than a gain. The song's proclamation of the dispossessed's unity amidst hostility – "Stop the slaughter! Let's go home!" – is thus defensive rather than transformative.

This theme recurs subliminally in R.E.M.'s 1991 'Shiny Happy People' (UK 6; US 10), whose solidaristic celebration of countercultural collectivity – "Everyone around: love them" – is captured by the video's dancing, diverse crowd gradually engulfing the band. However, the song's subtext is the Tiananmen Square massacre, where "holding hands" offered no protection against tanks and guns. Carter the Unstoppable Sex Machine's breakbeat-propelled 1991 'The Only Living Boy in New Cross' (UK 7) embraces a countercultural collective – "the gypsies, the travellers... Clause 28-ers... grebos, the crusties and the goths" – with the band again subsumed by a dancing crowd in the video. "I've teamed up with the hippies now", Jim-Bob declares: "Give peace, love and kisses out/To this whole stinking world". Yet as these countercultural groups had all learned in recent years, peace and love offered little protection against the police truncheons and charging horses of the free West. James's 1991 glam stomp 'Sit Down' (UK 2) demands we "sit down in sympathy" because "It's hard to carry on when you feel all alone". Yet such a statement of solidarity is passive compared to standing *up* to oppression. At the end of history, collectivity has become a huddling together against a hostile, authoritarian, essentially unchangeable system.

As part of *Achtung Baby*'s retreat from stadium statement, U2's 1992 'One' (UK 7; US 10) appears to concern the sundering of a couple, or, as one of its three videos suggests, a father and son. Yet as 'One' continues its stately progress, the personal becomes political in its depiction of disappointment, the song's conflict peaking in – and resolved by – the declaration "We're one, but we're not the same/We get to carry each other, carry each other". Hard as it is to allow profundity in U2, this resolves the era's tension between individual and collective freedom in entirely countercultural terms – "brothers, sisters" – the limit to freedom being obligation to others, when to "carry each other" is a *privilege*, not a duty. What makes this line so moving is not just its assertion of solidarity, nor that its protagonists know they've come up short in this regard, but its awareness that people now *need* to carry each other to survive in society's harsh environment. Collectivity here, and in all these songs, isn't utopian but defensive, arising from a need to protect each other in *this* world rather than the projection of hope into a better world.

This connects to contemporary political developments. Bill Clinton's 1992 presidential campaign restored colour to the era's sepia tones, a sense of hope to the period's hopelessness, with his progressive compassion contrasting with George Bush's bloodless authoritarianism. Yet Clinton's vision was the political logic of the end of history, abandoning social democracy's limited utopia for a 'centrist' no-man's land between Reaganite neoliberalism and social liberalism, based on the presumption that the freedom of the individual and of the market were one and the same. The media called it 'triangulation', but always tending to triangulate rightwards, Clinton's 'third way' was another example of a politics which aimed too low and thus didn't represent the radical break from the Bush era that was claimed.

This may explain why Clinton-supporters R.E.M.'s fall 1992 Rock the Vote song 'Drive' (UK 11; US 28) should sound so mournful – "Bush-whacked", but hardly psyched about the alternative: "maybe you're crazy in the head". The song's monochrome video, depicting singer Michael Stipe borne on the hands of a concert crowd, is a lovely image of collectivity – "We get to carry each other" – and thus implicitly of solidarity's political potential. Yet in this liminal period of unrealised possibilities, it's also an image of helplessness, like a baby floating in amniotic fluid (think of the cover of *Nevermind*), unable to influence events, but, again, soothed by human contact as a buffer against an endemically, unavoidably harsh world.

In such an environment, everybody *was* free, as the fall of the Wall had guaranteed: free to consume ("it can't be wrong"), and free to express themselves within neoliberal democracy's defined parameters – riots, raves and occupations excepted. Radical political change, like utopianism, was deemed not just undesirable but dangerous at the end of history, and centrism presented a means of preserving the existing system, seemingly without tears. We have arrived, therefore, at the Long 90s. Make yourselves as comfortable as you can: we're going to be here for a good old while.

Chapter 10

"The Power and the Money": The 90s in Soundbites and Buzzwords (1993–2001)

Sometimes the concept of 'the contradictions of capitalism' can sound like a copout: at others it just sounds like the 90s. Bill Clinton and Tony Blair's centrism was supposed to resolve neoliberalism's contradictions, to combine social liberalism with economic liberalism and realise personal freedom through the free market. As such, centrism created a more inclusive environment, but it also normalised the notion of human society as a competitive and thus *hostile* environment. So while there's a familiarly 'fun' 90s of Britpop and boybands, bling and big beat, 'Barbie Girl' and the Spice Girls, there's also an enduringly 'dark' 90s of gangsta rap and jungle, Rage Against the Machine and Radiohead. Cher Horowitz, as sage of the fun 90s, gave such "whiny" "complaint rock" short shrift in *Clueless* (1996): which 90s you got was down to the individual. "I can be it/If I just believe it", R. Kelly attests on 1996's anthemic 'I Believe I Can Fly' (UK 1; US 2). That Kelly doesn't now seem such a great poster boy for the period says it all. The fun and the dark 90s were always a two-for-one, reasserted rather than resolved by the cartoon *noir* of Tarantino's *Pulp Fiction* (1996), the gritty 'in yer face' glamour of *Trainspotting* (1996) or the literal cartoon nihilism of *South Park* and its musical equivalent, Eminem.

It's not just that 90s metropolitan coffee-bar music was so serenely miserable – Portishead's 1994 *Dummy* (UK 2) or Moby's 1999 *Play* (UK 1), with its "trouble so hard" ('Natural Blues', UK 11) – but that even boosterist Britpop became anthemically morose when Blair finally replaced Major in 1997. Thus, the Verve's upliftingly downbeat 'The Drugs Don't Work' (UK 1) and Pulp's poppily paranoid 1998 *This Is Hardcore* (UK 1). Even self-help teen pop developed a morbid streak with East 17's 1994 'Stay Another Day' (UK 1) and the Backstreet Boys' 1999 'Show Me the Meaning of Being Lonely' (UK 3; US 6), hardly resolved by Steps' triangulation of sad songs and jaunty formation dances.[1] The video for Kylie Minogue's breezy 1994 'Confide in Me' (UK 2) flashes up supertitles like "Depressed?" "Desperate?" "Angry?" Commodifying these contradictions, the period's biggest seller, Toni Braxton's 1996 'Unbreak My Heart' (UK 2; US 1) was as familiar as a heartbroken power ballad – featuring the most joyless "whoo" in pop history (at 4:07) – *and* as a pumping handbag-house remix.

Where late-80s teen pop had gloried in insubstantiality, its 90s iteration exhibited a recurring anxiety about substance. Natalie Imbruglia's brisk 1996 ballad 'Torn' (UK 2) frets that "illusion never turned into something real", as the video set collapses around the shattered singer. Robbie Williams's entire post-Take That career was a neurotic pile-on of content and contemporaneity – thus 1998's muddled 'Millennium' (UK 1). Jennifer Lopez, meanwhile, felt compelled to assert 'I'm Real' (UK 4; US 1), against all evidence. Yet to view the 90s as postmodern insubstantiality, as Bracewell does,[2] is to smoke but not inhale – like Clinton's student marijuana experience – to ignore the complexities and stick to a surface that the media and political class span then and are still spinning now. This continuity has made it seem a *very* long 90s.

A clue to the cause of these contradictions lies in this chapter's title (thank you for your service, Coolio). In the 90s, the money *was* the power, with "the economy", as Fisher observed, "an operative fiction which secures capitalist hegemony".[3] So while there was a huge consumer boom in the 90s, there was a far bigger stock boom following the deregulation of the banks. While GDP soared – music industry profits hitting their historic peak in 1999 – real wages stagnated. While the US government ran a surplus, its citizens ran debt at unprecedented levels.[4] As, visibly, the rich got richer and the poor poorer, it could seem like Clinton's campaign slogan, "It's the economy, stupid", was a diss of those who couldn't make the money or possess the power and who – doh! – saw nothing natural about this selection. With such a war of all against all requiring a Leviathan, the authoritarianism of the 90s' small state was arresting: not just Major's clampdown on raves but 'progressive' Blair and Clinton's assaults on "welfare as we know it" (all spin, no doctor) and other forms of "anti-social behaviour" – like strike action or single motherhood. The sacralisation of the family was an aspect of this authoritarianism – Major's 'Back to Basics' crusade; wives at the podium; Clinton claiming "marriage is the foundation of a successful society" – but also its antidote, with families forced to provide the safety net that the state was withdrawing.[5]

With power in the 90s lying with the competitive individual – "ruthlessness disguised as character" in Adorno's terms[6] – the result was another transactional turn in pop, an affective hardness heard most harshly in gangsta rap but extending far beyond it. For R. Kelly to compare a woman to his bank account on 1995's 'You Remind Me of Something' (UK 21; US 4) – "I wanna spend it, baby" – or Kelis's prostitute to reassure Ol' Dirty Bastard's pimp she's 'Got Your Money' in 1999 (UK 11) was all in a day's work for 90s pop. In such a structure of feeling, a song that reasserted the unconditional against the transactional, Meat Loaf's 1993 'I'd Do Anything for Love (But I Won't Do That)' (UK 1; US 1), caused such confusion about what "that" might be – the emotional small print! – that Meat took to onstage explanations with blackboard and a pointer. Even Madonna decried the affective chill of those "so consumed with what you can get" on 1998's 'Frozen' (UK 1; US 2).

More typically, Destiny's Child's 1999 'Jumpin', Jumpin'' (UK 5; US 3) joyfully advocates cheating with rich "ballers", while Jay-Z boasts of having a "heart cold as assassins" on 2000's reptilian 'Big Pimpin' (UK 29; US 18): "I thug 'em, fuck 'em, love 'em, leave 'em.../But I don't fuckin' feed 'em". Concurrently, Shaggy's dancehall hit 'It Wasn't Me' (UK 1: US 1) provided a consultancy in spinning literally naked reality, its critical free ride paralleling Clinton leaving office with sky-high ratings, despite the Lewinsky sex scandal.[7] As the platonic ideal of neoliberal individualism, the powerful and the monied could, it seemed, do as they pleased.

As the mix of sex-positivity and sexism in these songs suggests, the 'progressive' 90s was a contradictory era for women: better represented than ever – with Mariah Carey, Celine Dion, Whitney Houston, Janet Jackson and Madonna dominating the charts – but unable to identify as feminist in the backlash against 'political correctness'. For this is the storied age of the *kinder whore* look, the 'Slut' T-shirt, the 'babe' and the snickering lads' mag.[8] While career opportunities for women increased, so did self-harming and eating disorders for girls. The 90s was, likewise, a period of both queer acclaiming (*Brookside*'s lesbian kiss; *Philadelphia*; British TV's *Queer as Folk*) *and* queer shaming (the George Michael and Ron Davies cottaging/cruising scandals), while only in the 90s could Clinton's 'Don't ask, don't tell' policy for gays in the military be regarded as a resolution.

While hip-hop and R&B were 90s music's creative and commercial core – their diffusion indicated by Eminem, boy-band NSYNC and skate-punkers Offspring's flip but acute 'Pretty Fly (For a White Guy)' (UK 1) – America's projects and Britain's sink-estates sank ever deeper into dystopia. Such a harsh environment was conventionalised top-down by "culture of poverty" propaganda and street-up by gangsta rap and speed garage's role as synecdoches for the social whole.[9] "No disrespectin' the threat of my clique" So Solid Crew hiss on '21 Seconds' (UK 1): "Raise up the dead an' ah/Worship the devil".

With nothing un-spinnable in the 90s, Mariah Carey's hateful 1993 power ballad 'Hero' (UK 7; US 1) insists that although "hope is gone", leaving an atomised "emptiness", the solution is "within yourself" to effect change. 90s pop and politics were full of such fantasy resolutions to centrism's contradictions. Teen-poppers S Club 7's 1999 'Bring It All Back' (UK 1) asserts that "life it ain't easy", but because "you are your own destiny", you can still "reach the top" – echoing Blair's claim that each person "makes the most of what is within them". While Ultra Naté's infectious 1997 house anthem 'Free' (UK 4) frets "You can never trust another/'Cause they're all out to get ya", her chorus affirms that, "You're free to do what you want to do". Rather than resolving 90s contradictions, this *is* the contradiction: competitive individualism presented as the solution to – rather than the cause of – a conventionally cruel environment. This negative worldview was spun as positivity ('dark' as 'fun'), while the power and the money were redistributed upwards.

"Party jam"

Gangsta rap isn't known for its conciliation, yet in its take on the party jam, the contradiction between the fun and dark 90s was resolved, however uneasily. Quitting N.W.A., Dr. Dre's early 1993 *The Chronic* (US 3) established gangsta's tone and style: cold-blooded but commercial, and while too hostile to be hauntological, its ghetto-funk grooves and eerie synth whines were seductively nostalgic. Featuring newcomer Snoop Doggy Dogg, the low-slung 'Nuthin' but a 'G' Thang' (US 2) is nonchalantly antagonistic, whether to competitive gangs ("Try to get close and your ass'll get smacked") or compliant women ("hookers and ho's"). Dre's estranged colleague Ice Cube's contemporaneous 'It Was a Good Day' (UK 27; US 15) is similarly sunny sounding, but Cube's day is good because he doesn't get carjacked, harassed by cops or beset by gangbangers. "I didn't even have to use my AK", he rhapsodises. With Cypress Hill's reptilian 'Insane in the Brain' (UK 21; US 19) another of summer '93's party jams, there's no sense that this harsh environment is *bad*, these tracks proffering not a protest *against* but a paradigm *of* society.

Consequently, Snoop's slinky 1994 'Gin and Juice' (US 8) sublimates the values of market capitalism: competitive individualism, consumerism and transactional relationships ("We don't love them ho's"). With pretty-boy Warren G lacking brother Dre's sternness, he and Nate Dogg's mellow 1994 'Regulate' (UK 5; US 2), while strung from a yearning Michael McDonald sample, is presentist not hauntological, flipping from gang violence to motel orgy in a heartbeat. That same summer, Ice Cube's 'Bop Gun' (UK 22; US 23) takes Funkadelic's 'One Nation under a Groove' – with Clinton and Bootsy in the video –

but flips its utopian hedonism to dystopian hostility: "Party over here/Fuck you over there!"

With Tupac signing to Death Row, his and Dre's 1996 'California Love' (UK 6; US 1) is a consummate party jam, yet one in which Dre compares his songs to bullets and his career to pimping, while, shirtless in the video, Tupac bristles, "we collide with other crews". On '2 of Amerikaz Most Wanted' (*All Eyez On Me*, US 1), Tupac and Snoop make the implications plain: the world is "nothing but a gangsta party", where "we live by the guns, so we die by the guns, kid". Lapped up by suburban homeboys, gangsta realism provided not merely vicarious thrills but a metaphor for neoliberal society's harshness. With Dre more 'party' than gangsta on Blackstreet's joyous 1996 'No Diggity' (UK 9; US 1), his now-enemy 2Pac's 'Toss it Up' (UK 15; US 10) apes 'Diggity' to declare it's "no longer Dre Day". Yet with gangsta's combination of hostility and hedonism flowing into R&B – Montell Jordan's 1995 'This is How We Do It' (UK 11; US 1); Mark Morrison's 1996 'Return of the Mack' (UK 1; US 2) – it was *always* Dre day in the 90s.

"Music characterised by repetitive beats"

Commercially, the 90s was more the era of M-People than 'Common People', of pumping house rather than Supergrass's 'Pumping on Your Stereo' (UK 11), a decade culturally and musically suffused with dance, pre-eminent flag-waver for the fun 90s' perpetual party. Yet dance was itself a 90s contradiction, caught between radical roots and commercial cravings, fun mainstream and dark margins.

With the Conservatives' 1993 Criminal Justice Bill (CJB) pinpointing "music characterised by repetitive beats", rave renegades the Prodigy's 'Their Law' (*Music for the Jilted Generation*, UK 1) was a rebarbative response: "Fuck 'em and their law". The Prodigy resolved dance's contradictions by combining fun and dark, radical and mainstream on 'Firestarter' (UK 1; US 30), but in doing so, ceased to be dance. Another rave mainstay, Orbital defied the CJB in both the title of 1994's *Snivilisation* (UK 4) and in how *little* their epic soundscapes were characterised by "repetitive beats". Revealing the progressive potentiality within a medium critically deemed primitive and regressive, 1996's *In Sides* (UK 5) returns to the rural site of raves as expression of both Marcusian idyll and of protest. Combining rave and punk rebellions, Leftfield and John Lydon's 1995 'Open Up' (UK 13) channels Public Enemy to jeer, "Burn Hollywood, burn". Yet, despite Reclaim the Streets' pop-up raves on roads and motorways, the contradiction here was how *little* protest there was to the CJB, given its existential threat to dance culture.

Paradoxically, it was an indie band, Pulp, who captured this contradiction on 1995's 'Sorted for Es and Wizz' (UK 2). Jarvis Cocker, coming down from a pill in the early hours, wonders, "Is this the way they say the future's meant to feel?/Or just twenty thousand people standing in a field?" For there *was* no future in rave: without a utopian political project, dance culture had no resources for its own defence and was co-opted by capitalism long before the CJB became law. Promotors exemplified the period's power and money, creating superclubs like Cream (1992) and Home (1999), whose simulacras of sociality expanded into the countryside with Creamfields and Homelands in the late 90s, providing a corporate hauntology of rave's refusal.

Dance music soon lost both its radical associations and dark iterations to focus on the fun 90s. French duo Daft Punk liberated house from its disco denialism, reasserting its queerness, while offshoot Stardust's 1998 'Music Sounds Better with You' (UK 2) created a facsimile of transcendence from austere materials – a metaphor for the 90s. The subsequent dominance of disco-house became rote, its sentiments centrist – Armand van Helden's individualistic 1999 'You Don't Know Me' (UK 1); Roger Sanchez's wanly optimistic 2001 'Another Chance' (UK 1) – and while Basement Jaxx's 1999 'Red Alert' (UK 5) upped the excitement, it was as a palliative for passivity: "Don't worry... ain't nothin' goin' on but history".[10]

Trance was dance's lowest common denominator, all cheesy keyboard riffs, manipulative breakdowns and *very* repetitive beats, orientated towards conventional clubbing and ideology. Faithless's 1996 'Salva Mea' (UK 9) disingenuously demands, "How can I change the world/If I can't even change myself?" while Maxi Jazz's portentous rapping either reflects clubber solipsism – on 1996's 'Insomnia' (UK 3) – or promotes individualism, as on

1997's 'Reverence' (UK 10): "All ya have to do is love yourself/It's a fact you'll attract all the things that ya lack". The coerciveness of 90s common sense is captured by that insouciant assertion of fiction as "fact". 1998's 'God Is a DJ' (UK 6) carols the club as the place where a normatively harsh society's hurts can be healed and contradictions resolved. Until the club closes and you re-enter the competitive hostility of the conventional world. From its utopian roots, dance had gone from refusal of neoliberalism to acceptance.

"Slacker"

The slacker was an archetype of white American youth, contiguous with grunge and dramatised by the shiftless non-heroes of Richard Linklater's *Slacker* (1990), Douglas Coupland's *Generation X* (1991) and Kevin Smith's *Clerks* (1994). Yet it was rarely noted that slackers' dead-end jobs, disengagement and depression were responses to the betrayal of the Fordist promise of their childhoods and their subsequent exclusion from the fun 90s and from the power and the money.

Declaring, "I don't belong here", Radiohead's 1993 hit 'Creep' (UK 7) expresses as much loathing as longing for those who *do* belong in the competitive world: "You're so fucking special". Yet the song's crucial line is, "I don't care if it hurts/I just wanna have control". For in the 90s, control was ceded not to the state but to the market, where the trading of 'futures' boomed economically, while socially there was no future to trade on. Slackers had a front-row seat, therefore, on both the future's 70s' fetishisation *and* its 90s' cancellation.

The pejorative 'complaint rock' effected two very 90s tricks: denying there could be anything to complain about and personalising the political. The brilliance of Beck's wordplay on 1994's hip-hop/folk 'Loser' (UK 15; US 10) performs a flip rebuttal of slacker stereotypes, while mocking the media's excision of economics – "Savin' all your food stamps and burnin' down the trailer park" – in a moral economy of 'winners' and 'losers'. With sarcasm the slacker's only tradeable asset, the chorus's "I'm a loser, baby, so why don't you kill me?" is the 90s' weaponised performance principle internalised and spat back.

"Boyband"

Usually perceived as apolitical, the boyband was essentially centrist: perennially positive, competitively commercial and captive to the performance principle, making New Labour's 1997 campaign co-option of D:Ream's 1994 hit 'Things Can Only Get Better' (UK 1) entirely apposite. To the American, Boyz II Men model of 'new man' neediness, Brits Take That added self-objectifying sexuality – the flesh-filled videos for 1993's 'Why Can't I Wake Up with You' (UK 2) and 'Pray' (UK 1) – and a cheeky 'ordinariness'. This trace of sexual and class utopianism was largely contained by showbiz wholesomeness (the sepia 1930s video for 'Babe', UK 1; the jazz club video for 'Everything Changes', UK 1; Lulu). While Londoners East 17 rendered this social and sexual challenge more threatening – 1994's 'Steam' (UK 7) – they were still a *sensitive* bit of rough, like US equivalent the Backstreet Boys, acquiescent rather than adversarial.[11]

Framed as classless and sexless, Irish Boyzone's 1996 political statement 'A Different Beat' (UK 1) is a classic centrist proposition: performative social concern which ultimately affirms the status quo. "Let unity become" vies with the syntax of Blair's speeches: verb-heavy, content-light, structure… lacking. The utopian imagination of Westlife's 1999 'Flying Without Wings' (UK 1) can't get further than the quotidian – marriage and family – while the insistence that "you have to fight for every dream" asserts that, in an endemically hostile environment, the conventional is radical. The positivity of Five's 1999 breakbeat strumalong 'Keep on Movin' (UK 1) – "Better things are comin' my way" – is pasted over a suspicion that "life has no meaning". Spinning dark as fun, stasis as movement, the chorus provides a breezily bathetic summary of 90s politics – "I know it's not much, but it's OK/We'll keep on movin' on anyway" – that's inadvertently devastating.

"Cool Britannia"

Boybands with guitars, Britpop's contradiction was its combination of positivity and cynicism, a synecdoche for both the spun phenomenon of 'Cool Britannia' and the centrist political project itself. Although the 90s was claimed to mirror the 60s, it offered instead its mirror *image*, its affective reversal, replacing 60s positive-negativity with a new negative-positivity.

60s-suffused Oasis were full of upbeat invocations – "You and I are gonna live forever"; "You gotta make it happen", "We will find a brighter day" – but while their yearning *sounded* utopian, it only really voiced 'aspiration'. Moreover, Oasis's positivity was undermined by a recurring disengagement – Liam regularly losing interest in lip-synching, Noel eating chips in 1994's 'Whatever' video (UK 3), then sweeping up the studio. This often tilted into hostility: Liam staring down the camera; his hectoring bray of a voice; the 'Roll With It' (UK 2) lyric, "Don't let anybody get in your way". This was an apt sentiment for 'the Battle of Britpop' with Blur, therefore, which distilled Cool Britannia as competitiveness, class mobility and non-hauntological nostalgia.

Oasis's 1997 'D'You Know What I Mean?' went straight to no. 1 as Blair went straight to Number 10, and likewise sounded and looked like a celebration of collectivity – "all my people right here right now"; the video's crowd amassing around the band. 'D'You Know What I Mean?' never answers its titular question, as if spin were its own point, its only message being "get up off the floor and believe in life" – competition as survival in a hostile world. Oasis revealed the coolness in Cool Britannia: a chilly environment warmed by wan positivity; stasis spun as progress, and its cynical legacy is with us still.

"Comedy is the new rock'n'roll"

An acknowledgement of the mainstreaming of alternative comedy, this catchphrase captures the pop-careers of comedians – Vic and Bob; Newman and Baddiel's putrid Euro '96 positivity anthem 'Four Lions' (UK 1) – alongside 90s popular culture's determination to be 'fun'. That much of this was the opposite of fun indicates the cynicism that span this positivity, and the affectless flippancy that was the platonic ideal of the 90s subject. As David Stubbs summarises this structure of feeling, "this is the Nineties, can't we all lighten up?"[12]

The era's many novelty songs were a particularly grating facsimile of fun. 1993's Latex novelty figure 'Mr Blobby' (UK 1) embodied the performance principle in a conventionally hostile world: "No ride too rough, no test too tough". Euro duo 2 Unlimited's 1993 'No Limit' (UK 1) links dance ("techno techno techno") to hedonistic individualism ("We do what we want and we do it with pride"). The subject of Los Del Rio's cheesy dance craze, 1996's 'Macarena' (UK 2; US 1), asserts her independence by cheating on her boyfriend with his friends. Scandinavian trio Aqua's maddening 1997 'Barbie Girl' (UK 1; US 7) manages to triangulate critique and consent, piping, "I'm a blond bimbo girl in a fantasy world".[13]

This comedic core infused 90s teen pop (Spice Girls; B*Witched), Britpop (Jarvis Cocker's 70s loungewear; Supergrass's novelty sideburns and *Prisoner* video for 1995's 'Alright', UK 2), acid jazz (Jamiroquai's Jay Kay's penchant for absurd headwear), hip-hop (The Fugees' Wyclef and Pras) and lounge-pop, with Sweden's Cardigans a hipster Aqua on 1997's 'Lovefool' (UK 2). At worst, this collapse of cool into kitsch produced a wipe-clean irony separating signified from signifier: step forward, smirking, Chris Evans and Robbie Williams (2000's 'Rock DJ', UK 1). At its best, it encompassed comedy *and* content. The Beastie Boys' cool kitsch is captured aesthetically on Spike Jonze's 70s-cop-show video for 1994's 'Sabotage' (UK 19; *Ill Communication*, UK 10, US 1), but extends to critiques of misogyny on 1994's 'Sure Shot' (UK 27) and racism and homophobia on 1999's 'Alive' (UK 28).

Blur were constantly chasing this cool-kitsch ideal. The video for 1995 novelty 'Country House' (UK 1) stars comedian Keith Allen as the "City-dweller", owner of the titular pile. Yet the resultant Benny Hill romp is new-lad sexism as patronising populism, the song having nothing to say about the power and the money other than its failure to fulfil the financier (bless!). As Fat Les, Allen and Blur's Alex James' 1998 football song 'Vindaloo' (UK 2) gives boorish patriotism a multicultural veneer, 'solving' the 90s contradiction between national chauvinism and social liberalism. (Compare Cornershop's joyous ''Brimful of Asha', UK 1.) Yet Marge and Lisa's social conscience on *The Simpsons* doesn't cancel out Homer and Bart's conscience-free individualism: the former get to be po-faced, the latter get to be fun.

Britain's 'big beat' was a goonish take on the Beasties' cool kitsch, its aestheticisation of the past stripping out context in another non-hauntological nostalgia. Fatboy Slim's 1998 'Rockefeller Skank' (UK 6) reduces ghetto funk to pimp cool, captured by the video's novelty Afros and synthetic suits. 1998's 'Gangster Trippin" (UK 3) in unrelated to gangsta rap, while boasting a moronic exploding-furniture video Beavis and Butthead would consider "cooool". Even 1999's fetching ballad 'Praise You' (UK 1) obscures its sample's civil rights origins with novelty effects, fearful that sincerity might be considered pretentious. While at the time, Jonze's gonzo video's sendup of amateur dance troupes was the acme of cool kitsch, it's now exposed as hipster condescension to the unironically uncool and unintentionally kitsch.

Comedy was the medium that shifted slackerdom's dial from grunge negativity to pop positivity. Green Day's bubblegum-punk 1994 'Basket Case' (UK 7) rejects "whining", 1995's 'When I Come Around' (UK 27) mocks "feeling sorry for yourself", while their videos' exaggerated gyrations and gurning expressions keep seriousness at a safe distance. 'Minority' (UK 18), meanwhile, frames marginality as individualism: "Fuck 'em all, you are your own sight". Weezer's 1994 'Buddy Holly' (UK 12) replays grunge's disengagement and 50s fetish as fun, with its flip "I don't care about that", its Mary Tyler Moore reference and *Happy Days* video. Similarly slacker-lite, the Dandy Warhols repudiate grunge's narcotic negativity on 1997's affectless 'Not if You Were the Last Junkie on Earth' (UK 13), while reducing addiction to affectation ("heroin is so passé"). Brother-sister act Len's 1999 'Steal My Sunshine' (UK 8; US 9) regrets "indulging in my self-defeat", and thus "miss[ing] a million miles of fun", coming on with all the integrity of a grunge Aqua.

Juvenile jock-punk Blink-182 were the pop equivalent of *American Pie*'s frat house farce (1999). 'What's My Age Again?' (UK 17) posits frivolity as oppositionality: "No one should take themselves so seriously/With so many years to fall in line" (note the inevitability of consent). The by-product of music's comedy turn was to render those who insisted on emotional or social engagement humourless, 'politically correct' or simply 'sad' – and there were pills for that, both prescription and free market.

"I feel your pain!"

Bill Clinton's response to a campaign-trail heckler summarised his politics: performative compassion exploiting public pain for political profit, while repressing the political issue. During Clinton's presidency, harsh, reactionary policies were given a positive, progressive spin. Grunge's public displays of pain should therefore have been "off message", but similarly managed to exploit pain for commercial profit, while again repressing the political issues.

Nirvana struggled against this commodification of pain: rejecting the processed production of *Nevermind* for Steve Albini's rawer sound on 1993's *In Utero* (UK 1; US 1), its opening words were "Teenage angst has paid off well/Now I'm bored and old". The album is racked with pain, and while protesting that pain's co-option ('Milk It', 'Radio Friendly Unit Shifter'), uncomfortably cognisant that it's part of the spectacle. As Smashing Pumpkins put it on 1995's 'Bullet with Butterfly Wings', "Despite all my rage, I am still just a rat in a cage" (UK 20; US 22). Cobain's suicide was easily absorbed into the spectacle, while his politics – his awareness of the socioeconomic basis of generational pain *and* the pain industry – were repressed in his posthumous commodification. Only glimmers of political awareness would surface in grunge thereafter, with Stone Temple Pilots' 1994 power ballad 'The Big Empty' (*Purple*, UK 10; US 1) capturing the hollowness of commercial gain from personal pain – "My soul's worn thin" – while Soul Asylum's 1995 'Misery' (UK 30; US 20) accuses "all you suicide kings and you drama queens" of being a "factory" to "make misery" that's "incorporated".

"Passive-aggressive"

Grunge's post-Nirvana trajectory chimed with the newly vogue oxymoron "passive-aggressive": while the music was still aggressive, in a less punky way than Nirvana, its affective mode was passive. Soundgarden's 1994 'Fell on Black Days' sighs, "How would I know/That this could be my fate?" (UK 24). Even their attempt at social engagement, 'The Day I Tried to Live' (*Superunknown*, UK 4; US 1), was heard as a suicide note (lines like

"Pull the trigger, drop the blade" didn't help), while 'Black Hole Sun' (UK 12) can only envision society *annihilated* rather than transformed. The grunge 50s preoccupation represented by the 'Black Hole' video represents yearning for the period's orderly optimism alongside resentment at its calcified conservatism. Yet where 50s youth argued with parents, bosses and society itself, the parental accusation in the Pumpkins' string-drenched 1993 'Disarm' (UK 11) is so detached it sounds affirmatory. On 1996's 'Again', Layne Staley argues with *heroin* (*Alice in Chains*, US 1), an abusive relationship against which there's no rebelling, as Staley's eventual OD attested.

Where Fordist alienation was collective, post-Fordist alienation was individual. "How on earth did I get so jaded?" sighs David Pirner on Soul Asylum's 1993 'Runaway Train' (UK 7; US 5), as if he were aberrant rather than archetypical. Individualism was grunge's collective failure: Stone Temple Pilots shrug, "Friends don't mean a thing/Guess I'll leave it up to me" on 'Creep' (*Core*, UK 27; US 3); Smashing Pumpkins' 1993 suicide song 'Today' (*Siamese Dream*, UK 4; US 10) sees sociality as oppression ("Bored by the chore of saving face"); while Alice in Chains' 1994 'Nutshell' (*Jar of Flies*, UK 4; US 1), insists, "I fight/This battle all alone".

The most sonically corporate of these acts, Pearl Jam were paradoxically the least politically passive. From 1994 they refused interviews and stopped making videos –1994's 'Daughter' (UK 18) promo is a publicity shot overlaid with supertitles like "massive merchandising, advertising… and enormous demand!" They then took on first ticket touts, then corporate touts Ticketmaster. 'Dissident' (UK 14) examines the difficulties of refusing the system's logic: "When she had contact with the conflict/There was meaning/But she sold him to the state". 1995's 'Spin the Black Circle' (UK 10; US 18) hymns a gramophone rather than grunge needle, something to galvanise not pacify, restoring grunge's punk aggression without the passivity.

"Truth in sentencing"

Following 1993's California Street mass shooting and Waco cult siege, Clinton's 1994 Crime Bill was the New Democrats' "tough on crime" rhetoric writ legal, targeting not white-supremacist gun owners but black owners of very little. The bill's reduction of parole (imposing "truth in sentencing") caused mass incarceration to increase by 57%, with 1-in-6 black men having been imprisoned by 2001,[14] while the media – and Hillary Clinton – demonised this demographic as "superpredators". With the causes of crime dismissed, this legislative, economic and cultural repression made the projects' already harsh environment significantly harsher.

The cultural product of this environment, gangsta rap was wedded to a harsh "truth" – to "keeping it real" – in both their lyrics' sentences and prison sentences. While middle-class Ice Cube's claim that "I'm a motherfuckin' G" and 1993's 'Check Yo Self' prison-break video (US 20) are fantasy, the idea that gangsta rap was a hardboiled fiction is also a fantasy. "Word, I don't fantasize, I don't exaggerate", insisted the other Ice, T, on 1993's 'I Ain't New Ta This' (*Home Invasion*, UK 15; US 14). That Snoop was sentenced for murder in 1993, Shakur shot, sentenced, then killed in 1996 and Biggie Smalls murdered months later confirms the grim truth of gangsta, a rare 90s meeting of rhetoric and reality, signifier and signified.

At its worst, gangsta produced music as ugly as its social reality, like Cypress Hill's 1993 gun-glorifying 'I Ain't Goin' Out Like That' (UK 15; *Black Sunday*, UK 13; US 1). At its best, gangsta's sentences addressed a systemic truth. Dre's 1993 'The Day the N****z Took Over' (*The Chronic*) revels in the LA riots' refusal; Ice Cube's 1992 'Wicked' claims the protests "brought power to the people", while 'When Will They Shoot' states, "Uncle Sam is Hitler without an oven/Burnin' our black skin/Buy my neighbourhood and push the crack in" – economics as eugenics (*The Predator*, US 1). All this contradicts critics' claims that gangsta rap is apolitical and merely glorifies gang culture:[15] on 1993's *Home Invasion*, Ice-T lays out the 'Race War': "America was founded on that racist shit/The system wanna keep us at each other's throats".

Tupac was a scion of black radicalism – his parents both Panthers – but blooded by gangster culture, his lyrics vacillated between 'truth' as competitive individualism – "I represent the real 'cause I'm ill, G/Glock cocked 'til the day they kill me" –

and as a repressive political system. On 'Holler If Ya Hear Me' he demands, "How long will it last 'til the po' get mo' cash?/Until then, raise up!" (*Strictly 4 My N****Z*, US 24). 1995's 'So Many Tears' links being "stuck in the game" to "so many homies in the cemetery" (*Me Against the World*, US 1). Tupac's mentor, Coolio's summer 1995 'Gangsta's Paradise' (UK 1; US 1) articulates the gangster truth of the economic trap ("I can't live a normal life/I was raised by the street"), alongside its emotional and physical costs ("I'm 23 now but will I live to see 24?") and the system behind it: "power and the money, money and the power". Yet with no political project proposing to transform the projects, there's a fatalism to even such politically aware gangsta truths, articulated by Bone Thugs-n-Harmony's 1996 'Tha Crossroads' (UK 8; US 1): "Livin' in a hateful world, sendin' me straight to Heaven/That's how we roll". Once again, the harshness of this environment is just an unavoidable reality, not something to protest.

East Coast gangsta presented its truth as documentary realism, with gritty lyrics backed by dirty, crackle-strewn beats and visualised by black-and-white project-set videos. On Wu-Tang Clan's 1993 'C.R.E.A.M.', street-hustler and *Wall Street Journal* truths combine, "Cash rules everything around me" being both an excoriation and celebration of capitalism. However, gangsta godfathers Gang Starr's 1994 *Hard to Earn* (UK 29; US 25) pronounces sentence on "the system", while their 'Code of the Streets' lays out the vicious cycle of crime in a hopeless environment: "I gotta have it so I can leave behind/ The mad poverty, never having, always needing". Also in 1994, newcomer Nas's stunning *Illmatic* (US 12) gains distance on this conventionalised dystopia through cinematic verité – "My window faces shootouts, drug overdoses/Live amongst no roses, only the drama". Yet as both John Berger's *Ways of Seeing* and the film *Man Bites Dog* (1993) revealed, a camera is never a neutral observer of 'truth'. Despite Nas's lyrical dynamism, he offers a fatalistic deference to the system – "We're held like hostages" ('N.Y. State of Mind') – and of its emotional effect: "Things I do is real/It never haunts me".[16] The war of all against all means that 'reality' is beyond morality, and affectlessness a method of survival.

Although Notorious B.I.G. also brandished his street credentials, it was as origin story, not ongoing concern, his sense of the past giving Biggie critical distance, as on 1994's pre-crack, pre-gun ghetto evocation, 'Things Done Changed' (*Ready to Die*, US 15). Biggie's breakthrough, 'Juicy' (US 27), offers an 80s' hauntology of *Rap Attack* and tape decks, but never allows nostalgia to annul the gangsta life's negativity – having been "too used to packin' gats and stuff", now he's "livin' life without fear". Despite the pleasure Biggie takes in property, the truth of how he gained it means he's convinced he's going to hell on 'Suicidal Thoughts', "cause I'm a piece of shit". Such rare vulnerability in gangsta isn't precisely *political*, but it makes the presentism waver, to paraphrase Jameson.

Biggie's East Coast peers weren't all as reflective. Mobb Deep's 1995 'Survival of the Fittest' declares, "There's a war going on outside no man is safe from" (*The Infamous*, US 18) but its hostility to the competitive other seemingly celebrates this Hobbesian world. Concurrently, Wu-Tang's Raekwon's 1995 *Only Built 4 Cuban Linx* (US 4) inspired a Mafioso rap subgenre, adopting a mythic register for its consumerist world: "Infatuated by material things in this wild life of war" ('Verbal Intercourse'). Even Nas shifted from documentary to fiction for 1996's *It Was Written* (US 1), but while the commercial gloss of 'Street Dreams' (UK 12; US 22) resembled West Coast rap, the extraordinary 'I Gave You Power' utters a different truth: that of a disillusioned gun – "My creation was for blacks to kill blacks".

The real "truth in sentencing" is that felons return, hardened, to a harsh environment in which crime offers the only economic opportunities. On release, Tupac aligned with gangsta-suffused Death Row, dropping his analytic distance for solipsistic dissing. For its growing white audience, gangsta dramatised – and glamourised – the dominant ideology of 'survival of the fittest'. 2Pac's Dre-produced 'Can't C Me' warns, "Look what hell made... Fuck around with Tupac and see how good a n***a's aim is" (*All Eyez*). Dissing Biggie and his producer, Puff Daddy, on 1996's 'Hit 'Em Up' (B-side, 'How Do U Want it', US 1), Tupac threatens, "We gonna kill all you motherfuckers". He'd be dead himself within months, Smalls the following year, with Death Row's Suge Knight implicated in Smalls' murder. Gangsta's sociological truth was politically credited to a culture of crime, unconnected to Crime Bills. As prison sentences grew harsher, in the aftermath of the Tupac and Biggie beef, rappers' lyrical sentences grew milder, reorientating from murder to materialism.

"Cycle of dependency"

Reaffirming centrism's break with Fordism, Clinton's phrase from his Welfare Reform Act of 1996 reframed the state's relationship to its citizenry as negative, rejecting security as "dependency" and interconnection as a vicious cycle, and thereby rejecting the concept of collectivity.

Only months after playing Clinton's inauguration, R.E.M. released 1993's 'Everybody Hurts' (UK 7; US 29), in which the pain of the other is embraced as that of the self. This solidarity is beautifully realised in the Fellini-inspired video, where atomised units locked in private vehicles, with subtitled private thoughts, open their doors and collectively walk along the freeway.[17] R.E.M.'s stark 'Let Me In' on fall 1994's glammy *Monster* is addressed to Stipe's friend Cobain – "I had a mind to try and stop you" – in an affirmation of empathy that expresses a larger social interdependency. Despite its political demotic, Manic Street Preachers' extraordinary, bleak 1994 *The Holy Bible* (UK 6) is usually depicted as tracking lyricist Richey Edwards' personal pain (he disappeared soon after its release), yet as Rhian E. Jones points out, the album probes the personal as a synecdoche of political pain.[18] Lynskey interprets the screamed, repeated "Who's responsible? You fucking are!" on 'Of Walking Abortion' as an indictment of human nature: "Hitler reprised in the worm in your soul".[19] Rather, Jones argues, the track articulates collective responsibility – and thus human interdependence.[20]

Critically ringfenced as exploring Trent Reznor's personal problems, industrialists Nine Inch Nails' 1994 *The Downward Spiral* (UK 9; US 2) concerns the individual's relationship to society: for worse on 'Ruiner', while 'Closer' (UK 25) dramatises a desperate attempt to engage with an other: "Help me get away from myself" Reznor rasps. Even the druggy miserabilism of 1999's *The Fragile* (UK 10; US 1) keeps circling the concept that

'We're in This Together' – "When all our hope is gone, we have to hold on" – while 'Starfuckers, Inc.' satirises the affective free market: "I'll be there for you as long as it works for me". Elliott Smith's delicate anti-folk is, like Cobain's music, always viewed through the filter of his suicide. Yet Smith's yearning voice is a hauntological summoning of the 60s, its affirmative positivity captured not just by the title of 'Say Yes' but by its opening line's expansion from individual to collective *Eros*: "I'm in love with the world/Through the eyes of a girl".

By millennial nu metal, however, the ideological labour promoting competitive individualism was paying cultural dividends. Limp Bizkit's 2000 'Take a Look Around' (UK 3) ridicules grunge's vulnerability – "Do we always gotta cry?" – to advocate the survival of the fittest – "You better stay on top, or life will kick you in the ass" – which in the 90s passed for positivity. In retrospect, it's a surprise it took so long for competitive individualism to co-opt complaint rock. Linkin Park screech, "Shut up when I'm talking to you, I'm about to break!" on 2000's 'One Step Closer' (UK 24) and make mental health a survival of the fittest on 'Papercut' (UK 14) – "Paranoia is all I got left" – while on Korn's 2000 'Make Me Bad' (UK 25), the cycle of interdependency is a contradictory competition in pain. "I need my fix, you need it too/Just to get some sort of attention."

"Riot grrrl"

The third-wave feminist punk pioneered by Bikini Kill and Huggy Bear as 'riot grrrl' had its only commercial impact in minor hits by L7 (*Hungry For Stink*, UK 26) and Babes in Toyland (*Fontanelle*, UK 24). Riot grrrl effectively achieved its widest diffusion with Hole, who siphoned much of its spirit into grunge's best album, 1994's *Live Through This* (UK 13). While Hole were complaint rock, they jettisoned grunge's masculine passivity for feminist aggression. The fact that male critics (and Billy Corgan) attributed the album's songs to frontwoman Courtney Love's husband, Kurt Cobain, proved what the lyrics protested: women's definition in relation to men. Reversing this, Love depicts women as *raw material* for men, and with Corgan the rumoured subject of 'Violet' (UK 17), Love sarcastically demands he emotionally strip-mine her: "Go on, take everything, I want you to". Love's woman-as-exploitable-resource theme encompasses motherhood ('Plump'), the beauty industry ('Miss World') and female sexuality ('Doll Parts', UK 16). Reduced to a plaything, Love's insistence that "someday you will ache like I ache" isn't simply pain exhibitionism but a demand for an empathy so absolute that it *hurts*. Consequently, despite the conventional critical filter via Cobain's suicide, the lines on 'Asking For It', "If you live through this with me/I swear that I will die for you", say far more about Love than about her late husband. For in such a collapse of self/other polarity, there is, unlike contemporary male grunge, a surviving remnant of countercultural utopianism.

"Ho's and bitches"

"Who you callin' a *bitch*?" demands Queen Latifah on 1993's 'U.N.I.T.Y.' (US 23). With gangsta conventionalising that pejorative, Latifah challenges the targeting of anger at black *women* rather than white *power*. From "Bitches ain't shit but ho's and tricks" on Dre's 1993 'Let Me Ride', to 2Pac's concurrent 'I Get Around' (US 11) – "Hoes... they sweat a brother majorly" – a masculinity forged by systemic brutalisation and the politicised withdrawal of 'male' work defines and defends itself by its distance from the feminine. So, when Wu-Tang speak of "livin in the world, no different to a cell", they highlight not just the projects' literal and metaphorical proximity to prison but the absence of women in hardcore rap videos and lyrics. Even prisoners have mothers, sisters, daughters, as heard in TLC's 1995 'Waterfalls' (UK 4; US 1), with Left-Eye chiding gangster solipsism: "The system's got you victim to your own mind".

Ever contradictory, 2Pac could both produce 'Wonda Why They Call U Bitch' in 1996 (*All Eyez*)[21] and wonder "why we hate our women" on 1993's 'Keep Ya Head Up' (US 12). Deploying 'O-o-h Child' to give "a holla to my sisters on welfare", he insists, "Tupac cares if don't nobody else care". 1994's 'Dear Mama' (UK 27; US 9) is a touching tribute to Afeni Shakur: "There's no way that I can pay you back".[22] Similarly, on 1995's 'For My Sistas', Coolio asserts, "To every n***a that dissed ya and every n***a that hit ya/Accept my apologies for my brothas, my sista"

(*Gangsta's Paradise*, UK 18; US 9). The same year, the East Coast discovered women: Method Man's toughly tender 'I'll Be There for You/You're All I Need to Get By', with Mary J. Blige (UK 10; US 3), concedes "I love the fact you got a mind of your own". Also with Blige, Ghostface Killah's 1996 'All That I Got Is You' (UK 11) was his 'Dear Mama': presented as an MOR ballad in the video, Ghost sits (awkwardly) at a grand piano, an orchestra (and his dignity) behind him.

Southern duo Outkast's outstanding 'Ms. Jackson' the same year (UK 2; US 1) is sung to "my baby mama's mama", and while Big Boi acknowledges his parental responsibility resentfully, Andre 3000 does so rapturously: "Yes I will be present on the first day of school and graduation". Given Andre's campness and the music's softer sound, Outkast suggested a road forward for both rap and black masculinity that would not, ultimately, be followed.

"Ladette"

A key contradiction of post-Fordist capitalism is that its destruction of traditional male labour created space for women in the workforce and the pop marketplace. No longer content to merely front male-programmed pop or demurely strum acoustic guitars, from Kim Deal's Breeders (*Pod*, UK 22), to Belly's Tanya Donnelly, Sonic Youth's Kim Gordon to Stereolab's Laetitia Sadier and Mary Hansen, women now encroached upon traditional male musical domains.

PJ Harvey's startling 1993 *Rid of Me* (UK 3) utilised Albini's raw production to repossess the 'masculine' forms of punk, blues and classic rock. This paralleled the songs' desire to possess *maleness*: not just individual men – 'Legs' threatens amputation to prevent her lover leaving – but masculine *power* (the superheroine fantasy of '50 Ft. Queenie'): to "get girl out of my head" and shed feminine conditioning ('Man-Size'). If 1995's stunning *To Bring You My Love* (UK 12) tracks back from gender confrontation, its longed-for men are all *absent*, so Harvey's occupation of the emotional field tracks her occupation of 'male' musical fields – blues, desert-rock, swamp-rock and Spaghetti soundtrack. More radically, the narrative field of 1998's *Is This Desire?* (UK 17) is filled by an all-female cast of characters, with Harvey deploying a softer, more 'feminine', trip-hop sound for songs in which, uniquely, women aren't just un-sexualised, sex simply doesn't feature.

If there's no utopia in Harvey's vision of gender relations, Alanis Morissette's is actively dystopian. 1995's ornery 'You Oughta Know' (UK 22; US 6) is a pop diffusion of Harvey's aggressive victimhood ("the cross I bear that you gave to me"), but the passive 'You Learn' (UK 24; US 6) distils this as 90s negative positivity – "You lose, you learn/You bleed, you learn", etc. The individual here is a heroic survivor in a hostile world, boosted by the 90s' *Jagged Little Pill* (UK 1; US 1), Prozac. Tori Amos pulled and pushed at the boundaries of piano-tinkling Fordist singer-songwriter territory, incorporating post-Fordist hip-hop and dance, and defining herself as an unconventional "raisin girl" rather than regular 'Cornflake Girl' (UK 4). 1996's self-produced *Boys for Pele* (UK 2; US 2) is unequivocally feminist in a 'post-feminist' era, with 'Caught a Lite Sneeze' (UK 20) urging, "Need a big loan from the girl zone". 'Professional Widow' (UK 1) attacks the patriarchal family, although all that remains on the hit British remix is "It's gotta be big", tapping this paranoid era's defining (male) anxiety.

Britpop's women tended to deploy a more aggressive, punkier demotic than their male counterparts. Three-quarter female Elastica returned the gaze with insouciant blankness, while it was *men* who got their kit off in their videos – their pretty-boy drummer on 1994's 'Line Up' (UK 20); faceless models in 1995's 'Waking Up' (UK 13). Elastica's coolness is in pointed contrast to both the pain theatrics of grunge and the amateur dramatics of male Britpop, unmanning post-punk angularity and detached affectivity in drawlingly flinty confections like 'Connection' (UK 17). Shampoo were a more proley, poppy take on punk femininity, 1994's rapped 'Trouble' (UK 11) suggesting a Beastie Girls, while on 1995's 'Delicious' (UK 21) the duo are a feminist collective: "Come on we're not done/Or down on our knees!"

The contemporary concept of the 'ladette' walked a fine line between transcending traditional femininity and internalising the attitudes of lad culture. With a ladette having to prove she was fun, not po-faced (aka 'feminist"), Sleeper's Louise Wener skirted gender relations on hits like 1995's 'Inbetweener' (UK 16), returned the gaze with anxious, lash-fluttering eyes, and sneered at feminists in interviews. For Jones, Sleeper's 'What Do I Do Now' (UK 14) "paint[s] a curious portrait of the ladette as joylessly dutiful housewife".[23] When Wener asks, "Am I too familiar?/Was it when I said I wanted to have children?", her disempowerment reveals the reasserted gender traditionalism underlying the ladette.

"Off-Message"

In this period of managed consensus, this term denoting departure from the party line also fits those on the left who failed to get with the centrist programme. Hip-hop metallers Rage Against the Machine's 1993 'Killing in the Name' (UK 25) links the LAPD's racialised policing to white supremacy, calling out centrism's submerged authoritarianism with a defiant "Fuck you, I won't do what you tell me".[24] 1993's 'Bullet in the Head' (UK 16) links the money ("the products that they're sellin' ya") and the power ("the lies that they're tellin' ya").[25] The invocation to "rally round the family with a pocketful of shells" on 1996's 'Bulls on Parade' (UK 8) posits family values as a human shield for imperialism: indeed, Clinton's Iraq bombing sorties have been struck from the historical record. If such a negative dialectic was an effective evocation of dystopia, RATM offered a rare glimpse of utopia in 'People of the Sun' (UK 26), celebrating the 1994 Mexican Zapatista revolution.

Despite initially supporting Clinton, R.E.M. were increasingly aligning themselves with the complaint rockers. 1994's 'King of Comedy' satirises the sanctimony centrism attaches to self-enrichment – "Make your money with exploitation/Make it holy illumination" – while refusing to be bought and sold by market logic: "I'm not commodity" (*Monster*, UK 1; US 1). The now-disgraced Marilyn Manson's 1996 *Antichrist Superstar* (US 3) sufficiently subverted the commodity form to provoke congressional hearings. 'The Beautiful People' (UK 18) highlights the power and the money with a directness unheard in politics itself: "Capitalism has made [the world] this way/Old-fashioned fascism will take it away". Manson got blamed for the Columbine school massacre, but on 2000's *Holy Wood* (UK 23; US 13), he turned this back on politicians, with 'The Fight Song' (UK 24) asserting centrist authoritarianism ("death was on sale today"). 'Disposable Teens' (UK 12) calls out those who sold the 60s counterculture out: "You say you want a revolution, man/and I say you're full of shit".

The only protest to greet the arrival of hippie sellout, Tony Blair, at Downing Street in summer 1997 came, aptly, from a final remnant of the counterculture, crusty folkies the Levellers. On 'Beautiful Day' (UK 13) the generals hide out and politicians go to ground while "wealth redistribution, became the new solution". Unassimilably utopian in a pragmatic age, the Levellers were uncool at the time and have been excised from 90s nostalgia since, despite having more hits than Menswear (if worse clothes). Radiohead's now shifted from personal to political complaint rock, with autumn 1997's *OK Computer* (UK 1; US 21) an off-message state of the nation address. 'Paranoid Android' (UK 3) spits bile at the business culture Blair cultivated: "The yuppies networking/The panic, the vomit", and concludes with an invocation of apocalypse. 'No Surprises' (UK 4) urges, "Bring down the government/They don't, they don't speak for us", as crystalline glockenspiels chime soothingly.

With a demonstration at Seattle's 1999 World Trade Organisation Ministerial Conference becoming a bloody battle, and Naomi Klein's *No Logo* (1999) becoming the textbook for a new anti-capitalist movement, Radiohead's refusal of conventional rock forms on 2000's *Kid A* (UK 1; US 1) stood for a larger political refusal. This was made explicit on spring 2001's *Amnesiac* (UK 1; US 2), with 'You and Whose Army' daring Blair and his "cronies" to "take us on". 'Knives Out' (UK 13) likens capitalism's survival of the fittest to cannibalism, while 'Dollars and Cents' attests to centrism's mesmerisation by the money and the power. These musical and political refusals had no utopian element, being a refusal of what *was*, not a vision of what might be, thus Adornian rather than Marcusian.

"The class war is over"

Blair's claim that society was no longer divided between classes but between "progressives" and "conservatives", reassured the elites by removing economics from politics, while conveniently removing the economic underclass from politics' responsibility. "We're all middle class now" his deputy, John Prescott, proclaimed. Nevertheless, class remained an inconveniently visible and audible contradiction of neoliberal democracy's claim to have solved the problem of history.

Oasis's role in the centrist establishment as Blair boosters has eclipsed their initial self-presentation as "the outcast... the underclass" on 1994's 'Bring It on Down' (*Definitely Maybe*, UK 1). Even their video for 1995's 'Don't Look Back in Anger' (UK 1) presents a plebs vs. debs scenario, as the band invade a country house, while the archetypal aristo – *The Avengers'* Patrick Macnee – is reduced to the oiks' chauffeur. Glam revivalists Suede depict a landscape of "council homes" on 1993's 'Animal Nitrate' (UK 7), in which class is "a time bomb in the high-rise" on 1994's 'Stay Together' (UK 3). On 1994's stunning *Dog Man Star* (UK 3), the music's orchestrated ambition matches class aspiration to the lyrics' class antagonism. "The common breed" will "make them bleed" ('The Power'), while on 'We Are the Pigs' (UK 18), the dispossessed are in violent revolt: "Stay at home tonight... You wake up with a gun in your mouth". Even after regressing to boilerplate retro glam, 1996's 'Trash' (UK 3) insists class can't be so easily wished away – "It's in everything we do" – while walking a rakish line between essentialising and satirising prole stereotypes: "cheapness... tasteless bracelets and the dye in our hair".

Deploying stereotypes from within is one thing; to do so from without – as Blair and Blur did with working-class culture – is quite another. Blur's celebration of sliced-bread and Bingo on 1993's 'Sunday Sunday' (UK 26) is snide, as was calling a tour 'Sugary Tea', while 1994's admittedly nifty 'Girls & Boys' (UK 5) condescendingly carols "the herd" hedonism of Club 18–30 package holidays. Blur even put whippets on the cover of *Parklife* (UK 1), whose title track deploys *Quadrophenia*'s Phil Daniels to authenticate its class tourism (UK 10), while 'Bank Holiday' sneers at "fun pubs", "lager louts", bad diets and the proles' sexual morals. By 1996's *The Great Escape* (UK 1), Blur's satire of suburbanites could be complacently titled 'Stereotypes', a term, in the 90s, synonymous with 'realism'. Only the po-faced might suggest Marx's concept of 'ideology' had any bearing on such realism.

For Owen Hatherley, Blur are the target of Pulp's glorious 1995 'Common People' (UK 2):[26] the affluent seeking authentication by slumming it with the plebs, sublimating social class as style ("you think that poor is cool"), while their class privilege – and prejudice – is unaffected. The money and the power is emphasised as systemic here, the line "you'll never live your life with no meaning or control" sung at the furious, ragged edge of Cocker's range. Yet even 'Common People' signs on for a tour of class as culture (supermarkets, cigarettes, sex and chips). Crucially, however, Hatherley points out, the single/video edit excises the lines "Like a dog lying in a corner/They will bite you and never warn you/Look out, they'll tear your insides out." This class resentment runs through Pulp's magnificent *Different Class* (UK 1), where, in common with 'Common People', it's regularly misdirected into misogyny, and its Fordist melancholia is aesthetic rather than material. Nevertheless, Pulp provided a vital assertion that class was a social contradiction which couldn't be resolved rhetorically or performatively, as Blair and Blur, respectively suggested.

Unusually for Fordist melancholia, the Manics' magnificent, mythic 1996 'A Design for Life' (UK 2) acknowledges Fordism's contradictions. The celebratory "Libraries gave us power" is thus counterposed by the sarcastic "Then work came and made us free". From this dialectic, the chorus shifts to Benjaminian ambiguity, with "We don't talk about love/We only want to get drunk" mocking either class stereotypes or class apathy, when, defeated, deindustrialised and demonised, "we are told that this is the end". By contrast, the intoxication of Chumbawumba's 1997 'Tubthumping' (UK 2; US 6) isn't solely alcoholic, its itemisation of "whiskey drink" and "vodka drink" being part of a metaphor for the cycle of class struggle: "I get knocked down, but I get up again". With Labour having knocked down the 1995 Liverpool dock strike, Chumbawumba got up on their behalf to empty a bucket of water over Prescott's head at the Brit Awards. The class war was ongoing.

White rapper Eminem, meanwhile, articulated the resentment of an American underclass who, under neoliberal democracy, were excluded from the power and the money. "There's a million of us just like me", he snaps on 2000's Dre-produced 'The Real Slim Shady' (UK 1; US 4), "Who cuss like me, who just don't give a fuck like me". Except that Eminem plainly *did* give a fuck – pure nihilism would be less uncomfortable and less compelling than the vulnerability and volatility that mark his social origins. Eminem's career-best track, 2000's blistering 'The Way I Am' (UK 8), is a defence of his class as much as of himself, a bristling rejection of complacent bourgeois moralism. Eminem's depiction of a disturbed, obsessive fan on 2000's 'Stan' (UK 1) is both self-portrait and social portrait (he plays both roles in the video) and captures contemporary underclass despair. Yet it also reveals how this despair causes resentment to be misdirected, in this case, towards women, connecting Eminem to Pulp and a long tradition of misogyny.

Far from everyone being middle class now, neoliberal democracy's unequal distribution of the power and the money was creating a concomitant downward mobility. Edgerton notes that "armies of proletarianised office-workers and call-centre operatives… waiters and cooks… were making a mockery of the… notion that white-collar work was superior in status to a manual manufacturing job".[27] "We were brought up on the Space Race", Cocker mordantly notes on 1999's 'Glory Days': "Now they expect you to clean toilets" (*This is Hardcore*). The video for Westlife's 2001 cover of Billy Joel's 1983 'Uptown Girl' (UK 1) puts a bright, boyband spin on this situation. Updating the downtown boys from Fordist mechanics to post-Fordist waiters, Westlife's video presents them outsmarting smarmy city boys and going off with the uptown girl, the contradiction of class resolved not by economics but by attitude. The class war really was over.

"Bedwetters"

The contradiction between Blair's arrival in power and Britpop's concurrent switch to mournful balladry is resolved – or at least explained – by the Verve's grandiose 1997 ballad 'Bitter Sweet Symphony' (UK 2; US 12). Defining contemporary life as "Trying to make ends meet, you're a slave to money then you die", the song asserts the impossibility of change ("I'm here in my mould"), accompanied by a video depicting atomised vocalist Richard Ashcroft affectlessly cold-shouldering the world out of his way.[28] Such an invocation of alienation, stagnation and malignant individualism captured the political reality of the conjuncture rather too starkly at this moment of centrist political triumph.

The death of Princess Diana that summer conveniently diverted this structure of feeling into a culture of collective mourning. Elton John's tribute to Spencer, the execrable 'Candle in the Wind 1997' (UK 1; US 1), captured and crucially *contained* this affect. Exalting loss as victory, passivity as activity and *emoting* as emotion, the track provided a template for a bombastic, big-tent balladry as a social safety valve for the discontents of centrism. Robbie Williams' early-1998 Elton-esque ballad 'Angels' (UK 4) thus evokes a cruel world against which family – and sentimentality – function as a buffer: "I know that life won't break me… she won't forsake me".

With lighters-aloft balladry becoming latterday Britpop's dominant mode, Oasis manager and Blair donor Alan McGee's derisive term, "bedwetters", served only to highlight the harsh social environment from which such songs provided solace (while eliding Oasis's pioneering role in such pseudo-collectivity). Embrace's 1998 stadium-indie 'Come Back to What You Know' (UK 6) invites listeners to "Hang on to what you got/Keep it safe" in an unwelcoming world. Blur's 1999 breakup ballad 'Tender' (UK 2) upliftingly urges, "Come on, get through it", although not even a gospel choir can give the track's wan positivity substance or conviction. Spelling out this structure of feeling, Stereophonics' 1999 overpower ballad 'Just Looking' (UK 4) is paradoxically detached, a dismissal of utopianism: "Do I really want the dreams?... the more you fly/The more you risk your life" The video, depicting the band affectlessly driving their car under water, dramatises this passive acceptance of a normatively hostile world.

With the power (and the money) left to the politicians,

Travis made the disempower ballad their metier, from the cosily clever self-pity of "I'm seeing a tunnel at the end of all these lights" – on 1999's 'Why Does It Always Rain on Me?' (UK 10) – to the shrugging fatuity of "We all will live, we all will die/ There is no wrong, there is no right" on 'Side' (UK 14). As the millennium turned, U2 advised, "You've got to get yourself together", because everyone was 'Stuck in a Moment You Can't Get Out Of' (UK 2). This 'moment' was the Long 90s, but given the cosy passivity of such anthemically melancholy ballads, no one seemed much inclined to get out of it (least of all U2). "No change, I can't change, I can't change" as the Verve presciently, and depressingly, put it. Here we see capitalist realism in solution, poised to solidify into precipitate.

"Girl Power"

Wreaking minor class mayhem amongst aristos and authority figures, the Spice Girls' summer 1996 'Wannabe' video is one of pop's great 'ordinary' interventions into culture. However, as Ewing observes, 'girl power', half-inched from riot grrrl, "was never a utopian project"; like centrism, it was all about "surviving in the world as it was".[29] 'Wannabe' (UK 1; US 1) is thus a wan manifesto: "what I really, really want" is to be important as boys ("gotta get with my friends"). Yet mostly what they want to be is 'fun', in the 90s mode: "Zigazig ah!" Despite the video for 'Say You'll Be There' (UK 1; US 3) presenting the Spices as cartoon superheroes, its demands are markedly meek: that a guy simply stick around, wittily relayed by the girls roping and tying a hunk to the ground. While the video for 'Who Do You Think You Are' (UK 1) suggests a feminist statement, the song is simply a self-empowerment anthem, as befits such post-feminist Thatcherites: "The race is on to get out of the bottom… show me how good you are". Blair also acknowledged his lineage from Thatcher, and 1997's 'Spice Up Your Life' is practically a New Labour theme song (UK 1), trilling, "All you need is positivity", again spinning change in *attitude* over material change.

All Saints were marketed as girl power for urban sophisticates, their cargo-pants and strappy-tops look combining tomboy with 'babe' on 1997's 'I Know Where It's At' video (UK 4). Yet their superb Shangri-La's/slow-jam amalgam 'Never Ever' (UK 1; US 4) revels in traditional female victimhood, while, for all the sex positivity of their Labelle-cover 'Lady Marmalade' (UK 1), the Saints on 'Bootie Call' (UK 1) still "need a man to be a real man". Atomic Kitten's 1999 'See Ya' (UK 6) asserts a vague independence, while the rave-lite 'I Want Your Love' (UK 10) declares that "making lots of money and livin' in a dream" is the way forward, even as the space-kitsch of its promo suggests such a future's elusiveness. Billie Piper's bratty 'Because We Want To' (UK 1) renders individualism collective, with its girl-gang video and its paradigmatically 90s overclaim, "Some revolution is going to happen today".

It wasn't as if these newcomers invented girl power. Janet Jackson's 1994 'You Want This' promo (UK 14; US 8) prefigures the Spices with its hunks dumped in the desert, while the girl gang roars off along the freeway. By 2001's discofied 'All for You' (UK 3; US 1), Jackson is full sex positive – "Got a nice package alright/Guess I'm gonna have to ride it tonight" – as she and her dancing, dressed-down sisters occupy the subway and Time Square in the video. However, on 'Someone to Call My Lover' (UK 11; US 3), Jackson too is "looking for a guy-guy". Mariah Carey also went girl power, with her 1997 'Honey' video (UK 3; US 1) presenting her as a female James Bond, escaping the villain in strappy dress and heels, while on 1999's 'Heartbreaker' (UK 5; US 1), she and her gal posse do the dressed-down dance routine shtick at a movie theatre. Shania Twain's 1999 country-pop hit sniffs 'That Don't Impress Me Much' (UK 3; US 7) at an array of male suitors. With the video set in another desert, female power here is consumer power, with Twain haughtily examining the gender wars' stale goods (pompous ass, narcissist and boy racer, respectively). 'Man! I Feel Like a Woman!' (UK 3; US 23) posits female empowerment as the right to "colour my hair, wear short skirts" and "have a little fun" – and, in the video, strip down to a bustier.

Britney Spears' arrival in late 1998 with '…Baby One More Time' (UK 1; US 1) changed the game, offering a girl power that was both more coldly Aryan – via Max Martin's machine-precision production – and more coolly 'urban'. Although the lyric is, objectively, abject, the sound (woman-machine music) and vision (the schoolgirl video) are all cold, steely purposefulness, demanding attention, desire, remuneration – a corporate merger between capitalism and feminism. Equally, while Spears' colleague/rival Christina Aguilera's 1999 'What a Girl Wants' (UK 3; US 1) is more girl gratitude than girl power, the assertiveness of her vocal delivery and the video's girl-gang routine sounds and looks something like liberation. Spears' 2000 'Oops!... I Did It Again' (UK 1; US 9) is thus a victory march, an insincere apology to a hapless man for having captured his heart, functioning as a metaphor both for Spears' sexual and commercial power.

"Bling"

Named after ghetto slang for jewellery, the roots of 'bling' lie in Biggie's boasts about his new, luxury lifestyle on 1995's 'Big Poppa' (US 6) – "The back of the club, sippin' Moët is where you'll find me" – proclaiming himself and his crew "true fuckin' players". If a 'player' was initially a Lothario, here it meant someone with money and, as the 90s progressed, someone with power. The slippage is instructive, not just because the libidinal is never far from late capitalism, but because a hard-nosed individualism is written into all three meanings. With Smalls' producer Puff Daddy launching a business empire as Bad Boy, his signees, Junior Mafia's 1995 'Player's Anthem' (US 13) celebrates: "Caviar for breakfast, champagne bubble-baths". On Smalls' 1997 'Hypnotize' (UK 10; US 1), women coo, "I just love your flashy ways", while its Hype Williams video promotes the player lifestyle of champagne, linen suits, Benzes and yachts. Puff's early-1997 'Can't Nobody Hold Me Down' (UK 19; US 1) shifts the focus of its 'The Message' sample from the systemic to the solipsistic, boasting of being "young, black and famous with money hangin' out the anus". Puff and protégé Ma$e sporting shiny suits and throwing dance moves in the video is some deliberate distance from gangsta's project demotic.

Biggie's death sealed this shift from street life to high life, Adidas to Gucci, grainy hood video to glitzy Hype Williams promo clip. Puff's interpolation of the Police's 'Every Breath You Take' on summer 1997's Smalls tribute, 'I'll be Missing You'

(UK 1; US 1), triggers nostalgia rather than loss – which eludes Puff's mush-mouthed rapping. The primary impact is to push the Bad Boy brand, with Smalls endowing street authenticity. While credited to Notorious B.I.G., 1997's 'Mo Money Mo Problems' (UK 6; US 1) features a snippet of Smalls pasted onto Chic's liberation anthem 'I'm Coming Out'. In the video Puff and Ma$e dance in spacesuits, and brag "N***a never home/Gotta call me on the yacht", the track being about *their* liberation – with Smalls effectively their hostage – everyone else can just look on in awe. With the point of no-mark Ma$e being to push Puff's brand, the chorus of his 'Feel So Good' (UK 10; US 5) is "bad, bad, bad boy". The point of bling was that its 90s fun overlaid a dark realism. Thus Ma$e's "East, West, every state, c'mon bury the hate/Millions the only thing we in a hurry to make" is less a rejection of gangsta culture than a capitalist realist *recognition* of it.

Consequently, bling could infiltrate hardcore hip-hop without apparent contradiction. Hiring Puff as producer, Jay-Z launched a career of product placement, enumerating "Smelling like Miyake" and "Versace pants" on '(Always Be My) Sunshine' (UK 25; *In My Lifetime*, US 3). His 1997 'Wishing on a Star' (UK 13) lays out the African American dream from project to player – "I represent the lifestyle of those who thirst cream", invoking the Wu-Tang's "cash rules everything around me", but absent their ambivalence. On 1998's *Annie*-sampling 'Hard Knock Life' (UK 2; US 15) Jay's rap stares down the track's craven commerciality to assert his enduring gangsta credibility – "Hustlin' is still inside of me". Bling then was a none-more-90s contradiction, the money and the power declaring itself to be both authentic and adversarial.

"Player hate"

Product of bling's contradictions, player hate is a hip-hop take on the neoliberal 'politics of envy' and thus reduces systemic injustice to individual jealousy. Ma$e's frothy 1998 'Lookin' at Me' (US 8) proclaims poverty as a *choice* – "Bein' broke and alone is something I can't condone" – and as newcomer Missy Elliott coos the chorus for Puff's 1997 'It's All about the Benjamins' (UK 18; US 2), Biggie is exhumed to huff about such haters. Like nemesis Jay-Z, Nas amalgamated hardcore and bling, the project 'corner' with the club VIP room on 1999's 'Hate Me Now' (UK 14), with Puffy in sable-draped solidarity. The inability to comprehend criticism as anything but envy is lent pomposity by the track's *Omen* sample, absurdity by a video portraying Nas as Christ on the cross. If those with the money and power are the persecuted, then redistribution is *plainly* ridiculous – "Here's my cars and my house, you can live in that too" Nas scoffs. While this marks pop's all-time low in political analysis, it also provides an inadvertent critique of neoliberal culture. For pleasure in the money and the power is *tarnished* by paranoia, the hostile environment outside the limo remaining all too intrusively real, the denied substance of the 90s' signified intruding upon its determinedly surface-orientated signifiers.

"Tough love"

The increased representation of women in hip-hop and R&B in the 90s was a progressive reconfiguration of gender relations in popular music. Yet in an age of contradictions like Clinton's "tough love" approach to welfare, it was only logical that, in a deregulated affective marketplace, lovers should prioritise the welfare of the self over that of the other. Moreover, that this transactional affect should be rooted in residual gender relations indicated the conservativism that underlay the progressive veneer of this period.

Expressing this structure of feeling, the newly glammed-up TLC's 1994 'Creep' (UK 6; US 1) repays lowdown cheats by cheating on the downlow. Two 1995 sex positivity anthems – TLC's slow-jam 'Red Light Special' (UK 18; US 2) and Adina Howard's G-funk 'Freak Like Me' (US 2) – reject demure 'femininity' whilst also demanding reasserted masculinity: "I need a real man"; "There's just one thing that a man must do", etc. Lil Kim marries the traditional to the transactional on 1996's 'No Time' (US 18), "Gimme your loot/Your MAC-11 then shoot", while on Jay-Z's 1998 'Can I Get A...' (UK 24; US 19), Amil insists, "I like a lot of Prada, Alizé and vodka... if you ain't rollin', bypass". In this transactional hustle, tenderness gets lost in the tussle. Women's currency is sex, men's is money –

"that thing" which former Fugee Lauryn Hill's doozy 'Doo Wop' (UK 3; US 1) decries, targeting Lil Kim, Foxy Brown and Puffy ("Remember when he told you he was all about the Benjamins?").

Missy Elliott initially resisted this Fordist regression, presenting herself as post-human in tandem to production partner Timbaland's futuristically post-Fordist beats. Exemplifying Donna Haraway's cyborg feminism,[30] Missy moved beyond essentialised notions of feminine *form*, both physical and musical. Missy rapped as much as she sang, therefore, and donned an inflated trash bag on Hype Williams' video for 1997's 'The Rain (Supa Dupa Fly)' (UK 16), while declaring her financial autonomy: "Beep beep, who got the keys to the jeep?". The lubriciousness of 1997's 'Sock It 2 Me' (US 12) works in concert with Williams' computer-game video, with Elliott presented as science project rather than sex object. 1998's 'Hit 'Em Wit Da Hee' (UK 25), meanwhile, rejects the sex/money trade-off, "Just 'cause you cash a check and put it in da bank/That don't make me want to go out and sleep wit' you".

Missy was going against the grain, however. TLC's jerkily joyous 1999 'No Scrubs' (UK 3; US 1) decries "deadbeats" who "wanna get with me with no money". While there's a thrill to such power-levelling, lines like "live at home with your mama" again demand Fordist masculinity in a post-Fordist world. Newcomers Destiny's Child hired 'Scrubs' producer She'kspere for companion-piece 'Bills, Bills, Bills' (UK 6; US 1): "Can you pay my bills?" they taunt, knowing the answer. Destiny's disses of the post-Fordist male include the over-communicative 'Bug a Boo' (UK 9), formerly known as a 'new man'. Reversing the famous assertion of second-wave feminism, the political is reduced to the personal in this third wave. Soon, even Elliot was purring, "If you want me/Where's my dough?/Give me money, buy me clothes", on 1999's 'All N My Grill' (UK 20), while 'Hot Boyz' (UK 18; US 5) equates jeeps and platinum visas with attractiveness, with Timbaland's production blinged-up for the occasion. On TLC's folky-pretty 'Unpretty' (UK 6; US 1) the body negativity they decry as objects is the same that they dish out as subjects on 'I'm Good at Being Bad' (*FanMail*, UK 1; US 1), with its demand of "ten inch or bigger".

Jennifer Lopez's Destiny's Child-like 2000 'Love Don't Cost a Thing' (UK 1; US 3) rejects this transactional turn – "Credit cards aren't romance.../What I need from you is not available in stores" – sentiments somewhat offset by Lopez's blingy public persona. Concurrently, Destiny's *Charlie's Angels* theme, 'Independent Women Part I' (UK 1; US 1), rejects their previous transactional traditionalism – "I pay my car note and I pay my own bills" – though its equality is again accounted fiscally: "All the honeys making money.../All the mamas who profit dollars". In the gender wars, as in the gang wars, the currency of the 90s is still the power and the money.

"Jiggy"

Fresh Prince Will Smith's 1998 'Gettin' Jiggy Wit It' (UK 3; US 1) recycles several bling motifs as pop – playas and "haters", disco samples (Sister Sledge), product placement (Prada, BMW), shiny-suited dance routines and credible cameos (Nas ghost-writing some of Smith's *Big Willie Style*, UK 9; US 8). Repossessed from the pejorative 'jigaboo', 'jiggy' means 'rhythmic', 'sexy', 'flashy', 'fun' – a player without the gangster internship – and quickly entered popular parlance. Consequently, Faith Evans and Puff Daddy's 1999 'All Night Long' (UK 23; US 9) is an affirmation of the fun 90s – "Ain't nothing but a party" – underwritten by money and power: "Get the cash, and stock paper for the whole four quarter", Puffy boasts, standing on a catwalk. With bling's 'street' elements now excised – along with any critique of consumerism – Puff concludes, "Let's make 'em dance!".

Similarly upbeat, but with better music and politics, the fun proclaimed in Mary J. Blige and original gangsta Dr. Dre's fantastic early 2001 'Family Affair' (U 8; US 1) is uniquely socially aware for this era. Blige renounces gangster values – "hateration" – as a synecdoche of the conjuncture: "We don't need no haters/We're just trying to love one another". Such unexpected countercultural utopianism was a rare but welcome counter to the consumerist, pseudo-utopianism of jiggy.

"A bisexual man who's never had a homosexual experience"

Suede singer Brett Anderson's claim sums up the 90s' contradictory relationship to queerness. For while the era enacted the greatest queering of culture since glam, Major's Back to Basics moralism, New Labour's family sacramentalism and new lad's heteronormativity shrank the epistemological space available for any queerness more physical than an abstraction or more radical than an aesthetic.[31]

The queer 90s was: Nirvana declaring, "Everyone is gay" on 1993's 'All Apologies'; Bruce Springsteen's sweetly vague theme for 1993's film *Philadelphia* (UK 2; US 9); Manic Street Preachers' homoerotic guerrilla performance of 1994's 'Faster' (UK 16) on *Top of the Pops*; Ru Paul; David McAlmont's flamboyantly queer vulnerability alongside Suede guitarist Bernard Butler's girly-boy aggression on 1995's delightful 'Yes' (UK 8); Taylor Hawkins dragged up as Dave Grohl's girlfriend in Foo Fighters' 1997 'Everlong' video (UK 18); Marilyn Manson's homoerotic 1998 'Dope Show' promo clip (UK 12); Todd Haynes' assertion of grunge and Britpop's glam-derived queerness in *Velvet Goldmine* (1998) and British TV drama *Queer as Folk* (1999–2000).

The anti-queer 90s was Oasis's de-gaying of glam, the police toilet sting on George Michael, the hounding of Labour MP Ron Davies for cruising on Clapham Common, and Labour's failure to repeal Section 28. While Anderson's abstracted flirtation and Placebo's 1997 'Nancy Boy' (UK 4) offered queerness as *aesthetic*, the Michael and Davies scandals represented a grossly physical crossing of centrism's social liberal line. Manson's 1998 "norm life – we're white and oh so hetero" was a rare critique ('I Don't Like the Drugs'), but it was Michael who exposed the poverty of neoliberal progressiveness, his response to his arrest producing his career peak, 1998's 'Outside' (UK 2). A refusal of authoritarian moralism essayed with warmth and humour, the video features Michael dancing in a disco urinal, dressed as a policeman, while suggestively twirling his baton. Combining the fun and dark 90s to genuinely progressive effect, 'Outside' parodically plays up rather than attempting to resolve the period's contradictions.

"The information superhighway"

Innovation didn't terminate with Fordism. The internet initially appeared to possess utopian potential, with Mexico's Zapatista revolutionaries using it as a political tool, Napster's music-streaming service's wrong-footing the industry and Haraway's post-human feminism full of possibilities. Furthermore, as that futuristic talisman the year 2000 approached, a surge of post-Fordist innovation in hip-hop and dance suggested the opening of a parallel *sonic* superhighway. This wasn't "modernism's last stand",[32] as Reynolds argues: that would be Oasis's 1997 *Be Here Now* (UK 1; US 2), whose painted-on layers of guitars couldn't disguise Fordist rock's rusting undercarriage. This new music represented post-Fordism without either postmodernism or hauntology, unsentimentally deploying the past to create a sonic futurism that Fordism couldn't have dreamt of, even as the new music's sentiments fell short of Fordist dreams. Futurism without utopianism reflects the 90s contradiction of a 'progressive' politics without commitment to systemic change. Yet, that the radical ambitions of this vein of 90s pop transcended politics' timidity places it in a liminal space *inside* that contradiction, a dialectic that never synthesises, for all its electronic innovation.

Where pop derivations like the Fugees elided hip-hop's ontological oddity – see: 1996's 'Killing Me Softly' (UK 1) – the Wu-Tang Clan emphasised it. In sympathy with RZA's sonically fragmented, harmonically unresolved production, the ensemble's lyrics on Raekwon's *Cuban Linx* express an un-gangsta irresolution ('Rainy Dayz'), fracturing linguistic form ('Wu-Gambinos') while questioning quotidian project 'realism' ("Don't believe in heaven cause you're livin' in hell"). While GZA claims on 1995's *Liquid Swords* (US 9), "I'm not caught up in politics/I'm no black activist on a scholar's dick", the gangsta imagery is as cut up as RZA's production, likewise foregrounding its own apparatus ('Duel of the Iron Mic') to create a similar indeterminacy. On 1997's 'Better Tomorrow' (*Wu-Tang Forever*, UK 1; US 1), RZA's rap conjures a stream-of-consciousness dystopian utopia – "New World Order, slave trade, minimum wage, Medicaid" – as if unable to imagine the title's promise. With RZA's soundscape actually drowning out Inspectah Deck's verse on 'The City' and the ensemble a Greek chorus commenting on the production, *Forever* offers an alienated take on the alienation effect, foregrounding the apparatus of *social* production. Yet where Brecht's alienation effect is dialectic, without a positive vision, Wu-Tang's remains liminal, suspended in indeterminate sonic and political space.

Trip-hop was a British take on the Wu's approach. On 1995's *Maxinquaye* (UK 3), Tricky's fragmented lyrics express paranoia and atomisation ("emotional ties they stay severed", 'Suffocated Love') amid a conventionally dystopian landscape (the apocalyptic 'Aftermath'). 'Feed Me' rejects Fordism's utopia – "From cradle to grave…/The dream of yesterday becomes another lie" – even as its post-production ransacks Fordist raw materials. Tricky's unfocused anger is as post-Fordist as his post-human blurring of gender – Martina sings his raps; Tricky croaks an ectoplasmic echo; the pair swap clothes in their videos – popular music turned inside out, pullulating with potential, yet, again, indeterminate. American DJ Shadow's 1996 *Endtroducing....* (UK 17) is a literal blast from the Fordist past, composed of thousands of samples, but what could be a cosily melancholic collectors' hauntology is rendered adversarial by aggressive breakbeats and utopian by Shadow's futuristic methodology. Once again, the hauntology is liminal, however: as much an end as a beginning, as the title acknowledges.

In jungle, composed of 70s breakbeats accelerated to speeds unplayable by humans, the past is so distended it sounds like the future. With its rave elements endowing jungle with a residual utopianism, early ragga-orientated tracks like General Levy's 1994 'Incredible' (UK 8) were adversarial: "Cah we ah get dem critical, critical, critical". On Goldie's aptly named 1995 *Timeless* (UK 7), the effect is both edgily utopian and dreamily dystopian, its liminality readable as *openness*. Demurely renamed 'drum and bass', jungle became salon music, soundtracking fashion shows and adverts, and detached from a progressive vision, its foregrounding of the apparatus could simply seem fussy, as on Reprazent's 1997 *New Forms* (UK 8), thus the establishment endorsement of the Mercury Prize. Reprazent's innovation *was* vaguely utopian – "Together we can change it all" ('Share the Fall') – occasionally electrifying – "Something you've never heard before!" – but too often cold, presentist, *technocratic*.

Bjork expanded both dance's emotionalism and its experimentalism, the elasticity of her voice, body and production-techniques breaking through the rational and the physical, to embrace the musical and human other. There's a rare transcendence to 1995's *Debut* (UK 3): Marcusian joy in 1995's 'Big Time Sensuality' (UK 17); giddy optimism in 'One Day'. While Bjork's other here is privatised, the songs' emotions are open, expansive, epic. On 1996's *Post* (UK 2) the extraordinary, string-driven 'Hyperballad' (UK 8) evokes a supraphysical ecstasy as it ponders the limits of the human body in a liminal union of *Eros* and *Thanatos*. Bjork's creative peak, 1997's *Homogenic* (UK 4; US 28) voyages even further out in a frostily beautiful "emotional landscape", all gusting strings and icily creaking beats, with even the empathetic joy of 'Jóga' a "state of emergency". *Homogenic* expresses an ecstasy of agony at the barriers that besiege her. "I thought I could organise freedom", Bjork laments on electronic bolero 'Hunter': "how Scandinavian of me" – rejecting an affective Fordism, but from its emancipatory left. Yet, with no alternative vision available, the utopian *Eros* of the closing 'All is Full of Love' (UK 24) is undermined by social atomisation: "The phone is off the hook, the doors are all shut".

The union of the organic and electronic, human and machine, was always one of pop's most productive impulses, and much of the 90s' best dance came from crepuscular encounters between rock and rave. After appearing on 1996's *Trainspotting*, Underworld's startlingly *avant* 'Born Slippy Nux' became an anomalously huge hit (UK 2). A verbal cut-up whose dystopian, beer-monster chant of "lager, lager, lager, larger" is in dialectic with the music's rushing, surging utopianism, 'Born Slippy' never resolves harmonically or affectively. The Chemical Brothers were a dance adjunct to Britpop, 60s invocations in their artwork, videos and textures, and where their 1996 Noel Gallagher-featuring 'Setting Sun' (UK1) was a somewhat literal articulation of psychedelic dance, 1997's 'Private Psychedelic Reel' (*Dig Your Own Hole*, UK 1; US 14) was a lateral one. This swirling, mantric epic frames the countercultural past as the future it was always reaching for, stripped now not just of acid filigree but also of psychedelic utopianism. The visionary reel, for all its reaching, stretching, yearning, is 'private'. Technoexperimentalist Aphex Twin's 1999 'Windowlicker' (UK 16) creates sounds hitherto unheard in music, its restless rhythmic and electronic concatenation anchored by a cooing human hum. If this is the utopian push of the post-human, the video depicts the pull of its dystopian other, Aphex's face affixed to the bodies of voluptuous 'hoochies', its cartoon nightmare undercutting the track's transcendence, stranded in liminal space, a dialectic that can't achieve synthesis.

As Fordist guitar-music finally recognised its own obsolescence and incorporated electronics, its content became increasingly dystopian, as on Smashing Pumpkins' *Adore* (UK 5; US 2) and Marilyn Manson's 1999 *Mechanical Animals* (UK 8; US 1), whose *The Matrix*-featured 'Rock Is Dead' declares the termination of the adversarial: "Fuck all your protests and put them to bed". While Radiohead's 2000 'Idioteque' (*Kid A*) lyrically depicts dance hedonism as helplessness in an opiated dystopia, it was still the furthest rock had ventured into electronica, and thus pregnant with possibilities.

Inspired by both acid house and jungle, Tim 'Timbaland' Mosley's early productions were spectacularly odd interventions into the pop charts. On 1996's 'Pony' (UK 16; US 6), Ginuwine's vocal is mere background to Mosley's burping synths and off-kilter beats, while the swooning space-jazz of Missy Elliot's 1997 'Beep Me 911' (UK 14) is off-centredly eccentric. Then came Timbaland's hat trick, a pinnacle of post-Fordist creativity to rival anything produced under Fordism, although, again, its radical futurism, detached from utopianism, is all latency and liminality. On Aaliyah's 1998 'Are You That Somebody' (UK 11; US 21), her vocal coolly twines around the production's parries and pauses, her flirtation with potentiality seductive yet frustrated by Timbaland's vocal interjections, rhythmic and emotional resolution denied by the beats' lurching, looping agitation. On 2000's extraordinary 'Try Again' (UK 5; US 1), Aaliyah's serene vocal exemplifies the lyric's articulation of possibility, a future that Timbaland's foregrounded burbling acid synths promise but that his jerky, lopsided beats and amputated, circling guitar line deny. On Missy's astonishing 2001 'Get Ur Freak On' (UK 4; US 7), it's her lyric that foregrounds the apparatus, proclaiming Timbaland's innovation, while her own post-human moulding and modulation of language – "biggie biggie bounce'"; "what the drilly-oh" – matches the producer every jerky step of the way. With no tune, no hook bar a minimalist bhangra loop, the radical indeterminacy of 'Get Ur Freak On' just *hangs* there in its own sonic and sentimental space. That it doesn't – and cannot – resolve is testament both to the track's radicalism and, ultimately, its irresolution.

The information superhighway turned out to be a dead end, the dotcom crash leading to the internet's corporate consolidation. The non-event of the 'millennium bug' was paradigmatic of the new century's cybernetics – there would be no dramatic change, while the future would transpire to be an archive of the past. The sonic superhighway also turned out to be dead end. RZA stepped back from production and the Wu assumed more regular shapes; Tricky became so fractured as to be unlistenable; Shadow never followed up on *Endtroducing*'s implications, nor Aphex those of 'Windowlicker'; the Chemicals and Bjork retreated to more regularised musical forms; jungle became increasingly technocratic; Aaliyah died; Missy disappeared and Timbaland went pop; the Pumpkins and Radiohead brought their guitars back down from the attic. Unaligned to utopianism, 90s music's radicalism was all superstructure and no base – like the period's protests unaligned to any future-orientated political project. Music's processing of extant information was innovative, but with no *new* information to process, no vision of the future, it couldn't continue to create sonic change, could henceforth only consolidate and preserve, just as politics now would.

"The post-human"

Mainstream pop deployed dance's innovations to render the post-human humdrum – an everyday futurism without utopianism, a cyborg affectivity without human vulnerability. Madeover by the future Xenomania, Cher's 1998 'Believe' (UK 1; US 1) matches a middlebrow dance beat to sleek synthetics, its foregrounding of the apparatus via audible Auto-Tune parallelling Cher's own post-human physicality. The lyric spins a breakup into a self-esteem anthem, loss remixed as win, resulting in a song of robotic positivity that technocratically overrides reality. With Daft Punk

351

having pioneered such robo-disco, appearing in public only in cyborg costume, their marvellous 2000 'One More Time' (UK 2) is another Auto-Tune anthem, its lyric suggestive of a computer programmed to 'positivity', randomly generating affective data: "Celebrate and dance so free". In such post-human optimism, the promise of the future is folded into the present, because the cybernetic revolution is *now*, with technology solving all human problems.

Max Martin's post-Fordist factory streamlined this post-human pop through a machine-power far beyond Fordist capacity. Britney Spears' persona paralleled this, via fembot sentiments like 2000's 'Born to Make You Happy' (UK 1), while her affectless delivery rendered robotic even her declaration of agency on 'Stronger' (UK 7; US 11). Janet Jackson's 2000 'Doesn't Really Matter' (UK 5; US 1) served reminder she'd always been semi-cyborg, and with its space-age promo's CGI dance moves, sculpted bodies and Photoshopped smiles, the future is, again, both happening *right now* and is *fun*. Martin-produced boyband NSYNC are presented as puppets on the video for 2000's pummelling 'Bye Bye Bye' (UK 3; US 4) and as dolls for 'It's Gonna Be Me' (UK 9; US 1), the self-aware cyborg being the perfect role/riposte for 90s teen pop. S Club 7's bubblegum-robo-disco 'Don't Stop Movin'' (UK 1) posits the fun of the performance principle as being unending motion in a "crazy world", so "don't get left behind". The Auto-Tuned vocals and space-age video for Victoria Beckham's 2000 teaming with garage act, True Steppers, 'Out of Your Mind' (UK 2), capture Posh Spice's celebrity-cyborg persona, her exemplification of neoliberalism's merger of performance principle with pleasure principle.

Five's video for early 2001's Auto-Tune-disco 'Let's Dance' (UK 1) takes the self-aware cyborg to another level, foregrounding the capitalist apparatus by replacing a departed member with a cardboard cutout, while rejecting the robotic dance routines the power and the money impose on them. Yet the result is less alienation *effect* than alienation *affect*, not protesting so much as *professing* lack of agency, a disempowerment endemic to the 90s. This makes explicit what had been increasingly implicit: the post-human would not be the victory of humanity over the vulnerability of bodies and emotions, let alone over the need for endless labour. The post-human would be the victory of post-Fordist capitalism over *humanity*, both as a species – reducing us to data – and as "species-being" – human empathy, human value and human agency. This would enable optimal productivity within an ever-expanding performance principle, with the citizenry plugged intricately into the technocratic matrix, simultaneously slaved to and mesmerised by the power and the money, the money and the power.

Chapter 11

"Pop It Like It's Hot": Pop and Politics' Imperial Phase (2001–07)

The new millennium was all set to be the age of the cyborg and the technocrat: a brave new world beyond race, gender and class. In "a system architecture whose basic modes of operation are probabilistic, statistical", in Haraway's terminology,[1] we already inhabited the sleekly futurist world of Kylie Minogue's 'Can't Get You Out of My Head' video (UK 1; US 7). In this cybernetic era of smartphones and smart bombs, of simulacra and over-stimulation, the virtual realities of CGI and Photoshop, Ecstasy and Prozac rendered the real irrelevant, while the futures trade, a booming CD back catalogue and the advent of tech-friendly smart-pop obviated the need for a future. 'Pop' wasn't just the era's dominant musical genre – *Billboard* added its pop chart in 2005 – it was a synecdoche for post-millennial culture: digital, informational, commercial, presentist, 'poptimistic'.[2] With diversity, the internet and the iPod all evidence that the centrist system *worked*,[3] the occasional technocratic tweak was all the free market and its social corollary, 'freedom', required. Consequently, the cultural industries could afford to foreground their apparatus through product placement (Nelly pimping for Nike on 'Air Force Ones', US 3) and by placing the technocrats centre-stage in *Pop Idol* and *X Factor*'s celebration of the spectacle. Life as a talent contest was nothing if not democratic, for as *Big Brother* asserted: "*You* decide!"

Few of these marvels worked according to the manual, however. The probabilistic, statistical systems failed to predict the World Trade Center attacks of 9/11, while the matrix continued to glitch thereafter. The 'sexed-up' intelligence British and American governments produced on Iraq's 'weapons of mass destruction' insulted *public* intelligence, while making technocrats look like technophobes. The inability of spin's inventors to sell the Iraq War provoked the biggest political protests in decades, although *we* didn't decide about Iraq any more than anything else, and the British campaign slogan "Not in My Name" suggested we didn't expect to. Smart warfare proved to be shocking and aweing only in its incompetence, the conflict's "collateral damage" and "friendly fire" constantly available on 24-hour TV news and increasingly at the click of a mouse. For, as the internet took on its 2.0 form as social media – Facebook going from 12 to 58 million users from 2006–07 – it transpired to be a conflict zone, too. Žižek's *Matrix*-derived concept of "the desert of the real" captured the grimness of this virtual reality – its competitive flossing and aggressive 'flaming' – while the actual flaming of Iraq's deserts demonstrated the political reality of centrism.[4] As the oil and the ozone burned, anti-globalism protests and race riots testified against neoliberalism's claims to eco-friendliness and multicultural cosmopolitanism. As the boom bottomed out, consumer demand was maintained by a 'second life' of low-interest credit (what could possibly go wrong?), while centrism's cyborg model of citizenship was quietly replaced with that of the 'flexible worker'.

Like their political peers, pop's technocrats displayed a combination of complacency, ineptitude and authoritarianism – hunting down leakers; suing internet streaming services rather than developing their own; rendering CDs unplayable via anti-piracy software as unit sales steadily declined. This led to the micro-management of music – A&R departments matching artist to production factory; three-year gaps between releases to stimulate demand, plus the precision-tooling of post-millennial smart-pop. "Everything's calculated and sound precise/Another move another mill", as 50 Cent put it on 2005's 'Outta Control'

(UK 7; US 6). Given this merger of music and marketing, Natasha Bedingfield's desire for her song to "say what I mean" is thus *the same* as her search for "the killer hook" on 2004's 'These Words' (UK 1; US 17). With corporate containment always skewing conservative, even the *retro*-futurism of Missy Elliott and Timbaland's 2002 'Work It' (UK 6; US 2) wouldn't be repeated. With the track tame by his standards, Timbaland's future pop productions would be many things, but *futuristic* wouldn't be among them.[5] Pop, like politics in the new millennium, would consolidate rather than innovate, preserve rather than progress. With mp3s a technocratic triumph of space over sound quality – a voguely buzzy 'downsizing' – there wasn't much point in pushing the needle. Content became equally compressed, an increasingly small, mean thing, whether passively absent (Rihanna; Coldplay), actively unpleasant (Nelly; Ludacris), dumbed-down (Atomic Kitten; Kid Rock) or sexed-up (almost everybody).[6]

For while post-millennial pop displayed a historic level of diversity, the jewel in the centrist crown, the price of female assimilation was gender essentialism. Black Eyed Peas' 2005 'My Humps' (UK 3; US 3) celebrates the self-objectification of Fergie's "lady lumps" as fair exchange for male reward: "They say I'm really sexy", she coos, "They treat me really nicely". The song's writer, will.i.am, also provided burlesque troupe Pussycat Dolls with the grotesque 2006 'Beep' (UK 2; US 13), while he rapped the male-gaze 101: "You got a real big brain but I'm lookin' at ya [beep]". Not a good look. When in 2002 Nelly sang-spoke, "It's getting hot in here, so take off all your clothes" (UK 4; US 1), he wasn't talking to the fellas. Indeed, this diverse era was lousy with male-gaze songs, like Usher and Ludacris's crunked-up 2004 'Yeah' (UK 1; US 1) and R&B princeling Chris Brown's 2005 'Run It' (UK 2; US 1). There *was* some female clapback: on Ciara's 2004 crunk hit 'Goodies' (UK1; US 1), men can gaze but "the goodies stay in the jar". The same year, British teen-pop troupe Girls Aloud's ravey 'The Show' (UK 2) insists, "Nobody sees the show, not 'til my heart says so", with its spa-set promo's pretty boys passive objects for the Girls' gaze. Pink, co-opting 'masculine' rock into pop, snaps at a harasser, "I'm not here for your entertainment", with her 2006 hit 'U + Ur Hand' (UK 10;

US 9) acidly advising how best male gazers might meet their needs.

Even so, the era's 'reboots' of female stars always entailed them getting *even* sexier. Britney Spears' 'provocative' 2001 'I'm a Slave 4 U' (UK 4; US 27) was written by the era's other key producer, Pharrell Williams. While Christina Aguilera co-wrote 2002's 'Dirrty' (UK 1), her abject chasing of the gaze in the video exudes visible anxiety. This isn't to indulge in the slut-shaming common to the media, because an essentialised culture allows few options for female self-expression. It was thus inevitable that Mariah Carey's 2005 *Emancipation of Mimi* (UK 7; US 1) should announce her personal and career autonomy with a new, sexed-up image. Wholesome Nelly Furtado was similarly rebooted, on 2006's 'Maneater' (UK 1; US 16), and while it's hard to imagine a *less* sexy song title than 'Promiscuous' (UK 3; US 1), it better balanced the gender scales, with producer Timbaland as "promiscuous boy" to Furtado's "promiscuous girl".

While Beyoncé managed to look imperious in her underwear in 2003's 'Naughty Girl' video (UK 10; US 3), co-star Usher's reactions still framed her within the male gaze's confines. Equally, if newcomer Rihanna's hooded eyes initially looked askance at the gaze, by 2007's 'Hate That I Love You' (UK 15; US 7), she too was posing demurely in her underwear. Brit girl-poppers Sugababes similarly shifted from gaze-disdaining street kids to glamazon sexpots on 2004's 'In the Middle' (UK 8). Recurring personnel replacement rendered not just the Sugababes but *femininity* itself a faceless franchise – thus the perverse visual merger of Shakira and Beyoncé in 2007's 'Beautiful Liar' video (UK 1; US 3). In a rare instance of lesbian iconography, Russian pop duo TaTu's 2002 'All the Things She Said' (UK 1; US 20) split the difference between male-gaze titillation and diversity box-ticking. Post-millennial diversity was demonstrated by a flurry of such queer incursions into charts and minds. While this was for the better with Anthony and the Johnsons and 2005's marvellous, Mercury-winning *I Am a Bird Now* (UK 16), it was for the worse with Scissor Sisters (2005's 'Filthy Gorgeous', UK 5) and Mika (2007's 'Grace Kelly', UK 1), whose success seemed predicated on an epistemological narrowing of queerness to campness. With essentialism again the price of diversity, the maintenance of male queerness as masculinity's *other* retained a safe distance between homosexuality and heteronormativity.

This enabled hetero pretty-boys Pharrell Williams and Justin Timberlake to become poster boys for a vaunted 'metrosexuality', alongside doe-eyed footballer David Beckham. Yet as Pharrell and Snoop Dogg's dead-eyed ballers in 2003's leering 'Beautiful' promo (UK 23; US 6) and the rapey vibe of Timberlake's 2006 'SexyBack' video reveal (UK 1; US 1), misogyny wasn't incompatible with metrosexuality, it being an expansion rather than an evolution of masculinity. One of the era's biggest hits, James Blunt's 2005 folkie ballad 'You're Beautiful' (UK 1; US 1) is a case in point. Despite Blunt's heteroflexible falsetto, and a video flashing the most male flesh of its era, while touching on the epidemic of male suicide, 'Beautiful' is a stalker song whose subject is entirely defined by her physicality. R. Kelly and Russell Brand can thus be seen to represent what Žižek calls "the dirty obscene underside of power" in this period[7] – protected by the industry and presented a free pass by the public. With profit the only real currency of neoliberalism, tolerance for misogyny is thus the obscene underside to diversity.[8]

Post-millennial pop could unquestionably be thrilling – Timberlake's 2002, Timbaland-produced 'My Love', for example (UK 2; US 1) – but rarely was it innovative, musically, or imaginative, lyrically. Where songs weren't a content void (like 'My Love'), they represented a reckoning with 'reality' – "Me, myself and I/That's all I got in the end", Beyoncé's 2003 hit proclaimed (UK 11; US 4) – the capitalist reality of competitive individualism. In the epoch of Dr Phil's *Self Matters* (2001), the self-empowerment song – the carol of the competitive marketplace – was post-millennial pop's platonic form. "Losers lose, winners win", as 50 Cent put it on the Game's cheerily reptilian 2005 'Hate It or Love It' (UK 4; US 2): *you* decide – the system being no more rigged than reality shows. In a competitive environment, predicated on polarities of self and other – both symbolised and materialised by a state of war – it was only a short step from celebrating the self to denigrating the other. The diss-track was thus endemic to this era, typified by Jay-Z's 2001 takedown of Nas, 'Takeover' (*The Blueprint*, UK 30; US 1), and by Nas's detachedly deadening reply, 'Ether' (*Stillmatic*, US 5).

Amid such cold-blooded individualism, what warmth and collectivity there was came in the wan form of alternative rock, as it swooned into pop's waiting arms. Snow Patrol's 2004 power ballad 'Run' (UK 5) formulates a touchy-feely fatalism – "Light up, as if you have a choice" – that can also be heard in U2's 2005 'Sometimes You Can't Make It on Your Own' (UK 1) and Coldplay's 2005 'Fix You' (UK 4). These tracks tilt at transcendence, while reaching out for human connection in an affectless era, but their stadium-sized emoting ultimately advocates adaptation to an unchangeably hostile world – or 'Nature's Law' (UK 2) as Embrace's 2006 hit had it. Utopia is no longer imaginable; there *is* no alternative in rock, pop or politics.

Although *Big Brother*'s dystopian origin was rarely remarked, an awareness of the desert beyond the spectacular real still leaked from unlikely locations. The video for Girls Aloud's 2003 'Life Got Cold' (UK 3) presents them as post-humans in a dystopian landscape, while its lyric tells on the transactionality of networked social relations. Leeringly lubricious hip-hopper Ludacris's 2007 'Runaway Love' (US 2) laments violence against women, and with Luda's verses "trying to figure out why the world is so cold", Mary J. Blige's chorus offers a rare warm blast of empathy. Within undead indie, Maximo Park's 2007 'Our Velocity' (UK 9) invokes a world with "Poison in the air/A mix of chemicals and fear". In meathead nu-metal, meanwhile, Linkin Park's 2007 'Shadow of the Day' promo (US 15) sets its narrator's suicide attempt in a war-torn dystopia. Linkin's linkage was apposite: the threat to technocracy's "system architecture", Haraway attests, being *stress*, so if Iraq provided the political stress-point, the millennial mental-health epidemic was its cultural corollary. On Britain's first digital-sales chart-topper, Gnarls Barkley's gloriously giddy 2006 'Crazy' (UK 1; US 2), CeeLo's cry of "Ha-ha-ha, bless your soul/You really think you're in control?" might *sound* celebratory, but is all too pertinently cautionary.[9]

In a world without a future, we were all the flexible workers of flexible accumulation, occupying a perennial present without security or agency, exerting control only through what we consumed, whether binge-shopping at Primark or pimping our rides. Fisher named this condition "depressive hedonia" – "an inability to do anything else except pursue pleasure".[10] *Lord of the Rings* box-set marathon or vodka and Red Bull bender? *You* decide. Yet the circumscription of choice was indicated by *the* expression of the era, "having it large" deriving from McDonalds' corporate incitement to consumer excess. Celebrations of hedonism were hardly a new development in popular music, but even in rave these were usually allusive – and frequently utopian. Now, the stated aim was simply to get wrecked, from heavy rock (the Darkness's 2005 'One Way Ticket', UK 8), to pop (Pink's 2001 'Get the Party Started', UK 2; US 4), and from dancehall (Sean Paul's 2005 'We Be Burnin'', UK 2; US 6) to R&B (R. Kelly's 2002 'Ignition (Remix)', UK 1; US 2). 'Da Club' took over from the projects as hip-hop's staple location, your hosts here being 50 Cent and Dr. Dre (UK 3; US 1),[11] while Petey Pablo's 2004 'Freek-a-Leek' (US 7) provides the evening's menu: "Sniff a lil' coke, take a lil' X, smoke a lil' weed, drink a lil' bit" (US 7), do a lil' product placement.

There is *always* a comedown, however. With celebrities no longer post-human but *meta*-human, extraordinarily ordinary, they exemplified neoliberal subjecthood, being "rational, completely taken up with [their] own affairs, absorbed in... maximizing [their] individual interest", as Boltanski and Chiapello put it.[12] Increasingly accessible via what Richard Seymour calls the "contrived intimacy" of the internet,[13] these meta-humans also exemplified the system architecture's meta-stresses: witness the very public breakdowns of Mariah, Janet, Whitney and Britney in this period. The Streets' Mike Skinner's journey from communally celebratory hedonism on 2002's wonderful 'Weak Become Heroes' (UK 27) to isolated, suicidal anhedonia on 2006's dreadful 'Prangin' Out' (UK 25) racks out the faultlines of a fissured society. Those who, like Skinner and Amy Winehouse, overcame disadvantage only to descend into self-destruction were seen, as Jones points out, to lack 'class'.[14] This reframes Winehouse's refusal to clean up her act on 2006's 'Rehab' (UK 7; US 9) – "I won't go, go, go" – as less self-defeating than authority-defying: a rejection of technocratic solutions which, preoccupied with appearance, photo opportunity and spin, leave underlying issues unaddressed. That this ended so badly for Winehouse was a personal tragedy, but a synecdoche of a societal one.

Despite a busted boom, an unpopular war and the revelation that 'freedom' was being defended by torture at Abu Ghraib and Guantanamo Bay, Bush and Blair both won easy victories in the mid-2000s. Neoliberalism was now as embedded in our society as journalists in the Gulf, and equally proclaimed to be 'beyond' politics – as was an increasingly disengaged public. This produced an increasingly affectless culture that treated crisis as quotidian, audible in pop-punker Avril Lavigne shrugging "Cause life's like this" on 2002's 'Complicated' (UK 3; US 2), and on Destiny's Child's Kelly Rowland's 'Stole' the same year (UK 2; US 27), where a school shooting is a random tragedy rather than the result of, say, white-supremacist-appeasing gun laws. It likely wasn't coincidence that 'random!' became such a standard colloquial response in this imaginatively contained era. Nelly offered a useful historical overview on 2005's 'N Dey Say' (UK 6): "Before guns there was swords, and they was killing each other/Ain't much changed to this day".

Race war, gang war, gender war, War on Terror were all thus just everyday life in the new millennium, with its war of all against all available on 24-hour TV, accessible on the world-wide web and accompanied by a 'wicked' smart-pop soundtrack. Consequently, this chapter's title derives from Snoop and Pharrell's 2004 hit 'Drop It Like It's Hot' (UK 10; US 1), for while Snoop's line, "pop it like it's hot" could be heard as affirmation of the period's poptimism, it actually depicts shooting the competitive other in the head. It's an apt choice of image for an upbeat yet affectless era, whose energy derived from a conventionalised competitiveness and a dialectical fronting and flossing narcissism, underwritten by the legitimised violence of war in imperial-phase neoliberalism.

"Where Were You When the World Stopped Turning?": 9/11 in Popular Music

The September 2001 attacks on the World Trade Center should have shattered neoliberalism's glittering facade, revealing globalism as imperialism in business drag, neoliberal ecology's imbrication in the oil economy and – via Blair's unequivocal support of Bush – centrist comfort in neoconservative company.

Instead, 9/11 rebooted the system. With the welfare state replaced by a static technocracy in which contradictions were spun rather than resolved, both Blair and new president George W. Bush's approval ratings were slumping. After 9/11, the fear of an existentially threatening other gave crisis-value to the system we already had, which Bush called 'freedom' and which was now weaponised as a *warfare* state. In this climate of fear, the need to protect liberal democratic freedom allowed the *suspension* of liberal freedoms under 2001's Patriot Act. This then was next-level neoliberalism.

As America went backwards to defend the status quo, there was little dissent within politics or popular culture, with drama *The Wire* (2002–08) presenting surveillance as essential to 'civilisation'. "You're either with us or against us" as Bush put it. Even those who'd hitherto been other, like African Americans, now pitched up inside freedom's big tent. "Who the fuck knocked our buildings down?" demanded Ghostface Killah on Wu-Tang's 'Rules', patriotically asserting, "America, together we stand, divided we fall". Whitney Houston had her first American hit in several years with a melismatically melodramatic rendition of the 'Star-Spangled Banner' (US 6). Only Nas's late 2001 'Rule', with Amerie (*Stillmatic*, US 5), linked America's domestic othering – "confronted with racism, started to feel foreign" – to the attack on the Afghan other: "We all God's children". Framing this American War on Terror as imperialist and oil-driven, Nas declares, "blood and death" is "what America's about", and spits, "my country's a motherfucker".

Nas flew a solitary skull-and-crossbones in an ocean of American flags, however, for even the 9/11 dead weren't safe from enlistment in defence of American freedom. The bravery of New York's firemen made them national heroes, thus both the popular repurposing of Five for Fighting's 2001 'Superman, It's Not Easy' (US 14) and Alan Jackson's purpose-built 'Where Were You When the World Stopped Turning?' (US 28) that winter. "Did you burst out with pride for the red, white and blue?" Jackson demands, "And the heroes who died just doing what they do?" With Jackson's title claiming the 'world' as American, the title track of Springsteen's 2002 *The Rising* (UK 1; US 1) took a fireman's perspective, but even the

Boss's storytelling smarts were clogged by blood and oil here, descending into Old Testament justice, asserting "I want an eye for an eye" on 'Empty Sky'.

The Beastie Boys managed to memorialise the dead without the dead hand of xenophobia on 'Open Letter to NYC' (*To the 5 Boroughs*, UK 2; US 1), insisting on the American self as a plurality of others: "Home to the many… accepting peoples of all places". An optimistic take on American liberalism, the Beasties' view was hard-line Marxism compared to the reactionary credo of country singer Toby Keith. Early 2002's 'Courtesy of the Red, White and Blue (The Angry American)' (US 25) salivates, "Oh, justice will be served and the battle will rage…/'Cause we'll put a boot in your ass, it's the American way". Native Americans might well concur. Former scourge of trigger-happy presidents, Neil Young's 2002 'Let's Roll' (*Are You Passionate?* UK 24; US 10) sounded remarkably like Keith: "You've got to turn on evil when it's coming after you… go in after it and never be denied" – but in a hippie twist, universal love was now claimed for imperialism ("Let's roll for love"). Coldplay's 2002 'Politik' countered such fulminations with a fainthearted assertion of universal love (*A Rush of Blood to the Head*, UK 1; US 5), while Moby's 2002 'We Are All Made of Stars' (UK 11) invoked Joni Mitchell's 'Woodstock', although its claim of "slowly rebuilding, growing in peace" hardly reflected events in the Afghan desert.

The patriotic conception of America as its citizens' self produced a queasily comic variant in popular music. Veteran hair-metallers Bon Jovi compared their country's endurance to that of their own career on the title track of 2002's *Bounce* (UK 2; US 2): "I'll take the hit but not the fall/I know no fear, still standing tall". With Eminem having dressed up as Osama Bin Laden on 2002's brilliantly scabrous 'Without Me' (UK 1; US 2), he now claimed, on 50 Cent's 2003 'Patiently Waiting' (*Get Rich or Die Tryin'*, UK 2; US 1), that possessed of an office near the World Trade Center, "Some cowards fucked with the wrong building – they meant to hit ours". Such solipsism told a political truth, however: that the War on Terror was conducted to subdue the domestic self as much as the foreign other, 'shock and awe' inscribing the truth of neoliberal democracy in blood and bomb craters.

"We Gonna Rock, Then We Gonna Roll, Then We Let It Pop":[15] Post-Millennial Pop

"Imperial phase" was always an unfortunate phrase to denote commercial hegemony in popular music.[16] Yet the term is apposite for this period's smart-pop, both in its context – the literal imperialism of the War on Terror; the metaphorical 'imperial phase' of uncontested neoliberalism – and its conduct: the colonisation of musical territory. Imperial-phase pop annexed richly resourced hip-hop via the guest feature (50 Cent with Timberlake; Red Man/Nelly with Aguilera; Nas with J-Lo) and the proxy producer (Timbaland; the Neptunes). Pop colonised bankrupt R&B (Usher; Furtado), annexed the failed state of alternative rock (No Doubt's Gwen Stefani; Evanescence's 2003 'Bring Me to Life', UK 1; US 5) and subsumed the once-imperial state of dance in an act of union. Pop also subdued the spirited indie insurgency for which 'the Strokes' is a name, and whose first hit, 2001's 'Hard to Explain' (UK 16), was their best, still fresh from the fight. In the Sugababes' video for 2003's 'Hole in the Head' (UK 1), the girls symbolically seize the stage from a male guitar band. By 2007's 'About You Now' (UK 1), the Babes are flaunting the imperial booty of the Strokes' guitar sound. Here and on Rihanna's concurrent 'Blue Monday'-sampling 'Shut Up and Drive' (UK 5; US 15), indie is just a colonial outpost at pop's periphery, to be ransacked for resources and mobilised for markets at will.

Let's dispose of the indie/pop polarity, however. For even if pop can be claimed as the neoliberal self, the case for indie as its other is as redundant as the rockism this polarity perpetuates. Certainly, the crude Fordist rawness of revived indie was a refusal of the sumptuous excess of post-Fordist pop – the desert, the real – and while it was intermittently rousing – say, Electric Six's camply frenetic 2003 'Danger! High Voltage' (UK 2) – it was ideologically reactionary. Post-millennial indie fetishised the Fordist past as a sonic and material *lack*, whereas their forebears didn't just live in relative plenty, they were attempting to *transcend* the limits of Fordist sonics and sentiments. Post-millennial indie regarded old gear (White Stripes' migrainous minimalism), old geezers (Libertines producer Mick Jones) and geezerishness (the

Libertines' 2002 'What a Waster') as guarantors of authenticity, but sounded rusty and etiolated as a result (as on Sweden's Hives' 2002 'Hate to Say I Told You So', UK 23).

Through this retrofitted, romanticised *lack*, the Libertines evoke the 60s as halcyon days of criminal subculture and slumlords (2002's 'Up the Bracket', UK 29), rather than utopian counterculture and affordable housing. Disdaining the adversarial, the Libs offer hauntology as enervation – Pete Doherty often sounding like he's nodding out mid-song. While the Arctic Monkeys focus on the contemporary underclass, there's an affective alignment with the Libertines in Alex Turner's evocation of a grubby, "scummy" landscape ('When the Sun Goes Down', UK 1). Yet the Monkeys offer no real protest at this deficiency, it's just passively – if articulately – observed. Equally, the Strokes' performative refusal – disengaged in interviews; disdaining lip-syncing in videos – captures this conjunctural abnegation of indie's adversarial legacy, the confusion of affectless inertia for 'coolness'.

It was this abnegation that allowed *Pop Stars: The Rivals*-created Girls Aloud to claim – on a prefab 2003 Xenomania production – to be 'The Sound of the Underground' (UK 1), while co-opting rock aggression via eruptions of scuzzy surf guitar. Girls Aloud weren't so much claiming radicalism, here, as the collapse of the concept's relevance: post-millennial pop, like politics, was all about being 'progressive' rather than adversarial, reformist rather than revolutionary, and thus consolidating rather than innovating. 'The Sound of the Underground' is thus a winner's history, a declaration of the defeat of the indie insurgency and an assertion of pop's imperial dominance. While 'Underground' was rather good – and 2007's 'Call the Shots' (UK 3) was even better – this pop hegemony, like the political hegemony it paralleled, was a celebration and consolidation of the status quo.

The new pop order's charts-and-minds campaign not only converted rock critics into pop critics and interpellated indie kids as pop kids in short order, it changed music's very vocabulary. For it was now that 'pop' became a *genre* rather than an abbreviation of 'popular music', hegemonically asserting pop as music's own end of history. While, with its meritocratic base in talent contests, pop's mission, like imperialism's, was ostensibly to spread democracy, imperialism simply expands capitalism's operational terrain, as the Iraq War demonstrated: 'democracy' is the cover story. While the millennial 'mash-up' (e.g. the Strokes/Christina Aguilera's 'A Stroke of Genie-us') was decreed to liberate genres from tribal wars, this only occurred under the flag of the pop hegemon. The visibility of music-industry moguls on *Pop Idol* and *X Factor* and in promos for Pink's grim 2002 'Don't Let Me Get Me' (UK 6; US 8) and Gwen Stefani's great 2004 'What You Waiting For?' (UK 4) was a new foregrounding of pop's power apparatus. Yet judge Simon Cowell signing *X Factor* winners to his management roster was as transparent a demonstration of pop's imperative as the flood of American investors into post-invasion Iraq. Attempts to present resistance to pop as reactionary was thus a reality-defying spin worthy of Alastair Campbell.

Right after 9/11, Kylie Minogue's 'Can't Get You Out of My Head' (UK 1; US 7) launched this pop imperial phase. The track traces the conjunctural transition from cyborg to flexible worker, because, for all the video's futurism, Minogue is *human* here – vulnerable flesh amid the robot dancers' visors and space boots, lines around her eyes not retouched. Likewise, the track's electro-futurism is humanised by dabs of Fordist instrumentation. These human elements are coercive, however, the lyric attesting to pop's imperial power – you can't get it out of your head – while expressing not feeling but *brand*: Kylie's style, her sex appeal, her pop smarts. Public persona was always part of pop culture, but in a homogenised landscape of freelance producers and committee-written songs being passed from artist to artist,[17] a cultivated celebrity was how stars now individuated themselves. Celebrity and imperial pop are thus inseparable, and while Minogue was too private to pursue this strategy, there were plenty more-flexible workers who would. Usher's video for 2001's 'U Got It Bad' (UK 5; US 1), for instance, features his real-life partner, TLC's Chilli, while proffering press commentary on their private life not as a protest but as an assertion of cultural relevance.

Justin Timberlake's immaculate 2002 'Cry Me a River' (UK 2; US 3) triumphantly asserted his post-NSYNC 'brand' by tapping his celebrity persona to connect more closely with his public. With Timbaland's just-weird-enough production rendering pop hip, and Timberlake's yearning falsetto rendering revenge sweet, the song's nastiness ("it's your turn to cry") is nothing compared to the video, whose acted 'ex' marks the spot Britney Spears occupied in Timberlake's life. Only amid peak neoliberalism could hacking into someone's home and home-computer, filming having sex in their bed, then stalking them in the shower be considered to 'humanise' the perpetrator. That it was the *audience* being stalked, their computers that were being hacked, simply felt thrillingly intimate in this gazing and gazed-upon society. It was thus interpellation rather than innovation that was smart about smart-pop and which was imperialist about its imperial phase.

Like Timberlake, Beyoncé also launched her solo career as an assertion of her human factor. The lyric of 2003's fantastic 'Crazy in Love' (UK 1; US 1) proclaimed a loss of emotional control, driven by an organic Chi-Lites horn sample that simply *surged* from speakers in an age of cyborg electronics, while its rap feature was by Beyoncé's rumoured lover Jay-Z. Yet Beyoncé neither *sounds* remotely disempowered, nor looks it in the video, which is essentially a four-minute testimonial to her imperial sexual and celebrity power. 'Crazy in Love' is an assertion of humanity that's really an assertion of hegemony, yet such is the charge of the song's *Matrix*-style harvesting of human energy that the experience of being colonised is curiously thrilling.

If smart-pop's carefully crafted humanisation was key to its hegemony, sometimes the imperial hand showed too prominently through the proxies. Britney Spears' 2002 'Overprotected' (UK 4) attempts to reverse her reputation as what Ewing names a "cyborg hit-delivery system".[18] Yet with Spears declaring her agency – "I need me" – on a track custom-built by men and featuring her customary machine-mangling of the word "me", it's hardly the most persuasive of humanisations. 2007's 'Piece of Me' (UK 2; US 18) is both more persuasively personable in addressing her media presentation ("She's too big, now she's too thin") *and* more post-human – the electro sound, the glitching of Spears' vocals, even the electronic altering of her body in the video (and again, it's written by men).

By contrast, Jennifer Lopez was the model flexible worker – singer, actor, businesswoman and, most contemporary of all, curator of her own celebrity. Over old-school hip-hop beats, Lopez's lyric for 2002's 'Jenny from the Block' (UK 3; US 3) reifies being 'real' as "like breathing", though Lopez's reality in the promo is both mediated – mock paparazzi footage of her and celebrity lover Ben Affleck – and rarefied – lounging on a yacht, shopping for jewels. What Lopez is really announcing is the hegemony of the *capitalist* real. Black Eyed Peas' resident flexible worker Fergie's 2007 'Glamorous' (UK 6; US 1) also wants it both ways: flaunting her "first-class", "fast-lane" diamonds and champagne lifestyle while insisting she's "raw as hell" – it rhymes with "Taco Bell". Only in imperial-phase neoliberalism could product placement front as authenticity, credit due. However, Fergie's refrain "If you ain't got no money, take yo' broke ass home" telegraphs the distinction between celebrity and citizen formerly known as 'class'. This explains such absurdities as gilded Gwen Stefani longing to be a 'Rich Girl' (UK 4; US 7) in 2005 – she's empowering our broke asses. Yet, with both celebrity culture and self-empowerment songs being the products of public *dis*empowerment, these tracks feel more like the victor flaunting the spoils than sharing the wealth.

Celebrities' role as meta-humans made them not just a rarefied elite but representatives of the social whole: ostensibly for better (as neoliberal society's ideal) but, increasingly, for worse. Mariah and Britney's breakdowns, Whitney's lost decade, Eminem's rehab spell, Amy Winehouse's public pain and Pete Doherty's dead man walking were the collateral damage of pop imperialism. Yet, with all publicity being good publicity, celebrity crisis also provided human-interest stories to fuel pop's ruthless war machine. The video for Will Young's 2003 'Leave Right Now' (UK 1) is set at a media opening, with a distraught-looking Young confessing to camera and ignoring the glad-handing and schmoozing as the simmering tensions gradually erupt into violence. While the video presents this as protest, the fact that Young is using the *public* as his confidant means his distress is being deployed as celebrity-culture surplus value. Similarly, Spears' self-written 2004 'Everytime' (UK 1; US 15) was trailed as a response to Timberlake's 'Cry Me a River', but comes across as a cry for *help*, the video showing Spears trapped in the celebrity machine and her publicly pressed private life erupting into violence. The Streets' rehab-set video for 2006's 'When You Wasn't Famous' (UK 8) is as awkward as the track is ungainly, but both its candidness about Skinner's problems and its coyness about an unnamed crack-bingeing pop star fuel the celebrity machine. This, then, reveals the pessimistic underside of poptimism, the systemically destructive impact of celebratory, celebrity-fetishising pop in its imperial phase.

"Can Anyone Write a Protest Song?": Iraq, the Other and Music

When the Manic Street Preachers asked this question on early 2002's 'Let Robeson Sing' (UK 19), the answer appeared to be negative – not least from themselves. This once most political of bands, like many of their peers, remained mute on the War on Terror, and thereafter disengaged from contemporary politics altogether. The politics of the past is always safer ground for reneged radicals, as the Manics' 2004 'The Love of Richard Nixon' (UK 2) revealed. A passive melancholia now replaced political militancy: "With grace we will suffer/With grace we will recover", James Dean Bradfield sighs on the enervated 'There by the Grace of God' (UK 6). Another question asked in 2002, "Can Bono Save the World?", on *Time*'s cover, seemed, amidst U2's unwonted political silence, less ironic than indicative of the neoliberalised media's redundancy.

The Iraq War was a catalyst, however, prompting the first real refusal of the neoliberal order since Seattle. Radiohead's rawly brilliant 2003 '2+2=5' uses Orwellian language to evoke the war as the endpoint of neoliberal operations rather than the detour depicted by centrist apologists (*Hail to the Thief*, UK 1; US 3). "You have not been paying attention", Thom Yorke intones, and no one had – including George Michael, who imagined we'd previously had "democratic" to be "fresh out of" on his dreadful but worthy anti-war song, 'Shoot the Dog' (UK 12). Michael, Ms Dynamite and Coldplay's Chris Martin spoke out against the war at the 2003 Brit Awards. Yet when female country trio the Dixie Chicks, promoting their mildly anti-military 'Travelin' Soldier' (US 25), criticised both the Iraq War and the American president onstage in London that year, they detonated a political furore: a domestic blacklist from country stations, death threats and – worst of all – a feud with Toby Keith.

The political mood was shifting, however. Even as Bush declared "Mission Accomplished" at America's apparently easy victory in spring 2003, Black Eyed Peas' 'Where Is the Love?' (UK 1; US 8) was calling the CIA "terrorists" and dissecting the War on Terror's self/other polarity – "If you only have love for your own race/Then you only leave space to discriminate". Extraordinary stuff in itself, the song also rejects the neoliberal norms the war was defending: "People gets colder, most of us only care about money-makin'". As the Iraqi insurgency rebooted the war, music became increasingly politicised. On Green Day's 2004 'American Idiot' (UK 3), the wordplay of "alien nation" defines America not as its citizens' self but its other, all alienated work and managed consensus. 'Holiday' (UK 11; US 19) shows how those departing that consensus were othered, whether foreign (France) or American ("Kill all the fags that don't agree"). Eminem's dramatic, Dre-produced 2004 'Mosh' (*Encore*, UK 1; US 1) redeemed his previous flippancy, positioning Bin Laden as product of American imperialism, decrying "blood for oil" and rejecting the War on Terror's othering: "Don't matter what colour/All that matters we're gathered together". Yet while it *sounds* like Eminem is inciting revolution – "We gonna fight, we gonna charge, we gonna stomp, we gonna march" – in the video he's leading the masses not to storm the citadels of power but to sign the form at the voting booth. In the ensuing election, Bush was re-elected in a landslide.

As the war dragged on, however, and evidence of torture at Abu Ghraib tarred the hawks, the doves were released, and in 2005 the Dixie Chicks scored their biggest-ever hit with their response to the furore, 'Not Ready to Make Nice' (US 4). While the song addresses the controversy in liberal terms of free speech, the video depicts oil staining everything, while that a "Mother will teach her daughter/That she ought to hate a perfect stranger" reaffirms othering as the ideological oil that powers neoliberalism. In another indicator of the altering climate, Neil Young now changed his tune – if 'tune' rather overstates the case – and created an unlistenable concept album, 2006's *Living with War*, in opposition to Iraq (UK 14; US 15).

The War on Terror's demonisation of Muslims was laterally protested by a profusion of Middle Eastern and Indian sounds invading Western charts and minds. This was the *true* mash-up, complicating the concept of the Western self, with Springsteen using Qawwali singers and Middle Eastern instruments on 2002's 'Worlds Apart', Panjabi MC's 2003 bhangra 'Mundian To Bach Ke' (UK 5) sampling Busta Rhymes, and Jay-Z's remix making the implicit explicit, "We rebellious, we back home, screaming, 'Leave Iraq alone!'" This world-music influence endowed an affirmative otherness even to apolitical songs like Britney's brilliant Bollywood-string-driven 2004 'Toxic' (UK 1; US 9), Black Eyed Peas' Indian-suffused 2005 'Don't Phunk with My Heart' (UK 3; US 3) and 50 Cent's Middle Eastern-orientated 2005 'Candy Shop' (UK 4; US 1).

With the developing world's deserts invading the Western 'real', the sand-strewn video for U2's 2004 'Vertigo' (UK 1) was no coincidence – though given their political silence, it just sits there, scratching. While Gorillaz' cartoon video for their Middle Eastern-infused 'Dirty Harry' (UK 6) is a militarised desert of the *unreal*, the lines "I need a gun to keep myself among/ The poor people who are burning in the sun" questions who most threatens whom in the new world order. With dancehall's popularity representing another developing-world incursion, Bob Marley's son Damian's 2005 'Welcome to Jamrock' (UK 13) stands in solidarity with Iraq, with Babylon relocated from Middle East to Midwest. Sean Paul's spate of hits – 2003's 'Get Busy' (UK 4; US 1); 'Baby Boy' with Beyoncé (UK 2; US 1) – invoke not just Jamaica, but via their jerky Punjabi Diwali *riddim*, the East, a meta-other that's dialectically also the Western self.

America's international war on the other had some considerable domestic form. Critically regarded as frivolous fun, the timing of Outkast's glorious 2003 'Hey Ya!' (UK 3; US 1) is telling. The song not only reverses 60s appropriation of black music, but its video reimagines beat bands as black – alongside their audience of screaming girls. With Islam demonised, critics' hailing of Kanye West's joyous 2004 'Jesus Walks' (UK 16; US 11) as an affirmation of Christianity was politically and aesthetically tin-eared. The track's parade-ground drum, gunshots and the self/other dialectic in "We at war... with terrorism, racism/But most of all we at war with ourselves" makes clear that 'Jesus Walks' is rather more than a hip-hop hymn. The video depicts a black chain gang and white overseer, while the only crosses visible are burning KKK symbols of white supremacy, which symbolically fall to the ground. "We ain't goin' nowhere", West promises.

Preoccupied with the foreign other, Bush's half-hearted response to Hurricane Katrina revealed an enduring elite disregard for the African American self, which West condemned on live television. With Bush boasting the most colour-blind cabinet in US history, West's statement posed awkward questions about the political efficacy of a 'diversity' divorced from economics. U2 and Green Day's 2006 Skids cover 'The Saints Are Coming' (UK 2) was a less racially charged but still critical response to federal conduct of Katrina, its ironic video depicting Iraq troops redeployed to New Orleans attesting to Bush's political priorities. With anti-immigration rhetoric ramped up amid the War on Terror, the White Stripes' assertion on 2007's 'Icky Thump' (UK 2; US 26) that America was a *nation* of others – of immigrants – was politically sound but, like U2 and Green Day, missed a deeper systemic point.

Immigrants, the economically 'left-behind' and what was left of the left were as *other* to imperial-phase neoliberalism as terrorists, or indeed the civilians of 'rogue nations'. This hostile other was routinely posited as covetous of what the neoliberal self possessed – "You're either with us or against us" – an ideology that trickled down from politics into popular culture in attitudes to 'losers' and 'haters'. "You want to hate on me 'cause I'm the one that's chosen", as So Solid Crew put it on winter 2001's 'Haters' (UK 8): note that providential "chosen". This depiction of the competitively hostile other is as audible in the period's positive, self-empowerment songs as in its negative disses, each of which is considered now, in turn.

"Success Is My Only Motherfuckin' Option": The Self-Empowerment Song

Reality TV was a live demonstration of neoliberal democratic 'opportunity', (multi-)cultural 'meritocracy' and 'freedom' as competitive individualism. *Big Brother* (2000–) was driven by informal competition, while the music-focused *Pop Stars* (2001–02) was a formal competition – spinning off into *The Rivals* – and *Pop Idol* (2001) added the public vote to democratically decide the winner. 2002's *Pop Idol* victor Will Young's purpose-built 'Anything Is Possible' (UK 1) is the self-empowerment meta-song, with its self-belief ("I can do anything") in dialectic with the quotidian hostility of the competitive other (less Gareth Gates than "a world full of strangers"). Like its singer, the song is a flexible worker: a love song, a carol of gratitude to 'the people' ("'cause you believe in me") and a hymn to the system that offers such opportunity ("I'll never doubt again"), inspiring the listener to try harder, dream bigger, work more.

While Eminem's mighty 2002 'Lose Yourself' (UK 1; US 1) seems worlds away, it also concerns prevailing in a talent competition. While Eminem's barrier to success is material rather than emotional (his mobile home, his inability to "provide the right life for my family"), he insists that even class can be overcome by individual determination: "do not miss your chance to blow". Eminem being Eminem, he can admit to vulnerability in this strategy, but being "chewed-up and spat out and booed off stage" simply strengthens his Nietzschean will to power. The lyric's language of "opportunity" – "This world is mine for the taking" – harnesses the track's rock aggression as affirmative of, rather than adversarial to, the system.

American Idol-winner Kelly Clarkson's 2004 'Breakaway' (UK 22; US 6) avoids the charged issue of class for the stock 'small town' origin story, where overcoming barriers is again a mere matter of will: "I'll make a wish, take a chance, make a change". Yet the American Dream-come-true of reality TV only enables select 'ordinary' citizens to (often briefly) join the establishment – the system stays the same: endemically stacked, enduringly hierarchical. "Some people wait a lifetime for a moment like this", claims Clarkson on 'A Moment Like This' (US 1), when most will never get *near* such a moment. The song was covered by 2006's *X Factor* winner Leona Lewis (UK 1), accompanied by a video that was effectively an advert for the competition and also for 'competition' as the motor of neoliberal democracy.

This conventional competitiveness increasingly diffused

into alternative rock. Emo-ers Jimmy Eat World's late-2001 'The Middle' (UK 26; US 5) is another will-to-power anthem: barriers are "only in your head", so if you "try everything you can/Everything'll be just fine".[19] Those who weren't just fine had only themselves to blame. Inspired by campaigning with centrist presidential candidate John Kerry, Foo Fighters' 2005 'Best of You' (UK 4; US 18) relays the neoliberal mantra that social problems are caused by insufficient competitiveness ("Is someone getting the best of you?"). Once again, any sense of a system, or indeed of *society*, disappears in the providential individualism of capitalist realism's winners.

With every rapper bar Kanye embodying the African American dream of ghetto-to-glamour, hip-hop was system-built for self-empowerment. "To try and to fail, the two things I hate", raps Jay-Z on the Kanye-produced 'Izzo (H.O.V.A)' (UK 21; US 8), claiming self-empowerment as political: "I do this for my culture". Yet entrepreneurialism as the route to racial equality renders *racism* a losers' discourse rather than a political system, particularly given Jay-Z's hostility to his competitive others. One such other, Nas, was in such unwonted agreement with his nemesis that he bit Jay's kids-choir trick for his own self-empowerment track, 2003's 'I Can' (UK 19; US 12). "I know I can/Be what I wanna be/If I work hard at it", the children chant. Yet with Nas's lyric depicting the kids' African ancestors' being denied American *dignity*, let alone American dreams, racism here is implicitly resolved by willpower and the performance principle. Similarly, 50 Cent's dramatisation of his journey from street hustler to celebrity hitmaker in 2003's *Get Rich or Die Tryin'* is a testimonial that capitalism works – or that crime pays, which comes to the same thing. Again, 50's claim that he's rapping for his "n****s on the block" on 'Many Men (Wish Death)' is undermined by his hostility for the "faggot-ass n***a tryna pull me back".

Developing from UK garage, grime was Britain's answer to gangsta, and likewise began as an oppositional genre: "I'm a problem for Anthony Blair", spits Dizzee Rascal on 'Hold Ya Mouf' on his dazzlingly innovative debut, 2003's *Boy in da Corner* (UK 23). Yet by 2004's 'Dream' (UK 14), Dizzee was also deploying the showtune rap trick – via *South Pacific*'s 'Happy

Talk' – and, like Jay-Z, claiming success as a question of will: "All the youngers cotchin' on the stairs in the flats/You can go far if you put your mind to it". With Kanye lacking poverty to prove himself against, an automobile accident finally gave him the requisite obstacle to overcome and "turn tragedy to triumph". 2003's Chaka Khan-sampling 'Through the Wire' (UK 9; US 15) is rapped through West's wired-up jaw. In 2007, Kanye channelled the post-millennial re-up of Nietzsche (with some help from Daft Punk) in asserting that what doesn't kill him makes him 'Stronger' (UK 1; US 1), boom and bust as an affective mode. With these testimonials treading a thin line between attesting to the system's openness and asserting providential uniqueness ("Bow in the presence of greatness"), Kanye's self-boosting would be mere boasting were it not presented as a spur to others' self-empowerment.

By this token, Eve and Gwen Stefani's announcement that "I've got my foot through the door and I ain't goin' nowhere" on late 2001's Dre-produced 'Let Me Blow Ya Mind' (UK 4; US 2) is an empowerment claim for *all* women. British garagiste Ms Dynamite's delightful 2002 'Dy-Na-Mi-Tee' (UK 5), meanwhile, makes the brag-rap communal, vividly depicting going "through all the things a teenage girl goes through" and now making "beats for the streets". Although it's more inspiring than the male equivalent, this is still a restatement of empowered individualism. Similarly, while the vibe and the video for Sugababes' seductive 2002 'Stronger' (UK 7) is collective, its punchline is "I'm going to do this for me". While Christina Aguilera's 2002 power ballad 'Beautiful' (UK 1; US 2) is intended to be inspirational, to insist that "I am beautiful, in every single way" sounds narcissistic (not to mention embracing patriarchal criteria of female value), even when expanded in the last chorus to "we". Aguilera's harnessing of rock aggression to self-empowerment on 2003's 'Fighter' (UK 3; US 20) – with Jane's Addiction guitarist Dave Navarro – would be more effective were her words not so unwieldy: "'Cause if it wasn't for all that you tried to do/I wouldn't know just how capable/I am to pull through".

Kelis's 2007 ''Lil Star' (UK 3) stages a debate between self-defeat – "There is nothing special about me", she laments – and self-empowerment, via CeeLo's motivational chorus. "Just keep trying and trying", he coos, echoing the promise of reality TV: "You sure look like a star to me". The contrivance of meta-human celebrities performing 'ordinariness' attests to self-empowerment's spuriousness. As wages stagnated and the cost of living rose, society's losers, left-behinds, its homeless and its haters were the waste material of Western 'freedom'. That their predicament should be framed as a personal rather than political failure added insult to their injuries. Indeed, Žižek argues that Giorgio Agamben's conceptual category of *homo sacer* – those "excluded from the human community" – was expanded in this era of perpetual war against the other.[20] You could see and hear this not just in the cultural framing of 'losers', but increasingly in responses to business rivals, ex-lovers and internet interlocutors.

"Brush the Dirt off Your Shoulder": The Other-Disempowering Diss

The factor-X of reality TV contests was cruelty, a conventionalisation of neoliberal ideology's hostile environment. Although this cruelty was exclusively that of the shows' judges – the elite – it was always the competitive other that was posited as antagonistic in popular culture and towards whom adversarial energy was directed, rather than the establishment. This represented a soft-power iteration of 'divide and rule', while the real locus of ordinary people's power – solidarity – was almost unknown in this era.[21] Jay-Z's 2004 'Dirt off Your Shoulder' (UK 12; US 5) moves seamlessly from a residual reminder that he "came from the bottom of the bottom", to its hook's articulation of the other as mere dirt to be brushed off your clothes. Rendered anthemic by an ebullient Timbaland beat, Jay-Z's dirt-brushing gesture in the video was widely imitated by the system's upholders: politicians. Centrism's 'flexible worker' model of citizenship had thus absorbed the cyborg's jettisoning of human empathy.

The business-end of such othering was presented by the rap diss-track. The feuds between Jay-Z and Nas, and Ja Rule and 50 Cent, were an aggressive means of branding in a competitive marketplace, where each new release was now a 'comeback', every style-change a 'reboot'. The gun metaphor also captures the popping and capping of this brutal form of banter – "Pop it like it's hot" – a performative version of the drive-by disses that put Tupac and Biggie permanently out of business. Yet the co-option of hip-hop beef as business was demonstrated by Jay and Nas's decision to swap collision for collaboration – it's all publicity, it's all good. Celebrity diffusion of this misanthropic demotic through the diss-track hardly defused the streets' black-on-black violence, however, the othering of the African American self. M.O.P.'s 2001 party jam 'Cold as Ice' (UK 4) renders the rebuke of its Foreigner sample a rebarbative boast: "I'll bury you bastards, I custom-make caskets… get placed in a bodybag, with that ass zipped up". DMX's 2002 'X Gon' Give It to Ya' (UK 6) refers not to gifts of genitals but of bullets, while even Cam'Ron's concurrent slow jam 'Oh Boy' (UK 13; US 4) comes with a body count of brothers.

The mainstreaming of misanthropy had been exponential since the 80s, but misogyny has a rather longer history, with sisters long singled out as the original sinners (rapper Eve all too pertinently named). Ludacris's late-2001 'Area Codes' (UK 25; US 24) has hilarious fun with neologisms like "hoe-liday" and "hoe-roscope", while the reliably vile 50 Cent reduces women to commodities on 2003's 'P.I.M.P.' (UK 5; US 3) – "Man, bitches come and go, every n***a pimpin' know" – gender-built for sexual obsolescence.[22] Even Outkast's Andre 3000 lets forth a torrent of "bitches" on 2004's 'Roses' (UK 4; US 9), as he wishes violent death on his ex. These songs' assignment of malignity and covetousness to women renders half the population *homo sacer*: beyond empathy. Hence 50 Cent's 2002 'Wanksta' (US 13) bristling, "She tryin' to get in my pockets, homie, and I ain't gon' let her", Ludacris ludicrously presenting child support as venality on 2002's 'Move Bitch' (US 10) and Kanye and Jamie Foxx's grievous 2005 'Gold Digger" (UK 2; US 1). Testament to the conventionalisation of cruelty – and the distance still to travel for female equality – the critical and public uproar against these othering songs was non-existent.

Such an argument shouldn't single out hip-hop: the Strokes' entire shtick was a misanthropic individualism – "Alone we stand, together we fall apart!" ('Someday', UK 27) – that regularly tilted into misogyny ('Last Nite', UK 14), living up to the title of 2003's 'Reptilia' (UK 17). On metrosexuals the Killers' 2003 'Mr

Brightside' (UK 10; US 10), the privileging of the patriarchal gaze transforms male paranoia into female reality – Eve's original sin again. This misogynist move is repeated by emo sensitivos Fall Out Boy's 2005 'Sugar, We're Goin' Down' (UK 8; US 8): "I'm just a notch in your bedpost, but you're just a line in a song". Equally, the reptilian affect of Dizzee Rascal's 2003 'I Luv U' (UK 29) gets rather overlooked in his critical adulation: "It's a real shame you got had by the whores/It's a shame that kid probably ain't yours". The video for Timberlake and Timbaland's 2006 'What Goes Around… Comes Around' (UK 4; US 1) literalises 'Roses', with Scarlett Johansson's cheating ex killed in a car crash, and Timberlake's sick smirk as he sings, "You got what you deserved", the "dirty, obscene underside" of post-millennial pop. The pair manage to top this on Timbaland's 2007 'Give It to Me' (UK 1; US 1), Justin blaming Janet Jackson for humiliating her at the 2004 Superbowl, while even nice Nelly Furtado lays into the inoffensive Fergie.

Sisterly solidarity here is a casualty of competitive individualism. Avril Lavigne's 2002 'Sk8r Boi' (UK 8; US 10) steals the centrist move of spinning the reactionary as progressive. She loves the scruffy "skater boi" the normie girl disdains, but then he gets famous – so *ha*! Lavigne's 2007 'Girlfriend' (UK 2; US 1) reveals how such schoolyard cruelty has become social reality: "She's, like, so whatever/You could do so much better". Kelis's marvellous 2004 'Milkshake' (UK 2; US 3) also invokes the schoolyard, while dispiritingly equating female self-assertion with competition ("Damn right, it's better than yours"). 'Milkshake' was written and produced by men (the Neptunes), as was the Pussycat Dolls' 2005 'Don't Cha' (UK 1; US 2) (by CeeLo), which taunts, "Bet you wish your girlfriend was…" hot/a freak/raw/fun like the Dolls' Nicole Scherzinger. Given such a hypersexualised 'raunch culture', the exasperation of Pink's 2006 'Stupid Girls' (UK 4; US 13) is understandable, but its itemisation of triviality, attention-seeking and sluttishness is entirely un-sisterly. "What happened to the dream of a girl president?" Pink tuts, "She's dancing in the video next to 50 Cent". Pink's feminism disregards patriarchy as a *system*, where again, '*you* decide' what you derive from life's talent competition.

The kiss-off to the straying male ex, exemplified by Joss

Stone's 2004 'You Had Me' (UK 9), was claimed as female empowerment but was a falsification of feminism. Kelly Clarkson's 2004 breakup song 'Since U Been Gone' (UK 5; US 2) mimics both the Strokes' guitar sound and their misanthropy to jeer, "Thanks to you/Now I get what I want". Like the growth of brokers betting *against* stocks, a loss has become a net win. More vengefully, Lisa Kekaula and Basement Jaxx's 2004 'Good Luck' (UK 12) gloats, "You'll end up old and lonely/If you don't get a bullet in your head". Lily Allen's 2006 'Smile' (UK 1) is simply vindictive – "When I see you cry/Yeah, it makes me smile" – with the video depicting her laughing as her ex is beaten up and has his flat wrecked. Beyoncé's 2006 'Irreplaceable' (UK 4; US 1) sneers at her lover-turned-scrub, "It's my name that's on that Jag/So remove your bags, let me call you a cab". These songs perpetuate sexual relationships as an existential competitiveness, a zero-sum game, the empowerment of one necessitating the disempowerment of the other. Amidst this othering of individual, flawed, men, patriarchy itself remains untroubled.

Such confusions arise because centrist social liberalism treats structural divisions as either resolved – reducing oppression to individual experience, prejudice to individual choice – or as cultural rather than political, as with class. The depiction of the working class in the *Catherine Tate Show* (2004–07) and *Little Britain* (2003–06) as "the feckless poor and the malingering disabled", in David Alderson's words,[23] (thus as *homo sacer*), constructs an observing self which is middle class, metropolitan and 'civilised' (*homo superior*). This provides ideological justification for both the economic exclusion of the working- and under-class other *and* the economic success of the middle-class self. "The demonization of the working class is the ridiculing of the conquered by the conqueror", as Owen Jones puts it.[24] Indie's reneging on its radical origins was confirmed by it partaking in such bourgeois shoulder-brushing. The video for the expensively schooled Strokes' 2004 'The End Has No End' (UK 27) conveys hipster condescension to the state-educated: it's the individual themselves "keeping you dumb", not politics or the media. *You* decide.

Britain's Kaiser Chiefs' 2004 'I Predict a Riot' (UK 22) casts a middle-class gaze on a working-class Saturday night via stock 'chav' stereotypes: aggressive, track-suited men, whoreish "floozies", with "If it wasn't for chip fat, they'd be frozen" the hoariest cliché of all. The song's middle-class self is defined by the achingly twee phraseology ("It's not very pretty, I tell thee") and its pert piety ("They're not very sensible, really").[25] Alderson argues that the joke of *Little Britain*'s "only gay in the village" – that Daffyd is fighting battles that have already been won – "undermines the legitimacy of protest or complaint".[26] Kaiser Chiefs' terming the everyday culture of denigrated *homo sacer* a "riot" places the discontent of the dispossessed beyond 'civilised' behaviour. In an age of race riots and anti-globalism protests, technocratic politicians could thus brush such dirt off their shoulders.

The term 'reboot' recurred throughout the 2000s, applied to commercial enterprises, film franchises and flexible workers alike. "If you got glitches in your life-computer, turn it off and then reboot it", Andre 3000 recommends on Kelis's 2004 'Millionaire' (UK 3). However, rebooting only restores a computer to its pre-malfunctioning state: it doesn't renew it. 'Reboot' is an apt term for post-millennial neoliberal politics, therefore, with its cancelled future, its perpetual presentism, its institutional consolidation and its spinning of stasis as progress. Operation Iraqi Freedom was thus the mother of all reboots for a stalled system, despite the war's – and the war leaders' – increasing unpopularity. There was no alternative.

Amidst neoliberal hegemony, pop's rare expressions of discomfort at the conjuncture had an air of resignation. Kanye's 2004 'All Falls Down' (UK 10; US 7) rues being "addicted to retail", while itemising his expenditure and product-placing his own merchandise. Although West attempts to give this a racial dimension – "We floss because they degrade us" – he's aware that, from crack to sneakers, "white man get paid off of all of that". Internet-sensation Sandi Thom's 2005 'I Wish I Was a Punk Rocker (With Flowers in My Hair)' (UK 1) mashes up history to summon a meta-past "when revolution was in the air", rather than the contemporary "world that doesn't care". It's neither a great song nor a particularly pointed protest, without the depth to achieve hauntology. Yet that it got so pilloried by the liberal press spoke volumes about the agendas of the guardians of centrism.[27]

In what Žižek calls "post-politics",[28] Iraq functioned as a metaphor as much as a material illustration of politics' distance from ordinary people, a problem for professional politicos and their media peers, unrelated to the real world of networking, producing and consuming. The video for Gorillaz' 2005 'Feel Good Inc.' (UK 2; US 14) presents a surveilled populace narcoticised by corporate entertainment, immune to the megaphoned incitement of activists. On Arcade Fire's electric, surging 2005 'Neighbourhood #3 (Power Out)' (UK 26) the imprecation "Don't have any dreams, don't have any plans" is a hipster variant on Coldplay's "Some things you have to believe/ But others are puzzles, puzzling me" on the same year's flaccid 'Speed of Sound' (UK 2; US 8). On another stadium indie song, the cosy melancholy of Snow Patrol's 2006 'Chasing Cars' (UK 6; US 5) advocates withdrawal from the political sphere – "We don't need anything or anyone… forget the world". The video depicts singer Gary Lightbody symbolically flat on his back – in a street, in an underground station, by a motorway – passive, as the world speeds indifferently by.

Such political disengagement was the perspective of the system's middle-class winners; the structure of feeling of the growing hordes of losers, haters and *homo sacer* being somewhat different. Scary, masked nu-metallers Slipknot invoke a soon-to-be-familiar phrase on late-2001's 'Left Behind' (UK 24), capturing a disdained demographic whose churning *ressentiment* is expressed on 'Duality' (UK 15) – "All I do is live with so much hate" – and spills out into the accompanying video of their fans tearing a suburban house apart, plank by plank. Pop it like it's hot. The spokesman of the excluded, Eminem claims on 2002's 'Cleanin' Out My Closet' (UK 4; US 4) that "If I could capture the rage of today's youth and bottle it…" What came next wasn't clear, however, and Žižek argued that fascism was the more likely result of the era's accruing resentments than revolution.[29] If Žižek was premature in this prediction of where the heat would pop, he wasn't the only one looking the wrong way. Because, for all this era's defensive othering – of Muslims, of women, of the working class – the next crisis wouldn't come from the envious, resentful other but from within the complacent self of centrist neoliberalism.

Chapter 12

"Go Out and Smash It": The Financial Crash and Austerity Pop (2008–15)

The collapse of the West's entire financial system in 2007–08 was, in the era's terminology, an 'epic fail', the worst economic crisis since the Wall Street Crash in 1929. Despite the crash being the direct consequence of centrist deregulation, the elites, having gained better control of the news cycle since Iraq, made the story the economy's rebuilding as much as its collapse. This enabled the new leaders of the Western world, Gordon Brown and Barack Obama – deregulation's architect and supporter respectively – to become the crash's heroes, and a few 'rogue traders' and 'predatory lenders' its villains. Crisis was thus conventionalised, establishing, in Streeck's words, "disequilibrium and instability [as] the rule rather than the exception",[1] thereby 'resolving' capitalism's enduring contradiction of boom and bust. For, in an approach that Naomi Klein named "disaster capitalism",[2] crisis – a war, a hurricane, a financial crash – enables the capitalisation of chaos, a loss to become a net win, the damage to be recycled back into the system. Or as Katy Perry put it on 2010's 'Firework' (UK 3; US 1): "After a hurricane comes a rainbow". Disaster capitalism was absorbed as a cultural structure of feeling, with this period's pop regularly citing Kanye's – and Nietzsche's – assertion that "What doesn't kill you makes you stronger". On Kelly Clarkson's 2012 'Stronger' (UK 8;

US 1), she insists she'll "come back swinging" after a breakup, her emotional loss capitalised as a net win.

While the elite thrived on disaster capitalism, doubling its wealth over the next decade,[3] the public, forced to pay for the crash by a swingeing, service-slashing austerity, simply survived. A year after its public-funded bailout, Goldman Sachs awarded its executives huge bonuses, with other banks following suit, just as Britain's privatised Network Rail was revealed to be costing the public five times what the state-owned service had. The public had been paying for the free market all along: who knew? In short order thereafter, a 2009 climate summit confirmed capital wouldn't be held accountable for an ecological emergency requiring rather more than recycling, Obama failed to introduce equal access to healthcare, and a damning British 2010 income disparity study was deemed unworthy of action. Yet, when Britain's cities erupted into riots in 2011, the governing coalition condemned this as "criminality", with draconian prison sentences dealt out accordingly. Moreover, the success of TV's *Keeping Up with the Kardashians* (2007–21), *The Apprentice* (2004–17) and *Dragons' Den* (2005–) indicated apparent acceptance of the financial and regulatory disparity between elites and citizenry, and the endurance of the idea that willpower was all it took to overcome it.

Capitalism is neither omniscient nor omnipotent, however, and the flaw in Klein's thesis is that it makes too neat a drama out of a crisis, positing capitalism as intentionalist rather than opportunist. In this regard, the musical elite's confusion following the crash is revealing. "There's only two types of people in the world", Britney Spears asserts on 2008's 'Circus' (UK 13; US 3), "the ones that entertain, and the ones that observe", thereby affirming a natural order of inequality, the social contract 2.0. A fall 2008 summit of hip-hop's establishment on Jay-Z, T.I., Kanye and Lil Wayne's 'Swagga Like Us' (US 5) co-opted M.I.A.'s anti-establishment 'Paper Planes' to assert their property rights (while removing the cocking guns and ringing tills from the original). Kanye, having "slaved" – and read his Hegel – claims he deserves to be the "master", while Jay-Z's claim that "you can't buy class" asserts his preferment as providential. A subsequent 2009 summit between Jay-Z, Kanye and Rihanna upped the elite swagga, claiming to 'Run This Town' (UK 1; US 2), while flossing about living "the life everybody ask for" on "Millionaires' Row". If the video suggests some defensiveness, with the public portrayed as a baying mob, Rihanna's deadpan, dead-eyed purr of, "Life's a game, but it's not fair", jettisons all pretence of a meritocracy. Indeed, Rihanna's 2009 'Hard' video (US 8) presents her armed with sheer tights and a machine gun, insisting she'll defend her "need" for "the money, the cars, the clothes; the fame". Post-crash, the haters have become the elite's public rather than, as previously, their peers. Marx calls this a 'class system'.

"As of late, a lot of shit been goin' sideways", Canadian rapper Drake complains on his second hit, 2009's 'Successful' (US 17). Viewing the conjuncture personally rather than politically, Drake is simply peeved that, following the crash, he's being denied the respect he feels is his due: "Y'all don't get it, do you?", he seethes on 2011's 'The Motto' (US 14). At least Drake merely misdiagnoses the problem – indie poppers OneRepublic, on 2010's 'Good Life' (US 8), deny there *is* one: "Please tell me what there's to complain about?" Insulated in the celebrity club even *after* his assault on Rihanna, Chris Brown sneers at those left out in the cold on 2011's 'Look at Me Now' (US 6): "I don't see how you can hate from outside of the club/You can't even get in!" Lil Wayne's guest-rap, meanwhile, does a Marie Antoinette: "If you ain't eatin', call a waiter". When the public proved uncompliant with such privileged complacency and Britain erupted in riots for five days in 2011, panic about who ran these towns resulted in the elite and their middle-class enablers demanding the military be called in to crush the masses.

A more effective means of pacifying the public came in the form of a phalanx of less flossy, more 'ordinary' stars, with newcomers Adele, Ed Sheeran, Ellie Goulding and 2009 *Britain's Got Talent* winner Susan Boyle all being 'relatable' celebrities. Having overcome crisis themselves – be that economic, mental or physical – these ordinary stars were living demonstrations of disaster capitalism's 'resilience mode' (to adapt Robin James' concept of "resilience discourse").[4] "Don't say victim", *X Factor* winner Leona Lewis chides on 2009's 'Happy' (UK 2): "So what if it hurts me?/So what if this world just throws me off the edge?" Rather than invoking Traverso's distinction between the vanquished and the victim, victimhood here is being valorised as victory, loss as net win. Likewise, Adele's riproaring 2011 'Rolling in the Deep' (UK 2; US 1) transforms heartbreak into heroism via the gospel soar of her vocal – redemption in the crucible of crisis – and the push of the track's aggressively assertive drums. Jessie J's 2011 overwrought acoustic ballad 'Who You Are' (UK 8) insists "Tears don't mean you're losing/Everybody's bruising". The video depicts Jessie besieged by indoor rain, wind and lightning, while she remains stoic, broken but unbowed. Although this return of affect was a win after the detachment of the previous conjuncture, its co-option into such coercively pacifying 'emoting' – rather than, say, protest – was a net loss.

Another of these 'ordinary' stars, Katy Perry expanded her bubblegum brand with a resilience-mode hat trick. 2012's ravey, Max Martin-produced 'Part of Me' (UK 1; US 1) served triple duty as a kiss-off to Perry's ex Russell Brand, to her critics and to crisis: "Throw your bombs and your blows/But you're not gonna break my soul". On electropop power ballad 'Wide Awake' (UK 9; US 2), Perry is "born again out of the lion's den", while punching out Prince Charming in the video (no fairytale utopianism for *her*). On 2013's arena-pop 'Roar' (UK 1; US 1), emotional damage has taken Perry "from zero to my own hero", with the video featuring her as survivalist in a jungle that, unlike capitalism's jungle, is welcoming, cooperative, *cute*.

Having also previously presented herself as 'ordinary', Taylor Swift's brilliant 2014, Martin-produced electropop rebrand 'Blank Space' (UK 4; US 1) transcends its troll of her critics to enact a value-added resilience mode. As an emotionally damaged Swift welcomes her latest lover into her life, the chorus's "Because we're young and we're reckless/We'll take this way too far" positions the pair as traders in emotional futures, embracing risk, with the losses ("a nasty scar") fed back into the system as part of "the game". And because "you love the game" – "you" being both the lover and the public – the affective cycle of boom and bust will go round again. A new lover drives up at the video's end.[5]

This resilience mode has three formal mechanisms: audible Auto-Tune, the 'woah-oh' refrain and the build-breakdown-revival sequence of EDM (electronic dance music). Auto-

Tune was developed to repair the problem of uneven pitching, which can make a vocal sound uncertain, vulnerable. Cher's 'Believe' creatively misused this as a sound effect, making the repair process audible on a song denying a breakup's damage. Auto-Tune disguised Kanye West's dodgy pitching on 2008's *808s & Heartbreak* (UK 11; US 1), but its misuse now deliberately foregrounded the original damage – as if he was being punched in the throat mid-song – while also audibly 'solving' it. Vulnerability is thus valedictory, with Auto-Tune temporally compressing the affective cycle of bust and boom. There's no question this was hugely influential in hip-hop, but the more interesting question is *why* West's use of Auto-Tune resonated where T-Pain's upbeat usage didn't.[6] While not all artists experienced Kanye's emotional crash, the effects of the economic crash were widely visible, thus Auto-Tune's resilience mode becoming so widely audible.

The woah-oh refrain could be called 'the Coldplay effect' – for instance, 2011's 'Paradise' (UK 1; US 15, from 2:00-2:30) – were it not derived from Coldplay's own influences, the Police and U2's transformation of post-punk refusal into 80s stadium-pop affirmation. With no tricky words to remember, the woah-oh refrain is an easy prompt for audience participation, temporarily empowering the masses in pseudo-collectivity. Indeed the refrain was a unifying factor across austerity's popular music, and can be heard on Swedish House Mafia's 2011 'Save the World' (UK 10), *X Factor* boyband One Direction's 2012 'Live While We're Young' (UK 3; US 3) and Wiz Khalifa and Charlie Puth's 2015 lighters-aloft hip-pop ballad 'See You Again' (UK 1; US 1). That Coldplay's music gradually merged with EDM in this era is no accident. 2014's Avicii-produced 'A Sky Full of Stars' (UK 9; US 10) is a meta-resilience song: while the narrator is torn apart, he still has "such a heavenly view".

Dance music has always soundtracked recession – disco after the oil shock; acid house after Black Monday and, following the crash, EDM. Essentially a 90s revival, EDM's rebranding from 'trance' distanced it not just from drugs, as Reynolds notes,[7] but from rave's refusal – and, crucially, its utopianism. James argues that EDM's tension-generating builds ('the soar'), abrupt breakdowns (when the beat crashes out) and euphoric regeneration ('the drop'), once the beat kicks back in, enact the capitalist economy's cyclical "crises and overcomings".[8] On EDM kingpin David Guetta's 2007 'Love Is Gone' (UK 9), the EDM cycle thus 'solves' the damage of vocalist Chris Willis's heartbreak, which is paralleled by the resilience mode narrative of its diner-set video.

The ultimate genre of the post-crash era, EDM embraced both resilience and 'ordinariness'. One of the first EDM/pop crossovers, Rihanna's 'Don't Stop the Music' (UK 4; US 3) hit the charts as Britain's Northern Rock hit the rocks in late 2007, and the video shows Rihanna as part of a gang of ordinary female clubbers. When Rihanna addresses the DJ directly, demanding he help "shake the stress away", it's as part of the crowd, and this empathy between artist and audience, celebrity and citizen would become a feature of the genre. EDM empowered the crowd, with everyone cheering at the breakdown – *collapse* becoming the sound of life lived to the full – then whooping victoriously as the beat drop resolved the crisis.[9] In the video for Calvin Harris and Alesso's 'Under Control' (UK 1), the end of the world is enacted as a club narrative – steady build up, abrupt breakdown, a long, tension-building pause… before, finally, the crisis is resolved, the beat drops, the earth lives another day and everybody dances. With most EDM videos set in clubs full of ordinary hedonists, the austerity consensus was thus an affirmative collectivity: "We're all in it together", as Britain's chancellor George Osborne asserted.

Rather, with the Liberal Democrats joining the Conservatives in Britain's coalition government and Labour supporting austerity, politics itself seemed like a club – an elite one, safe behind the class system's velvet rope. Prime minister David Cameron's 'Big Society' reasserted the logic of austerity: that the public had to fend for themselves, his 'society' thus a small, mean thing. Even as Danny Boyle's epic 2012 Olympics ceremony celebrated the welfare state's cornerstone, the NHS, the coalition was pushing through the regressive Welfare Reform Act – and Labour was abstaining. With the Olympic ceremony also starring paradigmatic crisis-survivor James Bond as a symbol of plucky Britishness, Adele's darkly uplifting theme for *Skyfall* (UK 2; US 8), weeks later, was a hymn to resilience amidst recession, a carol to calm amid crisis.[10] "When it crumbles", she intones, "We will stand tall/Face it all together". Osborne couldn't have put it better.

In the back-to-front logic of the era, we were constantly being told things were "that next shit now" when they weren't: from Barack Obama to Lady Gaga to, in this case, Black Eyed Peas' overheated claim for 'Boom Boom Pow' (UK 1; US 1). In reverse order, these were rather good, reheated electro, an adroitly cartoonish recycling of Madonna and competent centrism with value-added drone-bombing. These figures moved nothing forward, particularly not, in the case of the first African American president, African American communities.[11] If anything, between the raids on the back catalogue and on the welfare state, we were moving *backwards* as a society.

Where, under Fordism the proletariat had been powerful, neoliberalism – exacerbated by the credit crunch – created a new 'precariat', that, in 2013's Great British Class survey, accounted for 15% of Britain's population. Klein calls this group "the disposable poor".[12] Maligned in the media as malingering 'chavs' and criminal 'hoodies', such emphasis on a 'culture of poverty' denied both political responsibility and human empathy for such anti-social *homo sacer*. As Owen Jones observed: "Demonizing people at the bottom has been a convenient way of justifying an unequal society throughout the ages".[13] Even the deification of Cheryl Cole, Rhian E. Jones points out, entailed a dialectical denigration of her class origins.[14] Meanwhile, ageing, economically insulated Fordist proletarians (14%) – not yet known as 'gammons' – nursed a growing resentment about the decay of their environments and depletion of their services. Soon after this survey, Cameron quietly dropped the 'Big Society'.

With the left failing to offer an adequate critique of neoliberalism in the crash's wake, the right stepped into the ideological breach. The reactionary US Tea Party (from 2009) and the racist UKIP (breaking through from 2013) articulated a politics of resentment focusing on the 'cosmopolitan elite' and the racial other – conveniently combined in America in the figure of Barack Obama. UKIP didn't just gain traction in decimated post-industrial areas but underwrote the media's racialised response to the 'England riots', the coalition's rubbishing of multiculturalism and 'migrants' and the historic ignominy of Labour's 'Controls on Immigration' mugs. Despite the 'post-racial' diversity represented by the Obamas and the Olympics, it was notable that austerity's 'ordinary' new stars were mostly white, while hip-hop, R&B and grime effectively disappeared as distinct, commercially viable genres during this period.

Feminism also appeared to be in retreat: thus Chris Brown still having a career, Kanye rapping about "raping the game" without kickback and Robin Thicke and Pharrell's 2013 'Blurred Lines' (UK 1; US 1) getting a free pass on an assault on sexual consent (long before knowledge of Thicke's sexual assault of Emily Ratajkowski). Meanwhile, the poster girl for post-millennial feminism, Beyoncé's 2008 'Single Ladies (Put a Ring on It)' (UK 7; US 1) simply recycled the social damage of the single woman ("it") into the heteronormative system ("a ring"). While the success of a female rapper was a feminist statement, Nicki Minaj's lines on Guetta's 'Hey Mama' (UK 9; US 8) – "Yes, I do the cooking/Yes, I do the cleaning… Yes, you be the boss/ Yes, I be respecting" – could have come from 1954 rather than 2014 (were it not for the video's twerking). Meanwhile, although gay marriage was legalised in this era, queers largely disappeared from popular culture. *Will and Grace* was dropped from schedules from 2007 to 2017, Mika's brief chart glory hardly constituted 'diversity' (and was over by 2009), while Sam Smith only publicly identified as gay from 2014.

The political situation after the crash seemed, initially, irredeemable, with no formal political opposition to austerity, the riots recycled into a law-and-order agenda and student protests and Occupy fizzling out without obvious achievements. Amidst austerity, disaster capitalism produced a disaster politics that enabled, funded and span the system's destructive dynamism as the way of the world. Yet no hegemony is ever complete, and new possibilities did emerge from the crash's wreckage – and not just for disaster capitalism – impulses that were contradictory, sometimes confused, but which still represented a looming change in the Long 90s' political consensus.

"Yo, We're Living in the Years of the Credit Crunch": The Crash and the Charts

In the crash's demoralised aftermath, Coldplay's spring 2008 'Violet Hill' (UK 8) was one of the first songs to acknowledge what had occurred. It invokes a world run by a "carnival of idiots", where "the banks became cathedrals" and the elite watch from their citadels as the masses freeze in the streets. However, on Coldplay's string-charged, war-drum-driven 'Viva La Vida' that summer (UK 1; US 1), the elite has been deposed by the revolution and – sung in the first person – the track is more empathetic than antipathetic to the rulers, "that was when I ruled the world" sounding downright elegiac. Such a liberal recoil from the radical would soon become very familiar.

Lil Wayne's summer 2008 'Got Money' (US 10) is ostensibly just another hip-hop jam about a baller flashing his bankroll at 'da club', but the video reframes it, featuring Wayne as a bank robber, who's applauded as he's arrested and throws the public the liberated loot. Wiley's late 2008 showtune-grime 'Cash in My Pocket' (UK 18) performs a similar trick: the song's venality in saluting "skrilla in my wallet" becomes satirical when camply mimed by data-traders in its one-take video. Just as Dizzee Rascal appeared to have cashed in his potential (see: 'Holiday', UK 1), he released late 2009's 'Dirtee Cash' (UK 10), whose identification of the political moment titles this section. Although Dizzee's analysis – "So they got bad credit livin' on direct debit" – risks blaming the "livin' large" public for capitalism's mess, he rightly predicts a recession and empathetically asserts that he remembers what "the bottom" looks like. Travie McCoy and Bruno Mars' 2010 hip-hop reggae 'Billionaire' (UK 3; US 4) is another recognition of the recession, and while it posits celebrity philanthropy as the solution, such confusion is comprehensible when the state, as per McCoy's invocation of Katrina, is the enabler of disaster capitalism.

As Coldplay's ambivalent interventions suggest, indie-rock was now making a tentative return to its social responsibilities. Always the exponents of the 'ordinary' – sonically, visually, conceptually – the National's 2010 'Bloodbuzz Ohio' summons the shaky superstructures of debt and derivatives now crashing down on ordinary Americans: "I still owe money/To the money/ To the money I owe" (*High Violet*, UK 5; US 3.) For many, the credit crunch came in the form of foreclosures, as the noughties' nexus of speculative home-building and unsustainable mortgages collapsed in the subprime crisis that's captured on Arcade Fire's 2010 *The Suburbs* (UK 1; US 1). "When we watched the markets crash/The promises we made were torn", laments the perennially forlorn-sounding Win Butler on 'Half Light (No Celebration)'. The bursting of the suburban building bubble represented the final collapse of residual Fordist dreams of security and social mobility, reverse-engineered by post-Fordist risk-addiction, with suburban poverty increasing by 64% across the 2000s.[15] As Jameson notes, from enclosure to foreclosure, capitalism has been one long land grab: the dispossession of the public by the private, of the ordinary by the elite.[16]

When protests against this latest land grab finally erupted in 2010 with Britain's student demonstrations, and again in 2011 with America's Occupy Wall Street, Britain's huge Stop the Cuts march and riots across the UK, they all enacted a ritualistic repossession of public space. With Occupy claiming to represent "the 99%" in opposition to the elite "1%", these movements were the dispossessed reclaiming what was theirs. It wasn't just a matter of *demonstration* – bodies on the ground – but of occupation: reclaiming rather than requesting. Students occupied Conservative HQ, Stop the Cuts culminated in invasions of businesses and banks, and Occupy created an encampment in New York's Zuccotti Park for three months. All these occupations were forcibly ejected by the custodians of capitalist order.

Rather than now-compromised grime, it was another garage derivative, kinetic, innovative dubstep, which captured the roiling tension that resulted in Britain's riots. You can hear it in the language of Magnetic Man's 2010 'I Need Air' (UK 10) – "making me blow", "suffocate", "losin'" – in the circling tension of its 3-against-4 rhythm and in its emphasis, again, on space: sonic, physical, emotional. You can see it in the video for Magnetic Man and Katy B's edgy collaboration, 'Perfect Stranger' (UK 16), with its face-off between estate residents and police. Emanating from the same sink estates as dubstep (and grime), blue-eyed

B-boy turned soulboy Plan B's 2012 'Ill Manors' (UK 6) presents a tableau of austerity Britain's decimated public space. He mocks this space's demonisation by politicians as a "jungle" of "illegal migrants" and "chavs", and their presentation of the riots as a cultural rather than political concern. Rather than being a passive protest, Plan B asserts class ownership of this space, and articulates its accumulating class threat: "We're poor round here", he hisses, "run home and lock your door".

These eruptions of public resistance prompted a more rebarbative reaction to the crash from indie-pop, its new radicalism somewhat countered by its sonic containment within Coldplay's stadium-indie conventions. Imagine Dragons' 2012 'Radioactive' (UK 12; US 3) is virtually an answer-track to 'Viva La Vida', with a huge woah-oh refrain and a revolution-themed video – except the Dragons are unequivocally on the side of the dispossessed. The collapsed city in Bastille's equally Coldplay-esque 2013 'Pompeii' (UK 2; US 5) is clearly a crash metaphor, with singer Dan Smith asking, "Does it almost feel like nothing changed at all?", and his repeated assertion that we're clearing "rubble" rather than "sins" suggesting the ongoing repair of the existing system rather than a systemic rethink. The similarly Coldplay-esque OneRepublic redeem themselves on 2013's 'Counting Stars' (UK 1; US 2), with its evocation of the anxiety visited upon the public ("Lately I've been losing sleep") and satire of financiers: "Take that money, watch it burn". Again, however, there's a liberal recoil, the refrain returning to Nietzsche/Kanye: "Everything that kills me makes me feel alive". For all such inchoateness, there was, by the 2010s, an increasing understanding that the crash wasn't just another crisis, to be processed and recycled, but the faultline of a failing system insulating the elite 99%, while leaving the ordinary 1% exposed.

'Someone like You': 'Ordinariness' in Post-Crash Pop

While the post-crash discourse of 'ordinariness' clearly related to class, it did so in cautious and contradictory ways. When grimester Tinie Tempah attests on 2010's 'Written in the Stars' (UK 1; US 12) that "Everyone's a kid that no one cares about/You just have to keep screaming 'til they hear you out", he's effectively denying class (and race) as a system, structural inequalities being nothing self-empowerment can't cure. Adele's class origins were initially politicised: late-2007s 'Hometown Glory' (UK 19) posits "the people against the government" and spits "We ain't gonna stand shit". Yet, as Jones points out, Adele was kept at a "classy" distance from the 'chav' archetype,[17] and she only achieved mass appeal when her ordinariness was depoliticised as democratising heartbreak. 2011's stark piano ballad 'Someone Like You' (UK 1; US 1) is an exemplification and internalisation of austerity, going beyond resilience, to emotional subalternity. "Sometimes it lasts... sometimes it hurts instead" is 'whatever doesn't kill you makes you stronger' without the 'stronger'. Fisher observed a contemporary structure of feeling that "to hold power is to inherently be oppressive, therefore... it's better to be the wounded, the abject".[18] Although this clearly relates to class as a system of power, in transforming victimhood into valediction, resilience and ordinariness combine here as a passive acceptance of disempowerment within an unchangeable system.

This conjunctural ordinariness was also deployed as an articulation of authentocracy, transcending class divisions to be "someone like you". Despite his public-school background, singer-songwriter Ed Sheeran pushed such ordinariness as his ontology, with a touch of Adele's valorising victimhood: "I haven't got a house, plus I live on a couch/So you believe the lyrics when I'm singing them out", Sheeran raps on 2011's folk-hop 'You Need Me, I Don't Need You' (UK 4), embracing his audience on the verses, rejecting the elites on the chorus.[19] He's someone like you. Yet Sheeran's fondness for piling on detail as authenticity bona fides undercuts his pitch for victimhood on 2014's Ellie Goulding-dissing 'Don't' (UK 8; US 9), his obsessive-defensive cataloguing coming over as controlling, a gender-inflected assertion of class power.

The authentocracy of this 'ordinary' mode is formalised by its deployment of organic instrumentation in self-conscious contrast to EDM's synthetics, thus the post-Adele preponderance of austere ballads like Bruno Mars' 2013 'When I Was Your Man' (UK 2; US 1) and Sam Smith's abject 2014 'Stay with Me' (UK 1; US 2). Thus also the revival of something resembling 'folk', encompassing Sheeran, fellow public-school folkies Mumford and Sons and their far better, bearded-hipster variants Bon Iver and Fleet Foxes. Ellie Goulding encompassed ordinariness in terms of both musical authentocracy (acoustic guitars) and class (her accented vocals). Revealing the contrivance that underlies the organic no less than the electronic, however, her 2010 'Starry Eyed' (UK 4) and 2011 'Lights' (US 2) hedge commercial bets by underpinning the acoustics with an EDM undertow.

Country also now made a comeback, and hard as it is to remember, Taylor Swift was initially marketed as 'ordinary', winsomely asserting on 2008's 'White Horse' (US 13), "This ain't Hollywood, this is a small town". Such non-metropolitan authentocracy carefully skirts class (Swift's father was a stockbroker) and is formalised in Swift's country phase by banjos and mandolins. Swift was possessed of a particular skill in creating an intimacy with her audience through her vivid, storytelling lyrics, plangently vulnerable vocals and self-effacing yet magnetic screen presence: she was someone like you. Swift's contrast to her rival on 2009's 'You Belong with Me' (UK 30; US 2) is rooted in a regular girl relatability: "She wears high heels/I wear sneakers". Travelling the same yellow brick road from country to pop, Miley Cyrus was marketed as 'ordinary' despite being country royalty Billy Ray's daughter and Disney child star of *Hannah Montana*. Like Swift, on Cyrus's video for 2009's '7 Things' (UK 25; US 9), she's in jeans and sneakers, merging with a gang of girls-next-door who lip-sync her lyrics, performatively dissolving the divide between celebrity and citizen,[20] the 1 and the 99%.

That there was such a preponderance of pop videos featuring ordinary people lip-syncing a celebrity's song in this period indicates a post-crash populist strategy. Witness Maroon 5's 2012, Max Martin-produced 'woah-oh' song 'Daylight' (US 7), or Pharrell's grating 2013 old-school soul pastiche 'Happy' (UK 1; US 1). Here, "bad news" is rhetoric, not reality, and millionaire Pharrell will, thankfully, "be just fine". In tandem, videos deployed documentary conventions to democratise the elite. When fans invade the recording studio in EDM kingpin David Guetta's 2010 'Gettin' Over You' video (UK 1), visiting pop royalty Fergie looks initially non-plussed, then shrugs, and celebs and plebs all dance together democratically. Maroon 5's

2013 'Sugar' video (UK 7; US 2) documents the band flash-mobbing civilian weddings to rapturous receptions – but reads like patronage rather than democracy, the elite giving their blessing to the masses. Self-effacing Justin Timberlake doesn't even feature on 2014's 'Not a Bad Thing' video (UK 21; US 8), which depicts attempts to find a regular couple who got engaged on the Long Island Railroad. It transpires that the guy popped the question to a Timberlake tune: it *is* all about Justin, after all.

As is becoming evident, celebrity attempts at relatability were regularly undermined by an endemic solipsism. On the video for 2008's 'Whatever You Like' (US 1), rapper T.I. relates to a female fast-food worker by flexing his elite lifestyle, while Mariah Carey's 'Touch My Body' video (UK 5; US 1) invites a visiting nerdy engineer to explore her multi-million-dollar 'property'. In each case, these levelling encounters turn out to be the regular person's fantasy, reasserting the social contract 2.0 between celebrity and citizen: one to live, one to dream. Jay-Z and Alicia Keys' 2010 'Empire State of Mind' (UK 2; US 1) finds Hova torn between conceding the social reality of the system – "Some of y'all won't make it" – and asserting a self-empowerment that's indistinguishable from self-regard. On the similarly piano-based 'Runaway' that year (UK 23; US 12), Kanye's relatability is as uncertain as his pitching, while the democratisation of us *all* being "douchebags" is a redistribution of mental health rather than of wealth.

Similarly, while Pink champions "all my underdogs" on 2011's 'Raise Your Glass' (UK 13; US 1), on 2010's 'Fuckin' Perfect' (UK 10; US 2) she keeps drifting from defending the downtrodden – "The whole world's scared" – to the delusion that she's *one* of them: "They don't like my jeans/They don't get my hair". Initially 'ordinary' internet sensation Justin Bieber's declaration, "We could be homeless/We could be broke" on 2012's 'As Long as You Love Me' (UK 22; US 6), is, rather than empathetic, a failure to read the room post-crash. The video for Drake's 2013 'Started from the Bottom' (UK 25; US 6) depicts him as a drugstore drone, but he can't help but mix this with glimpses of his elite lifestyle, while his proclamations of ordinariness are interspersed with brags like "half a million for a show". Drake is many things, but *relatable* is not among them.[21]

Eminem was one established star who could convincingly stand with the dispossessed, his ordinariness framed in the class terms absent from the songs explored so far. His 2009 'Beautiful' (UK 12; US 17) shifts from solipsism – "I'm just so fucking depressed" – to solidarity – "Feel your pain, you feel mine" – but the promo clip politicises that pain, depicting the damage that deindustrialisation has inflicted on Detroit. That Eminem articulates the desire to "Be just like you/Blend in with the rest of the room" is in stark contrast to collaborator Rihanna. Where Eminem is at home in the supermarkets and pool halls of 2010's 'Love the Way You Lie' video (UK 2; US 1), Rihanna is glamorously, glaringly out of place. So on the same year's 'Not Afraid' (UK 5; US 1), Eminem can convincingly assert, "We'll walk this road together, through the storm" to his fans, although it's unclear what they'll "take a stand" about.

It wasn't until 2013 that ordinariness was expressed in explicit, adversarial class terms, on New Zealand teenager Lorde's 'Royals' (UK 1; US 1). That the song entirely bypassed the industry, going viral on artist-platform Soundcloud, was thus entirely apposite. 'Royals' derides the flossy lifestyles of the elites – "Cristal, Maybach, diamonds on your timepiece/ Jet planes, islands, tigers on a gold leash" – in collective terms: "We didn't come from money". The dispossessed from "torn-up towns" driving Cadillacs in their dreams is thus an implicit threat of *re*possession. As against the frenzy of a Jessie J or a Lady Gaga, Lorde's singing is restrained, distanced, *thoughtful*, while, compared to EDM, her backing is quiet, austere. 2014's 'Team' (UK 29; US 6) similarly depicts the 99% from "cities you'll never see onscreen", refusing to be recycled into the system, insisting on their damaged presence. Again, this is presented in *collective* terms: they're on each other's team, in opposition to the elite, a reappearance of the formation formerly known as 'class'.

However, as the biggest stars of the pre-crash era were black, and with 'metropolitan' a cipher for 'multicultural' and 'small town' for 'white', Lorde's critique could be – and was – construed as being racial rather than social. Note the language of Flo Rida's "I got power, feel so royal" on 2011's 'Good Feeling' (UK 1; US 3), the title of Kanye and Jay-Z's collaborative *Watch the Throne* (UK 3; US 1), or Jay bragging about his art collection on his and Beyoncé's TMI 2014 'Drunk in Love' (UK 9; US 2). Yet celebrity solipsism and wealth-flaunting were hardly unique to black stars: it was Bieber who *literally* spat on his fans, after all. This reveals the limitations of 'ordinariness' as a critique. In skirting class as a system and emphasising culture rather than economics, 'ordinariness' was as readily mobilised by the culture-wars right as by a still fledgling left.

"Drink a Little More": Hedonism and Austerity[22]

With everybody cracking a bottle and raising a glass, austerity was both soundtracked and salved by a hedonistic club culture which fused the austerity motifs of 'ordinariness' and 'resilience'. Elite artists were democratised by a real or performative immersion in the club experience; ordinary clubbers gained validation from the valorisation of their culture. Black Eyes Peas' glorious, Guetta-produced 2009 'I Gotta Feeling' (UK 1; US 1) is the meta-song of this austerity hedonism, inviting everyone to its pre-drinks – "Jump off that sofa/Let's kick it off!!" – its video democratically merging band and ordinary clubbers, while Fergie ventriloquises popular frustration: "I feel stressed out, I wanna let it go". While the crash hardly invented hedonism, it incentivised it: what was new here was a nothing-to-lose nihilism that absorbed disaster capitalist affect, and whose demotic – "Go out and smash it… let's burn the roof!" – was that of crisis: a crisis conventionalised, and recycled back into the social system.

It was some time since the economic base had been so visible through the cultural superstructure. While it was also some time since Usher or Pitbull had worked a 9-to-5, on their 2010 'DJ Got Us Fallin' In Love Again' (UK 7; US 4), Usher's exclamation, "Thank God the week is done", is an expression of solidarity between celebrity and citizenry. Likewise, while Ne-Yo's renting days were long behind him, on 2014's 'Time of Our Lives' (UK 27; US 9), he's relatably saving his rent money to "have a good time before my time is up". Pitbull pops up again to empathically salute, "Everybody going through tough times… been there, done that". With grime effectively merging with EDM in this period,

Roll Deep's 2010 'Good Times' (UK 1) asserts, "I'm gonna leave the day behind", while Tinie Tempah celebrates 'Drinking from the Bottle' with EDM kingpin Calvin Harris in 2013 (UK 5), because "this crazy life can be a bitter pill to swallow".

In contrast to previous insensitive or defensive celebrity reactions to the crash, this hedonistic approach undoubtedly helped ordinary people through the hard years of austerity, while offering a welcome testament to the power of collectivity. Yet instructing people to forget their troubles, to 'drank!' and dance was hardly the response of the revolutionary vanguard to social crisis. Encouraging the masses to lose their heads could be regarded as the way the pop elite's Romanovs ensured they'd retain their own. In this way the imagery of austerity dance – "Go out and smash it!" – doesn't just sublimate crisis but the anger at its inequal distribution.

While austerity didn't invent the association of dance and damage, in previous eras plot-loss, sleep-loss and comedown were fed back into the culture's repetitive cycle, being invisible in dance's 80s utopian phase, and only occasionally indicated in its 2000s inebriation phase (the Streets, Plan B). After the economic comedown, however, hedonism's damage was reified as a feature rather than a bug. The druggy disorientation of Lady Gaga's 2008 'Just Dance' (UK 1; US 1) is ramped and camped-up in the video, while another newcomer, country-raver Ke$ha boasts of brushing her teeth with bourbon on 2009's 'TiK ToK' (UK 4; US 1) and looks totally trashed in Taio Cruz's 2010 'Dirty Picture' video (UK 6).

Across peak-EDM year 2010, this nihilism was steadily cranked up like an EDM build. First comes oblivion: Flo Rida, Sia and Guetta's 'Club Can't Handle Me' (UK 1; US 9) lining up the shots to achieve a total "K-O", while Tinie Tempah's 'Pass Out' (UK 1) promises, "We won't come down/Until we hit the ground and pass out". Then comes carnage: on Jason Derulo's 2011 'Don't Wanna Go Home' (UK 1; US 14), the revellers "burn [the club] down to the floor". Next comes acceleration: on Guetta and Usher's 2011 'Without You' video, pavements and walls crumble (UK 6; US 4), while Labrinth and Tempah's 2012 'Earthquake' (UK 2) depicts "rubble and dust... Cause we throw bombs on it".

This is the language of crisis, indeed of insurrection, yet rather than being adversarial, this destruction is recycled back into the system – like the crash, like the 2011 riot detritus swept away by virtue-signalling broom-wielders. That Sia proclaims herself "bulletproof" on Guetta's 2011 'Titanium' (UK 1; US 7) squares this resilient circle: she'll survive whatever is thrown at her because she has "nothing to lose". As affirmations go, this is a low bar. The same nihilism is evident in Florence Welch celebrating "living on such sweet nothing" on Calvin Harris's 2012 'Sweet Nothing' (UK 1), while in the video, scenes of physical violence and libidinal clubbing merge seamlessly. If this was all in a weekend's play amidst austerity, it was also all in a week's *work*, this hedonistic, aggressive "go out and smash it" demotic being absorbed into business, with meetings full of talk of "smashing" and "crushing" strategies and campaigns. This modality was also absorbed into entertainment, with *Breaking Bad*'s protracted cycle of violence tracking this era (2008–13), before 'resolving' in a concluding ecstasy of destruction. For all this conventionalisation of crisis and sublimation of the system's damage, however, the very excess of dance's – and the larger culture's – "go out and smash it" ethos still subliminally attested to a broken system.

"All Eyes on Us": Observing Gender[23]

Robin James argues that the gaze – hitherto male – was de-gendered in this era as a result of social media. With Facebook reaching saturation in the mid-2000s, Instagram making the visual central from 2010 and the smartphone selfie democratising PR from 2011, this pervasive self-objectification, James argues, gave the subject ownership of their own objecthood.[24] Certainly, in pop, Rihanna and Beyoncé both looked beyond the gaze; Rihanna indifferently, Beyoncé defiantly. Cheryl Cole simultaneously invited and confronted the gaze with conspiratorial amusement – see 2014's charming 'Crazy Stupid Love' with Tinie Tempah (UK 1) and note her wink at the end – and 'I Don't Care' (UK 1). Yet, whether it was ordinary people commodifying themselves for cultural capital or celebrities doing so for *actual* capital, this self-objectification operated within a market logic that was both socially competitive and economically exploitative via platform capitalism's harvesting of data.

Three tracks capture this culture of self-objectification. Mike Posner's 2010 indie-pop novelty 'Cooler than Me' (UK 5; US 6) observes, "You need everyone's eyes just to feel seen", encapsulating the insecurity underlying self-promotion's apparent complacency. The Chainsmokers' 2014 EDM novelty '#Selfie' (UK 11; US 16) captures how the virtual image of a person, "living her best life, from the best angle, in the best light" in Seymour's terms,[25] was beginning to eclipse their physical or emotional reality. From 2012, Labrinth and Emeli Sandé's bravely pretty attempt to look 'Beneath Your Beautiful' (UK 1), or your projected image – essentialised as beauty for women, strength for men – ultimately offers all the insight of a no-make-up selfie. The emphasis remains on *looking*, on *regarding* rather than *relating* to others.

Lily Allen's 2008 'The Fear' (UK 1) describes the event horizon of female self-promotion in the attention economy: "I'll take my clothes off and it will be shameless/'Cause everyone knows that's how you get famous". Allen isn't castigating individuals here but social conditioning: "It's how I'm programmed to function". The video for Beyoncé's 2009 'Run the World (Girls)' (UK 11; US 29) attempts to reclaim such sexual self-presentation as social power, with women in suspender belts facing down male soldiers bearing guns and riot shields. Yet rather than skewering patriarchal fear of female sexuality, the video's clunky symbolism highlights the song's hyperbole: the "girls" "making these millions" are a tiny minority. Moreover, positing personal enrichment as the path to gender equality perpetuates class inequality.

In Britney Spears' video for 2011's 'I Wanna Go' (US 7), she performatively rejects the gaze by smashing paparazzi cameras and then offering her sexuality in excess of the gawping gazers' demands. Spears has a point, but her 90s' grooming as a sex object, subsequent breakdown and loss of legal autonomy loom over the song. In the restricted parameters of the post-crash resilience mode, Spears' ambition is simply to survive in the existing dispensation; she can't envisage a world beyond it. So while Nicki Minaj's 2014 'Anaconda' (UK 3; US 2) ostensibly repossesses Sir Mix-a-Lot's 1992 'Baby Got Back', there's no substantive difference between the female objectification in either song's video, bar the ownership of the bodies on display. Drake, playing a mouth-breathing male-gazer, is tartly reminded of this by Minaj when he mistakes self-objectification for invitation.

While, superficially, Lady Gaga's 2009 'Bad Romance' (UK 1; US 2) represents yet another pop video featuring women dancing in their underwear, a closer look reveals Gaga being drugged and then *forced* to dance to promote herself for (clothed) men. It's a neat metaphor, wrapping celebrity, the music industry and patriarchy into neoliberal culture's "bad romance".[26] Patriarchy is symbolically defeated in the video's final image of a man's charred remains on a bed, next to an insouciant, smoking Gaga. Satisfying as this is, its extremity indicates a rhetorical, gestural revenge that's some distance from the "wild thinking'" and "loud and furious refusal" that Jack Halberstram claims for "Gaga feminism".[27]

With Madonna's post-feminist manual well-thumbed in this era, one recurring facet of post-crash feminism was a level of lesbian imagery previously unseen in pop. This included Katy Perry's 2008 immaculate confection 'I Kissed a Girl' (UK 1; US 1), Fergie *actually* kissing a girl in the 'I Gotta Feeling' video, Rihanna's 2010 'Te Amo' (UK 14) – where's she's the object of the *female* gaze – and Gaga's 2011 'Born This Way' (UK 3; US 1) asserting, "No matter gay, straight, or bi/Lesbian, transgender life". Yet there's a recurring sense of queerness being co-opted here. Perry's lyric doesn't just affirm her heterosexuality ("I hope my boyfriend don't mind it"), it essentialises the feminine as cutely girlish, while justifying her adventure in terms Robin Thicke could endorse: "Us girls [are] hard to resist/So touchable". Rihanna's collaboration with Shakira on 2014's ska-pop 'Can't Remember to Forget You' (UK 11; US 15) ambivalently transcends this containment. The video begins with a nearly naked Shakira limpidly inviting the gaze's objectification, but when Rihanna arrives, despite them inevitably lolling in their underwear, the pair smoke cigars, while their facial expressions challenge rather than invite, undermining the lyric's heteronormative affirmation, "I'd do anything for that boy".

The difficulty in degendering the gaze is indicated by the contemporary explosion of male-gaze songs which didn't just objectify women but also fetishised the objectifying *process*. In a last gasp of old-school R&B, Ray J's early 2008 'Sexy Can I' (US 3) asks permission to snap women's pictures, with the video alternating Ray's camera's gaze on breasts and pouting mouths and his confidential glances to camera, interpellating the viewer as male. Flo Rida and T-Pain's excruciating crunk hit 'Low' (UK 2; US 1) concerns the purely physical appeal of a 'shawty', with a video largely comprised of masculine, to-camera collusion. Even sensitivo Bruno Mars, on his 2010 ballad 'Just the Way You Are' (UK 1; US 1), defines his love object solely by her physicality, an approach repeated on One Direction's 2011 'What Makes You Beautiful' (UK 1; US 4).

With Usher abandoning R&B for EDM, 2012's 'Scream' (UK 5; US 9) is the more insidious for its infectiousness, a rehearsal for 'Blurred Lines'. "I try to fight it, but you're so magnetic… Now relax and get on your back". Sexiness here is not just an invitation to objectification but to sex itself. The corporate country of Florida Georgia Line's 2012 'Cruise' (US 4) employs another remaindered R&B star, Nelly, to authenticate the male gaze. Giving guest Jay-Z one of his few 2010s hits, Timberlake's 2013 'Suit & Tie' (UK 3; US 3) combines female objectification and cultural appropriation: "Let me get a good look at it… now I know why they call it a fatty". Employing the 'Cry Me a River' playbook, Maroon 5's 2014 'Animals' (UK 27; US 3) seeks 'edginess' by objectifying women. The lyric is creepy enough – "Preying on you tonight/Hunt you down/Eat you alive" – the video repellent. Adam Levine's blood-streaked slaughterhouse worker may be an animal, but as he surveils his prey from the street or looms over her bed, *she*'s inanimate, meat.

Even if we accept the 'two wrongs make a right' approach, an equal-opportunity gaze will always collide with conventional gender power relations. Despite Gaga's claim on 2009's 'LoveGame' (UK 19; US 5) that she "want[s] to take a ride on your disco stick", the body that's objectified in the video is *hers* – the male dancers remain fully clothed. When on Katy B's 2010 brilliant pop-dubstep 'Katy on a Mission' (UK 5) a man bars her way to the dancefloor, she takes charge of both his gaze and his drink, the result somewhere between control and capitulation. Spears' 2011 'Hold It Against Me' (UK 6; US 1) gender-flips the Bellamy Brothers' bovine 1979 joke ('If I Said You Have a Beautiful Body Would You Hold It Against Me', UK 3), while its video features the vanishingly rare sight of *men* dancing in their underwear: yet the song's female gaze is almost traditionally demure. Similarly, 'ordinary' Carly Rae Jepsen, in the video for 2012's pop-country 'Call Me Maybe' (UK 1; US 1), is embarrassed when the neighbourhood hunk clocks her perving on him. Notably, the chorus's considerate qualifier ("maybe") doesn't confuse his tops-off self-objectification for invitation: fortuitously, as he transpires to be gay.

In a more ambitious reversal, Beyoncé's 2008 acoustic ballad 'If I Were a Boy' (UK 1; US 3) flips the gender in its infidelity narrative. Yet in both the song and the Beyoncé-as-policeman video, gender is essentialised rather than defamiliarised – male as cold, selfish, faithless; female as warm, nurturing, loyal. What's more, Beyoncé still gets to stand in her bra; her male co-star stays fully clothed. 2009's 'Diva' (US 19) is a more confrontational gender flip, claiming "a diva is a female version of a hustla", while in the video Bey swaggers, smokes cigars – smoking being the era's shorthand for feminist rebel – and blows up cars. Celebrating "divas getting' money" and declaring, "This is a stickup", Beyoncé implies her hustle has gamed the system.[28] Again, while the financial empowerment of a lucky few *may* inspire the unluckier many, this is a variant on the American dream, of the neoliberal promise of 'opportunity', ideologies that austerity was concurrently demonstrating to be bankrupt.

There's more sense of the systemic in the double-diva team-up of Beyoncé and Gaga on 2010's 'Telephone' (UK 1; US 3), its video a *Thelma and Louise* tale of women overcoming patriarchy both indirectly – as a lesbian couple – and directly, by executing a misogynist. Leaving aside the video's inevitable dancing in underwear quotient, the real problem is that, as James points out, the symbol of patriarchy here is a black working-class male.[29] Jessie J's 2010 'Do It like a Dude' (UK 2) refuses the male gaze while mockingly mimicking masculinity, yet the song's demotic – "grab my crotch", "hood", "B.I.T.C.H." – is hip-hop, as are its beats. Moreover, with the chorus proclaiming, in grime-slang, "We can do it like the mandem, mandem", masculinity is again defined as a facet of black, working-class culture. Lily Allen's

2013 'Hard Out Here' (UK 9) disdains the male gaze just like Jessie – "Don't you want to have someone who objectifies you?" – and flips gender more drastically than Beyoncé – "grow a pair of tits". Yet Allen also uses hip-hop culture as a synecdoche of masculinity, bragging about cars, chains and "bitches", while in the video, she's flanked by twerking black dancers. The issue here is not cultural appropriation but the cultural *association* of working-class black masculinity with patriarchy. This association, while emerging from the liberal feminist left, intersected with the machinations of the illiberal racist right to become a factor in the revived 'culture wars' in the wake of the crash.

"Don't Worry 'bout Her Race, She Ain't in No Competition":[30] Austerity Pop and Race

Despite this being a supposedly 'post-racial' age, a racialised *ressentiment* was fomented among the 'white working class' in the American rustbelt and Britain's left-behind areas, by the Tea Party, UKIP and a rising online right exemplified by *Breitbart News* (under future Trump associate, Steve Bannon, from 2012). That this resentment focused on culture rather than economics was highly convenient for both capitalists and their centrist enablers, meaning that austerity's tag-team blame game never targeted the *actual* culprits.

Consequently, on the political watch of an African American president, two exemplary African American musical forms, hip-hop and R&B, entered a relative recession. Noughties stars 50 Cent, Ludacris and Nelly's chart appearances were reduced to guest spots on pop tracks, while Jay-Z's singles only charted spottily from 2010, and his wife Beyoncé only made the US top 10 twice out of eighteen attempts from 2009 to 2013. While the couple's albums still topped the charts, album sales were in decline year-on-year from 2008 – the result of recession, on-demand streaming, and from 2013, Spotify. R&B effectively disappeared as a distinct genre, Chris Brown and Usher surviving by switching to EDM, while the fact that Sheeran, Timberlake, Bieber and Sam Smith continued having R&B-styled hits suggests more was occurring culturally than hip-hop's failure to read the room amid austerity.

Like R&B, hip-hop shed its defining features, namely breakbeats – switching to EDM's four-to-the-floor – and rapping. Kanye shifted to Auto-Tuned singing. Drake sang as much as he rapped: 2010's EDM-driven 'Find Your Love' is completely sung (UK 24; US 5), as is 2013's 80s pop delight 'Hold On, We're Going Home' (UK 4; US 4). With even Kid Kudi's innovative 2009 'Day 'n' Night' (UK 2; US 3) being sung, most disorientating of all, Snoop's scant hits – 2007's 'Sensual Seduction' (UK 22; US 7); 2010's 'Wet' (UK 4) – feature his Auto-Tuned singing. This isn't to fetishise rapping but to regard it as the expression of a specifically African American culture. 'Rap' is, after all, the genre's *name* in America, and *Billboard* produces a Hot Rap Songs chart to this day. On 2009's 'D.O.A. (Death of Auto-Tune)' (US 24), Jay-Z complains "Y'all n****s singing too much/Get back to rap", and in a rare acknowledgement of economics beyond his bank account, credits this to the recession. While Jay was right, he could have benefitted from Auto-Tune on his *own* singing, and the track's messiness is indicative of hip-hop's contemporary loss of confidence (and note its measly chart placing).

The biggest hip-hop hits of this era were by non-African American artists. These comprised internet novelties like Korean Psy's 2012 'Gangnam Style' (UK 1; US 2) – caricaturing 'urban' vocal and dance styles over EDM beats – and white DJ Baauer's 2013 hit 'Harlem Shake' (UK 3; US 1), the first chart-topper from YouTube streaming. The video for Asian Americans Far East Movement's hedonistic 2010 'Like a G6' (UK 5; US 1) shows white people lip-syncing "Feelin' so fly", while Silentó's 2015 'Watch Me' promo (UK 19; US 3) features white people throwing 'urban' dance moves. *Billboard*'s biggest seller of 2013, Macklemore and Ryan Lewis's 'Thrift Shop' (UK 1; US 1), ostensibly chimes with the class critique of Lorde's 'Royals', in promoting a street culture of recycling rather than "getting tricked by business". Yet Macklemore's pious dismissals of "that pimped shit" clearly target African American culture, although the question of whose heritage is being recycled by a white old-school hip-hop track renders this critique ironic, at the very least.

Hip-hop's hegemony had once seemed like a cultural victory, but as its exponents and sound disappeared, the concept of cultural appropriation became more relevant. On 2010's 'Baby' video, Justin Bieber impresses a black girl with his moves in a throwdown (UK 3; US 5), and while rapper Ludacris yokes him (at 3:17), it's Bieber who has yoked African American culture, rapping about his 'swag' on 2012's 'Boyfriend' (UK 2; US 2). The body positivity of Meghan Trainor's dreadful 2014 doo-wop/hip-hop hit 'All About That Bass' (UK 1; US 1) is similarly immersed in black vernacular ("uh, that booty-booty"). Likewise, the demotic of Australian rapper Iggy Azalea's 2014 'Fancy' (UK 5; US 1) – the "realest", "bad bitch"; "who dat"? – and Azalea's drawling 'blaccent' blur the distinction between tribute and parody. Then there was Miley Cyrus's twerking.

The 2015 revelations of Bieber's youthful racism and Azalea's use of the N-word in tweets wasn't so much a contradiction as a reminder of a recurring disconnect in dominant ideology between a usable culture and the people who produce it. Again, this reveals the problem of prioritising culture over economics. It was economics that caused so many African Americans to be "excluded from the human community" and to be treated as disposable *homo sacer* by the repressive state apparatuses of the law and the judiciary. As Keeanga-Yamahtta Taylor points out, 'law and order' was the moral and physical guardrail against the crash's fallout: "the police function primarily as agents of social control in a society that is fundamentally unequal".[31] With the 2012 murder of Trayvon Martin prompting the formation of Black Lives Matter, protests erupted in Ferguson, Missouri, following the police murder of teenage Michael Brown in 2014 and continued for months. Again, this entailed the dispossessed reclaiming public space, as had Occupy and the England riots. With African Americans' median income declining at three times the rate of whites', black Americans refused to recycle their community's damage back into the system, refused to mourn and move on and thereby conventionalise their systemic devaluation. Taylor points out that, "when the Black movement goes into motion, it throws the entire mythology of the United States – freedom, democracy, and endless opportunity – into chaos".[32] Out of crisis, therefore, emerged hope.

"Love in a Hopeless Place": Melancholic Hedonism in Post-Crash Pop

A less overtly political resistance to austerity ideology was expressed by a new strain of melancholic popular music. Emanating from the same hedonistic culture as EDM, this music represented another refusal to mourn and move on, rejecting the recycling of loss that both Freud's 'mourning' and the resilience mode commend, refusing to accept a conventional 'closure' which closes off possibilities – whether emotional or political. As against the "go out and smash it" impulse, this melancholic music emphasised rather than sublimating the damage of an economically besieged, hedonistic culture – and did so in a mythic register that signified rather more than narcotic comedown. Reflective rather than immanent, therefore, this music was the first manifestation of what would come to be known as 'millennial angst'.

Having been in at the ground floor of the resilience mode, Rihanna's 2011 'We Found Love' (UK 1; US 1) was the first mass-diffused expression of this melancholic mode. Although produced and written by EDM kingpin Calvin Harris, the music is atypically mournful: mid-paced, hauntologically layered, its soars sucking the music into a void, unbelievably tense but also uniquely traumatic. Rihanna's voice is uncharacteristically resonant here, ethereal, mantrically repeating the line "We found love in a hopeless place". The video connects the economic and cultural fallout of the crash – a run-down council estate and a rave – as equally "hopeless places". With Rihanna looking convincingly 'ordinary' this time, it's curiously satisfying to see her riding a shopping trolley, queuing in a chip shop and clutching a can of Stella. The video's presentation of chemical recreation recycled into addiction, and hedonism sublimated as *anhedonia* (emotional numbing), depicts the damage of austerity as long-term rather than transitory.

Taylor Swift's 2012 'I Knew You Were Trouble' (UK 2; US 2) shares with 'We Found Love' its melancholy, its focus on hedonism and a reflective video voiceover. Starting with indie guitars, 'Trouble' effects Swift's stylistic and imagistic transition from country to pop *mid-song*, via a dramatic dubstep drop (at

3:08) that never lifts off, that's anti-euphoric, disorientating, deconstructive. This mirrors the song's emotional trajectory, with its thrill-seeking male subject representing an austerity culture that "lives too fast and burns too bright", and whose nihilistic hedonism morphs into anhedonia. Depicting Swift waking up alone in the ghostly, bleak aftermath of a rural rave, the video, like the song, is rueful rather than resilient, haunted rather than hedonistic: there's no rebuilding from this emotional crash, just an enduring damage in this hopeless place.

Even Ed Sheeran's flippant 2012 'Drunk' (UK 9) disconnects its hedonism from the resilience mode by recycling its totemic phrase as "What didn't kill me never made me stronger". Swedish singer Tove Lo's 2013 'Habits (Stay High)' (US 3) manages to make "Where the fun ain't got no end" sound like a prison sentence as she attempts to cure heartbreak through hedonism. In the quirkily queasy video, the Steadicam clinging to Lo's face accentuates the gaze's voyeurism − she looks vulnerable, damaged, unsexy, *particularly* when she's having sex, the shakicam gaze registering affective 'wrongness' in this hopeless place. Usually heard singing anthems to hedonism, Katy B was suddenly 'Crying for No Reason' (UK 5) in 2014, "Unable to sweep all my issues to somewhere I can't find" − to recycle her damage. 2014 proved to be peak anhedonia. On junglists Rudimental's 'Bloodstream' (UK 2), guest Sheeran keeps demanding, "Tell me when it kicks in", his high forever denied, while on Sia's 'Chandelier' (UK 6; US 8), the "party girl" swinging from the chandelier is "holding on for dear life". The tortured figure of Swedish EDM DJ Avicii haunts all these songs, the dance superstar who lived this anhedonia − and ultimately died of it.

In tandem, two rap tracks deconstructed austerity hedonism while starting to reconstruct hip-hop. Plan B's 2010 'Stay Too Long' (UK 9) revives rap's long-lost aggression, the tautening tension in his spoken verse equivalent to the EDM build (rising a semitone per stanza). As he goes from boozing to brawling, coking to cheating (a semitone per *line* now), there's a shouted "Yo!", then silence, a break with no rebuild, presaging the narrator's descent into hell on the accompanying *Defamation of Strickland Banks* (UK 1). Kendrick Lamar's 2012 'Swimming Pools (Drank)' (US 17) signalled hip-hop's reassertion as an African American form.

411

Still nodding at EDM's synthscapes, but slower, darker, jerkier, it's the sound of hardcore rap resurfacing. Lamar's repetition of the era's ubiquitous cry of "Drank!" captures the hedonic social pressure, which, he claims, ultimately rejects the social by retreating into narcotic solipsism and a consequent "appetite for failure".[33] If this is another hopeless place, there is, in Lamar's response, a suggestion of love in it too.

Lana Del Rey's viral YouTube success with 2011's mournful 'Video Games' (UK 9) announced an approach that was neither hedonistic nor resilient – thus 2011's 'Born to Die' (UK 9). Even the EDM remix of 2013's 'Summertime Sadness' (UK 4; US 6) doesn't jettison Del Rey's Fordist melancholia, the past's rebuke to the present's emptiness. Del Rey's influence is audible on Rihanna's 2012 ballads 'Diamonds' (UK 1; US 1) and 'Stay' (UK 4; US 3), in which *both* lovers are "the broken one", the damage displayed rather than recycled ("It's not much of a life you're living"), while in the video Rihanna is *crying*. Rather than this former replicant's tears being washed away by rain, they recur in early 2015's 'FourFiveSeconds', with Kanye and Paul McCartney (UK 3; US 4), in which Rihanna also gives her most emotional vocal to this point. Acoustic, slightly slapdash, its monochrome video makes the celebrities appear (relatively) ordinary, its lyric relaying the everyday crisis of people's lives, but again with an implicit hope.

With his moniker, the Weeknd, a play on both hedonism and disempowerment, Canadian Abel Tesfaye began self-releasing dark, dreampop-tinged R&B mixtapes in 2011. His 2014 breakthrough, 'Love Me Harder' (US 7), with former child star Ariane Grande, made for a curious follow-up to Grande, Jessie J and Nicki Minaj's hectic 'Bang Bang' (UK 1; US 3), despite both being produced by star-maker Max Martin. Dropping the tempo and the brashness, Tesfaye's falsetto purr of "Take the pleasure with the pain" reverses the resilience mode. On the Weeknd's solo 2015 'The Hills' (UK 3; US 1), the beats are slower still, the bass an EDM drop sucked into a black hole, and from the literal car-crash video to the line "When I'm fucked up that's the real me", the track evokes a hedonism that's anything but escapist: "Drugs started feeling like it's decaf". Co-produced by Martin, 2015's 'Can't Feel My Face' (UK 3; US 1) is the best Michael Jackson song since *Thriller*, its buoyant melody and featherlight falsetto delivering the sucker-punch: that having gone beyond hedonism into anhedonia, Tesfaye finds it's just as pleasurable. Such melancholia functions as a counter to the consensus, shattering the spell of surfaces, prompting introspection, from whence come reassessments: love discovered in a hopeless place.

The last time there was a financial collapse of this magnitude, in 1929, it prompted a top-to-bottom rethink of politics, the abandonment of laissez-faire and its replacement with a whole new socio-economic system – Fordist welfare capitalism. Securing capitalism against a restive, potentially revolutionary workforce, Fordism's safety net ensured that bare survival would become a thing of the past. Nearly a century later, with laissez-faire restored via neoliberalism, the capitalist class used the collapse of its financial system as an opportunity to accelerate the upward redistribution of wealth, thereby reintroducing bare survival, the retro revival no one was demanding.

Where the system had always previously absorbed and neutralised its critiques in the crucible of crisis, as Boltanski and Chiapello demonstrate, the complacency of capital and its political cheerleaders in the aftermath of the crash critically weakened neoliberalism's hegemony. For while the "established middle class" (25%) were insulated against austerity, that class's lower – and younger – cadres of "emergent service workers" (19%) were finding that the "rewards" of "participation in capitalism" – home ownership; "meaningful work"; career development – were diminishing. "Consent" to capitalism was thus reduced by the crash to the lowest functional level of "financial constraints".[34] If even the middle class weren't all middle class now, the economic situation couldn't be so easily ignored by the media, the precariat so readily swept from relevance by a broom-wielding bourgeoisie, or the "disposable poor" left to die in cardboard shelters or shot dead in the street by the lawless enforcers of 'order'. There was now an opportunity to politicise the pain of the damaged, dispossessed and denied in this broken system, to desublimate the anger of "go out and smash it" and reorientate its destructive energy into adversarial political action.

Chapter 13

"Longing for Change": The Rebirth of Radical Pop and Politics (2015–20)

Between 2015 and 2016, the political consensus that had held since the 1990s began to break down. Veteran American socialist Bernie Sanders' surging presidential campaign and British left-winger Jeremy Corbyn's surprise victory in Labour's leadership election in summer 2015 gave a face, a voice and a name to a long-marginalised constituency: the radical left. With Corbyn and Sanders returning state intervention and wealth redistribution to political discourse for the first time in decades, politics became a realm of creativity rather than consolidation, of activism rather than technocracy and of an optimistic rather than a pessimistic worldview. There was a tangible social energy and sense of possibility in this period, a widespread conviction that there *was*, after all, an alternative. If all this wasn't sufficient rejection of the capitalist realist, austerity-perpetuating establishment, it was followed in summer 2016 by the Brexit vote and Donald Trump's defeat of Hillary Clinton, a rejection of the centrist consensus from the right. The political bill for the financial crash had finally come due.

For the Long 90s' political and media establishment, legitimacy and rationality were located at the political centre, and to depart from that axis was to encounter the 'post-truth' of the alt-right's trolls, tradwifers, incels and white supremacists. While the centrist rationale presumed an evident reasonableness – "Why don't you just meet me in the middle?" as Maren Morris asked on Zedd's hit (UK 7; US 5) – it was predicated on a politics of stasis and preservation, a guardrail that was no longer holding. With Corbyn and Sanders attracting the kind of crowds politics hadn't seen in decades, the media lumped them in with Trump and Nigel Farage as incendiary 'populists'.[1] Although Britain's post-industrial areas *were* a source of support for Farage as well as Corbyn, and America's decimated Rust Belt as likely to stump for Trump as Sanders, this was only an 'own' in the media's own terms. For in framing popular resentment as cultural rather than political, racial rather than fiscal, centrists elided the system that punished the provincial poor while enriching their own metropolitan elite (Clinton didn't even bother campaigning in the Rust Belt). If Brexit was thus "a rejection of the cosmopolitan culture of the cities",[2] then social liberal Corbyn's 2017 obliteration of Theresa May's Conservative majority remained a mystery. These combined and uneven developments represented, in Gilbert's terms, "an active rejection of a particular political consensus and the social groups most associated with its propagation".[3] Fingers in ears, centrists instead tacked right on immigration, while concentrating on reports of anti-Semitism amongst Corbyn's supporters.

Although the radical right provoked a popular rejection of the status quo – Trump's "Make America Great Again" – they were themselves, in Seymour's terms, "the morbid symptoms, the excrescences of [the] declining authority" of centrist neoliberalism in the crash's hinterland.[4] For while Trump was an interloper into technocratic politics, he was still a scion of the elite 1%, for whom the centrist guardrail was erected, and he gave a voice (a face and a name) to the neoliberal id, in all its venality, paranoia and authoritarianism. With Trump's plan to build a wall to deter Mexican migrants paralleling May's 'Hostile Environment' – the Immigration Acts of 2014–15 and forced repatriation of the Windrush generation – the authoritarian right was essentially a malignant, metastasized neoliberalism. In this authoritarian atmosphere, Black Lives Matters' response to systemically racialised policing was only the first of a series of grassroots movements that surged out of social media and into the streets, alongside the feminist #MeToo (from 2017) and ecological Extinction Rebellion (from 2018). These movements entailed a popular engagement with politics unseen since the 80s, and which centrists, used to a high ground unconnected to principle or action, dismissed as "virtue signalling", a term borrowed from the right, who, in turn upped their trolling and gaslighting of this resurgent left.

The rebirth of radical politics didn't replicate the 1970s' imbrication of pop and politics. Corbyn and Sanders weren't cited in song, while May's brief tenure was commemorated only by Sleaford Mods (negatively). Trump appeared only as an absence – Rihanna, Panic! at the Disco and Adele ordering him to 'cease and desist' using their music at his rallies – just as, politically, he was a nodal point of negativity rather than propagator of policy. Clinton supporters the National sighed, "This is so embarrassing, ah, we're pissing fits" regarding Trump's election on 2017's 'Turtleneck' – a typically centrist preoccupation with 'optics': "just another man in shitty suits" (2017 *Sleep Well Beast*, UK 1; US 2). While Pink's 2017 'What About Us' (UK 3; US 13) is frustratingly unspecific, Sanders-supporting hip-hoppers Run the Jewels don't need to name Trump on 2016's '2100' (*RTJ 3*, US 13), which captures his essence as human absence: "These motherfuckers sick/They don't give a shit".

As this book has demonstrated, the political doesn't only reside in public figures and institutions but in the cultural unconscious, expressed through music's affect and vocabulary, grain and genre. Absent during austerity, disco's revival was an expression of this period's new optimism, audible in the utopian collectivity of DNCE's 2015 'Cake by the Ocean' (UK 4; US 9). It's audible too in Justin Timberlake's 2016 sugar rush 'Can't Stop the Feeling' (UK 2; US 1) – "We're flying' up, no ceiling, when we in our zone" – and visible in the video of Timberlake dancing with service workers in a car park. A revival of sunny dancehall brought Sean Paul back to the charts for the first time in an austere decade, on Sia's 2016 'Cheap Thrills' (UK 2; US 1). Likewise, Rihanna's dancehall-driven 2016, 'Work' (UK 2; US 1) rejects the austerity consensus by disdaining both the performance principle – her lazy, exaggerated Barbadian drawl rendering the title "wah-wah-wah-wah-wah" – and transactional affect. "You took my heart and my keys and my patience" Riri chides duet-partner Drake, while that reliable tracker of centrist affect has no answer but stasis: "We got to slow the motion", he urges.

Yet there *was* no slowing this motion, and after the emotional austerity of the post-crash years, humanist possibility and positivity flow through this period's music. British girl group Little Mix's bouncy, 2015 80s-pop 'Black Magic' (UK 1) offers to solve every ill, while, the same year, boyband One Direction exult that "nobody can" 'Drag Me Down' (UK 1; US 3). Corbynite George Ezra's 2018 folk-pop 'Paradise' (UK 2) and 'Shotgun' (UK 1) espouse utopianism and humanism respectively, while Bruno Mars' 2017 new-jack paean to positivity 'That's What I Like' (UK 12; US 1) chimes with Sanders' "Not me, us" in the line "Is it you? Is it me? Say 'us' and I'll agree". The abrupt halt to EDM's hegemony reflected the public rejection of austerity, with David Guetta struggling to have hits and Calvin Harris surviving by switching to upbeat 90s house. Harris's 2018 Dua Lipa feature, 'One Kiss' (UK 1; US 26), keeps repeating the keyword of the conjuncture, "possibilities", while his 2019 Rag'n'Bone Man collaboration 'Giant' (UK 2) asserts, "living is togetherness, togetherness, togetherness". Both the sentiment and the euphoric sound here are indicative of this revived humanism, of a collapse of divisions between self and other.

It wasn't as if the emotional and psychological damage of austerity was forgotten, however: it's audible in the millennial angst of Lana Del Rey and the tallying of society's mental health in the Weeknd. On his glorious, 80s-pop-suffused 'In the Night' (US 12) the heroine is "dancing to relieve the pain". Indeed once-normative hedonism was increasingly negative in this period's post-EDM pop. On SeeB's 2015 tropical-house mix of Mike Posner's 'I Took a Pill in Ibiza' (UK 1; US 4), Posner ruefully warns: "You don't wanna be high like me". On Snakehips' 2015 'All My Friends' (UK 5), Tinashe spits, "All my friends are wasted/And I hate this club/Man, I drink too much/Another Friday night I've wasted". Even once club-centric Flo Rida opines, "we don't have to go out" on 2015's 'My House' (US 4). On the XX's bruised 2017 dreampop delicacy 'A Violent Noise' (*I See You*, UK 1; US 2), years of "staying up too late/Trying your best to escape" have left the trio "too high", nowadays finding the club's "music too loud".

It was apt that the exemplary EDM cyborg Lady Gaga should humanise her image and sound at this moment. First came 2016's rock-orientated 'Perfect Illusion' (UK 12; US 15), with Gaga's rawer, un-Auto-Tuned vocal rejecting a digital identity that's "caught up in your show", while its 'realist' video featured her (relatively) dressed down. The follow-up, country-pop ballad 'Million Reasons' (US 4), was a dress rehearsal for Gaga's turn in 2018's re-remake of *A Star Is Born* and its soundtrack's more organic stylings. The film peaks with folk-rock power ballad 'Shallow' (UK 1; US 1), from whose lyric this chapter takes its title. Over an austere, plucked acoustic guitar, and with a concert crowd creating a live, collective feel, Bradley Cooper, as alcoholic rock star Jack Maine, rasps, "Are you happy in this modern world?" With Gaga's aspirational singer, Ally, turning the question back at him, the tacit answer is negative, and the pair then harmonise on the line "I find myself longing for change", before Gaga's vocal soar lifts that longing to transcendence. The song is only shallowly understood as concerning 'success': "the shallow" is life without existential depth, the post-crash "modern world" in which utopia is politically irresponsible and the future just more of the same. The pair's longing to escape precarity, both economic (Ally) and emotional (Jack), is a reassertion of hope, of a utopia that's "far from the shallow". The film presents this utopianism as negated when Ally allows her desire to be contained within the shallow imperatives of consumer capitalism.

This period was defined by attempts to transcend the limits which austerity had set on possibility, whether political, emotional or musical. The hip-hop renaissance exemplified by Kendrick Lamar was a musical corollary to BLM, countering the alt-right's ethno-nationalism with a revived black nationalism, using rap's sonic and sentimental heritage – 'boom-bap' beats, social comment, rapping itself – as a spur to progression and innovation. That Eminem was demanding, "What the fuck happened to hip-hop?" on 2018's 'Lucky You' (UK 6; US 6), just as Nielsen data revealed hip-hop to be the most successful form of popular music, simply indicated rap's biggest white star's commercial and cultural irrelevance.[5] Even on Southern-derived 'trap', the genre's unremarked sonic innovation – foregrounded 808 drum machine beats and distant, spooky synths – and unvarnished evocation of project life were an expression of a specifically African American culture (for better or worse). That Rae Sremmurd and Gucci Mane's 2016 viral hit "Black Beatles" (UK 2; US 1) announces, "I'm a fuckin' black Beatle, cream seats in the Regal", captures this renewed cultural confidence.[6]

In tandem,[7] drug-gang drama *Top Boy* (2011–23) and grime asserted black Britishness as an iconography and demotic sufficiently pervasive to be parodied by Big Shaq on 2017 meme-sensation 'Man's Not Hot' (UK 3). Not even this book can claim *Top Boy* co-star Dave's 2018 'Funky Friday' as political (UK 1), yet alongside tracks like Russ Millions' 2019 dance-craze 'Gun Lean' (UK 9), resurgent grime represented a vital rejoinder to the Brexit Party, Blue Labour's "legitimate concerns" and the Conservatives' 'Hostile Environment' as to what constituted Britishness. If the contrived controversy greeting Stormzy's assertion of Britain being racist represented the endurance of the past, Dave's impromptu onstage two-header with a young white fan at 2019's Glastonbury Festival represented the future: a material – and moving – exemplification of modern, multicultural Britain.[8] At such moments, social and political change seemed visible, tangible and achievable.

In narrating the period 2015–20 through the popular modality of celebrity – stars, personalities, names – this chapter positions popular musicians as lodestones of collective hopes and desires – expressed through their work rather than their personalities – as well as lightning rods for cultural fears and resentments. Trump was a celebrity long before he was a politician – first as a media playboy, then as star of *The Apprentice* – and that 'Trump' is a name for a politics of hate and paranoia means it's also a name for the cult of personality at its most pernicious. Consequently, each name in this chapter is invoked as a synecdoche, for the way in which they coalesce a particular political or cultural current of this period, mostly for better, but also, occasionally, for worse.

Justin Bieber: Self and Other

That Bieber felt the need to reboot his career in 2015 tells us rather more about the temper of the times than it does about the putative 'personality' behind the Bieber brand. Narcissism and disregard for others had, after all, been normative for celebrities and civilians alike for several decades. That Bieber's behaviour was now deemed unacceptable – the self-regard of a 'main character' – indicated a new structure of feeling, captured by Bernie Sanders' catchphrase, "Not me, us".

Jack-U's 2015 'Where Are Ü Now' (UK 3; US 8) was a collaboration between Bieber, dubstep producer Skrillex and M.I.A.-associate Diplo. Hiring hot producers is a standard comeback strategy, but the production here doesn't just sprinkle Bieber with hipster fairydust, it inscribes *change* into the music's very form. Eerie and fractured, 'Where Are Ü Now' was artier than anything in pop since dubstep's brief 2010 chart run. Suddenly, at 1:10, an ethereal sound enters – Bieber's voice futzed to dolphin frequency – occupying the space where the chorus would once have been. Soon named the 'pop drop' and widely imitated, this technique, rather than being a just-in-time delivery of EDM's beat-drop resolution, evokes the opposite: vulnerability, openness – it *never* resolves. The lyric expresses an affective generosity that's new both to Bieber and to post-millennial pop: "Turned your doubt into hoping"; "Gave you the shirt off my back". If this humility was still hedged with entitlement, another Skrillex production, fall 2015's 'Sorry' (UK 1; US 1), fixed that. Starting with another pop-drop and full of ghostly shrieks and random clunks, 'Sorry' is more recognisably pop, possessed of a dancehall beat as warm as its sentiment: "Let me redeem... myself tonight", Bieber entreats. Seen as a new personal humility (Bieber didn't feature in the video), this paralleled a new political recognition of the other by the self, of the social realm as more than a marketplace of competing needs: "Could someone call a referee?" Bieber quips.

Having a humanising makeover? Who you gonna call? Ed Sheeran co-wrote Bieber's empathic 'Cold Water' (UK 1; US 2) with Diplo and MØ, promising, "If you feel you're sinking, I will jump right over/Into cold, cold water for you". The 60s unconditional was back, the "not me, us" vibe enhanced by another Bieber-less video. The culmination – and contradiction – of this trajectory was a dressed-down, hipster-moustached Bieber in 2020's 'Intentions' promo clip (UK 8; US 5) visiting – patronising? – a women's shelter. Bieber's humility here becomes meta-human, Christ-like (with miracles, in capitalism, always monetised), the cult of personality as philanthropy. Yet it's still a world away from spitting on fans from hotel balconies.

Bieber collaborators Major Lazer, DJ Snake and MØ's 2015 'Lean On' (UK 2; US 4) is in similar vein, with its pop-drop, dancehall rhythm, multicultural (Indian) video and empathic chorus, "We all need someone to lean on". Indie-poppers Chvrches' 2015 *Every Open Eye* (UK 4; US 8) matches the best parts of EDM to "the best part of ourselves" on their giddy 'Make Them Gold': "We are falling but not alone… I will pull you on". Sheeran pops up again on Rudimental's late-2015 'Lay It All on Me' (UK 12), acknowledging social crisis – the recurring "If you're hurting" – but instead of advocating austerity's resilience, now offering solidarity: "I won't let you go it alone". The monochrome video extends this self/other elision, multi-racial figures meeting the camera's gaze, while Rudimental's 2017 album title, *Toast to Our Differences* (UK 5), captures this structure of feeling.

Empathy was British diva Jess Glynne's metier, her 90s house vibe eschewing escapism and meeting crisis with solidarity. Flitting between Glynne's warm, husky, low register and euphoric upper range, 2015's 'Hold My Hand' (UK 1) declares, "I don't want to walk on my own anymore". 'Don't Be So Hard on Yourself' (UK 1) adds perky disco strings to its house push, its sentiment ostensibly addressed to Glynne herself, but outreached to her other – "I'm just tired of marchin' on my own" – enhanced by its video's affirmation of multicultural Britain. Glynne's soaring late-2015 piano ballad 'Take Me Home' (UK 6) is in 'Someone like You' territory, but the encounter with the other here is healing rather than alienating, as she's "caught before I hit the ground" – literally uplifting. Glynne reciprocates the reassurance on 2018's upbeat 'I'll Be There' (UK 1): "I'm gonna come through, you'll never be alone".

Coldplay always fancied themselves inclusive, so this was their moment (again). Despite its title and the involvement of EDM producers Stargate and Avicii, 2016's 'Hymn for the Weekend' (UK 6; US 25) has nothing to do with hedonism, the invitation to "drink from me" and "shoot across the sky" being metaphors for the dissolution of distinctions between subject and object. The effect is enhanced by both Beyoncé's backing vocal and another India-set video. Achieving the same affect by different means, no one guessed the mesmerising pop-drop on Calvin Harris and Rihanna's 2016 tropical house hit 'This Is What You Came For' (UK 2; US 3) was sung by Taylor Swift ("You-ooh-ooh", from 0:15–0:30). Yet so empathically indistinguishable are the women's voices, it's unclear quite where one ends and the other begins.

Frantz Fanon developed the concept of 'self and other' from Hegel's 'master-slave' dialectic to account for both racism *and* its inevitable overthrow. So the issue's political pertinence extends far beyond the interpersonal – particularly when fascists like Richard Spencer were claiming 'pure' national selves against an 'impure' racial other. On 2016's hauntingly liminal, DJ Mustard-produced 'Needed Me' (US 7), Rihanna calls herself "a savage" and hisses at the attempted imposer of 'civilisation': "Fuck your white horse and your carriage". This postcolonial language reflects the fact that a hierarchy of master and slave, of self and other will not hold, the relationships being interdependent – "You needed me" – rather than purely adversarial, the ultimate endpoint being Fanon's state of "absolute reciprocity".[9]

Kendrick Lamar: Black Radicalism and the Rebirth of Hip-Hop

Black Lives Matter had become a significant force in American culture and politics by 2016. Again, it was all about names: Trayvon Martin, Michael Brown, Eric Garner, Rekia Boyd, restoring identity – and humanity – to ordinary people gunned down on public streets because of their race. But it was also about *extra*ordinary people, names like Kendrick Lamar, who came up from the Compton streets to capture this political moment. "We hate the po-po [police]/Wanna kill us dead in the street fo' sho'", he spits on 'Alright'. Yet Lamar isn't just a street observer, he's a street analyst: "Motherfucker you can *live* at the mall", he raps, ridiculing the idea that minorities can consume their way to equality. What really made Lamar the man of the moment, however, was that his critique was *optimistic*, with his assertion "we gon' be alright" articulating a new faith in the future.

'Alright' featured on Lamar's third album, *To Pimp a Butterfly*, in spring 2015 (UK 1; US 1), which didn't just return black politics to hip-hop, but Black Pride. Abandoning rap's assimilation into pop, Lamar's backing encompasses all of African American music – gospel, jazz, soul, funk – while 'King Kunta' invokes Alex Haley's slave hero and a host of storied African American names: Ralph Ellison, Richard Pryor, Michael Jackson, George Clinton. Yet the signifiers of black nationalism on 'The Blacker the Berry' – Wallace Thurman's 1929 novel of the same title; the boom-bap beats – are deployed as much in critique as celebration. "So why did I weep when Trayvon Martin was in the street?" Lamar demands, "When gang bangin' make me kill a n***a blacker than me?" Biography is plural rather than personal here, although it's Lamar's Blood credentials that give his breaking the *omerta* on gang violence authority, testifying to the devaluing of black lives by self-employed rather than state-employed gangsters.

Not that Lamar lets the state off the hook, it being precisely gangster culture's solipsistic focus that prevents confrontation with power rather than peers. "You hate my people", Lamar declares: "You sabotage my community, makin' a killing" – flooding the ghetto with crack – and thereby "made me a killer". That ambiguous "you" insists that black lives do not exist – or expire – in some morally remote 'elsewhere' but are imbricated with white lives, and that both are imbricated in the racialised system of capitalism. This was stunningly asserted by Lamar's performance at the 2016 Grammys. Amid the elite ballgowns and dinner jackets – signifiers of a 'civilisation' always locked in an antonymy with 'savagery' – Lamar shuffled onstage as one link in a chain gang. This served a reminder of civilisation's historical and enduring realities – the systemic chains locking African Americans in a regular shuttle between project and prison.

Lamar was the obvious choice to helm the soundtrack for 2018's *Black Panther* (US 1), which, with its all-black cast, was the consummate cultural expression of this revived black nationalism, becoming the year's second highest-grossing film. Like the film – a Marvel comics franchise unconnected to the historical Black Panthers – Lamar's soundtrack addresses issues of *leadership* rather than politics, however, reflecting his newfound role as spokesman.[10] In tandem, his music moved back from conscious hip-hop to more commercial pop, as on the gorgeous, EDM-influenced 'All the Stars' with SZA (UK 5; US 7). After asking himself on 'Black Panther', "What do you stand for?/ Are you a activist?… Are you a king?", Lamar appears to plump for the latter. Lamar's Weeknd collaboration, 'Pray for Me' (UK 11; US 7), is the only time political issues are addressed on *Black Panther* – "Life a livin' hell/Puddles of blood in the streets" – before returning to the pressure of leadership. "If I gotta be/ Sacrificed for the greater good then that's what it gotta be", Lamar states, but collective ambition is eclipsed by individual messianism, Lamar's previous statement that "this plot is bigger than me" forgotten. This, then, is the problem with the cult of personality: a preoccupation with celebrity is a cultural modality that detracts and distracts from the political.

Beyoncé Knowles' celebrity was triumphantly reaffirmed with early 2016's 'Formation' (US 10), rendering her, after a commercial slump, not just relevant but riveting, a tracks-stopping combo of Southern trap and queer 'bounce' with a Black Pride message. Only days after Lamar's Grammy appearance, 'Formation' was given prime-time exposure via a Superbowl performance in which Beyoncé and her dancers dressed in (historical) Black Panther outfits. The sense of motion at this moment was intense, visceral, and 'Formation' captures it. The song is an assertion of unmediated African American culture – "I like my negro nose with Jackson 5 nostrils" – but alert to the reactionary forces amassing against it. The track's iconic video features the provocative anachronism of African American women living it up in antebellum mansions, alongside the contemporary accusation of Beyoncé atop a submerged car in a drowning New Orleans. Such was the potency of 'Formation' as an event, as a *possession* of the spectacle, that its adherence to

Beyoncé's staple black capitalism – "Your best revenge is your paper" (money) – receded into the background.

'Formation' and Beyoncé's accompanying *Lemonade* (UK 1; US 1) were a vindication of smart-pop's creation-by-committee approach, transforming contrivance into transcendence. By the same token, Beyoncé transcended the cult of personality: for while *Lemonade* was trailed as exploring problems in her marriage to Jay-Z, it used the public preoccupation with celebrities' personal lives to provide not a kiss-and-tell but a panorama of African American culture and history. That *Lemonade* was followed months later by Knowles' sister Solange's *A Seat at the Table* (UK 17; US 1) testified to a creative fecundity plainly spurred by the possibilities in contemporary politics. Musically tapping 70s soul, 'Mad' is a radical rejection of a racialised resilience mode. An acquaintance asks Solange, "Why you always blaming?… Why you can't just face it?" Solange doesn't just affirm that "I got a lot to be mad about" – roping in future Trumpian Lil Wayne – she makes the blaming *collective*, inciting: "Be mad, be mad, be mad".

The same anger courses through Brooklyn/Atlanta duo Run the Jewels' propulsive, bracing 2016 *Run the Jewels 3* (US 13). "Born black, that's dead-on-arrival", spits Killer Mike on 'Talk to Me', ridiculing the "All-Lives-Matter-ass white folk" and their attempt to frame BLM (and Lamar) as racist via the liberal fantasy of a level playing field. Yet the alt-right had learned from the 'woke' left, mobilising a white victimhood that got legitimated by Trump's 'both-sidesing' of one-sided fascist violence at 2017's Unite the Right demonstration in Charlottesville. On 'Hey Kids (Bumaye)', Mike calls out these "fucking fascists" and, invoking Fanon, envisions popular resistance building to revolution: "Say hello to the masters, on behalf of the classless masses/We showed up, ski-masks, picks, and axes to murder asses/Lift up our glasses and watch your palaces burn to ashes".

Such was the adversarial energy of this era that Childish Gambino – aka Donald Glover – got caught up in it. Neither Glover's gorgeously soulful 'Redbone' (US 12) nor the TV comedy he wrote and starred in, *Atlanta* (2016–22), provided a precedent for summer 2018's extraordinary 'This Is America' (UK 6; US 1) and its literally explosive promo. Chanting, "We just want the money, we just want to party", Glover parodies pre-BLM hip-hop culture, with its dance crazes – a troupe of beaming children mimicking Glover's Jim Crow contortions – and consumerism: Glover dancing atop an automobile; the line, "Get your money, black man". This frivolity, Glover implies, is constantly punctuated by violence from law-enforcement ("Police be trippin' now"), from white supremacists (the choir Glover guns down echoing 2015's Charleston church shooting) and from gangsters ("Guns in my area... I gotta carry 'em"). That such an uncompromising production could be so successful revealed the radicalisation not just of artists but of the public in this period.

Renaissance woman to Glover's renaissance man, Janelle Monáe starred in Oscar-winning indie *Moonlight* (2016) and broke through musically with 2018's *Dirty Computer* (UK 8; US 6), which came with its own 'emotion picture', depicting a dystopian, authoritarian – indeed Trumpian – surveillance state. Where Monáe's devastating 2015 'Hell You Talmbout' emphasised the dead by insisting we "say her name", 'Crazy, Classic Life' doesn't just demand not to be killed ("police like a Rambo") but to be able to *live* (BLM was concurrently organising minimum wage campaigns). In similarly Marcusian spirit, 'Screwed' proclaims sexual liberation as political liberation – "You fucked the world up now, we'll fuck it all back down". That 'we' is crucial, with the track 'Americans' asserting a *collective* utopianism: "We will win this fight, let all souls be brave/We'll find a way to heaven", like the Fanonian vision of the "white man and a black man *hand in hand*".[11] Despite the dystopian tide of the alt-right – "hate all around you" – with *Dirty Computer*, *Black Panther* and Beyoncé's Coachella performance all occurring in the same year, this utopia felt *alive*, possible, graspable.

The Weeknd: The Mental-Health Epidemic

The rediscovered humanism of this era produced both an explosion of positive, upbeat music *and* a deeper mining of the melancholic seam of the austerity era. Neither the construct 'the Weeknd' nor its creator, Abel Tesfaye were quite human, let alone humanist – as his 2023 drama, *The Idol* would prove. Yet the Weeknd's best music depicts social crisis as damaging (weakened) rather than, as per the resilience mode, strengthening – although both occur in the crucible of hedonism (the weekend). If Tesfaye often appears to take nihilistic delight in psychological damage, it's an *active* negativity rather than resilience's passive positivity, a pursuit of sensation that pushes the psyche beyond the pleasure principle, in Freudian terms.

It isn't necessary to accept Freud's notion of mourning as closure to accept his warning about melancholia's seductions.[12] Sad pop, like Scottish internet sensation Lewis Capaldi's 2019 ballad 'Before You Go (UK 1; US 9), rarely achieves the Weeknd's dialectical depth: "time can heal", Capaldi mourns, "but this won't". Sam Smith's 2015 piano ballad 'Lay Me Down' (UK 15/1; US 8) articulates a near-ecstatic victimhood: "I don't want to be here if I can't be with you tonight". James Bay's 'Let It Go' (UK 10; US 16), with his tremulous vocal and very 2015 clean electric guitar, faces crisis without defeatism but also without dynamism: "Everything that's broke/Leave it to the breeze". Rihanna's stunningly sung 2016 old-school soul ballad 'Love on the Brain' (US 5) rejects resilience only to embrace masochism: "It beats me black and blue/But it fucks me so good/That I can't get enough".

This masochistic melancholia is audible in mumble-rapper Juice Wrld's 2017 breakup song 'Lucid Dreams' (UK 10; US 2), its delicate dreampop guitars closer to the XX than to hip-hop, as memories of his lost lover leave him "better off dead". Juice's OD in 2019 rendered such wrenching lines eldritch. Weeknd cohort Lil Uzi Vert's 2017 breakup track 'Xo Tour Llif3' (UK 25; US 7) keeps repeating, "Push me to the edge/All my friends are dead". If the reference is to 'dead presidents' (dollars), this is materialism at its most morbid, connecting to the singer taking Xanax to "blow my brain out". Another dream-hop breakup track, XXXTentacion's 2018 'Sad!' (UK 5; US 1), is equally passive – "I won't fix, I'd rather weep" – its melancholia preserved in amber by his being murdered at age 20.

Rather than wallowing in melancholy, the Weeknd goes beyond the pleasure principle by pushing pleasure to its limits. Created with Daft Punk, 2016's 'Starboy' (UK 2; US 1) directly addresses Tesfaye's now vast audience from the citadel of his stardom. Yet the boilerplate boasting – "Made your whole year in a week" – reads as critique, presenting capital accumulation as competition: "I'm tryna put you in the worst mood"; money earned "just to hurt you"; possessions accumulated "just to tease you". Most startling, though, is the song's accusatory chorus – "Look what you done/I'm a muthafuckin' starboy" – positing the public's investment in celebrity as masochistic, beyond the pleasure principle. Tesfaye may well mean it but, isolated amongst his riches in the video, the suggestion is that *stardom* is also beyond the pleasure principle. Not that there's much pleasure to be found in the other, either. On 'Party Monster' (UK 17; US 16), Tesfaye recounts indifferently bedding someone's girlfriend, ("dick game that's the meanest"), so his insistence that "I'm good, I'm good, I'm great" rings hollow, particularly punctuated by his and Lana Del Rey's background mutter of "paranoid, paranoid".

Amid this misogynistic and misanthropic othering, there's always a strain of tenderness in Tesfaye's music, with 2018's 'Call Out My Name' (UK 7; US 4) offering the candid, "I said I didn't feel nothing baby, but I lied". While 2019's 'Heartless' (UK 10; US 1) initially ramps up the hardness – "Never need a bitch"; "runnin' through the pussy, need a dog pound" – and again links this to capital accumulation ("All this money and this pain got me heartless"), suddenly, there's a near cry for help: "I don't do well when I'm alone".

This vulnerability recurs on 2019's stunning 'Blinding Lights' (UK 1; US 1): presented as 80s retro, and breaking sales and streaming records, it's superficially the Weeknd at his most upbeat. Unlike other 80s revivalists, however, Tesfaye and returning producer Max Martin catch the period's coldness, the sinister shimmer of the synths capturing the paranoia of 'Billie Jean', while the agitated rhythm tracks A-ha's anxiety on 'Take on Me'. "The city's cold and empty", Tesfaye sings, while he's "going through withdrawals". Set in the ultimate city of the spectacle, Las Vegas, the video's flashing neon signs, speeding cars and exponentially accelerating hedonism are intercut with violence, and it begins and ends with Tesfaye dripping with blood and shaking with psychotic laughter. The image is apposite, not for the psyche of Abel Tesfaye particularly, but for the collective psyche in a socio-political environment in which the advertised strategies for survival – hedonism, consumerism, celebrity – aren't just delusional (dazzled by the spectacle's blinding lights) but actively dysfunctional. This, then, is the social landscape of the mental-health epidemic.

Lana Del Rey: Millennial Angst

There's a peculiar injustice in millennials being regarded as 'entitled' by those who hold the world's title deeds, and whose aggressive defence of their status and the status quo can only itself be called 'entitled'. For it was previous generations' strip-mining of the world's raw materials that left the poisoned legacy of a burning planet, a housing crisis, the "bullshit job" and a withering welfare system.[13] What's audible in millennial-angst music isn't piety but a profound sense of *loss*: not of something remembered but, in this retro, YouTube, internet meme era, something *re*-remembered. For white rapper Mac Miller to regard hope as a hauntology on early 2020's 'Good News' (US 17) – "I know maybe I'm too late, I could make it there some other time" – is the more heartbreaking for emerging after his fatal overdose. Millennials feel that they arrived after it was all over: Anne-Marie's claim on the Sheeran co-written '2002' (UK 3), "No, it's never been better", couldn't sound more like a denial (just saying).

What millennials *do* have is *information* – too much of it, and much of it too awful to take in – and so the internet has become a regular reference point in popular music. Maroon 5 invoke their "socials" on the Pokémon-inspired video for 2016's 'Don't Wanna Know' (UK 5; US 6); the 1975 titled their 2018 album *A Brief Inquiry into Online Relationships* (UK 1; US 4). The internet captures the millennial condition: an endless archive of a lost past (like Joni Mitchell's tree museum), alongside an agonising, frame-by-frame capture of the perennial present. The future is notably absent, however: endlessly buffering, likely to cause the OS to crash.

On American duo Twenty One Pilots' late 2015 hip-hop-reggae 'Stressed Out' (UK 12; US 2), the narrator remembers being "told when I get older, all my fears would shrink". Singer Tyler Joseph then itemises the 'adulting' wake-up calls of student loans, existential stress and the performance principle – "Wake up, you need to make money" – as against the demotivating fact of the future's cancellation ("We used to dream of outer space"). One of many millennial ironies is that the automation that was to create a futurist utopia of expansive leisure amid collective plenty instead created a presentist dystopia of expanding labour amid competitive austerity.[14] The Pilots' reggae-pop 2016 'Ride' (US 5) *tries* to be optimistic ("I just wanna stay in the sun") but is perpetually dragged back to pessimism ("I'm falling"), pondering the social solidarity that's central to this era, but too floored by anxiety either to connect or to act: "I've been thinking too much", Joseph keeps repeating.

Dance duo the Chainsmokers ditched EDM's pummelling beats and hedonistic euphoria in this period for dreampop guitars and comedown introspection. 2016's 'Don't Let Me Down', with Daya (UK 2; US 3), is a song of emotional precarity: "Stranded, reaching out… I think I'm losing my mind". 2017's 'Paris' (UK 5; US 6) representatively combines retro hauntology ("Getting drunk on the past") with presentist technology ("Posting pictures of yourself on the internet"), while offering a mild rebuke to millennial stereotypes: "We'll get away with everything/Let's show them we are better". Summer 2016's mesmerising trap-dreampop 'Closer', with Halsey (UK 1; US 1), is packed with images of precarity – his broken-down car, her stolen mattress, the Rover she can't afford – and saturated with generational nostalgia, from its Blink-182 invocation to its dubstep undertow. The repeated refrain, "We ain't ever getting older", testifies not to eternal youth but to an enforced infantilism, when the forward-motion of 'maturity' has been fractured and both personal and global futures are, at best, uncertain. The song's pop-drop emits a wordless sigh at the state of the world. Halsey returns with Benny Blanco and Khalid on 2018's 'Eastside' (UK 1; US 9) and over more damped, cleanly shimmering guitars, she rues how "dreams of a house and a family" – the 80s' 'property-owning democracy' – have turned into "dead-end jobs" and "bills to pay". The home-movie video footage is heart-wrenching.

Millennial resentment towards the boomers who frittered away the planet's resources is understandable, if politically unhelpful. On Portugal the Man's fantastic, falsetto-driven 2017 soul pastiche 'Feel It Still' (UK 3; US 4), hippies are hypocrites – "Givin' in to that easy living" – the counterculture, again, a counterfeit: "I'm a rebel just for kicks now". Rather than chiming with right-wing critiques of the 60s, however, what comes across is a trans-generational loss which empathically unites boomer and millennial: "Goodbye to my hopes and dreams.../It might be over now, but I feel it still". Fordism filtered through post-Fordist techniques, the track's memory of a memory of utopian thinking is flippantly devastating. The 1975's 2018 'Give Yourself a Try' (UK 22) offers a more direct generational *rapprochement*. With the narrator "a millennial that baby-boomers like", that "your vinyl and your coffee collection is a sign of the times", captures the millennial fusion of the past (nothing says 'Fordist' like vinyl) with the technological present (nothing says 'hipster' like complex coffee machines).

What's arresting about the phenomenon of Lana Del Rey is the backlash regarding her 'inauthenticity', when her being a construct is the core of her appeal. This is not to damn her as 'fake', or to faint-praise her as 'postmodern', for Del Rey has a depth and resonance that her previous incarnation, Lizzy Grant didn't, and captures a specifically Fordist hauntology in an unmistakably millennial mode. The liminality of Del Rey's look and sound – both 50s *and* 60s – enhances their luminosity, that sense of a memory of a memory. With her generation's retro-presentism, Del Rey allies an aching sense of historical loss to an entirely contemporary escapism, from the technological (computer games) to the organic (getting high at the beach). "Let's leave the world for the ones who change everything", she sings on 2015's 'Swan Song' (*Honeymoon*, UK 2; US 2), tartly but sweetly trolling boomer centrists.

2019's 'The Greatest' is the culmination both of Del Rey's vision and of millennial-angst music. It evokes a generation raised on lack ("I'm facing the greatest loss of all"), who compensate with nostalgia and hedonism ("The culture is lit and I had a ball") but who can't escape an emotional, economic and ecological precarity: "I guess that I'm burned out after all" (*Norman Fucking Rockwell!*, UK 1; US 3). The greatest irony of all is that, rather than this angst leading to passivity, as in the media stereotype, millennials were the *activists* of the Sanders and Corbyn campaigns, and provided the new intake of radical politicians in whom hope for the future now resides. This confirms Traverso's articulation of an angst that, "instead of paralyzing actions", represents "a militancy... which [draws] its strength from *within* melancholy" – from within loss.[15]

Kanye West: Authoritarianism and the Alt-Right

Although Kanye West initially contributed to Hillary Clinton's campaign, he became, from 2016, the most prominent Trump supporter in popular music. While this could be seen as symptomatic of a purely personal breakdown – West was sectioned later in 2016 while shouting "Trump, Trump", and would later be diagnosed as bipolar – it was a psychic collapse that West shared with 46.1% of American voters. West's reactionary public statements expressed a structure of feeling enabled but not created by Trump, as austerity's losers found in "red-pilling" – *The Matrix*'s term for confronting the unmediated 'real' – a "potent self-medication", wherein conspiracy, in Seymour's words, "puts a name to an otherwise nameless misery and rage".[16] That West appeared to be red-pilling to the max was not a contradiction of his elite status but an *expression* of it, given the public's rejection of established hierarchies in this period.

Power is the currency, subject and substance of fascism, with the authoritarian right arising to protect the elite in austerity's overtly unequal society. If the "Power is Power" tagline of *Game of Thrones* (2011–19) was an expression of this fascistic power fetish, the show's popularity was evidence of the public's *dis*empowerment, as was their fetishisation of fame – of *reputational* power. With Kanye the creator and star of his own personality cult, 2016's *Life of Pablo* contained no hits (UK 30; US 1) and is famed, primarily, for 'Famous', West's diss of Taylor Swift. Following West's interruption of Swift's 2009 MTV Awards acceptance speech and his subsequent recantation of his apology – #sorrynotsorry – he now added insult to injury. "I feel like me and Taylor might still have sex", Kanye raps, and as the listener's jaw drops, he trumps this with, "Why? I made that bitch famous". West then goes on to claim, with eye-crossing solipsism, that the grievances of the women he *has* had sex with derive not from his own behaviour but from their being "mad they ain't famous". The track's real topic, therefore, is West's embodiment of fame, his reputational and commercial power, and his ability, therefore, to make or break people.[17] That West's sales were declining album-on-album, however, while Swift's were increasing, makes this insistence on his power merely a morbid symptom of his own – and the elite's – declining authority, accounting for his – and their – increasingly authoritarian attitudes.

On 2018's sinister-sounding 'Yikes' (UK 10; US 8), West expresses antipathy to #MeToo, while on 'All Mine' (UK 11; US 11) he gives rein to a traditional misogyny unassuaged by his adoption of a gratingly 'feminised' falsetto. West's seemingly random assertion that slavery was "a choice", the same year, connects quite logically to the fascistic fetishisation of individual power – and thus a denial of institutionalised systems of inequality. West concurrently reaffirmed his support of Trump, and in 2020 ran for that ultimate personality cult and locus of power, the presidency, funded by Trump supporters.

Taylor Swift: Post-Humanity (The Comeback)

If Taylor Swift was initially the wronged party in the Kanye beef, her response to 'Famous', summer 2017's 'Look What You Made Me Do' (UK 1; US 1), rather suggested they deserved each other. The track's preoccupation with public perception, its competitive othering ("I don't trust nobody and nobody trusts me"), its refusal of responsibility ("look what *you* made me do" – emphasis added) and its *Game of Thrones* invocation (of Arya Stark's kill list) are quite as Trumpian as West.[18] Having had her reputation trashed – and her power diminished – by West duplicitously claiming she'd signed off on 'Famous', Swift concludes there's no point in behaving decently in what she unquestioningly accepts as a social war of all against all. Claiming "the old Taylor" is "dead", Swift confides: "I got smarter, I got harder in the nick of time".

You can hear this new hardness not just in once-winsome Swift's affectless tone on 2017's *Reputation* (UK 1; US 1) but in the album's booming, aggressive – and ironically West-influenced – production. Even the love song '...Ready for It?' (UK 7; US 4) is sinister in both sonics and sentiment – "I keep him forever like a vendetta". What's most arresting, however, is that the song's video presents Swift embracing her cyborg doppelgänger. The post-human, with its supersession of human emotions, had, post-millennium, been superseded by the 'flexible worker' as the ideal of centrist subjecthood. Yet here and throughout *Reputation*, Swift serves a reminder that post-human affectlessness was simply absorbed into flexibility as competitive individualism. On 'I Did Something Bad', consequently, love is a zero-sum game: "You gotta leave before you get left". That Swift had previously presented herself as a victim rather than an agent of such transactionality (as on 2012's 'All Too Well', *Red*, UK 1; US 1) makes this affectlessness no less post-human, however sarcastically it's celebrated: "They say I did something bad/Then why's it feel so good?"

That Swift is representative rather than renegade in her affective post-humanism is illustrated by the declaration on Imagine Dragons' reptilian 2018 'Natural' (US 13) that, "You gotta be so cold/To make it in this world". Ariana Grande's 'Thank U Next' (UK 1; US 1), the same year, offers an affectless list of her ex-lovers – "They say I move on too fast" – whose loss is 'resolved' by the ultimate post-human non-emotion, 'self-love'. "I turned out so amazing", Grande coos: "Ain't no need for searching". Even in a society where the false flag of 'progressive' has turned the concept of progress upside down, as in Marx's *camera obscura*, the notion that such affective post-humanity was an evolution for our species-being was what centrists liked to call 'post-truth'.

Kesha: #MeToo

That the American president famously boasted that his flirtation technique was to grab women's genitals, whilst a raft of sexual misconduct allegations trailed him into the White House, was indicative not just of Donald Trump's personal failings but of an embedded, enduring societal misogyny. The #MeToo movement was launched a year into Trump's presidency, with its focus on collective solidarity aligning it with both BLM and the Sanders campaign.

It's telling, however, that, while attracting huge public and celebrity support, #MeToo has so little to represent it musically that it can be distilled to a minor hit by a once-major artist, Kesha, whose career and mental health were capsized by sexual harassment.[19] Kesha's first significant hit in *five years*, 2017's power ballad 'Praying' (UK 26; US 22) laterally addresses her accusation that EDM producer Dr. Luke abused and assaulted her (the case was settled out of court in 2023). It's also telling that 'Praying' was Kesha's *final* hit, making its assertion, "You said that I was done, but the best is yet to come", heartbreaking at both a personal and political level. It's even more telling that, despite the song's vengeful promise – "When I'm finished, they won't even know your name" – Dr. Luke is, as of this writing, still working, while Kesha's singles from 2019 to 2023 have failed to chart in any territory.

Cardi B: The Projects' Trap

A 'trap house' is a drug den, the 'trap' the drug economy, and as Biggie, 50 and Jay-Z had long testified, dealing and rap presented the primary escape hatches from the projects' poverty trap. While originating in the South, the first real trap hit was New Jerseyite Fetty Wap's 2015 'Trap Queen' (UK 8; US 2), which, as befits a street-up, emergent culture, broke via social media. Lyrically the track is a reassertion of 'keeping it real', with project hard times and financial bottom lines the economic base on which trap's superstructure arises: "In love with the money, I ain't never letting go". The venality here is balanced by a vulnerability gangsta rap had rarely expressed, via trap's Auto-Tuned sing-speak, while the eerie, dreamy synths keep it ethereal.

Georgia trio Migos's viral 2017 'Bad and Boujee' (UK 30; US 1), with Lil Uzi Vert, introduced the 'Migos flow', a stuttering triplet cadence tapped by everyone from Lamar to Drake. Another track fetishising the fiscal, the lyric seems always on the verge of saying something larger – "We came from nothin' to somethin', n***a" – a liminality enhanced by the psychedelic production, which is even more outré on 2017's reversed, ricocheting trip-trap 'T-Shirt' (US 19). Fellow Georgian Future's croaking, half-sung flow, its vulnerability enhanced by Auto-Tune, was responsible for a string of US number 1 albums and for Post Malone (the era's Eminem, without the talent). On his 2016 Drake collaboration

'Used to This' (US 14), Future's mesmerised itemisation of the material – "Drop-top Porsches… /Mansion in the hills, I got used to this" – suggests, rather, his *awe* at this outcome, "You know how far we came if you know where we been" being more haunted than hubristic.

Future's startling 2017 'Mask Off' (UK 22; US 5) boasts, "From food-stamps to a whole 'nother domain, ya/Out the bottom, I'm the livin' proof". Yet this achievement doesn't sound like much fun: blearily listing narcotics, Future sounds numbed – "I can barely move" – the track's 'realness' surreal, a threshold between dream and nightmare. On 2016's 'Low Life' (US 18), with kindred spirit the Weeknd, Future creates dystopia from utopia: "I turn the Ritz into a poor house… /Turn a five-star hotel to a trap house". Rather than the low life being elevated by capitalist success, the high life is degraded by it, disavowing liberal notions of 'civilisation'. Trap here becomes an elaborate troll, effected by that most disorientating of strategies – *living* the racial stereotype, keeping it real by making racial profiling real. "Yeah, they stereotypin'", Future sniggers, "'Cause they know a n***a keep ten rifles". In an era of festering ethno-nationalism, such a maxed-out bling and gangrenous gangsta shtick may be as effective a means of arguing with fascists as Trotsky's injunction to acquaint them with the pavement.

The persona and production of Cardi B captures all these facets of trap: its larger-than-life quality, its provocation of conservatives, and its combo of psychedelic spookiness and sidewalk crudeness. Yet, where previous trap productions were often lo-fi, Cardi's are high end, without approaching conventionality. While Cardi's strident drawl tracks trap's sing-speak, her timbre is diamond hard but distendedly blurry, as she creates neologisms – like the title of 2017's magnificent 'Bodak Yellow' (UK 24; US 1) – and tosses out testaments to springing out the trap: "I used to live in the Ps, now it's a crib with a gate". 2018's 'Bartier Cardi' (US 14) renders her demotic even more weirdly opaque – a mesmerising Migos flow of variants on 'Cardi', 'Cartier' and 'body' – while the synth drones psychedelically trip-trap across the speakers. Amidst Cardi's flossing, however, she exhibits, like Future, a disorientated wonder at the way class turns the world upside down: "I been broke my whole life, I have no clue what to do with these racks", she confides on 2018's 'Money Bag' (*Invasion of Privacy*, UK 5; US 1). While Sanders-supporting Cardi's politics remained radical, her music grew more conventional, the lyrics more audible, the mystery dissipating. 2018's 'Money' (US 13) was too materialist in every sense – "Nothing in this world that I like more than checks" – failing to regain her immaterial, liminal heights, her lateral expression of Black Pride.

A more 'conscious' exit from the trap came from an outsider to the genre, J. Cole. On 2017's 'Neighbors' (US 13), Cole falls foul of racial profiling when his Southern neighbours assume his studio is a trap house because the "only time they see us, we be on the news, in chains", resulting in a raid by an armed SWAT team. Where Future's response to such profiling is lateral, Cole's is literal, berating "a racist society that make/Every n***a feel like a candidate/For a Trayvon kinda fate". Not renowned for his humour, Cole is critical of trap's playing to stereotype. On 'ATM' (UK 28; US 6) – "Addiction to Money" – Cole uses mumble rap and trap beats to critique the genre: "In love with big wheels and quick thrills". Similarly, 2019's marvellous 'Middle Child' (UK 9; US 4) uses the Migos flow in a critique of trap consumerism: "What good is the bread if my n****s is broke?/What good is first class if my n****s can't sit?" Cole situates trap's individualism collectively, in "a long bloodline of trauma", which its inheritors are trying to escape, and he counsels: "I hope you know money won't ease the pain". Cole thus effectively offers a materialist analysis of trap's materialism.

Stormzy: Black Britain and the Grime Renaissance

The first we saw of Stormzy, on his YouTube video for 'Shut Up' (UK 8), was the way we'd always see him: in streetwear, in the open air, interacting with a crowd but also with us, the viewers, the fourth wall collapsing. This approach had some affinity with 90s hardcore-rap videos, with its all-male cast and tough-talk – "Dare one of you man, try get loud/All of my mandem move so foul". Yet where hardcore clips projected the projects in darkness and presented their denizens as threatening, Stormzy's video is shot in (weak) estate sunlight, warmed by Stormzy's smile and his social interaction (the last shot is him dissolving into laughter). The clip for 'Wickedskengman 4' (UK 18) adds women and white people, with the assemblage formerly known as the audience entirely aware they're equal stars of the show. Corbyn-supporter Stormzy conveyed the same connection with the polity as the Labour leader at this time, a crucial awareness that celebrity merely gives a name, a face and a voice to a structure of feeling.

This was how resurgent grime rolled: cheap-as-chips videos going viral on YouTube, independently released tracks, the genre's intricate beats and raps a rebuttal of claims that music ceased to innovate beyond the millennium. Even with a budget, Stormzy's video for 2017's 'Big for Your Boots' (UK 6) is just an artier take on his standard approach, shot in London estates and streets, its 'stars' ordinary, multi-ethnic Brits, glaring back at the camera's gaze, Stormzy intermittently riding atop a car like a politician. Positioned now in Brexit's hinterland, Stormzy's lyrics are more socially aware: "Man know that I kick up the yout'", he yelps – inspiring them; *inciting* them – defiance in his dissidence: "Try tell me I'm way too big to rebel!"

If you want to know what 2015–20 was about, watch the video for Stormzy's 2017 'Blinded by Your Grace, Pt. 2' (UK 7). Filmed in another London council estate, the clip returns to the shit-chatting and false starts of Stormzy's YouTube beginnings. Ostensibly, the song – extending grime into gospel – expresses gratitude to God for getting a "broken" Michael Omari out of such estates. Yet Stormzy's towering physical presence amidst the tower blocks, holding a neighbour's child in his arms, standing side-by-side with the crowd, roots him in the community he came from. "One time for the cause", Stormzy drawls, and as the enraptured crowd sing along, it's clear the grace of the song's title is *collectively* held, that this multicultural crowd of young people is the exemplification of hope, of the era's longing for change, the desire, as the track's breakout refrain has it, "to find a way/To another day". This was a realistic, rough-and-ready – even grimy – utopianism, but it was utopianism nonetheless, and we'd seen too little of it for far too long.

Stormzy was an effect as much as the cause of grime's resurgence, however, with veteran Skepta exemplifying its reasserted street origins after its corporate ransacking amidst austerity. Departing his major label, Skepta independently released 'That's Not Me' (UK 21) as a trailer for 2016's eventual Mercury-winner, *Konnichiwa* (UK 2), while filming its video for £80. "Yeah, I used to wear Gucci", Skepta snaps, "I put it all in the bin 'cause that's not me". Despite *Konnichiwa*'s title track's sideswipe at David Cameron – "Nobody's votin' for your corrupted agenda" – Skepta is rarely *overtly* political, yet his music is the sound and vision of a beleaguered black British citizenry, "Out there tryna survive on the streets/Tryin' not to get killed by the police". On 'Man', Skepta' boast that "I shut down Shoreditch carpark/And I got bars like Camden Town" prefigures grime's mapping of black Britain, post-Brexit, from Ramz's 2017 'Barking' (UK 2) to Dave's 2019 'Streatham' (UK 9) to AJ Tracey's 'Ladbroke Grove' (UK 3), a landscape which is also – English Defence League notwithstanding – simply 'Britain'. Similarly, the demotic of grime – "wagwan" [what's going on], "peng ting" [pretty girl] – deriving from Caribbean patois, is termed Multicultural London English (MLE) by socio-linguistics scholars.[20] For this vibrant demotic has diffused into all demographics and – unofficial, unlicensed, free – is thus ultimately utopian.

While grime stars articulated this double-consciousness of black Britons, Britain's racialised double standard was demonstrated by May's government's enervated response to the 2017 Grenfell fire – called out by Stormzy at 2018's Brits. This contrasted to the energy the government put into repatriating 'illegal' immigrants, many of them members of the Windrush generation who founded black Britain back in the 1940s.[21] All this was a symbolic and material assault on multicultural Britain, fanned by the media, but grime kept producing more artillery in its counterattack. And not just Grime4Corbyn. Dave's 2019 epic 'Black' rivals 'Blinded by Your Grace' in the grime-gospel stakes (and has the same producer, Fraser T. Smith), depicting the precarity of black Britons, who "need to do double what they do so you can level them", because "black is bein' guilty until proven that you're innocent" (*Psychodrama*, UK 1). After performing the track at the 2020 Brits, Dave called new prime minister Boris Johnson "a real racist", with Johnson's spokesperson Priti Patel issuing a denial the next day. In this febrile atmosphere, Northampton rapper Slowthai crucially insisted on 2019's *Nothing*

Great About Britain (UK 9), "I'm a product, yeah, you made me… it breaks and you can't fix it without me", invoking the Fanonian interdependence of self and other.

Stormzy returned with the brilliantly insouciant 'Vossi Bop' in 2019 (UK 1), which took the council estate video to new heights – dancing kids darting in and out of the frame, emitting both joy and defiance; locations seamlessly shifting, the cast claiming the capital as their estate. As Stormzy snarls, "Fuck the government and fuck Boris", he and the dancing kids are suddenly outside the Houses of Parliament. However, the accompanying album, 2019's *Heavy is the Head* (UK 1), contained little political material, and as that year's election loomed, Stormzy was preoccupied, like Lamar, with questions of leadership – the haters ('Big Michael'), the competitors ('Audacity', UK 6) and the pressure ('One Second'). 'Crown' (UK 4) manages to turn representativeness into uniqueness: "If I do it out of love, it's not to benefit myself", while Stormzy's iffy singing, unrelatable content and the video's setting in a church go against what originally won him that crown. Again, this is the problem with personality cults, the risk of preoccupation with the *process* rather than the *purpose* of political leadership.

Ed Sheeran: The Regional and the Metropolitan

Ed Sheeran is a pop populist: musically accessible – 2017's 'Shape of You' (UK 1; US 1) is one of the biggest-selling songs of all time – ordinary in looks and demeanour, Sheeran effaces the distinction between citizenry and celebrity, reassuringly awkward in formal scenarios and entirely at ease with ordinary people. Sheeran could thus appeal to both regional social conservatives *and* metropolitan social liberals: populism without prejudice. The managed amnesia regarding these years elides Corbyn achieving the same synthesis in the 2017 election. Whether or not this pop populism makes Corbyn-supporting Sheeran's music any *good* is as relevant as whether Corbyn had decent music taste.

Sheeran's collaborations with hip-hop and grime artists weren't just grafted-on guest spots,[22] Sheeran having incorporated hip-hop beats and grime flows from the get-go, collaborating with Wiley while still self-releasing records. Yet, unlike occasional collaborator Taylor Swift, Sheeran maintained his regional credentials amidst increasing mainstream success. 2017's 'Castle on the Hill' (UK 2; US 6) combines folk and stadium rock with dance rhythms to hymn a regional upbringing. "These people raised me/And I can't wait to get back home" salutes the "folk-body blood of the land"[23] while tapping metropolitan millennial affect – lacking decent housing in the cities and regarding parents' regional places as 'home'. The song is corny and contrived, yet it's effective. The same year's 'Galway Girl' (UK 2) was the most parochial pop had sounded since the 80s (even the Corrs were slicker). The video's use of the rare subjective gaze catches only Sheeran's occasional reflection, while we empathetically *experience* him drunkenly falling over and then being knocked out, dissolving the barriers between self and other, as well as those between metropolitan celebrity and regional citizen. Sheeran's final 2017 single, 'Perfect' (UK 4), concerns reconnecting with someone from his provincial past, again endorsing the pull of place and the reassurance of regional identity. Adding an artist and calling it a 'remix' was the industry's latest revenue-maximising ruse, and a Beyoncé duet of 'Perfect' (UK 1; US 1) restarted the song's sales while presenting the metropolitan and the regional in literal – rather fetching – harmony.

By 2019, the political mood had changed, second-referendum mania re-polarising the polity into provincial and metropolitan camps. Sheeran's multicultural 2019 *No. 6 Collaborations Project* (UK 1; US 1) appeared to be an attempt to steer through this. Released on the eve of the winter 2019 election, Sheeran's Stormzy collaboration, 'Take Me Back to London' (UK 1), is a potential provocation, with its grime beats and Sheeran echoing Stormzy's flow. Yet, with Stormzy asserting, "I don't mix with the glitz and the glam" and Sheeran doing his everybloke "Give me a packet of crisps with my pint" number, the metropolis here is just another home. As the song hit the chart, however, the election result revealed that the cultural gulf between Britain's polarised demographics was beyond politics' – let alone pop's – ability to bridge.

Drake: Centrist Confusion

Politically, it was assumed that Hillary Clinton's accession would be a cinch, first as Democratic candidate, then as president. Politically skilled, part of an established dynasty, Clinton was the centrist legacy candidate. Instead, by complacently pursuing the technocrat logic of 'more of the same', Clinton was close-run from the left by Sanders in the primaries – losing much of her poise in the process – and then defeated from the right by Trump in the 2016 election. Centrists' sense of injustice had been building since Sanders' candidacy (and Corbyn's accession) but now went into freefall, blaming variously the left, the right, the public – everyone but themselves – for this parlous political situation.

Culturally, Drake, or Aubrey Graham, by breaking through immediately after the crash, amid declining record sales and attenuating celebrity respect, was haunted by a sense of being denied his due. This dubious identifying feature was unconnected, he claimed, to entitlement (despite his uncle being in the Family Stone), while his sense of loss was seemingly unassuaged by winning. "They're never gonna finish Drake", he declares on 2016's 'Summer Sixteen' (UK 23; US 6), though who 'they' are is unclear, as is why or how they're trying to "finish" him. On 2016's trappy 'Pop Style' (US 16), with fellow paranoid egotist Kanye West, Drake complains, "I can't trust no fuckin' body/ They still out to get me 'cause they never got me".

Despite being a love song (of sorts), Drake's brilliant 2015 'Hotline Bling' (UK 3; US 2) captures the centrist sense of a perfect setup that no one had any business to mess with. Drake delivers the title line in a delightful burble that evokes a cellphone's 'bling' – its promise not material riches but sexual pleasure. It's thus a *booty call* that provokes Drake's sense of loss, expressed here as petulance, control-freakery (stalking his FWB's socials) and slut-shaming ("Wonder if you're bendin' over backwards for someone else"). In this orgy of oversharing, Drake's unawareness of how *seen* it makes him somehow adds to the track's attraction, though this rests heavily on its sample. That the bones of Timmy Thomas's 1973 'Why Can't We Live Together' are so visible in 'Hotline' attests to the attenuation of desire over the intervening forty years: from Thomas longing for a future of universal love to Drake pining for a lost past of transactional sex. Utopia here has been outsourced, then bankrupted.

In the video for 2018's 'God's Plan' (UK 1; US 1), Drake is a capitalist Jesus blessing people with cash (not unlike Bieber). The public's tearful reactions indicate the desperation created by the post-crash recession, but the video treats this as a matter of individual misfortune and individual generosity, because, in centrist essentialism, there *is* no system. However, with Drake transpiring to have abandoned a child he'd conceived, the video now looks distinctly like damage-limitation, paying off the public. Drake's enduring desire for the high ground – "Settled into my role as the good guy", he states on '8 out of 10' (US 21) – regardless of his actions on the ground, again mirrors centrism. 2018's 'I'm Upset' (US 7) finds him "offended" by the "disrespect" of being asked for child support (did he not have *people* to proofread his pronouncements?) And still the demands for appreciation arrived like terrorist ultimatums – "You gotta feel me before they try and kill me", on 2018's 'In My Feelings' (UK 1; US 1); "Give me my respect, give me my respect!" on 'Nonstop' (UK 4; US 2). Pathetic as this was, at least Drake said the quiet part loud, expressing the naked *id* of a centrism that was a graceless loser and would soon prove a gruesomely sore winner.

Despite centrism's self-exposure under pressure, and despite the energy of the emergent radical currents, it was residual centrism that, through no virtue of its own, emerged the victor from this period's political struggles. The UK Conservatives' December 2019 landslide was a pyrrhic victory for the centre, the spectre of a left-wing Corbyn administration allayed by a right-wing government of pure perniciousness, Boris Johnson as Trump's pale transatlantic shadow. A centrist restoration could meanwhile be conducted within the Labour Party, while it waited for the Conservative right to collapse from its own contradictions. Joe Biden's win in America, however, was a pragmatic victory, restoring storied centrist rationality and legitimacy and apparently banishing the 'post-truth' of Trump to history's dustbin.

It was Sanders' concession of the Democratic nomination to Biden in spring 2020 that represented the termination of this period's radical politics and which – prompting the immediate collapse of the American left – felt like the concession of hope. Corbyn's defeat, likewise, caused the British left's fragile coalition to crumble in depressingly short order. This again indicates the problem with the cult of personality. It's not just that the burden of representation causes figureheads to puff up with the attention or buckle under the strain – the fact that Sanders and Corbyn did neither is testament to their leadership qualities. Leadership's function is to give a face, a voice and a name not just to a constituency but to a *movement*, whereas, in the cult of personality, a collective project stands or falls with that individual. It's for this reason – and the ideological labour of the right and of restoration centrism – that 2015–20 has left almost no legacy in formal politics; only the music and the memories remain.

This makes it crucial that those memories, and that music, be kept alive, that this era's utopianism be remembered and can thus be re-accessed in less hopeful times. For this was a period that, while polarised, saw a dissolution of long-established, ideological barriers between self and other, for which Bieber's 'Sorry' and Jess Glynne's 'Hold My Hand' can stand. This was a time when radical black politics rebutted the malignant ethno-nationalism nurtured by austerity and so Beyoncé's 'Formation' stands with BLM here, as does Kendrick Lamar's 'Alright': "we're gonna be alright". For the adversarial spirit of the left in this period was – whatever the winners' histories will relate – entirely affirmative. Arising from Britain's parallel revival of innovative popular music and transformative popular politics, Stormzy's 'Blinded by Your Grace' articulates the multicultural utopianism of the British left in this conjuncture.

For this was a time when longing for change seemed not utopian but practical, when a different future seemed not just possible but graspable, when the greater good ceased to be merely an abstraction but a material policy offer, from "For the many, not the few" to the Green New Deal. The period from 2015 to 2020 was a time of hope, therefore, a hope driven by politics and captured by pop: a time when it felt like there *was* an alternative.

Conclusion:
Remixing Pop and Politics

The present is an arbitrary point at which to conclude any historical account. History doesn't reach narrative closure: three decades after the declared end of history, the status quo isn't static, and the neoliberal settlement isn't settled – although endless ideological labour goes into informing us that politics has found its final form.[1] Political control has become detached from consensus and political power from popularity (making all those anti-populism editorials the gift that keeps on giving), because neoliberalism is all out of ideas. The restored establishment has no solutions to the recession, to inflation, to the housing crisis, or to the increasingly tangible climate crisis – all of which would involve a confrontation with capital. Politics has become a matter of technocratically managing dystopia: not just the dramatic dystopia of disease and war, but the boring dystopia in which everyday activities like work, travel and shopping have become alienating and dehumanising experiences. "It is what it is" is the mantra of contemporary politics: social change is not the business of governance.

Rather than this meaning we're all doomed, it means, paradoxically, that everything is still to play for politically. That's the nature of the Marxist dialectic – it's both "an affirmative recognition of the existing state of things [and] at the same time... the recognition of the negation of that state, of its inevitable breaking up." This is because, Marx continues, the dialectic, "regards every historically developed social form as in fluid movement, and therefore takes into account its transient nature not less than its momentary existence".[2] This process doesn't occur organically or abstractedly but through the actions of *people*: ordinary people.

Music acts as a material instance of – and an inspirational metaphor for – this fluid movement of history. For, despite the insistence of those whose cultural or political narrative ended in the 90s, music has continued to develop in the last three decades. Its rate of change has been slower than under Fordism and is determined by data's ones and zeros rather than dramatic year zeros – but it is change, nonetheless. These developments aren't merely the product of capitalism's dynamism, but of the actions of musicians – of ordinary people. Even as Big Tech and the small state attempt to crunch us down to data, the post-Fordist process of processing and its cycle of recycling hasn't fixed innovation in the mix: technocracy's predictive systems haven't produced complete predictability. Contemporary music's innovations may not always be allied to utopian politics – Central Cee being a case in point – but in its refusal to recognise any arrival at a "final form", music remains a field of possibility, a perennially regenerating resource of hope, in Williams' terms.

Via the very embedding in the past that boomer pop-paradigmers decry, contemporary music points towards the future – note the title of Dua Lipa's 2020 *Future Nostalgia* (UK 1: US 3). The centrality of sampling and quotation in contemporary music, alongside the perennial accessibility and audibility of music's entire back catalogue, means the past is always alive in our present, history always tangibly in the mix. Music is thus a material expression of our existence within what Walter Benjamin called "open time".[3] Within such a temporality, the future isn't fixed, the present is in fluid movement, and the past provides an inexhaustible, infinitely renewable resource.

If time is open, therefore, the fact that history repeats itself, in Marx's famous claim, doesn't need to be either tragic or farcical. The third decade of the twenty-first century has seen the greatest incidence of industrial action in thirty years in both Britain and America. The right-wing press has spun this as a return to the 'nightmare 70s', with governments redeploying the spectre of inflation to divide strikers from the rest of the working public. These strategies have failed because such a historical repetition is a reminder of a time when ordinary people possessed power, and when governments sought *solutions* to social and economic problems, rather than leaving them to the market. Remembrance of the past, as Traverso argues, doesn't need to be mournful – a reminder that things have only got worse – nor does it need to be escapist, the indulgence of an enervated hauntology. Instead, the past can reacquaint us with the *possible*: striking miners, after all, caused the collapse of the Conservative government in 1974. In pop and politics alike, the presence of the past makes change a living, material occurrence: it opens time up and reacquaints us with what Traverso calls "the utopia of the future".[4]

As Grafton Tanner warns, while the past is "teeming with lost realities", it's also swarming with available myths – with 'tradition' – which can be deployed as a dead hand upon the present.[5] For the right, 'Union Joe' Biden pre-emptively banning rail workers from striking in late 2022 is also a historical repetition – of Reagan breaking the PATCO strike in 1981 – while Rishi Sunak's government's 2023 Strikes (Minimum Service Level) Act echoes Thatcher's late-70s anti-union legislation, which led to the 1985 miners' strike that finished off Fordist militancy. Yet there's no tragedy even in these repetitions for the left: authoritarian measures only reveal the fear that strikes – the organised power of ordinary people – provoke in the establishment. Whether this wave of strikes is ongoing or over by the time this book appears, these actions remain an intervention in history. Such struggles represent, for Marcuse, "a refusal to accept as final the limitations imposed upon freedom and happiness by the reality principle" – by capitalist realism – "a refusal to forget what can be".[6]

The worldwide lockdown of 2020–21 was an exemplification of this open temporality: with the performance principle suspended, time moved both more quickly *and* more slowly than the normative neoliberal pace. For Marcuse, "time is society's most natural ally in maintaining law and order, conformity, and [the postponement] of freedom".[7] The untrammelled id is beyond time (there's little limit to a child's capacity to play), while the superego, the enforcer of the performance principle – and of 'grown-up politics' – is forever calling time on pleasure. 2020 was a lost year on the capitalist clock, but a *found* year in human affect, its open time offering a glimpse of what freedom might look like – a window onto utopia.

This freedom was underwritten by the cornered Keynesianism of an ideologically opposed political elite, who leveraged lockdown to reassert the neoliberal verities of austerity as reality and authoritarianism as responsibility. In breaking up public assemblies and closing down parks, while exempting itself from such social strictures, the establishment asserted its re-established power. This elite exceptionalism was just as evident culturally as it was politically.

"We're all in it together", declared *Wonder Woman*'s Gal Gadot, introducing a video of celebrities singing John Lennon's 'Imagine' in March 2020. Yet not only did the participants' inability to agree on a common key attest to an ingrained atomisation, but mansion-dwelling elites urging ordinary people in rented flats to imagine a property-less world served notice we *weren't* all in it together. Drake's morale-boosting dance for April's 'Toosie Slide' (UK 1; US 1) offered us a grand tour of his Toronto mansion, as his fans underwent an eviction crisis. Despite the democratic clips of ordinary citizens in Ariana Grande and Justin Bieber's video for their doo-wop-derived duet 'Stuck With U' that May (UK 4; US 1), Bieber couldn't help showing off his mansion's huge grounds and private gym. Trap's typically amoral boasting didn't even pretend to be morale-boosting: Internet Money, Gunna and Don Toliver bragged on August 2020's 'Lemonade' (UK 1; US 6), "gotta thank God that I'm livin' comfortably... my old life was disgusting", while millions queued for food banks.

More subtly invidious was the cultural elite's management of citizens' expectations. Grande and Gaga's proclamation, "I'd rather be dry, but at least I'm alive" on their housey May 2020 duet 'Rain on Me' (UK 1; US 1) is a distinctly low-bar boost, with Gaga's bossy, spoken "Rain on me" spinning passivity as agency. Billie Eilish's July 2020 'My Future' (UK 7; US 6) closes the future down by personifying it ("Can't wait to meet her"). Was such self-isolating 'self-love' really the best strategy for surviving social distancing? Korean boyband BTS's Sheeran-penned July 2021 'Permission to Dance' (UK 16; US 1) conventionalises the pandemic's psychological damage – "If you don't let it faze ya/You'll know just how to break" – the broken citizen as ideal citizen. Cometh the crisis, cometh the dance revival, with David Guetta's 2022 Bebe Rexha co-sign 'I'm Good (Blue)' (UK 1; US 4) rebooting EDM's sonics and sentiments – "Imma have the best fuckin' night of my life" – but with a pandemic twist to austerity's resilience mode. Rexha's lines, "Don't need the finer things in life… /Don't got a lot, but that's enough for me" echo economists' insistence on the citizenry's need to accept a lower standard of living. This despite FTSE 100 chief executives pocketing 133 times the average wage, and the world's ten richest men doubling their wealth during the pandemic.[8] Breaking elite ranks, Kendrick Lamar called out this unequal distribution of austerity on 2022's 'N95' (UK 6; US 3): "Y'all getting' fucked… this ain't Monopoly", when some are "sleepin' in a box".

Where trap's melancholy realism once sounded resistant, it now sounded like resignation. Juice Wrld's posthumous 2020 'Hate the Other Side' (US 10) addresses the projects' PTSD – "My heart's still tryna recover from pain all my life" – but turns it on peers, not power: "I was taught to love my brothers and hate the other side". This is reiterated by Roddy Ricch on *Please Excuse Me for Being Antisocial* (UK 13; US 1): "The streets left me cold-hearted, they hurt me still". Yet Ricch's vulnerable, falsetto "eek" throughout 2020's 'The Box' (UK 2; US 1) doesn't disguise its aggressive antipathy to his competitive others.

So, that the Weeknd was, by summer 2021, safe for the Superbowl suggests how melancholia's refusal had been repressively sublimated during lockdown. While turning a pop cliché into a paean to autoerotic asphyxiation, 'Take My Breath' (UK 13; US 6) was less transgressive than passive: "You're offering yourself to me like sacrifice". Musically and lyrically, Sheeran's November 2021 'Overpass Graffiti' (UK 4) is a vanilla Weeknd: life as a "dark parade", with loss passively accepted because "the cards were always stacked against us". Harry Styles' April 2022 'As It Was' (UK 1; US 1) is a further dimming of 'Blinding Lights', matching both its 80s sugar rush and its melancholy – "Seems you cannot be replaced" – but with Styles' forlornly breezy falsetto rendering such resignation a relief from responsibility, thus loss as a balanced account.

By 2021, Grime4Corbyn was such a thing of the past that, on Dave and Stormzy's 'Clash' (UK 2), pop's first Corbyn reference was a descriptor of one of Dave's conquests (whether she supported or resembled the former Labour leader isn't revealed). Grime became more 'UK drill'-orientated, closer to trap's solipsism, so on Russ Millions' 2021 'Body' (UK 1), Tion Wayne boasts, "I got a million in savings/But you can still get shaven" (murdered). However, the title of Dave's 2021 *We're All Alone in This Together* (UK 1) affirmed ordinary people's sociality while satirising elite double standards. Moreover, Dave claims individual success is "like flying first-class on a crashin' plane", and on 'Survivor's Guilt' admits that "I feel the worst at my happiest/'Cause I miss all my n****s that couldn't be in this life I built". This isn't just about *Dave's* stardom and conscience; he's presenting himself as part of a community: "Poverty is killin' us, the government's killin' us". This is a key reminder of the pandemic's dialectic, therefore, of the fact that as much as it locked politics down, it also opened possibilities up.

Lockdown revived a collectivity prohibited not just by the practicalities of a pandemic but the politics of restoration neoliberalism. Reading and listening groups expressed the inherent sociality of popular culture, while mutual aid groups, #MeToo campaigns, food banks and neighbour support-networks demonstrated the power of solidarity. If there was a danger that such voluntarist interventions let the state off the hook, they also exposed the state's callousness. Footballer Marcus Rashford forced the British government to U-turn on school meals for poor families, and this was neatly deployed as a metaphor on AJ Tracey and Digga D's February 2021 'Bringin' It Back' (UK 5): "I locked up the food [drugs] for the kids like Boris/And then I let it go like Rashford". Tracey also invokes the acclamation of the NHS on the Live Lounge All-Stars' 2020 Foo Fighters cover, 'Times Like These' (UK 1): "I'll clap at 8… time to pay back all the health docs lent me". Again, the public risked being used as a decoy from the welfare state's defunding, with the government refusing nurses a pay rise at the pandemic's peak. Live-Lounge participant Sam Fender's indie-rock 2021 'Seventeen Going Under' (UK 3) excoriates this separation of state from citizenry – "I see my mother/The DWP sees a number" – the track building like a monument, Fender's vocal's mounting affective abandon asserting austerity's atomising inhumanity.

BLM's resurgence erupted from this reasserted collectivity, with masked demonstrators repopulating the streets where the police shot down George Floyd in May 2020 and spreading across America and Britain. If SAINt JHN's April 2020 'Roses ' was a rote, trap-life money-raiser (UK 1; US 4), J. Cole's May 2021 'My Life' (UK 13; US 2) was a coruscating conscious-rap revival: "Where I come from, people you grow up with layin' in a coffin". BLM's protests diffused throughout culture, and throughout British football's 2020-21 season, players took the knee in tribute during the national anthem, booed by portions of the crowd, with one MP calling the gesture "Marxist". However, as corporations began to brandish BLM insignia, Lamar's 2022 'Savior' (*Mr Morale & the Big Steppers*, UK 2; US 1) cautioned: "Capitalists posing as compassionates be offending me". Centrist emphasis on 'optics' over policy facilitates a purely presentational anti-racism – thus Labour leader Keir Starmer taking the knee for a photo opportunity – when, as Taylor argues, "the police function to enforce the rule of the politically powerful and the economic elite".[9] Police brutality is thus an expression of, not an exception to, that rule.

The pandemic also produced a resurgent female empowerment, which while again presentational rather than practical, provided necessary pushback to right-wing attempts to lock down feminism, as witness conservative reactions to leftist senator Alexandria Ocasio-Cortez and the overturning of the *Roe vs. Wade* abortion ruling in 2022. Beyoncé's April 2020 'remix' of Megan Thee Stallion's 'Savage' (UK 3; US 1) reclaims misogynist pejoratives like "bitch", "ratchet" (wretched) and "moody". Although Latto's September 2021 'Big Energy' (UK 21; US 3) liberates the 'big dick energy' internet meme for women, it leaves Freud's patriarchal concept of the 'phallus' as power symbol unchallenged. Doja Cat's October 2021 'Woman' (UK 13; US 7) confronts female conditioning, "'Cause the world told me, we ain't got that common sense/Gotta prove it to myself that I'm on top of shit". Yet that the toxic Dr Luke produces much of Doja's work – as well as 'Big Energy' – means these songs operate within a male-produced epistemology, still semi-locked down.[10]

Because libidinal capitalism has always sexualised female bodies, sex positivity can seem like a shaky political strategy.

Cardi B and Megan's foregrounding of female desire on August 2020's 'WAP' (UK 1; US 1) was relatively mild: "Bring a bucket and a mop for this wet-ass pussy" they demand. Yet that the track provoked such conservative hostility suggested its rejection of retrograde models of femininity was hitting home. Still, there's an attendant risk of accepting the right's assertion that assertive sexuality is feminism's political horizon. The sex positivity of Ariane Grande's October 2020 'Positions' (UK 1; US 1) and ensuing '34+35' (UK 3; US 2) with Megan and Doja doesn't render Grande's pride in the roles of cook, dutiful daughter-in-law and ditzy student ("bad at math") the less retrogressive.

With Megan and Cardi B openly bisexual, sex positivity intersects with queerness, but also with the conventionally reactionary. With Drake's claim to be a lesbian on 2021's 'Girls Want Girls' (UK 2; US 2) receiving zero kickback, an imagistic 'lesbianism' is still readily incorporated into chauvinistic, heteronormative discourse. "How can I be homophobic?" Central Cee demands on 'Doja' (UK 2), "My bitch is gay!" Male homosexuality can't be as readily incorporated, however. So, while corporations sport rainbow flags for Pride and queer films win Oscars (2016's *Moonlight*) and plaudits (2017's *Call Me by Your Name*), male queer *desire* has tended to be both inaudible and invisible. Into the space opened up by lockdown stepped the newly 'out' Lil Nas X. March 2021's 'Montero (Call Me by Your Name)' (UK 1; US 1) isn't particularly explicit, but that lines like "Shoot a child in your mouth while I'm riding" and a promo featuring Nas lap-dancing for the devil didn't prejudice the track's chart placing suggests unapologetic assertion can carry perception with it. Lil Nas was similarly assertive in response to criticism, comparing the video's impact on children to that of the commercial availability of guns. With Lil Nas's 'That's What I Want' video (UK 10; US 8) providing a critique of (illusory) heteronormativity, this was extended to gender normativity on Sam Smith and Kim Petras's autumn 2022 'Unholy' (UK 1; US 1). With its video depicting the sexual and gender ambiguities beneath conventional surfaces, the song's success represented pop again leading public opinion, while shaming formal politics.

With the pandemic pausing the performance principle and providing the longest reprieve from 'the grind' in most people's lives, lockdown created a liminal space for the first rethinking of work since the 70s' three-day weeks. The viral success of postal worker Nathan Evans' sea shanty 'Wellerman' (UK 1) was effectively a tribute to the delivery drivers who were briefly acclaimed as pandemic 'key workers': "Soon may the Wellerman come/To bring us sugar and tea and rum". The track's multiple-participant TikToks expressed a yearning for something denied not just by lockdown but by the ubiquity of bullshit jobs – work with meaning and dignity. In a material example of what Olin Wright calls "real utopias", pandemic furlough payments were a glimpse of what a universal basic income (UBI) might look like.

These impulses culminated in 2021's Great Resignation, when 4.7% of British and 3% of American workers quit their jobs after lockdown,[11] largely in low-paying, insecure sectors. Ed Sheeran and Lil Baby's spring 2022 '2Step' (UK 9) addresses this structure of feeling – "We forget that we're here right now" – rejecting being "stuck in a constant race", while warning, "Keep the pressure on, you're bound to break". Beyoncé's house-infused summer 2022 'Break My Soul' (UK 2; US 1) also refuses to be broken on the wheel: "Just quit my job… damn they work me so damn hard".[12] On that autumn's 'I Drink Wine' (UK 4; US 18), Adele rasps, "They say to play hard, you work hard/ Find balance in the sacrifice", whereas, contrary to this post-Fordist compact, alienation has instead amplified: "I don't know anybody/Who's truly satisfied" she sighs. However, with the left politically isolated – Corbinned – the Great Resignation was a mass expression of *individual* frustration and, unaligned to campaigns for UBI or a shorter working week, the greatest resignation was 2022's inevitable mass return to work. However, the Great Resignation almost certainly prompted employers to allow working from home to continue, while, as a mass withdrawal of labour, it was a precursor of the ensuing wave of strikes.

Lockdown's liminal temporality hardly invented nostalgia, but it did produce a past that was more than a palette of styles or an escape portal from a grim present, with three of the period's most luminous hits not just harking back to, but hauntologically engaging with, that past. As part of Taylor Swift's rerecording of her entire back catalogue – a rather literal enactment of 'open time' – her epic 2021 remake of 2012 stadium-pop ballad 'All Too

Well' (UK 3; US 1) testifies in context and content to mourning's incompleteness, the present-ness of the past. "I was there" she repeats, enraptured: "I remember it all too well". Lana Del Rey's music has always been imbued with this unresolved past, but her 2023 release of a 2014 track, the luminously shimmering 'Say Yes to Heaven' (UK 9), lyrically summons Lennon's 1969 'Give Peace a Chance', while reaffirming the counterculture's unconditionality, the affective openness of the 60s thereby revenant even in the locked-down 2020s.

In-between, Kate Bush's magical 1985 'Running Up That Hill' returned to the charts in summer 2022 (UK 1; US 3), driven by its deployment in 80s-set TV horror series *Stranger Things* (2022). Rather than this being a purely circumstantial event – a depthless hit of 80s nostalgia for an extra-diegetic overlay to the action – the song was integral to the series' plot, which dramatised the lyric's longing to "exchange the experience", to sideline the self and feel what the *other* feels, with music presented as the medium of that sociality. Moreover, that a boomer song from Gen X's youth was zoomer-driven to contemporary success suggested that, for all the post-crash period's generational resentments, we were all commingled – remixed – within an increasingly open time.

We don't listen to music chronologically, whether it's chosen or randomised – prompted by biorhythm or algorithm – and neither do we *hear* it chronologically. Whether in a shop or a hipster café, coming from a phone on a bus or a muscle car on the street, heard in a film soundtrack or in a TikTok, we're besieged by music from a randomised temporality. We're lost in music, spun round by it (like a record, baby). Music is both representative and constitutive of the hauntological presence of history, of the constant incursion of the past upon a porous present. Moreover, as memory is communal rather than purely personal, public rather than entirely private, this temporal openness interconnects with *social* openness, with the solidarity and collectivity that music has captured and conveyed over the decades, mixing and remixing us all.

This is *not* to argue that music transcends its historical period. This book has attempted to show something very different – that music *testifies* to its historical period, outlasting but not eclipsing the times that produced it, retaining some residue of the past's reality, its affectivity, its hope. In the 60s, Marcuse observed that what culture "recall[s] and preserve[s] in memory pertains to the future",[13] and it's in *this* manner that music is transcendent – and is utopian.

The period that's been revenant most regularly since the millennium has been the 80s, which provides the model for both our pop and our politics. Yet, as recalled in Chapter 8, the 80s always exercised a contrary pull to its neoliberal push, in both pop ('Running Up That Hill', for one example) and politics (the miners' strike, for another). *Black Mirror*'s 'San Junipero' (2016) distils the depoliticised positivity of 80s revivalism, but there was always a visible skull beneath the period's perfect skin (as the Weeknd understands). Thatcher and Reagan's free-market fundamentalism forged a society in which individuals compete for resources and power, "all for themselves, after all", in Depeche Mode's terms. Yet with the collective world a recent memory, this "competitive world" was always resisted in politics and pop, whether directly – Billy Bragg's 'Between the Wars' – or indirectly – Don Henley's 'Boys of Summer' summoning the Dead Head sticker on the yuppie Cadillac. Even in the most upbeat 80s pop, the engineering of neoliberal affect is audible, as on A-ha's 'Take On Me'. So with the 80s' meaning locked down by the descendants of Thatcher and Reagan who run our lives, this book has attempted to open it back up.

For all its glossy newness, the 80s was forever looking back to the 50s. Nostalgia isn't a neoliberal-era phenomenon, as Jameson, Fisher and Reynolds can seem to suggest, and, as evoked in Chapter 1, the 50s has long been the right's halcyon age of order and responsibility. Yet it's an unstable location for conservatives to erect their ideal home, because their suburban – white, middle-class – idyll is constantly disrupted by the refusal of rock'n'roll, r'n'b and doo-wop, now as much as it was back then. Little Richard, Chuck Berry, Jerry Lee Lewis and the rocker Elvis contradicted their society's complacency that work, sexuality, race and gender were stable concepts. The fuss and holler that Eddie Cochran's 'Summertime Blues' raises against the performance principle couldn't be more immediate, for while the nature of work has changed, its alienation of human nature remains. Equally, while the specifics of sex and gender prohibition have changed, prohibitions remain, and while the modalities of racial repression have altered, its repression remains. The right's desire to turn the clock back to the 50s, therefore, means that the period's struggles are revived along with its repression, and, like Little Richard, they rip it up.

The 50s' duality is captured by the notoriously nostalgic early 70s that's relayed in Chapter 5. Yet if 70s' tame teen pop and adult MOR paralleled politics' conservative restoration, they were countered by glam, as the direct descendant of rock'n'roll's rebellion, but also as a cultural assertion of contemporary working-class power, stomping across history's stage in platform boots. 70s musicians were, in T. Rex's terms, "children of the revolution", their nostalgia a confrontation with political reality, rather than a refuge from it, with Slade, Suzi Quatro, Bowie and Roxy Music capturing queers', women's and proles' refusal to accept their allocated place. In transatlantic tandem, 70s ghetto funk drew on a hauntological heritage of soul, r'n'b and gospel, both to protest the projects' present *and* to celebrate a living historical legacy. Consequently, to tap into the early 70s is to encounter historical memory at its most combustible, to mainline a shot of pure musical adrenaline. A key objective of this book has been to reverse the 70s' negative reputation and to take the pulse of its teeming possibilities.

The 90s had a duplicitous relationship to the past, with its revivals of 70s glam, metal and funk, via Britpop, grunge and gangsta, as Chapter 10 records, excising their utopianism. This parallels 90s' politics' conventionalisation of a harsh environment, where the sharp-elbowed and shell-toed jockeyed for "the power and the money", as Coolio coined it. If Britpop played out this competitive individualism performatively – Blur vs. Oasis – gangsta did so deadly realistically – Tupac vs. Biggie. Consumerist bling should have resolved these contradictions, but 90s positivity was always perturbed by the haters – the losers, the underclass, the left – who rejected its pacifying spin. So, paradoxically, it's in the negative, 'complaint rock' of the Manics, Radiohead and Rage Against the Machine that the 90s' resources of hope reside. Innovations in trip-hop, jungle, techno and R&B – for which Missy Elliott's 'Get Ur Freak On' stands – couldn't progress without a utopian political vision, yet their frustrated futurism destabilises the 90s' duplicitous relationship to the *present*. For in centrist nostalgia, the 90s appear closer in the rear-view mirror than they are, as Meat Loaf put it: this book puts the period at a critical distance.

With 90s complaint rock drawing on punk, the epoch of the Sex Pistols seems to float free from the sedate mid-70s and processed 80s that flank it. Chapter 7 presents this period as a liminal space between Fordism and post-Fordism, both a closing down – of industries, genres, hopes – and an opening up: of new forms (new wave, post-punk), new techniques (Donna Summer's electronic disco; Human League's synthpop) and new space for women and queers. Journey's claim "some will win, some will lose" fits both these understandings, therefore. With Miley Cyrus's 2023 retro-disco 'Flowers' (UK 1; US 1) repossessing Gloria Gaynor's collectivist 'I Will Survive' as individualism, *Small Axe*'s 1979-set *Silly Games* (2020) provides a cultural counterpoint. As the DJ turns off Janet Kay's reggae hit 'Silly Games' (UK 2), the whole party takes over the singing in collective unity. Just as the late 70s' cold stream infects its warm stream, so punk and disco have eclipsed the period's suffusion with reggae. For the Specials' 'Ghost Town' is this period's pop paradigm: a punky reggae party that looks backwards and forwards, both celebrating and mourning collectivity, while simultaneously refusing and resigning itself to neoliberalism.

There's a reason for the arrival of time-travelling TV drama *Life on Mars* in the mid-2000s, alongside a postmillennial post-punk revival. Viewed from the imperial phase of neoliberal hegemony historicised in Chapter 11, the collective, creative 70s possessed a hauntological otherness that didn't yet translate to politics. For, with the War on Terror making social stasis seem like social security, a disengaged public prioritised culture over politics. Yet, with pacifying smart-pop proving an attractive carapace for a 'poptimism' that normalised ugly affects, politics were never far beneath the period's shiny surface. If this age of war's aggressive individualism was explicit in Snoop and Pharrell's 'Drop It Like It's Hot', it was just as tangible in Justin Timberlake's misogynist

'Cry Me a River'. Far from being critiqued, the elites were elevated above the public's ground zero in this era, with Beyoncé and Jay-Z's 'Crazy in Love' video essentially a celebrity culture victory-lap. No epoch now is too close – or too closed – for nostalgia, which functions as Stockholm syndrome for its generational captives. So that this era's affects have aged quite so badly is actually its resource of hope, revealing neoliberalism's imperial phase as hubristic rather than hegemonic.

At the time this was unreadable, however, which is why, in this historical remix, the financial crash segues straight from the Iraq War. For as Chapter 12 recalls, neoliberalism's crises now became quotidian, its disaster capitalism absorbed into the body cultural as a resilience mode, exemplified by EDM, whose hedonic escapism hegemonised charts, minds and bodies amidst austerity. Although Black Eyed Peas' exhortation to "Go out and smash it" was metaphorical, it became literal when riots, demonstrations and occupations erupted in 2010–11. As the issue of economic inequality reopened in politics, so a culture of 'ordinariness' recalibrated the inequal celebrity-citizen relationship, exemplified by Adele, in equal parts pacifying and politicising. As austerity extended precarity to the *middle* class, meanwhile, a new pop melancholia articulated an implicit millennial protest, with Lana Del Rey its poster girl. More explicit protest came from Black Lives Matter, however, in whose wake, Kendrick Lamar and the Weeknd revived repressed hip-hop and R&B in defiance of alt-right racism. Full of competing, contradictory currents, this era is revealed as an interregnum, the old refusing to die while the new struggled to be born.

The reason this book has emphasised such interregna, separating them from the seismic epochs either side, is because it's in periods when history has seemingly paused that time is at its most open, and that possibilities teem in pop and politics. With the late-50s/early-60s period summoned in Chapter 2 long regarded as a lacuna between Elvis's resignation and the Beatles' ascension, its creative vibrancy and retrospective recurrence – think: *End of the F*****g World* – reveal it as a liminal space. This era is hauntological because it is haunted, the establishment's repression of rock'n'roll's rebellion imbuing its restoration balladry with an uncannily yearning luminosity.

The wistful "oohs" and "aahs" of supposedly evanescent doo-wop, soul and girl groups expressed a revenant utopianism which seeped out in obsessive dreams like Roy Orbison's and morbid visions like Skeeter Davis's 'The End of the World'. This interstitial pop's dialectic of loss and hope paralleled the civil rights movement, combining with it on Sam Cooke's 'A Change Is Gonna Come', whose melancholic accounting of history was the condition of its utopianism. As pop struggled to imagine what *could be* against the repression of what *was*, this period can now be seen as the spectre of the coming counterculture.

On the other side of the 60s, in the interregnum charted in Chapter 4, the utopianism was more direct, more confrontational – and more directly confronted. This was the period of Black Panthers, Che Guevara posters, Woodstock's "half a million strong" and songs entitled 'Power to the People' and 'Stop the War Now'. With its radicalism defined by the dissolution of divisions between self and other – the Viet Cong, women, nature – Sly and the Family Stone's statement "I am everyday people" is exemplary of the era. These impulses were "forces of chaos and anarchy", as Jefferson Airplane satirically put it, and this countercultural revolution was aggressively countered by the authoritarian forces of stasis and order. A quieter counter-revolution was conducted by capital, meanwhile, co-opting the counterculture in a politically ambivalent space where singer-songwriters and heavy rockers made their homes. While capital's longer game was revealed by Thunderclap Newman's revolutionary 1969 'Something in the Air' being redeployed in a post-millennial mobile-phone advert, such co-option is always volatile. For "Hand out the arms and ammo/We're gonna blast our way through here" is a reminder of a militant past when revolution was a political risk rather than commercial rhetoric.

Nothing sounds volatile, let alone militant in the mid-70s interregnum that's revisited in Chapter 6, a period whose sleepy soft-rock, stodgy MOR and escapist disco parallels its place-holding, line-holding politics. Representing a pause in the 70s' maverick momentum, this period is an oasis – probably at midnight – from the scorched earth on either side of it. Amid the worst recession since the war, the immaculately appointed productions of ELO, 10cc, Elton John and Queen were the very essence of inflationary

461

pop. Yet what once seemed like a soporific soundtrack to political stagnancy can now be heard as an affirmation of relative plenty, underwritten by a consensus social contract, and thus representing the last gasp of Fordist collectivity. The Eagles' 'Take It to the Limit' isn't recommending any drastic action, therefore, just hunkering down and holding on, while in these final days of Fordism, the Carpenters' 'Only Yesterday' doesn't yearn for the past, it hopes for the future. It's this forgotten futurism – from Kraftwerk to David Bowie to Stevie Wonder – and the optimism that was its condition of possibility which provides not just this period's poignancy, but also its resource of hope.

The seductions of Fordist melancholia are countered by the late-80s interregnum that's revived in Chapter 9, representing a hauntological *post*-Fordism. This era's rave, grunge and old-school hip-hop were all revenant subsequently, while also representing refusals of the neoliberal hegemony declared to be the end of history. Rather than rethinking after Black Monday, politics enacted a superficial softening, paralleled by the performatively socially aware pop of Janet and Michael Jackson, Paula Abdul and Madonna, who were ultimately no less a capitalist consensus than the factory-packed likes of Tiffany, Rick Astley or Kylie. Rozalla's declaration that "Everybody's free – to feel good" presents this period's political pessimism as cultural optimism, competitive individualism as radicalism. This neoliberal ideology, alongside an illiberal authoritarianism stifled the period's political alternatives, along with the radical potentialities of 'alternative rock', acid house and hip-hop. Nevertheless, 'Smells Like Teen Spirit', 'Voodoo Ray' and 'Fuck Tha Police' still radiate an adversarial energy that remains a resource of hope. In dark times, play the video for Public Enemy's 'Fight the Power' – equal parts rally, party, and revolution – and anything and everything will feel possible.

The time which most encapsulated such a sense of possibility was the high 60s invoked in Chapter 3, whose surging optimism is still audible in beat, soul, folk-rock and psychedelia. While this optimism was underwritten by the Fordist state, the counterculture's utopianism soon eclipsed such liberal pragmatism, resulting in confrontation. Endless ideological labour has been devoted to condemning, co-opting, twisting and trashing the counterculture, because the 60s expanded the parameters of the possible, and our smaller, meaner society is the consequence of the closure of that imaginative space.[14] The counterculture's radicalism rests on its affirmation of the collective over the individual, for which the Beatles' "I am he as you are me/And we are all together" is a synecdoche. 60s music tapped into the collective consciousness that Freud called "oceanic feeling": an "inseparable connection of the ego with the external world... a limitless extension and oneness with the universe".[15] Rowbotham describes just this feeling at the time, when "the energy of the external collectivity became so intense, it seemed the boundaries of closeness, of ecstatic inwardness had spilled over on to the streets... the libido defied borders".[16] This utopia isn't located in some distant future, but is *here, now* – material, tangible, graspable.

Some vestige of this vision felt in reach again in the 2015–20 period recalled in Chapter 13, when the discontents of neoliberalism were demonstrated by the combined and uneven developments of Brexit, the radical left candidacies of Corbyn and Sanders and the reactionary tide of Trumpism. While the right channelled these discontents into a negative politics of resentment, the left harnessed them as a positive politics of hope. This period's "longing for change", in Lady Gaga's words, was again expressed through a reaffirmation of collectivity over individualism – "Not me, us" – and of ordinary people over the elite: "For the many, not the few". The era's energy wasn't just derived from formal politics but street politics, via BLM, #MeToo and Extinction Rebellion's rejection of the longstanding neoliberal consensus. Pulsing with possibilities, this period's excitement and imagination was as audible in pop as it was visible in politics. No one could hear Stormzy, Kendrick Lamar or Cardi B and insist that nothing had changed since the 90s: this was change *occurring*, possibilities taking shape. So, although this period's radical politics were defeated, its music remains irrepressible, a resource through which we can reaccess its radical hopes.

Music is the expression of an entire society's structure of feeling, however, and with the power of the political class restored, and pandemic collectivity eclipsed by patriotism and a punching-down chauvinism towards refugees and trans people, othering has made quite the comeback. Across 2023's pop charts, Olivia Rodrigo's 'Vampire' (UK 1; US 1) gives her transactional, "fame-fucker" ex as good as she got ("you sold me for parts"), and with love again a zero-sum game, SZA's 'Kill Bill' (UK 3: US 1) boasts "I just killed my ex… his new girlfriend's next". Meanwhile, Drake's 'Slime You Out', with SZA again (UK 10; US 1), wraps up misogyny and transactionality in a typically unedifying bundle. These are love songs, sung by celebrities, but they normalise an aggressively competitive individualism and affectless lack of compassion. Whereas, Taylor argues, political "success or failure [is] contingent on whether or not working people see themselves as brothers and sisters whose liberation is inextricably bound together".[17]

The huge crossover success of two country songs in summer 2023 takes this othering to right-wing conclusions. The lyric and video for Jason Aldean's 'Try That in a Small Town' (UK 9; US 1) conflate leftist protest and violent crime (BLM footage was later edited out of the video), while threatening violent retribution from those "raised up right". Going viral on YouTube, unknown Oliver Anthony's austere, acoustic 'Rich Men North of Richmond' (UK 23; US 1) articulates class politics – "selling my soul… for bullshit pay" – but a class politics that's divisive rather than collective, individualistic rather than solidaristic. The song rests on right-wing shibboleths like "the obese milkin' welfare" and "your dollar ain't shit, and it's taxed to no end", while hinting at the QAnon conspiracy.

Despite these negative, competitive currents, the positive, collectivist politics of 2015–20 keep resurfacing, with the long wave of industrial action accompanied by autumn 2023 and winter 2024's Palestinian solidarity demonstrations. The spectre of a world that could be free has not been quelled, therefore: not by history, nor by the end of history; not by legacy centrism, nor by the authoritarian right. These combined and uneven developments confirm we're living through another interregnum, a period of open time, with the consequent potential for either the imposition of fascism *or* the institution of real utopias duking it out in the political mix.

Paralleling this political openness, the way we experience music now, rather than being a retreat or a loss – as rockists and

Fordist melancholics claim – is instead an advance and a gain. For we're perpetually exposed to an affective archive of music from the hauntology that is history: as revenant original recordings, as atemporal cover versions, and as evocative sampled snippets from a randomised past. Music is thus continually mixing and remixing history with the contemporary, and this recurring past doesn't just feel *alive*, but alive with *possibilities* – and encountering them, so do we. Because it's popular music's capacity both to evoke *and* to inspire desire – feelings, dreams, hopes – that is its power: a power that isn't just aesthetic or affective but is entirely, joyfully, *adversarially* political.

Notes

Introduction: The Top 10

1   Stuart Maconie, *The People's Songs: The Story of Modern Britain in 50 Records* (London: Ebury, 2013), p. 356.
2   John Street, *Music & Politics* (Cambridge: Polity, 2012), pp. 6–8.
3   David Hesmondhalgh, *Why Music Matters* (Chichester: Wiley Blackwell, 2013), pp. 142–6.
4   Tom Ewing, *Popular* website, 23 February 2020: https://popular-number1s. com/2020/02/23/the-black-eyed-peas-ft-justin-timberlake-where-is-the-love/
5   "A political song… is one that self-consciously recognizes the ideological content and seeks to draw the listener's attention to it." Street, p. 44.
6   Raymond Williams, *The Long Revolution* [1961] (Cardigan: Parthian, 2011), p. 69.
7   Theodor Adorno, 'On the Fetish Character in Music and the Regression of Listening' in *The Culture Industry* (Abingdon and New York: Routledge, 1991), p. 39; p. 40.
8   Karl Marx, 'Preface to A Contribution to the Critique of Political Economy' [1859] in *Early Writings*, trans. Rodney Livingstone and Gregor Benton (London: Penguin Classics, 1992), p. 426.
9   Ellen Willis, *Beginning to See the Light: Sex, Hope and Rock-and-Roll* (Minneapolis: University of Minnesota Press, 2012), pp. xvi–xvii.
10 Stuart Hall, 'Notes on Deconstructing 'the Popular'', in *Cultural Theory and Popular Culture: A Reader*, ed. John Storey (Hemel Hempstead: Harvester Wheatsheaf, 1994), p. 456; p. 459.
11 Karl Marx, *Capital: A Critique of Political Economy*, Vol 1 [1887], trans. Samuel Moore and Edward Aveling (London: Lawrence & Wishart, 1954), p. 29.
12 Alan Sinfield, *Literature, Politics and Culture in Postwar Britain* [1997] (London: Continuum, 2004), p. 202.

13 Theodor Adorno and Max Horkheimer, *The Dialectic of Enlightenment* [1944], trans. John Cumming (London: Verso, 1997), p. 144.

14 Sigmund Freud, *The Standard Edition of the Complete Psychological Works, Vol. XIV: On the History of the Psycho-Analytic Movement, Papers on Metapsychology and Other Works*, ed. and trans. James Strachey (London: Hogarth Press, 1957), p. 36–7.

15 Herbert Marcuse, *Eros and Civilisation: A Philosophical Inquiry into Freud* [1955] (London: Ark, 1987), p. 44.

16 Karl Marx, 'Economic and Philosophical Manuscripts' (1844), in *Early*, p. 326.

17 Marx, 'Economic', p. 327.

18 Fredric Jameson, *Archaeologies of The Future: The Desire Called Utopia and Other Science Fictions* (London: Verso, 2005), p. 199.

19 Marcuse, *Eros*, p. 149.

20 Eric Olin Wright, *Envisioning Real Utopias* (London: Verso, 2010), *passim*.

21 Marx, *Capital*, p. 26.

22 Raymond Williams, *Towards 2000* [1983] (Harmondsworth: Pelican, 1985) p. 13.

23 Luc Boltanksi and Eve Chiapello, *The New Spirit of Capitalism* [1999], trans. Gregory Elliott (London: Verso, 2005), p. 10.

24 Williams, *Towards*, p. 5.

25 Karl Marx and Friedrich Engels, *The German Ideology* (Amherst: Prometheus: 1998), p. 67.

26 Walter Benjamin, 'Theses on the Philosophy of History' [1940] in *Illuminations*, trans. Harry Zohn (London: Fontana, 1973), p. 263

27 Karl Marx, *The Eighteenth Brumaire of Louis Bonaparte* [1852] (New York: International Publishers, 1963), p. 15.

28 Enzo Traverso, *Left-Wing Melancholia: Marxism, History and Memory* (New York: Columbia University Press, 2016), p. xv; pp. 25–26.

29 Benjamin, 'Theses', p. 257; p. 259.

30 See: Paul Ewart, 'Rethinking the 1970s', unpublished Ph.D thesis, 2024.

31 Marx, 'Preface', p. 425.

32 Marx, *Capital*, p. 411.

33 Antonio Gramsci, *Selections from the Prison Notebooks*, ed. Quintin Hoare and Geoffrey Nowell Smith (London: Lawrence and Wishart, 1971), p. 303.

34 Francois Hartog, 'Time and Heritage', *Museum* 277 (57: 3) 2005, p. 14; p. 10.

35 In a landmark legal case, Irish singer-songwriter Gilbert O'Sullivan sued hip-hopper Biz Markie in 1991 over sampling his 1971 'Alone Again (Naturally)', confirming copyright as protection of capitalist property rights.

36 Simon Reynolds, *Retromania: Pop Culture's Addiction to its Own Past* (London: Faber and Faber, 2011), p. 419; p. 185.

37 Reynolds makes this point himself of hip-hop, *Retromania*, pp. 352–4.

38 Fredric Jameson, *Postmodernism, or, The Cultural Logic of Late Capitalism* (London and New York: Verso, 1992), p. 20.

39 Mark Fisher, *Ghosts of My Life: Writings on Depression, Hauntology and Lost Futures* (Alresford: Zero, 2014): pp. 21–2. With the book's title derived from Japan's 1982 'Ghosts' (UK 5), the potential of the haunt of the past to be enervating as well as empowering is written into Fisher's 'hauntology'.

40 Marcuse, *Eros*, p. 233.

Chapter 1. "Raise a Fuss, Raise a Holler"

1 Marx, *Eighteenth*, p. 25.

2 *The Wonder Years*, S01 E04, 1:10.

3 Michael D. Dwyer, *Back to the Fifties: Nostalgia, Hollywood Film & Popular Music of the Seventies and Eighties* (New York: Oxford University Press, 2015), p. 64; Bernard von Bothmer, *Framing the Sixties: The Use and Abuse of a Decade from Ronald Reagan to George W. Bush* (Amherst and Boston: University of Massachusetts Press, 2010), pp. 17–20.

4 Jeremy Gilbert and Tim Lawrence, *Love is the Message* podcast, Series 2, E05, 20/09/2022, 'Motown to Salsoul pt. 1: Music in the Age of Fordism' (54: 30).

5 Williams, *Towards*, p. 247.

6 Perry Anderson, 'The Left in the Fifties', *New Left Review* I/29, Jan/Feb 1965, p. 11.

7 Dwyer quotes the 1972 *New York Times*: "Forget [your] problems and return or at least recall those happy high school times – the prom, no wars, no riots, no protests, the convertibles at the drive-in" (p. 84).

8 Alan Nadel, *Containment Culture: American Narratives, Postmodernism and the Atomic Age* (Durham: Duke University Press, 1995).

9 Marcuse, *Eros*, p. 35.

10 Nadel, p. 3.

11 'Mr Sandman's use in *Back to the Future* to signal this 50s containment ironically gave the song new life in the 50s-haunted 80s, before its incongruous appearance in Method Man's 1994 'Sandman' (*Tical*, US 4).

12 Gilbert and Lawrence, *Love* podcast: 'Motown pt. 1'.

13 John Clarke, Stuart Hall, Tony Jefferson and Brian Roberts, 'Subcultures, Cultures and Class: A Theoretical Overview' in *Resistance Through Rituals*, ed. Hall and Jefferson (London: Hutchinson, 1976). p. 71.

14 Marx, *Capital*, p. 79.

15 Jim Tomlinson, 'Inventing "Decline": The Falling behind of the British Economy in the Postwar Years', *The Economic History Review*, Nov 1996, 49; (4), pp. 745–6.

16 Glenn C. Altschuler, *All Shook Up: How Rock'n'Roll Changed America* (New York: Oxford University Press, 2003), p. 131.

17 Raymond Williams lays out the concepts of "dominant", "emergent" and "residual" culture and ideology in *Marxism and Literature* (Oxford: Oxford University Press, 1977), pp. 121–7.

18 Fats Domino was on Imperial, Elvis started off on Sun, Jerry Lee stayed there. Little Richard was on Specialty, Buddy Holly was on fake indies Brunswick and Coral (subsidiaries of Decca) and Eddie Cochran was on Liberty.

19 Iain Chambers, 'A Strategy for Living', in Hall and Jefferson (eds.) *Resistance*, p. 158.

20 Altschuler, p. 160.

21 Billy Bragg, *Roots, Radicals and Rockers: How Skiffle Changed the World* (London: Faber, 2017): "Before commerce made ownership the key transactional interest of creativity, songs passed through culture by word of mouth and bore the fingerprints of everyone who ever sang them" (p. 17).

22 Nik Cohn, *Awopbopaloobopalopbamboom* [1969] (London: Minerva, 1996), pp. 46–51.

23 Sinfield, *Post*, pp. 178–9.

24 Greil Marcus, *Mystery Train* [1975] (London: Penguin, 1991): "Whites wrote it; a white made it a hit. And yet there is no denying that 'Hound Dog' is a 'black' song… Can you pull justice out of *that* maze?" (p. 155).

25 Leroi Jones (Amira Baraka), *Black Music* [1968] (New York: Akashi Classics, 2010).

26 Karl Hagstrom Miller, *Segregating Sound: Inventing Folk and Pop Music in the Age of Jim Crow* (Durham and London: Duke University Press, 2010), p. 4.

27 Paul Gilroy, *Darker than Blue: On the Moral Economies of Black Atlantic Culture* (Cambridge Mass: Belknap, 2010), pp. 145–6.

28 Altschuler, p. 39.

29 Marcus, p. 20.

30 Frantz Fanon, *The Wretched of the Earth*, trans. Constance Farrington (New York: Weidenfield, 1991), p. 40.

31 Jack Kerouac, *On the Road* [1957] (London: Penguin, 1991), p. 180.

32 Herbert Marcuse, *One Dimensional Man* [1964] (London: Sphere, 1968), p. 63.

33 Tony Jefferson, 'Cultural Responses of the Teds', in Hall and Jefferson (eds.) *Resistance*, p. 82. The seepage of Caribbean reggae into the charts and the music of white Britons in the 60s indicates this developing solidarity.

34 Even if calypso was appropriated by skiffler Johnny Duncan and his cover of 'Last Train to San Fernando' (UK 2).

35 Nadel, p. 5.

36 Gramsci, p. 297.

37 Altschuler, p. 38; p. 40.

38 Laura Mulvey, 'Visual Pleasure and Narrative Cinema', *Screen* 1975 16 (3), pp. 6–18.

39 Dick Hebdige, *Subculture: The Meaning of Style* [1979] (London: Routledge, 1988), p. 17.

40 Theodor Adorno, *Minima Moralia: Reflections from Damaged Life* [1951] (London: Verso, 2005), p. 22.

41 Louis Althusser, *Lenin and Philosophy* [1968] (New York: Monthly Review, 2001), pp. 96–9.

42 Kristin Ross, *May '68 and its Afterlives* (Chicago: University of Chicago Press, 2002), p. 205.

43 Phil Cohen, quoted in Hall and Jefferson (eds.), *Resistance*, p. 32.

44 Karl Marx and Friedrich Engels, *The Communist Manifesto* [1872] trans. Samuel Moore (London: Penguin Classics, 1985), p. 94.

45 Hebdige, *Subculture*: p. 2; p. 19.

46 Althusser, p. 109.

47 Marx, 'Economic', p. 326.

48 Marcuse, *Eros*, p. 156.

49 Raymond Williams, *Orwell* (Glasgow: Fontana: 1974), p. 24.

50 Raymond Williams, *Culture and Society* [1958] (London: Hogarth, 1993), p. 198.

51 David Kynaston, *Modernity Britain, Book Two: A Shake of the Dice*, 1959–62 (London: Bloomsbury, 2014): p. 145; p. 150.

52 Anderson, 'Left', p. 4.

53 Mark Abrams, *The Teenage Consumer* (London: Press Exchange, 1959), p. 13.

54 Hebdige, *Subculture*, pp. 77–8.

55 Tony Jefferson, 'Cultural Responses of the Teds' in Hall and Jefferson (eds.) *Resistance*, pp. 82–3.

56 George Melly, *Revolt into Style: the Pop Arts* [1970] (London: Faber, 2008), p. 38: "The Establishment wants order. The entrepreneurs want money, and the way to make the most money out of pop is to preserve at least the semblance of order".

57 Altschuler, p. 150.

58 Otis Blackwell was forced by Parker to give Presley co-writing credits on 'Don't Be Cruel' and 'All Shook Up' (Altschuler, p. 55).

Chapter 2. "In Beautiful Dreams'

1   Ian MacDonald, *Revolution in the Head: The Beatles' Records and the Sixties* (London: Pimlico 1995), p. 42.

2   Cohn, p. 70.

3   Gramsci, p. 276.

4   von Bothmer, pp. 11–17.

5   Simon Reynolds, *Shock and Awe: Glam Rock and Its Legacy* (London: Faber, 2016), p. 350.

6   von Bothmer, pp. 11–17.

7   Marcuse, *Eros*, p. 236.

8   Ewart.

9   Thomas Frank, *The Conquest of Cool* (Chicago: University of Chicago Press, 1997), p. 27; p. 23; p. 24.

10 Frank, pp. 170–1.

11 Anderson, 'Left', p. 4; Tom Nairn, 'The Nature of the Labour Party (Part II)' *New Left Review* 1/28, Nov/Dec 1964, p. 17.

12 Anderson, 'Left', pp. 5–7; pp. 10–13.

13 von Bothmer, p. 14; pp. 46–54.

14 Anderson, 'Left', p. 11.

15 Gramsci, p. 276.

16 See: Orbison's 1961 bolero 'Crying' (UK 25; US 2); Brill Building clients the Drifters' 1960 'Save the Last Dance For Me' (UK 2; US 1) and the Shirelles' 1961 'Baby It's You' (US 8); the Shadows' 1961 'Guitar Tango' (UK 4); Shirley Bassey's MOR bolero 'What Now My Love' (UK 5). See also the Middle Eastern flavour of Gene Pitney's 'Mecca' (US 12).

17 Traverso, pp. 45–6.

18 'Leader of the Pack' was endlessly revenant: in 1972 (UK 3) and 1976 (UK 7); Twinkle's 'Terry' is a British rerun (UK 4) minus the parental conflict.

19 Gramsci, p. 275.

20 This reaches its abject peak in the Righteous Brothers' stunning 1964 'You've Lost That Lovin' Feeling'. Their facsimile, the Walker Brothers' 1965 'Make It Easy on Yourself' (UK 1; US 1) and 1966 'The Sun Ain't Gonna Shine Anymore' (UK 1; US 13) would be ghosts at the 60s' feast.

21 Stephanie Phillips, 'The Two Sides of Phil Spector' in Rhian E. Jones and Eli Davies (eds.), *Under My Thumb: Songs That Hate Women and the Women Who Love Them* (London: Repeater, 2017), pp. 21–3.

22 Sigmund Freud, *The Standard Edition of the Complete Psychological Works* Vol. V (1900–19) trans. James Strachey (Vintage: London, 2001), p. 645.

23 Mark Fisher, '"A social and psychic revolution of almost inconceivable magnitude": Popular Culture's Interrupted Accelerationist Dreams', e-flux journal #46, June 2013. https://www.e-flux.com/journal/46/60084/a-social-and-psychic-revolution-of-almost-inconceivable-magnitude-popular-culture-s-interrupted-accelerationist-dreams/

24 Freud, *Standard*, vol V, p. 641.

25 Indicative of this modernism, Orbison's song also gave its name to a dream-themed album (UK 6), which included versions of 'All I Have to Do…' and Mercer's 'Dream (When You're Feeling Blue)'.

26 Freud, *Standard*, vol. V, p. 647 (emphasis in original).

27 Freud, *Standard*, vol. V, p. 646.

28 Charlie Gillett, *The Sound of the City* [1970] (London: Souvenir, 1983), pp. 190-1.

29 Cohn, p. 111.

30 Greg Tate, 'I'm White! What's Wrong with Michael Jackson?' in *The Faber Book of Pop*, ed. Hanif Kureishi and Jon Savage (London: Faber and Faber, 1996), p. 641.

31 von Bothmer, p. 147.

32 Gillett, p. 204.

Chapter 3. "We are All Together"

1 Fredric Jameson, 'Periodizing the 60s', in *The 60s Without Apology* (Minneapolis: University of Minnesota Press, 1984), p. 207.

2 Stuart Hall, 'The Great Moving Right Show', *Marxism Today*, January 1979, p. 16.

3 Margaret Thatcher, March 27 1982 Speech to Conservative Central Council, Harrogate: https://www.margaretthatcher.org/document/104905

4   Slavoj Žižek, 'The Ambiguous Legacy of '68', *In These Times*, 20 June 2008: https://inthesetimes.com/article/the-ambiguous-legacy-of-68. Boltanski and Chiapello make a similar division between "social critique" and "artistic critique", pp. 36-40.

5   Frank, p. 138; p. 208; pp. 166–7.

6   Boltanski and Chiapello, pp. 489–92.

7   Editors, 'Introduction', in *60s Without*, p. 2.

8   Herbert Marcuse, *Counterrevolution and Revolt* (Boston: Beacon Press: 1972), p. 48.

9   Arthur Marwick, *The Sixties: Cultural Revolution in Britain, France, Italy and the United States, c. 1958–c.1974*, (Oxford/New York: Oxford University Press, 1998), p. 19.

10 Dominic Sandbrook, *White Heat: A History of Britain in the Swinging Sixties* (London: Abacus, 2007), pp. 523–4; p. 529.

11 Jeremi Suri, 'The Rise and Fall of an International Counterculture, 1960-1975', *The American Historical Review*, Feb 2009 114 (1), p. 51.

12 Keeanga-Yamahtta Taylor, *From #BlackLivesMatter to Black Liberation* (Chicago; Haymarket, 2016), p. 56.

13 MacDonald, p. 79.

14 Ian Penman, 'Four Moptop Yobbos', *London Review of Books* 43; (12), 17 June 2021: https://www.lrb.co.uk/the-paper/v43/n12/ian-penman/four-moptop-yobbos

15 Holly had hits with versions of 'Bo Diddley' (UK 4) and Chuck Berry's 'Brown Eyed Handsome Man' (UK 3).

16 Cohn, p. 148.

17 Dick Hebdige, 'The Meaning of Mod', in Hall and Jefferson (eds.) *Resistance*, p. 93.

18 Townshend was inspired by Gustav Metzger, who called auto-destructive art, "an attack on capitalist values and the drive to nuclear annihilation".

19 The New Vaudeville Band's 'Winchester Cathederal' (UK 4; US 1) and the Bonzo Dog Doo Dah Band are a bizarre Edwardianisation of the genre.

20 Sheila Rowbotham, *Promise of a Dream* (London: Allen Lane, 2000), p. xii.

21 Marcuse, *Eros*, p. xvii; p. xx.

22 Marcuse, *One*, p. 77.

23 Other garage-rock hits – Sam the Sham's 'Woolly Bully' (UK 11; US 2); Sir Douglas Quintet's 'She's About a Mover' (UK 15; US 13) – were possessed of neither the aggression nor the pop smarts of the Raiders; 1966's late entry, the Music Machine's 'Talk Talk' (US 15) had both.

24 Marcuse, *Eros*, p. 3.

25 Marwick, p. 12; Sandbrook, *White*, p. 531; p. 533.

26 Philip Norman, *The Life and Good Times of the Rolling Stones* (London: Random House, 1989), p. 42.

27 Paul Gilroy, *The Black Atlantic: Modernity and Double Consciousness* (London: Verso, 1993), p. 202.

28 Gilroy, *Darker*, p. 6.

29 The song was used by Joe Biden in his 2020 presidential campaign.

30 The line is a mangling of WH Auden's "We must love one another or die" from 'September 1, 1939'.

31 Jon Savage, *1966: the Year the Decade Exploded* (London: Faber, 2015), p. 114–5.

32 MacDonald, pp. 120–1; Savage, p. 114.

33 MacDonald, p. 139.

34 Dorian Lynskey, *33 Revolutions Per Minute: A History of Protest Songs* (London: Faber, 2010), p. 68; p. 83.

35 Mike Marqusee, *The Guardian*, 28 May 2005: https://www.theguardian.com/books/2005/may/28/highereducation.news

36 The Seekers' title song for Swinging London film *Georgy Girl* (1966) places more faith in the power of clothes ("Shed those dowdy feathers and fly a little bit") (UK 3; US 2).

37 Fordist *Thanatos* is a recurring folk-rock theme, as on Liverpool's Searchers' 1964 evocation of nuclear fallout, 'What Have They Done to the Rain?' (UK 13; US 29).

38 Cohn, p. 175; Savage, p. 65.

39 Sandbrook, *White*, p. 555.

40 Rowbotham, p. 133.

41 Marcuse, *Counterrevolution*, pp. 74–8.

42 Marcuse, *Eros*, p. 199.

43 All three songs were written by future 10cc-er Graham Gouldman.

44 Theodor Adorno, 'Society', handbook entry, 1965.

45 Marcuse, *Counterrevolution*, p. 51.

46 Tom Bottomore, *A Dictionary of Marxist Thought* (Oxford: Blackwell, 1988), p. 451.

47 Marcuse, *Eros*, p. 94.

48 Herbert Marcuse, *An Essay on Liberation* (Boston: Beacon Press, 1969), p. 37.

49 Joe Kennedy, *Authentocrats* (London: Repeater, 2018), pp. 12–14.

50 MacDonald, p. 177.

51 E.g. MacDonald, pp. 113–5; Savage, p. 112.

52 Marcuse, *Liberation*, p. 30.

53   Rowbotham, p. 138.

54   Rowbotham, p. 133.

55   Throughout psychedelia there are songs that feature children (Traffic's 'Hole in My Shoe', UK 2; Keith West's 'Excerpt from a Teenage Opera', UK 1); songs about the magic of childhood (the Stones' 'Dandelion', UK 8; US 14; Incredible String Band's 'Witches Hat'), songs about childlike adults (The Who's 'Happy Jack', UK 3; US 24; the Kinks' gardener in 'Autumn Almanac', UK 3), acid nursery rhymes (Donovan's 'Mellow Yellow', UK 8; US 2; Pink Floyd's 'Bike'; Traffic's 'Here we Go Round the Mulberry Bush' UK 8). Psyche also produced songs *for* children (the Beatles' 'Yellow Submarine', UK 1; US 2; Donovan's *A Gift From a Flower to a Garden*, US 19). These don't *have* to be twee like Pink Floyd's 'The Gnome', yet MacDonald sneers at "the natural (and… unquestionably healthy) desires of the childlike id", and rejects the very notion of a "Systemic Ego", let alone any possibility of escaping it (p. 149).

56   Marcuse, *Liberation*, p. 10.

57   Richie Unterberger, *Eight Miles High: Folk-Rock's Flight from Haight Ashbury to Woodstock* (San Francisco: Backbeat, 2003), p. 50.

58   Cohn, pp. 113-4; pp. 223-6; MacDonald, pp. 202-11.

59   Viktor Shklovsky, *On the Theory of Prose* [1917] (Illinois: Dalkey Archive Press: 1991).

60   Marcuse, *Eros*, p. 100.

61   Marcuse, *Counterrevolution*, p. 74; p. 77.

62   Reynolds, *Retromania*, p. 277; Cohn p. 155; MacDonald, p. 206; Sandbrook, *White*, p. 557.

63   Simon Reynolds and Joy Press, *The Sex Revolts; Gender, Rebellion and Rock'n'Roll* (London: Serpent's Tail, 1995), p. 171.

64   Marcuse, *Eros*, p. 161.

65   Mark Fisher, *Postcapitalist Desire: The Final Lectures* (London: Repeater, 2021), p. 76

66   Tarantino used the song satirically in *Once Upon a Time in Hollywood*, the "young girls coming to the Canyon" being murderous Mansonites.

67   Rhian E. Jones, 'You Shouldn't Take it so Personal', in Jones and Davies (eds), p. 33.

68   Rowbotham, p. 232.

69   Marwick, p. 491.

70   Sean O'Hagan, *The Guardian*, 20 January 2008: https://www.theguardian.com/world/2008/jan/20/1968theyearofrevolt.features

71   MacDonald, p. 209.

72 Mark Fisher, 'Acid Communism', in *K-Punk: The Collected and Unpublished Writings of Mark Fisher (2004–2016)* ed. Darren Ambrose (London: Repeater, 2018), p. 767.

73 The promotional film was a key queering of the 60s – replaying Oscar Wilde's trial with Jagger as Wilde and Marianne Faithfull as his lover Bosey.

74 This inclusivity was also reflected by a black influence rarely noted of psychedelia. The Beatles' 'Penny Lane' and 'With a Little Help from My Friends' share the Supremes' crotchet bounce; their 'Baby You're a Rich Man' (B-side, 'All You Need is Love') taps the four-square Motown beat. Procol Harum's Summer of Love 'Whiter Shade of Pale' (UK 1; US 5) owes much to Percy Sledge's 1966 'When a Man Loves a Woman' (UK 4; US 1).

75 Eric Burdon wrote late-1967's 'Monterey' about this integration (US 15) – "music being born of love" – while Hendrix penned 'Little Wing' (*Axis*): another figuration of the counterculture as female.

76 Sandbrook, *White*, pp. 520–3.

77 Adam Curtis, *Can't Get You Out of My Head*, Part Two, 'Shooting and Fucking are the Same Thing', BBC documentary, 11 February 2021.

78 Žižek, 'Ambiguous'.

Chapter 4. "Forces of Chaos and Anarchy"

1 Rowbotham, p. 196.

2 Reynolds and Press, p. 167.

3 Todd Gitlin, *Years of Hope, Days of Rage* [1987] (New York: Bantam, 1993), p. 420.

4 From 1964-70, the number of Americans living below the poverty line dramatically dropped from 22.2 to 12.6%.

5 Stuart Hall, 'Hippies', stenciled CCS pamphlet, October 1968, p. 16.

6 Gilbert and Lawrence, *Love* podcast, 20/09/2022, E11, 'Huh! Here Comes the Funk'. Jordan Cummings points out the Grateful Dead regularly played benefits for the Panthers: 'Forces of Chaos and Anarchy: Rock Music, the New Left and Social Movements, 1964 to 1972', unpublished PhD thesis, 2017, p. 47.

7 Quoted in Taylor, p. 45.

8 Marx, *Eighteenth*, p. 25.

9 Marx, *Eighteenth*, p. 56.

10 Tom Wolfe, 'The Me Decade', *New York*, 23 August 1976: https://nymag.com/article/tom-wolfe-me-decade-third-great-awakening.html

11 Joan Didion, *The White Album* [1979] (London: Flamingo, 1993), p. 19; p. 37.

12 Simon Reynolds, *Rip it Up and Start Again* (London: Faber and Faber, 2005), p. 41.

13 Michael Bracewell, *The Nineties: When Surface Was Depth* (London: Flamingo, 2002), p. 246.

14 Suri, pp. 59–60.

15 Tony Judt, *Ill Fares the Land* (London: Penguin, 2011), p. 94.

16 Carl Freedman, *The Age of Nixon* (Alresford: Zero, 2010), p. 133.

17 Jefferson Cowie, *Stayin' Alive: The 1970s and the Last Days of the Working Class* (New York: New Press, 2010), p. 32.

18 In terms of working-class cultural domination, see also Rod Stewart's summer 1970 'Gasoline Alley' (US 27) and the Hollies' autumn 1970 'Gasoline Alley Bred' (UK 14).

19 Frank, p. 192.

20 Fred Goodman, The *Mansion on the Hill: Dylan, Young, Geffen, Springsteen, and the Head-on Collision of Rock and Commerce* (London: Jonathan Cape, 1997), pp. 78–9.

21 Cohn, p. 227.

22 Suri, p. 63.

23 Tariq Ali, *Street Fighting Years: A Memoir of the Sixties* (London and New York: Verso, 2005).

24 MacDonald, p. 227.

25 Bernie Sanders would deploy the song in his 2016 and 2020 presidential campaigns.

26 Theodor Adorno, *The Jargon of Authenticity* [1964] (London and New York: Routledge, 2003), p. 100.

27 Wolfe, 'Me'.

28 Gitlin, p. 425; p. 424.

29 In the summer of 1969, an announcer at the Woodstock festival declared, "The one major thing you have to remember… is that the man next to you is your brother, and you'd damn well better treat each other that way because if you don't, then we blow the whole thing".

30 Burgeoning reggae was similarly solidaristic – Jimmy Cliff's 1969 'Wonderful World, Beautiful People' (UK 6; US 25); Desmond Decker's version of Cliff's 'You Can Get it if You Really Want' (UK 2) – or just joyful, as on Dave and Ansell Collins' 'Double Barrel' (UK 1).

31 This can be seen as part of the same process as Marvin Gaye's cover of Dion's 'Abraham, Martin and John' (UK 9), lushly orchestrated by

Whitfield, in which King is situated in a lineage of liberal reformers, his radicalism elided.

32 Jameson, 'Periodizing', p. 207.

33 Simon Frith, 'Rock and the Politics of Memory' in *60s Without*, pp. 59–69.

34 Reynolds and Press, p. 190.

35 Goodman, p. 206.

36 Ross, p. 183.

37 MacDonald, p. 228; Penman.

38 Adam Curtis, *All Watched Over by Machines of Loving Grace*, BBC, Part 2, 20:10; Marwick, p. 484; Fred Turner, https://harpers.org/archive/2019/01/machine-politics-facebook-political-polarization/; Richard King, *The Lark Ascending: The Music of the British Landscape* (London: Faber, 2019), p. 121.

39 Fredric Jameson, 'Postmodernism or the Cultural Logic of Late Capitalism', *New Left Review*, I/46, July/Aug 1984, p. 77.

40 Svetlana Boym, *The Future of Nostalgia* (New York: Basic, 2001), p. 41; p. 49.

41 Marx, *Capital*, pp. 667–70.

42 Marcuse, *Counterrevolution*, p. 60.

43 Boym, p. 41; p. 49.

44 Marx, 'Economic', p. 352.

45 Andy Beckett, *When the Lights Went Out: What Really Happened to Britain in the Seventies* (London: Faber and Faber, 2009), p. 239.

46 Marcuse, *Counterrevolution*, pp. 69–70.

47 Marcuse, *One*, p. 60.

48 Marcuse, *Counterrevolution*, p. 64.

49 'Irrealism' is "an embrace of the non-realist – be it the fantastical, the uncanny, or simply the aggressively unreal – as a way of criticizing reality, a juxtapositioning through which we can see the gap between what could be, what should be, and what is": Alexander Billet, 'A Theory of the Imagination and/or an Imaginative Theory: The Case for Critical Irrealism', *Imago*, 1, 2021, p. 22.

50 Fogerty pointed out that Donald Trump, who used the song, was just such a draft-dodging 'Fortunate Son'. Despite having signed away the rights, Fogerty managed to stop both Trump and Wrangler using it.

51 Sampled on Kanye West's 2010 'Power' (US 22), it's thus King Crimson's best-known track on Spotify.

52 Gilbert and Lawrence, *Love* podcast, E11, 'Huh'.

53 Lynskey, p. 256.

54 Lynskey, p. 252.

55 Gilroy, *Darker*, p. 41; p. 44; p. 177

Chapter 5. 'Children of the Revolution'

1   Paul Hegarty and Martin Halliwell, *Beyond and Before: Progressive Rock since the 1960s*, (London: Continuum, 2011), p. 98; Tom Ewing, *Popular*, 3 June 2007: https://popular-number1s.com/2007/06/03/lieutenant-pigeon-mouldy-old-dough/; Reynolds, *Retromania*, p. 428; Paul Trynka, *Starman, David Bowie, the Definitive Biography* (London: Sphere, 2011), p. 163; Bracewell, pp. 205–8.

2   *The Daily Mail*, 26 September 2013, quoted in John Medhurst, *That Option No Longer Exists: Britain 1974–6* (Alresford: Zero, 2014), p. 1.

3   Alwyn W. Turner, *Crisis? What Crisis? Britain in the 1970s* (London: Aurum, 2008).

4   Dominic Sandbrook, *State of Emergency, The Way We Were: Britain 1970–1974* (London: Penguin, 2011).

5   Wolfgang Streeck, 'The Crises of Democratic Capitalism', *New Left Review* 71, Sept/Oct 2011, p. 11.

6   Beckett, *When*, p. 58; Jim Tomlinson, 'De-Industrialisation Not Decline: A New Meta-Narrative for Post-war British History', Oxford University Press, Advance Access Publication, 12/10/2015. pp. 83–4; Cowie, pp. 35–42.

7   Beckett, *When*, p. 64; Cowie, p. 8; p. 36.

8   Cowie, p. 47.

9   Fisher, *Postcapitalist*, p. 170.

10 Hebdige, *Subculture*, p. 2; p. 19.

11 Maconie doesn't adequately challenge this take, p. 144; Turner recycles it (*Crisis*, pp. 82–3).

12 Cowie, pp. 108-9.

13 Turner, *Crisis*, p. 136.

14 David Edgar, *The Guardian*, 9 May 2012: https://www.theguardian.com/books/2012/may/09/seasons-in-sun-sandbrook-review

15 Lynskey, pp. 254–5.

16 Maconie, p. 216.

17 Curtis, *Can't*, 'Shooting', 1: 09

18 Glam as rejecting the 60s: Reynolds, *Shock*, p. 11; Ian Taylor and Dave Wall, 'Beyond the Skinheads', in *Working Class Youth Culture*, G. Mungham and G. Pearson (eds) (London: Routledge, 1976). Glam as postmodern: Reynolds, *Rip*, p. 377. Glam as apolitical: Hebdige, *Subculture*, p. 77; Simon Frith, 'The Art of Posing' in *The Bowie Companion*, ed. Elizabeth Thomson

and David Gutman (London: Sidgwick & Jackson, 1995), p. 176; Maconie, p. 152.

19 Reynolds, *Shock*, p. 16.

20 Beckett *When*, pp. 66–86.

21 Reynolds, *Shock*, p. 140.

22 Chris O'Leary, *Rebel Rebel: All the Songs of David Bowie from '64 to '76* (Alresford: Zero, 2015), pp. 261–2.

23 Herbert Marcuse, 'Repressive Tolerance', in *A Critique of Pure Tolerance*, Robert Paul Woolff, Barrington Moore, Herbert Marcuse (Boston: Beacon Press, 1969), p. 89.

24 Susan Sontag, 'Notes on 'Camp' [1964] in *Against Interpretation* (London: Vintage, 1994), p. 280.

25 Jameson, 'Postmodernism', p. 58.

26 Benjamin, 'Theses', p. 263.

27 Reynolds, *Shock*, pp. 324–5.

28 O'Leary, *Rebel*, pp. 198–202; Nicolas Pegg, *The Complete David Bowie* (London: Reynolds & Hearn, 2000), p. 39.

29 Adorno, 'Fetish', p. 39.

30 Sontag, 'Notes', p. 284.

31 Hebdige, *Subculture*, p. 19.

32 Bracewell, p. 206.

33 Jameson, *Postmodernism*, p. 1.

34 Gilroy, *Darker*, pp. 41–2.

35 Greg Tate, *Flyboy 2: The Greg Tate Reader* (Durham and London: Duke University Press, 2016), p. 186.

36 Cowie, p. 6.

37 Although the Eagles' friend Jackson Browne had co-written 'Take it Easy', post-60s defeatism is analysed rather than absorbed on 1974's *Late for the Sky* (US 14) while both evoking and featuring Laurel Canyon's famous denizens ('Fountain of Sorrow' concerns Joni Mitchell). 'Before the Deluge' charts the counterculture's utopianism ("making plans and thinking of the future"), fatigue in the face of capitalism's promise of "glitter and rouge" and capitulation to "the resignation that living brings". While it's empathetic about the sellouts – aka his friends and neighbours – the song suggests that the price of doing so is paid by the earth – the deluge isn't just the increasingly corporate turn in rock, but ecological catastrophe.

38 Barney Hoskyns, *Hotel California* (London: Fourth Estate, 2005), p. 245.

39 While O'Leary sees 'Diamond Dogs' as the "grey paralyzed Britain of late 1973 and early 1974", he also sees that, "the future wouldn't be the

revolution of the radicals or the utopia of the hippies but a quisling culture, one happily relieved from freedom" (*Rebel*, p. 320).

40 Beckett, *When*, p. 288.

Chapter 6. "Take it to the Limit"

1 Perry Anderson characterises the Labour government's Social Contract as, "an exchange of welfare concessions – above all, increased pensions – for wage restraints". *English Questions* (London: Verso, 1992), p. 177.

2 See: Adam Curtis, *All Watched over by Machines of Loving Grace*, Part 3.

3 David Edgerton, *The Rise and Fall of the British Nation: A Twentieth Century History* (London: Penguin 2019), p. 422.

4 Gilbert and Lawrence, *Love* podcast, 20/09/2022, Series 2, E07, 'Motown: Disco as Post-Fordist Entertainment'.

5 Marcuse, *One*, pp. 71–2.

6 Philip Norman, *John Lennon: The Life* (London: HarperCollins, 2008), p. 750; pp. 772–6.

7 Thin Lizzy's early-1977 'Don't Believe a Word' (UK12) – "especially if I tell you, I'm in love with you" – is a harsher 'I'm Not in Love', without much sense of satire.

8 Marcuse, *Counterrevolution*, pp. 49–50.

9 Adorno, 'Society'.

10 Amidst these, Ringo Starr's own superstar hookup with John and Taupin on early 1975's 'Snookeroo' (US 3) was an endearingly humble assertion of his enduring working-class sensibility.

11 Glen Campbell's Fordist facsimile of 'Rhinestone', late 1975's 'Country Boy (You've Got Your Feet in LA)' (US 11) expresses a similar desire for "stayin' in touch with the street" that pulls against superstar solipsism.

12 von Bothmer, pp. 54–6.

13 Herbert Marcuse, *Marxism, Revolution and Utopia*, ed. Douglas Kellner and Clayton Pierce (Abingdon: Routledge, 2014), p. 114.

14 Turner, *Crisis*, pp.186–90.

15 Cowie, p. 67.

16 E. g. Maconie, p. 220.

17 Marcuse, *Counterrevolution*, p. 48.

18 Hebdige, *Subculture*, p. 34.

19 White reggae can be traced through Chris Andrews' 1965 'Yesterday Man' (UK 3), the Beatles' vile 1968 'Ob-La-Di, Ob-La-Da', Paul Simon's 1972 'Mother and Child Reunion' (UK 5; US 4) – with Jimmy Cliff's

musicians – and Wings' sloppy 1973 'C Moon' (UK 5; US 10). The Eagles 1977 'Hotel California's rhythm and cod-Caribbean vocal inflections often go unremarked.

20   1974's 'Sad Sweet Dreamer' (UK 1); 1975's 'You Sexy Thing' (UK 2; US 3) respectively. See also: Maxine Nightingale's delightful 'Right Back Where We Started From' (UK 8, US 2).

21   Miller, p. 4.

22   Reynolds, *Retromania*, p. 335.

23   Medhurst, p. 9.

24   Tomlinson, 'Deindustrialisation', p. 81.

25   Dominic Sandbrook, *Seasons in the Sun: The Battle for Britain, 1974–1979* (London: Penguin, 2013), pp. xix–xx.

26   Medhurst, p. 7.

27   Dominic Sandbrook, *Who Dares Wins: Britain, 1979–1982* [2019] (London: Penguin, 2020), pp. 18–20.

28   Chris Rogers, 'From Social Contract to 'Social Contrick': The Depoliticisation of Economic Policy-Making under Harold Wilson, 1974–75', *The British Journal of Politics and International Relations*: 2009, Vol. 11, pp. 634–51.

29   Beckett, *When*, pp. 355–6. The debt predictions were double the reality, and sterling and inflation stabilised during 1977.

Chapter 7. "Some Will Win, Some Will Lose"

1   Margaret Thatcher, *Sunday Times* interview, 3 May 1981: https://www. margaretthatcher.org/document/104475

2   Thatcher and Reagan's aggressive renewal of the Cold War has been largely forgotten, but the pop charts provide a clear record of the fear their brinkmanship inspired. Bowie on 1979's 'Fantastic Voyage' emotively links the threat of nuclear annihilation to elite indifference to "fatherless scum" (*Lodger*, UK 4; US 20), Talking Heads' concurrent 'Life During Wartime' is a matter-of-fact account of post-nuclear dystopia (*Fear of Music*, US 21), while the same year the Stranglers' link a primed 'Nuclear Device' to right-wing politics (*The Raven*, UK 4). Hazel O'Connor's 1980 'Eighth Day' (UK 5) depicts nuclear war as consequence of technological overdevelopment; Kate Bush's 1980 'Breathing' (UK 16) posits it as political recklessness ("the fools blew it"); UB40 depict it as a consequence of nationalism on 'The Earth Dies Screaming (UK 10). With the Specials' 1980 'Man at C&A' complaining of public disempowerment – "I don't have a say in the war

games they play" – Ultravox's 1981 synth-punk 'All Stood Still' (UK 8) passively accepts this ("What can we do?"), while Heaven 17's 1981 'Let's All Make a Bomb' combines nuclear anxiety with 80s hedonism: "Ignore the sirens, let's have fun/Put on your best, go out in style".

3   Jon Savage, *England's Dreaming: The Sex Pistols and Punk Rock* (Year, publisher, place), p. 256; Hebdige, *Subculture*, p. 83.

4   Edgerton, *Rise*, pp. 451–2; Turner, *Crisis*, p. 200.

5   Hebdige, *Subculture*, p. 115.

6   Matthew Worley, *Punk, Politics and British Youth Culture, 1976–1984* (Cambridge: Cambridge University Press, 2017), p. 37.

7   Thatcher's January 1978 *World in Action* interview was a less melodramatic reprise of Powell's 'Rivers of blood' speech, invoking white Britons being "swamped" by other cultures.

8   Turner, *Crisis*, pp. 222–3.

9   Gramsci, pp. 302–3.

10 Sham 69's 'oi' associates The Angelic Upstarts were stalwarts of Rock Against Racism. Moreover, The Upstarts' 'Teenage Warning' (UK 29) and 'I'm an Upstart' (*Teenage Warning*, UK 29) made punk's threat to the establishment explicit.

11 Colin Hay, 'Narrating Crisis: The Discursive Construction of the "Winter of Discontent"', *Sociology*, 30 (2), May 1996, p. 255.

12 Colin Leys, *Politics in Britain: from Labourism to Thatcherism* (London: Verso, 1989), pp. 104–5.

13 The exceptions are Sylvester's sole hit 'You Make Me Feel (Mighty Real)' and Space's 1977 'Magic Fly' (UK 2).

14 Andrew Gamble, *The Free Economy and the Strong State* (Basingtoke: MacMillan Education 1988), p. 200.

15 Meat Loaf's rock'n'roll-suffused 'Paradise by the Dashboard Light' (*Bat Out of Hell*) is a fusion of camp and cock rock, addressing the revival of 50s family values, wherein the utopian freedom of Fordist cars and sex transmutes into incarceration in dystopian convention.

16 Hebdige, *Subculture*, p. 34.

17 A solidarity returned by Marley on 'Punky Reggae Party', flipside to 1977's joyous 'Jamming' (UK 9).

18 Reynolds, *Rip*, pp. xvii–xviii; Reynolds quotes Malcolm McLaren on new wave as middle class, p. 309.

19 Cowie, p. 73.

20 Mark Fisher, 'The Metaphysics of Crackle: Afrofuturism and Hauntology', *Dancecult: Journal of Electronic Dance Music Culture*, 5 (2), p. 45.

21 Synthpop musicians grew up on dystopian sci-fi films like *THX 1138* (Lucas, 1971), *Logan's Run* (Anderson, 1976) and *Rollerball* (Jewison, 1976), and dystopian sci-fi novels like Ray Bradbury's *Fahrenheit 451* (1953) and Philip K Dick's *Ubik* (1969). *2001: A Space Odyssey* (Kubrick, 1969), *Colossus: The Forbin Project* (Sargent, 1970) and *Demon Seed* (Cammell, 1977) specifically showed automation's utopian potential becoming dystopian.

22 Jameson, *Archaeologies*, p. 199.

23 Fisher, 'Metaphysics', p. 45

24 Albiez and Lindvig suggest that even 'Autobahn' is a satire of West German mores: 'Autobahn and Heimatklange: Soundtracking the FRG' in *Kraftwerk: Music Non-Stop*, ed. Sean Albiez and David Pattie (New York: Continuum, 2011), pp. 327–44.

25 E.g. David Stubbs, *Mars by 1980: the Story of Electronic Music* (London: Faber and Faber, 2018), p. 230; again this is questioned by Albiez and Lindvig, pp. 25–7.

26 The Russian for 'robot' – as in the track's "I'm your servant, I'm your worker" – is '*robotnik*', or worker – though again the reference point is the contemporary West rather than East.

27 On *The Pleasure Principle* (UK 1; US 16) the sci-fi mise-en-scene fades to reveal human emotions: alienation ('Observer'), vulnerability (the lovely, violin-driven 'Complex', UK 6), although these are the work of social 'Engineers' who declare, "We're all you need to know".

28 Michel Foucault, *The History of Sexuality Volume 1: An Introduction* [1976] (London: Allen Lane, (1979), pp. 92–102.

29 Hall, 'Great', p. 15.

30 Leys, *Politics*, p.117; p. 125.

31 Williams, *Towards*, p. 262.

Chapter 8. "It's a Competitive World"

1   'What a Feeling' was produced by Giorgio Moroder, from whom 80s pop usually has only two degrees of separation. Laura Branigan's 1984 'Self Control' (UK 5; US 4) was arranged by Moroder's engineer Harold Faltermeyer, who produced Frey's 'Heat is On' and had a solo hit with 1984's 'Axel F' (UK 2; US 3). By 1986 Moroder was churning out electro power ballads like Berlin's 'Take my Breath Away' (UK 1; US 1).

2   von Bothmer, p. 37.

3   Marcuse, *One*, p. 69.

4   In late 1983, GLC council leader Ken Livingston appeared with the *a capella* Flying Pickets on *Top of the Pops*, singing Yazoo's 'Only You' (UK 1).

5   Gramsci, pp. 245-6.

6   See: Gamble, pp. 55–7.

7   Edgerton, p. 458.

8   von Bothmer, pp. 81–2.

9   Traverso, p. 36.

10   Kiran Sande, *The Quietus*, 2 April 2022: https://thequietus.com/articles/31336-michael-bracewell-interview-souvenir

11   Maconie pp. 248–50; Andy Beckett, *Promised You a Miracle: Why 1980–82 Made Modern Britain* (London: Penguin, 2016), pp. 183–5.

12   Beckett, *Promised*, pp. 186–7.

13   Elvis Costello (1983's *Punch the Clock*, UK 3; US 24), Lloyd Cole and the Commotions (1984's *Rattlesnakes*, UK 13) and Prefab Sprout inhabit similar sonic space (1985's *Steve McQueen*, UK 21, produced by Thomas Dolby).

14   Stubbs, *Mars*, p. 274; Reynolds, *Rip*, pp. 489–90.

15   Dylan Jones, *The 80s: Music's Greatest Decade?* BBC, 25 October 2021: https://www.bbc.co.uk/programmes/m00110rn

16   Thereafter other African American acts added rock elements to their synthpop-soul mix: Michael Jackson on 1983's 'Beat It' with Eddie Van Halen (UK 3; US 1), Lionel Richie on 'Running with the Night' (UK 9; US 7) with Toto's Steve Lukather the same year.

17   Margaret Thatcher, *Woman's Own* interview, 27 September 1987: https://www.margaretthatcher.org/document/106689

18   David Harvey, *A Brief History of Neoliberalism* (Oxford: Oxford University Press, 2005), p. 23.

19   Traverso, p. 9.

20   Pet Shop Boys offer a queer variant on the same situation on 'Rent' (UK 8) – "I love you, you pay my rent" – while also mourning a past of material and emotional plenty – "Look at my hopes, look at my dreams/The currency we've spent". The monetary language suggests the distinction between the material and the emotional is no longer discernible, however. 'Rent' was memorably deployed in *Saltburn* (2023).

21   Soul was now co-opted into the 'good 60s', primarily by *deracinating* it. So there were Motown covers by Phil Collins (1982's 'You Can't Hurry Love', UK 1; US 10), Kim Wilde (1986's 'You Keep Me Hangin' On', UK 2; US 1), alongside Bowie and Jagger's brutal 1985 assault on 'Dancing in the Street' (UK 1). There were Motown pastiches by Human League on 1982's 'Mirror Man' (UK 2' US 30); the Maisonettes' 1982 'Heartache Avenue',

(UK 7); Wham!'s 1984 'Freedom' (UK 1; US 3) and 1985 'I'm Your Man' (UK 1; US 3). The fact that the visual images for 1986 re-releases of Gaye's 'Grapevine' and Sam Cooke's 'Wonderful World' (UK 2) and Jackie Wilson's 'Reet Petite' (UK 1) were white – or in Wilson's case, clay – all contribute to the defusing of race in this era.

22 Raymond Williams, *Resources of Hope* (London: Verso, 1989), p. 118.

23 The video features Plant's car breaking down – a neat figure for post-Fordism – the singer adrift in a post-industrial California ghost town, eerie rather than morbid, a sense of possibility rather than probability.

Chapter 9. 'Everybody's Free'

1 Francis Fukuyama, *The End of History and the Last Man* (London: Penguin, 1992), p. xi.

2 Williams, *Towards*, p. 14.

3 Guy Debord, *The Society of the Spectacle*, trans. Donald Nicholson-Smith (New York: Zone, 1995), p. 76.

4 With divorce ending one-fifth of marriages, end of history power ballads pledging eternal devotion include: Cheap Trick's 1988 'The Flame' (US 1), Richard Marx's 1989 'Right Here Waiting' (UK 2; US1), Maria McKee's 1990 'Show Me Heaven' (UK 1) – which makes implicit the spiritual/emotional collapse in this affect: "You've such amazing grace" – and Roxette's 1992 'Listen to Your Heart' (US 1), the first song to get to no. 1 on CD sales alone.

5 Traverso, p. 8.

6 The Eastern Bloc's "disfigured socialism" (Traverso, p. 18) functioned throughout the Cold War to contain the Western left, but also kept alive the idea that "human beings can live in radically different ways, by radically different values, in radically different kinds of social order" as Williams put it (*Towards*, p. 13).

7 Matthew Charles, 'Utopia and Its Discontents: Dreams of Catastrophe and the End of 'the End of History' in *Studies in Social and Political Thought*, 18, Winter 2010, p. 30.

8 Dennis Soron, 'Back to the Future: the Contemporary Left and the Politics of Utopia', *Labour/La Travail*, 47, Spring 2001, p. 206.

9 Edgerton, p. 491.

10 Debord, p. 12.

11 Reynolds, *Energy Flash: A Journey through Rave Music and Dance Culture* (London: Picador, 1998), p. 83.

12 See also: Stone Roses' 'Fools Gold' (UK 8), Inspiral Carpets' 'This is How it Feels' (UK 14), Charlatans' 1990 'Then' (UK 12) and the Shamen's rural-medieval video for 1992's 'LSI' (UK 6).

13 Williams, *Towards*, p. 262.

14 Adorno, *Dialectic*, p. 151.

15 From KRS1's rap on R.E.M.'s 1990 'Radio Song' (*Out of Time*, UK 1; US 1).

16 Debord, p. 43.

17 Fredric Jameson, *Valences of the Dialectic* (London: Verso, 2009), p. 142.

18 It was unfortunate that the property Black Box liberated was that of straitened African American vocalist Loleatta Holloway, who sued them.

19 Reynolds, *Energy*, p. xx.

20 Matthew Collin, *Altered State: The Story of Ecstasy Culture and Acid House* (London: Serpent's Tail, 1997), p. 267.

21 Julianne Escobedo Shepherd, *Pitchfork*, 9/10/2016: https://pitchfork.com/reviews/albums/22253-rhythm-nation-1814/

22 Jeremy Gilbert, 'After 68: Narratives of the New Capitalism', *New Formations* 65, Autumn 2008, p. 52.

23 Abdul from 1989's 'Cold Hearted', Jackson from 1990's 'Love Will Never Do' (US 1) and Minogue from 1990's 'Better the Devil You Know' (UK 2).

24 Mim Udovitch, 'Madonna', in *Trouble Girls: The Rolling Stone Book of Women in Rock* (New York: Rolling Stone, 1997), pp. 341–6.

25 Marcuse, *One*, p. 71.

26 Marcuse, *One*, p. 70.

27 If Yazz's 'Stand Up for Your Love Rights' (UK 2) was a response, it was scuppered by a determinedly heteronormative video, rendering those 'rights' meaningless.

28 Marcuse *One*, p. 58.

29 The acoustic-metal power ballad revived in this era with Poison's 1988 'Every Rose Has Its Thorn' (UK 13; US 1), Guns N' Roses' summer 1989 'Patience' (UK 10; US 4) and Skid Row's late 1989 'I Remember You' (UK 6).

30 Debord, p. 26.

31 Fisher, *Capitalist Realism: Is There No Alternative?* (Winchester: Zero, 2009), pp. 11–2.

32 Joshua Clover, *1989: Bob Dylan Didn't Have This to Sing About* (Berkeley and Los Angeles: University of California Press, 2009), pp. 129–30.

33 From Public Enemy's 'Brothers Gonna Work It Out' (*Fear of a Black Planet*).

34 Clover, p. 128; Lynskey, pp. 562–7.

35   Steven Best and Douglas Kellner, 'Rap, Black Rage, and Racial Difference', *Enculturation*, 2 (2), Spring 1999: http://enculturation.gmu.edu/2_2/best-kellner.html

36   From Vanilla Ice's 1990 'Play that Funky Music' (UK 10; US 4).

37   Run DMC were aware the tendency went both ways, having broken through with a rock song, 'Walk This Way', and utilised The Knack's 'My Sharona' on 1987's 'It's Tricky' (UK 16). Tone Loc parlayed a line in sub-DMC rock-hop on 1989's 'Funky Cold Medina' (UK 13; US 8) with a Foreigner guitar-line. Utah Saints satirically claimed the 'running man' dance as a Welsh invention on the video for 'Something Good' (UK 4), its final frame featuring MC Hammer 'appropriating' it.

38   Jeremy Deller, *Everybody in the Place, An Incomplete History of Britain 1984–1992*, documentary, 27: 10: https://www.youtube.com/watch?v=Jqc_1NVHE-0

39   Reynolds, *Energy*, pp. 83–4.

40   Mark Fisher, 'Baroque Sunbursts', in *Rave: Rave and its Influence on Art and Culture*, ed. Nav Haq (London: Black Dog, 2016), pp. 42-3.

41   Deller, 35: 45.

42   Reynolds, *Energy*, p. 424.

43   The Shamen's 'Phorever People' (UK 5) does the same with added presentism: "we don't have to look too far to find ourselves… the future is now, and phorever is here". Rave is expressing a structure of feeling; see, therefore, Queen's 1989 'I Want it All' (UK 3), wherein collective demands – "Here's to the future for the dreams of youth" – are Hobbesian: "move out of my way", "I want it all, and I want it now".

44   Commercial acid house often passed off capitulation as positivity. Yazz's 1988 response to being "broken down to the lowest turn" is 'The Only Way Is Up' (UK 1). The recurring phrase in Coldcut and Lisa Stansfield's 1989 'People Hold On' (UK 11) is "givin' in" and a passive assertion that "maybe there's enough for everyone". Bomb the Bass's 1991 'Winter in July' (UK 6) suggests, "Make the best of what's given you/Everything will come in time".

Chapter 10. "The Power and the Money"

1   See: Steps' 1998 'Last Thing on My Mind' (UK 6) and 1999 'After the Love Has Gone' (UK 2),

2   Bracewell, *passim.*

3   Fisher, *Postcapitalist*, p. 59.

4 Streeck, 'Crisis', p. 17.

5 David Alderson, *Sex Needs and Queer Culture* (London: Zed, 2016), p. 146.

6 Adorno and Horkheimer, p. 143.

7 Commemorated by Super Furry Animals' lovely 2001 'Presidential Suite' (*Rings Around the World*, UK 3).

8 See also: Steven Tyler's Aerosmith putting his teenage daughter Liv in a schoolgirl uniform, alongside future *Clueless* star Alicia Silverstone, on the video for 1994's 'Crazy' (UK 23; US 17).

9 Taylor, p. 9.

10 Disco-house was perfect for pop colonisation: Janet Jackson's sweet 1998 'Together Again' (UK 4; US 1), Madonna's grating 2000 'Music' (UK 1; US 1) and Kylie's great 2000 'Spinning Around' (UK 1) meant Steps' 2000 'Stomp' (UK 1) was barely a cash-in (unless you were Chic).

11 The Cheiron factory gave US variant Backstreet Boys a harder, more hip-hop sound, but the promo for 1998's 'As Long as You Love Me' (UK 3) frames the boys as passive puppets for powerful women's gaze.

12 David Stubbs, *1996 & The End of History* (London: Repeater, 2016), p. 95.

13 That this trick was revived in 2023's *Barbie* feature film was effectively an acknowledgement of the Long 90s' restoration.

14 Thomas B. Bonczar, Bureau of Justice report, August 2003: https://bjs.ojp.gov/content/pub/pdf/piusp01.pdf

15 Stubbs, *1996*, pp. 71–2.

16 From Nas's verse on Raekwon's 'Verbal Intercourse' on *Only Built 4 Cuban Linx*.

17 Tori Amos's 'Pretty Good Year' (UK 7) the same year charts similarly empathetic terrain, as does Red Hot Chili Peppers' 1995 'My Friends' (UK 29).

18 Rhian E. Jones, 'Unwritten Diaries: History, Politics and Experience through *The Holy Bible*' in Rhian E. Jones, Daniel Lukes, Larissa Wodtke, *Triptych: Three Studies of Manic Street Preachers' The Holy Bible* (London: Repeater, 2017), p. 49.

19 Lynksey, pp. 616–9.

20 Jones, 'Unwritten', p. 86.

21 Zahra Dalilah, 'Equality is in the Doing not the Saying: What Tupac Taught Me', in Jones and Davies (eds), pp. 145-53.

22 See also the Spice Girls' 1996 'Mama' (UK 1), Boyz II Men's 1997 'A Song for Mama' (US 7) and Jay-Z's 2000 *Oliver*-sampling 'Anything' (UK 18), a cross between 'Dear Mama' and his own 'Hard Knock Life': "As a man, I apologise for my dad".

23 Rhian E. Jones, *Clampdown: Pop-Cultural Wars on Class and Gender* (Alresford: Zero, 2012), p. 54.

24 RATM can't be held responsible for the phrase being later taken up by UKIP and Trumpists.

25 RATM's British equivalent Senser more simplistically asserted that "The real enemies are in the corporate office blocks" on 1994's 'Switch' (*Stacked Up*, UK 4).

26 Owen Hatherley, *Uncommon* (Alresford: Zero, 2011), p. 70.

27 Edgerton, pp. 477–8.

28 Younger viewers may see nothing untoward in the video, for in the intervening 25 years, the neoliberal walk – of which this is an early instantiation – has become how *everybody* now moves down the street.

29 Tom Ewing, *Popular*, 3 January 2014: https://popular-number1s. com/2014/01/03/spice-girls-wannabe-2/

30 Donna Haraway, 'A Cyborg Manifesto: Science, Technology and Socialist-Feminism in the 1980s', *Socialist Review*, 80 (1985), pp. 65–108.

31 Alderson, pp. 106–7.

32 Simon Reynolds, *Energy Flash* blog, 22 May 2009: http:// energyflashbysimonreynolds.blogspot.com/2009/05/nuum-and-its-discontents-4-party.html.

Chapter 11. 'Pop It Like It's Hot'

1 Haraway, 'Cyborg', p. 130.

2 See: Paul Morley's *Words and Music; A History of Pop in the Shape of a City* (London: Bloomsbury, 2003), with Kylie Minogue as its cyborg pop paradigm.

3 Reynolds quotes *Wired* editor Steven Levy's "capitalist mysticism" on the iPod Nano being "so beautiful that it seemed to have dropped down from some vastly advanced alien civilization" (*Retromania*, p. 113).

4 Slavoj Žižek, *Welcome to the Desert of the Real* (London and New York: Verso, 2002), pp.15-17.

5 'Work It' is usually taken to use the metaphor of work to describe sex, but its sexual metaphors are actually used to celebrate *work*. Thus the elephant's big trunk, and Missy's booty going "badonka donk-donk" testify via lyrical innovation to the same thing as Timbaland's music's foregrounding of its own apparatus: the pair's skills in their work.

6   Note also Robbie Williams' 2003 'Sexed Up' (UK 10).

7   Žižek, *Welcome*, p. 31.

8   The misogyny of Eminem's 2005 'Ass Like That' (UK 4) and Nelly's 2003 'Shake Ya Tailfeather' (UK 10; US 1) – "Is that your ass or your mama half reindeer?" – barely even deserve a footnote.

9   See also: Charlotte Church's 2005 'Crazy Chick' (UK 2): "I need professional help" is uttered flippantly but contextually seems less so.

10   Fisher, *Capitalist*, pp. 21-22.

11   Raving rappers include: Ja Rule's E'd up 2001 'Livin it Up' (UK 5; US 6); Ciara and Ludacris's 2005 'Oh' (UK 4; US 2); and Clipse's 2002 'When the Last' (US 19): "Club nights, one of the reasons I love life/Smoke somethin', drink somethin', get ripped/I'm here to party y'all". Afroman's 2001 'Because I got High (UK 1; US 13) and Eminem and D12's 2001 'Purple Pills' (UK 2; US 19) celebrate polymorphous narcosis: "Speed, shrooms, down the Valiums"; while Missy Elliott on 2002's '4 My People' advises: "People, go 'head and drink up/Get in the club, get fucked up" (UK 5). True to the quotidian aggression of this era, much of this music sounds more like an attack than a party – e.g. Busta Rhymes and Dre's late 2001 'Break Ya Neck' (UK 1; US 26): "bang your head til you break your muthafuckin neck".

12   Boltanski and Chiapello, p. 531.

13   Richard Seymour, *The Twittering Machine* (London: Indigo, 2019), p. 89.

14   Jones, *Clampdown*, pp. 78-80.

15   From DMX's 2002 'X Gon' Give it To Ya' (UK 6).

16   Tom Ewing, *Pitchfork*, 28 May 2010: https://pitchfork.com/features/poptimist/7811-poptimist-29/

17   'Can't Get You of My Head' was offered to Sophie Ellis Bextor; Timberlake's 2002 'Like I Love You' (UK 2; US 11) to Michael Jackson; Spears' 'Slave' to Janet Jackson; Rihanna's 2007 'Umbrella' (UK 1; US 1) to Britney and Mary J. Blige.

18   Tom Ewing, *Popular*: https://popular-number1s.com/2020/02/23/the-black-eyed-peas-ft-justin-timberlake-where-is-the-love/

19   With its video's premise that the fully-clothed partygoer is 'othered', Jimmy Eat World get to assert their progressive credentials whilst producing a video of massed young people in their underwear.

20   Žižek, *Welcome*, p. 141.

21   That the marvellous Super Furry Animals should be reduced to a footnote is regrettably appropriate, as the sentiments of 2001's 'Juxtapozed with U'

(UK 14) are so anomalous in this era, "you've got to tolerate all of those people that you hate".

22　That 'pimp' has now become a synonym for 'man' hardly makes the use of 'ho' the more edifying – as in Ludacris's 2005 'Pimpin' All Over the World' (US 9) – it just transactionalises the othering.

23　Alderson, p. 276.

24　Owen Jones, *Chavs: The Demonization of the Working Class* (London and New York: Verso, 2011), p. 247.

25　Jamie T's 'Sheila' (UK 15) is a far more sympathetic account of urban underclass life, channeling poet John Betjeman as the censorious middle-class self, and featuring a brilliantly heartbreaking video with Bob Hoskins.

26　Alderson, p. 277.

27　Charlie Brooker, *The Guardian*, 9 June 2006: https://www.theguardian.com/commentisfree/2006/jun/09/buyingmusic.comment. Jones is also rather hard on Thom, from the left, *Clampdown*, p. 89.

28　Žižek, *Welcome*, p. 100.

29　Žižek, *Welcome*, pp. 118–23.

Chapter 12. "Go Out and Smash It"

1　Streeck, p. 5.

2　Naomi Klein, *Shock Doctrine: The Rise of Disaster Capitalism* (London: Penguin, 2007), pp. 6–7.

3　Juliette Garside, *The Guardian*, 26 April 2015: https://www.theguardian.com/business/2015/apr/26/recession-rich-britains-wealthiest-double-net-worth-since-crisis

4　Robin James, *Resilience and Melancholy: Pop Music, Feminism, Neoliberalism* (Alresford: Zero, 2015), pp. 6–8.

5　Capitalism maintains itself because "pleasure […] is experienced in confronting uncertainty": Boltanski and Chiapello, p. 488.

6　T-Pain's use of Auto-Tune on 2007's 'Buy U a Drank' (US 1), like Lil Wayne's spring 2008 'Lollipop' (UK 26; US 1) is far more upbeat.

7　Simon Reynolds, *The Guardian*, 2 August 2012: https://www.theguardian.com/music/2012/aug/02/how-rave-music-conquered-america

8　James, p. 148.

9　Splitting the difference between democracy and monopoly (it worked for neoliberalism), EDM swallowed every genre from R&B – Chris Brown's Auto-Tuned 2008 'Forever' (UK 4; US 2) – to grime – Dizzee Rascal's

2008 'Dance Wiv Me' (UK 1) – to teenpop – Cheryl Cole's 2012 'Call My Name' (UK 1).

10   Indeed, it was now that a relic of World War II, another great emblem of British resilience, the 'Keep Calm and Carry On' poster, became ubiquitous.

11   Taylor, p. 12; p. 15.

12   Klein, *Shock*, p. 444.

13   Jones, *Chavs*, p. 10.

14   Jones, *Clampdown*, p. 78.

15   Alan Berube and Elizabeth Kneebone, *Brookings*, 16 August 2013: https://www.brookings.edu/opinions/americas-shifting-suburban-battlegrounds/

16   Fredric Jameson, 'The Aesthetics of Singularity', *New Left Review*, 91, March/April 2015, p. 130.

17   Jones, *Clampdown*, p. 81.

18   Fisher, *Postcapitalist*, p. 57.

19   Sheeran's invocation of grime and hip-hop renders the multicultural ordinary.

20   This formal evocation of 'ordinariness' filtered into: R&B, with Chris Brown's 2008's acoustic-driven 'With You' (UK 8; US 2), with its promo featuring a dressed-down Brown on a public bus, into boybands, with One Direction's 2012 Sheeran-written ode to the un-madeover, 'Little Things' (UK 1) and EDM, with Avicii's acoustic 2013 'Wake Me Up' (UK 1; US 4).

21   For the first time since the mid-60s, there were expressions of dissatisfaction with work in popular music. Natasha Bedingfield's 2008 'Pocketful of Sunshine' (US 5) video features people parachuting out of their jobs. Avicii's 2011's 'Levels' video features a drone sparking an epidemic of dancing at his office (UK 4), while his 2012 'I Could Be the One' video (UK 1) focuses on an overweight female office worker, whose escape is again hedonistic, but who's killed as she quits her job. Anna Kendrick's folky 2013 'Cups' (US 6) features a waitress in a diner of ordinary people, all collectively participating in the song's cutesy cup rhythm, after which she also quits her job (and survives).

22   The line is J-Lo's, from her and Pitbull's 2011 'On the Floor' (UK 3; US 1).

23   The line is from will.i.am and Britney's 2012 'Scream and Shout' (UK 1; US 3).

24   James, pp. 92–6.

25   Seymour, p. 96.

26   James, p. 130.

27 J. Jack Halberstram, *Gaga Feminism: Sex, Gender and the End of Normal* (Boston: Beacon, 2012), p. xv.

28 James, pp. 117–8.

29 James, pp. 134–5.

30 The line is Tinie Tempah's, from 2010's Labrinth-produced/featuring 'Frisky' (UK 2).

31 Taylor, p. 133.

32 Taylor, p. 218.

33 This melancholia is key to a brace of guitar-based acts that owed nothing to EDM, let alone hedonistic pop-rock: indie folk acts Arcade Fire, the National and Fleet Foxes, and the electro-indie melancholy of The XX's 2009 debut (UK 3). Grizzly Bear's "routine malaise" ('Two Weeks') evokes "a perfect cleft/We all fall through" ('While You Wait for the Others', *Veckatimest*, UK 24; US 8).

34 Boltanksi and Chiapello, p. 15.

Chapter 13. "Longing for Change"

1 Use of the term 'populist' quadrupled from 2010–19: https://journals.sagepub.com/doi/10.1177/0263395720955036

2 Jeremy Gilbert, 'This Conjuncture: For Stuart Hall', *New Formations* 2019 (96-97), p. 17.

3 Gilbert, 'Conjuncture' p. 19.

4 Seymour, p. 153.

5 John Lynch, *Business Insider*, 4 January 2018: https://www.businessinsider.com/hip-hop-passes-rock-most-popular-music-genre-nielsen-2018-1?r=US&IR=T

6 Spanish-language songs scaling the cultural wall of the American pop charts was a troll of Trump's plan for a physical wall to keep Mexican immigrants from American territory. These include: Luis Fonsi and Daddy Yankee's dreadful 2017 Latin/hip-hop fusion 'Despacito' (UK 1; US 1); Beyoncé's 2017 remix of reggaetón star J Balvin's 'Mi Gente' (US 3); Balvin, Bad Bunny and Cardi B's 2018 'I Like It' (UK 8; US 1) and Bad Bunny's 2018 reggaetón 'Mia' (US 5), featuring a flown-in Drake singing in Spanish.

7 That grime's revival was launched by its stars appearing as "backup dancers" for Kanye West at the 2015 Brit Awards could be seen as perpetuating a longstanding transatlantic hierarchy, whereas West's invitation was a recognition of a two-way relationship. Drake was also

influenced by grime, and his financing of, *Top Boy* from 2017 was further acknowledgement of British black culture's currency.

8   Cross-genre collaborations that went beyond the hip-hop guest-feature included Tinie Tempah and Katy B's late 2015 housey, uplifting 'Turn the Music Louder' (UK 1) and former Fifth Harmony singer Camila Cabello and Young Thug's 2017 Latin-trap 'Havana' (UK 1; US 1).

9   Fanon, p. 191.

10 The Black Panther character dates to 1966, and was the first black protagonist in mainstream American comics, thereby predating the political Black Panthers

11 Fanon, p. 196.

12 On the other hand, Ariane Grande's 2018 'No Tears Left to Cry' (UK 2; US 3) is a somewhat superficial reaction to the terrorist attack on her Manchester concert: "We're way too fly to partake in all this hate".

13 David Graeber, *Bullshit Jobs* (London: Penguin, 2018).

14 Ewart: "Technology was to be used to further the desires of the individual, rather than the collective, as Keynes assumed. The scale predicted in sci-fi films was inaccurate: the clue is contained in the names of transformative technologies: the microchip, the personal computer and the mobile phone."

15 Traverso, p. 20.

16 Seymour, p. 167.

17 It's thus a post-millennial 'Don't You Want Me', but more authoritarian – and less good.

18 Swift took legal action over an accusation that she parlayed white victimhood and deployed Nazi-esque imagery in the video: https://pitchfork.com/news/taylor-swift-criticized-by-aclu-after-sending-cease-and-desist-letter-to-blogger/s

19 Note that Self-Esteem has never charted in any territory.

20 University of Lancaster Press Release, 'Research shows that Cockney will disappear from London's streets within a generation', 7 September 2010: https://web.archive.org/web/20210326032914/https://www.lancaster.ac.uk/news-archive/D47105465E6D082B8025775300374D2E.php

21 David Olusoga, *Black and British: A Forgotten History* (London: Pan, 2016), pp. 493-6.

22 For example, Sheeran's collaboration with Chance the Rapper on 2019's 'Cross Me' (UK 4; US 25).

23 The line is Jack Kerouac's, from *On the Road* (1957), and is also quoted in Wah!'s 1982 'The Story of the Blues' (UK 2).

Conclusion: Remixing Pop and Politics

1   Fukuyama, p. xi.

2   Marx, *Capital*, p. 29.

3   See: Traverso, p. 222.

4   Traverso, p. 232.

5   Grafton Tanner, *The Hours Have Lost Their* Clock (London: Repeater, 2021), p. 251; pp. 30–2.

6   Marcuse, *Eros*, p. 149.

7   Marcuse, *Eros*, p. 231.

8   Graeme Wearden, *The Guardian*, 25 April 2023:https://www.theguardian.com/business/2023/apr/25/britons-need-to-accept-theyre-poorer-says-bank-of-england-economist. The number of US billionaires grew from 614 in March 2020 to 745 in October 2021, and their accumulated wealth from $2.95 trillion to 5 trillion.

9   Taylor, p. 108.

10 The work of centrist bellwether Drake is revealing in this regard. Following Megan's reclamation of another misogynist pejorative on June 2021's 'Thot Shit' (US 16), Drake, on September's ghastly novelty 'Way 2 Sexy' (UK 11; US 1), simply reasserts it, with the classist misogyny of "turnt up little thotty, ain't no wife about it/I'ma fuck her friends and send her back to Metro housin'" receiving virtually no kickback. On Drake and 21 Savage's 2022 *Her Loss* (UK 1; US 1), 'On BS' trolls feminism itself, with Drake declaring of tipping a stripper, "I blow a half a million on you hoes, I'm a feminist". With such offensiveness functioning within liberal discursive parameters, Drake barely got called out. On 'Circo Loco' (UK 7; US 8), Drake joined those (men) questioning the truth of Megan's shooting by rapper Tory Lanez: "This bitch lie 'bout getting shots."

11 Rani Molla, Vox.com, 11 January 2022: https://www.vox.com/recode/22841490/work-remote-wages-labor-force-participation-great-resignation-unions-quit

12 'Break My Soul' samples Robin S's 90s house 'Show Me Love' (UK 6; US 5), a demand for demonstrative affect in an increasingly affectless age.

13 Marcuse, *One*, p. 61.

14 Fisher, *Acid*, pp. 753–55.

15 Sigmund Freud, *Civilization and its Discontents* [1929], trans. Joan Riviere (Mansfield: Martino, 2010), pp. 13–14.

16 Rowbotham, p. 196.

17 Taylor, p. 215.

INDEX

Acknowledgements

Everything of value derives from the collective: individuals just voice it. Thanks therefore to discussions with Max Stevens, Sarah West, Paul Ewart, Rhian Jones, Gus Griffith, Shahd Daher, Josh Bowsher, Frankie Mullen, Ian Alderson, David Wilkinson, Tanya Fehmi, Patrick Henry, Shanthi Sivranasan, Thomas Travers, Lucy Lloyd and Patrick Griffith.

Thanks to my editor, Tariq Goddard, and copyeditor, Josh Turner, at Repeater. Additional thanks to Sean Albiez, David Pattie, Alexander Billet, David Wilkinson, Tom Gann and Owen Hatherley for commissions that sparked this project.

Parts of Chapter 3 appeared in *Tribune*, parts of Chapter 5 in *New Socialist* and parts of Chapter 8 in *Red Wedge*, *New Socialist* and *Key Words*. All of this book appeared on this writer's computer: the collective is not to blame.

Repeater Books

is dedicated to the creation of a new reality. The landscape of twenty-first-century arts and letters is faded and inert, riven by fashionable cynicism, egotistical self-reference and a nostalgia for the recent past. Repeater intends to add its voice to those movements that wish to enter history and assert control over its currents, gathering together scattered and isolated voices with those who have already called for an escape from Capitalist Realism. Our desire is to publish in every sphere and genre, combining vigorous dissent and a pragmatic willingness to succeed where messianic abstraction and quiescent co-option have stalled: abstention is not an option: we are alive and we don't agree.